UFOs
THE SECRET
HISTORY

UFOs
THE SECRET
HISTORY

BY MICHAEL
HESEMANN

MARLOWE & COMPANY
NEW YORK

Published by
Marlowe & Company
841 Broadway, Fourth Floor
New York, NY 10003

Library of Congress Cataloging-in-Publication Data

Hesemann, Michael.
    UFOs : the secret history / Michael Hesemann.
        p.   cm.
    ISBN 1-56924-701-3
    1. Unidentified flying objects. I. Title.
    TL789.H444   1998
    001.942—dc21   98-11980
                                                      CIP

Manufactured in the United States of America

To Natalie, the princess of my heart

CONTENTS

Foreword

Michael Hesemann has produced a vast and absolutely riveting piece of scholarship that covers the whole enormous subject of the UFO experience not only with careful and even-handed attention to the facts, but also with a level of insight that makes it literally electrifying to read.

This is not only a book for the student of the UFO controversy; it is for the general reader who wants to gain an in-depth knowledge of it. Enormous work of scholarship though it is, there are surprises on every page.

For example, there was a UFO crash reported in hundreds of Americans newspapers by a world-famous columnist—and then ignored. As recently as 1990, irrefutable evidence of another crash has emerged. Hesemann has located some subtle, profoundly convincing information that sheds light on this incident. Beyond the possibility that an alien spacecraft might have crashed and been recovered, it suggests that something even more strange may have happened.

Hesemann explores every aspect of the phenomenon with an even hand. In the process, he offers a number of compelling reasons why the "contactee movement" of the fifties should be reexamined, showing that there were mysteries of real importance behind the claims of "contact" with shapely Venusians. He also ponders another mystery: why were all the early contact stories about beings that looked human, and all the later ones about creatures that appeared alien?

It is fascinating and provocative questions like these that animate the subtext of this book.

There is a stunning discussion of the principle of anti-gravity that strongly suggests that a technology of major importance was sucked into the classification system in the fifties and has never reemerged. If so, then one of the most important of all technologies—which could replace the costly, slow heat engine with something really efficient and really powerful—is being concealed from the public. The case that Hesemann makes for this is a convincing and very disturbing one.

He documents the fact that the United States Air Force never went out of the UFO business at all after Project Blue Book, and suggests the strong possibility that a unit once stationed in Fort Belvoir, Virginia, may still be actively involved, and doing much more than merely collecting information. He shows that the Air Force lied about the existence of this unit to a United States Senator as recently as 1992.

In fact, a large part of this book reads like something that the Air Force might have written if it decided to disgorge its secrets. How Hesemann accomplished this I do not know, but I do know him to be a very careful "hands-on" researcher, as well as a voracious and thoughtful reader on the subject. I do not believe that there is another researcher alive with his vast range of contacts, or with the international scope of information that he has achieved. Thus you read, for example, of the UFO-related activities of the U.S. government in other countries, not only from the American perspective, but also from that of the direct witnesses. What emerges is evidence of a vast and inexplicable human effort to conceal every possible shred of evidence of an alien presence in our world.

It becomes evident, as case after case is discussed, that certain elements of accepted wisdom about the UFO experience that are used by the skeptics as arguments for their position are not only false, but have apparently been contrived as a sort of propaganda.

For example, the notion that no professional astronomer has ever taken a photograph of a UFO turns out to be completely false. Not only have professional astronomers taken such pictures with amazing frequency, but as it turns out the first picture ever taken of a UFO was made in 1885—through a telescope by a professional astronomer!

With his world-spanning approach, Hesemann draws his information from many different sources, so many, in fact, that even the most concerted efforts at suppression fail. Thus we meet the distinguished Brazilian astronomer who took professional quality photographs of UFOs as they hovered over a great city—providing the world with proof positive that something very real and very strange was present. But that proof was suppressed, if not by an actual effort to keep the story out of the western media, then by the sheer inertia inherent in the situation.

And this is only one of many such stories. The fact is that, as Hesemann makes clear, science has had more than enough professionally gathered data available for years to justify its taking UFOs seriously.

Not only does this book deal with the vast amount of information that is available from modern times, it offers an illuminating review of the historical record. It turns out that much of the record has been ignored, but it suggests the presence of a persistent but subtle intervention in human affairs that must be addressed rationally if our history is ever to be understood.

For example, Hesemann has uncovered records of crucial interventions at small historical moments that on the surface do not seem particularly important. But a more careful reading of the history books reveals that one after another of these events led to an enormous turning of the wheel of human life. Indeed it becomes clear that an effort of breathtaking subtlety and insight has been under way for thousands of years, and that our world as it is presently constituted has been formed in no small part by these interventions.

Hesemann delves into the thorny issue of alien abductions with the same thoroughness and grasp of the material that he applies to the rest of this most complicated and difficult of all human experiences. Drawing on cases from countries all over the world—cases that are rarely even mentioned in the American and English literature on the subject—he opens a door into this very hidden corner of reality that has never been opened before. Juxtaposing one such case against another, he constructs a picture of close encounters that offers richer than usual insight, and leaves the reader stunned by the provocative nature of the questions that the problem raises.

The picture that emerges from a reading of this book is very different from the one that we tell ourselves represents our history. The very deepest meanings of human life are brought into question. The sheer scale and longevity of the intervention suggests, for example, that human history and the human species, far from being an outcome of natural forces, are something that has been carefully designed.

But by whom, and for what purpose? Hesemann's work leads the reader to extraordinary questions, questions that have never been asked before, but must be asked now, with the greatest possible urgency. For we must gain an understanding of what it is that has come into our midst, that obviously seeks to control our history and our lives, and is powerful enough to command secrecy even from the greatest human states that have ever been created.

As one who has read literally hundreds of books about the UFO experience, I can state without hesitation that this is the first one ever to deal with the subject on this large a scale, and to do so coherently. What emerges is a picture not only of a mysterious presence shaping and molding human history, but also one that penetrates deeply into the lives of individuals who lie far from the center of the world historical stage. And yet, the modern abduction of a seemingly unimportant individual may not be all that different in its eventual effect than was a tiny intervention in a seemingly obscure battle between warring city-states three thousand years ago.

This strange, enormous force that we have characterized as alien is seen to possess more insight into human affairs than we have. We observe the struggles of peoples and governments to understand, with ancient chroniclers explaining what they saw in terms of the mythology of their eras just as we explain them in terms of interstellar spacecraft and aliens.

As he speeds through the ages of man, capturing a chronicle here, a case study there, Hesemann builds a picture of a presence that is not only alto-

gether different from the images of gods and ghosts that were used to define
such phenomena in the past, but also from the modern idea that our visitors
are curious aliens recently arrived from another world.

One cannot help but be awed by the mystery that presents itself. It is so
large-scale and of such long duration, that the conclusion that human history is a history of intervention becomes impossible to escape.

He speaks eloquently of what it will be like for mankind as we come to
understand that somebody else is really here, and has been for a very long
time—that there is a mind other than human involved in human life and
human history. Thus this is a book about what is going to come to many
people as a great shock, but which will also propel us into becoming what
Hesemann calls a "cosmic species."

In the end, then, this is a story about the promising future of a very amazing species, the few billion souls collectively called mankind. We are seen
struggling out here in the immense dark for some spark of meaning that will
explain not only the meaning of our visitors, but also the meaning of
mankind.

Hesemann addresses mysteries like these with facts about the process of
human evolution and historical change that suggest that we have indeed
been put on the path that we walk, and kept there by gentle prodding from
the beyond. In the end, this is an incredibly hopeful book about the meaning and value of mankind, and the enormous potential of the human spirit.
A book of mysteries, then, that becomes a blueprint for future understanding.

—Whitley Strieber

Introduction

For confirmed skeptics, UFO sightings are no problem. In their opinion these can only be the mistaken identification of weather balloons, helicopters, meteorites, rockets, satellites or planets, etc. Otherwise, in the skeptics' opinion, UFOs are actually hoaxes invented by fame-hungry swindlers to acquire prominence. On the other hand, there is a front of uncritical UFO fans who are frequently victims of their own wishful thinking, and see in everything a manifestation of ambassadors from a "cosmic brotherhood," who have come to the earth to save humanity from destruction.

And then there are a few who deal with the phenomena in a sober and unprejudiced manner, and because of that are often thrown into the same pot with members of the superstitious "UFO cults" (by the self-appointed "popes" of authority). But there are numerous well-documented cases, confirmed by earnest witnesses, which indicate that, in fact, something is going on in the sky, which cannot be explained by conventional means, and behind which more and more recognized experts see the activity of extraterrestrial intelligence.

Experts define "UFO" as "unidentified flying object" whose appearance, flying characteristics, general dynamics and luminescent properties cannot be explained in a conventional manner. The astrophysicist J. Allen Hynek, who was for years advisor to the U.S. Air Force in the matter of UFOs, worked out a classification system for UFO sightings, which covers the entire spectrum of the phenomenon:

1. NL. Nocturnal light. A light that appears during the night.
2. DD. Daylight disc. A disc observed during daylight; mostly disc-shaped although spheres, cigars and triangles have been described.

3. RV. Radar visual. The sighted objects were also picked up by radar.
4. CE-1. Close encounter of the first kind. The UFO is seen at a distance of 400–500 feet.
5. CE-2. Close encounter of the second kind. There was a change or effect on the surroundings.
6. CE-3. Close encounter of the third kind. The crew was seen.

As spaceships of extraterrestrial origin, the UFOs have to cover distances which are unimaginable for us. This can only be possible through capabilities in the field of physics and technology that are beyond our understanding and which still lie in the realm of magic for us.

But UFOs are not only a challenge for astronomers, physicists and engineers; they also confound psychologists, sociologists and anthropologists. The reaction to the sighting of a UFO is, in the opinion of psychologists, determined by the psychological constitution of the observer. The sociologist, on the other hand, sees the reaction to a sighting mainly from the social and cultural background of the observer. For the anthropologist, there are parallels to myths and legends from the past, often connected with religion. He wants to understand the modus operandi of the extraterrestrials and investigate the public's general reaction to their appearance. Thus, probably one reason for the cautious approach of the alien visitors is that they are here on account of scientific curiosity.

An open contact would disturb our society and its dynamics and influence it to such an extent that the results of the aliens' observations of it would be contaminated. Our anthropologists also try to keep to a minimum their influence on a society they wish to observe. Extraterrestrial intelligences would perhaps, therefore, prefer to restrict their contacts to individual encounters so as to camouflage their reconnaissance as far as possible. Perhaps they have even deliberately staged the meaningless scenarios reported by the so-called contactees, so that their reports do not find general acceptance and they are mostly regarded as fools or psychopaths. Another protective measure would be, apart from this suggested disinformation, the induction of amnesia in the witnesses, as has been often described in cases of alleged alien abductions.

Although the UFOs quite obviously represent one of the biggest challenges for science, they are too often only laughed at, or simply ignored. One reason for that is that the whole spectrum of the UFO phenomenon is rarely presented in a serious manner and, when UFO sighting cases are reported in the press, they are usually taken out of their context. For this reason alone, we should be thankful to the cultural anthropologist and historian, Michael Hesemann of Düsseldorf, for having taken the trouble to write this book and highlight the interrelationships of all these incidents. We should be particularly thankful to him for his presentation of a whole pile of documents, originally top secret, which have been released during the last couple of years, and which represent the true history of unidentified flying objects. These are impressive documents and from them we see the

concern and anxiety with which the governments, especially the big powers, have reacted to the sudden appearance of these alien intruders.
Hesemann's thorough and gripping presentation of the facts bears witness
to this.

—Johannes von Buttlar

Preface

During every moment of our lives we are being watched from space. Permanently, inexorably, 7 satellites are circling around the earth, which, at least in theory, are capable of following every step that we take. At an altitude of 23,750 miles above the earth's surface they are stationed geosynchronously, which means that all 7 together have 100% of the surface of the earth under observation, right round the clock. Defense Support Program (DSP) is the cover name of this supersecret operation whose task it is to observe all military movements on the earth and, as early as possible, detect enemy jet fighters or missiles in flight against the United States of America. But in insider jargon DSP has another meaning—Deep Space Platform.

The DSPs are successors to the MIDAS satellite systems which, since the end of the 1950s, were in place to protect the United States from surprise attacks by intercontinental atomic missiles. But it was only in 1991, during the Gulf War, that the public at large learned for the first time of the existence of this system. It had been announced that the "Deep Space" satellites had detected the Iraqi "scud" missiles directly after they had been launched. That these satellites were capable of detecting other objects also had been revealed in 1974 in the astronomical journal *Sky and Telescope*. There it was said that the DSP satellites were equipped with more than 6,144 sensors which, besides being able to detect visible light, could also register the influence of infrared, X-ray and microwave spectra, as well as meteorites coming towards the earth.

But that was not all. Lee Graham and Ron Regehr, 2 engineers of the aircraft construction company Aerojet—which as a contractor had developed the DSP program for the U.S. Department of Defense—said that the space platforms regularly detected another kind of intruders from space. These were called "Fastwalkers," flying objects that came tearing through space at incredible speeds to enter the atmosphere of the earth and, after a while, to return to their cosmic homes. According to Lee and Ron, the satellites detected these objects on an average two or three times a month. What makes this particularly interesting is the fact that almost as a rule, every time a Fastwalker enters the atmosphere, it is followed by sightings of mysterious flying objects—unidentified flying objects, UFOs, down on Earth.

On September 19, 1976, shortly after the entry of a Fastwalker, the alarm sirens of the Sharokhi Air Force Base near the Iranian capital Teheran started howling. A UFO, a huge disk-like object, had been detected by radar and also seen by a number of pilots of civilian airlines. At once, 2 fighters of the type F-4 were started to pursue this mysterious object. They soon found the bright disk which was surrounded by blue, green, red and orange-colored lights. At that moment, all the instruments on board the first interceptor stopped functioning, and the pilot lost radio contact, so that he had to return to the base. The second pilot, however, saw a smaller object coming out of the bigger one and flying towards him. When he tried to fire a rocket at it, his firing panel failed to work and now he, too, lost radio contact with the ground station. He then carried out a quick turning and diving maneuver and managed to land. A few hours later, the UFO was seen above Morocco. The next day detailed reports were sent by the American embassies at Teheran and Rabat to the State Department in Washington, and Henry Kissinger personally gave orders to carry out further research. Apparently he, too, had heard about the DSP detection from the generals at the Pentagon.

A detailed description of the Teheran incident can be found in Chapter 17 of this book. The detection of the UFO by the space platform of the Pentagon came to light only a few years ago. After Graham and Regehr had established that the DSP had reported over a hundred fastwalkers, they asked the Pentagon whether a fastwalker had been detected by the space platform at the time in question. The Pentagon affirmed it.

In addition, the UFO researcher Joseph Stefula received from an official source the information that one of the DSP satellites had registered an object on September 19, 1976, that flew past it at a distance of only 2 miles. The observation lasted 9 minutes. Stefula was at the same time given a computer printout of this detection and observation from the North American Air Defense Command (NORAD). This showed that the flying objects that came from space are doubtlessly controlled by intelligence. NORAD had already, some years ago, conceded that the complicated infrared sensors of their radar network registered daily 800 to 900 objects whose flying characteristics corresponded neither to those of any terrestrial satellites nor to any usual ballistic trajectories. Even if 99% of them are meteorological phenomena, electromagnetic impulses, space garbage or other anomalies, it would still mean that every 3 hours a UFO is maneuvering in our airspace.

We can only imagine what anxiety this situation caused to those who were responsible for the security of national air space. They were helplessly confronted with a situation over which they had no control whatsoever. Unknown beings with unknown intentions were flying regularly in the atmosphere of the Earth and the top people at the Pentagon and in other defense ministries had no other choice except to take note of the situation passively. Only one thing was certain. One could not expose oneself and risk losing the confidence of the public through a confession of impotence. And for this reason UFOs were declared to be secret: the biggest military secret of our century.

But since the beginning of this decade, the 1990s, the veil of silence has been gradually lifted. There are increasing signs that in military and government circles a decision has been made to get the public accustomed gradually to the frightening truth that we are not alone in the universe. The idea was that this should be done through the implementation of an educational program.

On September 13–15, 1993, a meeting of leading UFO researchers was held at the ranch of Laurance Rockefeller in Wyoming. The participants of this meeting were planning to approach the Clinton administration with a plan to release selected information about UFOs during the oncoming years. At the same time the "Fund for UFO Research" prepared an extensive briefing paper about UFO topics for congressmen. This collection of "The Best Available Evidence," written by Antonio Huneeus and Don Berliner and financed with $20,000 donated by Laurance Rockefeller, was completed by the end of 1995. A thousand copies were printed and sent to U.S. senators, congressmen and White House personnel. Further copies were hand-delivered to key politicians in Europe and the U.S. by Marie Galbraith, wife of the former U.S. ambassador in Paris, France.

Meanwhile, Dr. John Gibbons, President Clinton's chief advisor in scientific matters and director of the White House office for scientific and technological policies, asked the CIA for a background report about the UFO phenomenon in preparation for a meeting with Laurance Rockefeller. Since Gibbons did not have any top secret clearance and could therefore see none of the secret briefing papers of the President in matters of national security, the agency withdrew from the affair in a most elegant manner. They entrusted Dr. Bruce Maccabee, UFO researcher and optical physicist of the U.S. Navy, with the compilation of a 10-page report. The document bore the title *"Briefing of the U.S. government on a way to solve the UFO problem, as determined by civilian researchers during the last twenty years."*

To discuss the implications of open contact with an extraterrestrial civilization, the Human Potential Foundation—financed by Laurance Rockefeller—organized an international conference in Washington D.C. on May 27–29, 1995, under the motto "When Cosmic Cultures Meet." The host of this conference—at which I had the honor to be one of the speakers—was Washington insider Commander C. B. Scott Jones (U.S. Navy), who was in close contact with Gibbons. Jones hoped to counter the secret fears of the policymakers who believed that the announcement of an alien presence might cause a panic. He intended to counter their fears with the considered opinions of the esteemed experts he had invited, mostly psychologists, anthropologists, sociologists, political scientists and historians. And indeed, representatives of several Washington offices participated in the conference, including John Peterson of the Arlington Institute, a Washington-based think tank with excellent White House connections, Jerome Glenn of the American Council of the United Nations University and Dr. G. Robinson, legal advisor to NASA. Shortly before the conference, Jones informed Gibbons about information he received from a confidential source: "I was told that there are on average 400 monthly uncorrelated space events detected by the U.S. Space Command. These are events that originated from earth and go into space."

Another approach, also originally sponsored by Rockefeller, was launched by the "Center for the Study of Extraterrestrial Intelligence" (CSETI) and its founder, Steven Greer M.D. Its "Project Starlight" has the intention of "presenting the best available evidence and witness testimony in a manner which would constitute a definitive disclosure regarding the reality of the UFO/ET subject. This is to be done in a scientific, nonsensational and hopeful manner, assiduously avoiding an alarmist tone or emphasis."

After a couple of private meetings on the highest level and personal briefings *"for White House staff, a sitting Director of Central Intelligence, senior military leaders, senior United Nations leadership, members of the Senate and House of Representatives, international leaders, and leaders in foreign governments,"* Greer changed his policy. He had to realize *"that this subject was being managed in a way which kept the majority of our constitutional leadership uninformed on the subject. It became clear that we should collect the best evidence and witnesses and provide unmistakable and unambiguous information to these leaders so that they could make a decision on how to proceed. Obviously, unless the leadership was informed, there could be no chance of their disclosing any information to the public, or of even convening an open hearing and inquiry."*

To inform the Washington leadership, CSETI organized "The Washington Briefings," a series of presentations given by 20 firsthand witnesses of UFO encounters and UFO-related projects of the U.S. government. They were chosen from a group of 120 men and women of the highest rank and leading positions inside the industrial/military complex who were willing to testify under oath at a congressional hearing, if one should take place in the future. These briefings, under the chairmanship of Apollo 14 astronaut Edgar Mitchell, were conducted between April 7–11, 1997, in the Westin Hotel in Washington D.C., with a second, smaller session, at the Pentagon. Nearly 30 congressional offices were represented by either members of Congress or of their staff. Also present were VIPs from the executive branch, foreign embassy staff members as well as government scientists and representatives sent to the briefing by two state governors' offices. Another "Project Starlight" Briefing will be held at the United Nations

Headquarters in the not-too-distant future. Whatever may come out of this conference and the following personal communications will make it impossible for the Washingtonians to ignore the UFO subject any longer. The facts have been "put on the table." The time has come to decide how to proceed, how to deal with them.

This book has a similar intention. Its purpose is to reconstruct as thoroughly and realistically as possible, from a contemporary point of view, the true and secret history of the UFO phenomenon and our way of dealing with this completely new situation.

For the appearance of extraterrestrials in terrestrial airspace signals for us the beginning of a new era, the end of our planetary isolation, and has been perhaps the most important occurrence in the last 2,000 years of human history. We are possibly in the same situation as the Aztecs were, hardly 500 years ago, when the first ships of the Spaniards reached their coasts. Whether we will suffer the same cultural paralysis, the same shock, as this powerful Amerindian culture suffered; whether the confrontation with extraterrestrial intelligence will be a curse or a blessing for humanity, depends on how well we are prepared for this event.

An undertaking like this book could never have been accomplished if UFO researchers and experts from all over the world had not given me their support, their documents, their secret files, research reports and photo material. Extensive personal research on 3 continents helped me to round off the picture and fill in the gaps. I am particularly thankful to Natalia Zahradnikova for her wonderful encouragement and inspiration, and Jonannes von Buttlar for the Introduction he has written for this book; to my old friends Colman VonKeviczky, Wendelle Stevens and, in memoriam, Anny Baguhn for their pioneering work. They deserve a place in the "hall of fame" of a cosmic mankind. I thank also Erich von Däniken, for photo material; Bob and Terry Brown and their lovely daughters Heather and Krystal, Giorgio Bongiovanni, Cecilia and Robert O. Dean, Sgt. Anthony Dodd, Timothy Good, Dr. Steven Greer, Cynthia Hind, Antonio Huneeus, Jaime Maussan, Howard and Connie Menger, Detlev Menningmann, Hans Petersen, Roberto Pinotti, Marina Popovich, Fred (in memoriam) and Glenn Steckling, Valerii Uvarov, Karl and Anny Veit of the "German UFO Study Society," as well as Mohammad Ramadan and Michael Geoghegan of the United Nations, who have all recognized that we can meet the challenge of the UFO phenomenon only as one united humanity. My special thanks are also due my publisher John Weber of Marlowe & Company, my agent John White and my translator, Marine Eng. L. Subramanyan (and his two charming grandnieces Lakshmi and Lalitha Sundaram for their untiring typing).

Writing this book was a very intensive project, although a very fascinating one. I hope and believe that it has been worth the effort and that this book will go on its way and fulfill its purpose in the world.

For the encounter with extraterrestrials holds for us the biggest chance that can be offered to us, standing as we are on the threshold of the third millennium. It carries with it the potential of a new Copernican revolution, a redefinition of our position in the universe. Perhaps we must first understand that the earth is really one of millions of inhabited planets in the infinity of space to understand that we are one people, children of this earth, and that we can solve our problems only when we are united. It is only when we throw off our tribal way of thinking, and think of ourselves as human beings and act accordingly, that we can be in a position to accept this great challenge, the dialogue with the universe.

—Michael Hesemann

CHAPTER I

The Year the Ice Was Broken

Rostock, Mecklenburg-Pommern [Pomerania], Germany, August 24, 1990, 8:20 p.m.: first four, then six and finally seven orange spheres appear in the evening sky, flash brilliantly one after the other, and disappear—UFOs— Unidentified Flying Objects. Over a hundred persons observed this occurrence, including Soviet physicists working at the Greifswald nuclear power plant. And what's more, two Russians, a West German married couple on holiday, and five members of a German family from Berlin were able to film this strange squadron with their video cameras, from three different perspectives. And it is exactly this that makes the incident unique.

It happened only five weeks before the reunion of West and East Germany. One of the Russian witnesses, Valerii Vinogradov (45), related:

> I was watching TV, when my wife, who was busy in the kitchen, called out to me, 'Valerii, there's something happening outside. People in the courtyard are all talking about UFOs!'
>
> It was a warm evening and the window was open. You could hear the excited voices of people discussing something. I looked out of the kitchen window and saw a small group of people on the lawn. Another group of teenagers stood in front of the Youth Club on Mendelejew Way. Some of our neighbors were leaning out their windows and looking in the direction of Eldena. But all of them were looking upwards.
>
> There, against a clear twilight sky, I saw a strange sight. A group of seven shining spheres was hanging motionlessly in the heavens, halfway up from the horizon. The spheres were loosely ordered; three were together and the other four were separate . . . the objects flickered a bit . . . I ran to the living room and got my video camera . . . through the viewfinder I could clearly see that they were spheres . . . they shimmered and began to move very slowly.

Gradually they stopped shimmering and then they suddenly disappeared. It looked as if they had dissolved into the sky.

In Vinogradov's videotape one can see two groups of these mysterious objects: five spheres on the left, which finally vanish at a high speed towards the north, and to the right another group, at first difficult to recognize, initially consisting of four, then seven objects. The Russian couple Ludmilla and Nikolai Ivanov, who lived in the same high-rise complex, were able to tape the objects from the second floor. Nikolai (42) was a project engineer at the Greifswald Nuclear Power Plant and his wife Ludmilla (37) was a doctor at the Greifswald Clinic. Their video runs only for a total of seven minutes, but shows the most salient features of the spectacle that lasted for twelve minutes in the sky. According to Nikolai Ivanov,

> The objects were over the Baltic Sea, in a northeast direction. There were two groups of stationary spheres of lights, which seemed to revolve around their own axes. At first the group on the left was clearly discernible, but then it vanished completely and the group on the right became distinctly visible. A few seconds later there was a flash of light where the first group had been and the objects became sharp and clear again. I could see seven separate ball-like lights.

Unfortunately Ivanov's video ends here. The battery in his camera ran down before he could shoot the the rapid departure of the UFO squadron. The most interesting sequence of the tape is the "flash of light." A thorough analysis of the video was carried out by experts in photography working for the international UFO-research group MUFON [Mutual UFO Network], led by the astrophysicist and DASA (German Aerospace Agency) research engineer Illobrand von Ludwiger. The experts came to the conclusion that the flash was caused by the explosion of a missile fired at the objects, either by the Soviet or the East German army.

Was this incident an extraterrestrial inspection of the notorious nuclear power plant at Greifswald? The newspaper *Bild* reported that the incident on the 24th of August was neither rare nor unique: *"For weeks now UFOs have been haunting the Baltic coast. More than 50 thoroughly convinced witnesses have reported this excitedly to the police and army."* The UFOs were seen above Rostock and Usedom. Gerald Schaub, on vacation from Berlin, said, *"They stood there for about three minutes, then moved forward rapidly."* Franz Kliern of Greifswald even photographed *"ships that looked like dishes with a conical structure on top."*

Fifteen tourists staying at the vacation home "Solidarity" were almost panic-stricken. One of them, Renate Grundmann, reported, *"The thing stood there above the waters for a minute. Then it lit up and vanished."* Forty schoolchildren and their teacher watched the objects from a children's hostel at Murkau-auf-Rügen. One of the boys related: *"We noticed that smaller objects rushed towards the group and others flew away from them."* The NVA (East Germany's National People's Army) told my colleague, the UFO researcher Detlef Menningmann from Hamburg, that the objects had not been picked up by radar and naturally denied having shot at them. But they also definitely ruled out all possibilities of military maneuvers by the Soviet Army or the NVA.

The most interesting confirmation of the sighting of August 24, however, came two years later, after I had presented Ivanov's video on Rainer Holbe's SAT-1 TV show "Phantastic Phenomena." It was the first time it appeared on German television. Shortly after the broadcast the couple Irmgard and Ingo Kaiser, living in Sauerland, called and reported *"We filmed that very same phenomenon during our visit to Rügen."* I met the Kaisers at the SAT-1 TV Studio in Cologne while making a film and Mrs. Kaiser related her experience to me on the telephone later.

We had spent our vacation in Sweden in our motor home and were on our way home. We stayed for a day at a small hotel at Lauterbach near Putbus on the east coast of Rügen. In the evening we went to the seafront with our new video camera to film the ferry coming in from the STASI (East German State Security Service) island Vilm. My husband noticed that a lot of people were looking at the sky. There was something there, which looked somewhat like the constellation Orion, but much smaller and brighter. A group of shining objects was hovering silently in the sky. I pointed the camera at them at once and started filming. The formation changed and finally the spheres shot off rapidly away from us and disappeared.

The most interesting point about Kaiser's film is that Lauterbach lies some 19 miles north of Greifswald. Now there were three films from two entirely different points of observation. A further inquiry revealed that whereas the Russian witnesses had seen the objects in a northeasterly direction, for Mrs. Kaiser they were observed "in the direction of the Baltic Sea", i.e. southeast.

Based on this it was possible for the computer experts of MUFON-CES (Mutual UFO Network—Central European Section) to determine the location and size of the objects by triangulation. Here is the result of their analysis:

The objects had stood above a small island, 3 to 5 miles north of Peenemunde, a Soviet military base at which the Germans, led by Wernher von Braun, tested the V-2 rocket during World War II. The first UFO group stood at an altitude of about 15,000 feet, the second group at 16,800 feet, 15 and 16 miles northeast of Greifswald respectively, both distances correct to +/− 650 yards. The objects must have been between 55 and 62 feet in diameter."

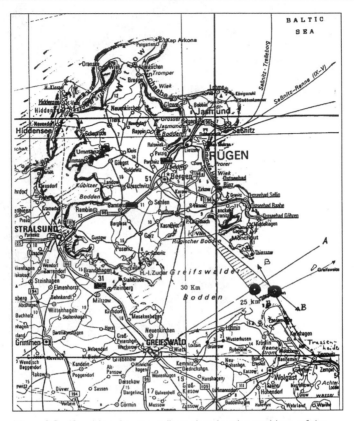

Map of Greifswald and surroundings, showing the positions of the
two UFO formations.

At a UFO Conference in Budapest in November 1993 I informed more
German journalists about the results of our investigations. Following the
press reportage of this information, a fourth witness with a video of the
objects turned up. On December 19, 1993 I met engineer Jürgen
Luchterhand (45) of Berlin in connection with the ORB [Brandenburg
TV] show "Live aus [from] Babelsberg." On August 24, 1990, he had
been on an excursion to the Baltic coast with his family. At the time in
question he was driving at a point some 3 miles south of the Greifswald
power plant, close to the Bodden Bay. With him in the car were his wife
Erna, his son Marc (13), his mother Elisabeth Narat (72) and his stepfa-
ther Veno Narat (60). Said Luchterhand,

> My son saw the lights first, then we saw them too. I wondered what on
> earth they were. We drove to the edge of the road, to where other people
> were also watching them—a group of people on a farm truck, and a moped

rider. At first we didn't think of UFOs at all, but the longer we watched the clearer it became to us that they must be something extraterrestrial. No one on earth can fly as fast as those things did, flitting from one position to another. Once we saw a flash like lightning directly on one of the objects. Each one was between 70 to 100 hundred feet long. Finally they faded out in groups.

Luckily Luchterhand filmed the occurrence from 8:43 p.m. until 9:03 p.m. with his Canon-Camcorder set at 8× zoom—as far as quality goes, his are the best shots of the Greifswald formation.

The evidence did not end there. In answer to an appeal inserted in the paper *Neuesten Nordsee Nachrichten* [*Latest North Sea News*] 17 witnesses from Usedom, Rügen and even as far as Neubrandenburg, reported having seen the objects. As of this point, with 6 videos, 8 photographs (even though rather poor in quality) and hundreds of eyewitnesses, the sighting on the Baltic is the best documented incident in the last 48 years of UFO history.

In spite of all desperate attempts by professional UFO-opponents and "debunkers" to find conventional explanations for the Greifswald formation, the true status of it is still "unidentified." The following is, however, certain:

Unidentified flying objects, large enough to be manned, obviously under intelligent control, carried out maneuvers over the Baltic Sea which no known aircraft is capable of performing. The ability to approach or retreat with rapidity, and abruptly stop, then hover at one spot in close formation for almost a quarter of an hour are not characteristics of airplanes, helicopters, balloons or signal rockets. But despite the wide publicity this case received—as opposed to other UFO sightings in Germany—in the newspapers *Bild* and *Super-Illu* as well as in the Television shows of MDR, ORB, RTL and SAT-1, the authorities failed to take appropriate steps and did not even investigate the incident. The public was too preoccupied with the imminent reunion of Germany to bother about UFOs near Greifswald, no matter how spectacular they might have been. And this sighting was only one high point in a whole series of UFO demonstrations over the European continent during the days of political upheaval between November 1989 and November 1990.

The "great 1989/1990 European wave of UFO sightings" began on November 7, 1989 at Esneux in Belgium, just ten days after the biggest world UFO congress to date, "Dialogue with the Universe," came to an end in Frankfurt. Attended by over 1800 people, that congress, held from October 26–29, was a "preparation for contact with extraterrestrials during the coming decade." A "global invitation" to the UFOnauts was read out— and the year 1990 was declared as "The Year of the UFOs." Almost prophetically!

On that November 7th two Belgian policemen were witnesses to the appearance of a *"large, silent object, which was surrounded by red and green lights, while two extremely bright beams of light were directed down towards the earth.*" But that was only a modest beginning—prelude to one of the most impressive and best documented waves of UFO sightings ever, a wave that made headlines all over the world, after 141 witnesses, including 8 police officers, saw "a huge triangular object," with "*a very bright searchlight at each corner . . . a pulsating light in the middle*" and a "*dome on top with shining windows*," near Eupen, at the border between Belgium and Germany. This happened exactly one month after the closing date of the UFO congress at Frankfurt, on November 29th, 1989, a beautiful, sunny day, late in autumn.

It happened in Lichtenbusch, on the E40, near Aix-la-Chapelle, at the border control point between Belgium and Germany. After the sun set at 4:45 p.m. a glorious starry sky spread over the land; only the western horizon was still lit by the last rays of the sun. The temperature was at about freezing point, the air was still. The border control official J—— sits in his booth as usual, checking passports. Shortly after 5:00 p.m. he notices something very strange. "*A low-flying object with two or three extraordinarily bright searchlights*" glided silently across the border, only about 500 yards away. A helicopter? An airplane? It was far too low and too silent. It seemed to follow the E40, in the direction of Eupen.

It was already dark now. The policemen Hubert von Montigny and Heinrich Nicoll of the Eupen police department were driving on the N68 towards Eynatten. Von Montigny looked at his watch. It was 5:20 p.m., just 20 minutes after their night duty began. As yet they do not know that this will turn out to be the most exciting night shift of their hardly unexciting careers. Suddenly their eyes were drawn almost magnetically to a bright spot of light beside the road. The light was glaring, like the floodlights at a soccer stadium. But there were no athletic facilities in that area, only meadows. And what's more, the light was coming closer and closer to them. When it was only 50 yards away from them it was so bright that "*one could have read a newspaper*," as von Montigny later declared. He rolled down his car window, looked out and saw "*a huge stationary dark platform hovering in the sky*" with "*three big floodlights*" on its bottom, which threw three cones of white light on to the ground below. "*It is at a height of about 400 feet and is absolutely silent*," registered Von Montigny. The policemen drove on slowly and continued their observations. They saw that the object, "the platform," had the shape of a broad-based equilateral triangle, with the corners at the base cut off perpendicular to the base, and that in the middle of the bottom it had a "*sort of red, circularly running light*" which flashed once or twice every second. They estimated its size to be about 80 × 110 feet, about 6 feet high at the edge. The dark triangle moved along, accompanying them at a speed of 30 mph, while they informed their headquarters about the object and asked, "*Are maneuvers being carried out at the moment with new types of aircraft?*" Eupen Tower answered: "*No. But we have a strange spot on our radar screen.*" The object was still unidentified. "*That must be Santa Claus!*" joked the colleague at the police station.

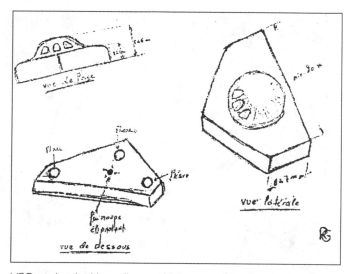

UFO as sketched by policeman Hubert von Montigny.

The two policemen in the car turned off the main road into a side road to see the UFO from another perspective, but it suddenly stopped moving, turned 180 degrees on the spot, and flew off in the opposite direction, towards Eupen. Surprised by this move, the policemen drove on to the "High Street," the ring road of Eupen. They saw the craft flying along the N68 towards Eupen, where a row of people were watching it, amongst them a truck driver, an engineer from Eupen, a caretaker, a married couple and a brigadier of the forestry department. Von Montigny and his companion Nicoll decide to call the police station again, and talk to the same colleague who had made fun of them only 20 minutes before with his "Santa Claus" joke. *"He'll have to believe us when he sees it himself!"* They challenge him, "Go and look out of the window, sir!" And in fact the police officer C—— saw the object motionless and shining, when suddenly it shot off into the heavens at an angle.

Von Montigny and Nicoll took up the chase and drove on in the direction into which the UFO had vanished. A little before Membach they saw it again, flying towards the Gileppe Dam and finally stopping at a position to the left of an illuminated tower above the reservoir. It was now about 2 to 3 miles away, but could be seen clearly. The policemen stopped their car and got out, and a few minutes later witnessed a strange spectacle. The mysterious craft sent out rays, two thin reddish beams that shot out simultaneously in opposite directions and left behind at each end a bright red ball. But soon after that the "fireballs" returned to the "mother ship" and revolved around it for a number of minutes, before the whole process repeated itself.

"The rays are very long," reported von Montigny to the station, *"about*

The UFO above Gileppe Dam.

three-quarters of a mile long. They are like harpoons on a line, which divers pull back." Nicoll, on the other hand, is reminded of balls attached by rubber bands to a bat, which are hit off by the bat but return to it.

A second triangular UFO appeared suddenly at 6:45 p.m., shooting up from behind a coniferous forest as if catapulted, and disappeared into the sky. The policemen could clearly make out a dome with rectangular *"windows, lit up from inside,"* on a *"not very thick plate."* The first object remained in its position above the reservoir until 7:23 p.m., then started moving slowly in the direction of Spa. That was the end of the show, which had lasted for more than two hours. Fascinated and out of words, the gendarmes went back to their car and returned to their normal duties.

What they did not know at this time is that while they were watching the strange happenings at the Gileppe dam, six other colleagues had seen the UFO demonstration from another spot. Policemen N—— and P——, both driving in a patrol car on the Route de Charlemagne towards Henri-Chapelle and Maison Blanche, saw a red ball shooting down vertically from the center of the three floodlights on the object and then abruptly, the objects raced off horizontally.

When the papers wrote about the incident at Eupen, 140 witnesses reported having seen the UFO. Besides that, the series of sightings continued. Almost every day, somewhere or other in the country, but mostly in the northeast part of Belgium, the mysterious triangle was seen. On December 5, it was once more detected by radar. The two F-16 interceptor fighters sent out by the Belgian Air Force returned without having seen anything in the area denoted. During the night of December 11, between 5:35 p.m. and

3:00 a.m., UFOs were seen at 24 places in the country.

In February 1990 an umpire had to stop a soccer game at Spa when a gigantic spaceship flew across the field at a very low altitude. It was reported in the papers that a married couple in Charleroi had watched a bluish disc appearing in their garden, after which the top power cable on the telephone pole burned out. While skeptical voices were loud in suggesting that the sighted objects could be early warning radar (AWACS—Airborne Warning and Control System), or perhaps even the American stealth bomber or an even more secret wonder weapon of the "Big Brother" across the Atlantic, the Belgian Defense Minister Guy Come stated: *"Every possibility of their being military aircraft has been thoroughly investigated by us and must be definitely ruled out."*

In fact this statement is confirmed by an internal status report of the DIA (Defense Intelligence Agency), an intelligence service of the U.S. Department of Defense. This report was officially handed over on May 1, 1991, to my friend Sgt. Cifford Stone. Copies of this report of March 1990, according to its distribution list, were sent also to the White House, the U.S. Defense Department, the State Department, the General Staff in Washington, the Commander of the U.S. Air Force, the CIA, NATO headquarters SHAPE in Brussels, the Commanders of the U.S. Navy and Air Force in Europe, as well as the Intelligence Center of the U.S. Forces in Heidelberg and the General Intelligence Center at Vaihingen near Stuttgart.

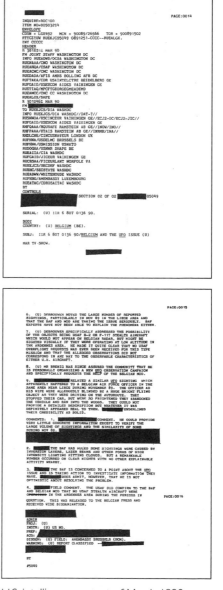

U.S. intelligence report of March 1990, about the incidents in Belgium.

This report says: *"The BAF and MOD are taking the issue seriously . . . The BAF has ruled some sightings were caused by inversion layers, laser beams and other forms of high intensity lighting hitting clouds. But a remarkable number occurred on clear nights with no other explainable activity nearby. The BAF is concerned to a point about the UFO issue and is taking action to investigate information they have. The USAF did confirm to the BAF and Belgian MOD that no USAF stealth aircraft were in the Ardennes area during the periods in question. This was released to the Belgian Press and received wide dissemination."*

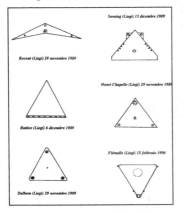

The various shapes of the UFOs seen over Belgium.

The suggestion of a group of debunkers, that the huge triangles were "Ultralight planes"—motorized kites—was not welcomed by the Belgian Air Force. Major Lambrecht declared in an official report, that after a thorough investigation *"not only the presence or test flights of B2 or F117 (stealth bombers) but also RPV (Remote Piloted Vehicles), ULM (Ultralight Machines) and AWACS (Airborne Warning and Control Systems) in Belgian air space at the time of the sightings could be ruled out."*

After all, it was always the military that—at least outwardly—denied the presence of UFOs and only too eagerly availed themselves of "debunker explanations." For it is much simpler to believe that a few civilians have mistaken ultralight aircraft for UFOs, than to confront the public with the presence in the country of an unknown power whose intentions are also unknown.

But in fact, what happened was something totally unexpected: the army approached the UFO researchers and sought their help in solving the riddle. What a few years ago had been called "glasnost" in the Soviet Union was now practiced in a NATO member country, and in fact in the matter of UFOs, i.e., a new openness, an honest and cooperative attempt to discover the truth.

And the UFO researchers who were chosen for the task were not the radical UFO opponents who were, during the era of secrecy regarding UFOs, always sent to the front lines as "useful idiots" to make the public believe that the government had the sky and the situation fully under control. No, this time it was a group of really serious UFO researchers, the privately founded "Belgian Society for the Study of Space Phenomena" [SOBEPS: Societé Belgique des Études des Phenomènes Spatiales], with headquarters in Brussels. To this society belong such personalities as Prof. Leon Brenig, a nonlinear dynamics physicist at the Free University of Brussels and Prof. August Meesen, physicist at the Catholic University of Louvain.

The Belgian Police Department ordered all police stations on December 12, 1989 to inform SOBEPS henceforth about all UFO sightings reported. After that, on December 18, there was an initial meeting between the SOBEPS members and Maj. Stas and Col. De Brouwer of the Defense Ministry. Following that, SOBEPS representatives were invited by the General Staff of the Air Force on January 10, 1990 to visit the NATO radar station at Glons. And on January 21, 1990 it became fully official: *"It is my pleasure to inform you that the Air Force is ready to do everything within its means to cooperate with you in your research work,"* announced André Bastien, personal adviser to the defense minister Guy Come, in writing to Michel Bougard, the president of SOBEPS. *"For the purposes of your investigations you are, therefore, authorized to contact the operating section of the Air Force staff."* With that the ice was broken. The UFO researchers had been presented with opportunities they had never even dared to dream of until then. And no later than two months after that they were able to gather the first fruits of the new policy of openness.

CHAPTER 2

Not a Terrestrial Craft

On Friday, March 30, 1990, at Ramilies near Wavre, Belgium, Policeman Renkin and his wife invited Mr. and Mrs. I—— to stop by for a casual visit in the evening. Mrs. Renkin, busy in the kitchen making snacks for the occasion, looked out of the window and saw something strange. A ball of light, three times as big as the biggest star, was floating in the sky over Ramilies, changing color continually between white, yellow, green, blue and red. Naturally, she had read about the UFO sightings in Belgium in the papers and her husband had also told her about the experiences of his colleagues in the police force. Was this one of those UFOs? She went to the living room and told her husband, *"Darling, have a look. There's something funny in the sky. I think it's one of those UFOs."* Renkin went to the window, pushed the curtain aside and saw it, too. *"I have to have a closer look at it,"* he said, and they went out together to see it better. It was making abrupt sideward jumps and also was flying in circles now and then. *"Look how quickly it moves from side to side, from left to right and back,"* said Renkin. *"That's definitely no plane!"* Slowly the ball of light in the west moved, then hovered above the townships of Perwez and Aische-en-Refail. It turned red and moved in the direction of Gembloux.

Renkin ran back into his flat to call the air force base at Beauvechain. *"Can you see it on the radar?"* They couldn't, because their radar station was closed during weekends, but they said they would ask the military space control station at Glons. *"Call me back after a few minutes,"* said Renkin, and ran out again to watch the object. Too impatient to wait for a call he ran back to the phone and rang up Beauvechain, where he was connected to the base at Glons. *"We are sending out two planes to investigate,"* said the officer on duty, Lt. Van Hauwermeiren. The time now was 11:05 p.m.

But before that, Lt. Van Hauwermeiren had called the police station at

Wavre. *"Send somebody out to check Renkin's statement."* At 11:08 p.m. Vossem, chief of police who is also coordinating the movements of patrol cars this evening, orders policemen Capt. Pinson and MDL Jamotte to go to meet Renkin. They drive over to the Renkins', and together with them they see two more objects appear, less bright, which form an equilateral triangle with the first, and also vary their colors all the time. A plane carrying passengers flies above the objects. The lights turn bright red and spring sidewards. At 11:25 p.m. Capt. Pinson decides to tell all patrolling cars to look for and observe the bodies in the sky. Patrolman Baijot and two colleagues from Perwez, MDL Chavagne and MDL Heyne, near Jauchelette, and two more policemen from Orp-Jauche, report seeing the phenomenon. At the same time the radar screen at Glons registers an unidentifiable object flying at the extremely low speed of 18 mph near Beauvechain towards the west. Soon dozens of reports come in from police and civilians who could see the mysterious objects over the Brabant district, amongst others from Brussels, Cauchelette, Judoigne and Throrembaisles-Beguines.

About a quarter of an hour later Renkin and the other policemen—at this point ten in number—saw the sudden appearance of three balls of light, which flew towards the first group and took up position near it. From time to time the UFOs sent out flashes of bright light. At 11:45 p.m. a seventh and then an eighth ball appeared. The radar screens at both Glons and the TCC/RP Radar Site at Semmerzake detected the new objects as well. When that happened, the conditions required for active military action were fulfilled. At 11:56 p.m. the space control at Glons gave starting orders to the 1st Fighter Squadron.

At 12:05 a.m. two F-16 interceptor fighters, the fastest fighting planes of NATO, thundered through the sky over Belgium. What the pilots saw can be read from an official report about the incident, written by Air Force Maj. P. Lambrecht of the general staff of the Belgian Air Force in Brussels. A copy of this report was sent to SOBEPS. It contains a detailed chronology of the events that occurred on the night of March 30, 1990, together with a number of enclosures, including the eyewitness reports of the policemen mentioned, and maps of the relevant areas.

According to the report, the fighter pilots had radar contact on a few occasions with the targets that the CRC Radar Site in Glons told them to find. The pilots were even able to activate the automatic pursuit system three times, but this led each time to a drastic change in the behavior of the objects. At 12:13 a.m. the first UFO was 7 miles ahead of one of the pilots, at a height of 9,000 feet, flying at a speed of about 150 knots. But as soon as the auto-pursuit system was switched on, the object accelerated within seconds to a speed of 970 knots and flew away from the plane. At the same time it dropped to a height of 5,000 feet, then shot up to 11,000 feet, only to sink immediately to almost ground level. With that the fighter was outmaneuverd, for at that low level radar contact breaks off. At 12:30 a.m. the object was spotted again, flying at 5,000 feet altitude and 740 knots speed. The automatic pursuit system was again activated and held contact for six second after which the radar was disturbed by jamming. This cat and mouse game repeated itself a few times until 1:00 a.m., when the objects vanished completely. The frustrated fighter pilots returned to the base with resignation.

Is there a conventional explanation for the unbelievable flying maneuvers of the UFOs? The official air force report says, "No!"

> The . . . speeds measured and the changes in altitude registered eliminate the hypothesis that aircraft had been mistaken for something else. The slow movements shown during other phases are also not characteristic of airplanes . . . The hypothesis that an optical illusion had been at play, in connection with a planet or a meteorological phenomenon, is in contradiction to the radar observations. This applies particularly to the flights at 10,000 feet and the overall formation of the objects. The geometric positioning suggests a planned maneurve. The theory of phenomena caused by holographic projections into the sky is also not tenable, for holograms cannot be picked up by radar, and laser projections are visible on the screen only when a reflecting element, such as a cloud, exists. During this particular night the sky was cloudless . . .

The possibility of "radar angels," phantoms on the radar screen seen occasionally and caused by temperature inversions, are expressly ruled out in the report. *"At the time in question no meterologically relevant inverted weather conditions prevailed anywhere in Belgium."*

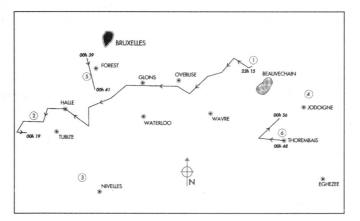

(T) Course of flight of the UFOs during the night of March 30/31, 1990, as reconstructed by the Belgian Air Force.

Observers on the ground had also watched the chase. At 12:30 a.m. five policemen driving on the N29 towards Namur saw a "flickering light," then two aircraft following it. The "light" was obviously evading the pursuit. Capt. Pinson at Ramilies saw the two fighters flying past "the big equilateral triangle" three times and "following their third passage" they started to circle around it, resulting in the objects taking off with incredible rapidity.

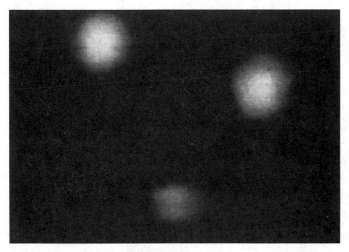

Still shot from the Alfarano video film.

At 1:18 a.m., however, according to Capt. Pinson, long after the F-16s had returned home four objects reappeared, again in formation. Finally, at 2:00 a.m., a further witness, Marcel Alfarano, filmed three balls of light over Brussels, with a fourth pulsating light in the middle; in two sequences, two brightly flashing lights are outside the triangle. These shots also clearly defy all conventional explanations.

What astonished Maj. Lambrecht most, according to his report, was the fact that *"although the objects broke through the sound barrier on more than one occasion, no shock wave was ever felt or a 'bang' heard. There is no explanation for that."* But even though he stopped short at classifying the objects as "unidentified," Maj. Gen. Charles De Brouwer did go a step further.

On June 22, 1990, he met with the French journalist Marie-Therese de Brosses of the renowned newspaper *Paris Match*, turned on the TV and played a video recording, the "black box" recording of the radar of one of the two interceptor planes, which clearly showed the evading tactics and acceleration of the UFOs. *"There is no logical explanation for their movements,"* declared De Brouwer. *"The top speed for F-16s is 700 knots at that low altitude, owing to the air density; if exceeded, there is danger of the turbines exploding. It just shook off our F-16s. And when it changed altitude and finally dove, it went off our radar."* This maneuver is far beyond the capacity of our planes. *"No machine is capable of flying at 1100 mph at that low height and crossing the sound barrier without a bang."* But there was one more important factor, which convinced Maj. Gen. De Brouwer that the objects his pilots pursued that night could not have been of earthly origin. *"It accelerated within one second from 183 mph to 1130 mph and dove from 10,000 feet to 5,500 feet. That represents an acceleration of 40 Gs."* (G stands for the gravitational force of the earth, 32 ft/s².) *"40 Gs would mean*

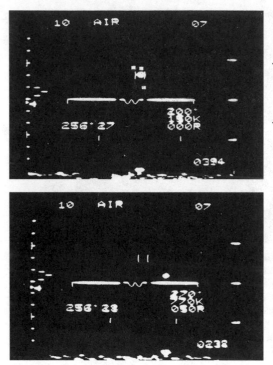

Pictures of the radar screen of the F-16, released officially by the Belgian Air Force, showing the position of the UFO (diamond-shaped spot) and the interceptor (-w-).

death for any human occupant of the vessel. The maximum that a fighter can tolerate is 8 Gs. At present there is no man-made machine, neither airplane nor other flying craft, that is capable of such a performance."

The first result of this unbelievable occurrence in the Belgian skies was a crisis meeting of the Ministries of Defense, Interior Affairs and Transport. It was decided that the public should be informed about the incident and called upon to help follow the UFOs. In cooperation with SOBEPS a "national UFO hunt" was organized during the Easter holidays. Between Good Friday (April 13, 1990) and Easter Tuesday (April 17, 1990) thousands of Belgians were on the watch: scientists with the most modern measuring instruments, magnetic-field detectors, telescopes, theodolites, infra-red and video cameras; laymen with telescopes and camcorders. SOBEPS set up 20 observation posts between Brussels and the German border; the state and the military police had a special UFO telephone, and the Royal Belgian Air Force kept two fighter planes ready for action around the clock, and even put the radar station at Glons at the service of the UFO seekers. But the apparently intelligent UFO crews seem to have been put off by the to-do and responded with polite aloofness. It was only towards the beginning of October that they let themselves be seen again with any frequency.

A year later SOBEPS published its 700-page report "UFO Wave over Belgium," the result of the evaluation of over 2,000 reports received by SOBEPS, in addition to dozens of photographs and films, which doubtlessly indicated that unknown and apparently non-terrestrial flying craft did indeed maneuver above that NATO country. In the epilogue Maj. Gen. De Brouwer confesses:

The Air Force has in any case come to the conclusion that a certain number of anomalous phenomena . . . [and] unauthorized flying exercises have taken place in Belgian air space.

Their military evaluation produced, however,

until now no evidence of aggressive behavior . . . one can, therefore, assume that no concrete threat arises from the maneuvers . . . The day will certainly come when we will be able to deal with this phenomena by means of highly developed detecting and recording devices, which will leave no more doubts as to their [the UFOs] origin. With that the veil that surrounds the mystery could possibly be lifted to a certain extent. It still remains a mystery. But it exists, and is real. That alone is an important conclusion.

Is the breakthrough in Belgium a unique instance? Obviously not. During the same period that the UFOs were active over Belgium, in Russia, too, the existence of unknown, non-terrestrial flying objects was officially confirmed—and by a person no less important than the Chief of Staff of the Soviet Air Defense Forces, Lt. General Igor Maltsev. The incident, which was to lead to the recognition of UFOs as such by a big power, occurred only a few days before the incidents in Belgium, on March 21, 1990, in the Sagorsk area, 30 miles northeast of Moscow, shortly after 9:00 p.m.

It was a quiet night and Maj. Stroynetski, officer on duty at the Sagorsk army base was preparing himself for an uneventful nightshift. But the peaceful silence of the oncoming night was rudely shattered by the shrill call of the telephone.

Against his will and rather sluggishly he reached out for the receiver and

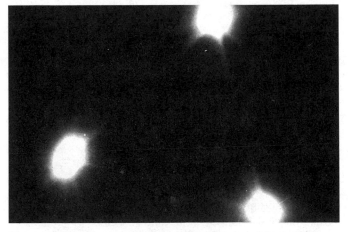

Picture of triangular UFO above Jaroslawl, Russia, in March 1990, taken by Y. Kapustin.

announced himself with a grim "Da!" [Yes]. At the other end of the line there was an excited voice. "There is a huge disc hovering over the highway to Jaroslawl, surrounded by colored lights!" "One of those UFOs again," said Stroynetski to himself. For days now citizens, civilians and army people had been calling Sagorsk base to report mysterious objects in the sky, which most of them were seeing on their way home from work. Sometimes they were pineapple-like bodies with lightly glowing "scales" on the outside and a sort of three-legged landing gear, sometimes discs with a clearly visible dome in the middle, about 35 to 45 feet in diameter. The dome was always red and had two dark "windows," and the rim of the disc had a number of small lamps. Another type resembled the Belgian UFOs: huge triangles with white lights on the sides and a pulsating red light in the middle. Because the sightings repeated themselves almost daily over the Jaroslawl highway, for days hundreds of spectators were waiting in the evening with binoculars and cameras to watch and photograph the UFOs.

A down-to-earth person like Maj. Stroynetzki would have considered the whole UFO fuss to be mass hysteria, if some of his best colleagues had not seen the mysterious objects themselves. And now they were there again, and during his watch! A second witness called, then a third and finally an officer belonging to the base. They all described the object in the same manner. Stroynetzki had no choice but to take action. He called the control tower of the air force. *"There are people calling again now, to report one of those UFOs. Have you picked it up on radar?"* Yes, they had, it is real. *"Then send a couple of fighters out. We'll get them!"*

At 9:58 p.m. the pilots of two MIG-29 fighter planes received orders to start. Within a few minutes the huge olive-green birds were out, racing against the stars, mission unknown. At 10:03 p.m. they received instructions: "There is an unidentified object at an altitude of 6,000 feet. Get on its tracks and find out its origin. Roger." Then, at 10:05 p.m. the object was in view of the pilots. *"Have two flashing lights at 1:30 position before me,"* announces one of the pilots, Lt. Col. A. A. Semenchenko. *"Waiting for further orders."* *"Order him to land,"* answers the tower. At that very moment the object dropped to a height of 3,000 feet and changed its direction of flight. Semenchenko tried in vain to contact the object over the radio. Then he saw with astonishment its incredible maneuver on the radar: from a distance of 12 miles from the MIG-29 the object "jumped" in less than a minute over a stretch of about 60 miles. This meant that it must have attained a speed of over 3,700 mph. For a moment Semenchenko's heart stood still. He had never seen anything like it before. Obviously the strange craft was equipped with a technology far in advance of anything comparable on earth. He had to catch up with it again. "Dive at it in a steep curve," instructed the tower. He did so and approached the UFO, which was now almost stationary, and got as close as 1,500 feet from it. Now he was able to see details, two blinking lights, a dark silhouette against the background of the city lights below. That was enough for the tower. *"Return at once to the base,"* ordered the air traffic controller. The MIG landed at the base a few minutes later.

Naturally the incident was thoroughly investigated by the Soviet Air Defense Forces, and over a hundred military personnel who had observed the UFOs were interviewed. The flight route was reconstructed on a map: an S-curve over the towns of Pereslavl, Zalesky, Novoselya, Sagorsk, Yakovlevo, Ploshevo, Dubki, Kablukovo, Fruzino and Kirsatch. The complete investigation report, enhanced with sketches and photographs, was sent directly to the Chief of Staff, Lt. Gen. Igor Maltsev. That was the usual procedure in cases of such gravity, and we would perhaps never have learned the details of the case if Maltsev had not—either on his own or acting on orders—taken a very unusual step: he informed the press. On April 18, the four-star general invited a reporter from *Rabochaya Tribuna*, the newspaper of the labor union, to his office at the Ministry of Defense in Moscow, gave him a copy of the report and made a declaration.

We observed a disc-shaped object with a diameter of 300 to 600 feet. It had two pulsating lights on the sides when it flew horizontally. During vertical movements the object rotated on its axis. It was capable of flying in S-curves vertically as well as horizontally. It hovered over the ground, then shot off at a speed higher than two or three times that of modern fighter planes. All witnesses agree that with increasing speed the lights blinked faster. The object moved at altitudes between 3,000 and 21,000 feet, its movements were silent and characterized by an incredible maneuverability. It looked as if the law of inertia of mass did not apply to it at all. In other words, they must have overcome the gravitational force of the earth. At present there are no earthly machines capable of performing such feats. Skeptics and believers both can take this as an official confirmation of the existence of UFOs. We can only hope that this open acknowledgment will put an end to the enormous speculation about this phenomenon and affirm beyond all doubt their presence. We now have good reasons to say that sightings of UFOs are not the result of hallucinations, optical illusions or mass hysteria. They were detected by radar, and photographs of the objects have been scrutinized by experts.

The *Rabochaya Tribune* of April 19, 1990 recommended that readers *"read these lines carefully . . . We hope that scientists will now take up the matter and examine the facts systematically. It could be the first step towards solving the mystery."*

That Maltsev was not alone in his opinion was revealed a few months later, when the Deputy Minister of Defense and Supreme Commander of the Soviet Air Force, Maltev's immediate boss Gen. Ivan Tretyak, was interviewed by the magazine *Literaturnaja Gazeta*. During this interview, published in the November issue of the magazine, Tretyak not only confirmed Maltev's declaration, but also revealed further details.

During a fairly long period, from 8:00 p.m. until 11:30 p.m. two pulsating lights were seen in the sky, moving at a fixed distance from each other. But it was not an airplane. We have eyewitness reports and photographs. Some of the observers were even of the opinion that the speed of the object influenced the frequency of pulsation of the lights.

Although the object was photographed and picked up by ground radar, it did not appear on the radar on board the interceptor planes. The board radar, Tretyak exlained, normally registers three signals: an optical signal, a thermic signal and the radar echo. But only the last appears on the screen. Whereas the UFO of March 21, 1990, gave out an optical and a thermic signal, it did not reflect radar signals. *"Obviously it had characteristics like the American stealth bomber, using shape and material which have an extremely low radar profile. That's what the American stealth program achieved."* He then made a remark that invites interpretation. *"I must add that the steps we took and are taking as an answer to that program will also help to solve the mystery of the UFOs."* Was he hinting that the Americans developed their stealth technique only after a thorough study of UFOs?

Asked why he had not given orders to shoot down the UFOs—after all, his predecessor resigned for not having prevented the amateur German pilot Mathias Rust from landing on the Red Square—Gen. Tretjak answered, *"It would have been stupid to start an unprovoked attack against an object, which probably had excellent and superior means of retaliation."* And if it had turned out *"that at least some of the UFOs are the products of a highly organized intelligence from a civilization developed far beyond ours . . . any martial action taken against these objects and their crew before we knew their intentions, would have had disastrous consequences."* Gen. Yevgeniy Tarosev, chairman of the scientific and technical advisory board of the Commonwealth of Independent States (CIS), took the same stand in a full-page article in the union newspaper *Trud* on August 22, 1992. Tarosev too affirmed that *"the Air Force detected UFOs and sent out fighter planes to intercept them"* and that there was *"information still kept secret about the interaction between the pilots and the UFOs . . . the reality of the UFOs is unquestionable, although their physical construction is still a mystery."* So far no instance of "definite hostility" on the part of the UFOs had been observed and, therefore, the Air Force pilots had been instructed to deal with the UFOs *"in a peaceful manner."*

We do not know what significant effect this "UFO glasnost" on the part of the Soviets had on the supreme commanders of the western military forces. But this much is certain: something must have happened in 1990 which brought a wind of change. Suddenly the UFO theme became an accepted subject in society. *"We are living in a period which signals the beginning of the era of openness,"* said the French professor of physics Jean-Pierre Petit in the prestigous paper *Paris Match*. *"The Berlin Wall came down first, and now it looks as if the wall of silence about UFOs is crumbling down. We are apparently entering a new phase regarding UFOs. The time of selling and swindling is over. At last the real scientists are coming on to the floor."* Prof. Petit is Director of the National Research Centre

CNRS (Centre National des Recherches Spatiales) and is a leading scientist of the country. His words mean something.

It was also the conviction of Elio di Rupo, the Belgian delegate to the European Parliament that it was indeed time to take up the case of UFOs anew. On the November 26, 1990, addressing the Parliament, he called for the *"establishment of a European center for the observation of UFOs."* Di Rupo, who had been Minister of Education and Arts of the Belgian province of Wallonia, stayed in contact with SOBEPS during the Belgian UFO wave and kept himself regularly informed about the latest developments in the field of UFO research. He supported the UFO researchers when they appealed to the European Parliament to finance the acquisition of a high-tech mobile unit, which could, with a crew of highly qualified scientists, be sent immediately to places in Europe from which unusual UFO acivities were reported. Details of this project were worked out by Prof. Brenig of Brussels University and outlined to the press in March. The cost of this monitoring unit was estimated at about $320,000. Foreseen as part of the equipment of the unit were very high-resolution cameras, radiospectrometers, light amplifiers and infra-red detectors. But even before this request was presented, something happened that gave the UFO sightings a truly European dimension, for suddenly the entire western part of the continent was drawn into the wave of sightings.

On November 5, 1990, exactly from 7:03 until 7:05 p.m., thousands of people from England to Germany, and Denmark to Spain, watched a squadron of glowing objects racing through the heavens. It was described later as the reentry of the remnants of the 3rd stage of a Soviet "Proton SL 12" carrier rocket, which had early in September put the communication satellite "Gorizont 21" into spatial orbit. But not all eyewitness reports can be explained by the reentry. Triangular UFOs, like the ones previously sighted over Belgium, appeared all over Europe at the same time and shortly after as well.

That they were not fragments of the rocket mistaken for UFOs is proved not only by the duration of observation—up to 5 minutes, whereas the reentry lasted for only 2 minutes—but also by the direction in which they flew. Instead of flying from southwest to northeast like the reentering rocket fragments, they often flew in a rather opposite direction, east to west. Among the witnesses were a number of airline pilots, including a British flight captain who saw 4 triangular UFOs in formation above the Ardennes. French news agencies reported that *"a large, shining metallic structure,"* shaped like a rhombus, with *"orange, yellow and green lights placed in a triangle,"* crossed the sky from Alsace in the northeast to Nantes at the Loire estuary in the south-

Press headline about the European UFO wave of November 5, 1990.

west. Pilots said the objects moved parallel to the ground; the Orly airport, Paris, registered *"a shiny object,"* and army pilots, according to statements made by the French ministry of defense, observed *"an unidentifiable shiny object."* After a careful investigation of the incidents, experts of the French National Space Research Center CNES (Centre National des Ètudes Spatiales, or National Center for Space Studies) in Toulouse came to the conclusion that they were *"self-propelled objects,"* which flew across France parallel to the reentering rocket fragments, but in the opposite direction.

At the police stations in north Bavaria and at the air traffic control station at Nuremberg the telephone lines were running hot. In England, following the UFO report of a flight captain of British Airways, a formation of "Tornado" jet fighters of the Royal Air Force was sent up. The pilots saw nine lights flying in towards them as if to attack them. But at the last minute they shot off over the formation, *"at almost supersonic speed."* Even three hours after the reentry, at 10:00 p.m., the pilot of an RAF "Phantom" jet flying over Rheindalen in Germany reported seeing UFOs in a "finger" formation. At the same time two Tornados over the North Sea detected two *"large, round objects, each equipped with five blue and a number of red lights,"* which at first raced towards them but when at a short distance in front of them, turned off and disappeared towards the North.

The incidents of November 5, 1990, convinced Di Rupo that it was time to act. On November 26, 1990, he handed over a petition to the president of the European Parliament, in accordance with Article 63 of the rules of that Parliament, asking for the following resolution to be passed:

The European Parliament

A. Considering that for many years now citizens claim having seen inexplicable phenomena in the skies above a number of European states;

B. Considering that during the last months reliable persons, scientists as well as military personnel, were witnesses of inexplicable phenomena, which were brought into association with UFOs (Unidentified Flying Objects);

C. Considering the large number of eyewitness accounts relating to the night of November 5, 1990;

D. Considering that a section of the population is disturbed about the frequency of these phenomena;

1. Calls for the formation of a commission to establish within a short period a European center for the observation of UFOs;

2. Proposes that this center should collect all reports of sightings made by citizens as well as military and scientific institutions and organize observation campaigns;

Anlage

Entschließungsantrag (B3-1990/90)
eingereicht gemäß Artikel 63 der Geschäftsordnung
von Herrn DI RUPO
zur Schaffung eines europäischen Beobachtungszentrums für "UFOS"

Das Europäische Parlament,

A. in der Erwägung, daß Bürger seit mehreren Jahren behaupten, unerklärliche Phänomene am Himmel über mehreren europäischen Staaten beobachtet zu haben,

B. in der Erwägung, daß in den letzten Monaten glaubwürdige Personen, Wissenschaftler und Militärangehörige ebenfalls Zeugen unerklärlicher Phänomene wurden, die mit "UFOS" (unbekannten fliegenden Objekten) in Verbindung gebracht werden,

C. in der Erwägung der großen Zahl von Zeugenaussagen aus mehreren Ländern der Europäischen Gemeinschaft, die sich auf die Nacht vom 5. auf den 6. November 1990 beziehen,

D. in der Erwägung, daß ein Teil der Bevölkerung über die Häufigkeit dieser Phänomene beunruhigt ist,

1. fordert die Kommission auf, innerhalb kurzer Zeit ein "Europäisches Zentrum für die Beobachtung von "UFOS" einzurichten;

2. schlägt vor, daß dieses Europäische Zentrum für die Beobachtung von "UFOS" alle einzelnen von den europäischen Bürgern und den (militärischen und wissenschaftlichen) Instituten gemeldeten Beobachtungen sammelt und wissenschaftliche Beobachtungskampagnen veranstaltet;

3. schlägt vor, daß dieses Zentrum von der Kommission sowie von einem ständigen Ausschuß aus Sachverständigen der zwölf Mitgliedstaaten verwaltet wird;

DOC-DE\PR\233233   - 13 -   PE 202.202/rev./Anl.

The di Rupo petition.

3. Proposes that this center be administered by the said commission as well as by a standing committee of experts from the 12 member states.

On January 25, 1991, the president of the European Parliament forwarded the petition to the Commission for Energy, Research and Technology (CERT) of the European Community. They decided, after a meeting on January 29, 1991, to compile a report, and appointed Prof. Tullio Regge, member of the Italian Socialist Party of Europe, to present the report. During five sessions which took place between January 20, 1992, and February 15, 1993, Prof. Regge made interim reports. From a statement made by him in an interview with the Italian magazine *Phenomena*, as well as his choice of assistants, we can see what conclusions he had come to: *"Thirty-nine percent of the UFO cases cannot be explained satisfactorily in a scientific manner."* He therefore called upon the European Parliament *"to exercise its political responsibility and inform the public about this important matter."* One of the persons whom Prof. Regge invited to assist him in compiling his report was Jean-Jaques Valesco, an engineer of SEPRA (Societé pour l'Évaluation des Phenomènes des Retour Atmospherique), which is subordinate to the CNES. Speaking at a UFO congress, organized by the Minister of Transport of the Republic of San Marino—the oldest republic on Earth—in April 1993, Velasco declared, *"It was requested that SEPRA should submit a dossier to the European Community, containing a solved, and an unsolved UFO case to demonstrate our methods."* In 1988 SEPRA took over GEPAN (Groupe d'Étude des Phenomènes Aériens Non-indentifiés), the CNES department established in 1977 for the sole purpose of observing UFOs. Although SEPRA's main activity is to follow reentries of satellites, etc. into the earth's atmosphere, it now also carried out the activities of GEPAN.

This is further guaranteed by the fact that Velasco was the last director of GEPAN. The best known and most startling "unsolved case" in the history of GEPAN occurred on January 8, 1981, in Trans-en-Provence in the south of France. It is perhaps one of the best documented and most intensively investigated cases of a UFO landing in the world. The traces of a landing, which a small disc-like UFO left in the garden of the farmer Renato Nicolai, were examined by the police and GEPAN within 48 hours. Prof. Bounias of the National Institute for Agricultural Research analyzed ground and plant samples. The result: *"Apparently an unusual and extensive occurrence took place, which heated up the ground to 300–600 degrees Celsius and probably left behind traces of substances like phosphates and zinc,"* wrote Velasco in his closing report. Prof. Bounias discovered significant biological and biochemical changes in the lucerne plants analyzed, such as a marked depletion of chlorophyll, according to the officially released "Technical Report No. 16: Analysis of a Trace." The Trans-en-Provence incident thus remained unexplained, as did a second case, the landing of a small metallic disc on October 21, 1982, at Amarante. Was SEPRA in a position to fulfill the requirements of Di Ripo's proposal? *"I believe that it would be better if the European Space Agency ESA itself took up the responsibility of establishing a UFO research center,"* declared Velasco on the San Marino Congress. *"SEPRA does not possess the right structure and it is difficult to impose the French model on the other European countries."* On October 20, 1993, Prof. Regge presented his preliminary *"draft of a report regarding the proposal to set up a European center for the observation of UFOs"* to the CERT commission. The draft had five pages, and was more or less a summary of what had been discussed during the previous sessions. In any case, he recommended:

 . . . It could . . . be useful to etablish a center to collect and coordinate information about UFOs. First of all it could counteract the stream of uninvestigated rumors, which upset the public . . . The center could make use of existing organizations and take the help of not only technical and scientific experts, but also of psychologists, in evaluating realistically and objectively the numerous eyewitness accounts relating to the matter.

EUROPÄISCHES PARLAMENT

AUSSCHUSS FÜR ENERGIE, FORSCHUNG UND TECHNOLOGIE

17. August 1993

ENTWURF EINES BERICHTS

über den Vorschlag zur Schaffung eines Europäischen Beobachtungszentrums für "UFOS" (B3-1990/90)

Berichterstatter: Herr Tullio REGGE

DOC-DE\PR\233233   PE 202.202/rev.

Draft Resolution and report by Professor Tullio Regge, dated August 17, 1993.

But Regge's report, scheduled to be presented finally on January 19, 1994, was not laid before the European Parliament after all. His colleagues in the Socialist Faction of the European Parliament had shortly before that urged him to withdraw his recommendation, after they had been violently attacked, especially by the British press. The European Parliament elections in the summer of 1994 led to a temporary pause in the matter.

During the night of March 30, 1993, three years to the day after the Belgian incident, a major wave of UFO sightings occurred over Great Britain, with many police and military witnesses. To quote Nick Pope who, at that time, was UFO desk officer at Secretariat (Air Staff) 2a of the British Ministry of Defense and responsible for handling official and civilian reports, the *"UFO flew directly over two military bases: it was seen by a guard patrol at RAF (Royal Airforce Base) Cosford and by the Meteorological Officer at RAF Shawbury, who described it as being a triangular-shaped craft only marginally smaller than a Boeing 747. It flew over the base at a height of about 200 feet, was making a low humming sound, and was seen to fire a beam of light at the ground. It was moving very slowly, but sud-denly shot off at several times the speed of a fast jet. Nothing was detected on radar. That this event took place is not disputed, and indeed it has been confirmed to the House of Commons by the Minister of State for the Armed Forces, in response to a Written Parliamentary Question."* This remarkable event changed the attitude in Great Britain concerning the UFO phenome-non considerably.

Pope himself, who had been a skeptic when he took over the Whitehall UFO desk in 1991, became a firm believer in the reality of the phenome-non and finally, after being transferred to another MOD office in 1994, wrote a remarkable book on the subject, *Open Skies, Closed Minds*, which was published in 1996. In his book, Pope described the sightings of March 30, 1993 in great detail, based on the reports which were sent to his office by the eyewitnesses. Shortly after the publication of Pope's book, on July 24, 1996, in reply to a question put in the House of Commons by a mem-ber of the Parliament, the British Ministry of Defense, for the first time, commented on both the events of November 5, 1990 and March 30 1993. To quote from the official "Hansard" (Parliamentary written answers) tran-scripts:

> Mr. Redmond: To ask the Secretary of State for Defense
>
> (1) what is his Department's assessment of the incident that occurred on 5 November 1990 when a patrol of RAF Tornado aircraft flying over the North sea was overtaken at high speed by an unidentified craft; and if he will make a statement;
>
> (2) if he will make a statement on the unidentified flying object sighting reported to his department by the meteorological officer at RAF Shawbury in the early hours of 31 March 1993?
>
> Mr. Soames: Reports of sightings on these dates are recorded on file and were examined by staff responsible for air defense matters. No firm conclu-sions were drawn about the nature of the phenomena reported but the events were not judged to be of defense significance.

With this answer, Nicholas Soames, Minister of State for H.M. Armed Forces, standing in for the Secretary of State for Defense, Michael Portillo, officially confirmed that both UFO encounters did indeed take place, were on file, were under investigation by MOD staff and still remained unex-plained!

This new attitude made another request from the European Parliament possible in 1995, this time from England, with the support of the former Admiral of the Fleet Lord Hill Norton. Once more the events of Belgium came into the limelight, after UFO researcher Derek Sheffield learned about their "British connection." In the early hours of March 31, 1990, according to Sheffield, the fast-moving triangular object that had been observed and pursued over Belgium continued its flight over the North Sea and was seen maneuvering near the coast of Kent, England. According to

Hill Norton, the two F-16 fighters of the Belgian Air Force which were chasing it lost sight of it five miles from Dover.

This caused Sheffield to file an official Petition to the Energy, Research and Technology Committee in which he requested an official investigation of the events of March 30, 1990 by the European Parliament. Furthermore, he recommended that for the case of future sightings, the European Community should fund a permanent UFO tracking center. The subject was taken up again after the European Parliament elections in the summer of 1994, and a Spanish official, Gabriel Sanchez, was commissioned to prepare a draft report for the European Parliament, *"The Creation of a European Observation Station for the sightings of Unidentified Flying Objects."* *"People are keen that this should be studied scientifically,"* said Sanchez in September 1995, when he presented his report. *"There is a mixture of opinion for and against."* He came to the same conclusions as Regge did and recommended that SEPRA be commissioned to coordinate and collect UFO information in Europe. British Euro-critics put the plan down to *"France wanting another EU-funded body within its own borders,"* as British MP Sir Teddy Taylor told *The Sunday Telegraph* of September 3, 1995. *"If by any chance there was a proven need to search for flying saucers, the European Parliament would be the worst outfit to find them. We would probably be left with a UFO mountain."*

Since then, the plans and petitions rest in Brussels, waiting for better times to come. But still, the European Parliament-approach from four Nations—Belgium, Italy, the UK and Spain—proves that indeed the events of 1990 caused a new attitude to be taken towards the UFO phenomenon. The "winds of change" which blew over Europe at the turn of the decade and brought walls down and caused iron curtains to fall, opened minds and eyes and ears to this newly accepted reality. For the first time in history, a large part of the public realized that "flying saucers" are a subject too real and too important to be dismissed. Finally, after decades of being ridiculed, they were taken seriously by scientists and politicians and the military; not merely behind closed doors, but publicly.

At any rate, this development is reason enough to review the history of the UFO phenomenon from a new perspective. Let us, therefore, go back to the beginnings.

CHAPTER 3

How It All Began

"There are more things in heaven and earth, Horatio, than are dreamt
of in your philosophy."

—William Shakespeare, *Hamlet*

Kenneth Arnold was an experienced pilot and a good businessman. He was
born on March 29, 1915 at Subeka in Minnesota. His father was quite a
prominent local politician and a close associate of the well known senator
Burton K. Wheeler. Kenneth had a typical American upbringing and education. He went to high school, was a Boy Scout, was selected in track and
field by the State of Minnesota to take part in the Olympics, had a lifesaver
certificate in swimming, and was a successful football player at college. At
the age of 23, Kenneth was a salesman for fire extinguishers with the firm
Red Comet and two years later established his own firm in the same field.
He had learned to fly quite early and since 1943 had made deliveries to his
customers mostly by airplane, that being the quickest and simplest means
of transport in the mountainous northwest of the USA. He booked between
40 and 100 flying hours every month. As a member of the Idaho Search and
Rescue Fliers, the businessman from Boise, Idaho occasionally earned a
few hundred dollars for spotting missing aircraft.

On Tuesday, June 24, 1947, Kenneth Arnold had installed fire extinguishers at the Central Air Service at Chehalis, Washington, and was chat-
ting with Herb Critzer, chief pilot of the company. The talk turned to a
recently missing C-46 Air Force transporter for which a reward of $5,000
had been set. The reward tempted Arnold. The plane had been lost near the
mighty Mount Rainier, which Arnold routinely passed by every day on his
flight home. So he decided to spend at least an hour there looking for the
lost aircraft. He had a lot of experience in flying over mountains and his airplane was new and particularly suited for such terrain. He felt confident
about undertaking the search, which was not without risk. He left Chehalis
at about 2:00 p.m. and about an hour later reached the Mount Rainier
region.

The weather was nice and sunny; not a single cloud in the steel blue skies. While searching the slopes and the high plateau for signs of the lost transporter, he suddenly saw a beam of light being reflected on the side of his plane. For a moment he was frightened. It could mean that he was on a collision course with another aircraft, whose presence he had not noticed. But there was no other aircraft in his vicinity, only a DC 4 flying slowly on her way from San Francisco to Seattle far away on the horizon. Arnold was puzzling over what could have caused the flash of light, when a second flash caught his eye. Now he knew where to look. From the direction of Mount Baker in the north, a formation of bright objects, flying at an incredible speed, was approaching Mount Rainier. Some of them shot out of the line for a moment and flashed in the sunlight. As yet they were about 120 miles away, too far for Arnold to make out their shapes, but they flew directly towards Mount Rainier. There were nine objects in a row, one behind the other, the biggest in the middle.

Kenneth Arnold, with his airplane.

Soon, however, he could see their forms clearly against the white snow covering the slopes of the mountain. To his surprise he could see no projecting parts like wings or tails on the objects. At first he had thought they were a squadron of jet airplanes, but he now began to have doubts. Were

Mount Rainier, Washington, where Arnold saw the flying saucers.

they some new kind of military aircraft? He had never seen aircraft until then that were capable of shooting past mountain peaks at that close range and speed. He looked at his watch. It was 2:59 p.m.

Arnold pushed up the side window to see the objects better. Soon the objects were over the ridge between Mt. Rainier and Mt. Adams. When the first object was exactly at the southern end of the ridge, the last had just reached the northern end. This meant that the formation line was at least 5 miles long. The objects were flat, not quite circular, and radiated a bluish white light from their upper surface. Arnold looked at his watch again: 42 seconds past 3:00 p.m. Within 1 minute and 42 seconds the chain had covered a distance of over 50 miles. Later he calculated the speed to have been about 2,000 mph, which was absolutely unbelievable.

The squadron passed by Mt. Adams and finally disappeared over the horizon. The show was over, and it had lasted only three minutes. Arnold was no longer interested in continuing his search for the lost C-46; the $5,000 reward suddenly left him cold. All he wanted was to get to Yakima and tell people what he had seen. He pondered over what the objects could have been. A new type of aircraft of the U.S. Air Force? A secret weapon, perhaps of Russian origin? In any case, it was his patriotic duty to report the incident to the authorities.

The press got wind of it the same day and the reporters were convinced

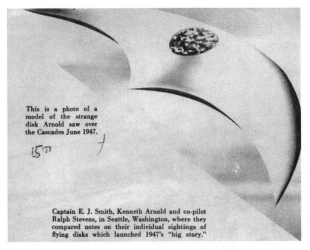

This is a photo of a model of the strange disk Arnold saw over the Cascades June 1947.

Captain E. J. Smith, Kenneth Arnold and co-pilot Ralph Stevens, in Seattle, Washington, where they compared notes on their individual sightings of flying disks which launched 1947's "big story."

An artist's impression of a UFO seen by Arnold.

that they had something that would make headlines—the matter was sensational and the witness reliable. At a press conference Arnold declared, *"They were flat as a plate and so smooth that they reflected the sun like a mirror. You can call me Einstein or Flush Gordon or just a nut. But I know what I saw. The things flew like saucers when you make them skip on water."*

That gave the press its cue and the catchy name "flying saucers" made its way around the world over the days that followed. A legend to suit the beginning of the atomic age was born. UFOs were everywhere and hardly a day went by without their making headlines somewhere. Hundreds of thousands of people claimed to have seen them, amongst them civil and military

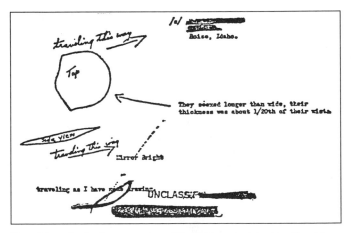

The objects he had seen on June 24, 1947, as sketched by Arnold for the U.S. Air Force.

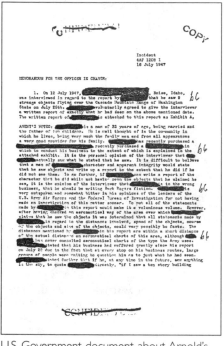

U.S. Government document about Arnold's sighting: "It is difficult to believe, that a man of [Arnold's] character and apparent integrity would state that he saw objects and write up a report to the extent that he did if he did not see them."

pilots, top ranking police and military officers. And that made the affair official. As often as people tried to put aside the flying saucer analogy as an optical illusion or humbug, Arnold's sighting could never be satisfactorily explained.

Within a few days a second witness turned up to support Arnold's story. An old golddigger from Oregon, who had read about Arnold's experience, declared that a few minutes after that he had seen the nine objects circling above the Cascade Mountains. While the "saucers" were flying around over his head, the needle of his compass went haywire. And it was not long before there was proof of the existence of those objects—the first photograph of a UFO.

On July 7, 1947, William Rhodes of Phoenix, Arizona was on his way to his workshop behind his house when he heard a noise, which sounded as if it came from a jet fighter flying very low. The enthusiastic amateur photographer had long waited for this opportunity. He ran quickly into the house to get his new camera and make a shot of the jet. But when he came out of the house, there was no aircraft in the sky. Instead, he saw a strange object flying, which was almost circular, without wings or projections, flat, with a light in the middle of its back. It must be one of those "flying saucers" he had read about in the papers, thought Rhodes, and pointed his camera at the approaching object. When it was about 2000 feet away he took the first picture of it. Instead of coming nearer, the object now veered and started moving away from him. Rhodes took a second picture of it before it accelerated and silently flew off towards the west, disappearing behind a blanket of thick clouds.

Rhodes developed the film the same day in his own darkroom and offered the photographs to the local newspaper, *The Arizona Republic*. Two days later they were published under the headline, "*Saucer flies in the Sky at Unbelievable Speed*." When Kenneth Arnold saw the photographs, he expressed his conviction that they must be genuine. It was exactly the same

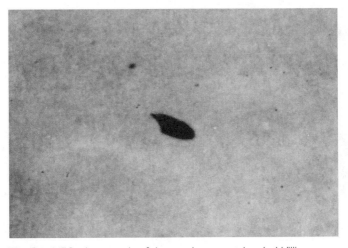

The first UFO photograph of the modern era, taken by William
Rhodes on July 7, 1947, at Phoenix, AZ.

type of "saucer" that he had seen, although he had never described them so
minutely to the press. Thirty years later the authenticity of the photographs
was confirmed by the UFO group Ground Saucer Watch in Arizona, using
state-of-the-art methods. With the help of a computer the GSW established
that the photographs depicted *"an object 30 to 36 feet wide, approximately
4,500 feet away from the camera."*

No wonder that soon after that the intelligence service of the Air Force,
Air Materiel Command (AMC), and the Federal Bureau of Investigation
(FBI) started taking interest in the matter.
*"The FBI appeared within 48 hours after I
published the news item,"* said William
Rhodes later. *"A civil official named Mr.
Ledding and a Lt. Col. Beam from the Air
Force were the interviewers. They confis-
cated the negatives and said I would get
them back soon. But that never happened.
Years later when I called the FBI, they
denied all knowledge of the incident."*

In reality the negatives had been sent to
the AMC and they are still in their possession. The interest of the authorities in the
matter of flying saucers became apparent
through their handling of this incident.

Up until September, 1947 the AMC had
collected 156 cases of sighting reports,
75% of which had to be classified as
unidentified. This meant that there were

This FBI memorandum of August
28, 1947, confirms the forwarding
of Rhodes's original photographs
to the U.S. Air Force.

no rational explanations for their nature or origin, enough grounds for the Department of Defense in Washington to make a first hand analysis. On September 23, 1947, no less a person than Lt. Gen. Nathan F. Twining, the legendary chief of staff of World War II fame and now commanding general of the AMC, sent a confidential report about *"AMC's opinion regarding flying discs"* to Brig. Gen. George Schulgen at the Pentagon. For 31 years this document was kept highly secret, until it was released under President Jimmy Carter.

AMC-Commander General
Nathan F. Twining

1. As requested by AC/AS-2, presented below is the considered opinion of this Command concerning the so-called "Flying Discs." This opinion is based on interrogatory report data furnished by AC/AS-2 and preliminary studies by personnel of T-2 and Aircraft Laboratory, Engineering Division T-3. This opinion was arrived at in a conference between personnel from the Air Institute of Technology, Intelligence T-2 Office, Chief of Engineering Division, and the Aircraft, Power Plant and Propeller Laboratories of Engineering Division T-3.

2. It is the opinion that:

    a. The phenomena reported is something real and not visionary or fictitious.

    b. There are objects probably approximating the shape of a disc, of such appreciable size as to appear to be as large as man-made aircraft.

    c. There is a possibility that some of the incidents may be caused by natural phenomena, such as meteors.

    d. The reported operating characteristics such as extreme rates of climb, maneuverability (particularly in roll), and action which must be considered evasive when sighted or contacted by friendly aircraft and radar, lend belief to the possibility that some of the objects are controlled either manually, automatically or remotely.

    e. The apparent common description of the objects is as follows:

        (1) Metallic or light reflecting surface.

        (2) Absence of trail, except in a few instances when the object apparently was operating under high performance conditions.

        (3) Circular or elliptical in shape, flat on bottom and domed on top.

        (4) Several reports of well-kept formation flights varying from three to nine objects.

        (5) Normally no associated sound, except in three instances a substantial rumbling roar was noted.

        (6) Level flight speeds normally above 300 knots are estimated.

    f. It is possible that with current technical knowledge—provided exten-

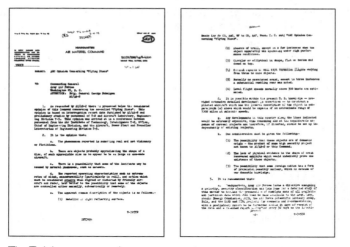

The Twining memorandum.

sive detailed development is undertaken—the U.S. could construct a piloted aircraft according to the general description of the object in subparagraph (e) which would be capable of flying at an approximate range of 7,000 miles at subsonic speeds.

g. Any developments in this country along the lines indicated in (f) would be extremely expensive, time consuming and would considerably take away from current projects, and therefore, if undertaken, should be set up independent of existing projects.

h. Due consideration must be given the following:

(1) The possibility that these objects are of domestic origin—the product of some high security project not known to AC/AS-2 or this Command.

(2) The lack of physical evidence in the shape of crash-recovered exhibits which would undeniably prove the existence of these objects.

(3) The possibility that some foreign nation has a form of propulsion, possibly nuclear, which is outside of our domestic knowledge.

3. It is recommended that:

a. Headquarters, Army Air Forces issue a directive assigning a priority, security classification and Code Name for a detailed study of this matter to include the preparation of complete sets of all available and pertinent data which will then be made available to the Army, Navy, Atomic Energy Commission, JRDB, the Air Force Scientific Advisory Group, NACA, and the RAND and NEPA projects for comments and recommendations, with a preliminary report to be forwarded within 15 days of receipt of the data and a detailed report thereafter every 30 days as the investigation develops. Data should be completely interchanged.

4. Awaiting a specific directive, AMC will continue the investigation within its current resources in order to more closely define the nature of the phenomenon. Detailed Essential Elements of Information will be formulated immediately for transmittal through channels.

N. F. TWINING
Lieutenant General, USA Commander

ATIC's intelligence specialists were confident that within a few months or a year they would have the answer to the question "'What are UFOs?'" wrote Capt. Ruppelt of the ATIC (Air Technical Intelligence Center—formerly the AMC) in his book *The Report On Unidentified Flying Objects*. The secret service officer Ruppelt was someone who knew what he was talking about. He had been in charge of the ATIC investigations regarding UFOs for many years. *"The question 'Do UFOs exist?' was never mentioned. The only problem that confronted the people at ATIC was, 'Were the UFOs of Russian or interplanetary origin?'"*

The first attempts to solve the mystery of UFOs as such was begun in the autumn of 1947, one can be sure, as a result of Twining's report. To start with, it was assumed that both Russian secret aircraft and extraterrestrial spaceships would approach the USA from the polar region. For the Russians it was the shortest route. For space vessels, considering the presence of the earth's magnetic field as well as the radiation belts, the polar region would be the most suitable place to enter the atmosphere. When the first reports of sightings from the Arctic and Antarctic stations and American bases in Alaska and Greenland came in, the evidence seemed to confirm the assumption. At any rate, the U.S. authorities decided to start tracking UFOs at the poles.

The leader of the project was a young officer, Capt. Wendelle C. Stevens

Capt. Wendelle C. Stevens, head of the first UFO tracking project in Alaska, during 1947–48.

(since 1963 retired Lt. Col.). After leaving the military academy in 1942, Stevens became a test pilot in the Army Air Corps, the forerunner of the Air Force. In 1945 he went for training in aeronautic technology at the Wright Field Air Force Base (later Wright Patterson AFB) at Dayton, Ohio, the headquarters of the AMC, before being assigned to the Foreign Technology Division of the Air Intelligence.

Stevens was transferred to Fort Richardson, Alaska, for his new task, and to assist him in carrying it out, he was given a group of specially trained technicians, fitted out with the most recent state-of-the-art equipment, all ostensibly for the sake of making meteorological observations. But it soon became clear to Stevens that he wasn't there to lead a simple weather research project. His instructions were to look out for anything that was unusual, to film it and then send his report, with the film, to AMC.

The B-29 bombers used by the team had been trimmed to make reconnoitering flights lasting from 12 to 16 hours. Special cameras were installed in them, as well as measuring instruments to register all changes in electric potential and magnetic field in their vicinity. At first they used 16 mm film cameras, then 25 mm and finally Wright Field sent them a 70 mm camera. For photographs they used Fairchild K 20 cameras, the best cameras at that time, which produced 8 x 8 inch negatives. Special emission scanners were put in, which could detect radio frequency fields, isolate and record them for 30 seconds, and then scan again to see if any changes had occurred during that period. It was Stevens's job to brief the pilots and crew before each mission, debrief them after their return, make them swear to secrecy, and finally send his report to AMC. The ground crew took out the photographs, cassettes and the measurement records from the instruments on board, packed them into boxes and flew them to Wright Field.

"It was obvious that the purpose of the project had nothing to do with

UFO over Anchorage, Alaska, in 1948.

meteorological measurements but with something else," said Lt. Col.
Stevens to me during an interview in 1990,

> something extremely "hot," kept under the highest level of secrecy. I heard
> some very fantastic stories from the crew about metallic, disc-like objects,
> which flew faster than any aircraft they knew. They were objects that could
> suddenly stop in flight, stand still in the air, or shoot up or down steeply. They
> could race towards you at a tremendous speed and then abruptly change direc-
> tion. Some of the pilots claimed having seen these objects landing on the ice
> or on the surface of the sea, or even diving into the water. They had also seen
> them emerge from the sea and shoot up.
>
> Once, one such object was observed just under the surface of the sea. It rose
> out of the water, hovered over the waves at first, then flew off at a high speed.
> The pilots told me that sometimes the discs flew fairly close to their planes and
> that this caused changes in the magnetic field and anamolous behavior of the
> instruments on board. All these reports tallied with one another, but were made
> independently, for the crew of one flight was not allowed to have contact with
> that of the previous or following flight. Thus I got a fairly good idea of the
> aeronautic feats that the discs could perform from competent observers. Some
> of my superiors had played with the idea that the things were the latest secret
> weapons of the Russians, but what the pilots saw went far beyond anything
> that had been manufactured on this earth.

The results of the Alaska project created a sensation at the AMC and the
Pentagon. Now, within only a few months after their first nationwide
appearance, there were detailed reports and film material to show the flight
characteristics of the "flying discs," which the AMC and Pentagon experts
could analyze. Towards the end of the year there were two factions in the
Defense Department. One faction still suspected the Russians or some other
terrestrial power; the other was sure that no terrestrial technology could
have developed the "saucers." For them there remained only the question
of the intentions and strategy of the intruders. And, of course, there was the
lure of possibly coming into possession of this fantastic alien technology.

The second World War had come to an end only three years ago. The former ally, the Soviet Union, had occupied one half of Europe, the first signs
of tension between East and West were signaling the beginning of the cold
war. It was necessary to find out why the "aliens" had come, and what they
were after in the U.S. If they were indeed extraterrestrials, the possibility
existed, through communication, exchange of information or goods, of
acquiring their technology, which would catapult the USA into the position
of being the most powerful nation on Earth. Should, however, the intentions
of the aliens be evil, one had to take counteracting measures before it was
too late. One had to act, and without delay. So the Pentagon worked out
plans for countrywide projects to detect and observe UFOs. But a tragic
incident had to occur before the first official project was taken further than
the planning stage.

On January 7, 1948, 2:45 p.m., at Godman Field Air Force Base, Kentucky the police and hundreds of civilians at Fort Knox and Madisonville had reported seeing a "gigantic flying saucer." The military administration office at Lexington confirmed the phenomenon. Col. Hix, commander of Godman AFB, having seen the object through his binoculars, sent three jet fighters to intercept it. Squadron leader was Capt. Thomas Mantell, an experienced pilot.

While thousands of people were watching the object, the three courageous Air Force pilots tried to catch up with it in the sky.

Capt. Thomas Mantell

Soon, however, two of them had to land, for lack of fuel. Mantell was left alone to pursue the object. The object was picked up by his radar. The pilot described it on the radio:

"... *It looks metallic and it's tremendous in size* ... *directly ahead and slightly above* ... *I'm trying to get close for a better look* ... *now it's starting to climb* ... *I'm going up to 20,000 feet.*"

That was at 3:15 p.m. Then his jet crashed. Mantell had apparently "blacked out" owing to lack of oxygen. His plane was not equipped with an oxygen supply, which was essential at altitudes above 15,000 feet, and Mantell had gone far above that. At the last second he must have put his aircraft nose down for a dive, but for him it was too late. With the pilot unconscious, the jet ended its dive on the ground. Mantell was dead, the aircraft totally wrecked. The remnants of the airplane were carefully collected and examined. According to unconfirmed rumors, they had been bored through with fine holes. For an experienced pilot like Mantell to risk flying at 20,000 feet without oxygen there must have been a very good reason. Perhaps he wanted to know more about something terribly important, something it was worth risking his life for, but the fact remains that the unidentified flying objects had claimed their first casualty.

The disc, however, flew further onwards. Witnesses from Lockburne Airport in Ohio described it two hours later as "*round or oval, bigger than a C-47, flying level but at a speed higher than 500 mph.*" They could follow its flight from the control tower for 20 minutes. It glowed, changed in color from white to yellow. No noise was heard.

The Pentagon reacted quickly. Maj. Gen. L. C. Craigie gave orders for an Air Force project to be started to find out whether the UFOs were a threat to the USA. Project SIGN started work at Wright Patterson Air Force Base on January 22, 1948. The investigations were to be thorough and serious and the best experts were selected for it. The location was well chosen: Wright Field was the headquarters of the Air Materiel Command (AMC) and the Air Technical Intelligence Center (ATIC). Given the second highest priority level of 2 A, the project was put under the technical intelligence division of

The remnants of Mantell's airplane. When his body was found, the salvaging crew noticed that his clock had stopped at exactly 3:10 p.m.

the AMC. During its 13 months of activity Project SIGN investigated 240 cases within the United States and 30 cases outside it. About 30% of the cases could be explained as optical illusions, mistaken aircraft, natural phenomena or hoaxes, but the majority of them, the remaining 70%, remained unexplained. Since the popular name "flying saucer" had a touch of the ludicrous, a matter-of-fact appellation "unidentified flying object (UFO)", was invented, and was soon in vogue.

Among the innumerable cases of sightings, including some by high ranking military and police officers, scientists, astronomers and pilots, there was one case that particularly astounded the SIGN experts. It was not yet clear whether the UFOs involved were of Russian or extraterrestrial origin, but now the supporters of the "interplanetary thesis" felt confirmed in their belief.

On the evening of July 24, 1948, an Eastern Airlines DC-3 started from Houston, Texas for Atlanta, Georgia. The pilots were Clarence S. Chiles and John B. Whitted, both experienced pilots. At 2:45 a.m. they had covered more than half the distance and were 20 miles southwest of Montgomery, Alabama, when Capt. Chiles saw a light coming towards them. At first he thought it was a jet fighter of the Air Force, but it was far too fast for that. Chiles pointed out the "light" to Whitted. It was already above them and

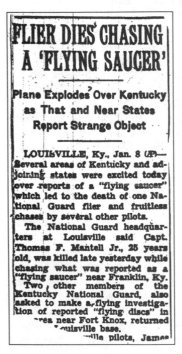

FLIER DIES CHASING A 'FLYING SAUCER'

Plane Explodes Over Kentucky as That and Near States Report Strange Object

LOUISVILLE, Ky., Jan. 8 (AP)—Several areas of Kentucky and adjoining states were excited today over reports of a "flying saucer" which led to the death of one National Guard flier and fruitless chases by several other pilots.

The National Guard headquarters at Louisville said Capt. Thomas F. Mantell Jr., 25 years old, was killed late yesterday while chasing what was reported as a "flying saucer" near Franklin, Ky.

Two other members of the Kentucky National Guard, also asked to make a flying investigation of reported "flying discs" in ʻʼrea near Fort Knox, returned ʼ ʻuisville base.

ʻʼille pilots, Jamʻʻ

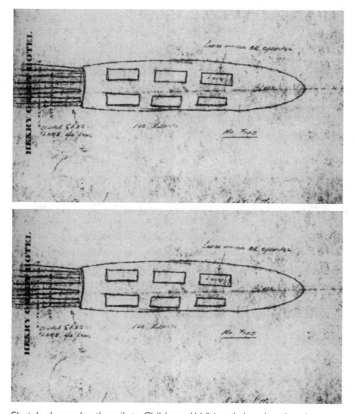

Sketch drawn by the pilots Childs and Whitted showing the cigar-
shaped UFO they saw on July 24, 1948.

Chiles steered to the left to get a better view of it. Finally he was able to
make out its details. A few minutes later it was only about 800 feet away,
when it suddenly moved to the right and then soared almost vertically
upwards, leaving behind it a turbulence in which the D-3 was caught. Capt.
Chiles described later:

> . . . a wingless aircraft, 100 feet long, cigar-shaped and about twice the
> diameter of a B-29 with no protruding surfaces. The cabin looked like a pilot
> compartment, except brighter. From the side of the object came an intense,
> fairly blue glow that ran the entire length of the fuselage, and the exhaust was
> a red-orange flame, with a lighter color predominating around the edges.
> Whatever it was, it flashed down towards us and we veered to the left . . . it
> veered to its left and passed us about 700 feet to our right and above us. Then,
> as if the pilot had seen us and wanted to avoid us, it pulled up with a tremen-
> dous burst of flame from the rear and zoomed into the clouds, its prop wash or
> jet wash rocking our DC-3.

Only one of the passengers had been looking out of the window at that time—the rest were sleeping or had the blinds drawn down—and he, too, reported the long, glowing object to the ATIC. It was a "strange, eerie streak of light, very intense." Minutes after that sighting a crew captain of the Robins AFB at Macon, Georgia, saw an extremely bright light flying over the base. ATIC received one more sighting report that night. A pilot flying near the border between the states of West Virginia and North Carolina had seen a *"bright star shooting in the direction of Montgomery."*

"According to the old-timers at ATIC, this report shook them worse than the Mantell incident," wrote Capt. Ruppelt, referring to that of Chiles and Whitted.

"It was the first time two reliable sources had been really close enough to anything resembling a UFO to get a good look and live to tell about it." The description of windows left only one conclusion possible, that the mysterious object was manned. One look at the map showed that the UFO, on its course as described by the pilots, had to cross Macon, Georgia—where, in fact, it was seen a few minutes later. *"The report of the crew captain at Robins AFB seemed to confirm the sighting, not to mention the report from near the Virginia-North Carolina state line."* The press spoke of a "gigantic spaceship" and also for the ATIC it looked as if the interplanetary hypothesis was confirmed.

On September 5, a confidential report of the ATIC was sent to the Pentagon—a so-called "evaluation of the situation." It was a voluminous document in a black envelope. Its covering sheet bore the stamp TOP SECRET. *"The situation was the UFOs; the conclusion was that they were interplanetary."* The report contained the *"Air Force's analysis of many of the incidents,"* recalled Capt. Ruppelt, who had seen a copy of the UFO File, and *"all of them had come from scientists, pilots and other equally credible observers. . . . "* The report went from one Pentagon office to another and finally landed on the desk of the Chief of Staff, Gen. Hoyt S. Vandenberg. He did not accept the concluding opinion. And he remained stubborn, even when experts from SIGN visited the Pentagon for discussions.

If the extraterrestrial hypothesis was true, what would the consequences be? Nobody knew whether the aliens were friendly or inimically disposed towards us. Vandenberg remembered only too well how the public panicked in 1938, when Orson Welles read his play on CBS radio about an invasion by men from Mars.

Indeed it was a very realistic play. H. G. Wells's *War of the Worlds*, presented as a radio entertainment program with music, realistically interrupted with news bulletins—"owing to urgent reasons"—with "real" switching over to "on-the-spot live reports." The timing of the broadcast, its date as well as its scheduling had also contributed to its effect. It was not only the eve of spooky Halloween, but also the "eve," metaphorically speaking, of the second world war. Anxiety and insecurity were in the air. Many listeners had been tuned in to another station, which was broadcasting a show by the very popular ventriloquist Edgar Bergen, and had switched over to CBS when the Bergen show came to an end—thus missing the proper announcement and introduction to Orson Welles's presentation. What they heard on switching over was indeed not very reassuring: the words of a CBS reporter apparently reporting live from "the landing site of the Martians in New Jersey." *"I see two shining discs peering out of a hole . . . could they be eyes? Is that a face? It could . . . good heavens! There's something winding out of the shadows, like a gray snake. Now a second . . . now one more . . . and yet another . . . look like tentacles. Now I can see the body of the thing . . . it's . . . ladies and gentlemen . . . it's indescribable. I can hardly look at it, it's just too dreadful!"* Statements from "astronomers," a "General Montgomery Smith" who declared a state of emergency, the "Vice President of the Red

Orson Welles, during the production of the *War of the Worlds* radio play broadcast on Oct. 30, 1938.

Cross" and a fictitious "Secretary of the Interior" lent the Mars crisis official character. One-fifth of the six million listeners, as later inquiries showed, believed what they had heard. Long before the broadcast was over, more than a million people began to pray, and desperately frightened, tried to escape from the invasion. Many of them barricaded themselves in their dwellings and sat with guns cocked ready to fire; even more tried to warn their dear ones over the telephone, until the overloaded lines broke down. And finally thousands of people rushed off in their automobiles to flee as far away as possible from New Jersey.

Chaos and panic are the nightmares of every crisis manager Gen. Vandenberg told himself. If the public were told that the UFOs could possibly be the forerunners of a real "Martian invasion," the consequences could not be imagined. Every single one of the literally thousands of UFO sightings each year could cause a panic like the radio play did. Even worse, no one even knew why the UFOs were here. Could the Air Force actually announce: "Ladies and gentlemen, we are witnesses to an extraterrestrial invasion. We do not know the intentions of the aliens, but whatever they are, we are powerless against them?" That would be a declaration of absolute capitulation by the U.S. armed forces and the results, the reaction of the population, could not be foreseen at all. There was only one way out.

Vandenberg invoked a new policy regarding UFOs. He ordered the SIGN team to continue their work, but to dissociate themselves from the "interplanetary hypothesis." Their report was declassified a few months later and destroyed.

The enthusiasm of the team had cooled down considerably, when, towards the end of 1948, they received hundreds of new reports of UFO sightings. One of these came from Germany. During the night of November 23, a pilot flying an F-80 type jet aircraft near the American base at Fürstenfeldbruck near Munich saw an object, shining bright red, in the eastern sky. The UFO seemed to be approaching the Bavarian capital. Following the inquiry of the pilot the local air traffic control station checked its radar and did, in fact, see an object flying towards Munich at the same altitude as the F-80, at the speed of 1,000 mph. Soon after that the control tower estimated that the UFO should be about 30 miles south of the city and the pilot confirmed this. He tried to get nearer to it, but then it shot up with the speed of lightning and was lost to sight. The radar showed that it had reached a height of over 60,000 feet! A second fighter pilot had watched the events and confirmed what the first pilot said. But despite this and many other interesting reports, the setback in Washington had dampened the dedication and élan of the research team. The UFOs had dropped in popularity.

CHAPTER 4

And Yet They Fly

In February 1949 Project SIGN's contract had run out, and one year of work had come to an end. SIGN's concluding report was sent under the code number F-TR-2274-1A, and classified as SECRET. This report disappointed the insiders, since only various possibilities were offered to explain the unidentified objects. Nothing conclusive was written, not even a tentative opinion, out of respect for the negative attitude in Washington. Naturally the possibility of interplanetary craft was still considered:

3. SpaceShips: The following considerations pertain:
   a. If there is an extraterrestrial civilization that can make such objects as are reported, then it is most probable that its development is far in advance of ours. This argument can be supported on probability arguments alone without recourse to astronomical hypotheses.
   b. Such a civilization might observe that on earth we now have atomic bombs and are fast developing rockets. In view of the past history of mankind they should be alarmed. We should, therefore, expect such visits at this time and be prepared for them.
   c. Since the acts of mankind most easily observed from a distance are A-bomb explosions, we should expect some correlation between the A-bomb explosions, the time at which the spaceships are seen, and the time required for such ships to arrive from and return to home base.

The fact remained that it appeared as if the greater part of military inventions and weapon tests were under the observation of UFOs. For years the missile testing grounds at White Sands in New Mexico had been the center of UFO activities, and this made people think. In 1950 the magazine *True* interviewed Commander Dr. McLaughin, who led the meteorological tests

Title page of the closing report of Project Sign,
February 1949. This report considered that UFOs
were extraterrestrial spaceships which visited the
Earth on account of the atom bomb trials.

at White Sands. He was not only convinced that he and his team had proven
the existence of UFOs, but also had an answer to the question of their origin. *"I am sure,"* he said, *"that the flying discs originate from another
planet and that they are controlled by intelligent beings."*

During 1948 and 1949 McLaughin and his team had seen UFOs over the
testing grounds on many occasions. One of the most impressive sightings
occurred on April 24, 1949, when a group of scientists, engineers and technicians were engaged in sending up a Skyhook weather balloon, 100 feet in
diameter. It was 10:30 a.m. on a bright and clear Sunday morning. In order
to test wind conditions, a smaller balloon was sent up first. One member of
the team tracked the balloon through a theodolite, another held a stopwatch
and a third jotted down the readings. The balloon had reached a height of
about 10,000 feet, when one of them gave out a loud cry and, excited,
pointed to his left. They all looked where he pointed—and saw a UFO. *"It
wasn't very big,"* said one of the scientists later, *"but it could be seen
clearly. You could easily see its elliptical shape and silvery color."* Within
a fraction of a second the men knew what they were seeing. Theodolite and
stopwatch were now used for tracking the UFO. They watched it for 60
seconds. Within 55 seconds it had dropped from an elevation angle of 45
degrees to 25 degrees, then zoomed up and disappeared towards the east.

No noise was heard, although the desert on that day was so quiet *"that one could hear a whisper a mile away."* When they evaluated the readings, they found that the UFO had travelled four degrees per second. It had passed a mountain range, which was used for orientation. They estimated its length at about 100 feet and its height about 40 feet. It must have been at an altitude of over 300,000 feet (56 miles) and flown at a speed of over 7 miles per second or 25,000 mph, which exceeded by far any speeds known on Earth.

On May 5, 1948, another meteorological team watched a UFO in the night sky carry out fantastic maneuvers. The disc-like object had a diameter of about one-fifth of a full moon. On another occasion the crew of a C-47, while observing a Skyhook balloon, saw two identical discs appear and circle around the balloon. Minutes after that the balloon crashed and when it was recovered, it was found to be slit open. Other scientists reported that UFOs had circled around V2 rockets during test flights.

The missile testing grounds at White Sands were equipped with all the instruments necessary for tracking rockets. Cinematic theodolite cameras were installed over an area of many square miles, whose cameramen were in full telephone communication with one another.

On April 27, 1950 these cameras filmed the flight of a remote-controlled missile, which went up to the stratosphere and then fell back to earth. Just as one of the cameramen was unloading his camera, he noticed an object racing across the sky. *"By April 1950 every person at White Sands was UFO-conscious,"* wrote Capt. Ruppelt, from whom we learned about this incident, *"so one member of the camera crew grabbed a telephone headset, alerted the other crews and told them to get pictures."* Before the others could reload their cameras the UFO had vanished, but luckily one camera had not been unloaded as yet and was able to film the flight of the object moving steadily at very high speed. A few days later all the camera station operators were told to look for UFOs and film them. Almost exactly one month later a UFO appeared again and this time the cameras were ready. Informed about a UFO over the telephone network, they all scanned the sky and two stations spotted the bright object and filmed it. The total footage was many yards long and when developed, showed that *"the object was at an altitude above 40,000 feet, moved at a speed of over 2,000 mph, and had a diameter of about 300 feet."*

Alarmed by these incidents in the vicinity of the testing and research ground of the Atomic Energy Commission, Col. Poland of the Army Intelligence Service (G-2) sent a memorandum in January 1949 to the Commanding General of the 4th Army and the director of the U.S. Army Intelligence at the Pentagon:

Agencies in New Mexico are greatly concerned about these phenomena. They are of the opinion that some foreign power is taking test snapshots with some superstratosphere [photographing] device designed to be self-disintegrating. It is felt that these incidents are of such great importance, especially as they are occurring in the vicinity of sensitive installations, that a scientific board be sent to this location to study the situation with the idea of finding a solution to this extraordinary phenomena with the least practicable delay.

That action was taken immediately is revealed by a report sent to the director of the FBI, J. Edgar Hoover, on January 31, 1949: *"Re: San Antonio letter to the Director dated January 31, 1949, which outlined discussion had at recent weekly Intelligence Conferences of G-2 (Army Intel), ONI, OSI and FBI in the Fourth Army Area concerning 'unidentified aircraft' or 'unidentified aerial phenomena,' otherwise known as 'flying disks,' 'flying saucers' and 'balls of fire.' It is repeated that this matter is considered secret by intelligence officers of both the Army and the Air Force."*

A top secret conference was held on February 16, 1949 at the research center of the Atomic Energy Commission in Los Alamos, New Mexico, to discuss the UFO phenomenon and the so-called "green fireballs," which had been reported in that region. Among the top scientists and military officers who took part in the conference was the astronomer Prof. Lincoln LaPaz from the University of New Mexico. He confirmed that the "fireballs" were not meteorites, but "reconnaissance probes sent out by a foreign power."

Investigations were also carried out by the Interplanetary Phenomenon Unit (IPU), of the scientific and technical department of the Director of Counterintelligence. This research team was brought into existence after the end of the second World War by the two legendary wartime generals Douglas MacArthur and George Marshall and was active until 1954, when a newly formed Air Force unit took over its duties. Although the existence of this unit was officially confirmed long ago, its files are still held strictly secret. Only in 1993 did an insider, Col. Philip J. Corso, reveal a few facts. According to him, it was a personal encounter of Gen. MacArthur with a UFO in April 1945 (!) at the Clark Field Air Force Base on the Philippines that led to the forming of the team, which at once started collecting information on and evaluating UFO sightings in the Pacific area at first, and later also those in the USA. Corso said that the IPU archives had files and reports on more than 20,000 cases. Under MacArthur he, Corso, was in charge of the "Division for Special Projects" of the Army Intelligence Corps of the Far East Command. From 1953 to 1957 he was a member of the National Security Council, the highest ruling military body under President Dwight D. Eisenhower. Corso is now convinced that *"the people have a right to know the truth about Gen. MacArthur's interest in UFOs."*

We do not know the results of the IPU investigations, but Gen. MacArthur certainly seems to have found them very disquieting: *"I believe that owing to the advances in science the nations of the earth should unite in order to survive and present a common front against attacks by people from other planets,"* declared the four-star general on October 6, 1955, during a visit to Naples. And again on May 12, 1962, addressing the cadets at West Point he spoke about *"the ultimate conflict between a united human-*

ity and the sinister powers from other planets in the galaxy.'' But the official policy of the U.S. Air Force regarding UFOs was quite different.

The project SIGN was renamed GRUDGE on February 11, 1949. "Nomen est omen"—the name "GRUDGE" did indeed reflect the government's disgruntled attitude only too well. But the top specialists were taken off the project and others were put on the job. *"With the new name and the new personnel came the new objective, get rid of the UFOs,''* wrote the intelligence officer Ruppelt. *"It was never specified this way in writing, but it didn't take much effort to see that that was the goal of Project GRUDGE. Everything was being evaluated on the premise that UFOs couldn't exist. No matter what you saw or heard, don't believe it.''* According to Ruppelt the reason for this "new look" was the rejection of the report produced by SIGN earlier. *"The Intelligence Corps had suggested an explanation, [for the sightings] but this was rejected. So they tried again, with a new hypothesis: UFOs don't exist. Until then, if an interesting case came up, and the Pentagon wanted an answer, all they could say was 'It could be true, but we're unable to confirm it.' But now they would quickly reply 'It was a balloon' and everyone felt happy about it.''*

At the Pentagon a new strategy had evolved. It was known that the Soviets were doing all they could to compel a UFO to land. The U.S. military knew what would happen if the Russians succeeded. They would copy the UFOs and possessing that superweapon, would attain supremacy on earth. The U.S. had to be ahead of them. On December 30, 1949, Maj. Jeremiah Boggs, spokesman of Air Force Intelligence, declared at a press conference, in the presence of the chief of the USAF Public Information Office, Gen. S. Smith: *"the Air Force is intent on getting hold of a UFO for studying, and has therefore instructed its pilots to bring one of them in, using all means available, even if they have to catch it by the tail.''* Only much later did it come out, that at that time the Air Force was already in possession of at least two UFO wrecks.

This, of course, was contradictory to the closing report of GRUDGE, which had been released three days before that. Its members had come to the dubious conclusion that all reports about UFOs could be traced back to

a. A mild form of mass hysteria or "war nerves";
b. Individuals who fabricate such reports to perpetrate a hoax and seek publicity;
c. Psychopathological persons;
d. Misidentification of various conventional objects.

Under the orders of Air Force Col. Harold E. Watson it was announced that *"behind almost every report analyzed was a crackpot, a cultist, a publicity hound or a joker,''* and with that the UFO riddle was apparently solved. But the facts were against GRUDGE; there were just too many new, credible cases. One of these happened in Oregon. The witnesses were respected and worthy citizens of a small rural community.

UFO photographs of Paul Trent, of McMinville, Oregon, May 11, 1950.

On May 11, 1950, at about 7:30 p.m., Mrs. Trent went as usual to a wooden shed in the backyard to feed her rabbits. She and her husband Paul were running a farm near McMinnville. It was still light, when Mrs. Trent noticed a silvery flash in the sky. She looked up and saw a big round object flying from the northwest towards the farm. *"I was not afraid,"* she said later, *"I found it beautiful. The thing was silvery, but with a touch of bronze. It looked as if it had something black on the top, like a big parachute without strings. The underside was darker, bronze and not so shiny."* A hallucination? She ran to the house and called her husband. "Paul! Come quick and bring the camera!" Paul was in the kitchen when he heard his wife calling him. He snatched his camera and ran out into the yard. *"The object was coming towards us,"* recalled Paul, *"it flew somewhat tilted, in a curve. It was very bright, shone like silver, and emitted no noise or smoke. It was flying nice and slow. I took my first picture. It flew further left. I went a bit to the right and took another picture. It literally glided, then disappeared slowly in the west."* And he noticed something strange; *"As the UFO flew past us, we felt a slight gust of wind. I don't know whether it had something to do with the UFO."*

When the photographs were finally developed and printed a few weeks later, Paul was delighted. They showed the object clearly, as they had seen it. The upper part was shining brightly; the base was a dark metallic color. At first the pictures made their rounds only in the circle of family and friends, and then a friend suggested that Paul should show the picture to the banker at McMinnville and ask him what it was. Until then the Trents had heard nothing about UFOs and were certain that they had seen a new aircraft of the Air Force. But the banker realized at once that it was one of those much-discussed UFOs. He phoned up a jounalist he knew, William Powell, who came at once to the Trents. Powell had the photographs examined in the laboratory of his newspaper and came to the conclusion that they must be genuine.

The pictures were published on June 8, 1950 and on the same day a number of witnesses reported that they too had seen the object. A few days later

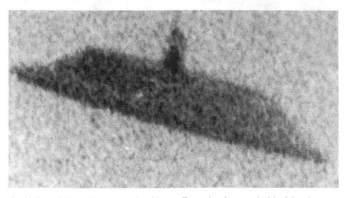

A similar object photographed by a French air marshal in March 1954 above Rouen, France. The photograph was published by the "RAF Flying Review," which described it as "one of the few authentic UFO photographs."

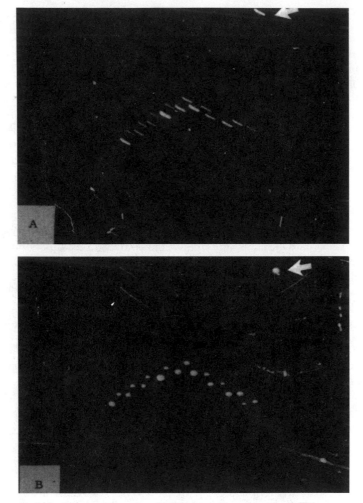

Carl Hart Jr.'s photographs of UFO formation at Lubbock, TX
August 31, 1951.

the Trents were visited by two FBI officials, who asked them for more information. Meanwhile two officers of the Air Force appeared at the offices of the newspaper and confiscated the prints of the photographs. The Air Force examined them thoroughly and arrived at the same conclusion reached by the University of Colorado's intensive examination 28 years later: the pictures did, in fact, show an unidentified flying object.

On the morning of August 15, 1950, Nick Mariana and his secretary Virginia Raunig drove to Legion Ball Park, a playground in Great Falls, Montana. Mariana was the general manager of the baseball team "Selectrics" and wanted to inspect the field once more for the game scheduled for the

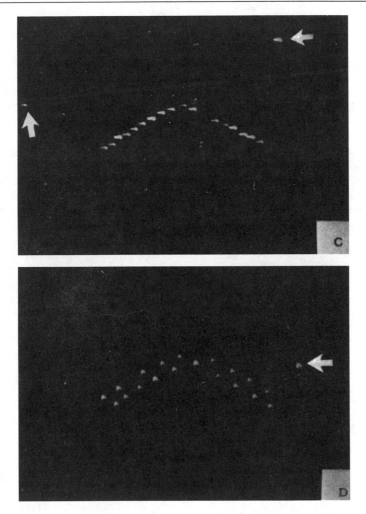

weekend. At about 11:25 a.m. Mariana saw something flashing in the sky. He and Virginia could see two silvery objects, which seemed to rotate and fly over the city at a speed of about 250 mph. *"Virginia, run quickly to the car and get the camera!"* he called out to his secretary and a few seconds later he was able to film the objects. On the 54-foot 16mm film he caught the objects flying over a water tower, flashing and then disappearing over the horizon. A few seconds later they saw two jet fighters shooting up from the nearby air base. Mariana, very excited, called up the local paper and described his experience.

A week later he had the developed film. He showed it to his teammates and one of them informed the Air Force. Mariana readily gave the film to the ATIC for investigation. When he got it back, the beginning was missing, where the rotation of the discs could clearly be seen. His statement about the two jet fighters would be verified later. A computer analysis made in 1979 showed that the objects were elliptical and at a very considerable distance.

When four university professors observe a UFO formation, which is also seen by hundreds of other people, and there are also photographs of the formation, we have at least a case worthy of note. On the evening of August 25, 1951, four professors of the Texas Technological College in Lubbock, Texas got together at the house of the geology professor Dr. W. I. Robinson. The others were Dr. A. G. Oberg, professor of chemistry; Prof. W. L. Ducker, head of the department of petroleum engineering; and Dr. George, professor of physics.

The four gentlemen sat in the garden, drinking tea and discussing micrometeorites, when one of them saw a light in the sky coming towards them. Soon they could see that it was a whole formation of lights, about 30 in number, arranged in a crescent. In a few seconds the squadron flew over the town. The intensity of the lights was about equal to a star, but the lights were much bigger and rounded in shape. The professors were too excited to observe the lights closely, but they discussed at length what they would do if the phenomenon occurred again. And during this very discussion the phenomenon repeated itself, something that they had never considered! This time, however, they were able to see clearly that the objects glowed with a bluish light and had a certain structure. Owing to this second sighting the professors felt that the incident could happen again. They decided that if any one of them should see the objects return, he should immediately inform his colleagues. Only thus could they, by triangulation, determine the altitude, speed and size of the objects. Prof. Ducker did in fact see them twelve more times during the following months, but the objects flew so fast that he could never inform the others in time.

"We felt no shock waves," said Prof. Ducker, "which any body moving at that speed at a low altitude should have created. With that in mind, one can only deduce that the formation was in the stratosphere, 10 miles above the earth. That would mean that the speed was about 18,000 mph."

The General Staff instruction JANAP 146 puts UFO reports under the espionage laws.

During the following week hundreds of people in and around Lubbock could see the objects in the sky. One of them, the 25-year-old student Carl Hart, succeeded in making five photographs of the objects. Owing to the heat he had drawn his bed close to the window, which he left open during the nights. On August 30, he had just gone to bed and lay looking at the clear sky, when he suddenly saw the light formation. He had heard about it from his professors. So he sprang out of his bed, snatched his camera, threw a bathrobe over his shoulders and ran outside. A few minutes later a second formation appeared at the horizon. Hart had set his 35mm Kodak camera at an aperture of f 3.5 and exposure time to one-tenth of a second. He was able to take two pictures. When another formation flew over the town half an hour later, he obtained three more pictures. When the press, armed with this abundance of evidence, challenged the results of Project GRUDGE, the Air Force could no longer keep quiet. The general staff was called to a secret meeting at the Pentagon to discuss further measures.

This gave birth to CIRVIS (Communication Instructions for Reporting Vital Intelligence Sightings), an instruction dispatched as JANAP (Joint Army, Navy and Air Force Publication) No. 146 to all the three armed forces. UFOs are mentioned explicitly in this circular, and the reporting of UFO sightings is described as *"of vital importance for the security of the USA, its territories and possessions"* and as *"requiring urgent defensive and/or investigative action by the . . . armed forces."* UFO reports are here assigned to MERINT reports, which stand under strict secrecy:

"All persons who are aware of the contents or existence of a MERINT report are governed by the Communications Act of 1934 and amendments thereto, and Espionage Laws. MERINT reports contain information affecting the National Defense of the United States within the meaning of the Espionage Laws, 18 U.S. Code, 793 and 794. The unauthorized transmission or revelation of the contents of MERINT reports in any manner is prohibited."

The punishment for violation of the Espionage Laws was a fine of $10,000 and/or imprisonment up to 10 years. With that the authorities believed they had the matter once more under control. Countrywide measures were taken to obtain more details about UFOs. Air Force planes were outfitted with suitable cameras; their pilots were told to film UFOs. And every one of them was given a

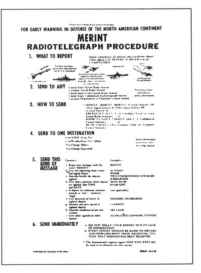

This Merint instruction for reports was displayed in all U.S. Air Force Bases and in all ships of the U.S. Navy.

sealed envelope containing secret instructions and bearing a note that it should be opened only in the case of a UFO sighting!

Project GRUDGE started working again on October 27, 1951. But since its name still had a strong negative image, it was renamed Project Blue Book and put under the leadership of the experienced Intelligence Corps officer Edward J. Ruppelt. Ruppelt was a World War II veteran, who had returned to active service when the Korean War broke out. Having graduated as an engineer, he was soon put in charge of analyzing new types of Soviet fighter planes. During secret meetings at the Pentagon connected with this subject, he was chosen as the right person to take over the restructured UFO project. Time showed that the choice was well-made. Time and again Ruppelt proved his competence as an objective analyst and he was able to reestablish the credibility of the Air Force in the matter of UFOs. And that was sorely needed at that time.

CHAPTER 5

The CIA Intervenes

"You really believe that they are of interplanetary origin?"
"I can't think of any other plausible explanation."
"This is not a purely private conversation. You don't have to keep silent.
Not anymore. Don, I have received instructions to help you, and you
have asked for ATIC reports about UFO appearances. What exactly do
you want?"
— Maj. Donald Keyhoe, *Flying Saucers from Outer Space*

The conversation quoted above took place in August 1952, in a small
room at the Pentagon. The persons concerned were Albert M. Chop of the
US Air Force Press Desk and Maj. Donald E. Keyhoe of the Navy. Chop
was privy to the official UFO investigation. He had been briefed on the
subject by intelligence officers before being transferred to the Pentagon.
Maj. Keyhoe had graduated from the U.S. Naval Academy and the officers' school of the Marine Corps. After his service period in the Marine
Corps he was the press spokesman for the civil aviation section of the
Department of Commerce. As a government representative he organized
nationwide campaigns for the South Pole fliers Admiral Byrd and Charles
Lindbergh. He wrote about his experiences in his first book *Flight with
Lindbergh*, with which his career as journalist began. As an expert he was
engaged in 1949 by the magazine *True* to make investigations for an article which appeared towards the end of the year under the title "Flying
Saucers Are Real." After 8 months of research Keyhoe came to the conclusion that the earth was being visited by beings from other planets. In
1950 his second book was published, under the same title as the magazine
article. Since he had found out that the Air Force must be in possession
of the most extensive information regarding UFOs, he continued his work
in Washington. He was, however, astonished when Chop offered to give
him the ATIC reports.

"What is behind all this investigation, in your opinion?" asked Keyhoe.
"I can't answer that," replied Chop, lighting a cigarette. After a moment of
hesitation he went on, choosing his words carefully, *"The Air Force does
not deny that some UFOs could be of interplanetary origin. But we have no
definite evidence to support that hypothesis." "What about the pictures you
have analyzed"? "Until now, none of the photographs has revealed details.*

No ATIC analysis has until today delivered undeniable evidence. . . . O.K.
I'll see what I can do for you. It could naturally take some time."
    A week later Chop called Keyhoe. *"Come on over here. I have three or*
four cases for you. You'll be surprised." Keyhoe got enough amazing material—41 cases from the ATIC archives—to use for his third book *Flying Saucers From Outer Space.* In an official letter to Keyhoe's well-known firm of publishers, Henry Holt of New York, Albert Chop wrote:
    "We in the Air Force recognize Maj. Keyhoe as a responsible, accurate
reporter. His long association and cooperation with the Air Force in our
study of unidentified flying objects qualifies him as a leading civilian
authority on this investigation . . . The Air Force and its investigating
agency, 'Project Blue Book,' are aware of Maj. Keyhoe's conclusion that the
'flying saucers' are from another planet. The Air Force has never denied
that this possibility exists. Some of the personnel believe that there may be
some strange natural phenomena completely unknown to us, but that if the
apparently controlled maneuvers reported by many competent observers are
correct, then the only remaining explanation is the interplanetary answer."
    After the conclusions of the Project GRUDGE report and the official statements of the Air Force, this declaration came as a surprise to Maj. Keyhole. What had happened?

    During the night of February 9, 1951, Lt. Graham Bethune, a 29-year-old pilot in the U.S. Naval Reserve, was flying a quadruple-engined C-54 transporter from England to the USA, with scheduled stopovers in Iceland and Newfoundland. Bethune had served at the Naval Air Station in Brooklyn, N.Y., then with a squadron in Norfolk, VA and finally at the Naval Aeronautic Test Center in Maryland. He was qualified to fly 38 different types of aircraft and had over 200 transatlantic flights to his credit.
    It was a quiet night, excellent flying weather. Although the moon had gone down in the west a good while ago, visibility was still good, the sky clear except for a few wispy clouds floating above the ocean.

U.S. Navy Commander Graham Bethune

Bethune could see the horizon distinctly and from time to time even make out the white foam on the crests of the waves 10,000 feet below. Bethune was in the cockpit, his copilot Lt. Fred Kingdon beside him, and the navigator Lt. J. P. Koger was in the seat behind. Sleeping in the cabin were their reliefs and about twenty passengers, mostly young officers returning to the States.
    They were flying at a constant speed of 200 knots towards Argentia in Newfoundland. Some three and a half hours after starting from Kevlavik,

A quadruple-engined C-54, like the one Bethune was flying during his UFO encounter on February 10, 1951.

Iceland, they passed over a weather ship lying at anchor near the coast of Greenland. They contacted the vessel over the radio and obtained the weather forecast, which indicated that it would continue to be clear and calm. So Bethune switched on the autopilot.

Scanning the sky for other aircraft, Bethune saw a faint yellow glow in the 1:00 position, perhaps about 30 miles away below the horizon. It must be the sky above a small city which was just out of sight below the horizon, thought Bethune. But that would mean that he was behind time and was on the wrong course, heading for the southern tip of Greenland. On the other hand they had just flown over the weather ship anchored near the west coast of Greenland and, therefore, they must be well past Greenland. *"Do you see the lights at 12:30 position?"* he asked Lt. Kingdon. *"Looks like a little city,"* replied Kingdon. *"Koger, please check our position,"* said Bethune to the navigator. *"Confirm: position 49.50 North, 50.03 West. We are flying as per schedule on course 230 degrees. Argentia, Newfoundland is 200 miles ahead of us. No land anywhere near."* It took another five minutes before the C-54 crew could see that the lights, now white, were arranged in a circular pattern. They were still about 20 miles away. *"Maybe they're a couple of ships tied together. Check the shipping schedules."* *"Our course does not cross any shipping route,"* replied the navigator. That was confirmed by calling up the weather ship; there were no vessels in the vicinity. *"Wake up Jones and Meyer,"* Bethune ordered Lt. Koger.

When the relieving crew entered the cockpit Bethune showed them the ring of lights at the 1:00 angle, less than 10 miles away. *"They're ships,"* said the naval pilots, rubbing their eyes, still sleepy. *"We've checked already, that's ruled out,"* answered Bethune, *"no vessel far and wide."* Now the pattern of white lights turned into a single ring, shining yellow, then changed in color to orange and finally red. At the same time the formation started coming up and moved with incredible speed toward the C-54. It then turned violet and approached them threateningly close. *"Hell! What is it?"* asked Jones in astonishment. *"It's rushing at us,"* cried Koger in a panic, *"it's going to collide with us!"* With presence of mind Bethune quickly switched off the autopilot and kept his hand on the joystick, ready to maneuver the airplane and avoid collision. The crew crouched down against the bulkhead of the cabin. Bethune's hand was trembling out of fear; he had never been so close to death before.

He knew that he had to act as quick as lightning, but at the same moment it was clear to him that every maneuver would be in vain. The shining ring could get at them in any position. The glow, he could now see, came from the rim of a gigantic circular disc, against which the C-54 seemed diminutive. He held his breath, and waited for death.

But suddenly the disc tilted and veered off from the transporter at a distance of less than two hundred yards away from it. It slowed down and hovered a hundred feet below the C-54, at the 1:30 position. It was a metal disc, surrounded by a fiery purple ring. The body was bathed in a cold white glow. The crew estimated its diameter at about 300 feet, more than twice

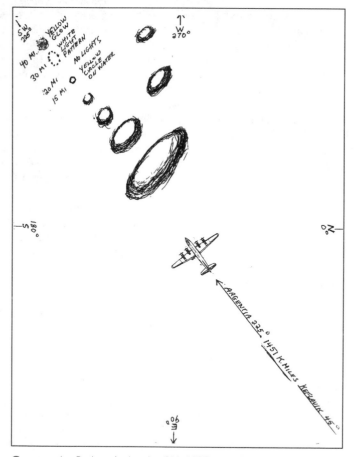

Commander Bethune's sketch of his UFO encounter.

the 120-foot wing span of their own machine. It must have approached them at the incredible speed of far over 1,000 mph. After a minute it tilted up slightly and shot off at an angle of 170 degrees, vanishing into the night within a few seconds. *"That's unbelievable!"* exclaimed Bethune with relief and astonishment, *"it must have taken off at more than 1,500 mph!"* *"What on earth could it have been?"* queried Koger. *"Certainly not one of our machines,"* answered Lt. Jones, still white as chalk from fear. *"It was definitely controlled by intelligence,"* pondered Bethune. *"It had spotted us and wanted to get a good look at us. But now we need relief!"*

Jones and Meyer took over the controls and Bethune and Kingdon retired to the cabin for rest. There was a serious discussion going on in there. Most of the passengers had seen the UFO and had followed what had happened through the portholes. Bethune asked the highest ranking officer present there, Commander M——, *"Did you observe the thing?"* Commander M—— replied: *"I did, but I didn't look. It was one of those flying saucers, and I don't believe in such things."*

Bethune went back to the cockpit and announced, *"Commander M—— thinks it was a flying saucer. We are to keep the matter to ourselves or they'll think we're a bunch of nuts!"* *"Too late,"* replied Lt. Jones, *"I've already radioed Gander and asked them if they saw anything on the radar screen."*

And, had they?

"Yes, they saw something near us, but they couldn't identify it. I told them we had seen it and that it certainly was no airplane."

Upon landing in Argentia the crew and passengers of the transporter found officers of the ATIC waiting for them. Each of them was interrogated for almost two hours separately. The questions left no doubt that those doing the questioning were fairly certain the pilots and passengers had seen an unidentified flying object. *"How close to you did they get? What was their rate of ascension? Did you notice any electronic interference? How did the glowing ring behave? Did you get the impression that it was manned?"* *"It was certainly controlled by an intelligence, and for a remote-controlled probe, it was rather too big, wasn't it?"* answered Bethune. *"I can't say anything about that,"* replied the man from the ATIC. *"But what does all this mean? Until now the Air Force has always declared that flying saucers don't exist."* *"I'm sorry, I'm not permitted to answer any questions!"* answered the intelligence officer laconically.

The report went to Project TWINKLE, a "daughter" of GRUDGE. When the file was released in 1990, Bethune, by that time a retired naval commander, could not believe his eyes. For in the final report about the incident it was stated that the huge object which had almost collided with his plane had only been a manifestation of the aurora borealis, the northern lights! At any rate, that was the conclusion arrived at by a student of astronomy for the ATIC.

One wonders whether this poor student ever made the grade. It does not seem to have occurred to him that the aurora borealis gets its name "bore-

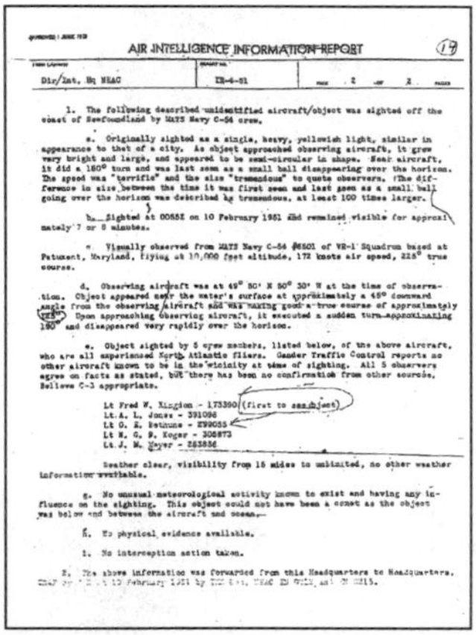

AIR INTELLIGENCE INFORMATION REPORT

Dir/Int, Hq NEAC | IR-4-51 | PAGE 2 OF 2 PAGES

1. The following described unidentified aircraft/object was sighted off the coast of Newfoundland by MATS Navy C-54 crew.

a. Originally sighted as a single, heavy, yellowish light, similar in appearance to that of a city. As object approached observing aircraft, it grew very bright and large, and appeared to be semi-circular in shape. Near aircraft, it did a 180° turn and was last seen as a small ball disappearing over the horizon. The speed was "terrific" and the size "tremendous" to quote observers. (The difference in size between the time it was first seen and last seen as a small ball going over the horizon was described as tremendous, at least 100 times larger.

b. Sighted at 0055Z on 10 February 1951 and remained visible for approximately 7 or 8 minutes.

c. Visually observed from MATS Navy C-54 #6501 of VR-1 Squadron based at Patuxent, Maryland, flying at 10,000 feet altitude, 172 knots air speed, 225° true course.

d. Observing aircraft was at 49° 50' N 50° 30' W at the time of observation. Object appeared near the water's surface at approximately a 45° downward angle from the observing aircraft and was making good a true course of approximately 225°. Upon approaching observing aircraft, it executed a sudden turn approximating 180° and disappeared very rapidly over the horizon.

e. Object sighted by 5 crew members, listed below, of the above aircraft, who are all experienced North Atlantic fliers. Gander Traffic Control reports no other aircraft known to be in the vicinity at time of sighting. All 5 observers agree on facts as stated, but there has been no confirmation from other sources. Believe C-3 appropriate.

Lt Fred W. Kingdon - 173390 (first to see object)
Lt A. L. Jones - 391098
Lt G. E. Bethune - 299055
Lt W. G. B. Koger - 308873
Lt J. M. Meyer - 283836

f. Weather clear, visibility from 15 miles to unlimited, no other weather information available.

g. No unusual meteorological activity known to exist and having any influence on the sighting. This object could not have been a comet as the object was below and between the aircraft and ocean.

h. No physical evidence available.

i. No interception action taken.

2. The above information was forwarded from this Headquarters to Headquarters, USAF ... 10 February 1951 ...

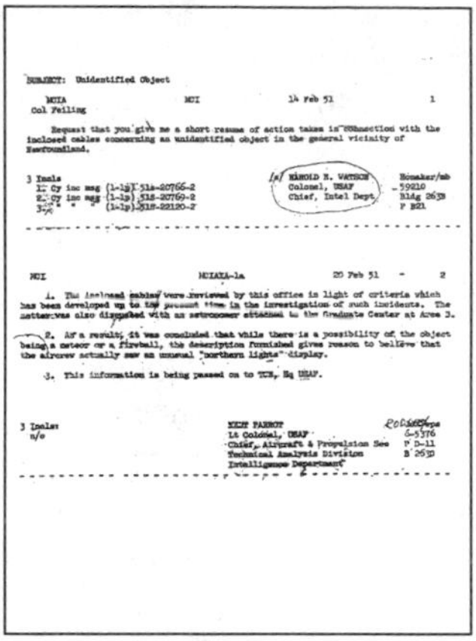

SUBJECT: Unidentified Object

MCIA | MCI | 14 Feb 51 | 1
Col Feiling

Request that you give me a short resume of action taken in connection with the inclosed cables concerning an unidentified object in the general vicinity of Newfoundland.

3 Incls
1. Cy inc msg (1-1p) 51A-20766-2
2. Cy inc msg (1-1p) 51B-20769-2
3. " " " (1-1p) 51B-22120-2

/s/ HAROLD E. WATSON
Colonel, USAF
Chief, Intel Dept

Homaker/mb
59210
Bldg 263B
P B21

MCI | MCIAXA-1a | 20 Feb 51 | 2

1. The inclosed cables were reviewed by this office in light of criteria which has been developed up to the present time in the investigation of such incidents. The matter was also discussed with an astronomer attached to the Graduate Center at Area 3.

2. As a result, it was concluded that while there is a possibility of the object being a meteor or a fireball, the description furnished gives reason to believe that the aircrew actually saw an unusual "northern lights" display.

3. This information is being passed on to TCB, Hq USAF.

3 Incls
n/c

KENT PARROT
Lt Colonel, USAF
Chief, Aircraft & Propulsion Sec
Technical Analysis Division
Intelligence Department

6-5376
P D-11
B 263D

ATIC report about the incident of February 10, 1951. Project Twinkle explained this "near-collision" as an unusual play of northern lights, although the UFO came from the southwest and appeared below the horizon.

alis", meaning "northern", because it is observed looking north, not southwest. Besides that, the aurora spectacle is always seen above and not below the horizon, where the light pattern was observed. *"Apart from that, the phenomenon is always mentioned in the weather report for the North Atlantic,"* declared Commander Bethune in the summer of 1992, when I interviewed him, *"and in our weather report there was no talk of northern lights!"*

Today Bethune is certain that what he saw was a spaceship from another world. During a later visit to Gander a military air traffic controller told him that the radar operators had estimated the top speed of the object at nearly 2,000 mph. When Lt. Jones landed in Argentia again a few days later, the captain of a VP-8 of the Navy told him that he and his crew had watched the same object during a night patrol. Overseas personnel of Lockheed who were in charge of the tower at Kevlavik, Iceland, told Bethune about a whole series of sightings of big disc-like objects over the North Atlantic, which were taken to be Russian secret weapons. Some people were even afraid that the Soviets were planning an attack on Iceland.

On the same day that they sighted the object, Bethune and his crew flew on to the U.S. Naval Air Station in Patuxent River, Maryland. On landing they were once more interrogated by Naval Intelligence. They were then asked to make a written report of the occurrence.

Five days later Bethune received a telephone call from a man who identified himself as a high-ranking scientist of the government. *"I have been informed about your encounter with a UFO and would like to ask you a few questions."* Bethune referred this to his superiors, who checked the credentials of the scientist. A meeting with him took place the next day. After

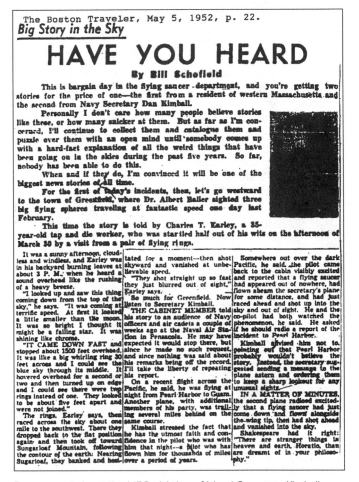

Press report about the UFO sighting of Naval Secretary Kimball.

Bethune told him in detail what he had seen, the scientist took out a few photographs from his attaché case and asked, *"Did it look like this?"* On seeing the third picture Bethune was startled. *"That's it! It looked exactly like that! But where do these pictures come from? So someone knows about them!"*

The scientist took the photograph back, saying, *"Sorry Lieutenant, I'm not allowed to answer any questions!"* He put the pictures back in his case, stood up and left. Bethune sat back, resigned. He knew that "they" were out there, but here he was confronted by a wall of silence. And he had no means of penetrating it. But there was another person who had enough political influence to push through the wall when he was given short shrift. In April 1952, the topmost naval official, Naval Secretary Kimball, had a UFO encounter while flying to Honolulu, Hawaii.

Two disc-like bodies raced towards his aircraft and were seen by the crew, officers and reporters on board. *"Their speed was incredible,"* declared the Secretary later to Maj. Keyhoe, *"my pilots estimated it at over 2,000 mph! The two objects circled around us before shooting off eastwards. About 50 miles behind us there was another naval aircraft, with Admiral Arthur Redford on board. I told my pilot to inform them about our sighting. A couple of seconds later Redford's pilot called us to say the objects were circling around their airplane. A few seconds later he called again to say they were out of sight. They must have covered the 50 miles in less than two seconds."*

Right after landing Kimball radioed a report to the Air Force and asked them what they would do about it. They replied that it was against rules to discuss a sighting case with the witnesses concerned, but Kimball was not one to be put off like that. He called Rear Admiral Calvin Bolster, Chief of the Office of Naval Research, and ordered him *"to investigate thoroughly all future reports from the naval side, independent of the Air Force projects."*

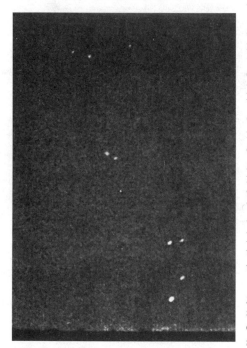

Soon Naval Intelligence had a case in hand which was documented by a film. On July 2, 1952, the naval officer Delbert C. Newhouse was driving with his wife and two children from Washington, D.C. to Portland, Oregon. He had been transferred to the flight logistics depot there to serve as photographic reporter. He and his family were passing through the broken, rocky landscape of Utah on Highway 30, going westwards through the Rocky Mountains. They left the little township of Tremonton behind them at about 11:00 a.m. and 10 minutes later, they saw a group of bright objects in the sky. Newhouse moved his car over to the shoulder and stopped to watch the objects' movements better.

Still from the film of deck officer Delbert C. Newhouse, July 2, 1952.

They looked so strange— definitely not any aircraft he knew of—that he immediately took out his Bell and Howell movie camera to get pictures of them. *"They were the color of red bronze, shaped like two*

saucers placed one over the other," he said later, *"and reflected the sun-light. They seemed to be as high as they were wide, and moved steadily."*
Newhouse filmed them in a manner that would help later with evalua-tion. When one of the objects broke off from the formation, he concentrated on it, and keeping his camera steady, let it "fly across the field of vision," hoping that would help to estimate the speed of the object. This he did three times. And finally the object returned to the formation, which had mean-while almost disappeared over the horizon. After developing the film he sent it to the Naval Photographic Laboratory at Anacosta for analysis.

The laboratory took 3 months—over 600 working hours—to analyze the 200-foot long film strip and finalize its report, in which all conventional identification possibilities were eliminated, i.e., aircraft (*"with the lens used, aircraft would have been identifiable up to a distance of 5 miles. At that distance their speed would have been 625 mph. . . . No squadron of air-craft is capable of flying in formation at that speed and carrying out such maneuvers"*); balloons (*"balloons would also be identifiable at a distance of 5 miles. But even at a distance of 4 miles their speed would have been over 300 mph, which is impossible for balloons."*); birds (*"no bird can reflect sunlight so brightly. The enormous speed of the objects also rules out this possibility."*). The final conclusion of the experts was simple: *"Unidentified objects under intelligent control."* A second analysis con-ducted by Project Blue Book led to the same result; *"We do not know what they are, but they are not airplanes, balloons or birds."* The film caused a big stir at the Pentagon. It was clear that it showed disc-like objects, which maneuvered at incredible speeds. The analyses suggested that they must have been at a distance of 6 miles—within 5 miles more details would have been visible—which put their speed at almost 900 mph.

Secretary Kimball planned to hold a press conference in October, at which time he intended to release the film and the reports from the experts. The timing would have been ideal, since during the summer a series of sightings had shaken the country.

On July 14, an airliner, a Pan American Airways DC-4, was on its way from New York to Miami. In the cockpit were Captain William B. Nash and his co pilot William Fortenberry. The night was clear and visibility excellent. The pilots were looking down at the lights of the big cities on the east coast, when they suddenly saw a reddish glowing light east of them in the air.

Even as they wondered what it could be, it became obvious that it was a group of six objects, flying in a row, approaching their jet at a low altitude and with great speed. Recalled Nash,

> They looked like glowing pieces of coal, and their shape was clearly defined and round. We estimated their diameter as somewhat greater than the wingspan of a DC-3, about 100 feet. They were 3,000 feet below us. When the row was just a bit ahead of us they tilted sidewards, their left edges, as seen by us, coming up and their top surfaces going right. Only the top seemed to be

lighted. In shape and proportion they resembled coins. After they had all tilted, the ones at the rear came forward past the leading object, so that their formation was now completely reversed. Suddenly two more objects shot into the picture and joined the previous six. There seemed to be a connection between their speed and their brightness, and they seemed to be brighter after tilting. We watched them, astounded, and probably with our mouths wide open, half expecting more such objects to appear. They were flying saucers and we had seen them. It all happened at 8:12 p.m. and lasted for only 12 seconds. We estimated the speed of the objects at around 12,000 mph.

As soon as they vanished the pilots reported the sighting to the control station at Norfolk. On landing at Miami in the morning, they called up the Air Force and set up a meeting with them. There they were interrogated separately. Hardly had the press heard about this incident, when another sensation was about to make headlines. During the night of July 19 a squadron of UFOs flew over the nation's capital, Washington, D.C.

It was the night of Saturday, July 19, at 11:40 p.m. It was a refreshingly cool night, a relief for everyone, since the capital, once again, suffered from one of its infamous heat waves. The scene of action was a long windowless

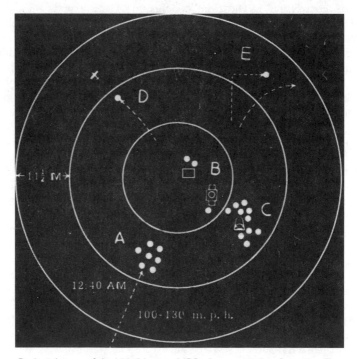

Radar picture of the Washington UFO demonstration from the files of the U.S. Air Force. Squadron "B" flies inside the security zone above the Capitol, "C" above the White House.

room, the air traffic control station of the city's National Airport. The semi-darkness made the radar screens easier to read. During that night eight operators were looking at the dimly lit radar screens, a job that requires concentration and skill. Controllers have to calculate the courses and interpret every signal ("blip") with greatest care, since any mistake can cost lives. It was an ordinary night with good visibility and a cloudless sky. Usually at that time of the day the air traffic was rather slow, and the air traffic controllers were prepared for a quiet 8-hour night shift.

Suddenly, on the main screen, Edward Nugent saw 7 blips appear, which changed positions with an incredible rapidity. Unable to identify the objects, he called his boss, Harry G. Barnes to his aid. He too saw the seven objects, in irregular formation, at a corner of the screen. That meant that they were about 15 miles south of Washington, but definitely getting closer to the city. For 5 minutes he watched them maneuver at speeds of about 120 mph, but they did not seem to follow any definite course. He asked two other experienced operators, Jim Copeland and Jim Ritchie, for their opinion. But they too were at a loss. He then asked a technician to check the radar apparatus, and when he heard that it was operating faultlessly, he called the control tower. There, too, the objects had been spotted, but not identified. The ground crew reported sighting "gleaming orange-colored lights."

Jim Ritchie saw one of the objects following an aircraft belonging to Capitol Airlines, which had just taken off. He asked the pilot, Casey Pierman, a man who had had 17 years of flying experience, whether he could see anything unusual around him. A few seconds later Pierman reported a bright light in the close vicinity of his plane, which suddenly shot off upwards. Ritchie too saw that on his screen. A few minutes later Pierman called, saying he could now see 6 glowing lights, which was also confirmed by the radar. Another pilot, coming in to land, saw a single light near his left wing, which too was seen on radar.

Shortly after that there was a big surprise for the radar operators: one of the blips made a 90 degree turn, which no aircraft can ever do. Another, doing about 100 mph, effected a complete reversal of direction within 5 seconds. The excitement waxed when Joe Jacko from the tower called. He had followed the movements of the objects on an Army Service Radar (AST), constructed for tracking objects moving at very high speeds. One of the objects had crossed a distance of 2 miles in one second, flying over Andrew Field towards Riverdale. From that he calculated its speed at approximately 7,000 mph! Barnes decided to inform the Air Force, and learned that they were trying to get reconnaissance planes to investigate. These, however, came three hours later; there had already been a UFO alarm in upstate New York and all the fighters had been sent there.

Luckily all the objects had vanished before the majority of the population was awake. Nevertheless a wave of hysteria spread once the story got around. An engineer of the radio station WRC had distinctly seen five gigantic discs that night, flying over the city. While he was watching them

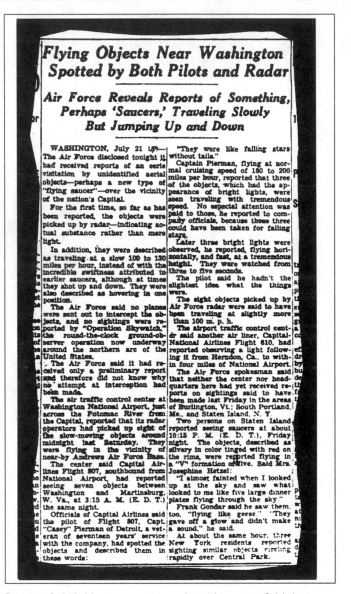

Flying Objects Near Washington Spotted by Both Pilots and Radar

Air Force Reveals Reports of Something, Perhaps 'Saucers,' Traveling Slowly But Jumping Up and Down

WASHINGTON, July 21 (P)—The Air Force disclosed tonight it had received reports of an eerie visitation by unidentified aerial objects—perhaps a new type of "flying saucer"—over the vicinity of the nation's Capital.

For the first time, so far as has been reported, the objects were picked up by radar—indicating actual substance rather than mere light.

In addition, they were described as traveling at a slow 100 to 130 miles per hour, instead of with the incredible swiftness attributed to earlier saucers, although at times they shot up and down. They were also described as hovering in one position.

The Air Force said no planes were sent out to intercept the objects, and no sightings were reported by "Operation Skywatch," the round-the-clock ground-observer operation now underway around the northern arc of the United States.

The Air Force said it had received only a preliminary report and therefore did not know why no attempt at interception had been made.

The air traffic control center at Washington National Airport, just across the Potomac River from the Capital, reported that its radar operators had picked up eight of the slow-moving objects around midnight last Saturday. They were flying in the vicinity of near-by Andrews Air Force Base.

The center said Capital Airlines Flight 807, southbound from National Airport, had reported seeing seven objects between Washington and Martinsburg, W. Va., at 3:15 A. M. (E. D. T.) the same night.

Officials of Capital Airlines said the pilot of Flight 807, Capt. "Casey" Pierman of Detroit, a veteran of seventeen years' service with the company, had spotted the objects and described them in these words:

"They were like falling stars without tails."

Captain Pierman, flying at normal cruising speed of 180 to 200 miles per hour, reported that three of the objects, which had the appearance of bright lights, were seen traveling with tremendous speed. No especial attention was paid to those, he reported to company officials, because these three could have been taken for falling stars.

Later three bright lights were observed, he reported, flying horizontally, and fast, at a tremendous height. They were watched from three to five seconds.

The pilot said he hadn't the slightest idea what the things were.

The eight objects picked up by Air Force radar were said to have been traveling at slightly more than 100 m. p. h.

The airport traffic control center said another air liner, Capital-National Airlines Flight 610, had reported observing a light following it from Herndon, Ca., to within four miles of National Airport.

The Air Force spokesman said that neither the center nor headquarters here had yet received reports on sightings said to have been made last Friday in the areas of Burlington, Vt.; South Portland, Me., and Staten Island, N. Y.

Two persons on Staten Island reported seeing saucers at about 10:15 P. M. (E. D. T.), Friday night. The objects, described as silvery in color tinged with red on the rims, were reported flying in a "V" formation of five. Said Mrs. Josephine Hetzel:

"I almost fainted when I looked up at the sky and saw what looked to me like five large dinner plates flying through the sky."

Frank Gondar said he saw them, too, "flying like geese." "They gave off a glow and didn't make a sound," he said.

At about the same hour, three New York residents reported sighting similar objects circling rapidly over Central Park.

Report of a Washington newspaper about the wave of sightings above the U.S. Capitol during the night of July 19–20, 1952.

in amazement, they tilted and disappeared vertically into the heavens. On Monday the magazine *LIFE* carried the headline, "Ghostly Demonstration Over Washington."

The Air Force had sent Capt. Ruppelt to Washington, and his research led him to conclude that the objects were UFOs. The importance of identifying them had reached its highest point yet—they were now part of world history.

On July 24, 1952, President Harry S. Truman and Chief of Staff Gen. Omar N. Bradley officially declared war on UFOs. *"Following the instructions of the President, the Defense Department gives orders to shoot down all UFOs which refuse to land upon being told to do so."*

The journalists hardly had time to discuss this spectacular order before there was a further demonstration over Washington. At about 9 p.m. on Saturday, July 26, the radar operators at the National Airport spotted five or six strange blips, objects moving south. The control tower at Andrews Field confirmed this. During the following two hours a number of sighting reports came in, some from airport personnel, others from pilots landing or taking off. The United Airlines flight No. 640 called saying its crew saw faint lights. The control tower answered, *"There are three blips coming towards you." "Yes, now they're getting nearer—now we see them very close to us—they are really magnificent."*

Officers at the Andrews tower confirmed having seen the three objects near the passenger plane. Barnes informed the Air Force and this time two F-94 jet fighters were in the air within two minutes, circling over Washington. One of the pilots reported seeing four lights near him. But when he tried to follow them, they out-maneuvered him. "It looked as if they were listening in to our radio messages," said Barnes later.

"Whenever I gave the pilots instructions, the blips raced off in the opposite direction." Finally they disappeared at a high speed. Shortly after that, "rotating lights which pulsated in changing colors" were seen over the Langley Air Base near Newport, Virginia, which lay in the direction that the UFOs had finally taken.

The following Monday all headlines were dedicated to the UFOs. One of the pilots, Lt. William Patterson, had declared at a press conference on Sunday morning:

"I tried to make contact with "them" below 1,000 feet, but they [the radar controllers] vectored us around. I saw several bright lights. I was at maximum speed, but even at that speed I couldn't close on them. I stopped chasing them because I saw no chance of overtaking them. I was alerted to other objects in my path. Later I chased a single bright light which I estimated to be about 10 miles away. I lost visual contact with it at about 2 miles."

"No flying saucer report in UFO history ever got more attention from the world than the Washington National Airport sightings," Capt. Ruppelt wrote later. Added to that were hundreds of telegrams from all over the country, sent to President Truman and protesting his orders. The population was on the verge of panic, and when Gen. Samford, chief of the ATIC, held a press conference on the 29th of July, he had to think a long time before he knew what to say. According to Ruppelt, *"Gen. Samford sat behind his big walnut desk in room 3A138 in the Pentagon and battled with his con-*

General Samford (middle, sitting) and Capt. Ruppelt (standing, middle) at the Washington press conference on July 29, 1952.

science. Should he tell the public the 'real truth'—that our skies are loaded with spaceships? No, the public might panic. The only answer was to debunk the UFOs."

That press conference was the biggest one since the end of World War II. Gen. Samford declared, before hundreds of journalists, that the UFOs above Washington had been radar disturbances caused by a temperature inversion. The direct visual observations were completely ignored as well as the fact that the inversion that night had measured only one degree Fahrenheit, far too low to affect radar at all.

Samford's declaration was in flagrant contradiction to the statements of the radar experts. *"I can say with certainty that they made circular movements, which no aircraft known to us is capable of doing,"* explained Barnes. *"In my opinion no natural phenomenon can explain those spots on the screen."* The blips definitely came from solid bodies. They weren't blurred as in the case of weather phenomena. The operators had estimated the size of the objects as 100 to 200 feet. *"The people involved were good radar men, men who deal in human lives. Each day they use their radar to enable thousands of people to come into Washington National Airport, and with a responsibility like that they should know a real target from a weather target,"* commented Capt. Ruppelt, and, therefore, labelled the National Airport sightings as "unidentified."

Indeed not all Air Force personnel were satisfied with Samford's declaration. *"One group was of the opinion that we then had enough evidence to support an official stand, that UFOs were real, and to be more precise, that they do not originate from this earth,"* writes Ruppelt in his book. *"The the-*

ory "possibly of extraterrestrial origin"—with a 'possibly' that approached 'they are' very closely, was the personal opinion of many highly decorated officers at the Pentagon, men whose personal opinions are almost already policy."
This group wanted to change the working methods of Project Blue Book.

They said we should not waste our time any longer investigating whether witnesses had seen anything unusual. Instead of that they wanted us to find out more about the UFOs. At first our work was to be carried out in strict secrecy, until we had all the answers, and after that the information was to be released to the public. The study of UFOs at that level was a big assignment and they wanted to engage scientists for the job . . . But Gen. Samford still gave the orders and he was of the opinion that we should carry out our work as before."

High-ranking Air Force officers decided that it was time to release a few good reports, to make the public familiar with the matter. After the Washington demonstration nobody knew what the next move of the UFOs would be. One could never be too sure; it was best to be prepared for all possibilities. It was against this background that Maj. Keyhoe's interview at the Pentagon was planned—a move given a lot of thought by the Air Force. But this strategy would soon change.

The number of sightings rose steadily and it seemed as if the UFO invasion would never end. In June alone over 250 sightings had been reported to the Air Force officially. Project Blue Book had official records of over 2,000 cases of sightings, of which 25% were designated as "unexplained." With that [data] the phenomenon had

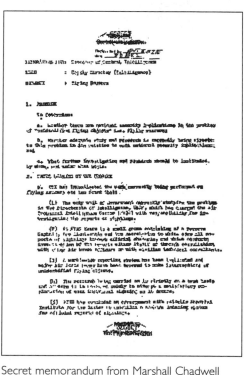

Secret memorandum from Marshall Chadwell to the Director of the CIA, dated September 11, 1952. "A worldwide reporting system has been instituted and major Air Force Bases have been ordered to intercept unidentified flying objects."

acquired a new dimension; it had become a matter of interest for the intelligence services. As early as September in 1952 the CIA started intervening in the investigations. Its aim was *"to determine whether there are national security implications in the problem of 'unidentified flying objects,' i.e. 'flying saucers'; whether adequate study and research is currently being directed to this problem . . . "* It was only in 1978 that some important documents of the CIA concerning this subject were released to the public, which enables us to reconstruct the proceedings. Thus we learn from two memoranda sent by Marshall Chadwell, Assistant Director of the Office of Scientific Intelligence, on September 11, and October 2, 1952 to the director of the CIA that:

- . . . a worldwide reporting system has been instituted and major Air Force Bases have been ordered to intercept unidentified flying objects.
- . . . The flying saucer situation contains two elements of danger which . . . have national security implications . . .
- The first involves mass psychological considerations and the second concerns the vulnerability of the United States to air attack . . .
- It is recommended . . . that the Director of Central Intelligence advise the National Security Council of the implications inherent in the flying saucer problem with the request that, under his statutory coordinating authority, the Director of Central Intelligence be empowered to initiate through the appropriate agencies, either within or without the Government, the investigation and research necessary to solve the problem . . .
- A national policy should be established as to what the public should be told regarding the phenomenon, in order to minimize the risk of panic.

This policy of censorship stood in opposition to two other endeavors. The first was that Secretary Kimball was in possession of the complete report of the analysis of the Tremonton film in October, but was awaiting the report from the Air Force before convening a press conference during which he intended to reveal and prove that UFOs were extraterrestrial spaceships. But in November Gen. Eisenhower, a Republican, was elected President and Kimball, a Democrat, had to make room for a Republican Secretary. His plans ended unfulfilled.

The second endeavor came from the ATIC—from Maj. Dewey Fournet and dozens of other officers. During the UFO wave Fournet was, as Officer-in-Charge of the UFO Project, a central figure in the evaluation of UFO reports. He was convinced of the existence of UFOs and opposed the policy of secrecy promulgated by the CIA. He had planned the press conference together with Secretary Kimball, at which they would reveal all that they knew. They would show that the UFOs were controlled by intelligent beings. And since their technology was so sophisticated as to rule out earthly origins, there was only one answer: alien spaceships were watching the earth. But for the CIA there was only one way to handle the UFO situation: *"complete control over Air Force investigations and a ruthless censorship to exterminate public belief in UFOs,"* as Maj. Keyhoe put it. So they decided to act quickly. Marshall Chadwell of the OSI wrote another memorandum on December 2, in which he said, *"At this time, the reports of incidents convince us that there is something going on that must have immediate attention. . . . Sightings of unexplained objects at great altitudes and travelling at high speeds in the vicinity of major U.S. defense installations are of such a nature that they are not attributable to natural phenomena or known types of aerial vehicles. OSI is proceeding to establish a consulting group of sufficient competence and stature to review this matter and convince the responsible authorities in the community that immediate research and development on this subject must be undertaken."*

Maj. Keyhoe, commenting on this, writes *"For this purpose the CIA arranged a meeting of Air Force representatives and scientists at the Pentagon to carry out a secret analysis of the UFO evidence. . . . But the scientists chosen by the CIA were known skeptics. Most of them knew practically nothing about UFOs and considered the subject nonsense. Since the CIA had complete authority, they could hold back evidence or trim it as they pleased. The CIA had no doubts about the success of such methods."*

The said meeting took place from January 14–17, 1953, with Dr. H. P. Robertson of the University of California as chairman—which led to its being referred to as the "Robertson Panel." Present at the meeting were the physicist Prof. Luis Alvarez, geophysicist Prof. Loyd Berkner, nuclear physicist Prof. Samuel Goudsmit, the astrophysicist Prof. Thornton Page and the astronomer Allen Hynek—and five CIA agents.

One of the ATIC officers told Maj. Keyhoe later:

We were all taken for a ride. The CIA did not want to prepare the public for the facts— the agents tried to bury the subject. They led the whole show and the scientists followed their lead. We presented over a hundred of the strongest verified reports. The agents bypassed the best ones. The scientists saw just 15 cases and the CIA men tried to pick holes in them. Fournet had sightings by top military and airline pilots—even scientists. The agents made it seem as if the witnesses were dopes, so the scientists brushed off the whole Fournet report, with the argument that it did not contain even the slightest evidence for the existence of interplanetary spaceships. Ed Ruppelt had plans for a special tracking system and that too was

List of participants at the CIA Robertson Panel on January 14–17, 1953.

rejected. I know those CIA agents were only following orders, but once or twice I nearly blew up!

In the official protocol, CIA Agent F. C. Durant wrote:

> Friday morning: At 10:00 Mr. Fournet gave a briefing on his fifteen months in Washington as Project Officer for UFOs and his personal conclusions. . . . Mr. Fournet, in his presentation, showed how he had eliminated each of the known and probable causes of sightings leaving 'extraterrestrial' as the only one remaining in many cases. Fournet's background as an aeronautical engineer and technical intelligence officer (Officer, Project Blue Book for 15 months) could not be slighted. However, the panel could not accept any of the cases sighted [sic] by him because they were raw, unevaluated reports. . . .

One notes the contradiction here. On the one hand, the very experienced Mr. Fournet has been able to rule out most of the possibilities of identification. On the other hand, his cases were new and not yet evaluated.

On the last day, the Robertson Panel approved an education program for the public. *"Integrating the efforts of all concerned agencies was that the program should have two major aims: training and debunking. . . . The debunking aim would result in reduction of public interest in flying saucers; they evoke a strong psychological reaction. This education could be accomplished by mass media, such as television, motion pictures, and popular articles. The basis of such an education would be actual case histories that were puzzling at first, but later explained. As in the case of conjuring tricks, there is much less intrigue if the 'secret' is known. . . . The National*

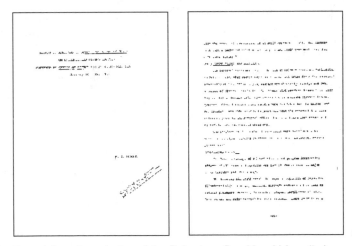

Extract from the minutes of the Robertson Panel in which an "educational program" was decided upon with the aim of "training and debunking."

Security Agencies should take immediate steps to strip unidentified flying objects of the special status they have been given, and remove the aura of mystery they have unfortunately acquired." *"We were instructed to work on a nationwide debunking campaign,"* said Press Spokesman Albert Chop. *"To publish articles in papers and give interviews on UFO reports to make UFO reports look ludicrous."* Capt. Ruppelt added, *"That was not the worst. We were ordered to hide sightings if possible, but if a strong report did get out, we had to publish a fast explanation, make up something to kill the report in a hurry, and also ridicule the witness, especially if we couldn't figure out a plausible answer. We even had to discredit our own pilots."* A few months later, Chop and Ruppelt resigned from the Air Force. *"We now had a new policy,"* wrote Ruppelt in his book, *"which said, 'don't say anything more'."* Officially, the UFO research work was now only in the hands of the Air Force, which, according to a memorandum of the Robertson Panel, apparently maintained only a dwindling interest in the matter.

In August, Ruppelt finished his work as leader of Project Blue Book. The last closing report was written and contained the results of the investigation. Of 1,593 reports which the Blue Book team had analyzed, they identified as

Balloons: 18.51 %;

Airplanes: 11.66 %;

Astronomical (planets, meteorites, etc.): 14.2 %;

Others (such as searchlight reflections, birds, inversion, etc.): 4.2 %;

Hoaxes: 1.66 %;

Insufficient data: 22.72 %

But still, 26.94 % had to be declared as unidentified flying objects, and that percentage represented 429 sightings.

On August 26, 1953, new instructions were given for the treatment of UFO reports [for the Air Force Regulation 200–2.]

"Procedures for reporting information and evidence pertaining to unidentified flying objects . . ." This report goes on to say, *"Air Force interest in unidentified flying objects is twofold. First, as a possible threat to the security of the*

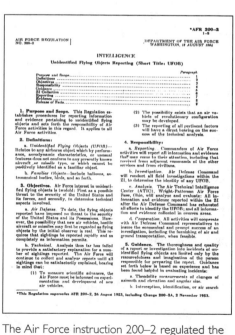

The Air Force instruction 200–2 regulated the procedures to be followed when UFOs were reported.

United States and its forces, and, secondly, to determine the technical aspects involved." The information policy is dealt with under paragraph 9, which is titled, ironically, "Release of Facts." It says, in response to local inquiries, "*it is permissible to inform news media representatives on UFOs when the object is positively identified as a familiar object. See paragraph 2b . . . For those objects which are not explainable, only the fact that ATIC will analyze the data is worthy of release, due to the many unknowns involved.*"

What this means is that only those cases that are hoaxes, jokes or misinterpretations can be given to the press. Under paragraph 7, "Reporting," it says that all UFO reports should be forwarded to the nearest ATIC service office by telex or radio. Also, the presence of evidence should be reported immediately, which according to paragraph 9, would include photographs, films, radar pictures and alleged or real material. This would include as well the wreckage of "flying saucers," which were to be taken by the quickest means of transport to Wright Patterson Air Force Base.

Project Blue Book was now only a showpiece project meant for the "education" of the public, consisting of a team of low-ranking officers and two secretaries. The sloppiness with which the research was conducted—identify at all costs, was the motto—is shown in an example given by Professor J. Alan Hynek, the astronomical advisor to Project Blue Book, in his book *A UFO Report* (1977).

"*17th October, 1958, Grand Rapids, Michigan: 24 spherical amber-colored objects, flying at a very great height. Two swarms, each consisting of 12 objects. Period, 25 seconds. Evaluation by the Air Force: Meteors.*" Said Hynek, "*It must be actually put in the Guinness Book of Records, under Astronomy.*" It was therefore no wonder that, by the time the project was closed, in 1969, the percentage of unidentified flying objects sank to 5.5 % of 12,618 cases investigated—a few years later, it was even lower and had sunk to an obligatory 0.8 %.

Nevertheless, the hunt for UFOs went on and at least the cadets of the Air Force were kept informed, as this subject was included in the curriculum of the United States Air Force Academy. One of the textbooks for the department of physics, called "Introductory Space Science," deals in detail with UFOs. It says there, "*We, too have fired on UFOs,*" and cites a case which Capt. Ruppelt dates back to 1952. At 10:00 one summer morning, the radar control of a military airfield picked up a UFO which was approaching the base at a speed of 700 mph. Two F-86 jet fighters were sent up to intercept the object at an altitude of about 3,000 feet. One of the pilots got as close to the object as 500 yards away and described it on the radio as very clearly saucer-shaped. When the pilot increased speed and approached the disk, suddenly it shot up vertically. When it had reached a distance of about 1,000 yards from him, the pilot started firing at it, but he could not hit the target. A few seconds later, it disappeared unscathed.

During the night of December 4, 1952, a frightened Air Force pilot landed at his base in Laredo, Texas. He too had been ordered to intercept a

UFO above Fort Knox Air Force Base, Kentucky.

UFO, but suddenly, the UFO had attacked him. The pilot had been chasing the object when, suddenly, it started coming towards him, and would have rammed his F-51 jet had he not, at the last second, been able to swerve out of the way and escape. The bluish shining object shot past him at an unimaginable speed. The jittery pilot, sitting trembling in his cockpit, was just considering returning back to base when he saw the object suddenly shoot up vertically and then come down in a circle towards him, as if it was going to attack him once more. The pilot switched off his lights and dived down spiralling, and once more, escaped. The object then turned away and flew towards the airfield at Laredo. Shortly afterwards it turned away again from the air base and finally disappeared vertically.

Another UFO encounter above Lake Michigan, which took place eleven months later, did not end so happily. The pilot concerned this time was Lt. Felix Moncla, one of the best pilots at Kinross Air Base at Lake Michigan. He was courageous, responsible and very quick in his reactions. He had "nerves of steel" and was absolutely familiar with the machine that he flew, an F-89 fighter. He had once boasted that, if he wanted to, he could fly the aircraft blindfolded. And it was for these qualities that he was always chosen for special and dangerous missions. But nobody thought that this mission was going to be dangerous. It was November 23, 1953, and a radar officer spotted an unidentified object above the security zone of the air base. All attempts to contact the unknown flier over the radio failed. The object carried out the most surprising maneuvers. The radar officer said to his commander, "That guy is crazy, but he must have a wonderful plane."

The commander stared at the radarscope. He checked with headquarters to find out if any planes were operating above Soo Locks. The answer was negative. At 9:18 p.m., Felix Moncla and his radar officer Lt. R. R. Wilson,

UFO chases B-57 interceptor fighter near Edwards Air Force Base, California, 1954.

started his F-89 fighter. The sky was cloudy. His mission was to identify the object. Surrounded by a thick bank of white clouds, he could see nothing. He flew blind, for the radar board showed him the direction of his target. The radar controller on the ground had both aircraft on his screen. When the jet approached the object, the object changed direction. It now flew in the direction of Lake Superior, and Moncla started chasing it at a speed of 500 mph. For nine minutes, the people at the ground station breathlessly watched the cat and mouse game on the radar screen. Moncla had overtaken the object. A skirmish in the air was now imminent, and the commander was just about to give his orders to the pilot to start firing, when something unbelievable happened. Both radar blips suddenly melted into one. "Hello, Moncla, Moncla come in," cried the commander into the microphone. "What has happened, F-89 . . . Give an answer, give an answer." Nobody answered. The blip took off at a terrific speed and disappeared from the radar screen.

The ground station had noted the last position of the F-89. They thought, as unbelievable as it sounded, that the F-89 had collided with the object and then crashed, whereas the object was still in a position to fly away. A frantic search action was started. Helicopters and fighters went into the air. American and Canadian Coast Guard boats were sent out, but without success. Not a single trace was found. No debris, no life jacket, not even a patch of oil. The F-89 had disappeared completely, and with it, the 2 pilots. Officially, the incident was at first denied. Then it was said that the F-89 had crashed, owing to unknown reasons, when it was following an aircraft of the Canadian Air Force. This declaration was at once denied by Canada, for at that time, that country did not have any RCAF aircraft over the Great Lakes area.

At about noon, on July 1, 1954, radar at Griffin Air Force Base, New York state, picked up a UFO. An F-94 Starfire was sent up to intercept. After a few minutes, the pilot could see a glowing disc-like object and flew towards it. As he gradually approached the UFO, and could see more details, the pilot described it, saying *"It's very bright. Oh, my eyes. I feel as if I've been paralyzed. It's a terrible heat."* Those were his last words. The burning airplane crashed on a house at the edge of the town Walesville, in New York state. Four people died in a sea of flames, a man, his wife and their two children, while five neighbors were injured very seriously. The radar operator said later that the UFO had disappeared at a tremendous speed. The Air Force could not deny this case, but did not want to say anything about the cause of the crash. In an official declaration, they finally agreed to a simple mechanical failure.

"We have stacks of reports of flying saucers," conceded the Air Force General Benjamin Chidlaw in 1953. *"We take them seriously when you consider we have lost many men and planes trying to intercept them."* And more than once, this had almost set off a third world war.

CHAPTER 6

The First Contact

It was late in the morning, just before 11:00, when the two cars reached Desert Center in the California desert. Desert Center is a small desert town on Highway 10 that connects Los Angeles with Phoenix, Arizona and lies very close to the outlet to National Road 177, leading to Parker, Arizona. The two vehicles came to a stop side by side. The driver of the second car leaned out of his window and asked the elderly gentleman sitting in the passenger seat of the other car, *"Professor, do we stick to our plans?"*

"Oh yes," answered The Professor with a slight Polish accent, *"follow us on to the 177. I have a feeling it can't be very far now."*

He looked rather tired, except for his eyes, which were shining with expectation. Deep down inside him, he sensed that this was the day it would happen and, with every passing minute, his conviction grew stronger. He had known it for two days. He had called his friends in Phoenix and arranged to meet them on November 20, 1952 at 8:00 in the morning, at the only coffee shop at Blythe on the state line between California and Arizona. He had started on his journey at 1 a.m. from Palomar Gardens, accompanied by his secretary, Lucy McGinnis, and Alice K. Wells, the proprietress of the Palomar Gardens Café, which was a frequent haunt of The Professor.

He himself did not drive, so the two women took turns at the wheel. Most of the time he spoke about how, in his opinion, the contact with "them" would take place, and what he had learned about "them" during his stay in Tibet. The first half of the California journey took the friends over winding mountain roads through the Indian reservations of Pala, Cahuilla and Santa Rosa, followed by the reproachful looks of deer, hares, rabbits and other such animals, whose nocturnal peace they had rudely disturbed. At about 5 a.m. they got onto Highway 10 near Indio in California. They finally reached the café at Blythe at 8:30 a.m., after having been delayed by a flat tire. There they met the young anthropologist Dr. George Hunt Williamson and his wife, as well as the Baileys.

The Baileys had visited The Professor in August at Palomar Gardens after reading an article in the magazine *Fate*, which stated that The Professor had seen many UFOs and made many photographs of them, mostly with his six-inch telescope.

The professor, George Adamski, was actually a philosopher, 61 years of age. He was born in Poland in 1891, and in 1892 his parents emigrated to the United States. Even as a boy he was interested in metaphysics. His parents were too poor to provide him with a really good education. He himself never got rid of the Polish accent of his parents. But, in New York, he was lucky to find a friend and mentor who helped him make a journey to Tibet. Years later, after completing military service during World War I and working at various other jobs in different places, he finally settled down in California. There he founded a mystic school called the "Royal Order of Tibet," where he taught the Royal Way: the way of life in harmony with the

George Adamski with his 16-inch telescope.

laws of nature. He possessed no academic qualifications, nor had he ever been a lecturer at any university. But, owing to his wide knowledge, which he passed on to others in hundreds of free lectures, his students and friends called him simply "Professor." Ever since he had acquired his 6-inch telescope—later on a friend presented him with one having a 16-inch mirror—he spent hours and hours looking into the clear night sky, to get a feeling for the infinite depth and beauty of the universe. In order to convey these impressions to his students he mounted a small camera onto the telescope and took pictures of planets, star clusters and galaxies.

It was his conviction that mankind was not alone in the universe. The old Sanskrit texts which he had studied in Tibet said that all planets in the universe carried life, and that visitors from these heavenly planets had come to the Earth ever since the ancient past to teach mankind. When the first reports about the mysterious flying saucers appeared in the newspapers, he felt that his convictions were being confirmed. From then on, he spent every clear night looking for UFOs, for extraterrestrial visitors. Doing so, he concentrated mainly on the moon. First of all, it seemed to him more sensible to point his telescope at an interesting object than just into empty space and hope for a chance discovery. Secondly, it seemed to him that visitors, considering the enormous distances in the universe, would use the moon as a midway station. Apparently, his conjectures were correct. At any rate, the result was dozens of UFO photographs of excellent quality. They were so interesting, that the government requested him to send his photographs to the Air Force in future. Captain Ruppelt wrote later: *"He literally overwhelmed us with photographs. Our experts examined them carefully and found no reason to suspect any kind of hoax."*

The Professor himself wrote later: *"Since then, day and night, through heat and cold, wind, rain, and fog, I have spent every moment possible outdoors watching the skies for spacecraft and hoping without end that for some reason, some time, one of them will come in close and even land."*

The year 1951 gave him cause to hope since the number of successful photographs had increased considerably compared to previous years. The spaceships seemed to be coming closer to the Earth and in larger numbers. For the first time, a photograph showed more than just lights and dark shadows. So he decided to publish these pictures in the magazine *Fate* to get into contact with fellow believers. In fact, he received hundreds of letters, and a number of the correspondents even visited him. Amongst them were the Baileys.

They told him about Dr. Williamson, who had studied anthropology and archaeology at the Universities of New Mexico and Arizona. Dr. Williamson was an expert in Amerindian cultures and was carrying out field research in the United States, Mexico, Canada and Peru. His interest in UFOs was kindled when friendly Indians in the reservations told him about their sightings, and how those sightings corresponded with their ancient legends which spoke of heavenly ships of star people, who had promised their Indian ancestors in the remote past that they would visit

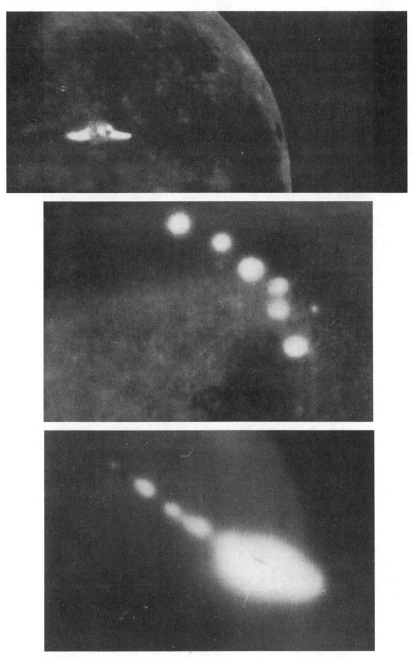

Three photographs of shining objects above the moon, taken by
Adamski in 1950 with his 16-inch telescope.

them once again. Being a radio ham, Williamson had spent the whole of 1952 trying to get in touch with "them" by means of radio telegraphy and Morse signals. Williamson believed that his efforts had not been in vain, for he did receive answering signals.

The Professor was eager to meet Williamson and when they finally did, 4 weeks later at Palomar Gardens, he was sure that he had found someone of the same mind as himself. Williamson told him that he had received signals which suggested that a landing would take place in California in the near future. The Baileys had also heard to close UFO encounters in the Mojave Dessert. "*I know, I am sure it will happen this year.*" The professor had answered, "*The UFO maneuvers over Washington were a sign that a new phase in 'their' approach is imminent and that they will soon land. And when that happens, I want to be there! During the days and nights during which I kept track of them, I probably learned more about them than any other person on this Earth.*"

He revealed to them that he had learned the art of telepathy during his stay in Tibet. "*Even if they don't speak our languages, telepathy is a universal language—communication by means of thought and pictures, without words. I will be in a position to communicate with them, and—please don't laugh—I feel that this will happen very soon.*"

"*When the time comes, please call us,*" said the fascinated Mrs. Bailey, "*we want to be there at all costs.*"

"*I will do that,*" promised The Professor.

Sitting at the café at Blythe, consuming his breakfast with his four new-found friends, who needed sleep as much as he himself did, he sensed a feeling of strong mutual trust. "*Professor, just tell us where you want to go, and we'll trust your intuition,*" said Mrs. Williamson, herself a well-known anthropologist. The Professor answered, "*I think that the best thing would be to go back on Highway 10, for, while driving here, we passed Desert Center, and there was a country road going left to Parker. I had a strong feeling that it would be somewhere around there.*"

Shortly after 11:00 a.m., as the car carrying the Professor started honking and flashing its lights, the two married couples realized that they had reached their destination, at least according to the intuition of The Professor. Williamson looked around. An old river bed crossed the road at the spot, but what was now left of the once sizable river was only a shallow brook that apparently came from the foot of the mountain that rose up from the landscape. The earth was not so sandy as in other parts of the desert, but strewn with pieces of rock, mostly with jagged edges and sharp corners, apparently of volcanic origin. The scattered bushes, amongst them silver-white desert holly with tiny bloodred berries, redeemed the terrain in front of the impressive looking Coxcomb Mountains from hopeless dreariness. It was winter, and a cold raw wind was blowing.

After inspecting the area, they decided to have lunch. So they spread out their blankets and opened their picnic baskets. Shortly after noon, they heard the noise of a motor. A twin-propellered Cessna came up from behind

The little dome shaped spacecraft appears between the hills—photographed by G. Adamski.

the mountains and flew slowly over their heads. Then suddenly, their attention was caught by another object. Above the same peak over which the Cessna had flown, they now saw a huge cigar-shaped vessel at a very great height hovering absolutely silently, its silvery surface reflecting the sunlight. *"Is it a spaceship?"* asked George Williamson excitedly.

"No George, I don't believe it is," answered Lucy McGiness, rather irritated. *"But that baby is high! And see how big it is!"* called out Mr. Bailey. Alice Wells joined in, saying, *"You're right, George. It's orange on top— the whole length!"*

They were all excited now, too excited to get their cameras, so instead they grabbed, one after the other, the two pairs of binoculars they had brought with them, to see if they could make out more details. Only The Professor remained silent and withdrawn. *"Someone take me down the road— quick!"* He said a little later, *"maybe the saucer is already up there somewhere, afraid to come down here where too many people would see 'them.'"* Lucy and Al Bailey jumped into the car and took Adamski to the place where he wanted to go, some 800 yards away from where the others were standing. They unloaded his equipment, set up the tripod and mounted the telescope. He then requested that the couple—much to their disappointment—go back to where the others were, and to pick him up an hour later.

Armed with his camera, he walked to the foot of a small hill, from where he watched the additional movements of the spaceship. Thoughts raced through his head. Would his great wish for a landing be fulfilled now? Would he get a chance to communicate with the aliens? Would they take him on board their ship; perhaps even take him to a foreign world? Still sunk in his thoughts, he saw a flash of light in the sky. Above the saddle between two hills, a small, strangely beautiful dome-shaped craft had appeared, of which he quickly took three photographs. They were there! If only they would come a little closer. What would they look like, the crew

Three original photographs which George Hunt Williamson took on that memorable day, November 20, 1952. The picnic, the examination of the footprints, George Adamski at the spot where the alien stood.

of the vessel? Would he ever get a chance to have a look at the inside of that ship?

Once more the thoughts of the Professor were interrupted when he saw a man standing at the entrance to a gorge between two small hills, some 400 yards away from him. A prospector, or a mountaineer who needed his help? Rather irritated, the Professor went towards him and felt something strange taking hold of him. He could now see the man better. He was wearing a brown suit, rather like a skiing suit. He was shorter than the Professor, and his blond, wind-tossed hair reached his shoulders. He smiled a smile that touched the bottom of Adamski's heart, dispersed all doubts and filled him with a feeling of trust for the stranger. When he was within a few feet of the man, Adamski was sure that he was looking at a visitor from another world. *"I felt like a little child in the presence of one with great wisdom and much love,"* he wrote later, *"and I became very humble within myself, for from him radiated infinite understanding and kindness, with supreme humility."*

He was about 5 feet 2 inches tall, and looked like a young man of about

28 years. He had a round face, an unusually high forehead and large gray-green eyes, slightly slanted. His cheekbones were high, the nose finely chiseled, the chin smooth without any sign of a beard, his skin slightly tanned. His long hair was the color of sand and glistened in the sun. His chocolate-colored uniform seemed to be made of one piece, wide on the top with a close-fitting, high collar, like a turtle-neck, but not turned down. It had long wide Raglan sleeves which ended in close-fitting cuffs at the hands, a sash or band at the waist about eight inches wide, the lower part with wide legs ending in close-fitting cuffs at the ankles, rather like ski trousers. The whole uniform had a certain sheen or lustre, and revealed no seams, buttons, buckles or zippers. There were no pockets either. His burgundy shoes were high, seemed to be of very fine, soft material, woven but somehow resembling leather. The shoes "opened" on the outer side near the arch of the foot. There were no laces, zippers or other fasteners there, but two narrow straps, which were probably stretchable.

"*Where do you come from?*" asked The Professor. But the stranger shook his head with an apologetic look on his face, as if to say that he did not understand him. Only sign language and telepathy were left. Adamski imagined a planet, pointed to the sun which was high up in the sky, and said "sun." Then he made a circle around the sun with his hand and said "Mercury," and a second circle around it and said "Venus," a third circle and said "Earth," and pointed down to the ground. The alien seemed to understand. He pointed to the sun, drew one circle around it, then a second circle and pointed to himself. The Professor was now sure that he wanted to say that he came from Venus (or of any other second planet of a solar system, we have to add).

A second question, "*Why do you come to the Earth?*" was then posed by The Professor with what he thought were suitable mental pictures and gestures. The stranger transmitted the impression that he came with friendly intentions, and that it had to do with the radiations extending out from the Earth. The Professor conveyed the mental picture of an atomic explosion and asked whether this had anything to do with such explosions on the Earth. The stranger assented. "*Are these dangerous?*" asked The Professor. "*Yes,*" said the stranger with a nod of his head, while his face expressed deep compassion. He pointed to The Professor, then a plant on the Earth and gestured to signify the whole Earth and indicated that all this would be destroyed.

Asked by the professor if he had come with the little space vessel which he had photographed, the alien pointed to a hill over

Sketch of the alien as seen by Lucy McGiniss through the binoculars.

which the bell-shaped craft was hovering. The Professor was surprised to see it there because, meanwhile, he had lost sight of it. The stranger further made The Professor understand that these smaller spacecraft came from a much larger mother ship stationed elsewhere, and that they were driven by a principle of magnetic attraction and repulsion. Further also that there were even smaller ships, mostly unmanned, and that some of these ships had also crashed. He also indicated that people on the Earth were responsible for these disasters.

Asked whether he believed in God, the stranger answered that there was a creator of the universe, but that our knowledge of Him was very shallow. His people had a wider knowledge in this respect and lived according to the Laws of the Creator, not the laws of materialism, as we did on Earth.

Extraterrestrials from various planets did, and would, visit our Earth frequently. Space travel was, in fact, quite simple, and was a regular activity among the inhabitants of various other planets. The inhabitants of these planets were principally humanoid, for the human form was a universal form. The differences were only in stature, color and in the shape of details. Their bodies were also mortal, but their souls would live on forever. They would go through innumerable incarnations to evolve themselves, and he himself had once, long ago, lived on Earth.

He went on to declare that further landings and contacts would take place, but at first not in very highly populated areas, for the population could get into a panic, and may even tear the visitors into pieces. Finally, he indicated to the professor that it was time for him to get back to his ship. While walking towards the ship accompanied by The Professor, he repeatedly pointed to his footsteps, as if to say that they were of particular interest. Soon they were standing near the extremely beautiful spacecraft, which resembled a big bell rather than a saucer, and whose translucent material appeared more crystalline and transparent than metal—rather like very thick glass. It floated above the ground, three spherical balls on the underside; there was a row of circular ports, covered by a dome from which a glowing white ball protruded. A gust of wind caused the vessel to wobble, and its surface broke the sunlight as a prism does, reflecting it as beautiful rainbow-colored rays. The Professor was excited and enchanted as never before. Certain that this was the most wonderful and the most important moment in his eventful life, he tried to absorb as much information about the wonderful craft as he could.

The alien warned him not to get too close to the ship, but the warning came too late. His right shoulder had come under the rim of the vessel, and his right arm was violently pulled upwards, only to be thrown back against his own body again. He could move his arm but it had become totally insensate. It took three months for it to heal again; but at the moment he was far more worried about the negatives he had in the right-hand pocket of his jacket. He took them out immediately and put them in his left pocket. Seeing that, the stranger requested Adamski to give him one of those cartridges, indicating that he would return it later. Adamski complied. The

Professor's requests to be allowed to photograph the alien and the ship were refused, as well as his request to have a look inside the craft. The stranger took leave of him, went around the vessel, seemed to step on to the rim— and disappeared from sight.

Adamski sadly watched the space vessel gliding over the peak and disappearing beyond the horizon. Later he wrote: "*I felt that a part of me was going with that spaceship. . . . There was an emptiness such as can be compared only with the feelings experienced when a very dear one departs.*"

Then he had to get back to his friends, who had been watching everything that had happened through their binoculars and were already coming towards him. Shortly afterwards he heard a loud thundering noise in the sky. A big B-36 of the Air Force circled the sky above the area, and finally took off in the direction in which the space vessel had disappeared. The roaring of the B-36 was in jarring contrast to the silence of both the space vessels that Adamski had seen.

He looked at his watch. It was 1:30 p.m. His encounter with the alien must have lasted almost an hour. While he was still pondering that meeting, Williamson had discovered the footprints of the visitor from space and asked his wife to bring the plaster of Paris from the car, which he always had with him, being an anthropologist and archaeologist. Now The Professor, too, could see why the alien had repeatedly pointed out his footsteps and indicated that they were important. The prints showed strange characters, which Williamson later identified as ancient sacred symbols of mankind.

Half an hour later, sitting in a café at Desert Center, the Professor told

Close-up of a footprint of the visitor.

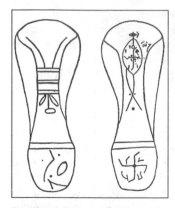

Sketches of the footprints.

them about his experience. "We must inform the press!" said Williamson. This was an historic moment, and since the Professor lived as a retiree in a secluded place, Williamson offered to do the necessary work. Apart from that, the professor was no longer interested in such worldly matters. His thoughts were still with the visitor from elsewhere. He had promised to return the film cartridge. That meant he would come back again. If only he knew when!

On November 24, 1952, an article describing the encounter in the desert appeared under the large headline *"Flying Saucer Passenger Names Atom Bomb as the Reason for Visit"* in the *Phoenix Gazette*. Williamson sent a copy of this article to the British UFO researcher, Sir Desmond Leslie, a grand-nephew of Sir Winston Churchill. Leslie was just then working on a manuscript for

Professor George Adamski in front of an idealized painting of the extraterrestrial visitor he met on November 20, 1952.

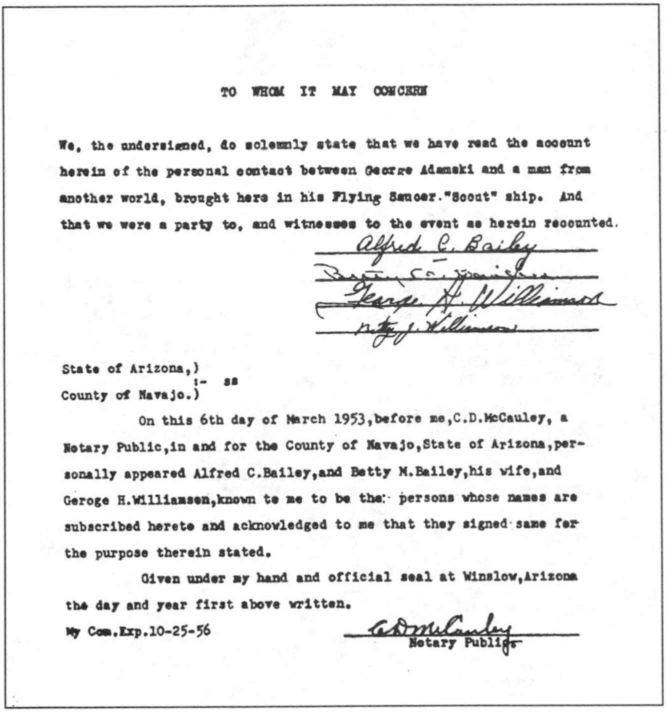

TO WHOM IT MAY CONCERN

We, the undersigned, do solemnly state that we have read the account herein of the personal contact between George Adamski and a man from another world, brought here in his Flying Saucer."Scout" ship. And that we were a party to, and witnesses to the event as herein recounted.

Alfred C. Bailey

Betty M. Bailey

George H. Williamson

Betty J. Williamson

State of Arizona,)
                 :- ss
County of Navajo.)

On this 6th day of March 1953,before me,C.D.McCauley, a Notary Public,in and for the County of Navajo,State of Arizona,personally appeared Alfred C.Bailey,and Betty M.Bailey,his wife,and Geroge H.Williamson,known to me to be the persons whose names are subscribed hereto and acknowledged to me that they signed same for the purpose therein stated.

Given under my hand and official seal at Winslow,Arizona the day and year first above written.

My Com.Exp.10-25-56

C.D.McCauley
Notary Public

Affidavit of the married couples Williamson and Bailey.

a book about UFOs, and he found the article so interesting that he decided to include the report in his book. He wrote to the professor, who promised to write a complete report for him about the events of that memorable November 20, 1952.

The book appeared early in 1953 under the title *Flying Saucers Have Landed*. Within a few months it became a best-seller, and over 100,000 copies were sold in the United States alone. The Professor became famous. But he was accused of being a liar and a fraud by some, and was threatened by others; he still remains, even posthumously, a controversial figure. Yet there are a number of indications which make his "incredible" story less incredible. On March 6, 1953, all the six witnesses who had been with the professor when he met the alien appeared before a notary public and signed an affidavit stating *"We, the undersigned, do solemnly state that we have read the account herein of the personal contact between George Adamski and a man from another world brought here in his flying saucer scout ship, and that we were a party to and witnesses to the event as herein recounted."*

In 1956 Richard Ogden of Seattle, Washington, asked the Air Force what their opinion was about Adamski's story, considering an Air Force B-36 had allegedly followed the said space vessel. The answer from ATIC was

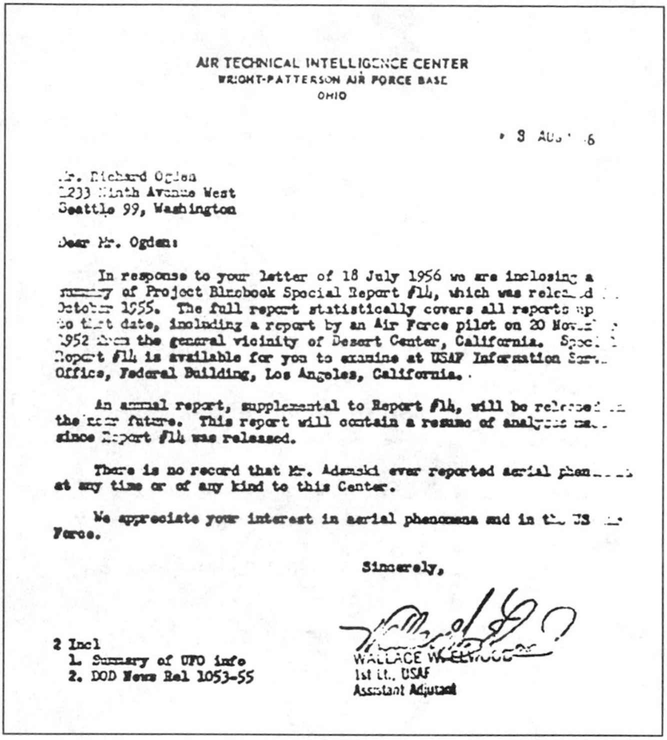

AIR TECHNICAL INTELLIGENCE CENTER
WRIGHT-PATTERSON AIR FORCE BASE
OHIO

> 3 AUg ' 6

Mr. Richard Ogden
1233 Ninth Avenue West
Seattle 99, Washington

Dear Mr. Ogden:

In response to your letter of 18 July 1956 we are inclosing a summary of Project Bluebook Special Report #14, which was released October 1955. The full report statistically covers all reports up to that date, including a report by an Air Force pilot on 20 November 1952 in the general vicinity of Desert Center, California. Special Report #14 is available for you to examine at USAF Information Service Office, Federal Building, Los Angeles, California.

An annual report, supplemental to Report #14, will be released in the near future. This report will contain a resume of analysis made since Report #14 was released.

There is no record that Mr. Adamski ever reported aerial phenomena at any time or of any kind to this Center.

We appreciate your interest in aerial phenomena and in the US Air Force.

Sincerely,

2 Incl
1. Summary of UFO info
2. DOD News Rel 1053-55

WALLACE W. ELWOOD
1st Lt., USAF
Assistant Adjutant

Confirmation of the ATIC that there was a USAF pilot's report in the files of Blue Book about a UFO sighting on November 20, 1952, in the "general vicinity of Desert Center, California."

unequivocal. Included in the files of Project Blue Book, there was a report from a pilot of a B-36 who had flown around the area near Desert Center on November 20, at the said time. The Air Force, therefore, had confirmed at least that little bit of Adamski's story.

But that was not the end. On December 13, 1952, the bell-shaped craft in which the alien had first landed in the Californian desert, and which Adamski called the scout ship, flew low over Palomar Gardens. Early in the morning, a loud howling noise in the sky, like that made by a jet fighter, had indicated that something was going on up there. At about 9:00 the professor saw a bright streak crossing the sky. He could then make out an iridescent, glassy-looking object, its surface shining in bright, variegated colors. It came closer and closer, as close as about 600 yards at a height of about 300 feet. Adamski took four photographs through his telescope before the object started moving again. The object then glided over the houses, crossed over Adamski's garden where it dropped a film cartridge, before it crossed over a gorge and finally disappeared behind the tops of the trees.

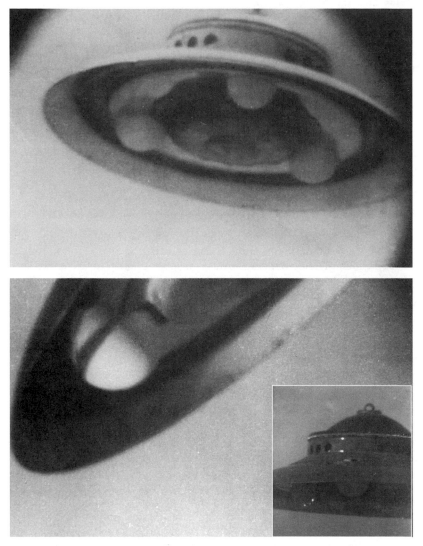

Three telescope photographs Adamski took on December 13, 1952, of a "scout ship" over Palomar Gardens.

One of Adamski's neighbors, Air Force Sgt. Jerrold Baker, was even able to take another picture of the object as it flitted past.

When Adamski got his film developed, he was very satisfied with the results. The photographs were sharp and clear, and every detail was recognizable, better than anything he had obtained so far. On the film which the alien had thrown down, there were a number of mysterious symbols like hieroglyphics. During the following years, various attempts were made to decipher these symbols. It was only in 1958 that it became known that a French archaeologist, Professor Marcel Homet, had discovered very similar-looking symbols in the Brazilian jungle.

On June 1, 1953, a meeting was held at the Veterans Administration Building in Washington D.C. where a group of U.S. Air Force Reserve Officers were briefed about flying saucers. Air Force Press Officer, Albert M. Chop, presided. Amongst the speakers were the physicist Harold Sherman, and the Air Force photography expert Pev Marley, who had worked on Hollywood projects like Cecil B. de Mille's *Greatest Show on Earth. "If these photographs have been faked,"* said Marley, *"then they are the most skillfully faked trick photographs that I have ever seen. The shadows on the flying saucer tally completely with the shadows on the ground, so that a double exposure is ruled out. To produce such cunning fakes, one would need very expensive equipment which Adamski, obviously, did not possess. I, therefore, consider these pictures to be genuine."*

Sufficient grounds, therefore, existed for the Air Force to investigate Adamski's story thoroughly. If the flying saucers had indeed been brought to the Earth in gigantic mother ships, as Adamski claimed to have seen and photographed on many occasions, then it should be possible to locate these vessels in orbit around the Earth. As a matter of fact, a later UFO sighting report seemed to confirm Adamski's statements and caused a stir amongst the highest military personnel.

Shortly before dawn, on December 6, 1952, a B-29 bomber of the U.S. Air Force was flying over the Gulf of Mexico on its way back to its base in Texas. The crew had just left a strenuous night flight to Florida behind them and the only thought they had in mind was to get home and relax. The moon was shining brightly, and they were flying at a height of about 20,000 feet. At 5:23 a.m. the bomber was about 100 miles south of the coast of Louisiana. The pilot, Captain John Harter, asked his radar officer Lt. Sid Coleman over the intercom to switch on the radar. Two minutes later Coleman, sitting in the rear of the machine, was looking at the screen, trying to make out the coastline. Then suddenly, a blip appeared to one side of the screen. At first, the radar officer thought no more about it. It might have been an airplane. But when the cursor went around once again, he jumped up in surprise. Within a second the blip had moved 15 miles.

Shortly thereafter, a second blip appeared and started moving towards the first which, in turn, was racing towards the B-29. It seemed spooky. For a moment it looked as if the two objects must inevitably collide with each other. Then Coleman saw that their courses were slightly different. He grabbed a stopwatch and called out to Sgt. Bailey, the flight engineer, to come over. Before the blips disappeared again he timed their movement. Their speed worked out to be exactly 5,000 mph. They looked at each other speechless for a moment, then Coleman picked up the microphone and informed Pilot Harter. *"Captain, have a look at the radar screen. We have just spotted an unknown object flying at 5,000 miles per hour." "Impossible!"* answered Harter, *"Check the equipment again."*

While Coleman was checking the calibrations, Bailey was watching the screen, fascinated. *"There's one more now,"* he called out, *"no, two!"* A fraction of a second later, Navigation Officer Lt. Cassidy reported on the intercom *"They're on my screen, too!"* Coleman was finished with the calibrations, and a few moments later there were four objects racing across the screen. Then came Harter's voice over the radio, *"I have four unknown objects at the 12:00 position. What have you got?"* *"They're on all three screens,"* answered Coleman. *"I've recalibrated. The equipment is in order."* Harter followed the tracks of the objects incredulously. When one of them came dangerously close to the plane on the starboard side, he warned the others, saying *"Unknown object at 3:00 position."* In the stern, Bailey jumped up and looked out through the starboard window. To his surprise, he saw a shiny blue object tearing past, from forward towards the stern. Hardly had the objects vanished before a new squadron was seen on all three screens, objects that were flying at a speed of almost 5,000 mph towards the B-29. The hearts of the crew almost stood still. At first they thought they were being attacked, but then they saw how the objects turned off at lightning speed when they were at a certain distance from the bomber and disappeared into the sky. When the third formation appeared, Bailey saw two spots of blue-white light racing past their aircraft.

Suddenly, the objects which had flown back and were astern of the bomber reversed and came on a collision course directly behind it. Harter could hardly breathe. At that tremendous speed, it would only be a matter of seconds before they had overtaken the bomber. But before he could pull on the joystick and try to out-maneuver them, they suddenly decelerated and started following the B-29 at slow speed. Shortly after, they turned off and flew sideways away from the machine. When Harter looked again at the radarscope, he saw something that had not been there before: a huge spot, some three quarters of an inch in diameter. The smaller machines flew towards this spot at a speed of 5,000 mph and merged into it. Then the "mother ship" started moving and, within a few seconds, disappeared from the screen.

A few minutes later, Coleman's frightened but clearly relieved voice came over the intercom: *"Captain, did you see that?"*

"Yes, I did."

"We timed them with a stopwatch," said Coleman, *"you won't believe it. They were doing 8,500 miles per hour!"*

"Oh yessir, I do believe it," said Harter, *"that's what I thought."*

The captain informed his base over the radio. On landing, two intelligence service officers were waiting to take down the reports of the crew. Soon it was obvious what the crew had seen. A gigantic mother ship had been in the atmosphere of the Earth and sent out a squadron of saucers which, after completing their mission, had returned to the mother vessel. Radar experts of the Air Force came to the conclusion that the mother ship must have had a length of at least 13,000 feet—some two and a half miles! It appeared, therefore, that these gigantic mother ships did exist. Now it was only a matter of locating them.

Early in 1953, the Americans started experimenting with a newly developed long distance radar system by which objects in the stratosphere could be detected. Right from the start, during the first trials, the technicians were surprised to find that a huge object was circling around the equator at a speed of nearly 16,000 mph at an altitude of about 7,000 miles. A few minutes later a second object was seen flying at a height of about 500 miles. The Defense Department was immediately informed.

The Pentagon immediately started a new project, codenamed Project Sky Sweep, to scan the skies systematically with the aid of telescopes and cameras from the testing grounds of White Sands, New Mexico. The person selected to lead this project was no less a personage than the advisor to the government on space matters, Professor Clyde Tombaugh, America's star astronomer and discoverer of the planet Pluto.

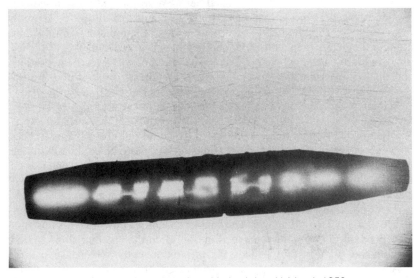

Telescope shot of a cigar-shaped mother ship by Adamski, May 1, 1952.

Officially, the astronomers were supposed to look out for smaller satellites of the Earth which could one day be used as starting platforms for spacecraft. This did not sound very convincing since the Defense Department had so far never bothered itself with such scientific research work, and the testing grounds at White Sands had been reserved exclusively for military projects. Added to that, the results and transactions of the project were classified as strictly secret. All that was revealed was that, up until then, two unknown objects had been discovered circling around the Earth. Officially, they were designated as little moons, but soon other astronomers refused to accept these objects as permanent and centuries-old satellites of the Earth; they knew that they had not been up there for very long.

In August 1954, the journal *Aviation Week* published a report that Prof.

Lincoln LaPaz, one of the experts employed by the government for investigating meteorological phenomena, had announced the sighting of two mysterious satellites which circled around the Earth at heights of 400 and 600 miles respectively. LaPaz was compelled by the Pentagon to disclaim his statement. Also, Tombaugh's discoveries were not supposed to be published at all, particularly because towards the end of 1954, the objects had vanished without leaving a trace. But during the following years, the objects kept reappearing periodically and were each time accompanied by a wave of UFO sightings.

The British aviation and astronautical engineer, Thomas Roy Dutton, a retired engineer of "British Aerospace," investigated hundreds of UFO sightings to find out whether they had any connection with the positions of the various planets. In doing so he found an interesting pattern. Sightings took place in certain cycles with surprising regularity. He summarized his conclusions as follows: There are ten mother ships stationed around the Earth, from which scout ships are sent down for short missions whenever a mother ship—taking into consideration the 24-hour rotation of the Earth around its own axis—was exactly above a geographical area in which the mission was to be carried out. Since Dutton was able, based on his theory, to predict the "time windows" for UFO sightings in certain regions on more than one occasion, one may consider the theory at least empirically confirmed.

Whereas these discoveries support Adamski only indirectly, the strongest evidence in his favor lies elsewhere. Cigar-shaped mother ships and bell-shaped scout ships, like those which Adamski had photographed in 1951 and 1952, have since been seen, filmed and photographed on many occasions in various countries.

Two of these photographs were taken by a ten-year-old boy at Coniston in Lancashire, England. Stephen Darbishire, son of a country doctor, had received as a birthday present a small Kodak camera, which he carried with him whenever he went out. On February 15, 1954, he and his cousin, 9-year-old Adrian Meyer, climbed on the top of a hill behind their house, on the other side of which lay the picturesque Coniston Lake. They suddenly heard a kind of humming noise which drew their attention to a bell-shaped craft, gliding over the park *"as if it was going to land"* about 300 feet away from them. Stephen quickly took two pictures of the object with his new camera, but unfortunately, in his excitement, forgot to set the correct distance, so that the photographs are a little out of focus. *"It was a firm, metallic thing,"* as Stephen described the object later. *"It had a dome, portholes and three balls on the underside. Somehow it appeared to be translucent."* The craft did not land, but after hovering for a few seconds, shot off and disappeared in the sky. The spacecraft on Stephen's photographs, even though slightly blurred, and that on Adamski's photographs, are as alike as two peas in a pod.

A British engineer, Leonard Cramp, did some research on this Darbishire case. He compared Stephen's photographs with those of Adamski. By

Photo by Stephen Darbishire, Coniston, England, February 15, 1954.

means of orthographic projections, he showed that both objects had the same proportions and size. These details tallied so well that there was only one explanation possible. The same object which had been photographed over Palomar Gardens on December 13, 1952, or its twin, had been photographed again at Coniston on February 15, 1954. That Adamski would have sent his "model" across the Atlantic to two schoolboys who were absolutely unknown to him and who had never heard of him would seem to be impossible, and again would seem to show that both sets of photographs were authentic.

This circumstance fascinated a very special UFO fan, the Prince Consort of England, Philip, Duke of Edinburgh. He arranged for Stephen to come to Buckingham Palace a month after the incident had taken place, so that he could make a personal and complete report of his sighting to one of the Prince's aides. A complete report of the interview was sent to Prince Philip who was then in Australia. At an official dinner in 1962, the Prince declared *"There are many reasons to believe that they* (UFOs) *do exist: there is so much evidence from reliable witnesses."* He later confirmed this statement of his in a letter, via Maj. Andrew Wigram, to Timothy Good, the British UFO researcher, and added, referring to Leslie and Adamski's book, *"Flying Saucers Have Landed has a lot of interesting stuff in it."*

There is a police report in the United Kingdom of a sighting of an Adamski-type UFO. The incident occurred on the frosty winter morning of December 12, 1978, not far from Skipton in North Yorkshire. At 4:30 a.m.,

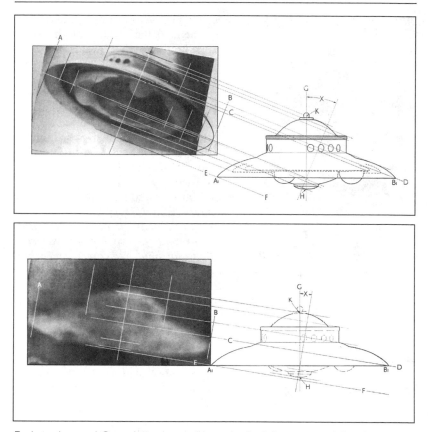

Engineer Leonard Cramp's "orthographic projection" demonstrated that the proportions of the craft photographed by Adamski and Derbyshire were identical.

a lonely police patrol car was driving on a remote country road along the Cononley Moor. In the car were Sgt. Anthony Dodd and Constable Alan Dale, who operated the radio. It was very dark and the road was lit only by the headlights of the car, the silence broken only by the noise of the motor and the occasional messages over the radio. Dodd loved that kind of mysterious stillness in the middle of a bare and unspoiled countryside, with dark houses snuggling up against the low hills as if seeking shelter from the cold winds, and the stone walls that divided the meadows from time immemorial.

It was the land of sagas and legends, of witches and elves, spirits and wills-o'-the-wisp, which lured unfortunate wanderers in the moor towards inescapable death. There was a magic in the air which, even thousands of years ago, the ancestors of the Celts must have been aware of, as is shown by the mighty sacrificial altar stones in the middle of the moor.

Suddenly, a loud static noise, hissing and rustling, tore Sgt. Dodd out of

Police Sgt. Anthony Dodd.

his reverie. They were just then driving into a curve when, to the right, a bright white light seemed to be diving towards them in a glide. They thought it was a burning airplane so they drove to the side and stopped the car to see what was happening and where it would land, in case help was required. It was, however, no airplane but a big shining disc which flew over their heads at a speed of about 40 mph. At its closest, it was hardly 100 feet away from them, so that they could see a number of details.

When I interviewed Dodd in 1991 for my documentary film *UFOs: The Secret Evidence*, he explained, *"It had a dome with ports all around it. The bottom was surrounded by colored lights like neon lights in blue, red, green and white which blinked in a sequence as if they were rotating, and in the middle there were three spheres or hemispheres. It was a huge thing, about 100 feet in diameter, and it made no noise whatsoever. What fascinated me even more was that the object was enveloped in a kind of halo which made its entire metallic structure glow white. It flew slowly over our heads and seemed to land at a place behind a group of trees. But we couldn't see or check that out because at that point it was too far away and in the middle of the moor."*

"What on Earth was that?" asked Constable Dale breaking the silence, brought back to reality by the penetrating cold. Sgt. Dodd's answer came minutes after that.

"I don't know, but it was wonderful."

From that day onwards Dodd started collecting all the information about UFOs that he could get, including, of course, the book *Flying Saucers Have*

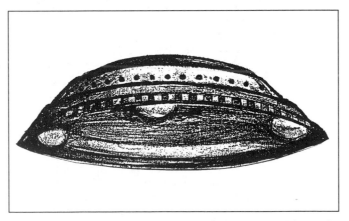

Detailed sketch of the object that Dodd observed during his patrol.

Landed by Desmond Leslie and George Adamski. His personal encounter with a saucer that resembled Adamski's saucer like a twin had convinced Dodd that Adamski must indeed have had an encounter with a UFO. Since retiring in 1988, Dodd has dedicated himself fully to his "cosmic hobby" as he calls it, and is today one of Britain's leading UFO researchers.

Adamski was the first person to have spoken about contact with aliens who resembled human beings. After him many others reported such encounters. With Adamski, the age of the contactees had begun.

CHAPTER 7

The Secret of the Saucers

It was not long before a second book by George Adamski appeared on the market. It bore the title *Inside the Spaceships* and its contents were far more fantastic than that of *Flying Saucers Have Landed*. For now the professor claimed not only to have met visitors from other worlds, but also that he had flown around in space in scout and mother ships, and that he had once circled around the moon in the company of spiritual teachers of an extraterrestrial civilization. It began when, on February 18, 1953, he felt an inner compulsion to go to Los Angeles.

In the hall of the hotel where he was staying in Los Angeles two men met him and, speaking in perfect English, said that they were extraterrestrials who were living incognito on Earth to study mankind. He drove with them into the California desert until they came to a spot where the familiar scout ship was hovering above the ground. Out of the craft came the stranger whom he had met on November 20, 1952, who now unexpectedly spoke English. He invited Adamski to get into the scout craft and they flew to the mother ship from where the professor had his first look at space. He was then taken to a "master" who explained to him that nearly all the worlds in the universe were populated, either by civilizations much more advanced, or by civilizations far behind, compared to ours on Earth. *"On our planet, and on other planets within our system, the form which you call 'man' has grown and advanced intellectually and socially through various stages of development, to a point which is inconceivable to the people of your Earth. This development has been accomplished only by adhering to what you would term the laws of Nature. In our worlds it is known as growth through following the laws of the Most Supreme Intelligence which governs all time and space."*

For those who know these laws, he added, interplanetary space travel presents no difficulty. Whereas our aircraft try to overcome the forces of nature, their spaceships utilize them. Every spaceship has its own gravitational field which is fed by electrical energy, which pervades the universe. The three spheres on the under side of the scout ships serve as *"condensers for the static electricity, sent to them from the magnetic pole in the center of the ship."* Even as the stranger did once before in the desert, the teacher warned Adamski about the use of atomic energy. The power and radiation released by nuclear explosions *"are endangering the life of men on Earth. A decomposition will set in that, in time, will fill your atmosphere with deadly elements . . . The radiation released from those bombs is now going out only so far, since it is lighter than your own atmosphere and heavier than space itself."* But further activities in that direction could raise the level to a "point of no return." The consequences: *"A large part of Earth's population could be annihilated, your soil could be rendered sterile, your waters poisoned and unable to bear life for many years to come."* Only today, 20 years after the discovery of the thinning of the ozone layer at the poles, can we understand the warning that was spoken in 1955. Also, Adamski's description of space was confirmed by astronaut John Glenn. Adamski had said that space was *"totally dark. Yet there were manifestations taking place all around us, as though billions upon billions of fireflies were flickering everywhere."* John Glenn, in 1962, described the glow-worms around his Mercury capsule: *"I am in the midst of a number of tiny bright particles whirling around as if they were glowworms."*

Adamski was not the only person who encountered aliens who resembled human beings. In 1954, two books were published more or less simultaneously, written by alleged contactees. Truman Bethurum, a simple roadlayer, claimed to have met the crew of a landed UFO in the Mormon Mesa in the Nevada desert in July 1952. In his book *On Board a Flying Saucer* he writes that eight or ten little men in uniforms had taken him out of the truck in which he was sleeping and brought him to their landed spacecraft, a disc which looked as if it was made of steel, about 300 feet in diameter. There he was greeted by the commander, a small beautiful black-haired woman who called herself "Aura Rhanes" and said that they were from the planet Clarion on the other side of the moon. During further encounters, she related to him fascinating things about her idyllic world devoid of wars and the concern of her people for the people of this Earth, who had just begun to experiment with atom bombs, without realizing the dangers associated with them. The encounters with the aliens changed his life. After the appearance of his

Truman Bethurum claimed he met an extraterrestrial crew in the desert of Nevada in July 1952.

Sketch of the UFO according to Truman Bethurum.

book, Bethurum became famous—at least in UFO circles—traveled throughout the country, spoke at congresses and canvassed for a community called the "Shrine of Thoughts," allegedly on the instructions of Aura Rhanes. He got so involved in his new life that his wife filed for divorce, citing as Bethurum's corespondent the lady from the planet Clarion—certainly something absolutely without precedent in the history of the courts of law!

The second contactee who came out into the open was a person of entirely different caliber. Dr. Daniel W. Fry was a top scientist, a rocket engineer, who as vice president of Crescent Engineering Company and chief of the research department, developed various kinds of equipment for steering controls of Atlas carrier rockets. Before that, he had worked for the Aerojet General Corporation, a contract firm of the United States Government, for whom he installed various control systems for experimental rockets at the high-security area in White Sands, New Mexico. It was there that on July 4, 1950, he intended to take a bus to Las Cruces, to join in the Independence Day celebrations there. But he missed the last bus, so he decided wander around a bit in the desert under the canopy of stars.

After a while, he saw something in the sky which gradually eclipsed more and more of the stars. A big, dark, oval flying craft descended slowly from the sky and finally landed about 60 feet in front of him. He was looking with astonishment at this product of an unknown technology when he heard a voice inviting him to come on board. He went towards the vessel, which had a sliding door that opened, and he walked in. The voice instructed him to sit in what looked like a pilot's seat and went onto explain that the craft was unmanned and remote-controlled, propelled by a strong gravitational field created by a massive flow of electrons between two field rings. The flying capacity of the vessel was demonstrated by a flight which took him to New York and back in 30 minutes at a speed of over 8,000 mph. During this flight the speaker introduced himself to Fry as A-lan. His people, he said, lived permanently in huge spaceships and moved about in the universe, without having any permanent home on any planet. He said they had actually originated from Earth, which they had left long, long ago. He talked about lost, highly technical civilizations on Atlantis and Lemuria, from which his forefathers were able to escape before those civilizations destroyed themselves through the misuse of technology. They were here now to prevent a repetition of this history on Earth.

A-lan spoke more about this during the second contact which took place on April 28, 1954, when Fry was staying at his vacation home in the mountains of Oregon. This time he was contacted by means of "electronic radio communication." *"The future of your children and grandchildren depends to a large extent on the success or failure of your own efforts,"* said A-lan. The technical and material sciences on Earth are over-developed in contrast to the mental and social sciences. Unless the latter were promoted intensively, unless they take the place that material science is now occupying, our civilization could collapse. His books, *The White Sands Incident* and *A-lan's Message to Mankind* led to Fry becoming a cult figure in UFO circles in America. When he spoke at the 1st Annual Flying Saucer Conference in Los Angeles in 1954, even his critics were impressed by his sober appearance and the high philosophical content of his message, as reporter Paul Weeks of the *Los Angeles Daily News* had to concede.

Rocket engineer Dr. Daniel Fry claims to have flown in a flying saucer on July 4, 1950.

Another person who spoke at the conference was George Van Tassel, an aircraft engineer who maintained a small airfield at Giant Rock near Yucca Valley in the California Mojave Desert. Tassel used to sleep outdoors in the summer, and one night in August 1953, he was awakened by an extraterrestrial, Solganda by name, and taken to a spacecraft which was about 36 feet in diameter, resembling the scout ships that Adamski had seen. Owing to that experience, as well as to a series of telepathically received messages, Van Tassel became a celebrity among UFO enthusiasts. When in 1955 he started inviting ufologists to Giant Rock, the UFO fans had a new Mecca. In the following years hundreds of them streamed to the California desert every year to hear the latest stories of contactees.

Then there was Dick Miller, who had joined up with Dr. George Hunt Williamson and had received messages from his space brothers, at first over the radio, later by telepathy. There was also the farmer Buck Nelson who claimed that his farm was literally crawling with Venusians and, as proof of this, sold the hair of an extraterrestrial dog. It was indeed a colorful bunch that met annually in the middle of the California desert—UFO enthusiasts, contactees who spoke of fantastic experiences with the

Three stills from a UFO film Fry took in 1964 at Merlin, Oregon.

aliens, opportunists, charlatans, mediums, occultists, sensation-mongers and sensation-seekers.

In the summer of 1957 a young visitor to Giant Rock related a story that made even the skeptics prick up their ears. His name was Howard Menger, and he came from New Jersey, where he and Van Tassel had met during a talk show about UFOs. Menger claimed he had had his first alien encounter at the age of ten on his parents' farm in Highbridge, New Jersey. A beautiful woman with golden hair had appeared to him, he claimed, who told him she came from *"very far away"* and that she and her people *"would always be near him and lead him."* This was not an empty promise, during the war he was contacted, aided and protected on many occasions by persons whom Menger recognized as aliens living on Earth.

Howard Menger, 1957.

Back in Highbridge after the war, when he had set up as a sign painter, he saw a pulsating ball of fire in the sky one day which gradually came nearer and hovered over a field. The light stopped pulsating, and he was able to make out a bell-shaped space vessel with portholes all around it. A door opened up like the iris shutter of a camera. Two men came out of it, dressed in uniforms that looked like blue-green ski suits, their shoulder-length blond hair blowing in the wind. Then a woman followed, also dressed in a similar uniform, and also with long blond hair. It was the same woman he had met when he was a child. She had not changed during the last fourteen years! *"When we live according to the laws of the Creator we are blessed by the gift of longevity,"* she told him in perfect English. But even death was only an illusion, only a change from one state into another, and nothing her people were afraid of. Menger was fascinated by the wisdom, beauty and radiating personality of the woman.

> You will have many more contacts which will further instruct and condition you. Each contact will be a step in this development. For instance, one contact will deal with 'diet', another will deal with marital problems in a social sense. You will learn a great deal about our technology and our science from certain of our people . . . you will learn to use your own mental powers and also to strengthen them. Then you will teach people the laws of the universe. Howard, your story must not come out until late summer of 1957!

She then asked Howard whether he was ready to take on the task—*"Are you willing to go on?"* When the young man assented, she took leave of him, after giving him a gentle kiss on the cheek. Then she and her two male companions went back to their ship and got in, the doors closed and the vessel took off vertically. When it was about 400 feet above the ground, there was a flash of light and it disappeared into the west.

It took Menger a few weeks to digest this experience. Then in autumn

1947 a young man, dressed rather fashionably, entered his sign shop and introduced himself as a real-estate agent. He chatted for a long time and suddenly said *"Howard, we know you're keeping your contacts with our Brothers a secret as you have been instructed."* He then said that he too was one of them and had been on Earth for a fairly long time. He wanted to show Menger a certain place, not far from Highbridge, but cut off and surrounded by woods, *"where no one can be harmed by the electromagnetic force which emanates from our craft."* Menger asked him what he meant. *"Even a small craft, the type we use for observation and reconnaissance, will nullify . . . anything electrical, such as the electrical systems of an automobile, radios, television and the like."*

Menger called that clearing in the midst of the woods "Field Location No. 2," because the second UFO landing was to take place there, and he did meet his friend from outer space there frequently after that. He was often witness to aliens being brought to the Earth to carry out missions, as well as aliens being taken back, who had finished their missions. *"You know, Howard,"* one of them explained to him, *"a lot of our people are among you, mingling with you, observing and helping where they can. They are in all walks of life—working in factories, offices, banks. Some of them hold responsible positions in communities, in government. Some of them may be cleaning women, or even garbage collectors."* The nightmare of the Generals of SHAPE headquarters was, at least for Howard Menger, a reality.

According to Menger, the extraterrestrials were coming to the Earth to help us achieve a new and higher level in our evolution, to help us develop a new cosmic consciousness. Humanity on this planet had to grow up and learn that it is one, that we are all children of the Earth, and only by so realizing this can the destruction of the Earth be prevented. The extraterrestrials feel themselves somehow bound to us, for they themselves belonged to the same species and were our very distant cousins. They have been for a long time in contact with our outstanding politicians and celebrities, but these people were reluctant to talk about this openly, for they were afraid that the economic system would collapse if they did so.

"The knowledge that you would gain would be related to a way of life that is completely unknown to you. Most of your sources of energy would be completely outmoded."

Spectacular mass landings would only lead to confusion, hysteria and panic and, therefore, they preferred the policy of gradual approach. *"We go carefully, directly to those persons who are advanced enough, so that humanity will get to know us slowly, without fear, panic or censorship. Every big movement has so far been started by the people."*

There is, in fact, evidence to show that Menger's incredible claim that extraterrestrials had contacted the chiefs of various governments could be true. For years, a rumor went around in UFO circles that U.S. President Dwight D. Eisenhower had been involved in a UFO contact at the Edwards Air Force Base (then Muroc Air Force Base) in California. This rumor was

Silhouette of an extraterrestrial in front of a glowing spacecraft, photographed by Howard Menger, 1956.

based on the fact that on February 20, 1954, during a visit to Palm Springs, California, not far from Muroc, the President had disappeared for a few hours from public life.

Officially he had come to California to play golf, and was staying at the ranch of his friend Paul R. Helms. That itself was a bit strange since he had returned only a few days earlier from a long hunting holiday in Georgia. What happened on February 20 is even today veiled in darkness. At any rate, the President had driven away without his bodyguard. Towards evening there was much unease among the journalists who had gathered there and many were worried that something had happened to the President. Then, when his press spokesman James Haggerty was called out from a private barbecue to Smoke Tree to make an official statement, the tension rose to breaking point.

In the press room of the Mirador Hotel in Palm Springs there occurred what *The Times* later reported as a demonstration of journalistic mass hysteria. The representative from United Press announced that Eisenhower was apparently seriously ill, but his colleague from the Associated Press outdid him by saying that the President had just passed away. He had to withdraw that statement when Haggerty, in a bad mood and in loud tones, announced that Eisenhower had broken the cap of a tooth on a chicken bone and that his host had immediately taken him to the nearest dentist, Dr. F. A. Purcell. The press was quickly satisfied by this explanation, and nobody asked why a visit to the dentist should have taken an entire day, and why it had to be done in "cloak and dagger" fashion without the usual bodyguards. At a hastily organized barbecue the next day, Dr. Purcell was presented as "the dentist who had treated the President," but Purcell's wife refused to make any comments to the author Willam L. Moore about what had happened. That was strange behavior for the wife of a provincial dentist who, one would expect, would have been proud that her husband had treated a President.

There were also other circumstances that made the official statement sound dubious. All documents from the period of Eisenhower's presidency are now to be found in the Eisenhower Library, amongst them detailed medical reports about the President. Although every visit to every doctor and every treatment had been meticulously recorded, there is no mention whatsoever about the dental treatment by Dr. Purcell. There is another

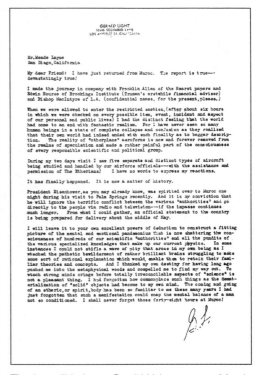

The incredible letter Gerald Light wrote to Meade Layne.

file which contains all letters written by the President thanking people at Palm Springs after his visit. These include letters to people who had sent him flowers, to those who had wanted to play golf with him and one to the priest who conducted the Sunday Mass which "Ike" had attended. What is missing is a letter of thanks to Dr. Purcell for his timely help. The tale of the tooth seems to have been a cover-up for the truth, but for what reason?

On April 16, 1954, the metaphysicist Meade Layne of San Diego, California, received a letter from his friend Gerald Light of CBS. What Light described in that letter certainly makes the "chicken bone affair" seem a political hush up.

My dear friend:
I have just returned from Muroc. The report is true, devastatingly true. I made the journey in the company of Franklin Allen of the Hearst Papers, Edwin Nourse of Brookings Institute (Truman's erstwhile financial advisor) and Bishop MacIntyre of L.A. (confidential names, for the present, please.)
When we were allowed to enter the restricted section (after about six hours in which we were checked on every possible item, event, incident and aspect

of our personal and public lives) I had the distinct feeling that the world had come to an end with fantastic realism, for I have never seen so many human beings in a state of complete collapse and confusion as they realized that their own world had indeed ended with such a finality as to beggar description. The reality of 'otherplane' aeroforms is now and forever removed from the realms of speculation and made a rather painful part of the consciousness of every responsible scientific and political group.

During my two days' visit, I saw five separate and distinct types of aircraft being studied and handled by our Air Force officials—with the assistance of and permission of the Etherians. I have no words to express my reactions.

It has finally happened. It is now a matter of history.

President Eisenhower, as you may already know, was spirited over to Muroc one night during his visit to Palm Springs recently, and it is my conviction that he will ignore the terrific conflict between the various authorities and go directly to the people via radio and television—if the impasse continues much longer. From what I could gather, an official statement to the country is being prepared for delivery about the middle of May.

I will leave it to your own excellent powers of deduction to construct a fitting picture of the mental and emotional pandemonium that is now shattering the consciousness of hundreds of our scientific "authorities," and all the pundits of the various specialized knowledges that make up our current physics. In some instances, I could not stifle a wave of pity which arose in my own being as I watched the pathetic bewilderment of rather brilliant brains struggling to make some sort of rational explanation which would enable them to retain their familiar theories and concepts, and I thank my own destiny for having long ago pushed me into the metaphysical woods and compelled me to find my way out. To watch strong minds cringe before totally irreconcilable aspects of science is not a pleasant thing. I had forgotten how commonplace such things as the dematerialisation of solid objects had become to my own mind. The coming and going of an etheric or spirit body has been so familiar to me these many years, that I had forgotten that such a manifestation could snap the mental balance of a man not so conditioned. I shall never forget these 48 hours at Muroc.

The official announcement which Gerald Light had hoped for was never made but, during the following years, again and again, there were indications that President Eisenhower had in fact witnessed a contact taking place by extraterrestrials. When Sir Desmond Leslie investigated the event in the summer of 1954, he met an Air Force officer who confirmed that President Eisenhower, during his holiday at Palm Springs, had visited Muroc to inspect landed extraterrestrial spacecraft.

The author Frank Scully who had bought a log cabin in the neighborhood of Edwards in 1954 learned from one of his carpenters that the President had indeed a few months ago visited the Air Force base. The carpenter, who was a civilian employee at the base, had wondered why this visit had not been reported in the papers during the following days. The actual purpose of the visit was, however, unknown to him.

Towards the end of 1982 a member of the British House of Lords, the Earl of Clancarty, released a document that had been sent to him. It was

a confidential report of a retired United States top test pilot. The pilot said he was one of six people at Eisenhower's meeting with the beings. He had been called in as a technical advisor because of his reputation and abilities as a test pilot. Five different alien craft landed at the base. Three were saucer-shaped and two were cigar-shaped . . . As Eisenhower and his small group watched the aliens first disembarked and then approached them. The aliens looked somewhat human, but not exactly. They were about the same height and build as an average man and able to breathe air without a helmet. The aliens spoke English and told Eisenhower they wanted to begin 'an education program for the people of Earth' to make mankind aware of their presence. Eisenhower told them he didn't think the world was ready for that, and was concerned that this revelation would cause panic. The aliens seemed to understand and agree, and then said that they would continue to make contact with isolated individuals, until Earth people got used to them so that the aliens didn't create panic and confusion. The President stood there as if paralyzed while they showed him various technical possibilities which could evoke nothing less than deep respect. They demonstrated their spacecraft for the President. They showed him their ability to make themselves invisible. This really caused the President a lot of discomfort because none of them could see "them" even though they knew they were there. The aliens then boarded their ships and departed. All of the witnesses were sworn to complete secrecy. The pilot said he had never spoken to another person about this, but now everyone involved except him was dead.

Seven years later, Tarna Halsey, wife of Commander Frank Halsey, nephew of the war hero and five-star Admiral "Bull" Halsey, asserted that during a private conversation, President Eisenhower had confirmed the story of the contact at Edwards Air Base. According to Tarna Halsey, a few months before that, Admiral Halsey and her husband had had a UFO contact experience and had reported this officially. At a later UFO contact, Mrs. Halsey was also present. After having seen the landings at Muroc Air Base, the President asked the Chief of Staff of the Armed Forces to give him a list of all high-ranking army officers who had had personal UFO contacts. The three Halseys were on the list. So the President invited them to the White House for a private conversation. During the conversation he let them know that he too, shortly before that, had had contact with extraterrestrials. He did not, however, mention the time or the place. He now wanted to know from them what they had experienced, and he listened very carefully to everything they said.

Finally, Tarna Halsey asked him, "*Mr. President, you know that these things happened and we know it too. Why don't you tell the American public about it?*" *My dear*," answered the President, "*even a President cannot always do what he would like to.*"

"*But, at the end of your next speech to the public, you can just say*

'Ladies and Gentlemen, I have an announcement to make,' and tell them about everything we have been talking about during the last half-hour."
"I am sorry, my dear," said "Ike," *"but that is just impossible."*

Instead, the FBI and the Pentagon started working with contactees, for one thing to get at information about the aliens through them, and for another, to keep control over what UFO evidence would get to the public and also to learn how the public would react to such information. One of the first persons who was to work with them was Howard Menger, who had caught the attention of the authorities as early as 1951.

Menger had at that time tried to put into practice what he had learned from the extraterrestrials about the propulsion of their spaceships. He believed that gravity is a push, not a pull, not a force of attraction, but the result of pressure caused by cosmic particles approaching the Earth. How could clouds weighing sixty tons glide through the atmosphere as if they had no weight at all? Only through changing the strength of the electric field, theorized Menger. He believed that high and low tides in the oceans were not the result of the gravitational pull of the moon, but that the moon, by its presence, shielded off the cosmic particles behind it.

To produce the effect that one feels as gravity, these particles need an electrical resonance field. In outer space this field is absent, so that the particles move in all directions, and therefore become ineffective, causing the so-called weightlessness. Bodies in space, no matter what their size and speed, build up variable magnetic fields. The magnetic flow is in effect determined by the stream of energized cosmic particles. Menger remembered how one of the visitors had said, *"We use the energy of the atom by taking the electron away and letting it go its own way until nature brings it back to where it belongs without destroying anything."* He discovered that high voltage current flowing at an extremely high rate in a circuit can cause an object to float in air. The electric field shields the object from the cosmic particles, and thus from "gravity", and also creates an ionizing effect which makes the object glow. With the help of suitable condensers he could control the current which was supplied by remote-controlled batteries. This led to the development of "Electro-craft X-1," a disc 4 feet in diameter.

When the model was completed, Menger put it to a test flight early in 1951. He was able to raise the disc to a height of about 600 feet, then made it shoot off to the east and back to the west, when it suddenly went out of control. The model did not react to the remote control anymore and was lost. It had cost him about $6,000 to build.

A couple of weeks later, two men came to his sign shop and brought with them metal pieces which Howard immediately recognized as parts of his electro-ship. The men showed him their identity cards, said they came from the FBI and that this object had crashed near the state line between Ohio and Pennsylvania about 625 miles away from Highbridge. Farmers had believed that it was a UFO and had called the FBI, who soon found out that it was of earthly origin. Through the manufacturers of the high-volt batteries, they were able to trace the purchaser, one Mr. Howard Menger of High-

Model of "Electro-craft X-1" with which Howard Menger experimented in 1951.

bridge, New Jersey. They warned him never again in the future to try anything like that without permission.

They were certainly interested in his work. They informed themselves thoroughly about his theories and also asked whether he was prepared to work for the government. Menger, as a patriot, assented. They promised to get back to him, but it took 9 years before that happened.

Meanwhile, Menger's contacts with aliens as well as with the FBI continued. Since 1956 the aliens had allowed him to bring witnesses during the contacts. In the beginning they were neighbors, then UFO friends from New York and New Jersey, later critical UFO researchers and finally, a man from the FBI. What these witnesses saw convinced even such skeptics as the Cambridge biologist Ivan T. Sanderson who at that time led the New York UFO research group, CSI (Civilian Saucer Intelligence). The neighbors said that strange lights appeared often above Menger's home. A lady neighbor asserted that in the company of Menger she had seen three flying saucers, one of which landed. "A man came out dressed in a kind of ski suit. He came over to them, about a distance of 20 feet, and Mr. Menger spoke with him." Some of the neighbors and visitors whom Menger took to Field Location No. 2 claim to have seen tall spacemen in shining ski pants. Others spoke of fluorescent "thought or observation discs" between 20 and 70 inches in diameter, which lay on the ground between the trees and, according to Menger, were there to register the mental vibrations of the visitors.

The psychiatrist Berthold Schwarz, whose interest covers all parapsychological phenomena, investigated the Menger case. He interviewed over 30 witnesses. The event which impressed him most happened when Menger's 12-year-old son Robert was lying on his deathbed with a brain tumor. A number of witnesses including Menger's first wife, another married couple, an engineer and an economist who often came to visit Menger, all saw one night a mysterious blue beam of light appear above Robert's bed, which pulsated and became brighter and brighter. A little later, the two men and the married couple left and when they went to their cars they saw four men in shining uniforms a few hundred feet away, standing on a hill in the midst of the meadow. It was a full moon night, and therefore they could see the men clearly, see how they moved in front of a group of trees and finally how they jumped over a fence in what looked like slow-motion tempo. At that moment Howard Menger was still sitting near his son and his wife had just accompanied the other visitors to the door.

When Dr. Schwarz interviewed the witnesses in 1971 they compared the motions of the four shining figures with the kangaroo jumps of astronauts on the moon. *"It is completely out of the question that the case was faked,"* said Dr. Schwarz when I interviewed him in 1993 at Vero Beach, Florida, *"all witnesses spoke in a credible manner and assured me that Menger was in no mood at that time to practice any joke. Besides, it was only ten years later that such jumps were brought into connection with astronauts."*

Photograph taken by a witness. Menger at Field Location No. 2, while a spacecraft appears in the southwest.

One of the witnesses whom Dr. Schwarz interviewed was a top-ranking physicist, today a professor of Physics and chief of the Department of Physics at Princeton University. Menger had driven him down to Field Location 2 where he saw a disc about 3 feet in diameter lying on the ground, which continuously changed in color. He was allowed to get close to it, up to a distance of about 6 feet, but Menger warned him, on account of its strong electromagnetic field, not to touch it. For 20 minutes he watched its behavior, when suddenly a small "light" rose out of it and circled around them for many minutes. *"I was terribly impressed,"* confessed the professor, *"I will never forget it. This experience really aroused my curiosity. It had a tremendous influence on my life after that."* When another witness went secretly at night to Field Location No. 2 with a few friends, they heard a human voice speaking to them (*"Who is with you, Rob? Don't be afraid."*). Then, a 12-foot high bright object shot up and threw out a small ball of light. The men were panic-stricken and ran away. The next morning, they went back and found broken branches where the light object had risen.

Other witnesses got in touch with the popular radio show presented by Long John Nebel (the Larry King of the late '50s) at the broadcasting station WOR, in New York City. Nebel loved to invite controversial persons and discuss things with them right through the night, and Howard Menger was one of his favorite guests. On January 10th, 1957, Long John interviewed a physicist who had gone with the Mengers, plus another young lady and her mother, to the clearing in the woods. He said that at first he had seen a light which *"glowed between the trees, became brighter and brighter and started pulsating."* Menger said suddenly, *"Wait here,"* and went towards the light. *"He didn't get very far, must have been about forty feet, then he stopped, and we heard two male voices talking to each other. The unknown voice sounded rather monotonous against Menger's, and the conversation lasted perhaps half an hour."*

On another occasion, in the summer of 1957, Menger had obtained a movie camera and took it with him when he went with a group of witnesses, amongst them an FBI employee, to Field Location No. 2. It was 9:30 p.m. and just getting dark. A disc-like object, with shining portholes, a dome on top and three spheres on the underside, appeared. It approached and finally landed at a distance of about 250 feet from them. A port opened, bright light streaming out of it, and two men came out and stood on either side of the opening. Then, a third person stepped out, dressed in dark overalls, and walked towards Howard, who, film camera in hand, had already gone to within a distance of 50 feet from the UFO. When the third person was about twenty feet away from him, he saw that it was a woman. On the belt of her space suit, she wore a light. She stood still and touched the light which then spread and enveloped her completely. And then, she was suddenly gone. Menger was perplexed, *"Where has she gone?"* he called out to the two men who still stood before the space vessel. *"She is back in the ship,"* they answered. Then, they too climbed back into the ship, the port closed and, with a blinding flash of light, rose up into the skies and disappeared.

Menger had experienced a lot things with the aliens but this was something new. His heart was racing with excitement when he got back to his group. *"Did you see that?"* he asked. *"Howard, did you get all of it on film?"* *"Most of it."*

"This film footage will disperse all doubts about your story."

"Yeah, yeah!" said the FBI man. He knew that he would have to report this to his superiors and he had an idea of what his instructions would be!

A week later the group got together again, this time to see the film. With his polaroid camera Menger shot a few of the single scenes, in order to be able to give them to the others. But as they sat down, silently thinking about how the public would react to this new evidence for the reality of alien contacts—a sense of victory was filling their hearts—the FBI man raised his voice. "Howard, I have bad news for you. I have strict instructions to send this film to Washington for analysis."

Although the others felt as though their world, or at least their dreams, were completely destroyed, Howard took it calmly. He was a thorough

Summer 1957, a UFO coming in to land about 15 minutes before sunset, flying over a deciduous tree at Field Location No. 2. The object lands, a hatch opens, a ramp comes down, a bright light shines out from the inside of the object. A woman steps out of the

patriot, had worked in the intelligence service during the war, knew what his duty to his country was, and he was proud to be, in some way, serving his country.

A little later, a government official contacted Menger. He asked him if he

UFO and walks towards Menger. On the belt of her space suit she carries a light. She touches this light and vanishes. Four scenes from an 8mm film which Menger shot in the presence of a number of witnesses, amongst them an FBI official. The film was later confiscated by the FBI.

was ready to put his knowledge and experiences at the service of his nation. He was asked to put down his experiences in a book that would include some of his actual experiences, but to make the story sound as if it was a futuristic vision. The aliens, and the contacts, were to be described in a manner which would dispel the fears of the reader and project them into a distant spiritual world. Everything having to do with Menger's Electro-craft was to be suppressed. The purpose of the entire project was to test the people's reaction to contacts with aliens and condition their reactions in a particular manner. That meant many visions, many messages, few proofs, no hardware, no technology. Menger agreed. He was convinced that the government had good reasons for such a measure.

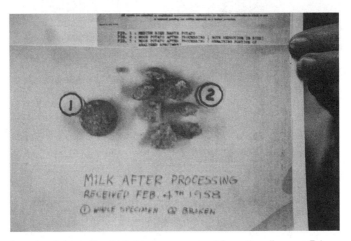

Sample of dry milk which Menger received from the aliens on February 4, 1958.

The earth as seen through the porthole of the spacecraft.

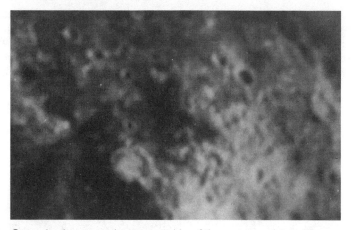

Crater landscape on the reverse side of the moon–a picture Menger took in 1956.

And he felt that he was fated to be an instrument anyhow, used either by the aliens, or as now, by the government. When his book. *From Outer Space to You* came out in 1959, Howard Menger had far more evidence to show than any other contactee before him. He had dozens of witnesses, photographs and films, dehydrated plants, samples of milk, and an extraterrestrial potato, which had five to six times more protein than the earthly potato (that is, 15.12% instead of 2 to 3%), although in 1959 the agricultural technology on Earth was not developed that far to assess it all. There were close-up photographs of the rear side of the moon, of the earth and Mars, which Menger claimed to have taken while on a flight in a spacecraft, to which he was invited in August 1956. The photographs of the moon show small craters which were otherwise photographed only years later by Soviet probes. On the photographs of Mars, there is a huge crater at the equator, perhaps the crater Schiaperelli, which was officially discovered and photographed by Viking I in 1976.

But all that did not bring Menger any happiness. The death of his son had affected his marriage very badly and the UFO ruckus disrupted his sign business. He had become an outsider and could not live on the royalties which the 8,000 copies of his book—3,000 printed in the first edition followed by 5,000 in the second—brought in. The lectures that he was invited to give all over the country were not exactly professionally delivered. Although he could talk for hours about his cosmic philosophy, he was a bad speaker and easily lost his train of thought to the frustration of his audience. On the one hand, his contacts had enriched his life in many ways. He discovered in himself unknown talents; he began to play the piano and compose songs inspired by his friends from space, but these things did not help him feed his family, which was what his wife complained about most. When, after a lecture, he met the pretty Connie Baxter (who looked a little

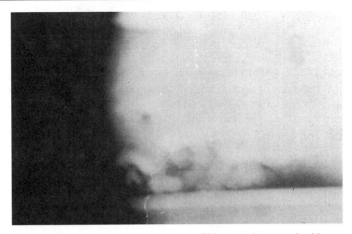

The crater Shiaparelli on the equator of Mars as photographed by Menger in 1956.

bit like the lady on the rocks from his childhood) he was convinced that he had found the right companion for his life. His first marriage ended on the rocks, the second was founded on them: he got divorced and married Connie in 1958! A year later, the contacts stopped. A 12-year phase had come to an end; the racket that followed the publication of his book had made peaceful landings on Field Location No. 2 impossible. The curious, who wanted more sensation, were disappointed and turned against Menger. If anything happened at all, they accused him of having faked it.

In April 1960, a Col. Amos T. Simpson of the United States Defense Department offered Menger the chance to work on a project for the government. It had to do with his "Electro-craft X-1." They organized a group of chosen scientists and engineers to build such an electro-ship before the Spring of 1961, this time big enough to be manned. Howard was thrilled and accepted the job. After that, he got precise instructions. The project was to remain strictly secret. In order to put an end to the publicity he was getting, he was to disavow publicly all his statements about his contacts. The ship would be built in Colorado Springs. The government promised him a sizable salary and a 1960 model Mercedes as a service vehicle.

After one year, during which Menger commuted between New Jersey and Colorado Springs, the discus-shaped electro-ship could be rolled out of the hangar. For Howard, it was one of the most beautiful things he had

Howard and Connie Menger today.

ever seen, "*A wonderful machine that taps its energy from the endless sea of energy that surrounds us and, under the control of a single pilot, converts it into high-voltage electricity.*" The test flight went through successfully. The job was finished, and Menger had enough money to start a new life. In 1963, he moved to San Sebastian, Florida with his family, which now consisted of four members, and opened a new sign shop. For another year, he still received his monthly check from the government, but it stopped suddenly. After making inquiries, he was told that the project had finally ended. Today, Menger lives in Vero Beach, Florida. He is now a retired and very respected citizen, the proud father of two grown-up children and is three times a grandfather. In 1990, he got an invitation to speak at a UFO conference in Phoenix, Arizona and his contact man at the Pentagon gave him permission to speak. Since then, he has talked openly. He experiments with high-voltage models in his workshop, a fully-equipped garage, and seeks investors for a new electro-ship. Since 1959, however, he has had no further contacts with extraterrestrials.

And George Adamski? In 1959, he travelled through Europe. He was invited for private audiences, officially by Queen Juliana of Holland, and unofficially by Pope John XXIII, yet at the banking capital, Zurich, hooligans compelled him to break off his lecture prematurely. He had been able to make dozens of films of flying saucers during their maneuvers, gigantic cigar-shaped mother ships, small telemeter discs—unmanned probes ranging in size from sixteen to sixty inches of diameter—and even a landed scout ship, in front of which a telemeter disc pendulated hither and thither. He had over three dozen witnesses for his UFO sightings and encounters with the "space brothers" who live amongst us. But it was only two months before his death on April 23, 1965, that he was able to present the final evidence. In the presence of the witness Madeleine Rodeffer, a government official, he shot the most sensational film of the early UFO era.

Mrs. Rodeffer had made the acquaintance of The Professor in March 1964. She was fascinated by his books, and invited him to give a lecture at Rockville, Maryland, a suburb of Washington D.C. They became close friends and from then on, whenever he had anything to do at the capital, Adamski made use of the Rodeffers' hospitality. This was not seldom; he had frequent invitations to confidential meetings with NASA and the Atomic Energy Commission and once he had to give a lecture to Air Force Reserve officers at Madeleine's house in Silver Springs, Maryland.

Towards the end of February 1965 he was once again staying with the Rodeffers at Silver Springs. Madeleine had organized a press conference for him. On the morning of February 26, he greeted her with the news that he, earlier that morning, had had a talk with a space brother who had announced a fly by. Mrs. Rodeffer loaded her 8mm film camera and both she and Adamski kept watch the whole afternoon. At 4:00 they noticed, looking out through the dining room window, a small telemeter disc above the tops of the tall trees which bordered the Rodeffer holding. Madeleine snatched her camera and she and

Adamski ran out to the veranda of the house and there, she found that she could not use the camera. She had received the camera as a Christmas gift from her husband only two months ago and did not not know how to use it. She gave it to George who knew how to operate such a camera. Just then a second, bigger object appeared. At first it flew at a distance, then came closer and floated above the street, hardly a hundred feet away from them. The demonstration lasted for about ten minutes. Its undercarriage, consisting of the three "condenser balls," as Adamski called them, was put out and withdrawn again, and the force field which surrounded the 27-foot diameter disc was increased and decreased, which gave it a ghostly appearance.

UFO still shot from the Rodeffer film.

"It was sometimes greenish-blue, then very dark brown or gray-brown and again like pure aluminum," explained Madeleine Rodeffer to me when I interviewed her in front of her house on July 5, 1993. It made no loud noise, just hummed and hissed very softly. Then, it glided, as though weightless, between the trees here and there. The force field seemed to vibrate and distort the form of the object. When it finally disappeared, Adamski felt like a child at Christmas when he gets all the toys he had wished for. As Madeleine put it, *"He was more excited than I, which means a lot. Again and again, he said, 'Can one ask for more proof? Madeleine, tell me honestly, what more can one ask for?'"*

The miserable part came when the film was developed. The Rodeffers had bought cheap film which was meant only for indoor shots with spot-lights. As a result, during the first run the UFO, lit by the evening sun, looked like a black blob. Only the overexposed parts showed details of the surface (see photograph).

William Sherwood, an optical engineer and film expert at Kodak East-man, analyzed the film frame by frame and came to the conclusion that the object must have had an actual diameter of 27 feet. *"What is remarkable, I believe, is the slight glowing of the underside,"* he said, and attributed it to the force field of the object. Had it been a model, this part specifically would have been darker. The distorting effect had already been explained by the engineer Leonard Cramp in the case of the second photograph of Stephen Darbishire from Coniston, England, as follows: *"Through the study of the effects of G (gravitational field) on light, we can expect to find that such a field acts like an atmospheric lens, which can lead to optical effects that can be enhanced by other field effects like the gravitative bending of light."*

When the British UFO researcher Timothy Good gave him the Rodeffer film for analysis, Cramp was impressed, *"It confirms completely my theory of atmospheric field effects. We have here a case of genuine optical distortion, in which the rays of light from the underside of the object and also from the dome reach the camera simultaneously, which otherwise optically and perspectively would have been impossible. Only a strong gravitational field can produce such an effect."*

Because of this, the Adamski-Rodeffer film became particularly interesting for those who were trying to find out the secret of the saucers. Indeed, it seemed to give a clue as to how the saucers were propelled and it gave support to the various theories based on electro-magnetic propulsion methods, a concept, which, at least theoretically, had already been developed during the 1920s.

CHAPTER 8

Project Magnet

On November 21, 1950, an intra-departmental memorandum, classified "top secret," was sent to the Canadian Controller of Telecommunications of the Department of Transport, calling for the investigation of UFO phenomena from an entirely new perspective. The writer of the memorandum had made discreet inquiries through the staff of the Canadian Embassy in Washington regarding the stand of the United States government in the matter of UFOs, and had learned the following:

a. *The matter is the most highly classified subject in the United States government, rating even higher than the H-bomb;*

b. *Flying saucers exist;*

c. *Their modus operandi is unknown, but concentrated effort is being made by a small group, headed by Dr. Vannevar Bush;*

d. *The entire matter is considered by the United States authorities to be of tremendous significance;*

I was further informed that the United States authorities are investigating quite a number of fields which might possibly be related to the saucers, such as mental phenomena, and I gather that they are not doing too well since they indicated that if Canada is doing anything at all in geomagnetics, they would welcome a discussion with suitably accredited Canadians.

That was exactly what the author of the memorandum wanted: to start a project to investigate and understand the propulsion system of UFOs. He had reason to believe that it had to do with the phenomenon of geomagneticism, which his own researchers had suggested could be a potential source of energy for the future.

Secret memorandum sent by Wilbert Smith to the Canadian Transport Department. "Flying saucers exist . . . the matter is considered by the United States authorities to be of tremendous significance . . . the most highly classified subject in the United States government, rating higher even than the H-bomb."

The writer was the electronics engineer Wilbert M. Smith, a high-ranking official of the Department of Transport of Canada. Smith had studied engineering sciences at the renowned University of British Columbia and had worked for the radio station at Vancouver, before entering the services of the Department of Transport in 1939. In Canada, the Department of Transport also handles telecommunication. In 1947, he was entrusted with the job of setting up a network of ionospheric measuring stations to study the dissemination of radio waves. As the leader of the project, he had to

study and become familiar with all phenomena that affected radio waves: the Aurora Borealis, sun spots, cosmic radiation, atmospheric radioactivity, all forms of geomagnetism. Soon, he came to the conclusion that geomagnetism could also be used as a source of energy. He constructed an experimental unit in 1949, and tested it in the standard laboratories of the Department. The results were promising. Sufficient energy was tapped from the magnetic field of the earth (approximately 50 milliwatts) which was enough to move the needle of a voltmeter. *"We believe,"* he wrote in his memorandum, *"that we are on the track of something which may well prove to be the*

Wilbert Smith

introduction to a new technology. The existence of a different technology is borne out by the investigations which are being carried on at the present time in relation to flying saucers."

Smith's interest in UFOs had been awakened during a visit to Washington to attend a conference in August 1950. Two books were released at that time, one titled *Behind the Flying Saucers* by Frank Scully and the other, *Flying Saucers Are Real* by Donald Keyhoe. Smith read both books with avid interest. Frank Scully's book was soon on all the best-seller lists. In that book, Scully claimed that the Government of the United States was in possession of three UFO wrecks which had been recovered in Arizona and New Mexico. The first saucer, according to Scully, crashed on March 25, 1948, east of Aztec, New Mexico. When the retrieval crew of the US Air Force and government scientists arrived at the crash-site, they found, lying on a rocky plateau above Hart Canyon, a Saturn-shaped object, 100 feet in diameter, with an 18-foot wide oval cabin in the middle. They were able to enter the ship through a broken hatch. Inside, they found the corpses of sixteen members of the crew, small humanoid creatures in strange uniforms, their skins burnt chocolate-brown. Dr. Silas Newton, geophysicist who had accompanied the retrieval crew, confided to Scully that the first investigations seemed to show that the saucers probably fly along the geomagnetic lines of force and were propelled by magnetic principles unknown to us. For Smith, this book was a revelation.

It appeared to me that our own work in geomagnetics might well be the link between our technology and the technology by which the saucers are designed and operated. If it is assumed that our geo-magnetic investigations are in the right direction, the theory of operation of the saucers becomes quite straightforward, with all observed features explained qualitatively and quantitatively . . . While I am not yet in a position to say that we have solved even the first problems in geomagnetic energy release, I feel that the correlation between our basic theory and the available information on sources checks too closely to be mere coincidence. It is my honest opinion that we are on the right track and are fairly close to at least some of the answers.

But at first, he had to verify how far Scully's statements in his book were true, and also had to find out from whom he could get more detailed information.

With the aid of the Military Attache of the Canadian Embassy in Washington, Lt. Col. Bremner, he was able to arrange a meeting with one of the most important scientists of the United States Government, the physicist Prof. Dr. Robert I. Sarbacher, at his office in the Pentagon. Sarbacher was not only a professor at Harvard University, Dean of the Technical College of Georgia and Director of Research at the Wedd Laboratories, but also scientific advisor to the Research and Development Committee of the United States Defense Department. Lt. Col. Bremner told Wilbert Smith that if anyone at all knew about the alleged recovered saucers, then it would be Prof. Sarbacher.

The meeting took place on September 15, 1950 and since Smith has kept his handwritten notes of the meeting all his life, we are now in a position to quote the conversation word for word:

Smith: *I am doing some work on the collapse of the earth's magnetic field as a source of energy and I think our work may have a bearing on the flying saucers.*

Sarbacher: *What do you want to know?*

Smith: *I have read Scully's book on the saucers and would like to know how much of it is true.*

Sarbacher: *The facts reported in the book are substantially correct.*

Smith: *Then, the saucers do exist?*

Sarbacher: *Yes, they exist.*

Smith: *Do they operate, as Scully suggested, on magnetic principles?*

Sarbacher: *We have not been able to duplicate the performance.*

Smith: *So they came from another planet?*

Sarbacher: *All we know is, we didn't make them and it's pretty certain they didn't originate on the earth.*

Smith's handwritten notes about his talk with government scientist Prof. Robert I. Sarbacher on Sept. 15, 1950.

Smith: *I understand the whole subject of saucers is classified.*

Sarbacher: *Yes. It is classified two points higher than the H-Bomb. In fact, it is the most highly classified subject in the U.S. Government at the present time.*

Smith: *May I ask the reason for the classification?*

Sarbacher: *You may ask, but I can't tell you.*

The Canadian Government was so impressed by what Smith had said, that the Deputy Minister of Transport for Air Services, Commander C. P. Edwards, sanctioned the start of Project Magnet on December 2, 1950, with the words, "Go ahead, and keep me informed from time to time."

From the beginning, Project Magnet was an official project of the Department of Transport but had the support of the Defense Research Board and the National Research Council. The scope of its work consisted of two goals: *"1) the collection of data, analyzing them and evaluating them, and 2) systematically and experimentally analyzing all known concepts in the hope of discovering discrepancies which may prove to be the key to a new technology."*

Among the scientists who worked for Project Magnet were such well known authorities as Prof. J. T. Wilson of the University of Toronto, Dr. James Wait, physicist of the Defense Research Board and Dr. J. D. Garland, expert on gravitation in the Department of Research. The first interim report was finished in 1952. It concluded, *"as appears evident, the Flying Saucers are emissaries from some other civilization, and actually do operate on magnetic principles."*

Since, however, Project Magnet was rather limited in its possibilities, the Defense Research Board created a UFO study group in April 1952, of which Smith was to be a member, as representative of the Transport Department. The group, which worked under the code name Project Second Story, was put under the leadership of the astrophysicist Peter M. Millman, of Dominion Observatory, and consisted of top-ranking military and intelligence service personnel. One of its tasks was to collect and provide Project Magnet with pertinent data.

Whereas very little was made known about the work of these projects, the Canadian Transport Department released, on the 9th of May 1968, an interim report from the year 1953, written by Smith. In that, the engineer came to the conclusion:

> From a study of the sighting reports it can be deduced that the vehicles have the following significant characteristics: they are a hundred feet or more in diameter; they can travel at speeds of several thousand miles per hour; they can reach altitudes well above those which would support conventional aircraft and balloons; and ample power and force seem to be available for all required maneuvers. Taking these factors into account, it is difficult to reconcile this performance with the capabilities of our technology, and unless the technology of some terrestrial nation is much more advanced than is generally known, we are forced to the conclusion that the vehicles are probably extraterrestrial. It appears then, that we are faced with a substantial probability of the real existence of extraterrestrial vehicles, regardless of whether they fit into our scheme of things. Such vehicles, of necessity, must use a technology considerably in advance of what we have. It is therefore submitted that the next step in this investigation should be a substantial effort towards the acquisition of as much as possible of this technology which would, without doubt, be of great value to us.

At the same time, he proposed the establishment of a UFO observation station which would be on the lookout for UFOs around the clock. Its aim would be acquiring data through controlled sighting, which could give information about UFO technology. This proposal, too, was accepted by the Transport Department. In November 1953, the station was put into operation. It was a fenced-off shed belonging to the Transport

Page out of the interim report of Project Magnet.

Department at Shirleys Bay, a lonely bight in the Ottawa River, ten miles west of the city of Ottawa, Ontario. It was equipped with state-of-the-art equipment including ionospheric reactors, electronic sound measuring instruments, a gamma ray counter, a gravimeter, magnetometer and radio receiver. The data measured by these instruments were continuously registered by a graphic recorder. Whenever the instruments detected any anomalies that could possibly be the result of the presence of a UFO in the vicinity, an alarm was set off. The people who were in charge of this station were the members of the well-proven crew of Project Magnet: Smith, Wait, Wilson and Garland, as well as John Hector Thompson, from the communications division of the Department of Transport.

Finally, on August 8, 1954, the project met with success. At 3:01 p.m., the gravimeter reacted violently. Everything indicated that a magnetically propelled flying object, therefore a UFO, was approaching the station. Smith and his two colleagues, who were there that afternoon, ran out excitedly, but all they could see was a heavy fog, which covered the Ottawa River landscape. Whatever it was that flew over Shirleys Bay, and however close it might have been, it was hidden from human eyes.

Though this was an embittering experience, Smith believed that his great hour had arrived. He informed the Press, declaring that, provided no mistakes were found in the instruments, he had just detected a flying saucer above the Canadian capital. A check showed that the instruments were operating faultlessly. Something very strange must therefore have flown over the station.

But the headlines in the papers the next morning put Smith's superiors in the Department of Transport ill at ease. They were suddenly faced with a situation in which an employee of the Canadian Government had officially confirmed the existence of UFOs. This could lead to diplomatic complications with the big neighbor, the United States of America, and an unfriendly reaction in Washington could not be ruled out. The powers that be in Ottawa acted quickly. Within two days, the UFO observing station at Shirleys Bay was closed down and Project Magnet was declared finished. Smith was unequivocally instructed not to give any comments in the future in the name of the Department of Transport. As a small gesture of goodwill, however, they allowed him to make use of the facilities of the Department for private research, which he continued to do until his premature death in May, 1962.

From 1955 onwards, Smith, now a conventional telecommunications engineer in the Department of Transport, devoted himself to another branch of UFO research: the contactees. He read with fascination the books written by George Adamski and George Hunt Williamson, and tried to get as much information as possible through the media. Commenting on Adamski's description of the propulsion system of the saucers, Smith wrote, *"Adamski's book . . . is scientifically fairly correct and is conforms with our work."* Adamski had also stated that the saucers were driven by the use of electromagnetic principles:

The undercarriage, consisting of three spheres observed on most of the saucers, serves as withdrawable landing gear, as well as a three-point, electrostatic propulsion control system. The vehicle is steered by controlling and regulating the discharge. During horizontal flight in the ionosphere of a planet, the vehicle travels along the geomagnetic lines of force of the planet, and the most important function of the spheres is to act as condensers for the static electricity, which is drawn from the atmosphere through the magnetic pole and led on further.

Soon after that, Wilbert Smith had his own personal confirmation that George Adamski had spoken the truth. Since 1956, he he led a group of people, amongst them two officers of the Air Force, who kept nightly watch for UFOs on the same lines as Project Magnet. On one occasion, half an hour after midnight, the entire group was able to observe, for about five minutes, a bell-shaped saucer identical to that which George Adamski had described. Neither Smith nor Adamski, however, was aware of the fact that the technology which they were trying to describe had been known on Earth already for several decades. In 1921 the young physicist Thomas Townsend Brown, experimenting with Coolidge tubes which generated X-rays, noticed a strange phenomenon. Whenever he switched on the tubes they moved slightly. Soon, Brown discovered the cause. The high-voltage which he switched on to operate the tubes created a certain pressure that acted against gravity. Further experiments with the "gravitator," a machine constructed by Brown, confirmed his observations. If a 100 kv electric current was switched on, the object lost 1% of its weight. Brown was sure that he had discovered a new electric principle, the effect of electricity on gravity. But in 1922, when he pursued his studies at the California Institute of Technology, none of the professors there, including the Nobel prize winner Dr. Robert A. Millikan, seemed to be interested in his discovery.

In 1923, however, when he transferred to Denison University at Granville, Ohio, he found competent support. The physicist Prof. Paul Alfred Biefeld, a Swiss-born fellow student of Albert Einstein, was fascinated by Brown's discovery and became his mentor. Together, they demonstrated experimentally that a condenser hanging by a thread showed a tendency to move in the direction of its positive pole when a high voltage current flowed through it. This phenomenon was then known as the Biefeld-Brown effect. In a further experiment, the condenser was suspended with its poles vertical and with a counter-weight. Upon switching on a high-voltage current, if the

T. Townsend Brown

positive pole was pointing downwards, the condenser moved downwards. If the positive pole was on top, however, the condenser moved upwards, working against gravity. The anti-gravitation effect, as Brown called it, could be enhanced by the following measures:

1. By bringing the condenser plates closer together;
2. by increasing the K factor (the capacity of the dielectric substance between the plates to store electricity at high voltage);
3. by increasing the area of the plates;
4. by increasing the applied voltage, and
5. by increasing the mass of the dielectric material between the plates.

Based on these experiments, in 1936 Brown constructed something that he called a "space vehicle," a flying machine based the electro-gravitative principle, which makes the aircraft of today look primitive. That "space vehicle" had no moving parts. Its propulsion and steering mechanisms were operated only by changing and amplifying the electric polarization. Conforming to the Biefeld-Brown effect, it always moved in the direction of the positive pole. For the vessel to change direction, this pole had to be shifted. The direction of motion was, after that, the resultant vector between the direction and strength of the negative and positive voltages. To determine the ideal shape for this vehicle, Brown experimented with various forms and finally came to the conclusion that the disc shape was the most suitable.

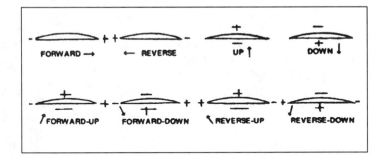

This flying disc required no moving parts, wings, propellers or any aerodynamic design. Brown had discovered the secret of the saucers long before the first reports about a flying saucer ever appeared in the papers.

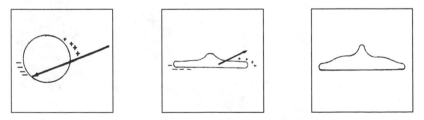

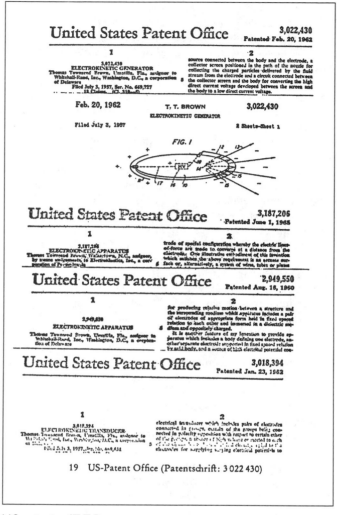

19 US-Patent Office (Patentschrift: 3 022 430)

U.S. patents of T. T. Brown.

Brown's spaceship could produce its own electro-gravitative field with which it could move and travel through space independent of the gravitation of the Earth. This meant that it could accelerate and decelerate, start and land, climb and dive and change direction at sharp angles and move in weightless space without its crew being affected, because they would always be in their own gravitational field. According to Brown, *"The field behaves like a wave with a negative pole on the top and a positive pole at the bottom. The disc moves like a surfboard on the rising wave which is continually kept in motion by the electro-gravitative generator. Since the orientation of the field can be controlled, the disc can fly in any desired direction and at any desired angle on its own continuously created wave."* Brown explained in 1938, *"On account of the high-voltage discharge, the disc would be enveloped in a light glow."* In addition to that, the field would affect plants and animals.

Brown was convinced that he had discovered the basis for a whole new spectrum of technologies. The magic word was electro-gravitation. Electro-gravitational effects were not governed by the principles of electromagnetism and occurred completely independently of these. More than that, he believed that for every electromagnetic phenomenon there was an electro-gravitative effect and since all of our electronics, telephone, telegraph, radio, television, generators and motors were based on electromagnetic principles, the newly discovered phenomenon opened up undreamed-of possibilities. But more than two decades were to pass before Thomas Townsend Brown was given the attention that his discovery deserved.

Way before that, his career had taken Brown to the research laboratories of the U.S. Navy. There he was responsible for fifty qualified scientists and had a budget of $50 million at his disposal. He also worked together with Albert Einstein. During World War II he led projects of the National Defense Research Committee which, after the end of the war, was renamed the Office of Scientific Research and Development, and was placed under Professor Vannevar Bush, the scientific advisor to the President. Later on, Brown worked for the aircraft construction company Lockheed. He was a member of various well-known professional associations like the American Association for the Advancement of Science, the American Geophysical Union of the National Academy of Sciences, the American Society of Marine Engineers, the American Institute of Aeronautics and Astronautics, and the American Physics Society. His studies in the matter of electro-gravitation were conducted by him only in private.

Only in 1947, when flying saucers had made headlines, did no less a person than Admiral Arthur W. Radford, supreme commander of the Pacific fleet of the U.S. Navy, become aware of Brown's research. He believed that Brown was the only physicist who was capable of solving the mystery of the propulsion system of the UFOs. That was the beginning of Project Winterhaven, which Brown led in Cleveland in 1952. While working there, he succeeded in developing a machine that was capable of overcoming its weight completely and hovering in the air.

In a further experiment, he suspended 2 disc-shaped bodies, each 2 feet in diameter and equipped with a variation of the 2-plate condenser, from a kind of carousel. When constantly supplied with a current of 50 Watts at 50 kilovolts, the discs started moving in a horizontal orbit of 18 feet diameter and a speed of 12 miles per hour. When he used discs of 3 feet diameter and applied 150 kilovolts, the size of the orbit increased to 51 feet diameter. The results were so impressive that they were immediately classified as secret, as the special journal *Interavia* later reported, under the heading "Towards Weightless Flight." Brown asserted that, given a sufficiently strong source

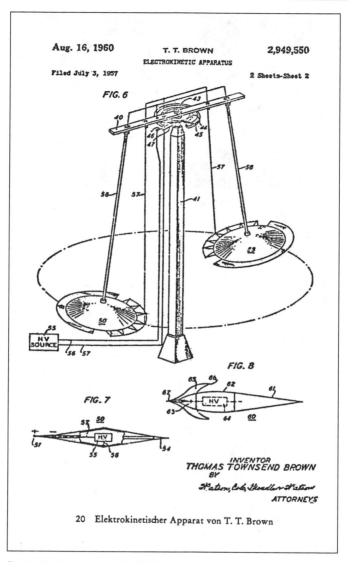

Electrokinetic apparatus by T. T. Brown, patented 1960.

of energy, he could construct a manned electro-gravitational flying craft. What that would look like was shown by Dr. Mason Rose of the University of Social Research in a paper published by him in 1952. His construction drawing resembles the flying saucers photographed by Adamski, and later by Menger.

This, of course, opens up the possibility that the first contacts had been deliberately staged by someone who already possessed such an aircraft.

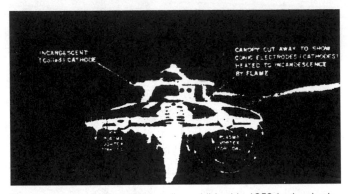

Prototype for an anti-gravitation disc published in 1952 in the thesis of Dr. Mason Rose.

Perhaps that is what happened, as Menger was told by someone from the Pentagon, in order to familiarize the public with the idea of contact with aliens.

Another explanation is also possible, however fantastic it may sound, that T. Townsend Brown had become a contactee without knowing it himself. Someone found that he was on the right track and someone gave him the right inspiration, for that someone wanted us to take up this new technology, since we were destroying the Earth by using our old technology. The fact is that T. Townsend Brown felt himself drawn to UFO phenomena as if by magic. He studied the photographs and reports of eyewitness accounts and contactees, particularly those of George Adamski, as shown by his drawings, for he intuitively felt that someone out there had long since put into practice what he could imagine only in his wildest dreams. Or, the third alternative was that Brown had personal access to alien technology.

On November 18, 1955, a conference dealing with the subject of gravitation was held in New York. Amongst the leading physicists who took part in the conference were Professor Edward Teller, the inventor of the hydrogen bomb, Professor Dr. J. Robert Oppenheimer, leader of the Manhattan Project which had developed the first atom bomb, Dr. Freeman J. Dyson and Professor John A. Wheeler, who had shown that nuclear fusion was possible. Ansel E. Talbert, the scientific editor of the *New York Herald Tribune*, summarized what had been discussed at the conference as follows:

"Many in America's aircraft and electronics industries are excited over the possibility of using its magnetic and gravitational fields as a medium of support for amazing 'flying vehicles' which will not depend on the air for lift. Space ships capable of accelerating in a few seconds to speeds many thousands of miles an hour and making sudden changes of course at these speeds without subjecting their passengers to the so-called 'G-forces' caused by gravity's pull are also envisioned. William P. Lear, inventor and chairman of the board of Lear Inc., one

T. T. Brown's handwritten analysis of Adamski's photographs in light of the latest discoveries "in the laboratory," dated January 5, 1958. It documents the great interest the inventor/genius had for the contactee. "It is a fact that the behavior of the laboratory model resembles that of the alleged ship from Venus and, what is more provocative, its construction is similar in very important details."

of the nation's largest electronics firms specializing in aviation, for months has been going over new developments and theories relating to gravity with his chief scientists and engineers. He is convinced that it will be possible to create artificial electro-gravitational fields whose polarity can be controlled to cancel out gravity . . . Eugene M. Gluhareff, president of Gluhareff Helicopter and Airplane Corp. of Manhattan Beach, Calif., has made several theoretical design studies of round or saucer-shaped vehicles for travel into outer space."

That the subject of UFOs was expressly discussed at this conference is shown by the words of William P. Lear, the inventor of the Lear Jet. *"I am convinced that the UFOs are a reality, and that they are most probably closely connected with the theory of gravitational fields. We are on the threshold of being able to prove the existence of these antigravitational forces."*
Major Donald Keyhoe mentions in his book, *The Flying Saucer Con-*

spiracy, the theory of the German pioneer rocket research scientist Professor Hermann Oberth, who was Wernher von Braun's teacher and is known in scientific circles as the father of space travel. Oberth declared that the entire behavior of UFOs indicated that they had their own gravitational fields. Oberth called them G-fields: *"Even during the most rapid changes in direction and speed, the passengers would remain unaffected. Further, the space vessels would be able to attain extremely high speeds, even the speed of light. Thirdly, the G-field would explain the noiseless flight of these vessels. The air surrounding them would be drawn along with them so that there would be no turbulence and, therefore, no noise. Fourthly, the changes in the glowing of the saucers which had been observed could be the result of the transformation of obstructing rays in radiation of extremely long wavelength, which would produce light and electricity."* A study conducted under the supervision of Lt. Plantier of the French Air Force in 1953 came to similar conclusions.

The Japanese physicist Professor Shunichi Seiki seems to have discovered a means of producing an artificial gravitational field. In his book, *The Principles of Ultra-Relativity*, published in 1972, he describes the possibility of converting the potential energy of weight (mass) into electromagnetic energy. This was based on the Kramer equation, known since 1934, which connects the fourth-dimensional gyration of atoms with external electric and magnetic fields. Seiki's model makes use of the spatial spin of electrons in the spectrum of magnetic nuclear resonance.

The material to be tested is placed in a high-frequency alternating field at frequencies which are typical for, and at variance with, the material in question. An absorption effect takes place. Energy is drawn out of the surrounding field.

Seiki demonstrated that the polar rotary impulse is affected by an electrical nuclear resonance just as the axial spin is influenced by the magnetic nuclear resonance. The polar rotary impulse creates in space a source field which is connected by a diverging equation with the energy operator directly and, therefore, also with the gravitational field. Seiki found a solution to the equations of motion in a rotating alternating current field which is loaded with a magnetic counterweight. Above certain resonance frequencies a condition of negative entropy is created and energy from the gravitational field of the Earth flows into the system. The negative forces thereby create an artificial gravitational field which counteracts that of the Earth.

Using three spherical condensers which were alternatingly loaded and discharged by means of three magnetic spools—in other words, exactly as George Adamski had described—Seiki created the rotating field. An external source of energy is required to start the motor. The total output of the machine was calculated at 3×10^9 kilowatts, which is far above the energy produced in a Saturn rocket. If a vessel powered by these means approached the Earth, according to Seiki, electronic and electrical machines would be put out of action and plants injured, effects which have been observed in connection with UFOs.

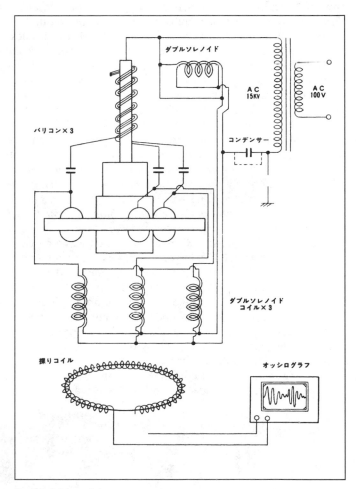

Prof. Seiki's model.

The theoretical models of Brown and Seiki show at least how the UFOs are propelled, why they have such extraordinary flying characteristics and why they have certain effects on the surroundings. But after top scientists conferred in New York in November 1955 to discuss gravitation, the subject of electrogravitation suddenly disappeared from the scene. We can only assume that further research was being conducted in secrecy under military protection. That at this period practically all armament and aircraft manufacturers were working on this technique is proved by a document called the study of "Electrogravitics Systems" dated February 1956, and which was discovered, appropriately enough, in the technical library of Wright Patterson Air Force Base, where the Air Technical Intelligence Center (ATIC) is located.

One reads in the document: *"Most major companies in the United States are interested in organizing groups to study electrostatic and electromagnetic phenomena."* Amongst them are Douglas and Glenn Martin [*"who say gravity control could be achieved in six years"*]; Clark Electronics [*"add that in their view the source of gravity's force will be understood sooner than some people think"*]; General Electric and Bell [*"Are convinced that practical hardware will emerge from current programs"*]; Lear [*"have a division working on gravity research"*] and Lockheed and Boeing. All leading universities were also conducting research in this field, including the Massachusetts Institute of Technology, the Institute for Advanced Study in Princeton (where Einstein was working), the Caltech Radiation Laboratories—in short, the cream of the community of physicists in the country.

Further it says, *"Major theoretical breakthroughs to discover the sources of gravity will be made by the most advanced intellects using the most advanced research tools. Aviation's role is therefore to impress upon physicists of this caliber the urgency of the matter . . . Some extremely ambitious theoretical programs have been submitted and work towards the realization of a manned vehicle has begun."* Convair was cited as being exemplary. Included in their experimental team were such advisors from nuclear projects as Dr. Edward Teller, the father of the hydrogen bomb.

What conclusions these top scientists arrived at is not known. The invitation given to Menger in 1960 to work on such a project indicates that it was a long-term program carried out under complete secrecy and also that it was finally successful. But whatever the scope of the project, it was carried out without the participation of Thomas Townsend Brown. But he, too, had begun to take an interest in UFOs when, during the early 1950s, he recognized that their flight behavior confirmed his theories.

Like Wilbert Smith in Canada, he founded a private organization in

Reconstruction of Adamski's disc by engineer Leonard G. Cramp.

Washington D.C. in order to obtain more data. Called the National Investigating Committee on Aerial Phenomena (NICAP), it soon became the best known UFO research organization in the United States. It was later led by Major Donald Keyhoe. Among the members of this committee were high-ranking military officers, including Admiral Roscoe Hillenkoetter, the former director of the CIA, showing that Brown was not the only person who believed that collecting data about UFOs was important.

Brown was sometimes accused of conducting the research solely from the point of view of electro-gravitation. During the following years he was increasingly convinced that someone, most probably a government official, was keeping an eye on his work, hoping to get useful information. The eagerness with which the authorities pursued information on UFO phenomena in order to understand the method of propulsion explains the special interest of certain departments for the activities of the contactees Adamski and Menger. Then came the Rodeffer film which, like nothing else before it, gave clear clues regarding the driving mechanism of UFOs.

On February 27, 1967, Madeleine Rodeffer showed her movie in the presence of two friends, Fred and Ingrid Steckling, to a group of 22 NASA employees at Goddard Space Flight Center at Greenbelt, Maryland (Building A1). The Stecklings also had something to show, which confirmed Adamski's contact posthumously. Fred Steckling was a young German who had come to Washington in 1962; right away he became a UFO witness. That made him go to the Library of Congress and look for literature. The first name listed among authors of UFO literature was, naturally, "Adamski, George." Fascinated by Adamski's incredible report, Steckling was bent on meeting the man who claimed to be in contact with extraterrestrials. Steckling wrote to Adamski, learned about his forthcoming visit to Washington and, when that took place, met the author. They became fast friends. Adamski took Steckling, who was then working as a pilot for an American airline, completely into his confidence. Then came the day when Adamski introduced Steckling to his "space brothers," extraterrestrials who, according to Adamski, lived and worked in Washington.

Fred Steckling

One year after Adamski's death, Steckling met one of these "space brothers" again in Washington. Concluding a long conversation, the German pilot said that he wanted to go to Germany in autumn to meet with some relatives and also some like-minded persons. "There too, we will always be with you," promised his friend from space. "Keep your movie camera ready." Steckling did what he was told.

After visiting some friends in Schifferstadt on September 7, 1966, he boarded at 11:00 a train running from Mannheim to Frankfurt. As always, he had his super-8 movie camera with him. When he looked out of the window by chance at 11:15 a.m., his attention was caught by a group of twelve long objects which flew in three rows of four each and seemed to accompany the train. Steckling was certain that this must be the demonstration his "space brother" had promised. The whole armada of flying cigars gleamed white against the clear blue sky. His son Glenn quickly opened the window, and Steckling leaned out and started to film. Now the other passengers also began to notice the cigar-shaped forms. They crowded at the windows and watched the maneuvers spellbound, until it was over two minutes later.

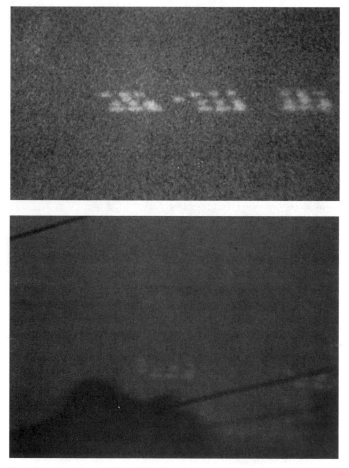

Fred Steckling filmed this UFO formation on September 7, 1966, between Mannheim and Frankfurt.

"You certainly have something very, very remarkable," said one of the astonished NASA scientists after Madeleine Rodeffer and Fred Streckling had shown their films. Two weeks later both of them were invited to the Pentagon, where they showed their films, on March 20, 1967, to a group of experts under the chairmanship of Lt. Col. George B. Freeman Jr. There, too, the audience was highly impressed. Madeleine and Fred were filled with new confidence. The theme of UFOs was at that time very popular, and the events of the two years following Adamski's death had almost caused a breakthrough.

CHAPTER 9

For What Should Not Be Cannot Be

During the night of August 2, 1965, thousands of people in the midwestern United States, from North Dakota down to Texas, saw whole formations of colorful disc-shaped objects flying over them. Motorists stopped their cars in the middle of the road and got out to watch the spectacular show in the sky. Whole families ran out of their houses to watch. Radio and TV programs were interrupted to announce that shining discs were flying above their stations. The Tinker Air Force Base near Oklahoma City announced that they had UFOs on the radarscope and that they were flying at an altitude of above 20,000 feet. A witness from El Reno described one of the UFOs thus: "*It looked like a bright source of light, mostly white. It seemed as if it was enveloped in a greenish glow. The UFO flashed and then shone red, white and blue when it flew off towards the west.*"

A few days later came the official declaration of the U.S. Air Force regarding this mass sighting: "*The observed objects could have been the planet Jupiter or the stars Rigel, Cappella, Betelgeuse or Aldebaran.*" It sounded good, but it became embarrassing for the person who made this declaration when astronomers stated that they could not accept this explanation. At the time of the sighting, none of the celestial bodies named was above the horizon!

There is also photographic evidence to show that the "explanation" by the Air Force could not hold water. During that night, 14-year-old Alan Smith of Tulsa, Oklahoma succeeded in taking a color photograph of the object. And what he saw with his own eyes, Alan describes as follows: "*An object in the shape of a baseball, it changed in color from white to red and bluish-green. Its lights pulsated. It gave off a high-pitched, shrill, whistling noise. As the noise became louder, the object became brighter.*" When the UFO was just over his head, he shot a picture with his 620 Kodacolor film.

Witnesses to this were Alan's father, 43, his sister, 18, and Daryl Swimmer, a neighbor. Alan's father estimated the altitude of the object at 6,000 feet and its diameter as 40 feet: *"The object appeared at first like a bright star, with a glaring white light, turned red and, when it came nearer, blue, then green, and finally creamy-white. All the dogs in the neighborhood began to bark and howl when it flew over us."* In the photograph, the UFO appears as a bright spot in the corner of the picture, but when sufficiently magnified, it shows details that the naked eye cannot make out. A computer analysis made in 1976 by the GSW showed that it was *"a three-dimensional solid discus-shaped object of medium size, whose diameter was between 30 and 40 feet."*

During the following months, the UFOs made their presence known by a very different and new method. During the night of September 23, 1965, hundreds of witnesses, including General Rafael Vega, commander of a military district, Mayor Valentin Gonzales and Governor Emilio Riva Palacie, saw a glowing disc-shaped UFO which hovered low above the Mexican city of Cuernavaca. At the same time, there was a complete failure of the electrical supply in the city and the lights went on again only after the UFO had flown away.

When Renato Pacini, conductor of the Indianapolis Symphony Orchestra, visited his brother in Rochester, NY, on September 9, 1965, he was picked up at the Syracuse airport by his brother. At about 5:20 p.m., after they had covered more than half the distance, Renato noticed a strange bright light in the western sky. He pointed it out to the others, who agreed that it was unusual. As they drove along, the light descended like lightning and then set off in the direction of Syracuse. They were able follow the light for some distance until it was too low and hidden by the treetops. A few seconds later there was a radio announcement that a blackout had occurred. In the entire Northeast of the United States, and even across the Canadian border, the electrical supply had failed. The area affected was about 55,000 square miles. A pilot who was just then flying in to land at a New York airport and saw the lights of the city vanishing said, *"I had a feeling that it was the end of the world. Balls of light and shining discs could be seen all over that area, particularly above power stations, during that entire night."* Pacini's report could also be verified: at the same time as he and the others saw the light, the city's representative for air traffic, Robert C. Walsh of Syracuse, was in an airplane flying about 1,500 feet above the city. Then it became dark suddenly.

"It was a weird feeling," said Walsh describing his experience, *"I thought I had lost my eyesight and thought for a minute about what I should do. Then I saw the vehicles moving in the streets and at least it was clear that I could still see. Sabotage occurred to me at the first, and then a number of other causes for the blackout. I contacted the control tower of the airport— I knew it had an emergency generator. I asked what had happened, but nobody had any idea. I decided to land."* Soon after landing, Walsh was discussing the occurrence with friends from the airport personnel when, sud-

denly, they all saw a big ball of fire in the sky, which seemed to rotate. According to the estimates of the pilots, the object was only 100 feet above the ground and had a diameter of about 45 feet. Then the object rose suddenly and vanished into the sky.

Similar occurrences followed during the next few weeks in the states of Minnesota, Texas, California and New Mexico.

The next wave of UFO sightings came in March 1966 in the state of Michigan. Hundreds of witnesses described how they saw objects of the size of an automobile, shaped like a flattened baseball, which often hovered over the villages at relatively low altitudes. Among the witnesses were twelve policemen, 80 female students from a college, and a professor. Once more the Air Force passed judgment, premature in thought and time. They explained the phenomenon as marsh gas which had caught fire. There was a storm of protest, and not only from the witnesses.

The press had now lost its confidence in Project Blue Book completely. Hundreds of angry letters arrived at Wright Patterson Air Force Base while other citizens approached their representatives in Congress. The congressional spokesman of the Republican Party, the future president Gerald R. Ford, demanded in a letter to the chairman of the Armed Services Committee, L. Mendel Rivers, on March 28, 1966, *"better explanation than that thus far given by the Air Force. . . . I think we owe it to the people to establish our credibility regarding UFOs, and to produce the greatest possible enlightenment on this subject."*

For the first time since 1953, the silence enforced by the CIA's "educational program" of "training and debunking" seemed to have been broken.

Enraged by the nonsense perpetrated by the Air Force, some well-known military officers dared to speak out: *"I have been long convinced that the saucers are interplanetary vehicles,"* declared the former Air Force Press Officer, Albert Chop, who was now

Two sketches by eyewitnesses in Michigan who described the UFOs as solid, metallic objects. Prof. Hynek (L) of Project Blue Book, called them swamp gas.

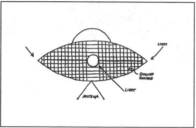

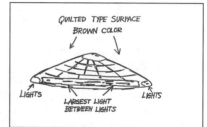

Congressman Gerald Ford demanded "the reestablishment of our credibility in connection with UFOs."

deputy director of the NASA department for public matters, "and *that extraterrestrial beings visit us.*" Rear Admiral Delmar Fahrney conceded that "*reliable reports indicate that unidentified objects with great velocities come into our atmosphere, and that they are controlled by intelligent beings.*" Lt. Col. Howard Strand, commander of Michigan Air Base, was convinced that "*UFOs are real and can come only from planets whose civilizations are older than ours.*" Admiral Roscoe A. Hillenkoetter, who until 1952 was director of the CIA, declared that "*the Air Force has continuously withheld the truth about UFOs from the public. The unknown objects operate under intelligent control. It is of pressing necessity that the public should know where they come from.*" High-ranking military officers and congressman joined NICAP to support the UFO researchers, and to bring about the release of information. And, in fact, the Air Force released at that time the twelve completed reports of Project Blue Book from the Ruppelt era, which had been previously classified as top secret. The Johnson administration promised the "Committee for the Freedom of Information," that it would take further steps but it was to stagnate at that stage.

The new magic formula created to console the UFO lobby said that the Air Force wanted a well-known university to carry out a scientific study of UFOs. Theoretically, this was not a bad idea at all. But none of the bigger universities wanted to pick up this "hot potato" for fear of losing its reputation. Finally, the University of Colorado agreed and a contract for research was signed between representatives of that university and the Air Force, with a budget of $313,000.

The dark, squat and beefy-looking physicist Dr. Edward U. Condon was put in charge of the research work. Condon was, from the beginning, an arch-skeptic. "*I will not believe in extraterrestrial saucers,*" he declared to a reporter even at the start of the investigations, "*until I have seen and touched one, entered it, brought it to the laboratory and studied it together with competent people. I would be only too happy to get one.*"

Dr. Edward Condon

Soon there was a scandal in Colorado. Two scientists of the UFO project, Dr. David R. Saunders and Dr. Norman Levine, were dismissed suddenly without notice for insubordination. They had published a memorandum found in the files which they could not accept. In that memorandum, the project coordinator Robert J. Low, on August 9, 1966, expressed some thoughts about the UFO project.

> In order to undertake such a project one has to approach it objectively. That is, one has to admit the possibility that such things as UFOs exist. But it is not respectable to give serious consideration to such a possibility. Believers, in other words, remain outcasts . . . the simple truth is that in admitting these possibilities we would lose more prestige in the scientific community than we could possibly gain by undertaking the investigation . . . our study will be conducted almost exclusively by nonbelievers who, although they couldn't possibly *prove* a negative result, could and probably would add an impressive body of data to the evidence that the observations have no reality.
>
> The trick would be, I think, to describe the project so that, to the public, the study would appear totally objective but, to the scientific community, would appear to be a group of nonbelievers trying their best to be objective, but having an almost zero expectation of finding a saucer. One way to do this would be to stress investigation, not of the physical phenomena, but rather of the people who do the observing—the psychology and sociology of persons and groups who report seing UFOs. I'm inclined to feel at this early stage that, if we set up the thing right and take pains to get the proper people involved, and have success in presenting the image we want to present to the scientific community, we would carry the job off to our benefit.

When Prof. Saunders published this document, he set off a countrywide scandal about the Colorado project. Condon barked at the professor, "*For that, you deserve to be ruined professionally!*" and dismissed him from his post.

Condon however, did not, hesitate even for a moment to act on the guidelines of Low's memorandum—and by implementing it encountered success. It is a well-known fact that no criticism is so shattering as one that makes something look ludicrous, and that was Dr. Condon's method. Every crackpot, every charlatan seeking fame was given importance and publicity—and then deflated in the concluding report with much sarcasm and a smirking satisfaction. An anonymous letter from California, which was particularly remarkable for the eccentricities in spelling that it exhibited, foretold a UFO landing at 11.00 a.m. on April 15, 1967, on the Salt Flats in Utah. Condon apparently had nothing more important to do than to call up the governor of Utah and arrange for a reception committee to be on the spot, complete with brass band. What did not appear, naturally, was the announced spaceship. The writer from California had had his laugh, and in Colorado, Condon slapped his thighs in joy. In the eyes of the press and the public the UFO affair had received one more deadly blow.

Shortly afterwards, Dr. Condon gave a great deal of attention to the former inmate of a mental asylum who introduced himself as Sir Salvador, representative of the Third Universe; he promised to bring about a UFO landing for the meager sum of $3 million in gold. A drug-addicted female student whose connections with the crews of alien ships was sexual was also a subject carefully studied by the scientific team.

Dr. Edward U. Condon was a man who loved anecdotes that paralleled his eccentric sense of humor. This applied to the "damn UFOs," as he always insisted on calling them.

But as Professor James McDonald of the University of Arizona said, *"After all, it was not the weak-minded, but pilots, policemen and other reliable witnesses whose UFO reports kept the matter going. In principle, Dr. Condon made no effort to go into the serious side of the matter."*

In December 1968 the "Scientific Study of Unidentified Flying Objects" was finally finished. Its budget, meanwhile, had been increased to $500,000. On January 8, 1969, the 965-page report came out as a paperback, obviously subsidized, at the ridiculously low price of $1.95 and published by Bantam Books. Presented on 236 pages separately and detailed were the reports of the investigation—59 cases of UFO sightings carried out by the Colorado scientific team. The report was self-contradictory.

The results given were astounding. In one third of the cases, the objects sighted could not be identified, whereby everything was done to avoid the word *"unidentified."* For example, *"One could find no clear explanation," "interesting, but inexplicable," "difficult to judge,"* and finally *"there appeared to be little convincing evidence that these sightings involved objects that were physically real."* [Case 38]. Or *"The case obviously provided no verifiable information about UFOs."* In such a way were embarrassing cases put aside. Nevertheless, for all who read it carefully, this report was a proof that unidentified objects did exist, whatever they were. *"I have been interested in UFO phenomena ever since I read the Condon report,"* said the French space expert Dr. Claude Poher of the French National Society for Space Research (CEFS), *"for if one really reads the entire Condon report and not just Condon's summary and conclusions, one finds that one is faced with a real problem."*

Indeed, some of the best cases made it clear that the UFO phenomenon exists, i.e., The Great Falls, Montana case (*"The case remains unexplained"*), and a report from 1957 about the crew of an Air Force B-47 observing a UFO which, at the same time, was picked up by radar (*"the phenomenon remains unidentified"*). In "the Lakenheath case," when UFOs were spotted on the radarscopes of a NATO Air Base in England, jet interceptors were sent out and the entire ground crew watched the brightly shining, solid, flying objects. The conclusion: *"it seems to be highly possible that at least one genuine UFO was involved."* The McMinville case of 1950 was even described as *"one of the few UFO reports in which all factors investigated, geometric, psychological and physical, appear to be consistent with the assertion that an extraordinary flying object, silvery, metallic, disc-shaped, tens of meters in diameter and evidently synthetic, flew within sight of two witnesses."*

Despite these and other such cases, in his "Conclusions and Recommendations," Condon claimed that *"UFO phenomena do not offer a fruitful field in which to look for major scientific discoveries . . . careful consideration of the record as it is available to us leads us to conclude that further extensive study of UFOs, in the expectation that such study will advance science, probably cannot be justified."*

A calculation of chances is given to show that a visit from extraterrestrials is improbable for the next 10,000 years. Also *"no indications could be found to justify the belief that extraterrestrial visitors have entered our air space. There are also no sufficient grounds to justify any further research in this direction."*

Condon's conclusions not only evoked a protest from UFO enthusiasts, but also found no great agreement among his colleagues in the scientific world. From the many disapproving statements made by American scientists—there was even a note of protest sent to Congress, signed by 19 university professors—only the following passage from an article written by the nuclear physicist Stanton T. Friedman and published by the journal *Physics Today*, No. 1/71, is cited here:

"After studying the UFO question for 11 years, I am now convinced that some of these UFOs are extraterrestrial vehicles. The problem about accepting them is a psychological problem, just as the acceptance of the Copernican conception of the world was, 300 years ago. . . . every generation of eminent scientists seems to make the same arrogant mistake, namely to believe that mankind has, during that epoch, reached the peak of scientific knowledge and technology . . .

If there really is any mental aberration in connection with the UFOs, then I am convinced that it exists among the scientists and journalists who make the persons who have seen UFOs look ludicrous; who give out authoritative judgments without examining the information; who think they know what science and technology will look like in the future; who claim to know how visitors from space will behave; and those who, without having informed themselves in any manner whatsoever, claim that scientists have never seen UFOs and that only uneducated fools believe in UFOs. The task of the psychiatrist is to find out why such a deep-rooted desire not to believe in UFOs exists, and not why people see UFOs."

Meanwhile, the U.S. Air Force had declared as "unidentified" a report about a UFO landing during which members of its crew came out of the vehicle. In fact, they had no other choice, for the report was a police report and the chief witness was a patrolman of the New Mexico police department, who saw the object in broad daylight.

The incident occurred late in the afternoon of April 24, 1964, on the outskirts of Socorro, a desert town in New Mexico. Police officer Lonnie Zamora was carrying out his duties as he had done every day for the past five years, since his last promotion. At about 5:30 p.m., when he had just

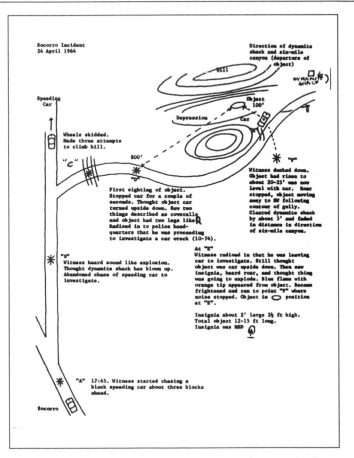

Map sketched by Lonnie Zamora to describe the Soccorro landing, taken from the investigation reports of the Air Force Project Blue Book.

passed the town court, a black Cadillac drove past in the opposite direction at excessive speed. "I'll get him," said Zamora to himself. Turning his car around, with squeaking tires he took up the pursuit. He was on State Road 85 with the Cadillac still ahead of him, when he heard a noise like thunder. In front of him, in the southwest direction and about three-quarters of a mile away, an orange and blue-colored flame shot across the sky. In that area there was a dynamite store and Zamora wondered whether there had been an explosion there.

So he decided to let the speedster get away and drove towards the dynamite store in case help was needed there. After driving up the first hill he looked in the direction of the store and saw a glowing white object at the bottom of a gorge about 500 feet away from him. "Oh my God!" said

Highway Patrol Officer Lonnie Zamora

Zamora to himself and thought that some terrible accident had occurred there.

He picked up his radio at once and called up headquarters using police code: "*Socorro 2 calling Socorro. Probably 10–44* [accident]. *I will 10–6* [be busy, shall leave the car and check the vehicle]." That was at exactly 5:51 p.m. When he looked once more at the bottom of the gorge, he realized that what he had taken to be a wrecked car was something very different. There was no doubt at all that there was a white, glowing, metallic object shaped like an American football down there, standing on thin black landing struts. Then he saw, close to it, two persons in white overalls. One of them turned around and looked in the direction of Zamora's car, and apparently frightened by it, started moving hastily. The police officer got back into his car and drove towards the object, intending to offer help if required. When he got closer he once more heard the noise of thunder and again saw a flame.

This time the flame was under the object. It was light blue in color, whereas the underside of the object was orange. As the object shot up vertically, the noise became louder. He could see a sign, a kind of symbol painted in red on the white side of the object: a semicircle, drawn horizontally, about 25 inches long. Inside it was an arrow pointing upwards with the shaft cut off at the level of the barbs. The experienced policeman was now frightened. He thought that the mysterious flying object would explode at any moment, and so he ran away with his arms protecting his face, past his car and up the hill. While running he looked back now and then at the object and saw how it rose within seconds out of the gorge and was at the road level. Once on the other side of the hill he felt a bit more safe, and, sheltered by the rocks and bushes, he looked back to see the "egg" flying away at a low height of about 15 feet above the ground. It missed the dynamite store only by about 3 feet, then gradually increased its speed and finally glided off into the sky. Zamora ran back to the car, grabbed the telephone and told his colleague Nep Lopez, "*Look out the window and tell me if you can see an object. It looks like a balloon,*" but a moment later he realized that Nep could not see the object at all because the window of Nep's office was facing north, and the object was heading in a southwestern direction.

After Zamora had informed headquarters as to his exact location, his colleague Sgt. M. S. Chavez came to the spot. He found Zamora in a pretty pitiful state—pale, sweating and jittery. He pointed to a group of burning bushes and kept repeating "That's where it stood, Sergeant, that's where it was." When they both climbed down the gorge to the spot where the object

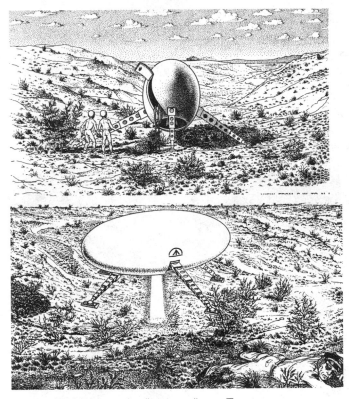

Sketch of the Soccorro landing according to Zamora.

had stood, they found four hollow impressions in the ground, 18 inches by 10 inches, which together formed the corners of a rhombus, obviously made by the four landing struts of the UFO. Now Zamora remembered that on arriving at the place, and before the explosion occurred, he had heard a kind of metallic clatter that probably came from the landing struts being withdrawn. Between these hollow impressions in the ground the men discovered two smaller imprints like those which a ladder would have left. *"I knew that Lonnie had seen something and the proof was there right before our eyes,"* declared Sgt. Chavez later. He knew what had to be done. First he told patrolman T. V. Jordan to photograph the landing spot. Then he informed the Air Force and the FBI.

The first investigators arrived the same day. Special agent D. Arthur Byrnes, Jr. of the FBI and Capt. R. T. Holder from the Air Force collected the evidence, took samples,

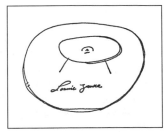

Zamora's sketch of the object and the mysterious symbol.

interviewed Zamora and Chavez and confiscated Jordan's as yet undeveloped film. The next day a preliminary report was sent to Project Blue Book at Wright Patterson Air Base in Dayton, Ohio, which had been written by Col. Eric T. de Jonckhekre. When, a day later, on April 26, the investigating team of Project Blue Book—Maj. Hector Quintanilla and the astronomer J. Allen Hynek—arrived at Socorro, the gorge where the UFO had landed had long become a stomping ground for dozens of journalists, UFO enthusiasts and the generally curious. They were greeted at first by a thunderstorm and when that subsided, they themselves had to give dozens of interviews before they could interview Zamora and Chavez. Hynek believed the policeman.

The Air Force photograph of one of the 4 imprints of the landing struts of the UFO. The stones were put there by an FBI official to mark and protect the spot.

Zamora had had a terrible shock. Chavez repeatedly impressed upon me that in all the years during which he had known Zamora officially, he had never seen him in such a state as he found him in, when he went to the spot in question. Zamora had been used to bad accidents, bloodshed, street fights and even murder. We are all unanimous here that he had experienced something that had frightened him thoroughly.

The taciturn policeman detested the turmoil brought about by the incident. If he now wrote out a ticket for a teenager, he had to hear "What are you giving me a ticket for? Don't you realize that any minute another flying saucer could land here?" As a faithful Catholic, he asked his priest for advice and, as a loyal policeman, he regretted from the bottom of his heart that he had broken off his pursuit of the speeding Cadillac and driven into the desert instead!

There were other witnesses. Opel Grinder who had a gas station on State Road 85 said that shortly after the incident a tourist couple had said to him "You've got funny-looking helicopters here." They said that an egg-shaped helicopter had flown across the road in front of them at low altitude and had landed in a hollow between the hills. "Apparently it was an emergency landing. In any case, the police were there soon after." As late as 1968 another witness, Larry Kratzer of Dubuque, Iowa, reported that, at the time in question, he had been in New Mexico with a business friend, Paul Kies, and was now in a position to confirm Zamora's story.

But there was a better proof for this amazing incident, the landing marks and the stone samples which the investigators took from the imprints left on the ground by the landing gear. The first analysis of the hollow imprints showed that they could have been left only by an object weighing many tons, as the report of Project Blue Book states. Two samples of dirt were given by Sgt. David Moody to the Materials Physics Division of the Air Force laboratories for analysis. The report of the tests, written on May 19, 1964, says: "Spectrographic analysis showed that the chief element was silicon. Other elements present were magnesium, aluminum, iron, sodium, potassium and calcium besides traces of manganese and titanium." The percentage in which these elements occur were not given.

Ray Stanford of NICAP, who had also gone to the spot on April 26, discovered traces of metal on a stone against which apparently a landing strut had rubbed. He took it with him to Washington and

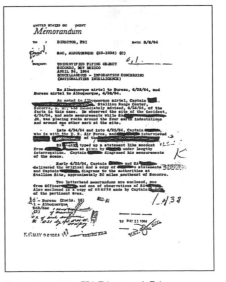

Report sent to FBI Director J. Edgar Hoover about the investigation activities of FBI agents in the Soccorro case.

gave it to Dr. Henry Frankel, chief of the metallurgical department of Goddard Space Flight Center of NASA in Maryland for analysis. On August 5, 1964, Dr. Frankel telephoned Ray Stanford and told him what he had found.

The particles are composed of a material that could not occur naturally. To be precise, it consists predominantly of two metallic elements, and there is something that is rather exciting about the zinc-iron alloy of which we find the particles to consist. Our charts of all alloys known to be manufactured on Earth, the U.S.S.R. included, do not show any alloy of the specific combination or ratio of the two main elements involved here. This finding definitely strengthens the case that might be made for an extraterrestrial origin of the Socorro object.

But instead of forwarding the promised written confirmation of these results, Dr. Frankel suddenly became silent. For two weeks Stanford tried in vain to get him on the telephone, and then Gordon Space Flight Center called him. At the other end of the line it was not Frankel, but a certain Thomas P. Sciacca Jr., who explained to Stanford that Dr. Frankel was no longer responsible for this matter, and added that his analysis had been wrong. The metal on the stone, according to Sciacca, was silicon, just simple sand. Stanford could just not believe that a top expert like Dr. Frankel could have misread a spectroscopic analysis. No chemistry student in his first semester would have mistaken silicon, which has an atomic weight of 28, for an alloy of iron, 56, and zinc, 65.

Prof. James E. McDonald, physicist and specialist of atmospheric science at the University of Arizona, learned from a radiation chemist that at the landing site molten sand had been found, which meant that it had been subjected to extremely high temperatures. The Air Force never returned the film taken from the policeman T.V. Jordan and gave as an excuse that exposure to radiation had turned the film completely black. The Socorro case gave Major Quintanilla of Project Blue Book a few more headaches. "*At first I thought it was a test of the latest moon landing vehicle of the NASA. That seemed to me to be the only logical explanation,*" he confessed later. "*That was perhaps the best documented case in the archives of the Air Force and I examined every possibility from top to bottom. I even asked the White House . . . nothing, nothing. Nevertheless, even today, I am not convinced that it was anything extraterrestrial. I just can't believe that.*" The case finally ended up in the files marked "unidentified."

Professor Hynek was more than impressed by Zamora's descriptions of the humanoids: "*I don't remember anything particular, no head covering or helmets. The people seemed to be of normal proportions, only rather small. They were either small adults or big children,*" wrote Zamora in his police report.

There was another case in the files of the Colorado study similar to the Socorro incident, in which another police officer also encountered "small adults or big children" who came in an oval space vessel, but he could remember this only under hypnosis.

State trooper Herbert Schirmer of Ashland, Nebraska, was on duty during the cold and clear winter night of December 3, 1967. His shift began at midnight. At about 1:30 a.m. he had inspected the stalls of the local cattle market. For no apparent reason, the animals were excited, mooed as if in panic and trampled around with their hooves. Later, at 2:30 a.m. he reached the crossing of the highways 6 and 63 at the outskirts of town when he noticed red blinking lights at the edge of the road, some 400 yards away from him. Thinking that it was a broken-down truck, he drove towards it to see if he could help. Stopping on the shoulder, he switched on his headlights to see better, and what he saw frightened him out of his wits. The blinking did not come from a truck, but from an object shaped like an American football that was hovering slightly tilted at about six feet above the ground.

It seemed to be made of polished aluminium. Around its middle was a row of round portholes, each about two feet high, out of which the red light blinked. Below the ports there was a kind of flange. Three landing struts were projecting downwards from its underside. While Shirmer was trying to make out more details, he heard a shrill noise like a siren and an orange-colored flame shot

Sketch of the UFO as seen by patrolman Herbert Schirmer on December 3, 1967.

down from the bottom of the object, which then rose up in the air. Breathlessly, Schirmer watched it ascend slowly with a slightly wobbly motion. It then crossed the road, accelerating and finally disappearing into the sky. He grabbed his logbook and wrote, "2:30 a.m. Flying saucer seen at the crossing of highways 6 and 63, believe it or not." He then drove on to the police station and, to his amazement, saw that the clock there showed 3:00 a.m. He had looked at his watch as a matter of routine when he drove towards the "broken-down truck" and his watch had shown 2:30 a.m. The whole incident could not have lasted for more than five minutes, and he would have needed at the most only 5 more minutes to drive down to the station. In addition to that, he felt funny, dizzy, weak, nervous and sick. Early in the morning, at 5:00, he returned home from duty. When he undressed to go to bed, he noticed a red scratch on his leg but was unable to remember how he could have gotten it.

The next morning, Schirmer's boss informed the Air Force about the incident, and he was told to contact the Colorado study group. A few days later, the physicist Prof. Roy Craig, the psychologist Prof. Leo Sprinkle of the University of Wyoming and their assistant, John Ahrens of Ashland,

Wyoming, came and interrogated Schirmer and his colleagues, his family and his neighbors. All were unanimous in their opinion that Schirmer was an honest and reliable person who had both feet on the ground, certainly not one to suffer from hallucinations or daydreams. His superior officer had already subjected Schirmer to a lie-detector test—Schirmer had begged for it when the story came out into the open—which the patrolman passed without the slightest difficulty. All the psychological tests that the investigating team from Colorado put him through also confirmed the impression of an honest young official who was convinced that what he had seen was real. But there was no supporting evidence. As Professor Sprinkle put it, *"On the other hand, unlike at Socorro, no landing imprints or effects of radiation could be found at the spot in question."*

Then there were these 20 lost minutes for which nobody could find any explanation, until the idea of hypnotizing Schirmer occurred to Prof. Sprinkle. He did this and, by regression, sent Schirmer back to the time when he encountered the UFO. He asked him to describe what was happening. What came out of this inquiry was in no way less fantastic than the claims of George Adamski and Howard Menger.

The craft literally dragged me and my car uphill towards it and, when I had reached it, a figure came out from under the ship and moved towards my car. When it stood near the door, another one came out carrying a box-like thing in its hand, with which it directed a kind of green light at and around the car. I wanted to take out my revolver, but I couldn't. I felt as if I had been paralyzed. Then one of them came to the car, grasped inside and touched me on the neck, when I felt a piercing pain. Then he stepped back and motioned with his hand. I got out of the car slowly, stood before him and he asked me "Are you the policeman of this place?"

I answered "Yes, I am."

Their leader had a very high forehead and a very long nose. His eyes were rather sunken and he had round eyes like us, except for the pupils. They were, I would say, like the eyes of a cat. His complexion was a kind of grayish pink. I didn't see any hair or ears, for they were covered by a kind of cape which was part of his uniform. A thin antenna was sticking out of a little box, which was attached to the other side of his uniform. His mouth was like a slit and, when he spoke to me, it was in a very deep voice as if it came out from deep inside, but his mouth didn't move at all.

He said: "Policeman, come with me." We climbed up a ladder and entered the ship and, once inside, he took me down to the lower deck. We stood there and looked at these things like oil casks in a circle, all connected by a black cable to one another. Then, in the middle, there was what looked like half a cocoon which rotated and gave out light in all the colors of the rainbow. He said "Policeman, that is our source of energy, reversible electric magnetism." We went back to the entrance and sort of glided up into the upper storey—simply 'sss!' as if one was in a lift. There was a kind of red light, and then this big rotating cone and all kinds of panels and computers. Then there was a map on the wall and a big

Schirmer on board the UFO. Sketch by W. Crom, after information given by the witness under hypnosis.

screen like a viewing screen. He went there, pressed a few buttons, pointed to a few stars and said 'We come from there.' There was writing on the map, which I couldn't read. It showed a sun and six planets. They came from a neighboring galaxy. That was all that he told me. He named no names, only showed it on the map. They observe us and have been observing us for a long time.

He said: "Policeman, we have come here to get electricity." They obtain their electricity from one of the high voltage towers here which is directly connected to the Ashland power house. This antenna thing at the edge of the vehicle moved when he pressed a few buttons. A ray came out and hit the big transformer and drew back. The high voltage tower burned for a whole minute until they somehow put out the fire.

The upper deck was a kind of observation deck with switching panels and chairs and a big viewing window. He said to me "Policeman, you will see the universe as I have seen it," and thereby showed me the stars.

He said "policeman, come with me," and we went back, directly down and out of the ship and went to my car. When we came to the car he said to me "you will not remember what you have seen and heard. You will only remember that you saw something landing and starting." And that was it.

But in spite of this amazing result, the Colorado study team came to the conclusion that its project staff was not sure whether the UFO experience of the policeman was real or not. Now, it must be noted that nothing worked against its being real except for the lack of traces of a landing, which in any case could not have existed since the object never actually landed; it hovered at a height of 20 feet above the ground. It was Schirmer's story that to them sounded too fantastic to be true. And what should not be, cannot be.

The insiders in Washington ignored the results of the Colorado study, knowing that it was, after all, a diverting maneuver meant for the public. They were no longer interested in the question of whether there was enough proof to justify the belief in the existence of extraterrestrial visitors. They were more worried about the implications of the actual presence of the visitors.

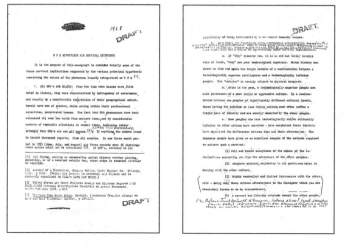

NSA study about "UFO hypotheses and survival questions," from 1968. "Some UFOs are related to extraterrestrial intelligence. This hypothesis cannot be disregarded . . . and has far reaching consequences."

"UFO Hypotheses and Survival Questions" is the title of a 7-page report which Prof. Lambros Collimabos, head of a group of elite scientists of the super secret National Security Agency, wrote in 1968 and which was released officially 11 years later under President Jimmy Carter. That paper, originally classified as top secret, discusses the five most important hypotheses about UFO phenomena and rules out three of them:

1. All UFOs are hoaxes: The fact that UFO phenomenon have been wit-

nessed all over the world from ancient times and by considerable numbers of reputable scientists in recent times indicates rather strongly that UFOs are not all hoaxes. If anything, the modern trend is towards increased reports, from all sources;

2. All UFOs are hallucinations: But a considerable number of instances exist in which there are groups of people and a radar or radars seeing the same thing at the same time. Sometimes a person and a military camera confirm each other's testimony. On occasion, physical evidence of a circumstantial nature was reported to have been found to support witnessed sightings. The sum of such evidence seems to argue strongly against all UFOs being hallucinations;

3. All UFOs are natural phenomena: If this hypothesis is correct, the capability of air warning systems to correctly diagnose an attack situation is open to serious question. Many UFOs have been reported by trained military observers to behave like high speed, high performance, high altitude rockets or aircraft. The apparent solidity and craft-like shape of the objects have often been subject to radar confirmation. If such objects should come over the Arctic from the direction of Russia on the United States, they could trigger 'false reports of missile attacks.'

4. Some UFOs are secret Earth projects: The U.S. Air Force reentry vehicle and an often publicized Canadian "saucer" project leave little doubt as to the validity of this hypothesis. Undoubtedly, all UFOs should be carefully scrutinized to ferret out such enemy (or friendly) projects.

5. Some of the UFOs are related to extraterrestrial intelligence: According to eminent scientists closely associated with the study of the UFO phenomenon, this hypothesis cannot be disregarded. This hypothesis has a number of far-reaching human survival implications. . . .

Obviously the writer of this paper had a fairly deep inside knowledge about the UFO phenomena upon which he bases his analysis. Reading between the lines, one surmises that highly critical situations had arisen, cases which the writer had obviously found recorded in the archives of the Pentagon. Thus, indirectly, through reference, the detection of UFOs by the air warning systems of the United States, and the sightings of pilots simultaneously documented by military camera, are officially confirmed as being facts—things which were known to us until now only through the statements of former Air Force officers. Even more interesting is his analysis of the implications of an extraterrestrial presence—or better, of open contact with extraterrestrials—which makes us guess why, in 1969, the National Security Agency decided to continue the policy of silence:

a. If "they" discover you, it is an old but hardly invalid rule of thumb, "they" are your technological superiors. Human history has shown us time and again the tragic results of a confrontation between a technologically superior civilization and a technologically inferior people. The inferior is usually subject to physical conquest.

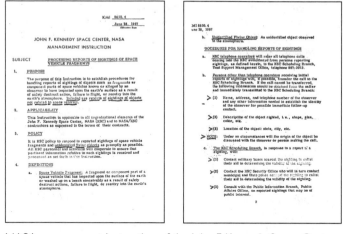

NASA management instruction of the John F. Kennedy Space Center for dealing with UFO reports.

b. Often in the past a technologically superior people are also possessors of a more virile or aggressive culture. In a confrontation of two peoples of significantly different cultural levels, those having the inferior or less virile culture most often suffer a tragic loss of identity and are usually absorbed by the other people.

c. Some peoples who were technologically and/or culturally inferior to other nations have survived—have maintained their identity, have equalized the differences between them and their adversaries. The Japanese people have given us an excellent example of the methods required to achieve such a survival:

1. full and honest acceptance of the nature of the inferiorities separating you from the advantages of the other peoples;

2. complete national solidarity in all positions taken in dealing with the other culture;

3. highly controlled and limited intercourse with the other side— doing only those actions advantageous to the foreigner which you are absolutely forced to do by circumstance;

4. a correct but friendly attitude toward the other people;

5. a national eagerness to learn everything possible about the other culture—its technological and cultural strengths and weaknesses. This often involves sending selected groups and individuals to the other's country to become one of his kind, or even to help him in his wars against his adversaries;

6. adopting as many of the advantages of the opposing people as you can, and doing it as fast as possible, while still protecting your own identity by molding each new knowledge increment into your own cultural cast.

While only strictly "controlled" and "restricted" contact with the aliens was maintained, as recommended by the NSA paper, it was looked upon as a necessity for "cultural survival" to keep this contact hidden from the public at all costs. More than that, it was intended to keep alien visits under control, through a clear demonstration of one's own unwillingness to accept too frequent visits and too public an appearance or, as the NSA report recommended: *"Investigation would become an intensive emergency action to isolate the threat and to determine its precise nature. It would be geared to developing adequate defensive measures in a minimum amount of time. It would seem that a little more of this survival attitude is called for in dealing with the UFO problem."*

The first step in this direction was to inform the top officials of the armed forces and the space authority NASA to ignore the findings of the Colorado study completely. On June 28, 1968, a service regulation under File No. KMI 8610.4 of the John F. Kennedy Space Center, NASA, came into force. Under the heading "subject" it says: *"Processing reports of sightings of space vehicle fragments"* but the first paragraph makes it clear that more is meant. *"Included are reports of sightings of objects not related to space vehicles."* In paragraph 4b, it says, *"Unidentified flying object: an unidentified object observed in the atmosphere."* If such reports came in from civilians to the KSC (John F. Kennedy Space Center), then they were to note down the name, address and telephone number of the observer *"and any other information needed to establish the identity of the observer for possible immediate follow-up contact."* Further, they were to take down *"description of the object sighted, that is its shape, size, color, etc."* A little later it says: *"Under no circumstances will the origin of the object be discussed with the observer or person making the call."* The KSC personnel taking down the report were, further, to *"a) contact military bases nearest the sighting to enlist their aid in determining the validity of the sighting; and b) contact the KSC security office. . . . ' "*

For UFO reports there was even a special telephone number, the command post of Patrick Air Force Base, telephone number 494-7001. In fact, although Project Blue Book had been officially closed with the Colorado study and *"no further investigations were being conducted regarding unknown flying objects,"* the interest of the authorities in UFOs had not subsided in the least. Air Force Secretary Harold Brown said in 1966, in answer to a question from Congressman L. Mendel Rivers, that the Air Force *"in evaluating these sightings . . . has used carefully selected and highly qualified scientists, engineers, technicians and consultants. These personnel have utilized the finest Air Force laboratories, test centers, scientific instruments and technical equipment for this purpose."* This elite team referred to by Harold Brown was a newly established group which worked under the codename Project Moon Dust and is probably still active today.

CHAPTER 10

Moon Dust

On October 20, 1969, Brig. Gen. Carrol H. Bolender, deputy director of the Department of Research and Development of the US Air Force, wrote a memorandum to end the Project Blue Book, in which he declared, *"reports of unidentified flying objects which could affect national security are made in accordance with JANAP146 or Air Force Manual 55–11, and are not part of the Blue Book system. The Air Force experience therefore confirms the impression of the University of Colorado researchers 'that the defense function could be performed within the framework established for intelligence and surveillance operations without the continuance of a special unit such as Project Blue Book.'"* And with that, Gen. Bolender confessed something which insiders had guessed long ago; that Project Blue Book was only an office for collecting reports, a kind of public relations project which had no military significance. The truly relevant cases went through other channels.

As a matter of fact, cases which could have affected the national security were never left to be dealt with by Project Blue Book. Under Air Force regulation 200–2 of August 12, 1954, another very special unit had been commissioned to deal with such cases: Air Intelligence Service Squadron (AISS) no. 4602 of the Air Defense Command, which had been established a year before and had its headquarters at Fort Belvoir in Virginia. This unit was responsible for the field investigation of the identity of possible UFOs within the sovereign territory of the United States. The reason for this decision, it was stated, was that the squadron possessed all qualities and means required for such investigations.

"The 4602nd AISS is composed of specialists trained for field collection and investigation of matters of air intelligence interest. The Squadron is highly mobile and deployed throughout the ZI . . . " [Zone

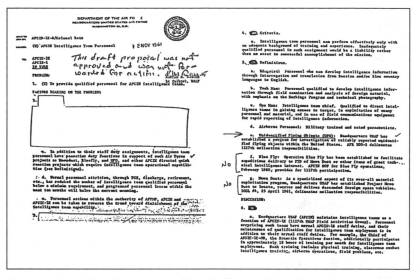

Memorandum of the Department of the Air Force defining the actions and activities of the AFCIN intelligence teams, the support given to Air Force Projects Moon Dust, Blue Fly and UFO.

Interior, or, the continental USA] The team had full authority and was fully in command of all investigations: *"All Air Force activities are authorized to conduct such preliminary investigation as may be required for reporting purposes; however, investigation should not be carried beyond this point, unless such action is requested by the 4602d AISS."* What was more, the AISS decided what would finally be sent to the ATIC and Project Blue Book.

During the following decades, AISS 4602d was to be renamed many times. In July 1957 it became the AISS 1006th and in April 1960 the USAF Field Activity Group 1127, later Field Activity Group 7602, then Air Intelligence Group 696 and, since 1989, AIG 512. It is still stationed at Fort Belvoir, Virginia. What, however, remained unchanged during all these years was their mission. The scope of this activity is outlined in a memorandum of the Air Force department dated 3rd November, 1961.

1. Unidentified Flying Objects (UFOs): *Headquarters USAF has established a program for investigation of reliably reported unidentified flying objects within the United States. AFR 200–2 delineates 1127th collection responsibilities.*

2. Blue Fly: *Operation Blue Fly has been established to facilitate expedition delivery to FTD of Moon Dust or other items of great technical intelligence interest. AFCIN SOP for Blue Fly operations, February 1960, provides for 1127th participation.*

3. Moon Dust: *As a specialized aspect of its overall material exploitation*

program, headquarters USAF has established Project Moon Dust to locate, recover and deliver descended foreign space vehicles . . . "

Under Paragraph 6 of the same document, "Discussion," the personnel requirements of these projects is set forth:

. . . These three peacetime projects all involve a potential for employment of qualified field intelligence personnel on a quick reaction basis to recover or perform field exploitation of UFOs, or known Soviet/Bloc aerospace vehicles, weapons systems, and/or residual components of such equipment.

. . . Intelligence teams are comprised of three men each, to include a linguist, a tech man, and an ops man (Intelligence Team Chief). All are airborne qualified. Cross training is provided each team member in the skills of the other team members to assure a team functional capability despite casualties. . . .

To what extent the scope of Project Moon Dust was repeatedly widened is shown by a telex sent out by the Defense Intelligence Agency (DIA) in 1973 through the Department of State to all U.S. embassies and consulates in the world. It instructs all U.S. diplomats to report all incidents concerning investigations of space objects of non-American or of unknown origin under the code word "Moon Dust." When documents mentioning "Moon Dust" and "Blue Fly" were rather inadvertently released in 1980 and these names became known to the public, the Air Force changed the code names.

How secret these projects still are was revealed when the UFO researcher Sgt. Clifford Stone attempted in 1992 to obtain more information about them, through Senator Jeff Bingaman. *"There is no agency at Fort Belvoir, Virginia, nor has there ever been, which would deal with UFOs. . . . In addition, there is no Project Moon Dust or Operation Blue Fly. These missions have never existed,"* answered Lt. Col. John E. Madison, Jr. from the U.S. Air Force, in November 1992. When Bingaman sent the Air Force twenty documents given to him by Stone, in which these projects are mentioned, the Air Force "rectified" its statement by conceding the historical existence of Blue Fly and Moon Dust, but "clarifying" that they had been closed down *"As the occasion never arose to use these air defense teams. . . ."*

Stone's documents show that the projects were still active in December 1989. When he had written to the Air Force Department asking for files pertaining to the said projects under the Freedom of Information Act, the Department refused to release them, claiming that *"release of the information could cause identifiable damage to the national security,"* as Col. William A. Davidson, in his letter of July 25, 1990, put it. To prevent another accidental release of documents in this way, all files connected with Moon Dust and Blue Fly were classified a higher level than they had been before. One more reason to do this was to divert attention from a particular case which Moon Dust and Blue Fly were working on just then, and which had already attracted far too much publicity. This incident was nothing less than the recovery of a crashed UFO within the territory of the United States, to be more exact near Kecksburg in Pennsylvania, which had to be covered up at all costs.

On December 9, 1965, at 4:44 p.m., thousands of people from North

Press report about a crash of an unidentified object at Kecksburg, near Pittsburgh, Pennsylvania.

Canada to Pennsylvania observed an orange fireball tearing across the evening sky towards the south east, followed by a trail of smoke. Pilots who were in the air in Michigan, Ohio or Ontario reported sighting the object, which they thought was a burning airplane that would crash into Lake Erie. But it crossed the Great Lakes and Minnesota as well. Over Ohio, witnesses saw it standing still for a few seconds in the sky and then change its course to the east, towards Pennsylvania. Exactly at 4:47 p.m. one Mrs. Jones from the little township of Kecksburg called the radio station WHJB in Greensburg and told the reporter John Murphy, *"A huge fireball has crashed in the woods about 1.5 miles from here."*

Mrs. Jones's children had been playing in the garden when they saw what they later described as a "burning star" suddenly appear in the sky, and a few seconds later, fall into the forest. She herself was visiting neighbours and saw, looking out from their veranda, blue smoke coming out of the forest, then a bright light like a 4-pointed star hovering above the trees. The radio station informed the police, who contacted Mrs. Jones and requested her to lead them to the crash site.

Reporter Murphy got into his car and drove towards the area in question. When he got there, there was already much activity. Two police cars were parked at the edge of the forest, and near that, a fire engine. The fire marshal had just interrogated Mrs. Jones and the children. He then went with one of the policemen into the forest. Sixteen minutes later the two men came out. To Murphy's questions the marshal replied tersely, "ask my lawyer."

What followed was a large-scale salvage action. Whatever it was that had crashed in the forest, the Army and the Air Force marched up to deal with it. The military and state police cordoned off the forest area, stationed armed guards at all the roads and ways leading into the forest and transported a whole lot of technical equipment to the crash site. The Air Force took over the premises of the local voluntary fire station and set up a commando post there. The firemen, now forbidden to enter the station, stood by watching while persons in military uniform brought in more equipment into the station, which included a huge radio transmitter. A little later, two large transport trucks, one of them bearing the insignia of the army, were seen driving into the forest. At about the same time, people living close to the nearby Latrobe Airfield saw a jet plane landing there, although the airfield itself had been closed to traffic for quite some time.

Soon after that, dozens of reporters from Pittsburgh arrived at Kecksburg

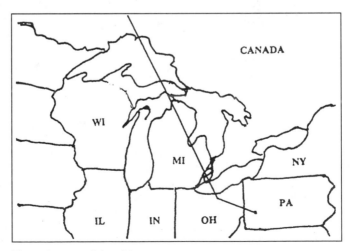

The trajectory of the object.

and were met by official silence. But the one thing that a police spokesman told the reporters said enough, "There's an unidentified flying object in the woods." When they then phoned up Project Blue Book, Major Hector Quintanilla replied by saying that an investigation team of the Air Force was already at Kecksburg.

Witnesses later described this team as being dressed in blue overalls and wearing blue berets. "Blue Berets" was a nickname for members of Operation Blue Fly and now they were in charge of the operation. The actual salvaging work was done by the 662nd Radar Squadron, a unit under the Air Defense Command stationed at Oakdale near Pittsburgh. Complete censorship followed after that. The very next day, the Air Force informed the press that they had recovered a meteorite that had struck the forest, but failed to present this meteorite to the press or to scientists.

But before the army had succeeded in sealing off the forest area, one civilian managed to get to the crash site. Bill Bulebush had heard over the radio about the accident and, being a passionate hunter who knew the forest thoroughly, set off immediately to find the wreck and render what assistance he could. He drove to the top of a hill, saw smoke coming up from a certain spot, drove towards it as far as he could and, finally, had to cover the last bit on foot. There he saw something that threw him for a loop. A metallic bullet-shaped object was sticking in the ground at the end of a trench, which it had obviously formed while landing. *"It looked like a big burned orange. It sparkled and twinkled, was about 9 feet wide and 12 feet long. Somehow it gave me the creeps and I got away quickly."* And when he read the Air Force explanation in the papers the next day, he knew they were lying. What he had seen had certainly not been a meteorite!

What Bulebush said convinced the local UFO researcher Stan Gordon that something else must have crashed into the forest. If nothing else, the speed with which the object had crossed the northeastern states worked against the meteorite theory. The speed could be calculated at about 5,000 miles per hour, but meteorites have speeds varying from 30,000 to over 120,000 miles per hour. Besides that, the trajectory of the object had been neither a straight line nor a smooth curve. It had taken a clear and sharp turn of 45 degrees over Ohio. *"What landed in Pennsylvania?"* asked the biologist and UFO researcher Ivan T. Sanderson in the March 1966 issue of the magazine *Fate*. He questioned the meteorite hypothesis based on the facts cited above. But 22 years elapsed before another witness was ready to say what actually had been recovered during the night in question.

James (Jim) Romansky was 19 years old at that time and was a volunteer in the Kecksberg Fire Department. He too, like thousands of others, had watched the fireball flying over the town, but when the sirens went off a little later, he did not connect the alarm with the fireball. For him it was a fire fighting job like any other. When he got to the station, he and the other firemen were instructed to form search parties and comb the woods near Kecksberg for the "wreck of an airplane, which had exploded in the sky and probably fallen in the forest."

Dozens of other fire fighting units had been called up from the entire countryside around the forest. Search teams were formed consisting of three or four men. Equipped with torches and walkie-talkies they went into the woods to look for the wreck. After an hour or so, Romansky's team heard over the radio that a team somewhere to the right of them had found something and needed assistance. So they went there and finally they, too, saw the object. It was sticking into the ground by its nose at the end of a trench. It had obviously landed at an angle of 20 to 30 degrees and, in coming down, had torn a path through the trees, and finally created the trench. The trench was about 25 feet long and about 6 feet wide and, at its lowest point, 6 feet deep. To Romansky's surprise there was nothing burning or smoldering. If it had really been the fireball that he had seen that afternoon, then the whole forest should have been ablaze. But there were no significant traces of burning at all.

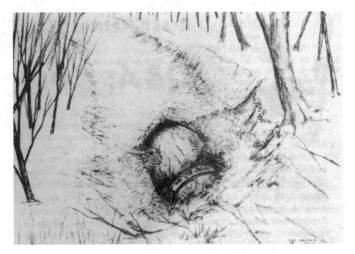

The object at the crash site. Sketch according to eyewitnesses' description.

The object itself looked strange. It had the shape of an acorn, made of shining silvery metal which had a light touch of gold in it. Its bottom was surrounded by a kind of ring or, as Jim put it, a kind of metal bumper on which strange writing could be seen. Romansky described it later. *"They looked like Egyptian hieroglyphics, but without any animal signs. There were straight and broken lines, dots, squares and circles."* What amazed him most was that the object was in such good shape. During his work in the fire department he had often enough seen wrecked aircraft, but what he now saw was something entirely different. There was no glass, no propeller or jet nozzle, no burst tanks from which any fuel had leaked out, not even the sign of a hatch or entrance. The men stood there and were looking at it from a respectful distance, when a policeman and an elderly gentleman in civilian clothes, the fire marshal, joined them. Soon after that the army arrived and instructed the firemen to leave the forest immediately.

When he and his comrades finally got back to the fire station, it was like being caught in a swarm of bees. The Air Force had taken over their station and posted an armed guard before it, who shouted at them "No entry for you here today." The place was crawling with armed military personnel, some of whom were carrying all sorts of equipment into the fire house. They managed to pick up bits of a telephone conversation between an officer at the station and, apparently, the North American Air Defense Command (NORAD) in Colorado.

A few days later the fire department received a letter of thanks from the Air Force. Although the object, which had at first erroneously been taken to be a crashed airplane had only been a fallen meteorite, the Air Force thanked the firemen of Kecksburg for their cooperation.

Romansky, of course, knew that what he had seen was not a meteorite. He was a mechanic by profession and knew something about metals. He had never seen metal like that out of which the object had been made. For him, the object was "something that was not from this Earth."

Later on he suffered from skin cancer. He could never free himself of the suspicion that the object had something to do with it, that it had been radioactive. In fact, witnesses did see containers being taken into the forest bearing the radioactivity warning sign on them.

NBC broadcasted a television special based on Romansky's report and Gordon's research as part of the series "Unsolved Mysteries." After it aired, hundreds of other witnesses came up with their reports of the Kecksburg incident, all of which confirmed the words of Romansky and Gordon. Thus, about a dozen witnesses said that late in the night they had seen a large army flat-bed transporter coming out of the forest, with a large bell-shaped object on it, covered by tarpaulins. The triple-axle truck had red warning lights on it. There was an escort of armed soldiers sitting in army jeeps in front and behind the truck. As soon as the convoy reached the highway, it accelerated and drove off, completely disregarding the speed limit. After that it was announced that the search operation had been completed. All this was confirmed by James Mayes, vice-captain of the Kecksburg fire department, to the NASA employee Clark McLelland of Kennedy Space Flight Center in January 1980. Said McLelland,

Mr. Mayes declared that a large military truck drove into the blocked off area and that hours later, it left with a large object on it covered by a tarpaulin. A number of residents of the area heard the droning of the truck late at night. Mayes's superior, fire department captain Robert Bitner, who went to the spot later, confirmed this too. Bitner was present when, late at night, a 10-ton military transporter came out of the forest. On its loading deck was a large object, about 6 feet high, 9 feet wide and 18 feet long. Mr. Bitner was standing about 25 feet away from the truck, which was surrounded by military guards. Finally, an escort of a number of army jeeps was formed and the convoy started moving.

The first destination of the convoy was Lockborne Air Force Base near Columbus, Ohio, where, according to a witness who contacted Stan Gordon, the personnel had been put on the highest military alert. This witness, Robert Adams (pseudonym), belonged to the military police and said that during the morning hours of December 10, his unit had received orders to surround a particular hangar and "to shoot anyone who tried to get in there without a top-secret access permit." A little later, an escorted army truck arrived, entered the base through the rear gate, and drove into the hangar. On its loading deck was an object "twice as big as a Volkswagen" that was covered with tarpaulins. At six o'clock in the morning Adams's unit was relieved, but his comrades told him that the truck had left the base at 7:30 a.m. and was now on its way to Wright Patterson Air Force Base, 100 miles to the west. There it was seen by another witness, who also contacted Stan Gordon.

He called himself "Myron" and remained otherwise anonymous. He worked as a truck driver for a cement factory belonging to his family at Dayton, Ohio. Two days after the incident occurred at Kecksburg, his firm received a large order for specially glazed bricks from the Wright Patterson Air Field. A representative of the base had had a look at the bricks in stock at the factory and finally ordered 6,500 double-glazed processed bricks, which, he said, "were for building a double-walled shield around a recovered radioactive object." Whoever delivered the bricks was to be reliable and discreet and, no matter what he saw, do his job and ask no questions.

On the same day at about 1:30 p.m., Myron and his cousin took the bricks for delivery, loaded on two trucks. At the entrance to the base they were informed that a high-ranking officer was waiting for them in a jeep and were led to a brick-built store. The building was about 85 × 55 feet, surrounded by wooden office cubicles and not far from a powerhouse. The driver of the jeep signed to them to park their trucks in a parking lot next to a large three-axle army transporter, which was standing there with a tarpaulin lying on it. Myron, putting two and two together, was convinced that the object in question must have been transported on that truck. Four or five men in white overalls, rubber boots and rubber gloves, wearing helmets, "were running around like frightened chicken[s]. But that had nothing to do with us; the reason was the damn thing in the building." Then the two men started unloading the bricks.

Myron's curiosity had been aroused. He just had to know what was going on. Pretending to go for a short rest, he crept up secretly to the door of the building and had a quick look at what was inside. There was a sort of circular metal scaffolding, with a balustraded walk around it at a height of about 9 feet. Two ladders led up to it, one up to the height of the handrail, the other going about 5 feet above it. In the middle was a kind of half-open

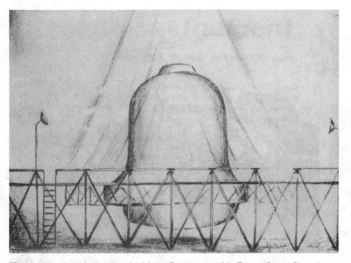

The object in a hangar at Wright Patterson Air Force Base. Sketch according to witness "Myron."

tent of parachute silk hanging from the ceiling, through which, thanks to the floodlights, the shadowy outlines of a large bell-shaped object could be recognized. It was perhaps about 9 feet wide and 12 feet high. Through a small opening in the tent, Myron could see that it was metallic, like some kind of whitish bronze.

When one of the men working on it came out and went past Myron, he could not keep himself from asking what it was all about. The technician obviously thought that Myron belonged to the project, and answered unhesitatingly, "We're trying to get inside it, but even with diamond drills and acid we can't crack the damn thing." A few seconds later a rough voice called to Myron "What are you doing here?" It was a guard. "Get away from here at once and forget everything that you've seen! Is that clear? If you ever open your mouth, we'll lock you up and throw away the key." Only after Myron had promised by everything that was holy did the guard calm down again. His parting words were, "In twenty years you'll know the truth anyhow."

But was the Kecksburg craft, indeed, of extraterrestrial origin? Not necessarily. There had been discussions that it very well might have been the returning Soviet "Kosmos 96" Venus probe, although this was doubtful. The Foreign Technology Division at Wright Patterson AFB denied that there was a record of such a retrieval. The Soviet Embassy denied that Kosmos 96 crashed near Kecksburg. And Stan Gordon found out that Kosmos 96 reentered Earth's atmosphere about 13 hours before the events in Pennsylvania and indeed crashed in Canada.

The wreck at Kecksburg was not the only unknown space vehicle that project Moon Dust recovered. In August 1967 a Blue Fly team recovered an object of unknown origin, which was later described as a satellite, in

SATURDAY MAY 6, 1978 4:15 PM.
THE STRANGE OBJECT FALLS IN BOLIVIA

The UFO crash in Bolivia. Sketch according to eyewitness reports.

Sudan. In July 1968 they found in Nepal an object that was made up of four pieces. In May 1978 they investigated an object in Bolivia. . . .

On May 6, 1978, at about 4:15 p.m., something crashed into a mountain near El Taire on the Bermejo River, the border between the Bolivian province of Tarija and Argentina. Thousands of people saw this happening and later described the object as being cylindrical in shape with a flaming tail. It had caused a supersonic bang that was heard up to 150 miles away and that cracked windowpanes as far away as 30 miles in every direction. The next day, the papers were speculating on what had come down in that godforsaken place. The explanations ranged from meteorites to UFOs and belated reentry of some Apollo capsule. All of them referred to statements of eye witnesses.

Then it was announced that the Argentinian authorities had sent the 20th unit of the border police to the area in question to look for wreckage on their side of the border. The search in that mountainous country could last for weeks, so swarms of reporters went to the nearest big town, Aguas Blancas, to take up quarters there and await further developments, as well as to interview eyewitnesses in the town. And in fact, there were a number of witnesses who claimed to have seen the object. Most of them described

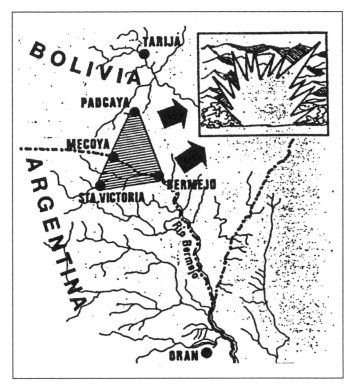

The region in which the UFO crashed.

Photograph of El Taire mountain. The crash site is marked with an arrow.

it as oval or cylindrical and metallic. The army, too, seemed to be convinced that it was a UFO. Corporal Natalio Farfan Ruiz, the commandant of a small border police unit at the little village of La Marmora (800 inhabitants), confirmed the crash to Argentinian reporters saying: *"It was about 4:30 p.m. when a cylindrical object made the earth tremble. Just imagine what would have happened if the UFO had fallen on the houses!"* Policeman Juan Hurtado had also seen what had happened: *"It looked like a gigantic wine container emitting a trace of white smoke. I saw it clearly. It flew directly above my head. I was on duty and at that moment was talking with three engineers from the mine in La Paz, when we saw the object crashing into the El Taire mountain. The impact was so strong that it threw me to the ground. The earth trembled at that moment."*

Finally, the Bolivian Air Force sent three single-motored AT6 airplanes—a model from World War II—to the area and discovered the crash site on the southern slope of the El Taire mountain. Whereas the pilots found it impossible to land anywhere near it, the newspaper *Clarin* of

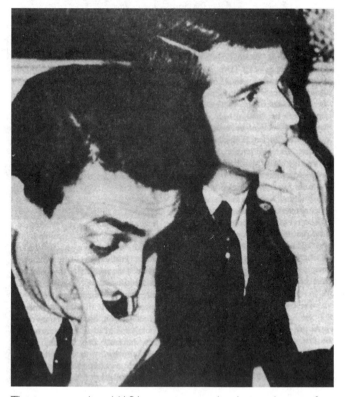

The two mysterious NASA experts proved to be employees of the military attaché of the U.S. embassy at La Paz, working for Operation Blue Fly.

Buenos Aires announced on May 14, that the object had been found. As proof, they quoted the police chief of Tarija: *"Our men have discovered the object and inspected it, but have received no instructions for further action. It is a dull metallic cylinder twelve feet long with a few dents. No one knows what is inside it, and we are awaiting the arrival of various technical commissions. A NASA expert is also expected to arrive tomorrow morning."*

As a matter of fact, no NASA expert came at Tarija. Instead, two U.S. Air Force officers, Col. Robert Simmons and Maj. John Heise arrived. According-ing to a newspaper, although these officers were officially on leave, they had been instructed to take the object to the United States in a Hercules C-130 transport machine, which was waiting for them at La Paz. When other news-papers made inquiries at the American Embassy regarding this secret mis-sion of Simmons and Heise they were met with a denial. Only two years later, 5 relevant documents were released by the U.S. State Department: they revealed that Simmons and Heise had been assigned to the military attaché

```
75 STATE 126725
                         SECRET
      SECRET
?AGS Ø1          STATE  126725
ORIGIN CES-47
INFO  OCT-01  APA-10  ISO-00  SP-Ø2  PM-C5  INR-10  ACDA-12
        NSCE-00  DCR-15  CIAF-00  DODE-00  L-03  HSAE-00
        NASA-31  SOE-02  SS-15  INRE-00  SSO-00  /Ø33 P
DRAFTED BY OES/APT/SA:REDDINGTON:D3U
APPROVED BY OES/APT/SA:REDDINGTON
ABA/AND/R:DTOYRYLA
ARA/ECA:JPUMPUS
S/P:WCATHRIGHT
PM/15P:MMICHAUD
INR/STA:DPALMER
OES/APT/SA:IMPIKUS
                    ---------------Ø21140  182ØØ4Z /4Ø
● 1519392 MAY 79
FRM SECSTATE WASEDC
TO AMEMBASSY LA PAZ IMMEDIATE
S E C R E T STATE 126725
P.O. 11652: GDS
CAGS:  TSPA. BL
SUBJECT: REPORT OF FALLEN SPACE OBJECT
REF: LA PAZ 3Ø24
  . PRELIMINARY INFORMATION PROVIDED IN REFERENCED CABLE
AND FBIS CABLES PANAMA 142357Z AND PARAGUAY 161931Z HAS
BEEN CHECKED WITH APPROPRIATE GOVERNMENT AGENCIES. NO
DIRECT CORRELATION WITH KNOWN SPACE OBJECTS THAT MAY HAVE
REENTERED THE EARTH'S ATMOSPHERE NEAR MAY 6 9AM FB MADE.
HOWEVER WE ARE CONTINUING TO EXAMINE ANY POSSIBILITIES.
YOUR ATTENTION IS INVITED TO STATE A1EGRAM A-6343.
    SECRET
    SECRET
AGT 22          STATE  126725
JULY 26. 1973 WHICH PROVIDES BACKGROUND INFORMATION AND
GUIDANCE FOR DEALING WITH SPACE OBJECTS THAT HAVE BEEN
FOUND.  IN PARTICULAR ANY INFORMATION PERTAINING TO THE
PRE-IMPACT OBSERVATIONS, DIRECTION OF TRAJECTORY, NUMBER
OF OBJECTS OBSERVED, TIME OF IMPACT AND A DETAILED
DESCRIPTION INCLUDING ANY MARKINGS WOULD BE HELPFUL.  VANCE
    SECRET
```

Telex of the U.S. State Department about the UFO crash in Bolivia, with the personal instructions of the Secretary Cyrus Vance.

of the U.S. Embassy in La Paz and did, in fact, fly to Tarija accompanied by an officer of the Bolivian Air Force, in connection with Project Moon Dust. The first of these documents was a telex sent by the U.S. Ambassador in Bolivia, Paul H. Boeker, to the State Department. In that, he quoted newspaper reports and requested the department *"to ask the relevant agencies whether they could explain what this object could be,"* adding *"during the last week, more and more UFO reports are coming from this region."* The answer was a telex classified "secret" dated May 18 in which the U.S. Secretary of State Cyrus Vance personally declared: *"Preliminary information has been checked with appropriate government agencies. No direct correlation with known space objects that may have reentered the earth's atmosphere near May 6 can be made. However we are continuing to examine any possibilities."*

He then referred the embassy to "State aerogram A-6343" of July 26, 1973, classified 'Secret,' *"which provides background information and guidance for dealing with space objects. In particular any information pertaining to the pre-impact observations, direction of trajectory, number of objects observed, time of impact and detailed description, including any markings would be helpful."* The next document was a "Moon Dust Message" of the office of the U.S. military attaché, dated May 24, addressed to the Division for Foreign Technologies at the Wright Patterson Air Force Base and the headquarters of the U.S. Air Force at the Pentagon, classified as "confidential NOFORN (No Forwarding To Foreign Nationals)." Under reference Moon Dust, the military attaché at La Paz reported that *"they had taken pains to verify the press reports."* In addition to that, they had asked the general staff of the Bolivian Air Force and the chiefs of the Bolivian Army who had declared—apparently after a first unsuccessful attempt— *"we have sent search troops to the area in question but have found nothing."* The army came to the conclusion that there could have been an object there, or maybe not, but to date they had found nothing. The attaché added that he would send two officials to Tarija and promised, *"We will keep you informed if anything turns up."* These "two officials," we can assume, were Simmons and Heise.

Regrettably, no further reports concerning the Simmons-Heise expedition were released and, to get a picture of what happened, we are forced to rely on reports in the Argentinian press. Apparently, however, nobody came to the conclusion that a meteorite had hit the earth. At the world-famous Smithsonian Institution there is a data bank of scientific occurrences, or an "alarm network," that keeps track of every volcanic eruption, every earthquake and every meteorite collision since 1973 with painstaking accuracy. The data bank reveals no mention of a meteorite falling during May 1978 at the Bolivian-Argentinian border. The Air Force documents reveal that the 1127th field activities group, which coordinated Project Moon Dust, was interested in another task besides the recovery of UFO wrecks and other space objects, represented by the code name HUMINT. This code name, short for Human Intelligence, means the collection of information from human sources through clandestine undercover methods—in contrast to interrogations, reading through files and correspondence, etc. In other words, it meant the collection of information about UFOs from reliable sources through a game of deceit. The method which was chosen to achieve HUMINT's goals was so bizarre that nobody outside the UFO community would believe it. It was the birth of the "Men In Black," subject of a Hollywood blockbuster movie in 1997.

This legend was born when the UFO researcher Albert K. Bender of the International Flying Saucer Bureau reported in September 1953 that "three men in black suits" had visited him at his house in Bridgeport, Connecticut. They had introduced themselves as agents of the government, revealed to him "the terrible truth about the UFO mystery," about which they, too, had known only for the past two years. If he would work with them, they promised they would give him bits of information, however, he was to keep it to himself. Bender kept to the rules, more or less, but never missed the opportunity to say that he knew something nobody else knew.

Finally, in 1962, Bender broke his silence after being pestered by Gary Barker, another UFO enthusiast who had, a few years before that, established the first publishing house in the United States specializing in UFO material. The result, Bender's book *Flying Saucers and the Three Men*, was so unconvincing that the author himself seems to have found it painful. He moved to California and vanished from the UFO scene completely. In this book, Bender claimed that the three men were extraterrestrials who had to camouflage themselves as human beings, for their true appearance would have frightened earthlings. Then there followed a story about his having been kidnapped by monstrous space beings who took him to the South Pole. UFO insiders decided that Bender had either lost himself in a world of fantasy or had become an expert in the game of "disinformation."

What remained, however, was the legend about the three men in black. Whenever a spectacular case was reported, they appeared mysteriously, intimidated witnesses, showed identity cards from fictitious government authorities and confiscated original photographs, films and negatives. With that they had achieved their purpose. All the original evidence was now in their hands, and the credibility of the poor witnesses was ruined, not only by being denied their evidence, but also by their ominous story explaining the disappearance of same: particularly when reporters, trying to verify the information given by the witnesses, found out that the official agencies which had ostensibly sent the agents did not exist at all!

Researchers have investigated over fifty such cases. Sometimes the men in black were as white as chalk and moved almost mechanically, then again they appear dark-skinned, with foreign accents. Almost always they left the impression that they were actually extraterrestrials. They spoke about having to go "because our energy is running out" or stared, as if paralyzed, at a ballpoint pen as if it were a ray gun. They often tried to imitate the clichés of movies of Hollywood's famous "noir" series, speaking with exaggerated politeness or rudeness like the celluloid Mafiosi. And to top it off, they drove black Cadillac or Lincoln limousines like the toughs in gangster films. *"Watch out, Mister. If you value your life and that of your family, you'd better not talk about what you saw."* Such words, spoken out of the corner of the mouth, seemed to be their style. Since no genuine secret agent would have ever behaved so ridiculously, the frightened UFO witnesses got nothing but derision from the public when they spoke about their experiences.

That was exactly the result that Field Activity Group 1127 wanted, and the method employed bore great resemblance to the methods of that group, namely the sending of 3-member teams to deal with operations. Apart from the highly qualified experts working in the team, persons of a completely different character belonged to the HUMINT side of it. J. R. Richelson writes in his standard work *The U.S. Intelligence Community*, *"It was part of their duties to coordinate all Air Force activities concerning the collection of information from human sources. This included secret collection as well as the interrogation of traitors. These tasks were carried out by a unit of specialists recruited from various special intelligence groups—these men were excellent tricksters and con men. It was their job to make people talk."* And that was an understatement.

In fact, the men recruited for this job were confidence artists and burglars, marriage swindlers, car burglars and fast-talkers, actors, imitators, costume and make up experts, and tricksters and eccentric geniuses, many of whom were serving prison sentences. Military discipline played only a secondary role here. It was more important to have people who knew how to dig up information, how to silence people effectively and how to make people believe what they were meant to believe. The last was the classic "disinformation," an expression that Lenin invented. Disinformation means misleading the opposition by deliberately feeding him with false information. To make this false information credible, it was essential to include something in it that was true and would bear investigation.

Soon the conning unit of Field Activity Group 1127 gained expertise in all these talents, and was sent to work in various fields, not only those concerning UFOs. But it was particularly in this field that they did exemplary work and contributed extensively to making the UFO subject increasingly obscure and ludicrous in the eyes of the public.

It was because of this that the media was ready to accept the superficial "debunking" of the final report of Blue Book and the Condon study. That suited the Air Force because it was a guarantee that they were still in control of the situation.

Meanwhile, their secret projects were still operating and, bit by bit, a solution to the UFO puzzle was coming closer and closer. An idea of what conclusions they actually drew can be found in the abovementioned U.S. Air Force Academy textbook *Introductory Space Science*, Volume 2. The cadets of the academy were the future leaders of the Air Force, and one could not afford to teach them anything that was not true.

Thus this book on space physics includes a chapter—Chapter 33—about unidentified flying objects. In 14 pages it describes the characteristics of

UFOs. It presents the story of the phenomenon and discusses the hypotheses. Although it appeared in the same year as the Condon report, 1969, it arrives at completely different conclusions about the true nature and meaning of UFOs. Like the National Security Agency paper, the author of this textbook also dismisses the hypotheses of hoax, secret weapon and natural phenomena. *"It is difficult to label this episode a hoax. . . . very few people accept this as a credible suggestion . . . does not seem to be very plausi-*

INTRODUCTORY SPACE SCIENCE

VOLUME II

PHYSICS

370

UNITED STATES AIR FORCE ACADEMY

Textbook at the U.S. Air Force Academy which includes a chapter about UFOs.

ble," and declares instead *"the most stimulating theory for us is that UFOs are material objects, which are either 'manned' or remote-controlled by beings who are alien to this planet. There is some evidence supporting this view."* There were various groups or types of "visitors":

"The most commonly described alien is about 3½ feet tall, has a round

head (helmet?), arms reaching to or below his knees, and is wearing a sil-
very spacesuit or coveralls. Other aliens appear to be essentially the same
as Earthmen, while still others have particularly wide (wrap around) eyes
and mouths with very thin lips. And there is a rare group reported as about
4 feet tall, weighing around 35 pounds, and covered with thick hair or fur
(clothing?). Members of this group are described as being extremely
strong."

The textbook further asks "Why no contact"?, and answers this question
with four alternatives:

"1. We may be the object of an intensive sociological and psychological
study. In such studies you usually avoid disturbing the test subject's envi-
ronment.

2. You do not 'contact' a colony of ants, and humans may seem that way
to many aliens (variation: a zoo is fun to visit, but you don't 'contact' the
lizards).

3. Such contact may have already taken place secretly.

4. Such contact may have already taken place on a different plane of
awareness, and we are not yet sensitive to communications on such a
plane."

Finally the book comes to the conclusion that *"the UFO phenomenon*
appears to have been global in nature for almost 50,000 years. . . . That
leaves us with the unpleasant possibility of alien visitors to our planet, or
at least of alien-controlled UFOs. However, the data are not well-corre-
lated, and what questionable data there are suggest the existence of 3, and
maybe 4, different groups of aliens (possibly at different stages of develop-
ment). This too is difficult to accept. It implies . . . a surprisingly strong
interest in Earth by members of other solar systems."

The armed forces of other nations had also come to the same conclusion.
The large number of competent observers left no other choice.

CHAPTER 11

Who Saw UFOs?

The training ship of the Brazilian Navy, *Almirante Saldanha*, was lying at anchor near the mountainous island of Trinidad in the South Atlantic, getting ready to sail home. The crew of the vessel had completed their assignment of collecting hydrographic and oceanographic data in the region of that island. On board the ship were scientists, top military personnel, professional photographers, reporters and leading heads of the hydrographic and navigation divisions of the Brazilian Navy, who had carried out this investigation in connection with the International Geophysical Year. Already in October 1957, the Hydrographic Institute of the Navy had established on that geologically interesting rocky island a station for oceanographic and meteorological studies, which was under the charge of the ship captain Carlos Alberto Bacellar. The *Almirante Saldanha*, with its crew of 300 men, had been converted into a research vessel and attached to that station for this mission.

On that day, February 16, 1958, the Navy photographer Almiro Barauna, a former press photographer and expert in underwater photography, was standing on the foredeck, watching the preparations being made for departure. He took a few shots of the proceedings with his Rolliflex 2.8 Model E camera. A little later he was standing on the lower deck, leaning against the railings and staring at the sea, when two officers came rushing up to him, very excited, and pointed to a bright object in the sky that was approaching the island at a very high speed. Then the dentist of the ship came out, stumbling in his excitement, and the men stared in fascination at the ball of light in the cloudy sky. It was 12:15 p.m.

After half a minute, the object was close enough to photograph. Barauna focused his camera and took the first picture. The UFO came nearer and nearer and soon one could see that its dark gray metallic fuselage was surrounded by a ring or flange, while a greenish phosphorescent glow enveloped its entire body. The flying characteristics of the object were remarkable. It moved like a wave, flying like a bat, intermittently leaping forward abruptly. Soon it reached the island and flew along the steeply rising rocky chain of the Calo-Crast range, when the photographer took his next picture. The third photograph was taken when the object circled around the highest mountain of the island, the 1,800 foot Desejado peak, before flying out again towards the sea with a sudden increase of speed. Meanwhile a good part of the crew had collected on the deck to watch this spectacle. Barauna was caught in the crowd, pushed here and there so that his fourth and fifth shots were failures. But the sixth photograph captured the UFO clearly, before it disappeared into the same direction from which it came.

Barauna (5) with six eyewitnesses: the photographer Faria de Arevedo (1); Admiral Saldanha da Gama (2); Amilar Vieira, Director of the Banco do Brasil (3); Commandant Paulo Moreira da Silva, Director of the Naval Hydrographic Institute (4); Commandant of the Trinidad Island Carlos Alberto Bacellar (6) and Alvizio Bancario (7).

The film was developed at once in the laboratory on board, in the presence of some of the officers. After the ship's arrival at Rio de Janeiro, the investigation of the case was pursued by the Navy. All witnesses—there were 48 people—confirmed that the photographs showed exactly what they had seen. The negatives were analyzed, separately and independent of each other, by the Hydrographic Institute, the photographic laboratories of the Navy and in Rio at the evaluating center for aerial photography. All three

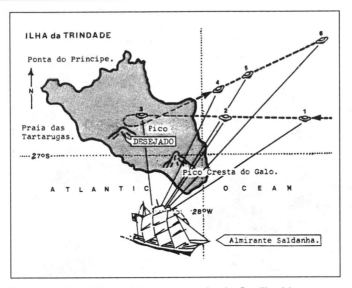

Reconstruction of the sighting sequence by the Brazilian Navy.

confirmed that the pictures were genuine. The diameter of the object was calculated at 120 feet, its height as 24 feet and its speed between 550 and 620 mph. Barauna was given permission to publish his photographs and they first appeared in the newspaper *Ultima Hora* on February 15. When other papers approached the Navy and asked for a statement from them, the Navy spokesman answered saying *"Señor Almiro Barauna shot the pictures in the presence of a large section of the crew of the* Almirante Saldanha," but he added that he was not prepared to make any statement about the sighted object itself.

On the same day, Naval Secretary Admiral Antonio Alves Camara flew over to the summer residence of the Brazilian President Juscelino Kubitschek near Petropolis, carrying 4 original prints and enlargements of the UFO photographs. According to press reports, the President was strongly impressed by the photographs and the analysis. In any case, he gave the secretary permission to confirm the authenticity of the photo series at the press conference which was scheduled for the next day. *"I have never believed in flying saucers before,"* said the minister to the reporters, *"but the photographic evidence from Mr. Barauna has convinced me."* Admiral Gerson de Macedo Soares, Secretary-General of the Navy, confirmed saying, *"I have no grounds to doubt this report made by reliable and scientifically trained witnesses. I personally believe now in the reality of UFOs, even if they do originate from other planets."*

The reaction in the United States to these photographs was, of course, very different. The newspapers published only one of the photographs and the Air Force declared it to be a fake or the picture of a weather balloon.

Official photo series of the Brazilian Navy showing a Saturn shaped UFO, taken by Navy photographer Almiro Barauna on January 16, 1958, on board the Ship Almirante Saldanha during a geo-physical expedition near the island of Trinidad.

The Brazilian government was offended and spoke about American arrogance. The flying saucers almost led to a disruption of relationships between the United States and Brazil. Besides that, Dr. Edward U. Condon did not show any interest or inclination to include this case in his studies, although all the photographs were shown to him by the Maj Colman VonKeviczky of the "Intercontinental UFO Research & Analytic Network."

COMO SE DEU A APARIÇÃO DO DISCO VOADOR DA ILHA DA TRINDADE;

No dia 16 de Janeiro de 1958,o Navio Escola Almirante Saldanha,da Marinha de
Guerra do Brasil,se encontrava fundeado na enseada da Ilha da Trindade,a cerca
de 800 milhas da costa do Espirito Santo.Eram então os menos 11 horas da manhã
o dia estava claro,a tripulação preparava-se para retornar ao Rio de Janeiro
quando de repente um grupo de pessoas que se encontrava na pôpa do navio,entre
eles o Capitão Aviador da reserva da Força Aérea Brasileira José Viegas,deu o
alarme.Num instante,todos os que se encontravam na coberta do navio,cerca de 3
50 pessoas,passaram xxxx a observar um estranho objeto prateado em forma de xx
prato,que se deslocava do mar em direção a ilha.o objeto em questão,não fazia
o menor ruido,era luminoso e se deslocava ora rapido,ora lentamente,subia,des-
cia,ondulava suavemente e quando aumentava a velocidade, deixava atraz de si
um rasto branco fosforescente que logo se desfazia.Na sua trajetoria,o objeto
desapareceu por detraz do morro Pico Desejado,e quando todos esperavam que ele
surgisse do lado oposto,ele retornou na mesma direção,parou alguns segundos
e em seguida disparou em incrivel velocidade desaparecendo no horizonte.
Durante a aparição,consegui tirar 6 fotos,sendo que 2 delas,devido ao pandemo-
nio que se formou no convez,não foram aproveitadas,as outras 4,mostram numa
sequencia (melhor) e finalmente desaparecendo no horizonte,aproximando-se da Ilha,parado no lado
do morro(melhor) e finalmente desaparecendo no longe.O filme foi revelado
cerca de 20 minutos após,a pedido do comandante que desejava saber se as fotos
estavam boas.Os negativos foram vistos por quasi toda a tripulação,e todos foram unanimes em identificar posteriormente as ampliações no Serviço Secreto
da Armada.Convem esclarecer,que o grupo de civis xxx se encontrava a bordo a
a convite da Marinha xxxxxxxxx para fazerem pesquisas submarinas e tirar foto-
grafias da fauna submarina da Ilha.
O grupo era composto dos seguintes elementos:
Chefe: Amilar Vieira Filho,Bancario,Mergulhador e desportista.
Sub-Chefe:Cap.Av.da reserva da F.A.B. José Viegas
Mergulhador: Aluizio
      "   : Mauro
Fotografo : Almiro Baraúna
Todos os componentes ,faziam parte,na época dos acontecimentos,do Grupo de
Caça Submarina Icaraí.
Dentre os cinco,somente Mauro e Aluizio não viram o objeto,uma vez que se en-
contravam no refeitorio do navio,e quando subiram atraidos pela gritaria,o
objeto já havia desaparecido.
Segundo rumores ouvidos á bordo,a aparelhagem eletrica do navio deixou de fun-
cionar durante a aparição do objeto, o que posso afirmar é que 3 vezes depois
da largada,o navio parou por 3 vezes,tendo os oficiais dado as mais estranhas
explicações versões sobre as paradas, Quando o navio parava,a luz xxxxxxx ia
aos pouco apagando até apagar de todo. Nessa ocasião,varios oficiais me dirigi-
ram para a convez munidos de binoculos,entretanto o céu estava já encoberto
por nuvens e nada foi possivel observar.
Devo acrescentar que se não fosse a indiscreção de uma reporter do Correio da
Manha,que apoderou das copias fotograficas oferecidas ao então Presidente
Juscelino Kubitschek, talvez ninguem viesse a saber desse fato, uma vez que a
Marinha já havia me "sondado" para saber quanto eu queria para não / dar publicidade as fotos.Convem deixar claro,que todos os oficiais com que tive
contacto durante todo o tempo do inquérito,foram gentilissimos comigo,deixa-
ram-se inteiramente á vontade,mas puzeram nenhuma objeção a divulgação do o
apenas insinuaram que sensacionalismo no caso,poderia causar panico na popula-
ção,daí o interesse das Forças Armadas em não dar publicidade a casos dessa
natureza..

30/1/67

OFICIAIS MARINHEIROS

Baraúna's report about the incident.

(ICUFON). In fact, the Condon committee, doubtlessly intending to preserve the impression that UFOs were sighted only by uneducated fools, did not present even one of the numerous documented cases of sightings made by leading scientists, astronomers, politicians and celebrities. It even ignored a very much discussed document of those days, namely a report from the Argentinian Navy in July 1965, in which officially the sighting of a *"solid, lens-shaped flying object, which lit up alternatingly red, green and yellow and flew in a zigzag course"* was confirmed by three of their bases in the Antarctic. Amongst the witnesses were scientists working on various research projects in that area. They had also taken photographs which were, however, being withheld as secret.

In 1976 the international organization MENSA conducted an opinion poll amongst its members in the United States, all 20,000 of whom had an Intelligence Quotient of higher than 130. The results showed that 67% of the members were convinced that UFOs are extraterrestrial spacecraft whose crew are here to study our civilization; 16% claimed to have seen UFOs with their own eyes.

A well-known Austro-German rocket research engineer, Franz A. Ulinski, of Wells, Upper Austria, saw UFOs on the 5th of June, 1971, looking out a window from his flat. Four shining UFOs, enveloped in a plasma-like fog, shot across the steel-blue sky. He reported this immediately to the Austrian military commander Hörschung and also made inquiries at the airport. At the time of the sighting, no military airplanes were flying in that area. *"They must have been relatively small bodies, about 30 feet in diameter,"* said Ulinski. During World War II Ulinski had been working with Wernher von Braun at Peenemünde and was quite experienced in the observation of military aircraft. After the end of the war, he continued to be in contact with people like Albert Einstein, Balier and von Braun. The reliability of this person, whom Braun described in a letter written to me as *"one of the early pioneers of rocketry,"* is unquestionable.

A well-known German scientist, Dr. W— was driving on the motorway on October 23, 1962, in the vicinity of Ahrensburg, when noticed a long object hovering in the clear sky. Driving on, he could see the shining, metallic, cigar-shaped object, which shone at first red, then bluish-green, for almost 15 minutes.

Dr. Walter A. Frank was a lecturer at the Institute for Central Asiatic Ethnology at the University of Bonn, Germany. During January and February, 1990 he was on one of his ethnological study tours in India. While in Jodhpur, Rajasthan, he saw a spherical flying object: *"I spent the night of February 8 in the hotel Ajit Bhavan. Before going to sleep I went out into the street once more to get some fresh air. The sky was uniformly covered with a thin layer of clouds through which the full moon and Venus, which was quite close to the moon, could be seen fuzzily. But near the moon there was a bright, clearly defined spherical object which neither moved nor made any noise. I thought at first that it was the landing light of an airplane or a helicopter. After I had watched it for about 10 minutes without its changing position it appeared strange to me. So I fetched my camera* (Canon A1 with Vivitar zoom, 28–200mm). *The light was still there, and I took two photographs of it. Immediately after I had taken the second shot, the light suddenly vanished as if it had been switched off,"* said Dr. Frank, describing his experience.

What happens when a scientist starts studying UFOs seriously is shown by the example of Professor Harley Rutledge, Chairman of the department of physics at Southeast Missouri State University at Cape Girardeau, Missouri. Prof. Rutledge was an arch-skeptic when he heard about a wave of UFO sightings in 1973 at Piedmont, some 80 miles west of Cape Girardeau. His curiosity was aroused, and so he drove down to Piedmont with his car loaded with measuring instruments. And there he saw his first UFO. *"The people* Prof. Harley Rutledge *were in such a panic that the women didn't dare to go out at night without a gun,"* said Rutledge later to reporters of local papers, *"and then I saw it with my own eyes—a shining object hovering over the parking lot of a nursery school. Believe me, they came into the town, followed people and beamed lights at them. The cars in the streets couldn't move, and TV reception was disrupted."*

This expedition made Rutledge change from "UFO-Saul" into "UFO-Paul"; debunker into defender. He then decided to investigate by scientific means the mysterious luminous objects. And with that, Project Identification was born, the first genuine scientific study of the UFO phenomenon. Instead of trying, like Condon in Colorado, to prove that a UFO sighting had to do with a hoax, thereby losing sight of what was really important, Rutledge started to study the objects themselves and collected material and data on his own.

The project lasted for 7 years. Over 620 voluntary helpers, most of them Rutledge's physics students, took part in it, manning 158 mobile observation stations. A variety of photo and film cameras with telephoto lenses, night and infrared film, Questar telescopes, electromagnetic frequency analyzers, highly sensitive sonic detectors and mobile radar units, were put on the job. The skies were scanned for a total of 427 hours. Rutledge himself led the project during 137 nights. The results: 178 sightings—during 158 of which Rutledge himself was present—with over 700 photographs. That put an end to all doubts. *"I don't believe in UFOs,"* said Rutledge to reporters, *"one believes in God. But UFOs, they are not a matter of belief, they are a fact."*

Prof. Rutledge divided the objects into two categories: those which do not break the known laws of physics, and those which *"do not look as if they were man-made and are capable of unbelievable maneuvers, such as accelerating from stationary conditions and stopping abruptly during flight at extremely high speeds."* From his own 158 observations, 28 belong to the second category, and 34 from the total of 178. Among them were cases *"in which apparently massive objects could accelerate so fast within one-fifth of a second, that they could hardly be seen with the naked eye. One which we tracked accelerated from standstill to a speed of over 7,500 miles per hour."* A similar event happened when Rutledge was flying over Clark Mountain near Piedmont with a friend, Drake Kambitch, in his Cessna 150, at a height of about 18,000 feet. *"We saw a strange object with orange, red and green lights,"* said the professor later, *"and when we flew towards it, it shot off vertically. It was just like a flash of lightning. Its speed must have been at least 6,000 mph, but there was no supersonic bang to be heard."* As a physicist, Rutledge knew this much: no earthly aircraft was capable of that performance, and no human pilot would have survived that acceleration: it would have been like being crushed by a weight of over 16 tons.

But what fascinated the scientist even more was the apparent interaction, the way the objects played with the observers. Witnesses often felt the presence of the UFOs even before the UFOs actually appeared, and had the feeling that they themselves, and their group, were the ones being watched. Sometimes it looked almost as if some kind of telepathic communication existed. If one was not sure whether it was a UFO or a conventional object, the UFO presented an answer by suddenly carrying out an impressive maneuver. If a witness imagined to himself a particular course of flight or maneuver, he could be sure that the UFO would immediately do what he had imagined. One experience confirmed to Rutledge that they indeed were watching him: *"Once a beam of light appeared on my office window at the university. I felt sure that it was there because of me."* On another occasion he noticed a gray bullet-shaped object outside his house, which then took on an olive-green color, *"but when I went to get my binoculars, it disappeared. It is unscientific, but I felt that it wanted to give me a small demonstration."*

Then he noticed something else. The UFOs were camera shy. Whenever he pointed his camera at them, they suddenly disappeared. When he spoke over the radio and alerted one of the other observation stations lying in the direction in which the UFO seemed to be moving, often enough the object turned off and disappeared in another direction, or hid itself in front of a star. *"Sometimes,"* said the physicist, *"it was a regular cat-and-mouse game. They loved to play with us. Sometimes they jammed our radio communications, sometimes the electric supply failed completely, sometimes the instruments went awry."*

Gradually, the more professionally Prof. Rutledge tried to get onto their tracks, the less frequent were the UFO sightings. So Project Identification came to an end, after the great initial success of 1980, mainly because the observed objects suddenly seemed to give Cape Girardeau a wide berth.

"It is definite that there is an intelligence behind the UFO phenomenon, which is at least equal to, probably far more advanced than, human intelligence," said Professor Harley Rutledge. *"They can be divided into 3 main types: the familiar discs, the bullet or rocket-shaped ones and finally the balls of light or pseudo-stars."* But he is restrained about theories regarding their origin: *"I have no evidence of where they come from, and if I am known to be somebody who believes in extraterrestrials, I will have to defend myself for the rest of my life."* About their propulsion system, too, he can only speculate: *"One possibility is electromagnetic radiation in the form of microwaves. Many of the physiological and physical effects, which witnesses have reported since the end of World War II, suggest microwaves in the spectrum from 300 to 3,000 megahertz, or even higher. Another possibility is gravitative force fields. Perhaps they use the magnetic field of the Earth."*

Prof. Rutledge was surprised by the reaction of his colleagues when his book *Project Identification* came out, published by Prentice Hall. *"I had reckoned with, under the best of circumstances, being laughed at and being avoided by my colleagues from then on,"* he confessed, *"but instead I have been repeatedly approached, congratulated, stormed with questions. Many say that I had literally opened their eyes and some of them discuss my book with their students during seminars."*

Pilots

Flight Captain Werner Utter, until recently a member of the 5-man board of directors of the German airline Lufthansa, had over 5,700 employees working under him involved in air traffic control and ground service. The well-versed Swabian was a pioneer in German aviation and, since the end of World War II, had flown at least 100 different types of aircraft. He estimates his total number of flying hours at about 29,000—including 1,200 Atlantic crossing with aircraft varying from transporters to jumbo jets. From 1971, Utter was chief pilot of Lufthansa, and piloted the former German President Heinrich Lübke on 8 state visits to Africa, South America, the Near and the Far East. With that background, his reliability and sobriety of mind can hardly be questioned. Nor is it surprising that he, too, has had his mysterious encounters. The latest incident occurred in 1980 on Ascension Day. Talking to journalists from *Neue Ruhr Zeitung*, Utter said, *"you may laugh about it, but I have it on audiotape. I was coming back from New York with a freight plane. It was evening, but still quite bright. Then this huge thing came right at me. The flight engineer, who was standing behind me and talking to the copilot, called out suddenly—you can hear it on the tape—'Watch out!', and then 'Hey, what's that?' It was a huge cigar which was coming towards us, at an altitude of 35,000 feet. I called to the pilot below and said 'That's a UFO.' The pilot below replied that he hoped it was not one of those flying saucers. . . . I thought it was going to get into my motor no. 1 (the outermost one on the left). If I alone had seen it . . . but the engineer saw it too and gave a cry of alarm."*

That was 3 miles behind Dover. The audiotape had been switched on by chance because just then air traffic control had been shifted from London to Maastricht. But this was not the only UFO experience in the life of the flight captain.

"It was during the fifties on a flight from Beirut to Baghdad, when we were just flying over Lebanon at an altitude of about 10,000 feet," he said, describing his first encounter with an unknown flying object, in October 1992, before millions of viewers in the SAT-1 broadcast "Fantastic Phenomena," *"when I noticed in the starlit sky a bright object like a ball of light. The ball came nearer and nearer. I got excited and switched on the board searchlights, because I thought another airplane was coming towards us. Suddenly there was a huge ball of fire between the cockpit and the inner motor, with a diameter of about 15 feet. It was a warm reddish light. The whole ball of fire moved. I didn't feel afraid. I was completely taken by its appearance. The whole cockpit was lit up. I looked at my copilot and he nodded that he saw it too. When I looked out again, the object had disappeared into the sky at a tremendous speed."*

On November 21, 1978, Utter flew a Lufthansa Boeing 747 from Frankfurt to New York. He was above Labrador at an altitude of over 36,000 feet, when he received the radio message of a TWA passenger plane. *"We have just sighted a light, possibly a UFO. It must now be crossing your path."* A few minutes later, at about 9:55 a.m. GMT, Utter and his crew saw it too. *"It looks like we have a flying saucer in sight,"* he spoke into his dictation machine, which he always carried with him on flights, *"it is very bright and sends out beams of light, sometimes red, sometimes white, sometimes vio let, like a huge spider."*

Utter is only one of many thousands of civilian pilots who have had UFO experiences during their careers. The German Lufthansa flight captain I. Heldmeier of Düsseldorf told TV journalist Rainer Holbe about his mysterious encounter during a flight over the Austro-Yugoslavian border. *"It was in January 1986. We were flying with our Tristar 345, carrying German tourists from the Maledives via Munich to Düsseldorf. Some 30 miles from Zagreb, 6 disc-shaped objects came flying towards us. At that time, we were at a height of 32,000 feet, flying over the Caravanks in the direction of the Steiner Alps. We saw these dark discs directly in front of us. They were surrounded by a greenish glow that seemed to be brighter forward than astern. The objects had a course opposite to ours, but at a higher altitude and roughly at a 60 degree angle to ours. We estimated their speed as being two or three times that of sound."* Heldmeier's copilot and flight engineer had also seen the UFO fleet.

Another remarkable case which took place in the summer of 1991 over the French-Belgian border was investigated by "Deutschlandfunk" (German radio) journalist Rudi Schneider. An air traffic controller of the Köln-Bonn airport was on his flight home from a vacation on the island of Ibiza, Spain. The crew of the Lufthansa Tristar on this Ibiza-Düsseldorf route invited him into the cockpit. After passing the Alps, on French territory, he noticed an object on the right-hand side of the aircraft. It was flat and disc-shaped, surrounded by a brightly glowing halo, and had three colored areas on its bottom. He showed it to the flight captain, and eventually the whole cockpit crew saw the UFO. *"Do we have any unidentified traffic?"* the flight captain radioed the French Air Traffic Control. The Frenchman denied it but informed the military. Shortly after, the air traffic controller informed the crew that, according to the military, they had nothing unusual on the screen.

At this moment the crew of an aircraft of the German airline Condor, following the Lufthansa airplane on the same route, but 2,000 feet above it, radioed those on the Lufthansa jet: *"Don't let them fool you. We see the thing, too."* Shortly after, a Lufthansa captain, flying 4,000 feet higher and more to the right, radioed a confirmation of the sighting. *"It's larger than your Tristar,"* the Condor Captain estimated, *"maybe about 300 feet in diameter."*

In the meantime the object repeatedly changed position and seemed to play a cat-and-mouse game with the 3 passenger aircrafts. *"I can't believe you don't have it on the screen,"* the Lufthansa Captain radioed the Air Traffic Control, and added: *"especially the military."* Civilian radar systems sometimes "filter out" anomalous signals automatically. *"Military is military, you know,"* the Frenchman replied.

Shortly after that the 3 German airliners left French airspace and reported to Maastricht Eurocontrol. The Belgians welcomed the Lufthansa airplane, saying: *"You are identified, and we do have this object on radar."* Seconds later, the disc speeded up and passed the 3 German aircraft with a speed of 5,000 knots (5,000 mph).

Such reports were not isolated cases, as was shown by Dr. Richard F. Haines, who was chief of NASA's Space Human Factors Office at Ames Research Center until 1988. Haines was able to collect over 3,000 cases of UFO encounters by civilian pilots from all over the world. Amongst them were flight captains of Air France, American Airlines, British Airways, PanAm, TWA, United Airlines, Varig, Alitalia, Aeroflot, Japan Airlines, Lufthansa and Swissair. Haines is further convinced that even these reports represented only the tip of the iceberg.

"Generally speaking, pilots keep quiet about these cases, for UFO encounters are still considered dubious and dismissed as being ridiculous," explained the scientist in an interview on the U.S. TV broadcast "UFO Cover-up Live," which was broadcast by CBS throughout the country on October 15, 1988. *"Many pilots fear official reprisals, the derision of their*

A pilot of the Venezuelan airlines Avensa allegedly took this controversial photo in 1963 above the Amazonian jungle. Debunkers claim it shows a button.

colleagues, pressure from superiors, doubts about their mental health. Others would rather avoid the paperwork which is bound to follow if they report any anomaly. And airlines don't want such reports to become public for they could damage their image. Who would like to advertise with the slogan 'Fly with us, for our pilots see UFOs?"

As it turns out, Swissair, one of the most renowned airlines of the world, has been an exception. It has shown the courage to acknowledge, or at least to put down on record, the UFO encounters of some of its employees. At any rate, we have a good dozen pilots' voyage reports from Swissair, in which UFO encounters of Swissair crews are described in detail, sometimes up to three pages. There are separate "Flight Crew Member Reports" for "Satellite reentry, Bright Fireball or other Atmospheric Phenomena," and naturally "UFO Encounters," which are forwarded to an official of the Cockpit Crew Administration. If the objects appear on radar, separate reports from the ground crew are collected. Thus we read in a case which occurred on April 14, 1977, referred to in the report as "UFO,"

> Just before 1:00 a.m., I saw a flash of light before us, but since neither Capt. Scherrer nor the stewardesses said anything I thought I had been mistaken. At 1:00 Maastricht asked us about our flight details . . . at 1:02 a.m. the traffic controller informed us about a strange radar echo at 1:00 position and 15 nautical miles distance. We had negative contact, but saw for a short time two echos on our screen, roughly 15 nautical miles away at 1:00 position.
>
> Soon after that, all three of us saw an object that flashed like lightning. During the following minutes, Maastricht kept us informed about the position of the target. The target, according to Maastricht, stayed in position for a time, then moved at high speed to a 1:00 or 2:00 position at a distance of 3 miles . . . still no sight contact. At 1:10, all of us saw an intense light just ahead of us . . . like lightning. Distance not measurable and completely silent. According to Maastricht, the target then moved in the southern direction and appeared, as the traffic controller said, to be playing its game with us at the tail and east of us. Maastricht contacted a military radar station which estimated the speed of the object at Mach 4–5 (4–5 times the speed of sound). Then I saw a fourth and last lightning-like light at a certain distance behind our right wing, still unable to say what it was exactly . . . Maastricht informed us further that they had observed a similar occurrence with an LTU airplane a few weeks ago in the same area without their having been able to find any logical explanation for it. Signed, Captain F. Schmid.

When Swissair asked for a comment from the traffic controller at Maastricht, he replied: *"The occurrences have been described by your crew in their report fairly correctly. I remember seeing from my position on the ground a fixed primary signal . . . the echos seemed (within the next 5 seconds) to move suddenly around the aircraft when it approached it. Then it moved in 3 or 4 springs (on the radar screen, that is, with each swirl of the cursor it seemed to have leapt to another position) in the direction of England."*

In another report dated September 12, 1968, Captain Ottiger of Swissair reported: *"UFO sighting. At about 3:33 in position 30 miles E Toulouse sighted object vertically above SR 651 (our flight 280), very high. Object appeared to be stationary, or moving insame direction at slower speed. Shape something as (drawn) below, in any case, diamond-shaped. Seen by all 3 pilots in cockpit, reported to Bordeaux radar, who reported no contact."*

Below that is Captain Ottiger's sketch of the UFO. It shows a Saturn-like object exactly like the one which the crew of the Brazilian training ship *Almirante Saldanha* saw over Trinidad. Further pilot encounters from the Swissair "Pilots Voyage reports" were:

- August 22, 1978: A bluish-white disc "of magnesium-like appearance" crossed the course of a Swissair aircraft.

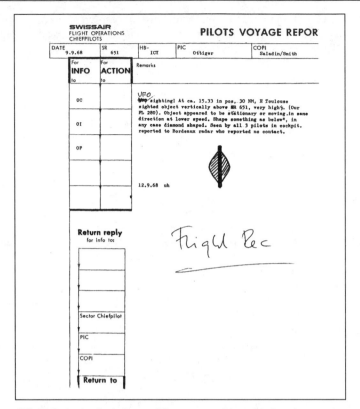

Official Swissair pilot's report. "Shape something as below, in any case diamond-shaped. Seen by all 3 pilots in cockpit, reported to Bordeaux radar who reported no contact."

- June 16, 1981: "Six to eight objects" between the airplane and the setting sun.
- June 26, 1986: A small gray, cigar-shaped object appeared in front of a Swissair aircraft in close propximity.

But the most interesting report about a UFO encounter from a civilian pilot does not come from Switzerland but from Japan. The incident occurred on November 17, 1986.

Japan Air Lines (JAL) flight 1628 started on November 16, from Paris, with a stopover at Reykjavik on the way to Tokyo. On board the Boeing 747 freight plane there were two crews, which relieved each other during the long flight. In the hold were about 200 cases of top quality French wine. Bad weather compelled them to stay in Iceland for longer than scheduled, but finally they were able to start again on the 17th. The pilot was Flight Captain Jenju Terauchi, a man with 19 years

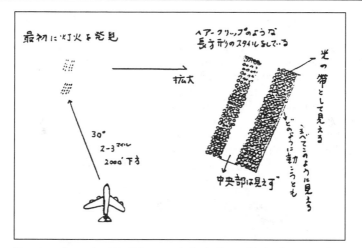

Sketches drawn by JAL flight captain Jenju Terauchi: the 2 reconnaissance ships approaching.

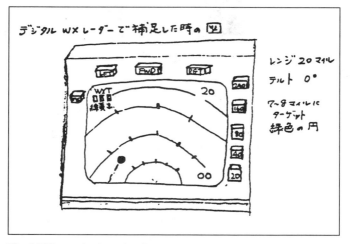

The UFOs on the board radar.

of flight experience. The route planned was the polar route over Greenland, northern Canada and Alaska towards Japan. A bright moon bathed the glaciers of Greenland with a ghostly blue-white light, but disappeared behind them when they had crossed northern Canada. When they reached a settlement called Shingle Point at the border between Canada and Alaska it was pitch dark. Only isolated lights from the outposts of humanity in the endless icy desert of the Arctic were still twinkling. In the east one could see a bit of the afterglow that follows sunset. Otherwise, the snow-covered land below them lay like black velvet. In the cockpit, too, it was dark, except for the lights of the control panel. Everything was quiet.

Then at 5:11 p.m. Terauchi saw two lights where none should have been, to the left and below his machine. Actually, he had become aware of them a minute earlier, but had ignored them, taking them to be military aircraft. But now, 60 seconds later, they were still there at the same spot. More than that, they appeared to be flying in formation with his own machine. Terauchi checked his instruments. He had switched on the autopilot, flew at a speed of 525 knots towards the southwest at an altitude of 35,000 feet, location about 90 nautical miles northeast of Fort Yukon, Alaska. Both lights seemed to be flying 2,000 feet below him and were keeping to the 10:00 position.

The UFOs directly before the airplane.

Then suddenly, after 6 minutes, they sprang to a position directly in front of him and he saw two pairs of rectangularly shaped sets of lights, one pair above the other. Captain Terauchi described it later as *"two spaceships from which white and amber-colored lights shot out, pulsating jets in the direction of a dark vertical field in the middle of each object."* They were so close that they lit up the cockpit brightly, and Terauchi even believed that he felt their warmth on his face. After a few seconds the objects ceased sending out beams and formed instead of that small circles of light like "a dozen small jets" which lit up, alternatingly bright and dim in the colors dull red, soft green, white, orange and brighter red. Both flying objects were now between 600 and 900 feet away, slightly higher than the Boeing 747, "had the size of a DC-8." After another five minutes, they changed their formation, flew side by side, sparkling and twinkling. *"Somehow I was reminded of Christmas decorations,"* said copilot Takanori Tamefuji. The board engineer Yoshio Tsukuba was also one of the spectators. For flight captain Terauchi it was clear: these were not terrestrial machines. *"I did not even feel threatened by their sudden maneuvers,"* he said later. *"There was something reassuring that came out of them."*

At 5:19 p.m. co pilot Tamafuji called up the tower at Anchorage:

JAL *stands for Japanese Air Lines; Anch. stands for Anchorage)*

JAL: *Anchorage center, Japan Air 1628, ah, do you have you any traffic, ah 7:00 above?*

Anch: *JAL 1628 you are hard to understand, say again.*

JAL: *Do you have any traffic in front of us?*

Anch: *JAL 1628 you are very hard to understand negative.*

JAL: *Ah, JAL 1628, roger and, ah, we, in sight, ah, two traffic [sic], ah, in front of us one mile about.*

Anch: *JAL 1628, do you have, ah, can you identify the aircraft?*

JAL: *Ah, we are not sure, but we have traffic in sight now.*

Anch: *JAL 1628, roger. Maintain visual contact with your traffic, and can you say the altitude of the traffic?*

JAL: *Ahm, at the same altitude.*

5:21 p.m.:

Anch.: *JAL 1628, you are still very hard to understand; Sir, are you able to identify the type of aircraft, ah, and see if you can tell whether it's military or civilian?*

JAL: *Ah, JAL 1628, we cannot identify, the type, ah, but we can see navigation lights and strobe lights.*

Anch: *Roger. Sir, say the color of the strobe and beacon lights.*

AL: *The color is white and yellow, I think.*

Anch: *White and yellow, thank you.*

The radio contact was poor, unusually poor as Tamefuji noticed. At 5:22 p.m. it went off completely.

At 5:23 p.m., the tower at Anchorage asked them to change the frequency for they could hardly understand them. But on a different frequency there was only static and hissing. Gradually, the copilot felt the thing was getting a bit uncanny. While the tower at Anchorage inquired of the Elmendorf Regional Operational Control Center (EROCC) whether they could see anything near the JAL machine on the radar, things were getting more urgent in the air.

The two objects had left the 11:00 position in front of the Boeing, then looked just like two lights at a distance in front of a huge silhouette, *"the outlines of a gigantic spaceship,"* as Terauchi described it later.

"I got the impression that they were two small ships returning to their mother ship, which was hanging there hidden in the night sky; but the rest of my crew could hardly make out more than the lights of the reconnaissance ships." The flight captain could see the Saturn-like shape of the mother vessel. Since no further information came from Anchorage, Captain Terauchi switched on the board radar. On the screen, one could clearly see the echo of a huge object at a distance of about 8 nautical miles in the 10:00 position. But it was not red like the echo of a conventional aircraft, but green such as only nonmetallic targets reflect. Either the gigantic space vessel was not made of metal, or it used a camouflaging technique like the American stealth bomber. That would explain why the air traffic controllers at Anchorage had not seen anything definite on their radar, whereas the far more sensitive EROCC radar had picked up something which, with certainty, was no normal aircraft. And now, Anchorage could also spot the target 8 miles in front of the JAL machine, somewhat in the 10:00 position. But, for the crew of the Japanese Boeing, the 2 objects were just 2 points of light.

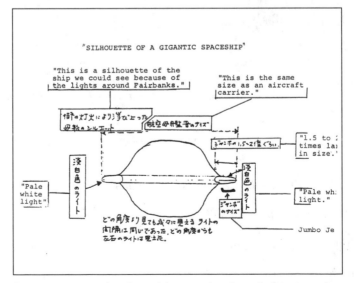

The "giant spacecraft, twice as big as an aircraft carrier," compared to the JAL Jumbo jet.

Meanwhile it was 5:26 p.m.

At 5:30 p.m. they could see the lights of a town on the horizon. They were 30 miles from Fairbanks, Alaska, and a few minutes later they had reached the town. One would almost have breathed a sigh of relief, believing that the uncanny encounter was a thing of the past. But then, one could not be sure: the "mother ship" still had to be out there somewhere, maybe immediately behind them. The almost prayerful silence in the cockpit was broken by Terauchi's voice saying *"There it is again!"* He had looked out of the left window towards the rear and could see the silhouette of the space vessel clearer than before.

The moon behind them lit up the Saturn-shaped UFO *"which was as big as two aircraft carriers."* The lights from the city of Fairbanks were reflected on the metallic stern of the spacecraft. It was a majestic spectacle. A shiver ran down Terauchi's spine: for the first time now, flight captain Terauchi was touched by fear: *"Request . . . deviate . . . from . . . object . . . request heading two four zero,"* stuttered copilot Tamefuji into the microphone, *"it's . . . ah . . . quite big!"* He had to repeat his request four times because the connection was so poor. Then after a minute the JAL 1628 was granted permission by the tower to change course.

JAL Pilot Jenju Terauchi

But even after this dodging maneuver, the huge UFO remained at the same position, at an angle behind the airplane. Even when he flew in a circle, with the permission of the tower, he was unable to shake off the UFO. It was no longer visible to the naked eye, but could still be spotted on the radar. At 5:38 p.m., the EROCC radar confirmed once more that *"there were definitely no military aircraft in the area."* But the unidentified radar echo was still in the neighborhood of the Japanese aircraft. *"JAL 1628, would you like our military to scramble on the traffic?"* asked Anchorage. Terauchi quickly refused the offer: *"Negative, negative."* "Whatever it is, we should not provoke it," were his feelings. After 10 minutes, however, when a United Airlines plane came flying in the opposite direction, the apparition came to an abrupt end. At 6:20 p.m., the Japanese plane landed at Anchorage.

The same evening, the Federal Aviation Authority (FAA) of the United States at Anchorage started investigating the incident. Three FAA officials interviewed the three witnesses from the JAL crew as well as the traffic controller at Anchorage and the radar operator of EROCC. Four months later, in March 1988, the authorities released their concluding report: *"The FAA is not responsible for UFO investigations, and since there is no proof of violation of the airspace, we have ended our investigations with this conclusion."*

On January 6, 1995, a Boeing 747 of British Airways with 60 passengers aboard was flying from Milan, Italy, to Manchester in England. At 6:47 p.m., when they approached Manchester airport, the pilots had a close encounter with what they described as a "luminous triangle."

It was a dark, clear winter night with a good visibility of more than 6 miles, with a fairly strong northwest wind. The airplane was over the Pennine Mountains, about 9 miles southeast of Manchester Airport, at an altitude of 4,000 feet, slowly descending in preparation for the landing. The first officer had just turned on the landing lights and was watching the lights of Greater Manchester appearing in the distance ahead of him, when his attention was suddenly diverted by something in his peripheral vision. Turning right, he saw a *"lighted object fly down on the right-hand side of the aircraft at high speed from the opposite direction,"* as he wrote later. It was big, nearly as big as a jet, and wedge-shaped, with what could have been a black stripe down the side. There was not a shadow of a doubt in him that the craft was real, metallic and much too close merely to speculate about it. *"Captain, we have traffic at 2:00 position, just above us."* Both pilots were able to track the object through the windshield and side window for about 2 seconds. When it shot by, the pilots instinctively "ducked," although the object was actually too far off for a collision.

"What was that?" the captain asked, with his heart beating madly. *"Whatever it was, we just escaped a catastrophe,"* responded the still breathless copilot. *"Why didn't those bloody bastards in the tower warn us?"* the captain railed, *"Are they sleeping down there?"* He grabbed the microphone, radioed air traffic control, but trying to sound as cool as possible, reported with British understatement:

B737: *"We just had something go down the right-hand side just above us very fast!"*

Manchester: *"Well, there's nothing seen on radar. Was it, er, an aircraft?"*

B737: *"Well, it had lights, and it went down the starboard side very quickly."*

Manchester: *"And above you?"*
B737: *"Er, just slightly above us, yeah."*
Manchester: *"Keep an eye out for something, er, I can't see anything at all at the moment so it must have, er, been very fast or gone down very quickly after it passed you, I think."*
B737: *"OK. Well, there you go."*
"How lovely," he said to his first officer with irony, *"they say there was nothing. Now everyone will say we saw one of these goddamned flying saucers."*

Since he had already reported the sighting, he had to file an official "Commercial Air Transport Airmiss Report" right after his safe landing in Manchester, which led to a 13-month long investigation by the "Independent Airmiss Working Group" of the Civil Aviation Authority. When on February 1, 1996, "Airmiss Report No. 2/95" was published, it caused a stir. Although all possible alternatives were considered—including *"the possibility that the object might have been a hang glider, paraglider or ultralight"* or an experimental aircraft of the Royal Airforce—the working group had to conclude: *"There is no doubt that the pilots both saw an object and that it was of sufficient significance to prompt an airmiss report. Unfortunately the nature and identity of this object remains unknown. To speculate about extraterrestrial activity, fascinating though it may be, is not within the Group's remit. . . . The incident therefore remains unresolved."* And indeed the crew described a highly unconventional type of craft. *"The captain remained convinced that the object was itself lit,"* The report added, *"Although he could not determine a definite pattern, he described it as having a number of small white lights, rather like a Christmas tree. He confirmed the high speed of the object, and though unable to estimate its distance, said he felt it was very close. Following the incident, the captain and first officer independently drew what they had seen, both agreeing about the shape. . . ."* They only disagreed on a single point: The copilot believed the object was illuminated by the landing lights of their own aircraft, whereas the captain was sure it was self-luminous.

Presidents

Interestingly enough, even a U.S. President, namely Ronald Reagan, saw a UFO from an aircraft. The incident happened in 1974 when Reagan was still governor of California. *"I was on board my airplane. I looked out of the window and saw this white light,"* he said to the journalist Norman Miller during his presidency. (Miller was chief of the Washington office of the *Wall Street Journal*.) *"It went around in a zig zag course. I went to the pilot in front and asked him 'have you ever seen anything like that before?' He was shocked, and denied it. Then I said, 'Let's follow it.' It was a bright white light. We followed it until Bakersfield, but to our astonishment, it suddenly shot up high in the sky. After landing I told Nancy about it, and we read everything about the long history of UFOs."* Asked about the incident by journalists, Reagan's pilot, Bill Painter, said, *"On board were Governor Reagan and a few security men. We were flying in a Cessna Citation. It was about 9 or 10:00 in the evening. We were above Bakersfield when Governor Reagan and the others pointed out a big light to me which appeared to be accompanying us. It looked as if it were a few hundred feet away from us, and seemed to be a fairly stable light before it began to accelerate and appeared to elongate. Then it shot off at an angle of 45° . . . from one moment to another it went from normal flying speed to a really fantastic velocity."*

Miller asked Reagan if he believed in UFOs. *"When I put this question to him, he looked at me almost frightened. He had suddenly realized what he had just said, what consequences it could have, and that he was speaking to a reporter. But he composed himself quickly and answered coolly, 'Let us simply say that as far as UFOs are concerned, I am a skeptic.' "*

His predecessor Jimmy Carter, who had observed a UFO as big and bright as the moon in the presence of numerous witnesses near Leary in Georgia during 1969, was more open, but that comes later.

Celebrities

A list of celebrities who were UFO witnesses would include a number of world-famous names. The American author Timothy Green Beckley cites in his book, *UFOs among the Stars*, close encounters and eyewitness reports of actors like Anthony Hopkins, William Shatner, Dan Ackroyd, Charles Bronson, Glenn Ford, Shirley MacLaine, Olivia Newton-John, Stuart Whitman, and Sammy Davis Jr.; of rock stars like Jimi Hendrix, David Bowie, Elvis Presley, John Lennon and Neil Sedaka; of athletic figures like Muhammed Ali, and of film directors like Steven Spielberg. From England, one can mention names like Redge Presley of the Troggs ("Wild Thing"), Doane Perry (of Jethro Tull) and also Prince Charles. Among the most prominent UFO witnesses is also the well-known Norwegian ethnologist and archaeologist Thor Heyerdahl, who, in June 1970, during his Ra II expedition, had a UFO sighting together with his crew. The Ra was an exact replica of an ancient Egyptian papyrus ship, with which Heyerdahl wanted to prove through practical demonstration, that at least theoretically, the ancient Egyptians were in a position to sail to America. This hypothesis, he was convinced, would not only explain the existence of pyramids, but also that of huge Negroid stone heads and statuettes in the Egyptian style in Central America. The Ra II was already 45 days under way, with 12 days to go to arrive at its destination at the Caribbean island of Barbados, when his radio operator Norman Baker at first spotted a flat circular bright object. Heyerdahl and the Mexican anthropologist Santiago Genoves saw it next. That was about 12:30 a.m. on June 30, 1970. In his book *Expedition Ra*, Heyerdahl describes the UFO as *"a round, pale disc, a ghostly, aluminum-colored gigantic moon which stood in the Northwest and appeared to come towards us. After about 10 minutes, it had covered about 30 degrees of the sky.*" The next morning, the crew of Ra II learned from a radio station on Barbados that at the same time, the disc had been observed by hundreds of people on the island, who saw it in the Northeast. Heyerdahl connected this phenomenon with two other sightings of flickering orange-colored lights, which his crew had seen on two successive nights, further out in the ocean. *"In any case,"* he writes, *"the feeling overcame me, that the universe had come to us."*

The well-known Tyrolean mountaineer Reinhold Messner also claims to have seen a UFO as big as a full moon. He was on his way back to Khatmandu, after an unsuccessful attempt to climb the 26,516 foot peak of Champlang. *"It came from Tibet and flew South over the snow-covered peaks of the gigantic massifs of the Himalayas into Nepal,"* said Messner, describing his mysterious encounter at a press conference on October 2, 1981. *"It moved very slowly. At first, it turned towards the east, then changed its course to southwest, and finally, turned north again, towards Tibet."* His companion, the British schoolteacher Doug Scott, saw it too, as well as the members of a British expedition which was also in the neighborhood. *"It could not have been a satellite,"* said Messner, *"because it moved in elliptical paths. The movement of the object was irregular."*

Messner's report reminds us of the experience of the famous Russian painter, writer and philosopher, Nicholas Roerich (1874–1947). Roerich was one of the great painters of this century, and over 7,000 of his paintings hang in museums in New York, St. Petersburg, Moscow and Nagar, India. Russia paid tribute to its great son by naming the Academy of Arts at St. Petersburg the Roerich Academy, and when Uri Gagarin saw our planet from space, being the first man to do so, he called out, *"The whole earth shines in Roerich colors."* Roerich's vision of freedom through culture and the movement inspired by his vision, "Banner of Peace," led to the signing of the Roerich Pact. Protecting important cultural objects of humanity, even during times of war, it was the antecedent of the Hague Convention signed in 1955 by 39 states.

In the summer of 1924, Roerich started on a 2-year expedition into the heart of Asia. Following ancient paths of pilgrimage, he wanted to see the gigantic mountain peaks and places connected with ancient legends, and to paint them. On August 5, 1926, the expedition was on its way back from Mongolia through the Himalayas towards Darjeeling, to set up camp in the Kukunor district, not far from the Humbolt range. *"On this morning, at about 9:30, one of our drivers noticed a particularly big black eagle that was circling above us,"* wrote Roerich in his travel diary *Altai Himalaya.* *"Seven of us followed the flight of this unusual bird. At that moment, another driver remarked, 'There is something high above the bird.' And he cried out, totally astonished. We saw something big and shiny that reflected the sunlight, a big oval which moved at high speed from the north to the south. When it crossed over our camp, it changed its direction towards southwest. Then we saw it disappear into the intensely blue sky. We even had time to pick up our binoculars, and recognized fairly clearly its oval form with a shining surface on one side of which the bright sunlight was reflected."*

On December 1, 1990, the "Russlan," the ingenious construction of the Soviet aircraft designer Oleg Antonov, began its ascent. The aircraft was to fly over the North and South Poles and thereby set a new record in nonstop flight. Leaving Melbourne, its flight route was over the South Pole, Rio de Janeiro, Casablanca, the North Pole, Osorusk and then back to Melbourne. The major part of the 31,200-mile flight of the 400-ton machine, which later broke 7 world records, was over the ocean. The 4 pilots on board were all experienced test pilots: Leonid Koslov, Juri Ressnizki, Oleg Pripuskov and Anatoli Andropov. And everything went well, except for one incident on the way. During the middle of a difficult passage, there appeared, at an angle to the jet, a shining sphere which seemed to take an interest in the Russlan. *"There's a UFO, what a wonderful example,"* noted the crew in the logbook.

Astronauts

And what about the astronauts and cosmonauts who have gone out into the cosmic ocean? Have they seen alien visitors? They have, although NASA denies this fact officially. About two dozen astronauts, and almost every other space mission, has sighted, filmed and photographed them. The pictures are there in the NASA archives, even if their existence is always denied. Amongst NASA insiders this is an open secret. *"Many astronauts have confirmed having seen UFOs,"* the German engineer Martin Rebensburg, a coworker of Wernher von Braun, told me, *"and not only American space travelers but also those of the Soviets say that they have been followed by UFOs."* Let us start with the Americans. The following is official since it comes from the Condon report:

> There are three visual observations made by astronauts while in orbit which, in the judgment of the writer, have not been adequately explained. These are:
> 1. Gemini 4. Astronaut McDivitt. Observation of a cylindrical object with a protuberance.
> 2. Gemini 4. Astronaut McDivitt. Observation of a moving bright light at a higher level than the Gemini spacecraft.
> 3. Gemini 7. Astronaut Borman saw what he referred to as a "bogey" flying in formation with the spacecraft.

Unfortunately, the Condon report failed to mention 2 photographs made by Gemini astronauts, which show very interesting details. During the Gemini 11 mission on September 12, 1966, astronauts Richard Gordon and Charles Conrad photographed a squadron of 4 yellow-orange shining oval bodies. The photograph shows the 4 objects being connected to one another by a luminous energy field. NASA's original explanation, that they were the Proton 3 satellite, was disproved soon by Bruce Maccabee, a physicist and photo expert of the U.S. Navy. Proton 3 was at the time in question too far away from Gemini 4 to have been seen at all. On November 13, 1966, Gemini 12 was escorted for a number of minutes by a V-formation of yellow-white UFOs. This astounding maneuver was filmed by the astronauts Edwin Aldrin and James Lovell. A series of mysterious occurrences happened during the moon missions, but more about that later.

On September 20, 1973, at about 4:45 p.m., 4 objects shining red, 3 oval discs and a sphere were photographed from Skylab 3. Again they seemed to be connected through a luminous forcefield. Finally in 1978 NASA released a collection of film clips from the Gemini and Apollo missions, entitled "Photographic anomalies, space garbage and UFOs." Considering that the space authority had until then officially denied all UFO sightings by astronauts, these pictures astonished even the skeptics. There one sees not only McDivitt's astonishing film, but also an Apollo film of a shining object which flits at a tremendous speed across the surface of the moon, as well as two gigantic Saturn-like objects parked on the surface of the moon (these films are part of our video documentation "UFOs: The Secret Evidence").

The modern space shuttle era is also full of UFOs. During the early hours of March 14, 1989, the radio ham Donald Ratsch was, as he usually did during NASA space missions, listening to the radio conversation between the STS 29 mission of the US space shuttle *Discovery* and the ground control station in Houston, Texas. Ratsch belonged to the Goddard Amateur Radio Club whose members follow NASA missions and record them on tape. But what Ratsch heard that morning at 6:42 a.m. EST took his breath away. *"Houston, this is* Discovery, *we still have the alien spacecraft under observance,"* said a voice obviously from the space shuttle to the Earth. After that there was silence for the next ten minutes. Apparently, concluded Ratsch, someone had changed over to another frequency, probably to a secret channel. A bad joke? Probably not. A voice analysis showed that it was not the commander of the Discovery, Lt. Col. John E. Blaha, an experienced Air Force officer who had reported the UFO, but a civilian on board, the crew's doctor James F. Buchli. That would also explain why the speaker had frankly spoken of an alien spaceship. It was possible that Buchli did not know the strict security regulations in the matter of UFOs, or had talked too much in his excitement. At any rate, the NASA spokesman, James Hatsfield, had to concede that the recording was genuine.

When, during the Bush era, the NASA budget was repeatedly reduced, space authorities decided to broadcast the flights of the space shuttles "live" over the government-owned television station PBS Channel 6 in order to stimulate the public's interest in space travel. Luckily Don Ratsch took the trouble of making video recordings of these live broadcasts, and of later examining them for unusual features. He made his first discovery on September 15, 1991, during the STS 48 mission of the shuttle *Discovery*. At 7:00 p.m. GMT (Greenwich Mean Time), a light appeared out of

Sphere in the Earth orbit, filmed by the astronauts of the Space
Shuttle Mission STS-37 in April 1991

the darkness of space, and a second light even made a turn before the camera. Space garbage? A meteorite? Ruled out on account of the change of
direction. The only possibility was an object under intelligent control. An
hour and a half later, Ratsch found something really sensational. The *Dis-*

covery was above Southeast Asia, flying at an altitude of 375 miles and had just crossed Burma at a speed of 17,500 miles per hour. Java was lying before her and on the horizon one could make out the lights of North Australia. At this moment, a light appeared from behind the Earth and seemed to fly along the horizon. Suddenly the object seemed to change direction and raced off at right angles into space. At the same moment something like a beam shot out in the sky to the spot where the object would have been, had it not changed course. The whole scene lasted for only a few seconds, but in spite of that, it turned out to be one of the most interesting proofs of UFOs.

Ratsch sent copies of the remarkable video recording to UFO researchers and NASA scientists and asked for their opinion. Whereas NASA officially explained it as ice on the windshield of the *Discovery*, thorough investigations showed that it was not so. The physicist Prof. Jack Kasher of the University of Omaha, Nebraska, and the Boston professor Dr. Mark J. Carlotto, computer analyst of The Analytic Sciences Corp. (TASC), a contract firm of NASA, were unanimous in saying: *"It is an object at a distance of about 1,800 miles which at first flew with a speed of 15 miles per second or the incredible speed of 54,000 mph, and then left the atmosphere of the Earth at a speed of above 187,500 mph. That means it accelerated to 14,000 Gs, or 14,000 times the gravitational force of the Earth, or 272 Mach, that is 272 times the speed of sound, an acceleration that no human being would survive."*

"There cannot be the slightest doubt that the object is at that distance," declared Prof. Carlotto. *"It is not an optical effect. It really comes from the other side of the horizon, and it leaves the atmosphere of the Earth, whereby its luminosity decreases considerably. Apparently it is surrounded by some kind of force field which makes the atmosphere glow by the effect of ionization. All this completely rules out the possibility of its being a particle of ice that has loosened itself and flies across the windshield. Apart from that, for the ice particle to take a turn, the* Discovery *itself must have made an abrupt change in direction, but she is technically not capable of such a maneuver. Furthermore, the positions of the stars which we can recognize above the horizon remain unchanged. That proves that the Shuttle was stable in its course."* And the beam which seemed to shoot at the UFO? Some speculated that it might have been a SDI weapon called "Brilliant Pebbles." This space age cannon is an electromagnetic accelerator, shooting with a speed of over a thousand miles per second, or nearly 4 million miles per hour. What we see in the film is not a beam but a camera effect, say the experts, caused by the electromagnetic impulse that effects the thrust. That is Star Wars technology in action. If one follows the track of the light, it appears to come from Central Australia and there, 12 miles from Alice Springs, is Pine Gap, a super secret U.S. base at which SDI technology has been tested.

But Carlotto and Kasher discovered surprising details in other space shuttle UFO films which Ratsch had recorded as well. On a film shot from the *Discovery* on September 16, 1991, one can clearly see a dome-shaped object, which flies beneath the shuttle and suddenly accelerates. On a clip from another shuttle mission, STS 44, in November, 1991, a dome-shaped UFO rushes by, at first to the right and then to the left of the shuttle, only to disappear after that. Enlarging the pictures, Carlotto discovered dark lines on its surface which can be interpreted as windows or ports. In another film, the UFO glides right across the picture with its dome on its underside. Naturally, the showing of these pictures in news features like "Hard Copy" and "Larry King Live" caused a stir in the United States. NASA reacted quickly. From then on, the Space Administration stopped sending live broadcasts of further shuttle missions. But owing to strong public demand, it decided to go back on air shortly after. And again it was Don Ratsch who screened hundreds of hours of NASA's live transmissions on PBS for anomalies, which he released in January 1997. The latest incidents:

• On October 17, 1993, NASA broadcasted the launch of the Shuttle, carrying out Mission STS 58. On a tail of fire, emitted by the booster rockets, the Space Shuttle ascended into the blue sky of Florida. Forming a giant "victory" sign, finally the booster rockets were ejected from the Shuttle, which, on a smaller flame, continued its flight into space, when suddenly its trail was crossed by a fast-flying formation of two luminous spheres.
• On October 21, 1995, at 6:05 a.m. GMT, the Shuttle was just flying over Brazil, when astronaut Cathrin Coleman informed Ground Control: *"We have an unidentified flying object."* Those who were watching the scene live on TV could see Coleman gliding to the next porthole, obviously to observe the UFO, when suddenly the transmission was interrupted.

Scene from the transmission of the Space Shuttle Mission STS-80 on December 1, 1996: A triangular UFO formation in the Earth orbit

- The most interesting Space Shuttle footage was recorded by Ratsch on December 1, 1996, during the STS 80 Mission. Over Central Asia, during a raging thunderstorm, at least 12 objects, obviously under intelligent control, seem to maneuver in the atmosphere of the Earth. In the beginning, two of them, one coming in from the left, the other approaching from the right, headed towards the center of the thunderstorm, where they stopped and hovered for a few seconds, before moving back into the directions they came from. The one on the right later joined a triangular formation hovering in orbit around the Earth, approached by other spheres of light. Then the three objects got closer to each other, when the Shuttle camera zoomed onto this scene, obviously to see more details. Shortly after that the objects separated again, still in a triangular pattern. *"There is no doubt these objects are under intelligent control,"* said Jim Dilettoso who analyzed the footage frame by frame. *"One of the spheres appeared under the clouds and rose up into the atmosphere. Another one seemed to enter the atmosphere, when it lit up."* Researcher Bill Hamilton of MUFON told me that for him the STS 80 footage is *"the best evidence yet to show that objects under intelligent control do maneuver in the Earth's orbit."*

The history of UFO encounters of Soviet cosmonauts began with the first man in space, Uri Gagarin. *"UFOs are a reality. They fly with incredible speeds and, if one will give me permission to do so, I will gladly tell you what I saw while in orbit around the Earth,"* were his words as cited by Russian papers.

I asked Dr. Mark Milkhiker, who had been deputy director of the Soviet Institute of Cosmonautics for over 17 years and is today codirector of the museum for cosmonautics in Moscow, whether other cosmonauts had had UFO encounters. Milkhiker, whose Mephistopheles beard and bushy eyebrows make him look rather like a mixture of Lucifer and Lenin, belongs to the great pioneers of Soviet space travel. Even as a student, he had constructed a rocket. He studied under the legendary space pioneer Aari Abrom Sternfelder and the founder of astrobiology Gabriel A. Tichov, and was involved in the development of space suits for cosmonauts. In short, he was an insider of the Soviet space program, who had worked with a number of cosmonauts. If anyone knew about UFO experiences, it was Milkhiker. *"Yes, and a couple of them confided their experiences in orbit to me,"* he said, answering my question, when I interviewed him after a conference in Tblissi, Georgia. *"For example, General Pavel Popovich, who took part in 3 space missions, told me that he had seen a triangular object. Also the cosmonauts Ivantschenko and Kovalyonok had had UFO encounters, which were even mentioned in the monograph* Investigations and Observations of the Earth's Atmosphere *by Saljut 6. I myself had a chat with the East German cosmonaut General Siegmund Jenn who spent a few days at the space station Saljut 6, of which Ivantschenko and Kovalyonok were the permanent crew, and he described the sighting in detail. Also the magazine*

Sputnik, *vol. 10/1989 quoted this incident in a report about UFO phenomena. The spherical object circled around Saljut 6, was watched for 47 minutes, was described by the cosmonauts over the radio, noted in the logbook, photographed and filmed. The object accompanied the station like a patrol at a distance of less than 3,000 feet."*

Cosmonaut Gen. V. Kovalyonok

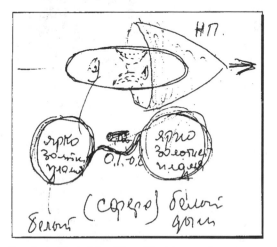

Kovalyonok's sketch of the object he saw in space on May 5, 1981, aboard Saljut

Col. Marina Popovich, the most famous female test pilot in the Soviet Union, knew more details about the incident. In her hometown, Marina is a living legend. After she had set 101 world flying records, amongst them flights in the stratosphere, she was lovingly christened "Gosposa Mig," Lady Mig, referring to the legendary Soviet fighter plane. Marina had test-flown practically every new model. Until her divorce, she was married to cosmonaut Gen. Pavel Popovich, whose UFO sighting she confirmed. She was then trained to be a cosmonaut, but has never been out in space. Even now, she lives at Startown, the cosmonaut settlement outside of Moscow, which no foreigner is allowed to enter because too many bearers of secrets live there. *"On March 12, 1981, Ivantschenko and Kovalyonok had begun their 75-day mission on board the space station Saljut 6,"* said Col. Popovich when I interviewed her in Moscow. *"On May 5, they saw two spherical objects connected by a kind of tube or tunnel. Then one of the spheres seemed to explode, whereas the other slowly approached the space station. For Kovalyonok that was reason enough to try to establish contact. He succeeded in making a film of the object, which had come within a distance of about 600 feet. The film must be somewhere in the archives of our space department. At that time, it was classified Top Secret, for, before glasnost, before the Gorbachev era, it was strictly forbidden for our cosmonauts to talk about their UFO experiences and sightings."*

But times change. On September 28, 1990, the union newspaper *Rabochaya Tribuna* interviewed via live radio the cosmonauts G. M. Manakov and G. M. Strekhalov, who were at that time on board the space station *Mir*. During this interview, for the first time ever, a cosmonaut described a UFO sighting to millions of listeners:

Rabochaya Tribuna: *What was the most interesting natural phenomenon that you saw on the Earth?*

Manakov: *"Yesterday, for instance, we saw what one would call an unidentified flying object. I called it such."*

RT: *"What was it?"*

M: *"I don't know. It was a big silvery sphere and iridescent. That was at 10:50 p.m."*

RT: *"Was it in the area above Newfoundland?"*

M: *No, we had already passed Newfoundland. We had a clear sky. It is difficult to say, but the object was at a great height above the Earth, about 15 to 20 miles. It was much bigger than a big ship."*

RT: *"Could it have been an iceberg?"*

M: *No. It had a completely regular shape, but I don't know what it was. Perhaps an enormous test object, or something like that. I watched it for about 6 to 7 seconds, then it disappeared."*

RT: *"Could you estimate its speed?"*

M: *"No, it just hovered over the Earth."*

This broke the ice, and the first cosmonauts started talking in public about their UFO encounters. One of the first was General Kovalyonok: rumors about his sighting got around, and he immediately became the target of UFO researchers who wanted to know more. Finally, on April 5, 1992, the Italian ufologist and contactee Giorgio Bongiovanni managed to meet General Kovalyonok in person and interviewed him on camera regarding his encounter:

Bongiovanni: *"I have heard you saw something in Outer Space that could have been connected with extraterrestrial intelligences. . . ."*

Kovalyonok: *"It was on May 5, 1981, at about 6 p.m. We were in space over South Africa, flying in the direction of the Indian Ocean. I was doing some physical exercises when I saw, through a window in front of me, an object I could not explain. It is impossible to estimate distances in space. A small object can appear large and a big object small. Sometimes a cloud of dust can look like a big object. I observed this object when suddenly something happened I couldn't explain, something which is impossible from a physical point of view. The object was disc-shaped, one-half of it surrounded by a conical kind of fog, and it flew with us. In front view it looked like it was rotating, and we observed these revolving movements in flight direction."*

Bongiovanni: *"How did it fly? Straight or did it make some unusual movements?"*

Kovalyonok: *"Just straight, but then a kind of explosion happened, beautiful to watch, of golden color. This was the first part, then, 1–2 seconds later, a second explosion happened, and two spheres appeared, two globes of the same color, golden, beautiful . . ."*

Bongiovanni: *"Was anything inside of the globes?"*

Kovalyonok: *"No, nothing. After this explosion there was just a white smoke, a cloud-like ball. Before we entered the shadow of the Earth we passed the terminator, the twilight-zone, but in the very moment we entered the Earth's shadow, everything was dark and we didn't see anything anymore."*

Bongiovanni: *"Do you believe the object was intelligently controlled?"*

Kovalyonok: *"I think the parallel movements, indeed, indicate intelligence and logic. This was not a coincidence, but the act of a precise will."*

Since 1995, my Russian coworker Valeri Uvarov has been able to interview the Cosmonauts Musa Manarvo, Gennadi Strekhalov and Pavel Popovich about their UFO encounters in space.

Astronomers

UFO debunkers often one bring up the argument that UFOs cannot exist *"because until now no astronomer has seen one"*. But like so many of the arguments of anti-ufologists, this too can be easily refuted. Apart from the fact that *"many professional astronomers are convinced that UFOs come from other planets,"* as Dr. Frank Halstead, astronomer and head of the Darling Observatory in the United States, said in an article in *The Tribune* on July 7, 1954, many astronomers have seen UFOs with their own eyes. The Swiss engineer Adolf Schneider could list 114 UFO sightings by astronomers in the period 1947–1982. That they have not been seen more frequently through the big reflector telescopes is easily explained. These are not constructed for viewing objects close to the Earth, but for viewing tiny sections of the sky, where galaxies and nebulae located at enormous distances away from the Earth can be focused upon. On the other hand, astronomers have often enough seen UFOs in the neighborhood of the moon or the sun.

Professor Clyde W. Tombaugh was the only astronomer of this century who had discovered a planet, namely Pluto in 1933, and was for that fact alone a legendary figure in his faculty. For years he served his country as advisor to the United States Government in space matters. Professor Tombaugh had seen a UFO in 1949. It was in the evening of August 10, and he was sitting with his wife and his mother-in-law on the terrace of his house at Las Cruces, New Mexico. They were looking at the sky when their attention was drawn at 10:45 p.m. to a formation of lights which glided across the heavens. The lights approached them absolutely noiselessly, and Tombaugh got the impression that he was looking at a cigar-shaped object, the lights being its lit-up windows.

Another prominent astronomer and UFO witness was the late English professor H. Percy Wilkins, an internationally recognized moon specialist. During a lecture tour in the United States, the astronomy professor flew on June 11, 1954, from Charleston, West Virginia, to Atlanta, Georgia. Looking out of the window he saw to his surprise two objects at a distance of about 3 miles flying in and out of the clouds. They were oval and had an estimated diameter of about 50 feet and looked like they were made of polished metal. *"Exactly like plates of polished metal which reflected the sunlight when they flew in and out of the clouds. Then a third object came out slowly from behind a huge cloud, remained motionless in the shadow of the cloud and looked, therefore, darker than the others. Suddenly it flitted away and dove into another cloud bank. A couple of minutes later, the other two did the same and I never saw them again. One thing is certain; if the UFOs were of solid metal and capable of moving at their own will, and at any speed and in any direction, then they must be constructed, steered and controlled by intelligences that are superior to that of humans."*

One of the best known American astronomers, Professor Lincoln LaPaz of the University of Las Cruces, New Mexico, saw an elliptical bright object that was moving back and forth behind the clouds on July 10, 1947. He was together with his family, in the vicinity of Port Sumner, New Mexico. The previously mentioned astronomer Dr. Halstead said in *The Tribune* article that two high-ranking colleagues had seen disc-like objects through their telescopes.

Professor Hall, chief of the well-known Lowell observatory in Massachusetts, tracked through his telescope, on May 20, 1950, at 1:00 p.m., a strange flying object whose speed, distance and size he tried to estimate. Two days later, Prof. Seymour L. Hess, of the University of Florida, sighted a similar object through the telescope of the observatory at Flagstaff, Arizona.

Things were not very different behind the Iron Curtain. On July 26, 1965, the Latvian astronomers Robert and Esmerelda Vitolniek, as well as Jan Melsers, saw through the telescope of their observatory near Orga a lens-shaped UFO with a diameter of more than 100 feet, around which 3 smaller spherical objects were circling. After about 15 minutes, the smaller objects flew away and then the mother ship followed. A few days later, the astronomical surveyor Ludmilla Tchekanovitch of Sukhumi in the Caucasus was at work, when a disc appeared which carried out quick maneuvers above the sea and then flew off into the mountains. Ludmilla could make out circular ports in the dome of the object where there was a bright light. At the astrophysical mountain station of the Soviet Academy of Sciences near Kislowodsk in the Caucasus, astronomer Anatoli Sazanov saw a huge UFO of about 500 feet in diameter on August 8, 1967, at about 8:40 p.m. A number of other scientists at the station were also witnesses.

On September 24, 1965, astronomer Dr. Larissa Zechanovitch of the Moscow Planetarium was on holiday at Novi Afon on the Black Sea. The sun had set just a little before that, and Larissa, still swimming in the sea, saw a black object in the sky which proved to be a disc with a viewing window, from which a yellow light came out. It came down to about 300 feet above the water, and about 1,000 feet away from Dr. Zechanovitch.

One of the few astronomers who speaks openly about his numerous UFO sightings through the telescope is the Argentinian Jesuit father, Dr. Benito Reyna, director of the Adhara Observatory at San Miguel, near Buenos Aires. *"I have often followed the movements of UFOs, with the naked eye or through prismatic binoculars,"* said Father Reyna, *"and they almost always follow satellites or rockets on their course."* Dr. Reyna is a well-known scientist, well-versed in the natural sciences and philosophy. Besides that, he is a biologist and professor of physics and mathematics at the respected El Salvador University of Buenos Aires, the biggest university in the country. In 1959 his name went around the world in faculty journals for being the only astronomer who could photograph the dust and gas cloud which rose from the landing of the Soviet Lunik 2 probe on the moon.

On December 1, 1965, Dr. Reyna and his assistants were taking pictures of the moon. Using a camera attached to a telescope, they took shots of the moon at 4-minute intervals. On developing the photographs they found on one of the pictures 3

The Argentinean astronomer Father Reyna, took this picture of 3 dark discs in front of the moon in 1966.

dark discs which hovered between the Earth and the moon. During the same evening the pictures were shot, hundreds of witnesses could see 3 lighted discs flying very low over the town of La Plata. That was the first time that Reyna could capture the flying objects on celluloid.

A year before that, the team at the Adhara observatory had observed something strange:

> During the clear night of November 14, 1964, we were tracking the satellite Echo 2 with a telescope," says the report from Father Reyna, "It flies from the North Pole to the South Pole at 8:37 p.m., almost on the same meridian as the observatory. At 8:45 there appears in the west, near the constellation Pegasus, and at right angles to Echo 2, a UFO. After getting close to the satellite, it swerves off and makes a semicircle (perhaps to avoid influencing the satellite through its magnetic field). After that it flies east, and in 3 minutes is in the neighborhood of Orion and disappears beyond the horizon. At 8:52 p.m., when Echo 2 was at the zenith, the UFO reappears from the southwest in the constellation Centaur and flies towards Echo 2. When it gets near to the satellite, it swerves off and goes northwest and finally disappears behind the horizon near the Andromeda nebula. For a third time then at 9:00 p.m. it appears once

more near Altair in cigar-shape and then becomes spherical. When it gets near Echo 2, it makes the same maneuver as before, turns south and flies off in the direction of Canopus, finally disappearing over the southern horizon at the same time as Echo 2. Many people inside and outside the observatory dome could see and follow its various courses. We could see it very clearly near the horizon.

One could see its upper tower absolutely clearly, green in color like mercury lamps. Its middle was yellow and its borders blue. Sometimes it covered the visual field of the telescope completely and seemed to be bigger than the full moon. The speed of Echo 2 is around 1,600 miles per hour. The UFO could have been 4 times as fast, considering the distance covered at the same height. We were fascinated and delighted by the appearance. The spectacle offered by the UFO was unique and wonderful."

And in a letter the Jesuit father goes further and says: *"one must bear in mind that the diameter of the UFO was three times that of the satellite. If you remember, Echo 2 had a diameter of 120 feet."*

In 1966 the same team sighted 5 UFOs in V-formation which crossed the heavens horizontally.

A year later, Professor Reyes Febles, chief of the Antares observatory in Montevideo, Uruguay, succeeded in taking 19 photographs of a saucer-shaped craft from which smaller discs came out. Professor Febles had intended to photograph the sun in order to evaluate its photosphere periodically and thus get information for a long-term project which he was working on. When he was adjusting his instruments, suddenly a strange flying object appeared in the visual field of the telescope. It seemed to be very big. Soon the astronomer could recognize details. The spaceship was oval, steel-colored, with two bays at each end, and spewed some gas towards the sun. It was approaching the Earth slowly. Prof. Febles had already taken a number of photographs when, from the left side of the vessel, objects of various colors shot out in all directions. It took about 17 minutes until they reappeared, and with the same speed, reentered the mothership, but this time through the right side. The craft hovered at a height of about 4,000 feet, stood at first above a cloud and then flew into it. The last photograph was taken when one of the clouds threw its shadow onto the object. At the same moment, according to the astronomer, one could look through an open port into the insides of the UFO. The appearance had lasted for an hour and fifty minutes, after which the craft disappeared into space at high speed.

The El Infernillo Observatory lies at a height of over 13,000 feet above sea level, high up in the Cordilleran range of the Andes mountains in Chile. It is part of the department of physics and mathematics of the University of Chile, with headquarters in Santiago de Chile. Its chairman is Prof. Gabriel Alvial Caceres, whose special field as the measurement of cosmic radiation. The professor believes in UFOs. In May 1968 he announced that *"since October of last year, our logbook alone has registered 15 UFOs, unexplainable starlike objects which move in space and can come to a standstill right in the middle of flight. Now we have at last succeeded in photographing one of them.*" That happened on May 17, 1968, at 1:35 a.m. According to Caceres, the UFO, a huge shining disc, had stood at a height of about 7,000 feet for one whole hour and blinked. In the photograph one can make out a dome-shaped object, high above the mountains, and the lights of the neighboring El Roblo observatory.

It is almost certain that German observatories have observed such phenomena but do not accept that they were UFOs. The German astrophysicist, Illobrand von Ludwiger, reports that the university observatory at Bamberg set up astronomical cameras night after night during the late fifties in order to photograph certain sections of the heavens over a period of one hour. As von Ludwiger emphatically states, during certain nights, apart from meteorites and airplanes, other bright objects also appeared on the plates, which could not be identified. One of these plates, he could recall clearly, showed a bean-shaped spot of light. The comment of the project leader at that time was simply "plate defect," but an assistant had added "no plate defect, since plate xy has also registered it." The chief of the People's Observatory in Munich, Hans Oberndorfer, conceded to the Swiss engineer Adolf Schneider that he had on occasion observed strange things, amongst them star-like points of light which suddenly went crazy and cut capers in the sky.

During the clear and starry night of April 13, 1980, the engineer and amateur astronomer Mauro Venturini of Munich wanted to take a photograph of the constellation Coma Berenices. Venturini was a member of the People's Observatory, and for 8 years, astronomy had been his hobby. He had just done a final check to see whether his subject, the star Gamma Coma Berenices was precisely in the center of the sight. At

"A huge space station" in front of the sun, photographed by amateur astronomer Akira Ishiguro through the 660mm (focal length) lens of his telescope.

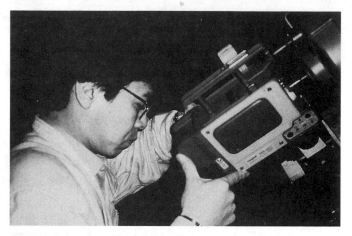

Amateur astronomer Yasumo Mizushima.

about 10:55 p.m., he looked up into the sky. He could hardly believe his eyes. Eight light yellow-colored discs with fuzzy-looking peripheries appeared at the level of the constellation Bootes and flew slowly and quietly from the northeast towards the southwest. Seven of the discs flew arranged like the mirror image of number one lying flat. The eighth accompanied the formation. *"Since the UFOs were flying in such a peculiar formation, the confusion with something else is ruled out,"* said the amateur astronomer to UFO researcher Herbert Mohren. He then added, *"before I saw this I never believed in UFOs but I must honestly say that I have changed from Saul to Paul and am now convinced of their existence."* The apparent size of the individual objects was about that of a coin held at arm's length. The length of the entire fleet was about 8 inches. The engineer Adolf Geigenthaler, the leader of a UFO study group in Munich, is convinced: *"Venturini saw how the UFO fleet floated there in a precise and unnaturally odd formation. A mistake is out of the question."*

Thanks to Yasumo Mizushima, a young Japanese amateur astronomer, there is a whole series of very interesting telescopic photographs of UFOs on the moon, and in the vicinity of the sun.

During a cool October night in 1985, Mizushima had connected, as he often did, his video camera to his two Celestron telescopes, one a C-14 and the other a C-8, mounted on a special tower in his garden. His target that day was the moon, whose surface he wanted to photograph in detail. It was a success. He obtained wonderful video tape of the craters and the "seas," of the valleys and mountain ranges of the satellite of the Earth. But then at 12:30 a.m. he had something very special in front of the lens. Two objects seemed to be maneuvering around the southeast side of the moon's surface. Their shadows on the moon were clearly discernible, which excluded the possibility of their being somewhere "out in space" between the Earth and

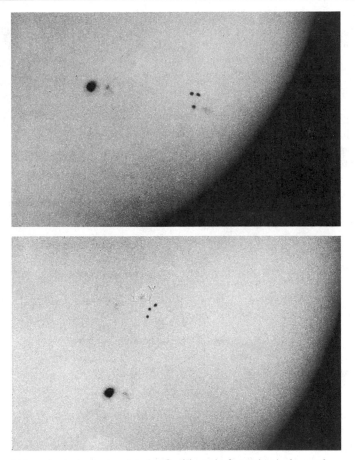

Ishiguro's photographs showing 3 objects in formation in front of
the sun.

the moon. They flew close above the sea of craters. Later Mizushima calculated that they must have been from 1,200–1,500 feet in size. That made
the matter clear—they were large flying objects, obviously operating with
intelligence, and were possibly using the moon as a base.

Mizushima had long been convinced of the existence of UFOs, and was
also convinced that they came from outer space. He had more than once
seen anomalous lights on the surface of the moon and once, on May 4,
1985, had even filmed an object. He had also spoken to other Japanese
amateur astronomers, who had also observed and photographed unusual
objects in space.

The most remarkable photograph was made by Akira Ishiguro of Yoko-
hama in April, 1991. Using a filter mounted on the objective of his telescope—60mm objective and focal length 660mm—to which he had

connected a polaroid camera, he made test photographs. On one of them something like a huge space station appeared above the disc of the sun, a space platform on which apparently 5 cigar-shaped objects had docked. And for Ishiguro too, that was not the first UFO photograph. Already in May 1989 he had captured on film 3 black oval objects which crossed the sun's disc.

There have been unusual observations such as these from the beginnings of astronomy. As early as 1762, the astronomer de Rostan of Basel could see "a gigantic flying cigar surrounded by a glow of light," which moved slowly across the sun. On June 17, 1777, Charles Messier, the famous French astronomer, observed a large number of dark circular discs in the sky. In 1844 his colleague Glaisher reported shining discs *"which sent out quickly flickering waves of light."* In April 1860 4 leading astronomers, Herrick, Buys-Barlott and de Cuppis of Great Britain, together with their Swiss colleague Dr. Wolf, watched from the Zurich Observatory as *"a large number of small black discs which came from the east flew past."* Mr. Marcel Trecul, member of the Académie Française, noticed, on August 20, 1880, *"a small object"* that separated itself from a *"huge air-cigar with pointed ends,"* and sparkled with a whitish-gold light. The renowned observatory at Greenwich announced on November 11, 1882, the sighting of *"a gigantic green disc at a height of somewhere between 40 and 200 miles."*

The first UFO photograph in history appeared in 1885 in the October issue of the Paris magazine *L'Astronomie*. The photographer was the Mexican astronomer José a y Bonilla, chief of the observatory of Zacatecas, which is at a height of about 7,500 feet above sea level, and was the second biggest observatory in the country. At about 8:00 in the morning of August 12, 1883, Prof. Bonilla began to observe the sun with his telescope, using a filter. He was just about to sketch the sunspots when his attention was diverted by a small shining object which suddenly came into the field of the telescope. It crossed the disc of the sun and had an oval

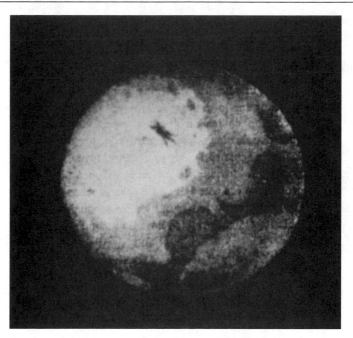

The first UFO photograph was published in 1885 by the journal *L'Astronomie*. It was taken by Prof. Bonilla on August 12, 1883, during an observation of the sun from the Zacatecas Observatory in Mexico.

shape. Only a few seconds later, this repeated itself and finally more mysterious flying objects appeared. It was a complete squadron. Within a period of two hours Prof. Bonilla could count 283 objects, which took, in each case, 3 to 4 seconds to cross the sun's face. After that the astronomer had to stop his observations because a pile of clouds hid the sun. He puzzled over what they could have been—for birds or insects the flying objects had moved too steadily. After a time, the sun was high up in the sky and he continued with his observations. This time he counted 48 objects. Bonilla noticed that many of the objects were circular, but others were long and shaped like spindles. All of them were phosphorescent in the darkness of free space. The time taken to cross the sun varied this time between a third of a second and 2 minutes. Finally Bonilla decided to attempt a photograph of these mysterious objects. With an exposure time of 1/100th of a second, he took a number of shots.

On the following day, August 14, they were there again. From 8:00 in the morning Bonilla could count 116 objects. With these, it made 447 objects in two days. The astronomer estimated their distance at 150,000 miles, at any rate *"less than that of the moon,"* which is 240,000 miles away. He telegraphed the observatories of Mexico City and Pueblo. He wanted his colleagues there to see the phenomenon and try to find out more about it.

An hour later Bonilla received their confirmation. They too saw the objects, exactly as he had described, and were convinced that they must be relatively close to the Earth.

And they returned. On November 30, 1888 Señor Ricci of the observatory in Palermo, Italy, observed *"a number of spindle-shaped flying objects crossing the sun's disc at a great height."* The interesting thing about these observations and the photo is that they demonstrate that the UFO phenomenon is not confined to our century alone.

CHAPTER 12

Sighted Since Millennia

His colleagues called him "The Caveman," for the prehistoric caves of Southern France and Northern Spain were his world. He spent day after day in the moist and chilly passages of the caves, squatting in rocky niches, creeping and crouching, sketching on paper what prehistoric people had painted on the cold walls thousands of years ago. Today, years after his death, Professor André Leroi-Gourhan is still revered by experts as one of the greatest authorities in the field of prehistoric art of the western world. His sketches and reproductions of the cave paintings of the Pyrenées are used and admired at all major universities.

The fascinating world which Leroi-Gourhan preserved in his work was little known until then. And even today, very few Europeans know that from about 30,000 BC till 10,000 BC, in the so-called Stone Age, a flourishing culture existed around the Pyrenées. During this period, which lasted perhaps well over 700 generations, the people, of whom the Basques of today are direct descendants, created masterpieces of painting and sculpture, which can even now be admired in the caves of Lascaux, Altamira and Les Eyzies.

When the French ethnologist Aimé Michel saw the reproductions of Prof. Leroi-Gourhan, he could not believe his eyes. Above the scenes depicting the daily life of the prehistoric people, above the pictures of hunters and animal herds, of mighty mammoths, muscular bison, shaggy horses and delicate deer, were disc-like objects floating in the air. On the rock paintings, thousands of years old, a phenomenon that excites people even today was depicted: unidentified flying objects. Would that mean, speculated Michel, that the flying discs had already existed in those days, and were even part of the daily life of early man?

The exact and lifelike depiction of human beings and animals leads us inevitably to believe that the initially inexplicable strange shapes were also meant to show something that was real,

concluded Michel in 1969.

In the caves there are up to 40 different types of strange objects, resembling in an astounding manner the manifestations in our skies which, during the last twenty years, have been called UFOs and which, according to the Condon report, do not exist.

The artists of the Paleolithic age drew whatever they wanted to depict, true to nature. They are absolutely reliable . . . the realities of prehistoric times are so remote from our epoch, that only those that are familiar with UFO literature can recognize the similarity between certain cave paintings and the appearances of our present day.

Indeed, what we see on the walls of these stone age caves is astounding. Spindle-shaped objects with long trails behind them fly over the landscape. Saucer-shaped bodies land, from which people seem to climb out. Others have long landing struts, domes, circular ports. Such representations are to be seen in 17 pre historic caves such as Altamira, Lascaux, Pech Merle and Les Trois Frères, names which mean something to every archaeologist. Do these wall paintings show something that the prehistoric people saw with their own eyes?

Cave paintings of Naux in the department of Ariege, southern France, approximately 12,000 BC, according to Prof. Leroi-Gourhan.

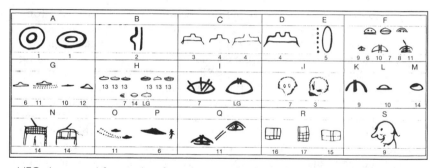

UFO shapes and forms taken from the reproductions of cave paintings dating back to the glacial age, sketched by Prof. Leroi-Gourhan, collected by Aimé Michels.

Or *"is it all pure coincidence?"* as Michel asks. *"For, as long as modern UFOs are nothing more than fantasy, invented by fools who have read too much science fiction . . . we must accept that early man filled his head with too much bad literature, or how else would he have gotten the idea of preserving for eternity flying saucers with an unheard of precision? If man had invented them, and a Condon report tries to prove that the similar appearances in the year 1969 were only weather balloons, temperature inversions, hallucinations and such, then we can equally well believe that UFOs from the time of the Magdalenian culture were airplanes and whether balloons."* But one finds similar motifs outside the Pyrenéean region as well. A rock painting in the Jabaren valley in the North African Tassili massif shows a woman greeting with outstretched arms 3 dome-shaped objects, which hover over a herd of cattle. One of the objects in the 10,000-year-old picture is depicted sending beams or rays to the Earth. Even more amazing is a rock engraving, which the Soviet archaeologist Dr. Vyacheslav Saizev discovered in the neighborhood of Fergana, in Uzbekistan. It looks like an illustration for a science fiction novel but, according to Saizev, is at least 7,000 years old.

It shows a man, his head enclosed in a kind of helmet with tubes and some sort of breathing mask, the hands in clumsy gloves holding something that looks like a music record or "CD." In the background, in front of strangely formed mountains, there hovers a disc with a ring around it. Under it is drawn a man with a spherical helmet, with two antennae sticking out from it.

In October 1959 Prof. Chi Pen-lao, lecturer in archaeology at the University of Peking, and his two assistants, Hui Chu-Ting and Dr. Wu To-wai, discovered caves in the heart of China, under the island of Yutuo in the Tungfing-hu lake; until then the caves had been unknown. They were actually looking for some ruins that had sunk with a part of the island 3,000 years ago. At a depth of about 100 feet, two divers found the entrance to a subterranean labyrinth which led deep into the granite rocks of the Hunan mountains. The labyrinth had sunk as a result of a strong earthquake. Well below the water surface, the archeologists found unusually well-preserved drawings engraved on a smoothly-polished granite wall, whose age Prof. Chi Pen-lao estimated at about 45,000 years. Quite obviously they must have been made by using hard tools, possibly of metal. What is more remarkable, the picture shows animals obviously fleeing from hunters holding tube-like weapons, seated in domed, saucer-shaped objects flying over the herd. Old Chinese legends talk of "fiery dragons" on which "sons of the heavens" rode, "heavenly vehicles" and "flying wheels." In the Yueh province one hears of "flying bells" which appear suddenly and mysteriously, silently carry out flying maneuvers, and then disappear.

At the outskirts of the town Yamaga, near Kumamoto in the Japanese province of Kyushu, there is the grave of a prince dating back to 2,000 BC. The walls of the burial chamber, built up of huge boulders, are painted. One of the pictures shows a king or prince wearing a 3-pointed crown, greeting with lifted hands 7 white discs floating in the sky. Since time immemorial the Japanese have called the grave "Chip-San" which, in the dialect of the Ainu, the original inhabitants of Japan, means "the place where the sun comes down." The Japanese archaeologist Dr. Yoshiyuki Tange said, *"We found out that these 'suns' in the old graves of Kyushu district were, thousands of years ago, symbols for 'flying saucers.' In fact one of the legends of the Ainu in Hokkaido describes such shining objects, which were called 'Shinta.'"*

"Shinta" literally means "cradle." The Ainu of Hokkaido believed that once upon a time, the god Okikurumi-Kamui came down from heaven in one of these cradles. Tange discovered one more prehistoric wall painting at Isumisaki on Hokkaido, which shows a group of people holding hands, watching a lens-shaped (or should we say cradle-shaped?) object descending in a spiraling course. This painting is also at least 4,000 years old. Japan's old chronicles speak of fiery suns, flaming objects, objects of the color of fire. A Japanese painting done in ink during the 9th century shows a fiery wheel in the heavens being watched by 4 priests; on the ground there is a winged human being apparently trying to escape their observation.

We find similar motifs and legends on the other side of the Pacific Ocean as well. In the Brazilian province of Minas Gerais, a 6 hour drive from Montes Claros takes one to the caves of Varzelandia. In 1963 an archaeological exploration led by Prof. Hernan Ebecken went deep into the caves and discovered some prehistoric graves of Indians, and a number of drawings on the rocks. One of them shows a dome-like object which is floating high up in the sky between the sun and the moon, and near it is a cigar-shaped flying object.

Another picture shows tilted discs flying over the landscape and a formation which, oddly enough, resembles the UFO fleet of Lubbock, Texas (see Chapter 5). The clever hoax of a joker, thought Prof. Ebecken but, to be absolutely certain, he scraped off some of the paint from the object and sent the sample to a laboratory at the University of Rio de Janeiro. The result: they are organic pigments whose age can be determined fairly accurately by the Carbon-14 method. In the opinion of the scientists, it is about 11,500 years old.

In fact, the Manacricas, a Brazilian Indian tribe, preserves memories of sorcerers who flew around in "shining round machines" and visited their people from time to time. The Kayapo, an Indian tribe from Rio Fresco,

Prof. Ebecken

south of Para in Brazil, has stories about the heavenly teacher Bep Kororoti (literally "he who comes from the universe"), who came to the Earth in ancient times and taught the Kayapo all sorts of things. They celebrated his coming as late as a few years ago with an annual festival, in the course of which one of them put on a suit of white bark to imitate the suit which Bep Kororoti was wearing when he visited the Earth. The clumsy suit covers the entire body and resembles an astronaut's suit. On the head is a basket-like helmet and the person carries in his hand a staff, a symbol of Bep Kororoti's thunder weapon, the "kop." When Bep Kororoti appeared, according to the tribal ritual, he was surrounded by dancing Kayapos who approached him with curiosity and then fled back in a wider circle. Was that the memory of an ancient encounter of the third kind?

We find similar legends also amongst the Indians of North and Middle America. The Huichol in North Mexico say that long before the arrival of the Spaniards a friendly tribe from the stars had visited them. *"They came down from heaven in vehicles like flat, polished gems. These star friends told us a lot about their home star, things we could not understand."* A 7,000-year-old rock drawing which was discovered in 1966 in the Mexi-

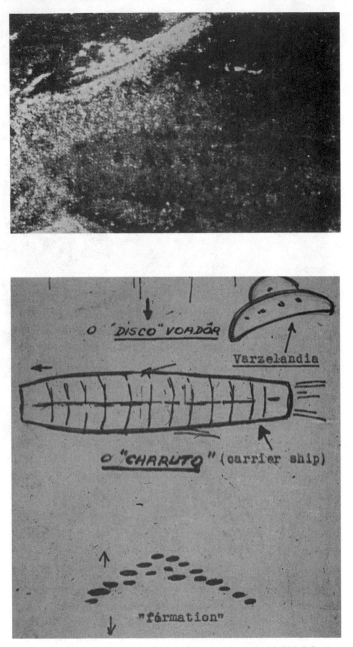

Wall paintings from Varzelandia, Brazil, approximately 11,500 BC, discovered by Prof. Ebecken in 1963, show disc and cigar-shaped UFOs and complete formations.

can province Querataro apparently depicts such a heavenly ship. It shows a big round object with a dome and circular ports. As it sends beams down to the Earth, human beings surround it, greeting it with raised hands. *"Beings who come in flying ships from heaven are . . . white gods, who fly in discs which reach up to the stars"* gave the ancestors of the Mayas their culture, according to the "Book of the Chilam Balam" (High Priest), a collection of old Mexican myths and prophecies put together at the time of the conquistadors.

The Hopis, whose reservation lies in the north of Arizona, also have legends about heavenly teachers, the Kachinas, a name that literally means "highly respected wise ones." *"They came from space, from a distant solar system with twelve planets called 'Toonaotakha,' "* related the Hopi Elder White Bear Fredericks to the researcher Joseph Blumrich, *"they cover these distances in their flying ships. The Kachinas are physical beings and, therefore, need the flying craft for their journeys, flying vessels of various sizes and with different names. One of them is Paatoowa, the object which can fly over the water. 'Pahu' means water in our language and 'toowata' is an object with a curved surface. Owing to this shape we call them also 'flying shields.'"* According to White Bear, the Kachinas had lived amongst the Hopis for a long time. Then one day they flew away but promised to return to Hopiland in the distant future. *"For this reason, even today we make Kachina dolls for our children, and men dressed in Kachina masks dance at our festivals. We want our children to get accustomed to the sight of Kachinas so that they do not get frightened when the Kachinas return."*

The neighboring tribe of the Hopis, the Navajo, talk about beings who came from the heavens, stayed on the earth for a long time and, finally, went back to their own world—and not without taking some members of the Navaho with them, at their own request! *"A petroglyph near Mishongnovi on the second Mesa shows flying saucers on their journey through space,"* said the Hopi elder Dan Katchongva, who had himself seen UFOs, to the Austrian Native American rights activist, Alexander Buschenreiter. *"The bow on which the dome-shaped object is resting represents travel through space. The Hopi girl on the dome represents purity. The Hopis who survive the Day of Purification,"* comparable to the Christian Doomsday, *"will be taken to other planets. We, the faithful Hopis, have seen the ships and know that they exist."*

The American anthropologist Dr. George Hunt Williamson found similar legends amongst the tribes who live around the Great Lakes. *"Before the arrival of the Europeans, round and silent aircraft used to come here, which could land on the lakes. When the white man arrived, the alien visitors departed in their spaceships, but promised to come back again."* From the Haida Indians who live on Queen Charlotte Island in British Columbia, Canada, one hears about *"great wise ones who came from the stars on fiery plates."*

And, finally, the Chippewa have a legend, according to which "a big

Pre-Columbian statuette from Ecuador, approximately 500 BC.

star with wings" appeared once above the tree tops. Some of the elders of the tribe took it for a sign from the Great Spirit, but others were frightened and fled. The star hovered for a month above the village and one day a "star girl" appeared before a young brave and said that she came from

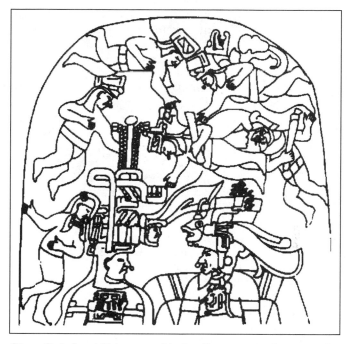

Olmec Stela from Villahermosa, Mexico. Six astronauts float around in the cockpit as if weightless, all wearing special headgear. The two pilots with complicated helmets are seated comfortably.

Aztec representation of the god Quetzelcoatl who, according to legends, visited the earth in a plumed serpent to bring culture to the Aztecs and Toltecs.

Publication of the International Academy for Sanskrit Research: the text of *Vimanaka Shastra* by Maharishi Bharadavaja, until recently believed to have been lost.

the Winged Star. Her people had come there from a very distant land and that the happy life of the people in the village would please them very much. They, the star people, wished to spend some time with the Indians. The brave presented this strange request to the council of elders. Spokesmen were then sent to welcome the strangers with fragrant herbs and peace pipes. The aliens lived for a few years amongst the Chippewa and taught them many things, after which they took leave and disappeared in their starship towards the south.

The most detailed description of these heavenly vehicles are to be found in the ancient writings of India where they are called Vimanas. One of these texts, the "Vimanica Shastra" (textbook of space travel), was published by Prof. G. R. Josyer, director of the respected Academy of Sanskrit Research at Mysore, India. This manuscript from prehistoric times is attributed to the ancient and wise Maharishi Baradhvaja, who, according to Indian tradition, lived around 3,000 BC; in the opinion of western Indologists, about 700 BC. Although the only existing version was written down in 1918 by Pandit Subbaraya Shastry, dictated by a sage, mention of the text itself had been cited by books published as early as 1875. The Sanskrit researcher Prof. Dilip Kumar Kanjilal considers it, on account of its archaic language and grammar, to be a work from the early times of India. Prof. Josyer also believes it is genuine and of inestimable value, and that its publication could reveal new knowledge for modern aircraft construction.

As a matter of fact, "Vimanica Shastra" describes a Vimana as "*an apparatus which moves under its own power like a bird, equally well on the ground, in water or in the air. That which can fly through the air from place to place, country to country, or planet to planet is designated by sages of space travel as Vimana.*" It has "*the secret means of making aircraft motionless or invisible, of overhearing conversations and other noises in enemy flying craft, of obtaining pictures of the insides of inimical aircraft, of determining their course, and making persons in inimical craft unconscious.*" It can make itself invisible and it glows in the night because "*electric energy collides with the wind*" [ionization?]; it glows even by daylight and can fly in a zigzag course.

Similar details are given in the "Samarangana Sutradhara," a work comprising 220 stanzas, the oldest version of which dates back to the 12th cen-

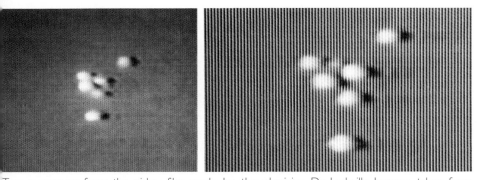

Two sequences from the video film made by the physician Dr. Ludmilla Ivanova, taken from Greifswald in former East Germany, on Aug. 24, 1990. One clearly sees the formation of the six spherical objects. In the middle, the seventh one is beginning to appear.

The film made by Dr. Ivanova was taken from this angle. Drawn in are the positions of both UFO groups.

D. Menningmann, with the married couple Ivanov and other witnesses of the incident at Greifswald.

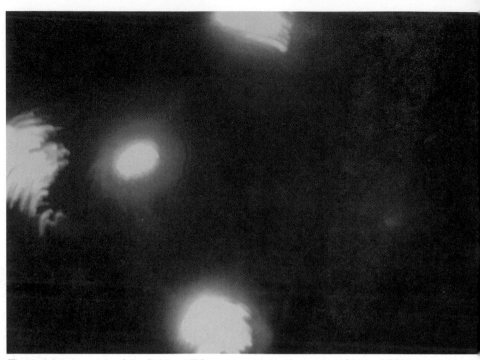

The best photograph of the Belgian UFOs was sent in by the witness P.M. to SOBEPS researchers It was taken on April 4, 1990, at Petit Rechin Vervier, Province Luttig.

By means of artificial coloring/computer analysis, the triangular basic structure of the object and the rotation of the lights becomes visible. Photo: SOBEPS.

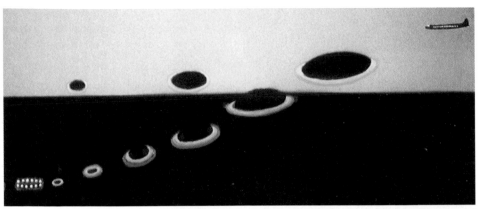

Reconstructed drawing of the UFO encounter experienced by Commander Graham Bethune of the U.S. Navy, while he was flying between Greenland and Newfoundland, Feb. 10, 1951.

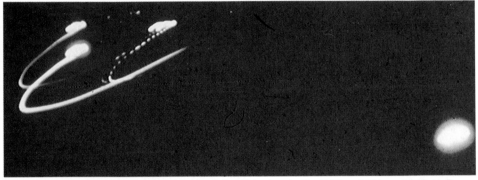

UFO formation over Honolulu, Hawaii, March 5, 1956, taken by Sgt. William L. Wannall, U.S. Air Force.

UFO over Holloman Air Force Base, Oct. 16, 1957. Photo: Ella Fortune.

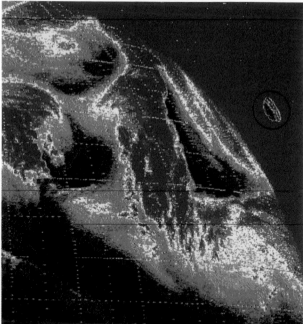

"Fastwalker" entering the Earth's atmosphere in close proximity to the "GOES 8" U.S. weather satellite —infrared photo of June 8, 1995, at 11:45 a.m. Photo: Antonio Huneeus/Philip Imbrogno

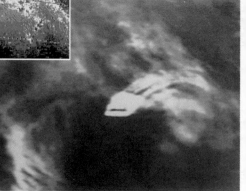

"Fastwalker" over Vladivostok, CIS— Official NASA photo from a Polar Orbiting Satellite, taken in 1992

Two UFOs above Westover Air Force Base in the U.S., Jan. 13, 1967. Photo: W. Varner, USAF

Official Air Force photograph of a UFO taken by H. Williams, pilot of a C-47 jet fighter, in July 1966 over Idaho.

Japanese interceptor chases UFO above Hya Kuri Air Force Base. Photo: O. Tsugaane, Japanese Air Force, Oct. 10. 1975.

UFO fleet above a Danish NATO base on Greenland. Photograph from the archives of Maj. Hans C. Petersen, Danish Air Force.

UFO above Wyborg, Denmark, Nov. 17, 1974, taken by H. Lauersen. This incident was investigated by Maj. Hans Petersen of the Danish Air Force. The vaporizing effect is explained by scientists as being the result of the surface of the UFO being cooler than -180 degrees Celcius. Because of that, the surrounding air becomes liquid and flows towards the Earth, which gives the object its jellyfish-like appearance.

Photograph officially released by the Spanish Air Force, taken by a German on June 22, 1976, from Maspalomas, Gran Canaria.

A similar light phenomenon was observed by thousands of people from Tenerife and Gran Canaria on March 5, 1979.

Two telescopic photographs of cigar-shaped mother ships, taken by George Adamski, Mar. 5, 1951.

The UFO landing at Gran Canaria on June 22, 1976. Reconstruction based on information given by Dr. Padron Leon.

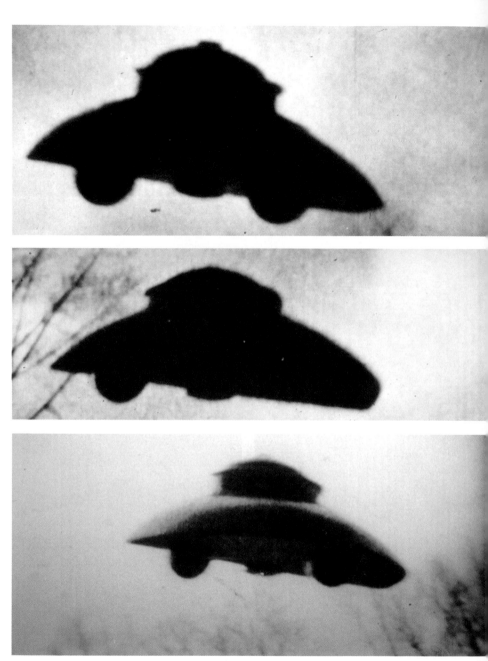

Three stills from the 8mm movie taken by government official Madeleine Rodeffer, on Feb. 26, 1965, at Silver Springs, Maryland, a suburb of Washington D.C., in the presence of George Adamski. One clearly sees the change of shape which is an effect caused by the electromagnetic force field around it.

The gorge at the foot of the Coxcomb mountains, north of Desert Center, California, where George Adamski met a visitor from another world on Nov. 20, 1952.

Madeleine Rodeffer, in summer 1993, standing in front of her house in Silver Springs, Maryland. Movie footage was shot from the veranda of that house.

One of the controversial photos taken by the Swiss contactee Eduard "Billy" Meier. Although debunkers claim they are fakes, a careful computer analysis by experts proved at least some of them to be genuine. On this photo of June 12, 1975, taken near Berg-Rumlikon, Zurich, Switzerland, the reflection of a beige-brownish rural road is clearly visible on the shiny bottom of the craft—indicating that it hovered at a distance, not close to the camera.

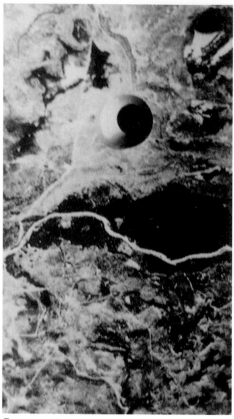

Encounter in the air with a cigar-shaped UFO. Photograph taken by the pilot Inake Osis, over Venezuela, Feb. 13, 1968.

Cigar-shaped UFO, photographed on Sept. 14, 1970, by N. Vidal, above La Reia, Argentina. It resembles the mother ship Adamski had photographed.

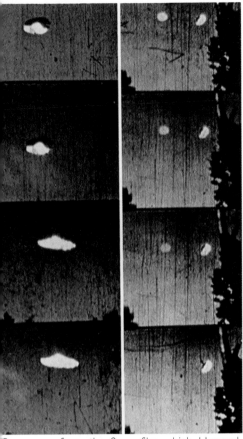

Police photograph of a UFO.; Deputy Sheriff Arthur Strauch took this photograph in the presence of 4 witnesses on Oct. 21, 1965, near St. George, Minnesota.

Sequences from the 8mm film which Howard Menger shot in 1956 at Highbridge, New Jersey.

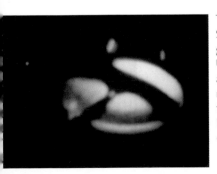

Tulsa, Oklahoma, August 1965. Fourteen-year-old Alan Smith photographed this colorful object during the great UFO wave. Neither an analysis carried out by the U.S. Air Force, nor a computer analysis by GSW found any indications of a hoax. On the contrary, "It has definitely been taken against the night sky. The object is very far from the camera. Behind the lights, there is a disc-like object about 30-40 feet in diameter," said the GSW computer analysis. (Enlargement)

A flight captain of the Brazilian airline VARIG took this photo in 1978 over the Amazon jungle, from his cockpit.

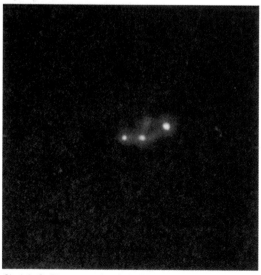

Skylab-3. Photograph of 4 disks, connected together by a force field.

Still shot from a film which an Australian TV team (Channel 10) took above New Zealand on Oct. 31, 1978.

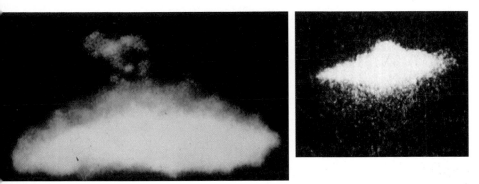

Telescopic photograph taken by the Argentinian astronomer Dr. Benito Reyna, from the observatory of San Miguel, near Buenos Aires, in 1966.

UFO above Chad, taken by a team of scientists on board a Concorde on July 30, 1973, during a solar eclipse, at an altitude of 51,000 feet.

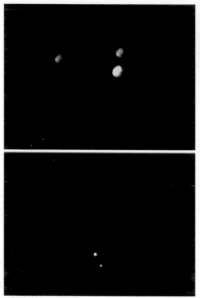

Official NASA UFO photograph. Gemini 4: a cylindrical object, June 3, 1966.

Gemini 12. Photograph of a UFO formation, Nov. 13, 1966.

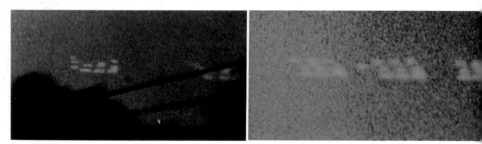

Two sequences from the 8mm film shot by Fred Steckling from a train, between Mannheim and Darmstadt, Germany on Sept. 7, 1966.

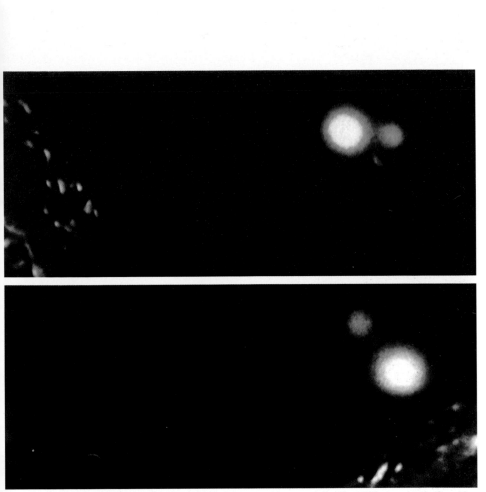

Two pictures from a film which the Apollo 11 crew shot on July 19, 1969, the day before the historic moon landing.

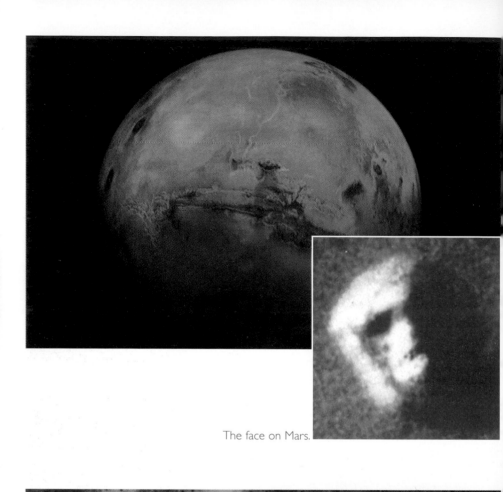

The face on Mars.

Do aliens have bases on Mars? In 1976, the Viking probe photographed pyramid-like structures and a face that looks like a human visage on the Mars region of Cydonia.

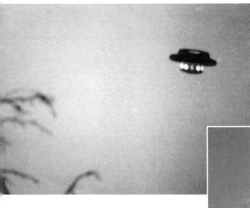

Daylight picture of a hat-shaped craft with blinking lights around its cupola, taken by Don Raul Dominguez on April 24, 1993 at Ocotlan, Jalisco/Mexico.

Saturn-shaped object photographed on Feb. 16, 1994 near Guadalajara, Jalisco/Mexico.

A white disc, surrounded by an orange halo, crosses the flight path of an incoming "SwissAir" plane over Zurich "Kloten" Airport on Feb. 6, 1979.

A fiery wheel and a human being with wings. Japanese ink painting from the 9th century.

Petroglyph in Isumisaki, on Hokkaido, Japan. It shows a mythical descent of the god Okikurumi in a "cradle."

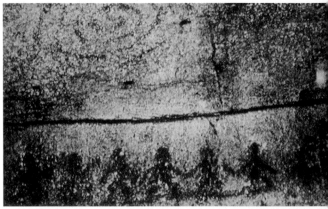

2,600-year old grave paintings from Yamaga, near Kumamoto, in the province Kiushu, Japan. In the language of the natives, it is also called "Chip san," "the place where the sun comes down."

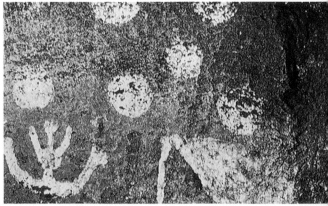

The Kayapo Indians of Rio fresco in Brazil celebrate in an annual feast the visit of "Bep Kororoti." His name means, literally, "from space." Photo: Archive E.V. Daniken.

7,000 years old? Wall painting in Fergana, Uzbekistan. Photo: Archive E.V. Daniken.

7,000-year old petroglyph, discovered in the province of Querato, Mexico, in 1966. One clearly sees domes and ports. Does it show the coming down of a white god in his spaceship?

God Shamash, in his heavenly ship. An Assyrian relief from the 9th century BC from Niniveh, now at the British Museum.

"The heavens opened up." Old Bible illustration of the encounter of the prophet Ezekiel. Photo: Archive E.V. Daniken.

Fresco in the church of a monastery in Cossovo
from the 14th century.

Statuette of Shamash from Ur in Sumeria, approximately
1,900 BC, now in the British Museum. Was Shamash an
astronaut?

The oldest official document in the world regarding UFOs comes from the archives of Pharaoh
Thutmosis III (1483-1450 BC). From the collection of Prof. Alberto Tulli of the Vatican Museum.

jwiſchen zum gehn tag vnd dem garaußz/das iſt zu morgens zwiſchen
5 auff der klainen vhr/iſt ein ſehr erſchröcklich geſicht an der Son wie
auffgang geweſen erſchinnen/vnd zu Nürnberg in der Star vnd vor
thor vnd auff dem Land von vielen manns vnd weyßs perſonen geſehen
1. Erſtlich iſt die Sonn mit zweyen Blutfarben halb runden ſtriche/ gleichförmig
Nonn im abnemen/mitten durch die Sonn erſchinnen vnd geſehen worden/vn
Sonne ſcheins/vnten / Vnd auff beden ſeyten Blutfarbe/vnd eines theyls Bleiche
ſen farbe auch ſchwarz farbrunde Kugel geſtanden / Deſelben gleichen auff ba
ten vnd ein aſcheyben vmb die Sonne herumb/ſein ſolche blutrote/vnd der andern
inzal viel/etwo drey in die lenge/ vnter weylen vier im einem Quarrangel/auch et
nig geſtanden/Vnd zwiſchen ſolchen Kugeln ſein auch etliche Blutfarbe Creuz ge
ozwiſchen ſolchen Creuzen vnd Kugeln ſein Blurfarbe ſtreyme hinden dick / Vnd
auff / etwas geſchmeydiger alls hocken thor/ Allenthalben mit ein vermiſcht gew
ipt vnter andern zweyen groſſen roen/eines zur rechten/vnd das ander zur linken h
ient/in welchen kleinen vnd groſſen Roen/zu dreyen/auch vier vnd mehr kugel gew
ſen alles hat mit einander anfahen zu ſtreyten / ſein die Kugel ſo erſtlich in der Son
en/herauzz auff die/ſo bey den ſeyten geſtanden/geſarn/ ſo ſein die ſo herauſſen g
ſampt den kugeln auff den klein vnd groſſen Rom/ im die Sonne hinein geſarn / zu

Leaflet from Nuremburg of the year 1561 showing what the citizensw of the town saw, including "Tubes from which red balls shot out."

Are the two UFOs observing the crucifixion of Christ in this fresco in a Georgian monastery church dating back to the 10th century?

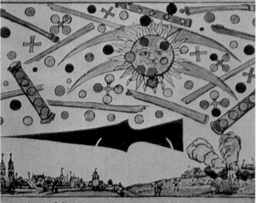

Ben de Roteßai ſo ſchr alls die Kugel vnter einander geſaen / vnd heſſtig alles mit
geſteitten vnd, eſochten/bey einer guten ſtund / Vnd wie der Streyt das ein w
Sonne hinein/vnd widerumb herauß am heſſtigſten bis vnd her geſaren/ſich b

A French Gobelin from the 15th century depicts the Virgin Mary and a disc-like object above the town.

UFO over Crimea, Sept. 22, 1983.

UFO over Shiraz, Iran, June 1978. Photographed by 16-year-old Yamshid Saidipour, which was published by various newspapers and was also included in the files of the DIA (Defense Intelligence Agency of the United States)

UFO over Las Lunas, New Mexico, not far from the Manzano mountains, one of the largest nuclear weapon arsenals of the United States. The photos were taken by Apolinar Villa on Sept. 24, 1972.

Drawing of a gigantic triangular UFO above Cabo Rojo in southwest Puerto Rico, seen on Dec. 20, 1988, and pursued by two F–14 Tomcat interceptors of the U.S. Navy. Before the eyes of thousands of witnesses the spaceship "swallowed up" both airplanes. Drawing by Jim Nichols.

Test flight of UFO in the desert of Nevada. Drawing by Jim Nichols according to information given by nucleur physicist Robert Lazar.

Artist Jim Nichols' painting of the Roswell crash. On July 7, 1947, the U.S. Army discovered the wreckage of a crashed spaceship and its four occupants. Three were dead, one was badly injured.

The author at the "debris field" near Roswell.

Life-size model of the surviving EBE of Rosewell exhibited in Montreal, Canada, based on real photos from the files of the U.S. Air Force.

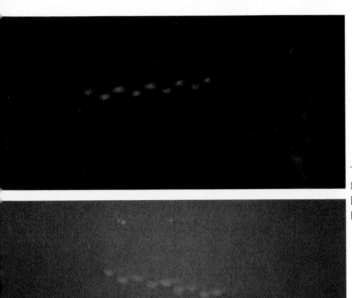

Two shots from the 8mm film which Martin D. shot on Aug. 2, 1979 in Hagen, Germany.

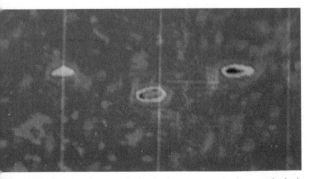

Sequence from Martin D.'s film, taken Mar. 6, 1980.

The GSW computer analysis (color contouring) concluded: These are 3 distinct objects in formation flight, about 2,500 feet from the camera.

A metallic disc chases a Phantom jet fighter above southern Germany. This photograph was made by high school director Dr. Karl Maier of Keltern-Weiler on Sept. 19, 1979 with a Polaroid camera.

Martin D. filmed a phosphorescent cigar-shaped object on Feb. 19, 1980, at about 10 p.m.

Cylindrical UFO photographed on June 4, 1980, at 2 p.m. by Martin D.

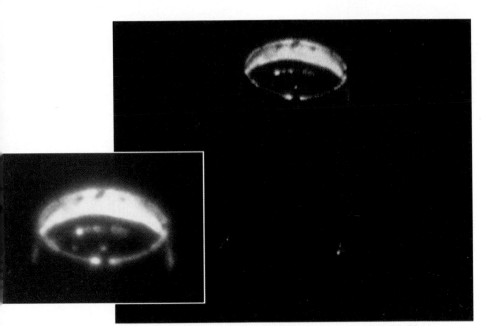

Apollo 12 - photo of a disc-shaped alien craft. NASA Photo No. AS12-50-7346.

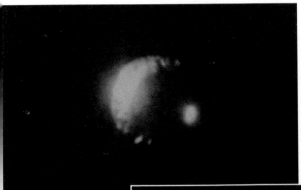

Official police photo of a disc-shaped craft taken near Lemittown, Puerto Rico at the end of 1980 by Police Officer Jose Cordero. In the first photo, the object passes the police vehicle at a low altitude...

...in the second, it flies away.

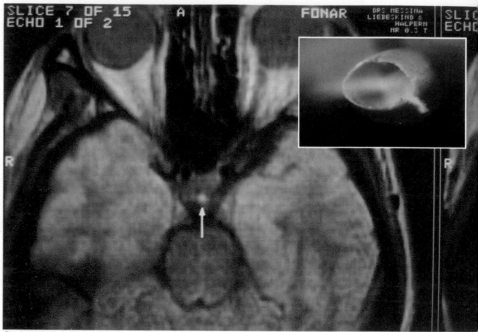

Brain scan showing "a 3 mm zone of intensity—an implant—in the skull of an abductee. (Pat Marcattilio)

inset: Implant under the electron microscope. (HUFON/Derrel Sims)

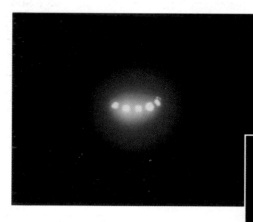

On July 7, 1981, at 8 p.m., four Puebla State Police officers photographed this craft hovering in front of them near Atlixco.

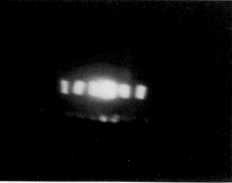

Three months later, on Oct. 31, 1991, Prof. Olquin and Dr. Carlos Perez photographed the same type of craft in Zacatelco, a small village between Tlaxcala and Puebla.

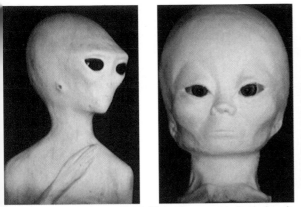

EBE typology. Left, reptiloid; Right, humanoid. Both heads were made according to descriptions given by eyewitnesses.

Jim Templeton's picture of his daughter and the "Cumbrian Spaceman" of May 23, 1964.

Big head, big eyes, slender bodies. Hundreds of witnesses all over the world have described the most frequently seen alien with these words.

Are we alone in the universe? Since October 12, 1992, dozens of electronic ears have been listening to signals sent out by extra-terrestrials, such as the one here at the "Very Large Array" (VLA) National Radio Astronomy Observatory near Magdalena, New Mexico.

tury AD, and which reads almost like instructions for constructing aircraft. *"The fuselage should be strong and durable, like a big flying bird, and of light metal. Inside it a mercury machine with its own heating apparatus should be installed. Through the latent energy of the mercury, which generates the driving whirlwind, a person sitting in the vehicle can cover long distances through the sky. On these principles, a Vimana the size of a temple can be built. The kinds of motion of a Vimana can be classified as follows: normal* (gradient) *ascent and descent, vertical ascent and descent, forwards, backwards, speed increasing with long distances . . . with the help of such machines, human beings can fly in the air and heavenly beings can visit the earth."* How these objects maneuver can be read in the epics of India.

The "Ramayana," an epic tale about the life and deeds of the Avatara Rama (incarnation of God Vishnu) composed during the 7th century BC—according to the Indian tradition even earlier—describes regular chases carried out with the help of Vimanas. Rama's Vimana *"had its own driving power. It was big. It had two decks and many chambers with windows"* and, at Rama's command, ascended into the clouds *"making a tremendous noise . . . high over hills and forested valleys . . . like an arrow shot from a bow, it races across the heavens, leaving forests and trees and water behind it and crosses the ocean . . . and reaches the island of Lanka."* And there the mighty Vimana of his opponent Ravana awaits him, *"glowing bright and frightening, throwing a jet of flame in the summer night, like a comet in the sky, surrounded by huge clouds."*

In the "Dronaparva," a chapter of the Indian national epic "Mahabharatha," written in the 8th century BC, one reads of *"Vimanas, the flying machines, spherical in form, which can hover at one position in the air. . . . Yudhishtira's Vimana came to a stop above the ground at a height of four fingers."* In flight, *"Vimanas had the form of hills . . . like a mass of blue clouds . . . in motion they resembled a swarm of migrating birds flying in formation."*

The "Ghatotrachapadma" describes a golden Vimana which, when it landed, looked like a beautifully shaped hill of antimony. And in the "Bhagavata Purana" (also called the "Srimad Bhagavatam"), one of the oldest holy texts of Vedic India, one reads of an aircraft built for King Salva by Maya Dhanava, a native of the lower planetary system.

This Vimana which Salva possessed was very mysterious. It was so unusual that it sometimes looked as if a number of aircraft were in the sky, and sometimes as if there was nothing there. It could appear, then become invisible, and the soldiers of the Yadus were perplexed about the position of the strange flying object. Sometimes they saw it on the ground and suddenly it was flying in the sky. Sometimes it looked as if it had landed on the peak of a mountain, then a second later it was floating on the water. This wonderful craft flew in the air like a glowworm in the wind. It never stood still, not even for a moment.

In fact, the Vimanas were vehicles of the gods and demigods who used them to travel "from heavenly planets" to Earth (there were a few exceptions when Vimanas were handed over to Earthlings). Interplanetary contacts were no seldom occurrences in the Vedic writings, for *"even as the common human beings travel on the surface of the Earth, so travel the demigods in heaven."*

The "Bhagavata Purana" describes how King Yudishtira celebrated a sacrifice with great pomp, at which *"demigods, the rulers of various planets,"* participated. And in the fourth canto it says that *"great sages, patriarchs and personalities of the heavenly planets came from their various planetary systems to Earth"* and on this occasion *"the domes of the city's palaces shone even as the domes of the beautiful aircraft which hover above the city. . . . The flying craft of the inhabitants of the heavens can be likened to the clouds in the skies ornamented by occasional flashes of lighting."*

In the same canto we read about the space travel of a maharaja. While he was flying through the universe, he could see, one after the other, all the planets of the solar system and, passing by, the demigods in their "Vimana" aircraft. The Puranas claim that at that time there were 400,000 people in the universe and that every planet was inhabited, either on the material or etheric plane. The spiritual knowledge of India itself, say the Puranas, was taught by visitors from higher planets. The American Sanskrit researcher Richard L. Thomson, in his standard work *Alien Identities,* shows on 480 pages the parallels between modern-day UFO phenomena and ancient Indian "divine encounters."

The oldest description of cosmic visitations can be found in the earliest writings of mankind, the Sumerian cuneiform texts. The city-states of Sumeria, which represent the earliest advanced culture of humanity, flourished between 3,800 and 2,000 BC in the south of present day Iraq. The first temples, and the earliest universities, hospitals and two-chamber parliaments arose in the country between the Euphrates and Tigris rivers, whose inhabitants were the first to possess a wide knowledge of writing, mathematics, literature, medicine, law and astronomy. The remarkable part of it is this: the Sumerian culture arose as if from nothing, had no early stages.

Where did the Sumerians get their knowledge? The cuneiform texts say from the "Anunnaki," their gods. But Anunnaki, translated literally, means "those who came from heaven to Earth" and, in fact, the myths of the Sumerians—which we know mostly from the copies found in the libraries of the Babylonians and Assyrians who took over their culture—describe space travel and the space vehicles of the Anunnaki.

One of them, the Etana epic, tells the story of Etana, king of Kish in the first centuries after the great flood. He journeyed through the skies "on the back of a heavenly eagle" and could thus get a bird's-eye view of the Earth. *"The earth was like a garden and the sea entered the land like channels that a gardener would make,"* he described it. Then, land and sea looked like "a cake in a breadbasket" and finally, the earth vanished completely. Etana became afraid, and asked his carrier: *"My friend, I do not want to go higher*

Heavenly ship on a royal seal of the Sumerians (Z. Sitchin, *The 12th planet*).

up in the skies, please stop, so that I can get back to the earth" and finally returned.

The Sumerian gods flew in heavenly ships, called "Mu" or "Din-Gir," from Heaven to the Earth, to every town in which they had a temple, which was their "home" here. Thus says a hymn to the Goddess Ishtar (Inanna),

> Oh mistress who,
> sitting in a Mu,
> joyfully swings high
> Up above in the sky!
> Over all places that lie
> On this earth you fly,
> Great Lady,
> riding in your Mu!

Their temple was a penthouse at the top of a Ziggurat, a temple pyramid. There, the priest regularly provided them with comfortable beds, costly clothing, fresh vegetables, beer (a Sumerian invention) or wine, delicious food and a young girl or, for the Goddess Ishtar or Inanna, a young man. Here, the God or Goddess received the King and the priests, gave them instructions, and taught them sciences. The Sumerians also knew why the gods felt responsible for the Sumerians. According to their creation stories, as told in the Atrahasis tablets, the Anunnaki created mankind 280,000 years ago, to serve them as "primitive workers." This they achieved by crossing *"the creature . . . that exists"*—the hominids, or forerunners of human beings—*"with the seed of the gods,"* thus creating a hybrid creature: half animal, half God.

The Sumerian creation story is considered to be the source of the Book of Genesis in the Bible and, in the First Book of Moses, Nephilim (literally, "those who came down") are mentioned: the "sons of God" who visited the Earth before and after the deluge. For quite some time now, researchers like Sir Desmond Leslie, Brinsley Le Poer Trench, the Earl of Cancarty and the great American orientalist, Zechariah Sitchin, have studied the episodes in the Old Testament and compared them with modern UFO reports. They have found astounding parallels. Thus, the Israelites, during their Exodus from Egypt, were led by a pillar of cloud during the day, and a pillar of fire during the night. When the Lord came down on the Sinai Mountain in a fire, to meet Moses and give him the Ten Commandments—as well as a number of instructions for the new nation—*"there was thunder and lightning, and a thick cloud on the mountain, and the voice of the trumpet was very loud,"* according to the Book of Exodus (19, 16). *"Now Mount Sinai was completely in smoke, because the Lord descended upon it in fire. Its smoke ascended like the smoke of a furnace and the whole mount quaked greatly."* (Ex. 19, 16)

The Prophet Elijah was taken up to heaven in a "chariot of fire" which rose into the skies *"by a whirlwind"* (2. Kings 2,11). The same thing must have happened to his predecessor Enoch, about whom the Bible only says, *"Enoch walked with God, and he was not; for God took him."* (Gen. 5:24). The Slavonic and Ethiopian Jews know of a Book of Enoch and meanwhile, fragments of this book dating back to the 2nd Century BC, found at Qumran near the Dead Sea, prove the antiquity of this text. According to a Jewish legend, Noah, Enoch's great-grandson, had saved this book from the flood by taking it with him into the Ark.

In this work, which consists of 108 chapters, Enoch, writing in the first person, describes how, during a certain night, he was visited by *"two very big men, such as he had never seen on Earth before,"* who invited him to go into the heavens with them. They then took him to a house made of *"crystalline stones, surrounded by tongues of fire,"* which took him to *"another house, bigger than the first,"* surrounded by lightning and circling stars. From there he saw—perhaps the first human being to do so—our Blue Planet from the sky. He gives unusually exact details about the orbits of the moon and the earth, about leap year days, stars, and astro-mechanics. Further he describes *"the places of lights,"* the *"estuaries of all the rivers of the earth,"* the *"winds of the heavens"* (today, one would say solar wind) the stars, and the sun. He then describes his journey to ten different "heavens"—planets?—on which human beings and animals lived. Then, he was taken to *"His Great Majesty"* who gave a message to mankind of the earth and warned him about the approaching flood.

But, in the Bible itself, there is a report that reminds us only too well of the descriptions of modern UFO contacts. It comes from the prophet Ezekiel who was in Babylon as a prisoner in 586 B.C. The following happened to him: *"in the thirtieth year on the fifth day of the fourth month, as I was among the captives by the river Che-bar, the heavens were opened . . . and I looked, and, behold, a whirlwind came out of the north, a great cloud and a fire infolding itself, and a brightness was about it, and out of the midst thereof as the color of amber, out of the midst of the fire. Also out of midst thereof came the likeness of four living creatures. And this was their appearance; they had the likeness of a man."* (Ez. 1,1–5)

Ezekiel relates how he saw a gleaming space vessel, then goes into detail and mentions concentric rings (*"behold one wheel upon the earth"*), and the body of the vessel (*"the likeness of the firmament upon the heads of the living creatures was as the color of the terrible crystal, stretched forth over their heads above"*) with a smaller dome above it (*"above the firmament . . . was the likeness of a throne"*).

A NASA engineer, Joseph Blumrich, has studied the description of the prophet and looked for technical information. His conclusion: *"It is the fully logical and sensible plan for the construction of a space vessel."* In his book *The Spaceships of Ezekiel* he published technical construction plans which he had made in accordance with the information given in the 2,600-year-old report. Four times, the hand of God overpowered Ezekiel (*"the hand of the Lord was strong upon me"*) and took him to various places including Tel-Abib, Jerusalem and a secret temple. Each time he received teachings and messages for his people: *"Then the spirit took me up, and I heard behind me a voice of a great rushing . . . I heard also the noise of the wings of the living creatures . . . and the noise of the wheels over against them . . . So the spirit lifted me up . . . Then I came to . . . Tel Abib."* (Ez. 3, 12–15)

The ancient Egyptians believed that their Gods sailed along the "celestial Nile," the Milky Way, in heavenly barques and visited the Earth regularly. Since for them, everything in Heaven had its parallel on Earth, they took statues of the Gods in barques on the Nile. They believed that their Pharaohs—descendants of the Gods—returned after death to their heavenly home in barques. Interestingly enough, the first government document about UFOs comes from Egypt.

The report, written on a papyrus fragment, was compiled by the court scribe of the Pharaoh Thutmosis III (1483–1450 B.C.) and discovered in the 19th century during excavations at Thebes. For years it was at the Vatican, in the private collection of Prof. Albert Tulli, the director of the Egyptian Section of the Vatican Museum. It was only after his death that Tulli's brother, Monsignore Gustavo of the Vatican Library, allowed the Egyptologist, Boris, Prince of Rachewiltz, to translate the text on the fragment. He identified it as being, without doubt, part of the Royal Annals:

In the third Winter month of the year 22 (counting from the coronation of Tutmosis III, therefore year 1462 BC) at the sixth hour of the day, the scribes in the House of Life noticed that a ball of fire came out of the sky. It had no head, but the breath from its mouth had an obnoxious smell. Its body was one rood long (approximately 135 feet) and one rood broad and it had no voice. The hearts of the scribes were filled with fear and confusion and they fell down on to the floor . . . (fragment destroyed) . . . they informed the Pharaoh. His Majesty ordered . . . was investigated . . . and he meditated over what had happened and what had been written down on the papyri in the House of Life. Now, after a few days had passed, behold! there were these things become more numerous in the sky than ever before. They appeared with more bright-

Biblical symbolic depiction of the vision of Ezekiel.

ness than the sun and stretched out till the borders of the four corners of the world . . . Powerfully they stood, these balls of fire in the sky. The army of the Pharaoh watched them with the Pharaoh himself in their midst. It was after the evening meal. Then, the balls of fire rose higher up in the sky towards the south. A wonder that was unknown since the establishment of this nation and the Pharaoh ordered that incense should be offered so that peace could reign on Earth . . . and whatever had happened was to be written, according to the order of the Pharaoh, in the annals of the House of Life . . . so that it would remain in memory forever.

We now go to the year 332 B.C. For 7 long months, the army of the victorious Macedonian king Alexander, to whose name historians later added "the Great," besieged the Phoenician city of Tyros. Tyros was a rich harbor city built on an island close to the coast, with which it was connected only by a narrow dam. The city walls were 50 feet high and were so solidly built that no machines of war at that time could do them any damage. The citizens of Tyros had engaged the best technicians and builders to construct the walls. Besides that, they had the most modern weapons for defense. The Macedonians had almost given up when a miracle occurred. Unknown beings interfered in history. The chronicler writes:

> Suddenly one day there appeared these flying shields, as they were named, above the camp of the Macedonians. They flew in triangular formation. At the apex was a very large one, the others were half so big. Slowly, they circled around Tyros while thousands of soldiers on both sides interrupted their fighting to watch the shields in astonishment. Suddenly, there came a flash of light from the largest ship, which hit the walls and caused them to collapse. Further flashes followed and destroyed walls and towers as if they had been built of mud, and made the way for the attackers free, who rushed into the town like an avalanche. The flying shields circled once more around the city until it had been totally stormed. Then, they just disappeared quickly, upwards into the blue sky.

When, three years later, the great Macedonian was trying to cross the river Jaxartes on the Indian border, the flying shields held him back. A historian writes that two strange flying machines kept diving at the army of the king, causing a panic among the soldiers, elephants and horses so that they refused to cross the river. The machines were described as big, shining shields, from which fire spewed, which came from heaven and returned to it.

Reports of strange appearances in the sky are known to us from the entire antique world. The Romans had seen the objects, too. Pliny writes that in the year 100 BC, *"a burning shield which sprayed sparks flew from the West towards the East at sunset."* According to the historians Julius Obsequence and L. Orosius, some time in 91 B.C. there raced *"at sunset a ball of fire across the sky, making a terrible noise. In Spoletium, a golden-colored ball of fire came down, before it again left the earth towards the east and was big enough to cover the disc of the sun."* After the death of Julius Caesar in 44 BC, people saw *"things in the shape of shields and bullets circling around in the sky."*

Palmyra in Syria was a rich commercial city during Roman times. It is described as a city of white marble, with a magnificent temple for the God Baal. Palmyra was situated like an oasis, on the old trade routes going to

Africa, Arabia, Europe and the land of two rivers. Costly wares were bartered and exchanged here and not a day went by without caravans coming in, loaded with goods from every part of the world as it was known then. On a certain day in the year 268 AD, according to the Italian historian Alberto Fenolio, there appeared in the sky above the city *"two great fiery spheres which rotated close to each other and suddenly went apart, during which they shot out beams of light in directions. One of them, as if it was itself in danger, came down and flew at lightning speed across the city so that the temperature suddenly rose and many palms were burned. The skirmish continued for a period. The spheres chased and shot at each other with lightning until one of the spheres disappeared in a huge cloud from which stones and pieces of the destroyed object fell down on the sand, while the other sphere disappeared into the heavens."*

In the 8th century AD, Germany was in the throes of war. The Christian Franks, led by Charlemagne, who had been crowned Holy Roman Emperor in the year 800 AD, was fighting in the region known today as Westfalia, against the heathen Saxons. The Franks were victorious and, in 772 AD, Eresburg, the chief shrine of the Saxons with its sacred ash tree "Irminsul," faced destruction. But the Saxons did not give up. While Charlemagne was fighting in Italy, they succeeded in retaking Eresburg in 776 AD and, encouraged by this, they laid siege to Sigiburg (today Hohensyburg, near Dortmund). In the *Annales regni Francorum* we find the following passage:

"But the might of God overcame them righteously. For, on a certain day, as they were getting ready to fight the Christians in the fort, the Glory of God made itself manifest above the roof of the church inside the fort, which many saw from outside as well as from inside, many of whom are still living today. They said they saw something like two big red shields surrounded by flames, moving above the church, and when the heathens outside the fort saw this sign, they were frightened and confused and fled to their camp."

Still in panic, they fled until they reached the river Lippe, where the Franks overtook them and wiped them out. As in the case of Alexander the Great, once more, flying shields had intervened in history. But who controlled them?

Einhard, Charlemagne's secretary and biographer, described in chapter 32 of his biography *Vita Caroli Magni*, a strange encounter of the Emperor in the year 810. On the way to Aachen, Charlemagne suddenly saw a great big sphere shooting down from the sky and then flying towards the east towards him. His horse was frightened by this and reared up, throwing the Emperor off his saddle and injuring him badly.

In the first section of Charlemagne's *Capitularien*, heavy punishment is ordered for the sylphs, the airy spirits who traveled around the country in their aircraft; they were held responsible for destroying the harvest of the farmers. How that came about is described by the Abbé Montfaucon de Villars, in his book, *Le Compte de Gabalis*. Zedekias, cabbalist and wizard, who was in contact with the sylphs, wanted to prove their (the sylphs) existence to the people. So he requested the sylphs to show themselves to all the people. They did this splendidly. One saw the creatures in human form in the air, often moving in battle formation, in air vehicles of remarkable construction. But, Zedekias's plan failed; the people were panic-stricken and, in their superstition, believed the sylphs were evil demons and magicians responsible for all the storms, hail and bad harvests. They were supported in this by the Emperor and the Church, who expressly condemned these intruders. Abbé de Villars said:

> When it became clear to the air beings to what extent they had excited the people and what animosity they had evoked, they lost their senses to such an extent that they landed their big ships and took some of the best men and women on board to teach them and dispel the bad opinion the people had about them. . . . But, when these men and women came back to the earth, they were regarded as demonic beings who had come to spread poison on the fields. So, they were quickly arrested and, after being put through the worst forms of torture prescribed for those who practice the arts of the devil, they were executed . . . Others also had to suffer the same fate. The number of the unfortunate ones who were executed by fire and water was very high indeed.

Besides that, at Lyons, three men and a woman were seen to come out of one

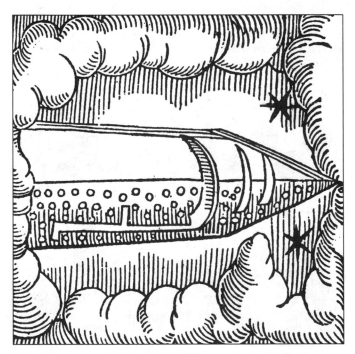

This object was seen in Arabia in 1479 according to the *Prodigies Chronicles* by Conrad Lycosthenes.

of these air vehicles. The whole town gathered around them and called out, "They're magicians! Grimond, the Duke of Benevent, Charlemagne's enemy, has sent them to destroy the state of the Franks!' The four innocent ones explained that they too belonged to the same country and had been kidnapped by strange beings, who had shown them unbelievably wonderful things and requested them to spread news of that.

Agobard, the Bishop of Lyons, came in time to prevent these contactees from being lynched by the people. He dismissed the whole affair as being simply unbelievable and impossible. The crowd had calmed down and the four went free. In spite of an injunction not to do so, they still kept talking about their strange encounter with the aliens, who came from a distant world called Magonia. But, after this bad experience with human beings, the sylphs withdrew for the time being.

Nevertheless, there were UFO sightings until the beginning of the modern era. On April 14, 1561, between 4:00 and 5:00 in the morning, hundreds of citizens in Nuremberg, Germany, saw a frightening picture on the rising sun. An eyewitness, the printer Hanns Glaser, described it in a leaflet he himself had printed: *"There were balls of blood red, blue and iron-black color or ring-like discs in large numbers in the neighborhood of the sun, sometimes three in a row, sometimes four in a square, also many isolated. Between these balls were also a large number of crosses in the color of blood."* There were also *"2 big tubes in which were 3 or even 4 balls"* as well as a long object like a big black spear."* On April 7, 1566, a number of black spheres appeared in the air

Leaflet printed by Samuel Caucius. "On August 7, 1566, at sunrise, many black balls were seen in the air which raced towards the sun."

above Basel, Switzerland. They travelled at high speed towards the sun, then disappeared.

In the 17th century, the Belgian Jesuit Father Albert d'Orville journeyed to Tibet—being one of the first Europeans to do so—which was then mainly a land of legends. In his diary, we find the following entry, made during his stay at Lhasa:

1661, November. My attention was drawn to something which moved in the sky. At first, I thought it was an unknown kind of bird which lived in this land, until the thing came nearer, and took the form of a double Chinese hat. While it flew silently, as if it were carried by invisible wings, it was certainly a wonder—magic. The thing flew over the town as if it wanted to be admired, flew twice in circles and was then enveloped in fog, and disappeared. No matter how much one strained one's eyes, it could not be seen. I asked myself whether the high elevation had played a trick on me, when I noticed a lama quite near, and asked him whether he had seen it too. After he assented with a nod of his head, he said to me, "My son, what you have seen was not magic. Beings from other worlds have been traveling through the oceans of space for centuries, and brought spiritual light to the first human beings who populated the earth. They condemned all violence and taught the people to love one another, although these teachings were like seeds sowed on stone and could not sprout. These beings, who are fair-skinned, always receive a friendly welcome from us. They land often in the vicinity of our cloisters. They teach us and reveal things to us which have been lost to us because of the cataclysms of the past centuries, which have changed the face of the earth."

Four years later, on the April 8, 1665, 6 fishermen of Stralsund, Germany and their companions noticed a similar appearance in Europe. After catching fish at about 2:00 o'clock in the morning, they saw, *"in the middle of the sky, a flat, round form like a plate and like a big man's hat upturned came before their eyes of colors like when the moon is eclipsed standing above St. Nicholas' church."* In the same year a print was published in Hamburg, Germany which shows a cylindrical and a cigar-shaped object in the sky over the town, described as *"a phenomenon observed in the sky by the author here in Hamburg from the sixth to the sixteenth of July during the current year 1665, to the report of the nobleman Herr Joseph Ernst von Raufenstein, Minister of the State and representative of Neuburg at the Regensburg Parliament. In the year 1665, truly signed by Hans Martin Winterstein. Lord give us peace in our days."*

A dotted line points out the house of the witness on the Jungfernstieg promenade in Mühlendamn. Thirty two years later, in 1697, *"a brightly shining circular machine with a sphere in the middle"* flew over Hamburg and other cities in North Germany

A similar thing happened in France. On June 7, 1779, the citizens dove of Boulogne, France saw a number of glowing discs in the sky. A gigantic sphere dove down from the sky on June 12, 1790, near Alencon,

On April 8, 1665, six fishermen saw above Stralsund the vision of
fighting ships, and then "a plate which was shaped like a hat fell
down from the heavens."

rubbed against a hill while landing and tore out some plants. When the
object had landed, the dry grass began to burn. Dozens of inhabitants of
the place ran there to put out the fire when they saw the glowing sphere.
The villagers stood around the strange object, astonished. A few brave
ones dared to approach it and touch it, when suddenly a door opened and
a man came out, who looked quite normal except for his strange clothing. He said something which they could not understand, before rushing
off into the nearby forest. Anxiously, the people withdrew from the
sphere. After that it exploded noiselessly and nothing was left except
powder. Nor could the mysterious man be found. The revolutionary government in Paris took the case so seriously that they sent a police inspector by the name of Liabeuf to Alencon.

On April 18, 1808, Signor Simondo, secretary of the Justice of Peace in
the North Italian town of Torre Pellice, was woken up by a continuous high-
pitched hum. When he looked out of the window, he couldn't believe his

Mysterious spheres above Hamburg. Woodcut dating from 1667.

eyes: he saw a shining disc rising from the meadow opposite. Before he could properly understand what was happening, the disc had risen and vanished in the sky at a high speed.

Strange flying objects flew over Embrum in southern France on September 7, 1820, in an awe-inspiring, unbroken formation. They flew first in a straight line then turned off at right angles, whereby they maintained the formation.

Near Sicily, the crew of the British ship S. S. Victoria saw, on June 18 1845, at a distance of about 900 yards, 3 shining discs coming out of the sea and rising up. They were visible for about 10 minutes. They were 5 times as big as the moon and it looked as if they were bound to one another by beams of light, as the captain wrote in his log book. As it turned out, this phenomenon had been seen by various ships within a radius of 1,000 miles.

When an exhibition was opened at Hyde Park, in London, on September 4, 1851, a large number of bright discs flew over the area from east to west . . . and these are only a few examples from the extensive UFO chronicles of the period of enlightenment and industrialization.

It was only towards the end of the 18th century that astronomers started observing the neighboring celestial bodies in a scientific and concentrated manner. While reading their reports, what strikes us in the higher-than-average frequency with which unusual appearances and flying objects have been seen in the vicinity of the moon. During a lunar eclipse on September 7, 1820, when the reflected light of the moon had diminished appreciably, French astronomers noticed strange objects close to it which moved in straight lines with military precision at equal distances from each other. During another eclipse, on August 7, 1869, similar objects wandered across the surface of the moon in straight and parallel lines. In 1873, the royal British Society of Astronomy reported that for many months, flashing lights had been seen on the moon, which they took to be intelligent attempts by an unknown race from the moon to establish contact. In April of the following year, Prof. Schafarik of the Prague observatory reported an object *"of such a strange nature that I do not know what to make of it. It was bright white and moved slowly across the face of the moon. I saw it even after it had left the disc of the moon. In other words, the object was no part of the moon because it left the moon behind and wandered out into space. What else can it be other than a flying machine?"* What was happening on the moon? It took almost another century until the first man landed on the satellite of the Earth and brought a possible answer.

CHAPTER 13

Russians Solve UFO Mystery

On October 9, 1989, an announcement circled the globe which, like so many others during that historical year, signaled a wind of change that was sweeping through Europe and the rest of the world. It was the year in which the Iron Curtain fell, in which human masses swept away the rigid structures of eastern dictatorships, the year in which the Brandenburg Gate in Berlin was opened. This climate of glasnost, the new openness which the Soviet Secretary-General Mikhail Gorbachev had insisted upon, made possible what was unthinkable until then. The official Soviet news agency Tass officially announced the landing of a UFO.

Artist's impression of the the Voronesh UFO landing, drawn by Detlef Menningman.

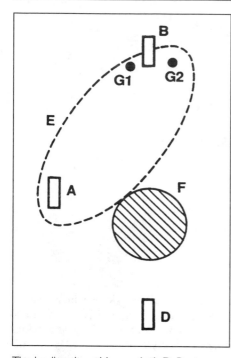

The landing site at Voronesh. A-D: Rectangular imprints of the landing feet; E: Flattened grass; F: Epicenter: here the radioactivity was found to be twice as strong as the surroundings; G1, G2: 40cm-deep vertical holes left by the ladder.

"Soviet scientists have confirmed the landing of an unknown flying object in a park in the Russian city of Voronesh. They have also identified the site of landing and found tracks of extraterrestrials who had gone for a short walk through the park. The aliens visited this spot at least 3 times, each time shortly after night had fallen, say the local residents. The citizens of Voronesh saw a big shining dome above the park. According to eyewitnesses, the UFO landed, a door opened, and 1, 2, or 3 humanoid beings and a smaller robot came out. The aliens were 9 to 12 feet tall with very small heads, say the witnesses. They walked around near the sphere or disc and then disappeared inside it. The onlookers were overcome by fear, which lasted for many days. 'We identified the site of landing with the help of bio-location,' declared Genrikh Silanov, chief of the Geophysical Institute of Voronesh, during an interview. "We found a circle of about 60 feet in diameter. Four 1½ to 2 inch deep indentations, each with a diameter of about 6 inches, were clearly recognizable and were located at the 4 corners of a rhombus. We took samples of strange-looking stones. At first they looked like dark sandstone, but chemical analysis showed that the substance could be found nowhere on earth. However, further investigations are necessary before we come to any final conclusions.'

Silanov used bio-location to find the route taken by the aliens when they walked on the earth. The eyewitnesses knew nothing about this experiment, but their description of which way the aliens went conformed with the scientific results. Further, the people of Voronesh reported seeing a banana-shaped object in the sky which carried a shining sign."

Voronesh is a small industrial town with 900 inhabitants, some 300 miles southeast of Moscow. The incident occurred on September 27, a warm day early in autumn, at 6:30 p.m. at Yuzhniy Park (South Park) on the Mendelejev road, in the district of Levonerezhniy. Two children from the nearby

The children of Voronesh: Lena Sarokina; Vasya Surin; Vova Startsev; Alyosha Nikonov.

"School no. 33," Vasya Surin, 11, and Genya Blinov, 11, were playing soccer in the park. Julia Sholokhova, 11, and a few other girls were playing hide-and-seek, and about 20 adults were standing near a bus stop on the road. Suddenly all of them saw a pink light in the evening sky from which a dark red sphere came out; and descended slowly. It lasted perhaps a minute until the sphere, about 30 feet in diameter, was floating and circling over the park at a height of about 50 feet. An invisible force field flattened the grass on the ground. Shortly after that the sphere shot off. A few minutes later a second UFO appeared and descended. Meanwhile, everybody around was watching it, fascinated, from a safe distance. They were watching it hover above a group of poplars, when a hatch opened and a huge being appeared who seemed to take stock of the area. The being did not have any head: instead of that was a hump between the shoulders with three shining eyes, of which the middle one seemed to look here and there. The hatch door closed and the object came closer with a humming sound. It stopped about 3 feet above the ground, hovered with a swaying movement like a falling leaf between the trees and shone brightly. Then it put out four landing struts, came down slowly and landed. The object was egg-shaped, about 45 feet long, 15 to 18 feet in diameter and bore on its side a sign, a sort of H with a middle stroke like the Cyrillic "zh," and it had ports. To those who were standing in front of it, it seemed more like a sphere. A trapdoor opened, a ladder came out and two frightening beings appeared.

One was about 9 to 12 feet in height, was dressed in a silvery space suit and moved stiffly like a robot. Behind it came an actual robot, a box with arms and legs and shining knobs on its breast. The "giant" made a noise upon which a shining rectangle, about 4 × 2 feet in size appeared on the ground and, shortly after, at a signal from the being, disappeared. Now the smaller robot pressed a button on the bigger one, and its eyes and 3 lights on its stomach began to shine. At this moment, one of the boys, Genya, began to cry out aloud. The bigger robot looked at him without turning its head— it directed its middle eye towards the boy. A beam of light shot out of that eye and hit the boy, who could not move for many minutes after that. Now the whole group cried out. For minutes after that, the UFO and the robots vanished from sight. Then they were there again, the giant now with a 4-foot long pipe in his hand. He pointed it towards a 16-year-old boy who dared to come a bit closer to the UFO than the others and, to the horror of the onlookers, the boy vanished. The "things" turned around and went slowly up the steps back into their ship. The port closed, the craft rose with increasing speed, tilted and shot off into the skies, finally disappearing. At that moment the 16-year-old boy reappeared all of a sudden. What was left of the craft were traces in the grass, indents of the 4 landing struts on the 4 corners of the rhombus. In the center was an oval patch of flattened grass, at one end 2 smaller holes where the ladder had been set on the ground—exactly like the case 25 years before that right after the landing at Socorro, New Mexico.

The first scientist to investigate the landing site was Prof. Genrikh Silanov, a physicist of the laboratory for spectral analysis at the Geophysical Institute of Voronesh. He measured the imprints in the ground, which were 6 inches in diameter and about 2 inches in depth. He reported later: *"The ground there was hard as stone, and we estimated that the object which had landed there must have weighed at least 11 tons."* In addition, at the middle of the rhombus he could measure increased radioactivity. The average level of radiation in the area was 10 to 15 micro-Rontgens per hour, but at this spot they measured 30 to 37 micro-Roentgens per hour. The middle spot showed other anomalies as well: increased magnetic field and a remarkable absence of microorganisms (about one-tenth of what was found in samples taken from the surrounding area).

Meanwhile, the aircraft engineer, Alexander Mosolov, who belonged to the local investigation commission for anomalous phenomena, interviewed the witnesses. A year later when the French astrophysicist Jacques Vallee visited Voronesh, Mosolov told him *"we began with investigations the very next day. We started with the schoolchildren and asked each one separately what had happened. We recorded every interview on video. Their reports confirmed one another in all details."*

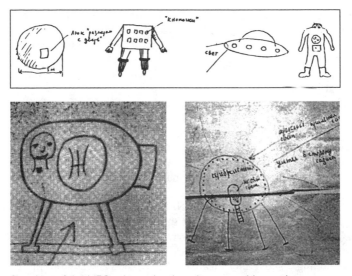

Sketches of the UFOs drawn by the witnesses at Voronesh.

The mayor of Voronesh, who had spoken to the children said, *"I don't have the impression that they invented the story. I believe them."* Col. Ludmilla Makarova of the local police conceded, *"I don't know what happened here and why, but the high radioactivity which we measured is proof enough that something unusual occurred at the spot."*

A UFO over Voronesh on November 8, 1989. (Photograph: A. Petrov)

More and more reports came in from witnesses who had seen the UFO flying over the town. Respectable citizens like Valentina Agibalova, manager of the state bank, Inna Nikitina, employee of the powerhouse at Voronesh, Yuli Sviridov, chief engineer of the Electrical-Institute, and Lt. Sergei Malvryev of the Voronesh militia, claimed to have seen the red-lit sphere at 7:00 p.m.

And soon it came out that the incident of September 27, 1989, was only one of a series: during the period September 21–October 30, seven different landings could be documented at Voronesh. The first had occurred on September 21 at 8:30 p.m. and had proceeded almost exactly as did the one that had taken place a week later. Here a sphere with a 15-foot diameter came down and landed in the same park. This time two giants and a robot stepped out, said the witnesses, four 13-year-old boys who were playing in the park: A. Lukin, Y. Levchenko, S. Borisenko and R. Torchin. A similar thing happened again 4 weeks after the first historic landing. This time on the 20th of October, 13-year-old Vova Startsev and his friends from the school were going home, when they saw a pulsating pink sphere which flew at an angle above their heads and bore the "zh" symbol on it.

"It flew low past the street-light and landed," said Vova. *"On the left side it had two antennae. It stood on four struts. A hatch opened, a ladder slid out and two beings and a robot came out. The two aliens carried the robot, set it on its feet and started it, after which it could move like a human being. It ran towards me followed by the other aliens. It was just about two feet tall and offered me its hand when I got frightened. I ran away and climbed up the nearest tree trembling with fear. The aliens had big heads, twice the size of ours, and three eyes in a row."* One of Vova's friends, Sergei Makarov, added that the beings had silvery suits with silvery buttons, and that their boots were also silvery. The color of their skin was dark brown and smooth. A blinding light shone out of the spacecraft, too bright to enable one to see what was inside the object. Finally the visitors went back to their ship, withdrew their landing struts, hovered for a few seconds above the lawn and then rose and disappeared.

Another landing occurred in the parking lot in front of a new nuclear power plant which was still being built, and caused the asphalt there to melt.

There was another landing at the Voronesh airport, and a witness, Igor Yadigin (29), even claimed that the tall crew of the shining sphere had telepathically projected a warning to him, showing pictures of an ominous repetition of the Chernobyl catastrophe, if this power plant were connected to the power supply system. Yadigin reported his experience to the local KGB office and he was told that they would send a report to Gorbachev. As a matter of fact the further construction of the power plant was stopped soon after that, perhaps owing to this occurrence.

Apart from the fact that the landings at Voronesh are amongst the best-attested encounters of the third kind in the 50-year-old history of this phenomenon, they had an almost historic character for another reason. Perhaps it was "the news of the year" as the *New York Times* described it, for through the experiences of Voronesh the public in the West was for the first time aware that UFOs appeared behind the Iron Curtain as frequently as they did in the West. And finally it drew the attention of western researchers to the Soviet UFO investigations, which by then had made appreciable progress. Two weeks after the "Tass" announcement, a 5-man Soviet delegation of experts, including "Tass" representative Sergei Bulantsev, took part in the UFO world conference "Dialogue with the Universe," held in Frankfurt, Germany. From then onwards an east-west dialogue regarding UFOs began, which continues even today.

It is owing to this fact that we are in a position to reconstruct the story of UFO research in the Soviet Union. For suddenly people in the Soviet Union started talking openly about things which until then had been kept strictly secret. It seemed as if the nightmare of Prof. J. Alan Hynek, the advisor of the U.S. Air Force in UFO matters, had come true. He had confessed during an interview with the magazine *Playboy* in 1969, that he was plagued by a nightmare. He was afraid of getting up in the morning and reading in the papers the headline "Russians Solve UFO Mystery." Night after night he dreamed that the Russians would come up with a surprising explanation for the UFOs, or even worse, report a first contact with alien civilizations. Hynek believed that both events would shake America to its foundations.

The story begins in early 1948, during the time of Stalin, when the dictator asked a leading scientist of his country to come to the Kremlin. The scientist was Professor Sergei Korolyev, a member of the Academy of Sciences. He was the Soviet counterpart of Wernher von Braun, and had designed the rockets with which the Sputnik and later Yuri Gagarin were taken into space. What Korolyev meant to Soviet science is shown not only by his innumerable decorations, including the Order of Lenin, but also by the fact that he was later on for many years President of the Academy of Sciences of the USSR. At the Kremlin, Korolyev was initiated into his task by high-ranking government officials. They had received a lot of material and analyses of press reports from the USA through the KGB, and Stalin wanted him to evaluate these within 3 days. The fundamental question was: do these objects represent a threat to the security of the Soviet Union? Korolyev was given an office at the Kremlin; it was strictly forbidden for him to take the files home, and a team of translators was there to help him.

There were piles of newspaper articles, long comments and reports about research done by the KGB. They dealt with the sighting of Kenneth Arnold, the Rhodes-photos, and American speculation about the flying saucers, such as whether they could be Soviet secret weapons which, of course, they were not. But the most interesting report was about one special event, the possible crash of a flying disc at Roswell, New Mexico, in the United States. That had been openly announced on July 8, 1947, by the press officer of Roswell Army Air Force Base, and withdrawn the very next day by the commander of the 8th Air Force at Fort Worth, Texas, Brig. Gen. Roger Ramey, saying that the UFO had only been a simple weather balloon.

The KGB regarded this as a cover-up story. The members of the 509th bomber group of the 8th Air Force which had recovered the wreck were considered to be the best-trained unit of the U.S. Army Air Force and had repeatedly been sent out on secret missions. They had dropped the atom bombs on Hiroshima and Nagasaki, had flown the latest types of aircraft, and were certainly capable of differentiating between a simple weather balloon and a flying saucer.

Three days later when Prof. Koroliev met Stalin he had formulated an opinion: *"Now, what are your conclusions?"* asked the dictator. The professor answered saying, *"I think we can rule out the possibility of their being secret weapons of the United States or of any other nation on Earth. I don't think that they represent a threat to the Soviet Union. There is no sign of any hostile intentions, but I am convinced that they are real, that flying saucers exist. I would therefore suggest, Comrade Secretary-General, the starting of a scientific study."*

"That's what the other experts said, too, to whom I presented this material for survey," said Stalin and expressed his thanks to Korolyev.

Later the professor learned who these other experts were: the academy member, Prof. Mstislav Keldysh, a mathematician and physicist, Prof. Alexander Topchiev, and two other top scientists who were later to become presidents of the academy of sciences.

As the United States knew already in 1952 through the double agent Yuri Popov, Stalin instructed the military secret service GRU (Glavnoye Razvedivatelnoye Upravleniye), the highest directorate of the intelligence service of the general staff, under the secret service number UZ-11/14, to get the following information immediately:

Re the UFOs:
a. *secret weapons of foreign powers*
b. *deliberate false information given out by imperialistic secret services.*
c. *manned or unmanned extraterrestrial intruders with the aim of investigating the earth, or*
d. *unknown natural phenomenon?*

At about the same time, the first UFO reports of the USSR started coming in. On July 16, 1948, the military pilot Arkadi Apraskin, a highly decorated World War II pilot, was flying in the neighborhood of the testing area Kapustin Yar in the Bakuntshak region. His mission was to fly a newly developed jet aircraft. He had been about half an hour in the air when, at a height of about 32,000 feet, he saw an object shaped like a cucumber, which sent out cones of light. Apraskin reported his observation to the tower, which confirmed that its radar had spotted it, too. *"Try to identify it and ask it to land,"* were his orders now, *"and if it resists, open fire."* He got as far as about 6 miles from the object, when it sent out a beam of light directly to his cockpit. The ray opened up like a fan and blinded him. At the same moment, the current supply to the control panel failed completely, and a few seconds later the motor also stopped running. Thanks to his consummate skill he was able to bring his machine down in a glide and land safely. While getting out of the cockpit, he saw the object departing at a tremendous speed.

The detailed report which Apraskin wrote about this incident went to Moscow. Soon after that a member of an investigation commission of the Ministry of Defense came to Kapustin Yar, interviewed the pilot and exmined his aircraft. He was then sent to a base in the Polar Circle where they showed him a report from a colleague who had also seen a UFO: Apraskin's experience was indeed not unique. During the following years, hundreds of similar reports arrived at the Defense Ministry, and many of them came from prominent pilots who were "heroes of the Soviet Union." One of them was the famous Polar flyer W. I. Akkuratov who sent the following report to the defense ministry personally:

> In August 1950 when we were stationed at Nishniye Kresti (Colima on the Arctic coast of northern Russia) and were digging in the ice, we noticed a disc flying over our settlement more than once over a period of 3 days and nights. It crossed the horizon in the south and was a bit smaller than the full moon. Normally this disc came at 3:30 p.m. and was observed by all the people in the settlement, especially by us pilots, with great interest.
>
> After we reported this to Moscow we received orders to follow the disc at the next opportunity in our seaplane "Katalin" and study it as thoroughly as we could. We went up to 21,000 feet, the maximum that the Katalin can do. When we approached the disc, we noticed that its size did not change, and that it was crossing from east to west slowly. It had the color of pearl, with blinking sides, without antennae or other protuberances. At 5:30 p.m. the disc rose higher and flew on towards the west beyond our visual range.

And in fact the other big power, the United States, could soon convince itself first hand that UFO sightings in the USSR were just as frequent as in the West. At the invitation of the Kremlin, the U.S. senator Richard Russel (Republican from Georgia), accompanied by staff officer Lt. Col. Hathaway of the Defense Committee of the Senate, and Ruben Efron, an advisor to the Committee, travelled right across the Soviet Union in October 1955. They went by train from Moscow through Bakuv, Tblissi, Dnieprpetrovsk, the Black Sea area and finally Kiev, and from there by plane to Prague, where they landed on October 12, 1955.

At about 7:10 p.m. on October 4, this delegation was in the train going from Atjati to Adzhyiabul when they saw *"a genuine flying saucer"*: a flat disc with two lights on the sides of a dome, surrounded by a ring rotating in the clockwise direction, which rose slowly, almost vertically, until it reached a height of about 6,000 feet. Then it accelerated very quickly and raced off in a northern direction where it disappeared. But the spectacle was not over. A minute later, a second saucer appeared and carried out the same maneuver as the first. Another thing that surprised the delegation: from a place in the

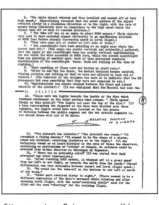

Official report about the sighting of "a genuine flying saucer," by a U.S. Senate delegation which was traveling through Russia. This incident convinced the U.S. authorities that UFO sightings were also made behind the Iron Curtain.

vicinity of the starting spot, some 1½ to 2 miles away from the train tracks, there were two searchlights directed almost vertically into the sky. Apparently a nearby military base had also seen the objects. A very excited train conductor came into the compartment suddenly, closed the curtains and told the Americans not to look out. After his arrival in Prague, Senator Russel told the Air Force attaché of the American embassy at Prague, Lt. Col. Thomas S. Ryan, about this incident, whereupon the latter immediately sent a report to the Pentagon. *"The significance of this report . . . is remarkable and lends credence to many 'saucer' reports,"* wrote Ryan in a memorandum classified as top secret.

Although sightings of "flying saucers" in the USSR were frequent, more concrete information about their possible origin could be gotten only towards the end of the 1950s, when the first inner space satellite monitoring systems were developed to keep track of the Sputniks. These radar systems were naturally capable of recognizing not only satellites but also meteorites—and another particular kind of flying craft. Thus they localized objects of many hundreds of feet in length which flew at heights of about 200 miles at speeds going up to 45,000 miles an hour.

The scientists responsible for watching these radar systems made a catalogue of flying objects and sent it to Prof. Korolyev who was working with the government commission on the matter of UFOs. The commission came to the conclusion, just as project Sky Sweep did a few years before that, that apparently mother vessels were placed in orbit, which brought the saucers to the Earth from throughout the universe. In 1965, at the international telecommunications congress in Moscow, a Soviet scientist declared to his western colleagues that they had found three unknown satellites in orbit around the Earth, but officially there was silence about these discoveries.

The Soviet policy of silence in the matter of UFOs began in 1952 with the speech given by M. Perwukhin, member of the presidium of the central committee of the Communist party of Russia. This speech, following the tradition of the times, included a blow directed at the arch enemy. With biting irony, Mr. Perwukhin said *"let me emphasize that flying saucers and green balls appeared first in America."* It was the unwritten law of the Soviet Union that such a speech determined the party line, which everybody had to follow, for the party was always right. After that, all the party media, and that meant all the media in the USSR, knew how they were to deal with the UFO problem. *"Flying saucers are mythical and appear all the time in the pages of the bourgeois press, when the ruling political group of one or the other of the capitalistic countries, on instructions from Washington, attempts to get the acceptance from their population for a new raise in the defense budget,"* said Radio Moscow on December 29, 1953.

The first attempts to discuss the UFO theme openly and scientifically were therefore frustrated. The father of the attempt to break through the silence was Felix Zigel. He was a professor at the Moscow Institute of Aeronautics and Astronautics, and also scientific instructor for the cosmonauts, whose textbooks on physics he had written together with Prof. W. Burdakov. During his work at the Institute, the only book about UFOs which had been officially published in Russian before glasnost fell into his hands. It was an anti-UFO book called *Flying Saucers*, written by the Harvard astronomer, Prof. Donald H. Menzel, who maintained that all UFO phenomena were misinterpretations of natural phenomena. But it was the cases that Menzel described, and not his interpretation, that fascinated Zigel. He felt that it was his responsibility as a scientist to investigate this phenomenon thoroughly.

This feeling became a compulsion when, in 1967, the Soviet Union experienced a wave of UFO sightings. At first he collected and analyzed dozens of Russian UFO sightings. Then, on May 17, 1967, he founded the first scientific UFO study commission, which was led by him and Maj. Gen. Portfiri Stolyarov. To this group belonged a whole group of famous scientists, military personnel, authors and celebrities, including Prof. Genrikh Ludwig; Dr. Nikolai Shirov; Dr. Igor Betuchev; Valentine Akkuratov, chief navigator of the Soviet polar flights and twice "hero of the Soviet Union"; Dr. Eng. Gregory Shivkov, and the "heroines of the Soviet Union" Dr. Ekatarina Riabova and Dr. Natalia Kravtsova. Together with the All-Unions Committee for Cosmonautics and the DOCAAF (Voluntary Organization for Support of the Army, Navy and Air Force), he conducted the first Soviet UFO congress on October 18 with over 400 participants, including highly respected scientists, astronomers and cosmonauts.

Whereas the Defense Ministry confirmed to Gen. Stolyarov the existence of voluminous files regarding UFOs, they refused to release them to him. Then he and Prof. Zigel were invited to the state-owned television station on November 10, 1967, to appear at the peak broadcasting time. There the general and the professor for the first time officially informed the public about the establishment of the Department of UFOs in the All-Unions Committee for Cosmonautics, with a staff of 18 scientists and Air Force officers, as well as over 200 ground observers in all parts of the land, and appealed to the public to help them in their work.

"The assumption that UFOs come from other worlds must be considered seriously," said Zigel. He cited the latest reports from military pilots and astronomers, and showed the sketch of a UFO landing in the Caucasus. *"It is important that we put aside all our prejudices about UFOs."* The broadcast triggered an avalanche. Claimed as a breakthrough all over the world-even the *New York Times* reported it in detail under the headline *"Soviet Astronomer Calls for World Study About Flying Saucers."* This set off a proper UFO fever in Russia, and thousands of letters, amongst them hundreds of sighting reports, came to the commission.

But this reaction met with the disapproval of the scientific establishment and the Communist Party. On November 22, an extraordinary meeting of the Academy of Sciences was called in Moscow, during which they came to the conclusion that *"the enormous publicity given to the UFO project affects the honor of all Russian scientists and makes them look ludicrous in the eyes of their western colleagues."* The UFO department was urged to stop its activities at once. On November 28, a crisis commission of the Department of General Physics and Astronomy of the Academy of Sciences, in consultation with the Central Committee of the Communist Party, laid down guidelines for critical evaluation: the tenor was that the belief in UFOs had no scientific basis, and that the observed phenomena could certainly be explained as arising from natural causes. From then on the press was forbidden to write anything about UFOs again.

After the UFO department was disbanded in March 1968, Prof. Zigel continued his research on a private basis. After all, he had collected an enormous amount of material, over 20,000 cases, enough to write a book. In 1976 he gave his manuscript "UFOs Over the USSR" to the Commission of the Councillor of the Moscow Institute for Air and Space Travel with the

UFO over a lake in the middle Urals, 1976. Photograph taken by S. Moskovskikh.

request for permission to publish it. That was a brave step but it brought him only the derision of his colleagues. Overnight he became for them a persona non grata. The investigating commission came to the conclusion that though his activities as lecturer were to be judged positively, his UFO research had, however, no scientific value. He was officially warned in regard to the lectures he had given on his own initiative.

On November 10, 1976, Zigel was expelled from the scientists' union Snabiye [Knowledge], for having created uncertainty and concern amongst their workers through his lectures. He was immediately forbidden to give any lectures or publish any books, and a special commission was even discussed to investigate whether Zigel was suitable at all for teaching at a scientific institution. Zigel then produced three "samisdat" (self-made) manuscripts with carbon copies—Xerox machines were a rarity in the Soviet Union in those days—and distributed them among friends and colleagues, who again made more copies of them for private distribution. The authorities seemed to approve of this procedure: perhaps because they were thankful that someone was relieving them of the burden of collecting and evaluating a lot of material.

"They can stand still in the middle of flight, and have also been seen flying at speeds of over 45,000 miles per hour," wrote Zigel in one of his manuscripts. *"They move without noise and create a vacuum around themselves which protects them from being burned when entering our atmosphere. They are described as crescent-shaped, spherical, disc-or cigar-shaped, They can appear and disappear as they please. They have the astounding capacity of paralyzing motors and electric supplies."* The Russian was convinced that they were controlled by humanoid beings, visitors from space, whom he divided into categories: *"Most of them are about 3 feet tall and resemble human beings. They have unusually big heads without any sign of hair, protruding eyes set wide apart, deep holes instead of noses, and skin sometimes wrinkled, which makes them look very old. The second species looks like us, and it would be difficult to make them out as aliens. A third group, seen seldom, is almost nine feet tall."* Witnesses also described robots or "walking computers" in all sizes.

Zigel was further convinced that people had been taken on board the UFOs and examined medically there. Only rarely did it happen that human beings were kidnapped and failed to return, as in the case of three Soviet citizens and a Pole. According to Zigel, what makes the UFO reports credible is the high educational level of the witnesses: 52% were academics, scientists, engineers or laboratory technicians; 7.5% were actually professional astronomers; the second largest group of observers (23%) consisted of civil military pilots.

As impressive as Zigel's study was, it required a special incident to make the theme of UFOs accepted again and discussed by scientists. This breakthrough came on September 23, 1978, when the Soviet party paper *Pravda* published its first UFO reports. That in itself was a sensation, since only a year before that the same paper had declared that *"UFOs had never been seen above the Soviet Union,"* and that *"citizens of the Soviet Union who reported they had seen so-called flying saucers were either weak in mind or liars."* Now however, the paper announced, without a suggestion of doubt " . . . *An intensely radiant 'star' which looked like a shining jellyfish, stood above Petrosavodsk. It moved slowly towards Petrosavodsk, throwing rays of light on the city. There were thousands of beams and it looked like heavy rain. A little later, the beaming came to an end, the source of light changed its brightness and moved towards Onezskoe lake. On the horizon were gray clouds, and when the object went in to these, a number of semicircles and circles of pink light appeared. The manifestation lasted 10 to 12 minutes."*

Photograph of the UFOs of Petrosavodsk, above the Onega Lake, in the early morning hours of September 20, 1977. This photograph was also published in the newspaper *Pravda*.

Naturally every speculation was avoided, and also the term "UFO" was not used. In spite of that, the report gave a good, though short impression of what had happened exactly one year before in Petrosavodsk—and what had been meanwhile examined with painstaking thoroughness by a commission of experts especially set up for that purpose.

It had happened on September 20, 1977. Early risers in Petrosavodsk (185,000 inhabitants), the capital of the Karelian Autonomous Soviet Republic, saw a bright light suddenly appearing amid the clouds at about 4:05 a.m. The star-like light came nearer and descended in a spiral trajectory, and soon looked like a ball of fire. It then reduced its speed and finally hovered for about 6 minutes in one spot. If anyone had not noticed it before, they noticed it now, for it made a terrible noise like the howling of a siren. The howling stopped and the object started moving silently towards the town. Soon, it looked like an reddish-orange hemisphere surrounded by a bright zone, in which there were many points of light like stars that twinkled and disappeared. The light began to pulsate. A beam of light came out like a telescope from the bottom of the object, vertically downwards, followed by a second, less bright beam. After a time, both the beams disappeared.

During the next few seconds, hundreds of thin rays of light, like thin arrows, were showered upon the earth. People who had, until then, watched the spectacle fascinated, now broke into a panic. They ran around the streets, throwing themselves to the ground. Some workers in the harbor thought that it was an American nuclear attack and shouted *"This is the end!"* "Tass" correspondent Nikolai Milov, who interviewed hundreds of people soon afterwards, said *"People looked as if they had suddenly become sick. They gave the impression of being mentally disturbed. People who had been sleeping said that at this moment they had been suddenly awakened and had had an unpleasant feeling. Some suffered from nightmares and depressions. Most of them said that they had felt 'electric currents' inside themselves."*

The thing now looked like a big jellyfish with golden tentacles, shining in beautiful colors. The white glow around the hemisphere had now shrunk to a shining ring. The beams of light came down to earth in a slight curve. They drilled thousands of holes in the asphalt and in window panes. Some of the people estimated the diameter of the object at about 300 feet. They said that it came down, closer and closer, and finally hovered above the harbor. By now it was shining so brightly that it hurt the eyes to look at it. Then a smaller and brighter object in the shape of an electric bulb detached itself from the jellyfish and flew over the roofs and between the houses along the street. Some of the people claimed to have seen this "bulb" returning to its mother ship and disappearing into it. A doctor said that while he was looking at the object his car had broken down. The air was filled with the smell of ozone.

Yuri Gromov, director of the meteorological station of Petrosavodsk, watched the phenomenon and said: *"The body gradually assumed the*

Sketch of the Petrosavodsk UFO, according to eyewitnesses' descriptions.

shape of an elliptical ring. It finally moved towards the bank of clouds above Onezskoe Lake, burned a red hole in the clouds and disappeared into it." The whole show had lasted for about 12 minutes. Whatever it was, at least the meteorologist Gromov ruled out the possibility of its being a ball of lightning or an aerial reflection. And at that time there were no aircraft or helicopters in the air space above Petrosavodsk. Gromov said: *"In my opinion it was either a UFO, the messenger of a higher intelligence with crew and passengers, or a field of energy that came from a UFO."*

During the next couple of weeks, over 1,500 letters were sent to the authorities and to the "Tass" agency, expressing worry and concern: *"How safe is it to stay in Petrosavodsk?"* or *"Is a journey to the Karelian capital*

Windowpane from Petrosavodsk, bored through by the UFO's rays.

Microscope snapshot of a circular piece of glass cut out of the pane by the UFO rays. Photograph by Prof. Manfred Kage.

dangerous?" or *"How high is the radioactivity?"* All these letters as well as the eyewitness reports in the archives of "Tass" were confiscated by government officials. All further references to this topic were forbidden, and scientists investigated the case in secret. Vasil Sakharchenko, the publisher of the magazine *Technique and Youth,* who had good connections with government sources, said, *"The Commission of Academy of Sciences has found*

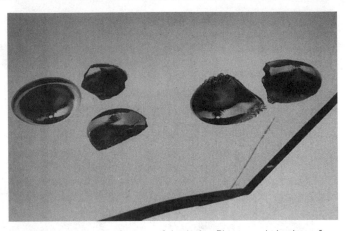

Detailed photograph of some of the holes. Photograph: Institute for
Scientific Photography, Prof. Manfred Kage.

*that the holes in the stones and window-panes give the impression that the
glass had been melted—The holes are the size of a coin.*" The window of a
factory in Petrosavodsk, perforated in such a way, were sent to Moscow for
analysis. The results of the analysis were given out only towards the end of
1981, by Dr. V. G. Azhazha during a lecture.

"*In many of the windows of the houses in the town of Petrosavodsk, there
appeared holes the size of 2 to 3 inches in diameter, whose borders showed
signs of melting. Circular pieces of glass of the panes of inner windows
were missing or lay on the ground or the window sill. The analysis was
interesting. Under the electron microscope, they discovered a crystalline
structure on the surface of the non-crystalline glass. They said it was normally impossible, but it was there. It remained a mystery. The only possibility was that mysterious objects had been active.*"

Years later, samples of these glass pieces were also shown to experts in the
West. In 1978 the astronomer Dr. Dale Cruikshank and the sociologist David
W. Swift of the University of Hawaii were allowed to see the glass pieces at
the Academy of Sciences in Moscow. They confirmed the existence of a crys-
talline structure at the edges of the holes, as did the chemist Prof. Manfred
Kage of the Institute for Scientific Photography at Schloss Weissenstein near
Stuttgart, who later examined one pane with a number of holes.

The sensation caused by the Petrosavodsk incident compelled the scientific establishment to take action. The president of the Academy of Sciences formed a special commission to be led by the academy member W.
Migulin. The commission took up the job of investigating the case, albeit
with little enthusiasm. After a superficial study they came to the conclusion that the holes were the result of a "*Still unknown natural atmospheric phenomenon, possibly in connection with human technology, for
instance a rocket launch.*" As a matter of fact, during the time in ques-

tion, at exactly 4:03 a.m., a rocket had been launched carrying the spy satellite Cosmos 955 at Plesetsk, about 200 miles *east* of Petrosavodsk. But it is obvious that this rocket could not have been the cause of the phenomenon: the shining jellyfish was sighted at first west of Petrosavodsk, and it moved *underneath* the clouds, long after the rocket had passed through the stratosphere. Of course, no rocket leaves behind thousands of holes in glass and asphalt. And as to what kind of atmospheric phenomena it could have been, nothing was said. All that had been established was that it was not an extraterrestrial object because *it should not have been one.*

Fortunately, Migulin confessed his own personal dissatisfaction about the matter in an interview with the Soviet journal *The Week: "I confess that the insufficient investigation of this case is our fault. Many serious scientists try their best to circumvent speculative problems. The story of science shows that little or no knowledge exists regarding such problems, simply because their investigation carries with it the danger of losing a lot of time, and even more than that, one's reputation. Neither I nor my colleagues*

Cigar-shaped UFO above the Onega Lake.

were, therefore, particularly enamoured with the task of examining this case when ordered to do so by the President of the Academy."

The investigation was conducted by researchers of the Leningrad Arctic and Antarctic Institute, the Geophysical Institute of Obrinsk, and a number of geologists, meteorologists and experts from the Air Force and Navy. Irrespective of what it was, they were at least able to trace the route of the mysterious object almost without a gap. Between 3:06 and 3:10 a.m., police officers in the Finnish capital Helsinki had reported sighting *"a bright ball of fire,"* which hovered over the airport for 4 minutes, and then moved eastwards. This was also confirmed by the radar at the control tower of the Helsinki airport. A little later the author Limik at Namoyevo, 20 miles northwest of Petrosavodsk, saw it through his telescope. He described the UFO as a lens-shaped object shining violet and surrounded by a shining ring. It had bright pulsating rays of light coming out of it *"like the tentacles of a Medusa"* (jellyfish). At 3:30 a.m. fishermen on Onezskoe Lake near Primosk saw a bright light in the sky which was surrounded by a kind of haze. At 4:00 a.m. employees at the observatory at Pulkovo saw the ball of fire in the north, as did a pilot in a passenger plane flying from Kiev to Leningrad. After its appearance over Petrosavodsk, they sighted the disc above Yandevar, south of the Karelian capital. At Polovina, 15 miles east of Petrosavodsk, people saw a cloud changing in color at 4:40 a.m. as if it had been lit up by a source of light inside it.

CHAPTER 14

UFO Glasnost

The incident at Petrosavodsk, and the fact that even the Academy of Sciences was taking the trouble to investigate it, made UFOs once more acceptable in Russia. The cosmonaut E. V. Khrunov stated in the issue 3/79 of the magazine *Technique and Youth, "The UFO problem exists and is very serious. Thousands of people have seen UFOs, but it is not clear what they are. We must investigate this question thoroughly. And it is quite possible that behind this question, the problem of communication with extraterrestrial civilization is hidden."*

But still there were limits to the openness. In 1978, the Assistant Director of the Department of Underwater Research of the Oceanographic Soci-

UFO above Murmansk, 1978.

ety of the Academy of Sciences, Prof. Dr. Vladimir Azhazha, formed a special group called the "UFO Initiative Group." During his first lectures on the subject at the Moscow State University, he called for the scientific and social recognition of UFO research. This had its effect in 1979, when Prof. Azhazha established a section called the "Search for Extraterrestrial Civilizations in Space Near Earth" under the Scientific and Technical A. S. Popov Society for Radio Electronics. Work started on July 17, 1979. The professor was successful in getting such personalities as cosmonaut Khrunov, Navy Vice Admiral Krylov, the Deputy Director of the Soviet Space Control Center Y. Nazarov and other well-known scientists to support the section. But when Azhazha and his colleagues tried to set up subsidiary groups in other parts of the country, they were repeatedly frustrated.

Prof. Vladimir Azhazha

To start with, the Popov Society forbade them to distribute circular letters to their branch offices. Then an article written for the magazine *Radio Technology* was censored, cut out at short notice. Following that, on orders from above, the name of the working group was changed to "Section for Investigating Anomalous Atmospheric Phenomena." Again and again lectures and seminars of the UFO researchers were deliberately disturbed. One seminar was abruptly stopped by the vice-dean of the state university only half an hour after it had begun, with the explanation that the room had already been promised to another group. As if to prove this, he had brought from the neighboring hall a few unruly students who started conversing loudly. But the harassment did not stop with such chicanery. The days of open UFO research were, for the present, numbered. Only 5 months after its inauguration, on December 12, 1979, the entire section was banned by the Moscow city committee of the Communist Party on the grounds that it was "anti-Soviet," whatever that meant.

An explanation for this followed in March 1980 in *Pravda*, the same newspaper which had only two years ago reported the Petrosovadsk UFO incident so objectively *Pravda* told the Soviet UFO believers now that there were no indications for the alleged existence of interplanetary visitors on earth. It cited the words of the president of the Academy of Sciences, Alexandrov, that the entire UFO business *"was based on rumors meant to mystify and mislead the credulous."*

As if to punish *Pravda* for its prevarication, during the years 1980 and 1981 the Soviet capital was subjected to a series of UFO sightings, including a landing in one of its more remote suburbs. The events of Petrosavodsk were literally repeated in Moscow. On August 23, 1981, at 7:12 p.m., hundreds of Muscovites saw a fleet of 17 mysterious objects in the sky above the capital. According to Prof. Azhazha: *"Two cigar-shaped spaceships, each about 3,000 feet in length, flew side by side at a height of about 10 miles and disappeared towards the north."* About an hour later, there followed a globular white and shining object, about half the size of the moon, which then reappeared after another hour at about 9:20 p.m. One of the witnesses was the well-known astronomer. Dr. Nikita Schnee who estimated the speed of this UFO at approximately 3,000 mph. *"When it flew by, I had the dreadful feeling that we were completely defenseless against the UFOs,"* confessed Schnee. Finally at 10:00 p.m. there appeared a "whale-like" space vessel which sent out blue light and carried out bizarre maneuvers above the city. Prof. Azhazha related, *"and between these 4 observations, there appeared again and again smaller objects. We counted at least 13."*

The amazing thing, however, was that after the UFOs had vanished, at least 60 window-panes in Moscow had big circular holes. An examination of about 40 of these damaged glass panes at the Moscow State Glass Institute showed that the molecular structure of the glass had been changed. Artillery experts only shook their heads when asked "How?" and wished that they, too, had a gun that could shoot such beautifully round holes through glass! Azhazha cited the report of a retired Moscow doctor, Dr. Bogatriev, who could not sleep during that night. When he got out of bed to get himself a glass of milk, he saw at only a distance of about 100 feet from his house, a strange indefinable "spot." Then he heard what sounded like a shot. A ring of fire about 3 inches in diameter burned a hole in his window. A moment later a circular piece of glass 4 inches in diameter fell to the ground in front of him. Azhazha added *"this mass demonstration of UFOs above Moscow posed a big problem for the authorities and the scientists, for they didn't know what they could do against it."*

But it was another dramatic incident which was finally to bring about a change. This happened on the evening of March 27, 1983, at the airport of Gorky, when a steel-gray cigar-shaped craft refused to respond to the attempts of the ground crew to establish radio contact with it. According to the radar, it flew at an altitude of 2,700 feet with a speed of 125 mph. They were able follow its movements for over 40 minutes. It first flew towards the southeast up to a distance of about 50 miles, then returned to the airport, finally to disappear in a northerly direction. The anxiety that this maneuver caused, particularly in military circles, led to the establishment of the first semi-official Commission for the Investigation of "Paranormal Phenomena" (which, of course, was a kind of euphemism for the undesirable "U-word") in February 1984. It was subsidiary to the Committee for Environmental Protection, which again was under the All-Unions Scientific and Technical Society. It could be proud of its list of members, which included a number of high-ranking military officers and members of the Academy, with V. S. Troitzky as chairman. The Deputy Chairman was the cosmonaut and twice decorated "hero of the Soviet Union," Gen. Pavel Popovich, as well as the academy member N. A. Sheltuchin. The secretary was the retired Air Force colonel, Dr. Arvid Mordvin-Chodro of Leningrad.

Prof. Felix Zigel was advisor to the committee until his death in 1988. At the same time, a network of local groups were set up all over the gigantic Soviet territory, in Gorky, Kiev, Leningrad, Novosibirsk, Tomsk, Dalnegorsk and Tblissi. In July 1984, the magazine *Sovietskaya Rossiya* (Soviet Russia) published an appeal of the commission to the people of the Soviet Union, to send reports of all UFO sightings to a particular Moscow postal address. The most spectacular incident reported happened in the early

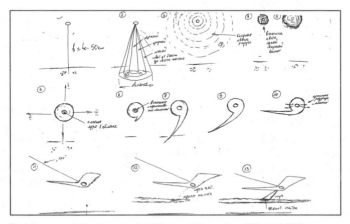

Sketches made by the copilot Gennadi Lasurin, of Flight 8352, showing the various phases of the UFO appearance, September 7, 1984.

morning of September 7, 1984 at exactly 4:10 a.m.

At that hour an Estonian airliner of the type Tupolev (TU 134) was flying on the route from the Georgian capital Tblissi to Tallin in Estonia with a stopover at Rostow. The crew of this flight included Capt. Igor Tcherkashin, an experienced pilot with over 7,000 flying hours to his credit, copilot Gennadi Lasurin (4,500 flying hours), the navigator Igor Michailovich Ognev, a recipient of the Order of Lenin Medal, and the flight engineer, Gennadi Koslov. At 4:10 a.m. they were 75 miles from Minsk. It was a still, clear night and, to the pilots, it seemed as if they were gliding through the universe. They felt at one with the twinkling stars, from which they were separated only by a sheet of glass. While they were watching the night sky in a pensive mood, the copilot suddenly saw a big star which did not twinkle but moved slowly to the right, upwards. It was a yellow object which was distended at its sides. He thought it was perhaps a refraction in the atmosphere but soon he had to abandon this thought for, out of this "solid light," a thin, fine ray dropped down vertically to the earth. Lasurin nudged the board engineer, saying, *"Michailovich, have a look at that."* As soon as he saw it, he called to the captain, saying, *"Captain, we must inform the ground control!"*

The spot of light changed into a cone of rays. Then, a second cone appeared, somewhat less bright than the first, then a third, very bright and broad. *"Let's wait,"* said the captain, shrugging his shoulders. *"Should we report at once? Let's wait a bit and see what happens. What is it, anyhow?"* The unknown objects were floating at a height of about 30 miles above the surface of the earth. The copilot quickly sketched what he saw. It was unbelievable. Everything on the earth which was struck by the cone of light was clearly visible. Houses and streets were illuminated as if in broad daylight. One can only wonder at how powerful these floodlights must have been!

Suddenly, the light was directed at the approaching airplane. The crew now saw only a glaring light, a point surrounded by colored concentric rings, and while the captain was still debating whether to report the incident immediately or not, something happened that put an end to all his doubts. The point of light suddenly flamed up and, in its place was a green cloud. "He's switching on his motors and getting away," thought the copilot. But Tcherkashin felt that the object was now coming with great speed towards them, cutting their course at an acute angle. *"Inform the tower!"* he told the navigator. Hardly had he spoken these words when the object came to a standstill. The tower at Minsk answered saying, "Tower Minsk here, regret we have nothing on the radar."

"There we have it," said Lasurin, annoyed, *"now they'll all say we're mad."* In the meantime, the green cloud had reached their aircraft, had dropped in height and now seemed to be taking stock of it. It appeared now left, then above, then again right of the aircraft. Finally, it took a position on the right and accompanied the airliner at a speed of 500 mph at a height of 30,000 feet. *"An escort,"* grumbled Tcherkashin with light irony, *"What an honor for us!"*

At this moment, the tower form Minsk Airport called, saying, *"I now have something on the screen. Where is your cloud?"* The navigator replied, *"At 2:00 position, right of us."*

"That's correct," was the answer from the tower. Flames were "playing" inside the cloud. They blazed up and went out, zigzagged from one point to another and the cloud itself underwent changes. First, it grew a tail, then, changed its elliptical shape to a rectangle. Then, it took on the shape of an airplane with a very pointed nose. *"Look!"* said the copilot, *"It's imitating us!"*

At this moment, the stewardess came to the cockpit. *"The passengers want to know what's flying at our side."*

Tcherkashin sighed. *"Say it's a kind of cloud, yellow because the lights of a city are reflected by it . . . uh, green . . . er, uh . . . say Aurora Borealis."*

Shortly after that, the tower at Minsk reported the passing of a genuine aircraft, another TU134 from Leningrad, flying in the opposite direction towards Tblissi. In its cockpit sat Flight Captain Vladimir Gotsiridze, copilot Uri Kabachnikov, navigator Josef Tomashvili and the board engineer Murman Gvenetadze.

Tower Minsk to Flight 7084: *"Can you see anything unusual in front of you?"*

Tomasvili answered: *"Negative, only an approaching plane, a TU134."*

Tower: *"Understood. That is flight 8352. Keep her under observation."*
It was only when they were 10 miles away from it that they could see the
"cloud plane" near the TU134. It looked as if they were in tandem flight.
"It's incredible," said Captain Gotsiridze. *"That, I've got to see closer!"* In
consultation with the tower, he changed his course and flew past this combination at a distance of about 3 miles. This was a tragic mistake which was
to cost him his life. A beam, about 8 inches in diameter, shot out of the
cloud and scanned the pilot's body from head to foot, as well as a part of
the body of copilot Kabachnikov, who was trying to protect his eyes from
the glaring light with his hands.

The UFO continued to accompany the first aircraft. As a pair, they flew
over Riga and Vilnius, spotted as such by the ground crew of the said air-
ports. When they reached the Tschudsk and Pskowsk Lakes, a conical beam
of light appeared from the middle of the "cloud plane," which lit up the
earth. They had a reference point. By projection from the point of observation, they calculated the length of the cloud itself at about 6 miles and, of
the core, between 300 and 1,000 feet. On the radar screen of the airport
Tallin, the TU134 was not seen "alone" when it came in to land. Finally, the
light went out and the "cloud-airplane" now looked like a kind of green
boomerang, which slowly moved off towards the sea, in the direction of
Finland.

Shortly after that, the Commission for Investigating Paranormal Phenomena was called in. There was a problem, primarily a medical one. The
pilot of the flight 7084, V. Gotsiridze, had become seriously ill after arrival
at Tblissi, probably as a result of an unknown radiation. At the medical
clinic of the Georgian capital they did not know how to treat him. In
Moscow, the wife of the vice-president of the UFO-commission, Col. Dr.
Marina Popovich, arranged admitting the pilot into the Botkin Clinic. There
too, no definite diagnosis could be made and finally, when Gotsiridze, back
in Tblissi, died in 1985, the cause of death was recorded as *"bone marrow
tumors, torn muscles, damage to and around the spleen, spreading necro-
sis of the tissue and a kind of myeloma."*

Shortly after that, copilot Juri Kabachnikov had to go to the clinic as
well. He suffered from dot-like burns at the back of his eyes and a series of
other complications, including frequent attacks of fainting. The clinic
declared him to be unfit for flight and put him on an invalid's pension,
which he drew until his death, a few years later. A medical report of the
Chief of the Department for Pathophysiology of the Research Institute for
Experimental and Clinical Therapy in Tblissi, dated June 23, 1986, says,
*"Juri Kabachnikov was exposed to an electromagnetic radiation of
unknown physical properties. Judging by the electrocardiogram and the
electroencephalogram, the damage was caused by a relatively thin beam
which injured spots in the brain and in the heart muscles. The anomalies
found are unique in medical practice and have never been described before
in medical literature. Signed, Prof. Konstantin Zindadze, M.D."* The stewardess who was in the cockpit at the time of the sighting suffered from a

severe skin disease for a long time. The pilots and crew of flight 8352, on the other hand, remained unharmed.

Whereas these injuries from radiation were kept secret until recently, a description of the occurrence, from the point of view of the Tscherkashin crew, appeared in the Union paper *Trud* on January 30, 1985 under the headline "Exactly at 4:10 A.M." This was accompanied by a commentary from the vice-chairman of the Commission for Investigating Paranormal Phenomena, N. A. Sheltuchin, and an appeal to the public to send similar observations to their address. Sheltuchin conceded, *"This case is very interesting and one can only draw one conclusion. The Tallin crew had something to do with what we call UFOs."*

That brought a whole load of letters—more than 33,000—that arrived at the given Moscow postal address. True, the people responsible for this (the writer of the article, the journalist concerned and the editor-in-chief of *Trud*) were all fired, but the newly-awakened interest of the Soviet public could not be stopped anymore. And soon, there was nobody left who had any interest in suppressing the matter. On March 11, 1985, Mikhail Gorbachev was elected Secretary-General of the Communist Party. The time of glasnost, openness, and perestroika, or Reform, had begun. During the same year, the chief of the Directorate for the Protection of State and Press Secrets, Vladimir Nasarao, passed a decree which said, *"as of today, the restrictions regarding the publication of reports about the UFO problem, which were in force in our country hitherto, are rescinded."*

Soon, the press had a very significant case to report. In February 1985, a freight train was rumbling through the night and was, of all places, at a location not very far from Petrosavodsk. The train was many hundreds of feet long and weighed over 1,600 tons, but had no freight on board. The engineer, Sergei Orlov, and his mechanic had been ordered to take the train to Petrosavodsk for loading the next morning. When he was driving through a forest of firs, Orlov, looking out from his cabin in the diesel locomotive, noticed a bright sphere which came out of the forest and started accompanying the train. He geared down and reduced speed a little later since the tracks were going uphill, when the sphere became brighter and took up a position in front of the locomotive. At once, the train started accelerating. When, after that, going downhill, Orlov tried to reduce the speed, he was unable to do so. Even the emergency brakes did not function and the train was being "drawn along" at a speed of 30 mph.

Orlov got frightened and radioed the nearest station, Noviye Peski, saying that he was unable to stop his train. The stationmaster, Olga Paushukova, set the traffic light to green and ran out to the platform. What she saw took her breath away. In front of the train, there was a transparent and glowing sphere, a fiery red disc that moved back and forth. Before reaching the station the object flew off, only to take up its position in front of the locomotive once again after a few miles. At that moment, the train stopped abruptly although Orlov had not activated the brakes. Orlov and his companion fell against the windshield. A few seconds later the train started moving again at normal speed. After it had covered about 30 miles, the sphere of light disappeared silently into the neighboring woods. When the train finally arrived at Petrosavodsk, the crew was in shock. An examination of the locomotive showed that it had more than 300 liters of fuel in the tank than it should have had. Apparently, the ball of light had helped the train save an appreciable amount of diesel fuel.

Cases like this, and the new openness allowed the press in the late 80s, caused UFO groups, committees and commissions to mushroom in all major cities of the Soviet Union. In April 1988, over 400 Soviet UFO researchers met at the Polytechnic Institute of the Siberian University of Tomsk for a week-long conference about "anomalous transitory phenomena in the environment." About 200 lectures were on the agenda and they were published in 3 volumes. During the second Tomsk conference about anomalous appearances, in April 1990, there were as many as 472 lectures. Unfortunately, violent controversies arose between the various groups of UFO researchers. This led to the splitting of the Committee for Investigation of Problems Concerning Exchange of Energy and Information in Nature which had been established in 1989. Academy member V. Kaznachayev became the new chairman, under the auspices of the All-Unions Scientific and Technical Society, of the Commission for the Investigation of Paranormal Phenomena.

On his own initiative, Professor Vladimir Azhazha, the undisputed expert of Soviet UFO research after the death of Zigel, founded during the same year the All-Unions UFO Center. Gen. Pavel Popovich was elected president and Azhazha, Maj. Gen. Nikolai Vassiliev of the Ministry of the Interior and the journalist Mikhael Yeltsin were elected as vice presidents. The *"Soyus-ufo-sentr"*—renamed the "Russian UFO Center" in 1992—stands

In the neighborhood of Moscow, 1989.

Russia, 1986.

under the aegis of the Union of Scientific and Engineering Societies. It has 120 local groups in 80 towns. In Moscow alone, 2500 people have attended its seminars and over 35,000 people from all parts of the country have taken its postal courses, "Introduction into UFO Research." Since January 1, 1991, the center has had its own rooms and offices at the Institute Steel Project at 18, Leningradski Chaussee.

This new openness gave the military courage to reveal, bit by bit, what the Soviet Armed Forces had learned about UFOs over the past decades. One of the first Air Force pilots to speak openly about his UFO encounters was the fighter pilot Lt. Col. Lev Vyatkin. This is his report:

On August 13, 1967, I took off in my jet fighter for a routine flight exercise. It was shortly after 11 p.m. I switched on the afterburner to increase acceleration and to get to a height of 30,000 feet. I maneuvered the jet in the

Yaroslavl, April 1990. Photograph: A. Nitowshchikov.

Saratov, September 1989.

Crimea, Ukraine, 1988.

Vidnoye, Russia, May 4, 1989. Photograph: A. Pavlov.

proper direction, reported to my commander and steered the plane slowly to the left.

It was a quiet moonless night. The bright stars lent the night an irresistible charm. The plane had just covered half the curve and was flying towards the sea. The lights of Yalta, the sea resort on the Black Sea, twinkled under me along the crescent bay. I made a routine check of the instruments. Everything was all right and the motor behind me was droning smoothly.

At this moment, I noticed something which I remembered vividly whenever

I tried later to find an explanation for what followed. After taking a look at the instrument panel, I looked up into the sky and there I saw a big, oval object, which was somehow hanging on to the port side of my plane. A strange object so close to me was reason enough for getting worried, so I asked the Flight Commander, Major Musatov, over the radio, "Who else is in the zone?" He looked at his radar screen and answered to my surprise that nothing else was in my vicinity and that all the other airplanes had already landed. I steered my

The Soviet flying hero Lt. Col. Lev Vyatkin.

machine slowly to the right, taking care not to lose sight of the strange object. I tried not to get too close to the object and at the same time, tried to find out in which direction it was moving. A few seconds later, its lights went out gradually.

By now, my plane had completed a full turn to the right and was again at its starting point. I deliberated as to what I should do next and decided to take a left turn as carefully as I could. But I'd hardly turned my Mig and increased my speed when I noticed a bright flash of light which came from above and went through the course I was taking. Then, a slanting milky-white beam appeared, which slowly moved and stood directed at the Mig. If I had not swerved out, the nose of the Mig would have flown directly into this beam. Instead of that, only my left wing passed through it. I went through at high speed, but kept the light in sight so that I was able to see something very strange. As soon as the wing touched the beam, the beam broke out into a million tiny sparks, like fireworks. "What had happened?" I asked myself. Is the beam something solid? The sparks fell towards the earth, and soon, the light and the beam vanished.

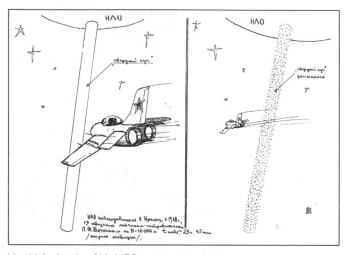

Vyatkin's sketch of his UFO encounter.

On the flight back to the base, I kept my eyes open for further surprises but everything was quiet, my flight ended safely. But, for many nights after that, the wing which had come in contact with this strange beam gave out a light like phosphorescence.

Such reports soon proved to be only the peak of an iceberg. The legendary MiG test pilot, Col. Marina Popovich, collected over 3,000 reports of UFO encounters from her comrade pilots. She presented the most interesting ones to the world in various lectures and also in her bestseller *UFO Glasnost*.

The legendary test pilot, Col. Marina Popovich.

And finally, the papers started writing about UFO incidents. For instance, the Union newspaper, *Rabochaya Tribuna*, reported in October 1990 that two UFOs had been picked up by radar above the Georgian capital, Tblissi, and had been pursued by a fighter plane, piloted by Maj. P. Ryabishef. This is the report of the pilot, as given by the paper: *"At 11:22 a.m. I was given the coordinates of the objects from the tower and also orders to follow them. According to the information given, the objects were at a height of about 3 miles. The weather was clear and cloudless. The visibility was excellent . . . Suddenly, something made me look back. At the rear of my*

machine, at the right side, I discovered two cigar-shaped objects of con-
siderable size. The first one seemed to be about 6,000 feet long and the
other one about 1,200 feet. They were flying one behind the other, and
could be clearly seen against the sky. The smaller one was silvery and
reflected the rays of the sun, whereas the bigger one was dull and matt.
They were too far away for me to see more. Finally, they flew away at an
extremely high speed. As the commanding post told me, the radar had
shown that they had been about 10 miles away from me."

Another consequence of the UFO glasnost was that high-ranking military officers started to reveal the truth about secret UFO studies which the
Soviet Armed Forces had been carrying out for years, although they had
denied it until then. These studies too had been triggered by the incident at
Petrosavodsk in 1977, although it took 2 years after that until enough data
had been collected for a statistical study, which finally led the Army to start
on a countrywide UFO research project.

The studies had been conducted by the scientists L. M. Gindilis, E. A.
Menkov, and I. G. Petrovskaya at the Institute for Space Research of the
Academy of Sciences. In 1979, they had carried out a statistical analysis of
observations of "anomalous atmospheric phenomena in the USSR," as a
result of a decision made by the Department of General Physics and
Astronomy of the Presidium of the Academy of Sciences. Their concluding
report was so spectacular that it was even translated into English by NASA
in 1980. That paper, after evaluating 256 sightings, concluded that the phenomenon showed certain stable statistical characteristics.

Twenty-five percent of the sightings had been made by scientists;
amongst them 7.5% were astronomers and 11% were pilots. The sightings
could be broken down into specific shapes: 19 % of the objects had been in
the shape of a star; 11% were spherical; 15.5% disc-shaped; 22.5% crescent-shaped, and 7.5% were long, flying fuselages, varying from elongated
ovals to cigar shapes and cylinders. The remaining 24.5% of the reports
cited other shapes such as triangles, squares, domes and dumbbells. This
led to the conclusion that *"the overwhelming majority of the cases could*
not be explained as being optical effects of the atmosphere and that they
were of a completely different nature." In order to understand this thoroughly, they recommended:

"Well-documented observations: The collection of such reports must be
done through the existing network of meteorological, geophysical and
astronomical observatories, as well as through other official channels. The
possibility of installing special apparatus for observation should also be
considered carefully."

This recommendation was put into practice. What followed was the
biggest UFO detection project that had ever been conducted.

"During the next few years, the Soviet Union became one big UFO
observatory," said Col. Boris Sokolov of the Ministry of Defense in March
1993 to the American TV journalist George Knapp. The project began in
1980 when a secret order from the defense ministry was sent to all military

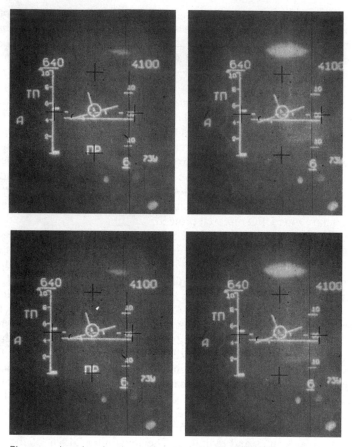

Photographs taken by the on board radar of an MiG-21 during a
UFO encounter in 1991, in the airspace near Voronesh.

bases in the USSR instructing all military units to report all UFO sightings
immediately. Pilots, soldiers and sailors were ordered to observe the objects
carefully and if possible to take photographs. All these reports went through
the usual official channels and finally landed on Sokolov's desk. There
were thousands of them. *"We had 40 cases of UFO encounters with our
pilots,"* recalled Col. Sokolov. *"At first they had orders to intercept the
UFOs and open fire if necessary. They tried this a few times, but the objects
accelerated, and when the pilots pursued them, they lost control of their
machines. In 3 cases, this led to their crashing and 2 pilots died. Then a
new order was issued. Upon sighting a UFO they were to change course
immediately and get out of the area. Later this order was also modified.
Finally they were told to observe the objects at a safe distance."*

Sokolov related that 30 radar stations had been set up to track UFOs and to find out where they came from. In doing this they followed the advice not only of Gindlis, Menkov, and Petroskaya, but also a recommendation which had been made by Soviet scientists during the 1970s.

In August 1971 a conference was held at Byukaran to discuss the search for extraterrestrial intelligence. As the American participants, Dr. C. H. Townes and Prof. R. Bracewell later reported, the Russians had very cautiously tried to discuss the necessity and possibility of a worldwide tracking of the UFO appearances in the sky. The *"program for investigating the possibility of communication with extraterrestrial civilizations,"* a paper published by the Academy of Sciences in 1975, was more concrete. On page 19 it says: *"Special efforts should be made to discover space probes that have been sent out by extraterrestrial civilizations to our solar system and which may even be in orbit around the earth. In order to discover such fast-moving objects, a permanent tracking system covering the entire air space should be in operation, supported by the newly developed network of radio-observatories (a system in which objects can be spotted from various stations over the radio radar antennae). During the first phase it should be possible to use, for this purpose, the existing radio radar stations developed for cosmic communication and radio detection."*

This paper was, of course, referring to, without expressly saying so, the detection of UFO mother ships in orbit around the earth since the end of the '50s. The astronomer and astrophysicist Dr. Sergei Bozhich stated that hundreds of UFO flights had been followed with the help of the most modern computers. This achievement was possible only by employing the latest detection instruments which had been placed at the various stations in the Soviet Union and the Arctic. Russian espionage satellites were also involved. During the first three years of this project, hundreds of UFOs were detected, and the following figures show those spotted above the five most important observing stations: Petrosavodsk: 94; Piotagorsk: 18; Nishnitagil: 23; Estonia: 44; Kiev: 36.

They found out that all UFO flights sooner or later end in space. Since a number of them shot off in the direction of the planet Saturn, as seen by the electronic eyes of the spy satellites, Dr. Bozhich believed that the UFOs had a base on one of the satellites of Saturn. But there was also another reason, other than the clarification of the question of their origin, that the Soviet armed forces secretly followed the maneuvers of UFOs. There was the well-founded suspicion that a great deal of the stealth technology of the new camouflage bombers of the USA had been derived from the study of UFO wrecks, and now they hoped that they, too, would see a UFO crash so as to recover the wreck and study it, and thereby overtake the Americans in their technology. But then something else happened that made the blood freeze in the veins of the top dogs of the Defense Ministry.

October 5, 1983, began for Col. Sokolov like any other day. Early in the morning he drove to the defense ministry in his Lada (car) and was sitting at his writing table reading the latest reports, when his antiquated black telephone rang. At the other end of the line was his commander, a four-star general. *"Sokolov, get ready at once. You will be picked up in ten minutes. An airplane is waiting for you. You will fly to one of our ICBM bases in the Ukraine. The rest you can read in the report which will be given to you on the way."* Sokolov had hardly digested this before he heard a knock on his door. A senior staff sergeant gave the colonel a file marked "strictly secret," which he opened only when seated in the car on his way to the airport. The more Sokolov read of this secret report, line for line, the clearer it became to him why all this was happening with such urgency.

The third world war had just then been averted at the very last minute. That morning, the commander of a base at which intercontinental ballistic missiles carrying nuclear warheads were stationed, reported an incident to the general staff that had occurred the previous evening between 4:00 and 8:00 p.m. During that time a UFO had appeared above the nuclear arsenal and hovered above it. Attempts to shoot this object failed because the automatic mechanism of the guns suddenly refused to work. During the entire period, the warning lights of the control equipment in the commando center of the base were burning brightly: the starting codes for the remote-controlled rockets had been mysteriously put out of operation. *"When the order to start the missiles was then received,"* Sokolov told George Knapp on camera, *"the chief of the general staff lost no time in calling in the UFO department."*

Luckily they all got off with a fright only, but the incident made the general staff aware that the implication and consequences of the UFOs could not be underestimated. And to avoid the risk of a third world war again in this manner, the defense ministry decided in the future to work together with the USA in the matter of UFOs.

The Soviets' intention was implied through the publication of a simple article, entitled "UFOs and Security." Published in the June 1989 issue of the *Soviet Military Review*. The official mouthpiece of the Soviet Ministry of Defense, it was published in English and distributed in the United States. To make the invitation for open communication sound as noncommittal as possible, they used the alleged inquiry of a citizen of Zimbabwe—whether UFOs really existed and, if so, did they mean a threat to world peace?—as a façade, before describing the problem in detail throughout 2 pages. In the answer it was conceded that there were over 10,000 cases of unexplained phenomena which could indicate the presence of extraterrestrial visitors. The authors left no doubt as to what they were really talking about:

> We believe that the lack of information on the characteristics and influence of UFOs increase the threat of incorrect identification. In such cases multiple flybys of UFOs along trajectories close to those of combat missiles could be regarded by computers as an attack . . . in SDI conditions such incidents could provoke immediate reaction from computers to destroy the 'targets,' say, by an X-ray laser, which means a powerful nuclear explosion. Or SDI computers could order a counterattack, which might prove unwarranted. It should be remembered that decisions will be made not by people but by impartial computers which know nothing about UFOs. There would be no time to determine

the cause of the conflict then, but those who are creating SDI should think about it now. The UFO problem remains unsolved . . . Back in 1968, Felix Zigel, the main Soviet researcher of the problem, said "The subject and aims of UFO research are sufficiently important to justify any effort. Understandably, international cooperation is vitally needed here."

During 1989 and 1990 there was such a wave of UFO sightings in the Soviet Union, (nothing comparable had occurred since 1967) that it emphasized the urgency of the appeal made by Zigel. A particularly interesting case from this period is to be found in a collection of 124 UFO files of the KGB which were given to the president of the All-Unions UFO Center, the ex-cosmonaut and Air Force general Pavel Popovich. The documents, copies of which came into my possession in 1994, treat 17 cases from the years 1982 to 1990. Amongst them is a case that occurred on June 28, 1989, at a military base near the nuclear test site of Kapustin Yar in the Astrakhan region (Caspian lowlands).

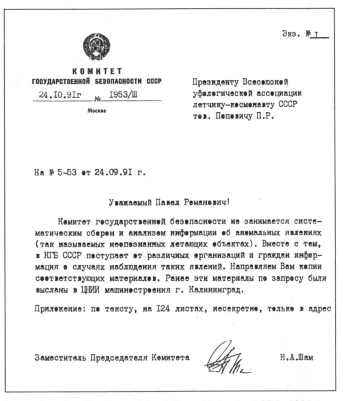

Instruction given by General Pavel Popovich to the KGB in 1991, to release 124 pages of secret UFO documents.

It was about midnight when members of two army units noticed a UFO which hovered for hours over the arsenal of the base. The KGB files contained the handwritten reports of the sighting, which 4 of the witnesses wrote after being interrogated by agents of the KGB. The report does not say what kind of missiles were in the arsenal, nor whether there had been any nuclear warheads.

I climbed up to the watchtower and watched the object at a height of 18 feet. I could clearly make out a glaring blinking signal, bright as a camera flash. The object flew over the stores of the unit and moved in the direction of the missile arsenal, about 1,000 feet away. It floated at a height of only 60 feet above the depot. The UFO glowed in a kind of phosphorescent green. It was a disc 12 to 15 feet in diameter with a semi-spherical dome on it.

While the object was hovering above the arsenal, a bright ray appeared on its underside where the light had been flashing before, and drew 2 or 3 circles. Then the object moved towards the railway station, still flashing. Soon, however, it came back to the missile depot and hovered at a height of 180–200 feet above it. Two hours after the start of the sighting, the object flew in the direc-

The most interesting incident mentioned in the KGB files occurred on June 28, 1989, at a military installation, the Kapustin Yar nuclear test site. The UFO hovered above a missile arsenal for over 2 hours.

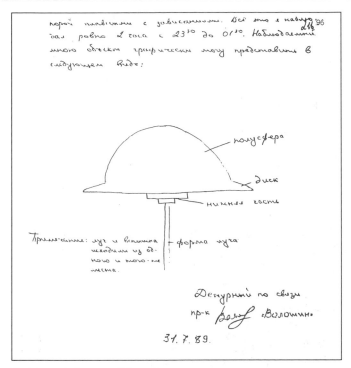

Sketch made by one of the witnesses.

Sketch made by another witness.

tion of the town Akhtubinsk and disappeared out of our sight,

wrote the communications officer on duty, V. Voloshin.

And the soldier G. Kulik added: *"Near the object in the sky I saw a fireball which arose from the earth and approached it. When the UFO moved towards me, I could physically feel its approach. Then it shot off into the sky. I saw an airplane that attempted to get close to the object, but the object accelerated so fast that it soon left the airplane behind".*

The maneuvers of a UFO above the radar station near Kuybishev (Samara) in the Tartar province, on September 13, 1990, did not end so harmlessly. Major A. I. Duplin, who was in charge of the watch at the time, reported:

"At 12:07 a.m. a big flying object was detected by the radar. The strength of the blip was comparable to that of a strategic bomber and its distance was less than 60 miles. I gave orders to check the object with the aid of our automatic identification system, when my chief sergeant Miketanok informed me that the system failed to function. At this moment—it was now 12:10, and 30 seconds,—the target burst and looked like a swarm of birds on the radar screen."

While the men at the radar station were still discussing whether it was an exploded rocket stage or a swarm of birds, the radar located a new target, that of a gigantic object hardly 25 miles away from the base. When it came closer, the officer in charge of the underground radar post ordered a team led by Capt. Lazeiko to look for the object in the sky. *"When we came out of the underground facility, an unknown object glided over our heads,"* said Capt. Lazeiko later on. *"It flew at a height of hardly 30 feet. We could see it very clearly. The area in the base is permanently lit bright as day by floodlights. It was an equilateral triangle with rounded corners. The underside of the object was smooth, but not mirror smooth. It looked as if it*

Artist's impressions of the three decisive phases of the UFO maneuvers above the radar station Kubishev, near Samara, on September 13, 1990: the triangular UFO approaches; lands; and fires a ray of light on the radar unit, which was destroyed completely by it.

had a layer of rust on it. It had no openings, windows or landing gear, but we saw 3 blue-white beams of light."

Meanwhile it was 12:20 and the commander of the watch, Chief Sgt. Gorin, sitting in his office, tried to call sentry No. 4, Corporal A. Blazhis, but he did not answer. Gorin sent 2 soldiers out to see what had happened, after he had checked that his radio was working properly. But Blazhis had disappeared. When Gorin heard that, he gave orders to search for the sentry. Half an hour later he was told that both Blazhis and another sentry, Corporal A. Varenitsa, could not be found.

Major Duplin continued the report saying *"After I heard that both corporals had disappeared, I gave orders to keep a close watch on the unidentified object, which meanwhile had landed near the fence of a mobile short-range radar unit (No. 12). At this moment, Captain P. Lazeiko reported that he had seen a flash of light and now the radar antennae of Unit 12 were burning, as if they were made of wood."* Another witness of the landing, Corporal S. Dudnik, described it as follows:

I was standing at the sentinel post No. 6 and watched the approaching flight of a big, black, triangular flying craft, each side about 45 feet in length. It landed after coming down vertically, rather slowly, and making a rattling noise. It was about 9 feet high. The flash of light, with which it shattered the radar antennae behind me, came out of the middle of the side of the object. I could see no opening there, but it seemed to be aiming at its target and I found myself directly in its line of fire. Oddly enough, nothing happened to me but the antennae collapsed and began to burn brightly."

Troop leader P. Beshmetov ran to Corporal Dudnik when the fire started. *"He stood there near the barbed wire fence, pointing his Kalashnikov at the black triangle which was hovering about 300 feet away behind the fence."* What happened after that Beshmetov described as follows:

The triangle left after 1½ hours and the commander of the watch ordered all soldiers to go back to their posts again. The color of the mobile radar unit was olive-green before that flash, but now it was black and covered with blisters.

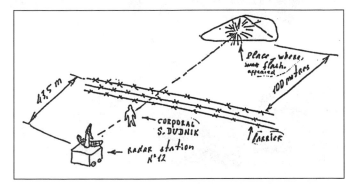

Eyewitness sketch of the incident.

Parts of the underside were melted. The upper radar antenna was broken and lay on the ground, 6 feet away from the unit. All steel parts had melted and only the aluminum mirror was left. The officers told Capt. Rudzit that the steel parts had been burned by a "beam" of oxygen, and they could not understand what kind of energy could cause steel to burn from a distance of 430 feet.

When I went to the warehouse, I met Corporal Blazhis. I was surprised to see him going to his post as if nothing had happened at all. I asked him where he had been all the time. He laughed and said that he had gone to the telephone to report the appearance of the object to Sgt. Romanov, when he suddenly lost consciousness. At the same time V. Varenitsa showed up, the other missing soldier. He, too, remembered nothing and was convinced that he had been standing at his post all the time! Corporal Blazhis' watch was running 1 hour, 57 minutes behind time and that of Varenitsa, 1 hour and 45 minutes. Besides that, the serial numbers on Blazhis' machine gun and bayonet had been completely erased!

The next morning the officers of the radar station inspected the spot where the UFO had "landed." According to Corporal Dudnik who had seen it at a closer range, the object had only hovered at a very low height above the earth. *"The place looked as if an explosion had occurred there."* The incident was reported to Moscow and on September 18, a commission arrived to investigate it. Although reports of the event appeared in various papers, amongst them the military paper *Za Rodinu*, the defense ministry denied the reports. But when photographs of the destroyed radar unit were published, the Kuybishev incident could no longer be kept secret. The Russian papers pointed out the UFO's resemblance to the triangular UFOs which had appeared at the same time in Belgium.

Official police photo of the burning UFO landing site at Frunze, Kirgistan.

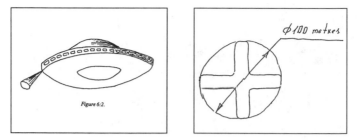

Sketch showing the object and landing spot, made by members of the militia.

Only a week later, on September 21, 1990, 3 members of the militia of the Ministry of the Interior near Frunske, Kirgistan, saw a UFO which set fire to a whole meadow. It began when somebody called the militia headquarters and said "*Come to the south entrance of the old airport. There is a huge UFO flying above it.*" A patrol car with 3 militiamen went to the spot. Shortly after they had crossed the city limits, the militia officer on duty, K. P. Kalugin, the chief of the militia investigation department, T. A. Zakov, and the militia radio operator, S. I. Savochin, saw the gigantic UFO—in their estimate it had a diameter of 300 feet—hovering at a height of between 400 and 500 feet. It looked like the planet Saturn, with a broad ring that had shining ports at the circumference; it seemed to rotate from time to time. From its side emerged a sharply defined cone of yellow light.

As soon as the patrol car approached it the UFO started moving south in the direction of the town Orto-Sai. For a time, the militia men lost sight of it, and then they saw a strange glow over a hill at the border of the town. They stopped, got out of the car and saw that the object had landed on the hill. It then rose slowly and flew away. It left behind 4 spots of burning grass, each 135 feet in diameter with a cross-shaped area in it, where the grass was unscathed. When the militia captain A. P. Sidelnikov inspected the landing site the next day, he discovered "honeycomb-like impressions," as he said when interviewed by the paper *Komsomolets Kirgizia* of the Communist youth organization.

Although the incidents at Kuybishev and Frunske served to remove the last doubts about UFOs being a reality, the most significant and spectacular incident had occurred years before that. It was an incident that gave more solid proof: metallic fragments which, beyond doubt, had not been produced on earth.

They came from a spherical UFO that had crashed at Dalnegorsk, north of Vladivostok, near the Siberian Pacific coast on January 29, 1986. Hundreds of inhabitants of this industrial city in the far east saw on that freezing winter day at 7:55 p.m., a ball of red light, about 3 feet in diameter, which seemed to be "made of some kind of glowing stainless steel," flying over the city silently and parallel to the ground, at a speed of about 30 miles per hour. Its destination was apparently the 1,835-foot Izveskovaya moun-

The Hill 611, above Dalagorsk, Siberia. The UFO crashed here (arrow).

Soviet scientists recover debris from the UFO wreck.

tain (often referred to as Mount 611, owing to its altitude of 611 meters), north of Dalnegorsk. Just before it reached the mountain, the ball changed course and rose at an angle of 60 to 70°, apparently to fly over the mountain. But, in all probability, this remote-controlled object missed the peak of Izveskovaya and crashed against the slope. Witnesses saw how it tore off a piece of rock about 18 feet wide, which fell to the earth with a loud noise. For almost half an hour, the ball tried again and again to rise, but fell back to the ground just as often, whereby its color changed gradually to a darker red. Then it seemed as if it had switched on a self-destroying mechanism. The object threw out flames which were as bright as a welding flame, exploded silently and burned for almost an hour until practically nothing was left.

On February 3, 1986, a team from the far east department of the "Investigation Committee of Anomalous Atmospheric Phenomena" of the "Scientific and Engineering Society" arrived at Dalnegorsk and examined the crash site.

There they found nothing more than a few pellets of lead and iron and— what later proved to be the most interesting find—some very fine, almost glassy, metal fabric. They also discovered some very significant magnetic anomalies as well as effects of extremely high temperatures. The silicated slate of the mountain was burned black and porous to a depth of 6 inches, partly broken into splinters by the heat, or flattened and turned to coal. The scientists estimated that it must have been subjected to temperatures of up to 25,000°C. More mysterious was the discovery that the slate at the site of crash had become magnetic, actually a physical impossibility. Besides that, an unknown radiation present at the site seemed to affect human beings. Their blood pressure and pulse increased, and they experienced dizziness and difficulties in balance. Later investigations showed that in the case of those who had been affected, the production of leukocytes, white blood corpuscles, had increased. The radiation also had the effect of increasing the quantity of bacteria. Birds avoided flying over the crash site.

The metal samples were examined in the various laboratories of the academy and also at 11 other research centers. Their results, published in various papers, were more than astonishing.

The "lead" pellets were shown by spectral analysis to actually be complicated alloys in which almost all known elements were found, as a metallurgist said during an interview with the journal *Socialist Industry*. One analysis showed that the pellets contained, apart from lead, 20% silicon, 15% iron, 10% aluminium, 2% each of titanium and silver, 1% of zinc, 1% magnesium, as well as traces of copper, calcium, sodium, vanadium, chromium, presidium, cerium, nickel, cobalt, lanthanum, molybdenum and potassium. Besides that, they showed openings that were characteristic of synthetic manufacture. The somewhat larger iron pellets, about 4mm in

The crash site at Hill 611. Photograph: ICUFON/V. Dvuzhilniyi

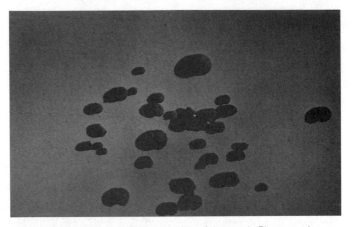

Metal balls that were found at the site of the crash. Photograph:
ICUFON/V. Dvuzhilniyi

Metal fabric found at the spot

diameter, included tungsten and cobalt and could be bored only with a diamond drill. X-ray analysis showed that the iron atoms had built a very
unusual crystalline structure. If one tried to melt them in a vacuum, the
structure changed to something equally strange and glass-like. Apart from
all this, they were, like all other finds from the site, extremely magnetic.

The most mysterious objects were the pieces of metal fabric. Optically a
glass-like porous, rough, and black encrusted mass, they presented a challenge to the scientists. *"It's impossible to find out what it is,"* said the
chemist A. Kulikov of the University of Vladivostok. *"It reminds one of
glass carbon. The conditions under which it can be produced are unknown.
Perhaps it was produced by extremely high temperatures."* His colleague,
Dr. Vladimir Vysotki, also a chemist at the University of Vladivostok, while
looking through the electron microscope found that it was a fine metallic

Clearly, an artificially made object. Microscope photograph of one of the metal balls of Dalnegorsk

network interspersed with threads of alpha-quartz, with a diameter of only 17 microns, one-fourth the thickness of human hair. Sometimes a dozen threads were plaited together like a rope and woven through the fabric, and in the middle of these was a fine thread of pure gold. *"That's a technology of the greatest precision,"* declared Dr. Vysotki, and speculated whether the quartz threads could be micro-cables. Quartz is a good insulator and gold, an excellent conductor. Other threads were alloys of gold, silver, zinc, lanthanum, silicon, sodium, cobalt and nickel.

For Dr. Vysotki it was clear: *"this fine metallic fabric is doubtlessly the product of a highly developed technology. A natural or terrestrial origin is out of the question, for no earthly production technique is capable of producing such fine material."* In addition, the metal fabric was immune to all acids. When heated to a temperature of 2,800°C, gold, silver and nickel vanished and were substituted by molybdenum, beryllium, and alpha-titanium. Heated in a vacuum, the material did not even burn. *"That shows that we are dealing with an artificial material,"* said the chemist Dr. A., Makayev who had investigated this aspect. *"Particularly interesting is the large proportion of organic material. It could mean that we are dealing here with some kind of artificial life. Perhaps this fabric is a dielectric substance which becomes a semiconductor upon heating and turns into a conductor in a vacuum."*

Whatever the object was, it was apparently missed by someone. During the following months, again and again, unidentified flying objects appeared over Dalnegorsk which seemed to be searching around the crash site. Dr. V. Dvulzhiny said in his report about the incident that at about 8:30 p.m., on February 6, 1986, 8 days after the crash, 2 yellow spheres appeared above

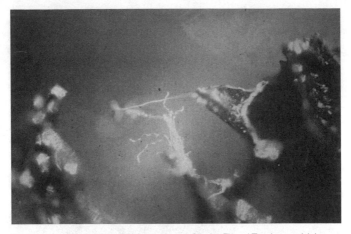

Microscope photograph of the metal fabric. Fine 17 micron thick
threads of alpha quartz stick out, in which still finer gold threads
were found. Photograph: ICUFON/V. Dvuzhilniyi

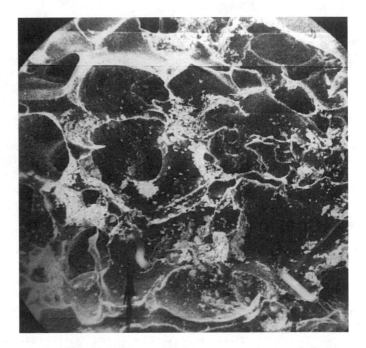

the city. They flew to Mount 611, circled 4 times there and disappeared at
lightning speed. After a series of sightings, on November 28, 1986, one of
the biggest UFO demonstrations in the history of the former Soviet Union
occurred over Dalnegorsk.

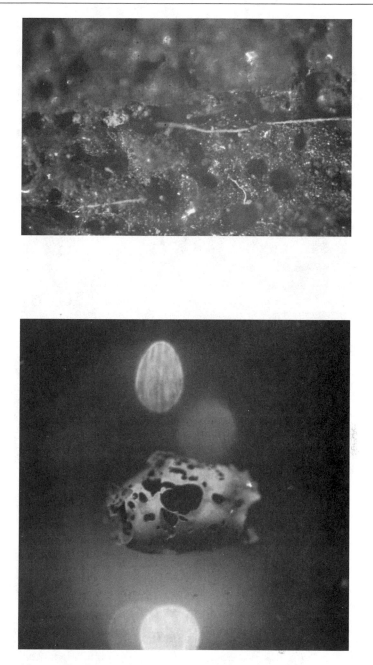

Above and at bottom, facing page, microscope photographs in various phases of the magnification of the Dalnegorsk fragments

UFO above Dalnegorsk, 1989.

On that Sunday, 33 UFOs flew at a low altitude over the east coast of Primorye. The flight took place between 9:10 p.m. and midnight. The objects crossed 5 regions and 12 cities. Witnesses described them as cylinders, cigars of a thousand feet in length, as well as spheres. Dalnegorsk was the center of

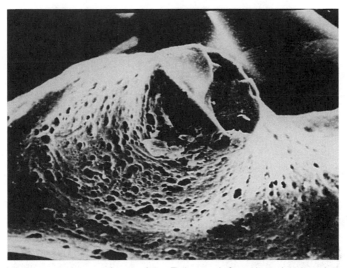

Microscope picture of one of the Dalnegorsk fragments shows web-like structure of the metal.

this activity. Thirteen objects flew low over Mount 611 in a radius of 1 to 2 miles, and directed searchlights towards the ground. Dvulzhiny, who had interviewed over a hundred eyewitnesses, said *"amongst the witnesses were men from the army and the militia, the border police and the Navy, as well as workers and academicians. The objects caused a two-minute interruption of all high-frequency receivers, television, telegraph. Computers stopped working and their programs were jammed. Apparently the UFOs were employing strong electromagnetic fields, many megawatts in strength."*

When the Secretary-General Mikhail Gorbachev visited a factory in the Urals in April 1990, workers asked him, *What about the rumors of unidentified flying objects?* According to the journal *Sovietskaya Molodezh* of May 4, 1990, his answer was that *"the UFO phenomenon is real and we should take it seriously and study it."* Perhaps he was thinking of something connected with Lenin, the founder of the Communist Party, of which he himself was to be the last secretary-general. The British author H. G. Wells once related a conversation he had had with Vladimir Illych Lenin when the two of them were discussing his book *The Time Machine*:

> I told Lenin that the development of human technology would one day change the face of the world, and that in such a changed world even the Marxist idea could become completely meaningless. Lenin looked at me and said 'You're right. It became clear to me when I read your book *The Time Machine*. All human ideas are measured according to the scales of our planet. They are

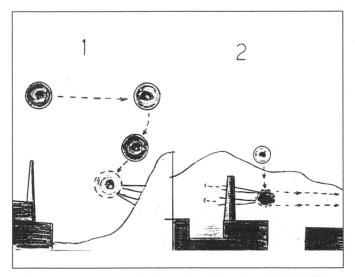

The UFO maneuver over Dalnegorsk on November 28, 1987. The trajectory of the objects, single sketches.

Dalnegorsk seen from Hill 611.

based on the assumption that technical potential, although it might be developed, will never exceed the terrestrial limit. If, however, we succeed in establishing interplanetary communication, then all our philosophical, moral and social ideas must be revised. In that case, the technical potential would be limitless, which would mean that violence would lose its role as a means and method of progress.

CHAPTER 15

Star Wars

The governor was more than punctual. His speech at the Lions Club at Leary, Georgia, was scheduled for 7:30 p.m. but the governor's limousine arrived at the club 20 minutes early, at 7:10 p.m., accompanied by the usual security escort. The reception committee, consisting of about 10 club functionaries and honored citizens of the town, rushed out of the clubhouse to greet the governor. The sun had already set and stars were beginning to appear in the azure blue sky, which was tinged red in the west from the last rays of the setting sun. The warm air made a person forget that it was already October. *"Governor, we thank you and consider it a great honor that you have come to us today,"* said the club president welcoming the governor.

He answered with his famous smile, *"Yes, it's nice to be back here in Leary. Isn't it a wonderful evening?"* He stood looking at the sky towards the place where the sun had vanished. Then he saw, close above the horizon, a bright light that was flying towards him. He had served in the Navy, knew the stars and was familiar with airplanes and helicopters. But this light behaved strangely, and while he silently observed the bright object, the other members of the club also noticed it. *"Governor, do you see that? What is it?"*

"I don't know." It came to a distance of about 500 yards from the group, and seemed to be as big as the moon. It was bright, had 3 lights on its surface and its color changed continually, going through the whole spectrum from violet to red. It hovered over the spot for a few minutes, shot back, then returned to the group, just to head back again, finally to disappear behind the horizon. The whole demonstration lasted for about 10 minutes. *"A UFO, a flying saucer,"* said one of the men. The governor only nodded, deep in thought, and he too had no better explanation for what they had seen.

One thing was certain for him. *"I will never make fun of people who say they've seen UFOs,"* he said, and has kept true to that statement all his life, even when he ran for the presidency in 1976. More than that, he promised, *"If I become President, I'll make every piece of information this country has about UFO sightings available to the public and the scientists."* He did become President and he kept his promise. During his period in office over 20,000 pages of documents from the U.S. Air Force and other services, which had been kept secret until then, were released. And further, through the Freedom Of Information Act (FOIA) 5 U.S.C. §552, passed by him, he declared that in the future, every U.S. citizen would have the right to ask for every document kept secret until then, from the relevant authorities, as long as this did not endanger national security.

With this policy of openness Carter made a number of powerful enemies, the most important one being the CIA director George Bush. Through dark

---

NATIONAL INVESTIGATIONS COMMITTEE ON AERIAL PHENOMENA (NICAP)®
3535 University Blvd. West
301-949-1267   Kensington, Maryland 20795

REPORT ON UNIDENTIFIED FLYING OBJECT(S)

This form includes questions asked by the United States Air Force and by other Armed Forces' investigating agencies, and additional questions to which answers are needed for full evaluation by NICAP.
After all the information has been fully studied, the conclusion of our Evaluation Panel will be published by NICAP in its regularly issued magazine or in another publication. Please try to answer as many questions as possible. Should you need additional room, please use another sheet of paper. Please print or typewrite. Your assistance is of great value and is genuinely appreciated. Thank you.

1. Name Jimmy Carter   Place of Employment

   Address State Capitol Atlanta   Occupation Governor
                                          Date of birth
                                          Education
                                          Special Training Graduate
   Telephone (404) 656-1776   Military Service Nuclear Physics
                                                           U.S. Navy
2. Date of Observation October 1969   Time   AM   PM   Time Zone
                                                            7:15   EST
3. Locality of Observation Leary, Georgia
4. How long did you see the object? _____ Hours 10-12 Minutes _____ Seconds
5. Please describe weather conditions and the type of sky; i.e., bright daylight, nighttime, dusk, etc. Shortly after dark.
6. Position of the Sun or Moon in relation to the object and to you. Not in sight.
7. If seen at night, twilight, or dawn, were the stars or moon visible? Stars.
8. Were there more than one object? No. If so, please tell how many, and draw a sketch of what you saw, indicating direction of movement, if any.
9. Please describe the object(s) in detail. For instance, did it (they) appear solid, or only as a source of light; was it revolving, etc.? Please use additional sheets of paper, if necessary.
10. Was the object(s) brighter than the background of the sky? Yes.
11. If so, compare the brightness with the Sun, Moon, headlights, etc. At one time, as bright as the moon.

35. Were you interrogated by Air Force investigators? By any other federal, state, county, or local officials? If so, please state the name and rank or title of the agent, his office, and details as to where and when the questioning took place.

    Were you asked or told not to reveal or discuss the incident? If so, were any reasons or official orders mentioned? Please elaborate carefully. No.

36. We should like permission to quote your name in connection with this report. This action will encourage other responsible citizens to report similar observations to NICAP. However, if you prefer, we will keep your name confidential. Please note your choice by checking the proper statement below. In any case, please fill in all parts of the form, for our own confidential files. Thank you for your cooperation.

    You may use my name. (x)   Please keep my name confidential. ( )

37. Date of filling out this report   Signature:

    9-18-73 INTERCONTINENTAL GALACTIC SPACECRAFT (UFO)   Jimmy Carter
            RESEARCH AND ANALYTIC NETWORK
            35-40 Seventy-fifth Street (Suite 4G)
            Jackson Heights, New York, 11372 U.S.A.

Questionnaire filled out by Jimmy Carter, when reporting his UFO sighting.

international intrigues, they staged the Teheran hostage affair and sabotaged all Carter's efforts to organize rescue efforts or mediation. As a result, Carter's popularity dropped beyond all hope of recovery and the hostages were freed—what a coincidence—on the very day when his successor in office, Ronald Reagan, and his vice president George Bush, were sworn in.

What remained was the media-created image of a naive peanut-farmer, which Carter had been only when he grew up on his parents' farm. He had joined the U.S. Navy as a young man, had graduated from the military academy as a nuclear physicist, and served as line officer on nuclear submarines. Although with this education and background he certainly fulfilled the qualifications of being a competent observer, NASA tried to convince Carter that the object he had seen, although it was *"as big and bright as the moon,"* had been nothing else but the planet Venus. At least for the President it was then clear how the public had been fooled and misled with such "intelligent" explanations over the decades. The picture given by the released secret documents justified the talk about a "Cosmic Watergate" of his predecessors.

For, until then, government authorities and the intelligence services had denied the existence of UFO secret files. This applied particularly to the CIA which had until then told all inquirers that *"the interest of the CIA in UFOs ended with the Robertson panel."* But it soon became clear that this was not so.

An ex-CIA employee, Ted Zachary, had given insider information to a UFO research group, the Ground Saucer Watch (GSW) of Phoenix, Arizona. And with this information, invoking the Freedom Of Information Act, GSW director William H. Spaulding asked the U.S. intelligence service for UFO documents. The coordinator of information of the CIA, C. F. Wilson, confirmed the existence of such files, but refused to hand them over "for national security reasons." With the aid of the New York Watergate-lawyer, Henry Rothblatt, Spaulding sued the CIA. The aggressive lawyer claimed that *"the CIA knows everything about UFOs"* and convinced the court to order a private chambers investigation to find out whether the national security was really endangered. The CIA was asked to produce over 20,000 pages of documents. The case ended in a partial victory for the plaintiff.

The procedures lasted for 14 months and, at the end, 925 pages—less than 5%—were released. These were more or less good photocopies of the originals, but full of blacked-out lines as proof, and the result, of censorship! *"These documents lead us to the conclusion that UFOs really exist,"* Spaulding told the press, and accused the government authorities of prevaricating and deliberately misleading the public. *"We possess information that categorically shows that the government does not tell the truth and that significant information is suppressed. We have caught them lying."* This referred especially to the claim of the CIA that they had not bothered with UFOs since 1953, whereas a CIA document of 1976 mentions that a foreign informant seeks the advice of *"the CIA UFO experts."* An internal memorandum of 1976 says *"at present the offices and personnel of the CIA are busy recording UFO phenomena. U.S. embassies have been instructed to*

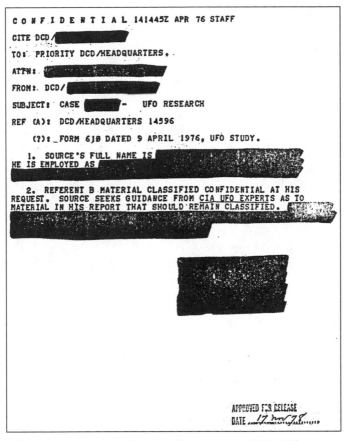

Official document released by the CIA, mentioning "CIA UFO experts" long after 1953

forward UFO reports to the CIA and to find out whether serious studies about UFOs have been carried out. The CIA has been informed that 4 countries have developed a kind of recording system for UFOs." As a matter of fact the documents that Spaulding received contained reports of over 200 UFO sightings from all over the world, including the Soviet Union. All this indicated that the worldwide UFO reporting system, which Marshall Chadwell, chief of the scientific department of the CIA, mentions in his memorandum of 1952 to the director of the CIA, had been in continuous operation for the last 25 years.

But the most important information that one gained from these released files was something quite different: according to them the UFOs demonstrated a great interest in the weapon technology of terrestrial powers . . .

UFO researcher Maj. Colman Von Keviczky of the ICUFON (Intercontinental UFO Research & Analytic Network) was the first to discover this, when he analyzed a wave of sightings and close encounters in the southeast of the U.S. The series of occurrences began on October 11, 1973, when two amateur fishermen, Charles Hickson, 42, and Calvin Parker, 19, were kidnapped by three alien beings and taken to a UFO.

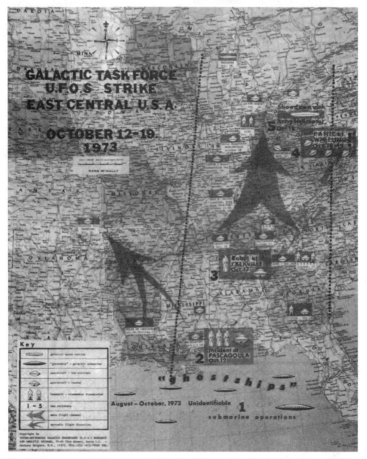

Strategic approach. Representation by Colman VonKeviczky of the UFO wave above southeastern United States, in October 1973.

The sun had set long ago, but the two friends still sat on a pier on the Pascagoula Bay, the estuary of one of the numerous distributaries of the Mississippi in the Gulf of Mexico, fishing poles in hand, waiting for a bite. Parker was actually the friend of Hickson's son. The 2 of them had often enough sat at that very spot, sometimes all 3 together, or sometimes only 2 of them, enjoying the peaceful view of the sea, the soothing sound of the waves and the cool breeze that came from the Gulf. But this evening they felt frustrated, for the fish would just not bite.

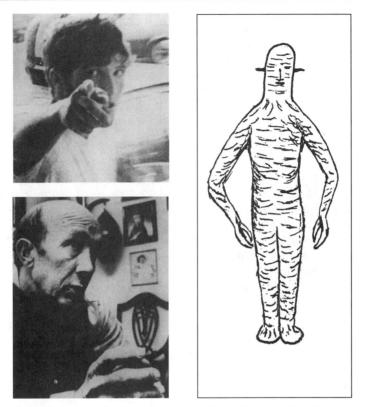

Calvin Parker, Charles Hickson and the alien, as they described him.

Charley swore saying, "I'm not going home until I've caught at least one damned fish!" He had hardly said this when he felt a tug on the line. When he felt that the fish had been properly hooked, he pulled the line in, unhooked the fish and threw it into a bucket. When he then turned around to get new bait for the hook he was paralyzed with fear for, behind him, only 50 feet away, he saw a glowing oval object from which came a barely audible hum. The UFO was hovering about 20 inches above the ground, had the shape of a football, with a dome on the top and a blue pulsating light on the side. At one end there were 2 windows. Now Calvin also turned around and was just as frightened. Charley's first thought was to get away from the spot as quickly as possible, but he was then caught by curiosity: what could be inside that thing?

At this moment, an opening appeared on the side of the object, from which a bright light emerged. Three beings came out of this opening. Calvin cried out aloud and Charley was trembling all over, thinking, *"damn, what do they want here?"* They were about 5 feet tall, moved stiffly like robots and seemed to be covered by a kind of gray and wrinkled skin, like that of an elephant. Instead of ears and nose, 3 pointed antennae were sticking out of the head which had no neck. Owing to the wrinkles, one could not make out whether they had eyes or not. They literally glided from the ship, hovered above the men who were paralyzed with fear, then grabbed them and took them into the space vessel. Calvin had meanwhile fainted.

The light inside was blindingly bright. Charley was still paralyzed and could not move. He could only register that something like an eye came out of a wall and seemed to inspect him. *"Why don't they just kill me?"* he thought. Scenes from the Korean War went through his head. And then he collected himself. After a time, the beings came back and took him out again. *"Perhaps it's not my day to die, after all,"* he thought to himself with relief as he was laid down on the cold ground. He could feel that he could slowly move his legs again. Then he saw Calvin. He stood there as if turned to stone: on one leg, an armed stretched out, the face distorted with fear. Charley crawled over to Calvin, but before he reached him he heard the humming noise again. He turned his head towards the spaceship and saw it rising slowly, and the shooting off into the sky. At the end he heard a voice in his head saying "We come in peace, and are no danger to you."

He finally reached Calvin and shook him. Slowly Calvin came back to himself and fell to the ground giving out a loud cry. It took a few minutes before he recognized Charley again. Then he shouted excitedly, *"What do we do now? Who are they? What are they going to do with us?"*

When the pair of them had finally calmed down, they drove to the nearest telephone booth and called the Keesler Air Force Base at Biloxi, Mississippi. *"Sorry, that's not in our jurisdiction,"* said a tired female voice after he had described his experience to her, *"call the sheriff."* The fisherman burst out *"My God! What if it's only part of a huge invasion?"* The sheriff took down the report and, although the men had expressly said that they did not want any publicity, he informed the local press. The next day, papers all over the country reported this incident. After this, two UFO researchers came to Pascagoula: the astronomer J. Allan Hynek, former advisor to the U.S. Air Force in UFO matters, now running the private Center for UFO Studies (CUFOS) at Evanston near Chicago, and Prof. James Harder of the University of California at Berkeley, who was working with the UFO research group APRO (Aerial Phenomena Research Organization). Both were soon convinced that the men had indeed gone through a traumatic experience and were not acting. A test with a lie-detector and hypnotic regression carried out by Prof. Harder confirmed this impression, as did also an official press release from the U.S. Coast Guard a few weeks later. According to this report, on November 6 two fishermen in the Gulf of Mexico had seen a strange glowing object that was flying at a height of about 4 feet above the water and at a speed of 5 to 6 miles per hour. They informed the Coast Guard. A search boat was sent out and its crew also saw a metallic object that projected an amber-colored beam of light over the sea. But the object escaped every effort of the boat to get near it.

Professor Jim Harder, of the University of California, Berkeley, and Astronomer Prof. J. Alan Hynek, examining the Pascagoula case.

One month before the Pascagoula incident, on September 8, 1973, 2 U.S. military policemen, Sergeant Burns and Sergeant Shade, had a UFO encounter at Hunter Army Airfield in Georgia. At about 2:20 a.m., in the course of a routine patrol of the installation perimeter, they *"noticed an object traveling at what appeared to be a high rate of speed from east to west at approximately 2,000 feet altitude and crossing the post perimeter,"* they later wrote in their report, released under the Freedom of Information Act. *"Ten minutes later, they resighted the 'object' when it appeared at tree-top level and made an apparent dive at their vehicle, seemingly just missing the vehicle."* It apparently came so close that, as the report explicitly states: *"There was no damage to the vehicle."* But this did not end the eerie chase. *"The object reappeared at another location and hovered for approximately 15 mintues in front of them,"* the report continued, and *"the unidentified object appeared to have brilliantly flashing lights, blue, white and amber in color. They then returned to the main post area and were followed by the unidentified object 50 to 100 feet away at treetop level until it finally veered off and visual contact was lost. The object made no noise. The sighted UFO was described as round or oval in shape and between 35 and 75 feet across."*

Six days after the Pascagoula landing, on October 17, 1973, Jeffrey Greenhaw, chief of police at Falkville, Alabama, received an excited call from a woman at 10:15 p.m.

Police chief Jeffrey Greenhaw at the spot where he shot the 4 Polaroid pictures of the alien (or alien robot).

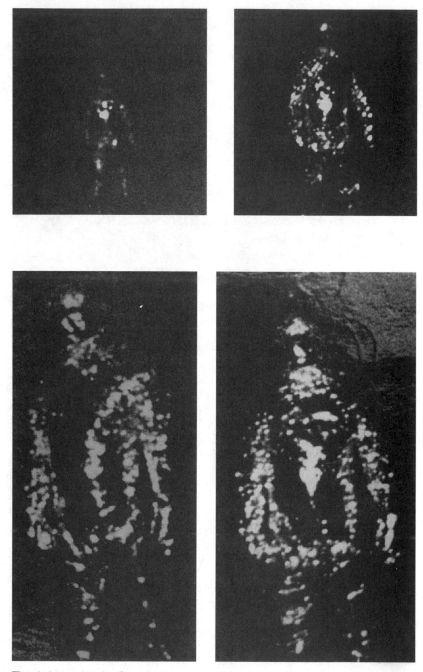

The 4 shots taken by Greenhaw.

saying that a spaceship had landed west of the town. Although he did not believe in UFOs he decided to go and investigate the report. He took his Polaroid camera, got into his car and drove out. At the alleged landing spot there was nothing. But Greenhaw then decided to look around in the fields before returning.

The moment he turned into the first field track, his searchlights picked up a metallic-looking figure. The policeman stopped, got out of the car and shouted *"Hey, Stranger!"* The figure did not react but marched with stiff steps straight towards the police car. The thing was getting uncanny. Greenhaw took out his camera and shot 2 photographs of the figure. About 6 feet away from the car the figure stopped. Greenhaw related later, *"At that moment I had one feeling—get away from here—but I felt as if I had been paralyzed and was too afraid to move. I wanted to pull out my gun, but I was afraid of what would happen after that. Then I collected myself and took 2 more photographs."* After that he put the camera in the car and switched on the blue light. When he looked up again he saw the figure running off towards the south with arms stretched down stiffly, the left and right side of the body alternately swaying forwards and backwards. Greenhaw: *"I thought it had springs under its feet, for with every step it covered about 9 feet."*

The policeman jumped into the car, started it and turned, but the car started skidding. By the time he had his vehicle under control again and could finally take up the pursuit, the creature had disappeared. After a vain search, the police chief returned to his station. The next day, he showed the 4 photographs to his wife, his brother and a number of policeman, and finally a reporter. He was met only with skepticism and derision. He did not know at that time that these pictures were to ruin his life. It was as if from that moment that there was a curse upon him. Unknown people sent him threatening letters, ransacked his car and burned his house down. Then to crown it all off, his wife left him. This blow, added to the terror from the unknown, and contempt from his neighbors, was too much for him. He became a nervous wreck, unfit for duty as a policeman. There was nothing else left for him to do but to give up his job and leave Falkville for ever. He lost everything he had possessed, and started a new life in another town—as a carpenter.

When VonKeviczky examined this case, it occurred to him that Falkville was only 15 miles away from Redstone Arsenal near Huntsville, Alabama, the largest center for space technology in the United States. Could the aliens' visit have something to do with that? As a matter of fact, according to an article which appeared in the magazine *Newsweek* on September 30, 1974, a laser tank was being developed at the Redstone testing ground during the period in question. Furthermore, Colman VonKeviczky was able to show that at the same time, dozens of sightings occurred along the Mississippi.

Only a day after the Falkville incident, a cigar-shaped object demonstrated to a helicopter of the U.S. Army that it possessed a "ray" technology far superior to that of lasers. Witness to this incident was Col. Lawrence E.

Coyne, an experienced helicopter pilot (over 3,000 hours of flight) who was on a routine flight with 3 other crew members on October 18, 1973.

At 10:30 p.m. the helicopter UH-1H of the U.S. Army Reserves took off from Port Columbus, Ohio, on the way to its base, the Cleveland Hopkins military airport. Col. Coyne was in command and with him were Lt. Arrigo Jezzi, Sgt. John Healey and Sgt. Robert Yanaczek. They were flying at an altitude of about 2,400 feet at a speed of 90 mph.

It was a clear and quiet night. At 11:02 p.m. Yanaczek noticed a red light just above the southeastern horizon. At first he thought it was an airplane, but it did not blink. After watching it for a minute, he called it to the attention of Coyne. Half a minute later the object changed its course and headed directly towards the helicopter. Coyne reacted immediately and brought the helicopter down in altitude by almost 600 feet. At the same time he established radio contact with the control tower of Mansfield airport which was in the neighborhood. Mansfield replied, but the contact broke off immediately and every attempt made by Coyne to reach them on another frequency failed. The red light was still on a collision course. Then it stopped suddenly, remained hovering in the air at an angle of about 45° from the nose of the helicopter.

Now the men in the helicopter could make out the shape of this object. It looked like a cigar with a bulge on the top, between 50 and 60 feet in length, gray and metallic in color. Janaczek could see a row of windows around the dome-like bulge. The red light that they had seen was at the front of the UFO and another white light was at the back. A green pyramid-like beam, like that of a searchlight, came out from the nose of the object and fell on the helicopter. The entire cockpit was lit up at the moment in an eerie greenish color. *"My God, what's happening to us?"* yelled Col. Coyne. His compass went crazy and started rotating slowly. All attempts to reach any ground station over the radio were in vain. Then as the object began to rise up into the sky, the helicopter was drawn up with it as if it were bound to it by invisible chains. Although the controls had been set for descent, the helicopter rose by about 900 feet per minute until it reached an altitude of 4,000 feet. The crew of the helicopter then felt a kind of jolt and saw to their relief that this mysterious flying object was leaving them. During the 5 minutes that all this had lasted, they did not hear the slightest sound. The green light went out and the UFO flew with tremendous speed westwards, then changed direction to northwest, accelerated, became brighter and shot off. Now, the crew was able to get radio contact with the FAA flight service station again. They eventually landed at the base without further incident.

Apart from Coyne and his crew, there were other witnesses to this occurrence. At 11:00 p.m., Mrs. C—— and her 4 children were returning home from Mansfield when they saw a bright red light that was flying south. Soon it disappeared behind the trees on the side of the road. Five minutes later, they saw it again, now as 2 lights, red and green, which rose up at a high speed. Mrs. C—— became curious and parked the car at the side of the road

The UFO encounter of Capt. Lawrence J. Coyne, as described by witnesses.

and got out. She could see that another light was flying in the opposite direction, coming from the southwest and, in contrast to the silent flight of the first object, clattered loudly. She could now see the first object more clearly. It was *"as big as a school bus, and shaped like a pear."* When it was almost above the helicopter, it sent out a green beam to cover the helicopter. *"It was as if the rays shot out of the object,"* said the children. *"Everything was colored green—the helicopter, the trees, the road, the car."* Anxiously she ran back to the car and drove away as fast as she could. The last thing they saw was the unknown object flying away towards the northwest.

It took only 2 years until the aliens demonstrated their capabilities at one of the most sensitive areas of the American defense system—at the nuclear arsenals of the Strategic Air Command (SAC). Over 2,000 installations are

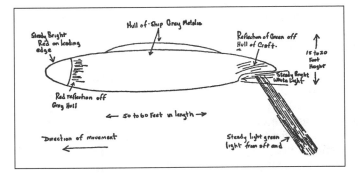

The UFO, as sketched by Capt. Coyne.

under the command of the SAC, and in most of them, intercontinental ballistic missiles (ICBMs) equipped with nuclear warheads are stationed. Since they are meant primarily to act as deterrents—their actual use would make the target area uninhabitable for decades—they are very carefully safeguarded and only the President can give orders to start them. Only through a 7-digit code, transmitted to the SAC, can the ICBMs be unlocked, the start button be pressed. This code is kept in a black suitcase, always handcuffed to its carrier, one of the security officials who accompany the President wherever he goes. Each ICBM is programmed with a special code which determines its target. But what happens when someone erases or changes these codes?

"That's impossible," the national security experts say. But they were proven wrong on more than one occasion.

Such a situation arose in the autumn of 1975 when a number of unknown flying objects more or less simultaneously maneuvered over a number of ICBM bases of the SAC in the northern states, and landed many times near the nuclear weapon silos. These incidents are documented—in secret files which were released under the FOIA as well as in a report about the sightings compiled by Col. Terence C. James of the U.S. Air Force Department on October 4, 1977, for the UFO researcher and ex-CIA employee Todd Zechel. The sightings began on October 27, 1975, when the alarm sirens at Loring Air Force Base in the state of Maine started howling. An unidentified flying object had violated the air security zone above the missile depots.

At 7:45 p.m. Sgt. Maj. Danny Lewis had seen the object when he was patrolling along the 12-foot high barbed wire fencing that surrounded the arsenal area of about 200 acres. Another sergeant, Steven Eichner, chief of a B-52 bomber crew, could see it a bit closer and described it as *"like a stretched-out football. It hovered still and motionless in the air. It had a red-orange color and was the length of about 4 trucks. It seemed to be surrounded by some kind of haze for the color seemed to change. It was like the shimmering of hot air in the desert. But it was a solid object."* At this time Sgt. Major James B. Sampley of the 2192nd contact squadron working at the tower picked up an echo on the radar screen showing an object within the security zone. He looked out of the window and saw an object that was circling around the northern side of the base at a height of about 300 feet, and then coming down to a height of 150 feet. When he informed Col. Richard C. Chapman, the commander of the 42nd bomber squadron, about this, he immediately called out alert stage 3. NORAD, the North American Air Defense Commando, could not send an interceptor at once to investigate. The object flew around the security area for 40 minutes and then disappeared in the direction of Canada.

Exactly 24 hours later the UFO returned. Again at 7:45 p.m. 3 members of the military police saw the object, also picked up on radar, with lights flashing white, orange and blue. During the next hour, it flew down to an altitude of 150 feet, crossed the runway, hovered for a few minutes above

ATTEMPTS TO IDENTIFY THIS AIRCRAFT HAVE SO FAR MET WITH NEGATIVE RESULTS.

2. IN THE INTEREST OF NUCLEAR WEAPONS SECURITY THE ACTION ADDRESSEES WILL ASSUME SECURITY OPTION III DURING HOURS OF DARKNESS UNTIL FURTHER NOTICE.

ACTIONS ALSO SHOULD BE TAKEN TO RE-ESTABLISH LIAISON WITH LOCAL LAW ENFORCEMENT AGENCIES THAT COULD ASSIST YOUR BASE IN THE EVENT OF A SIMILAR INCIDENT. BASES SHOULD THOROUGHLY REVIEW AND INSURE ALL PERSONNEL ARE FAMILIAR WITH ACTIONS TO TAKE IAW THE HELICOPTER DENIAL PORTION OF YOUR 207-XX PLAN.

SUBJECT: DEFENSE AGAINST HELICOPTER ASSAULT.

1. SEVERAL RECENT SIGHTINGS OF UNIDENTIFIED AIRCRAFT/ HELICOPTERS FLYING/HOVERING OVER PRIORITY A RESTRICTED

AREAS DURING THE HOURS OF DARKNESS HAVE PROMPTED THE IMPLEMENTATION OF SECURITY OPTION 3 AT OUR NORTHERN TIER BASES. SINCE 27 OCT 75, SIGHTINGS HAVE OCCURRED AT LORING AFB, WURTSMITH AFB, AND MOST RECENTLY, AT MALMSTROM AFB. ALL ATTEMPTS TO IDENTIFY THESE AIRCRAFT HAVE MET WITH NEGATIVE RESULTS.

2. WHILE AFFECTED BASES ARE NOW RETURNING TO NORMAL SECURITY POSTURES (AT THE OPTION OF THE LOCAL COMMANDER), ALL SAC SECURITY POLICE UNITS ARE REQUESTED TO MONITOR AND REPORT ALL SIGHTINGS OF UNIDENTIFIED AIRCRAFT/HELICOPTERS FLYING/ HOVERING IN THE VICINITY OF WEAPONS STORAGE AREAS, AIRCRAFT ALERT AREAS AND MISSILE LAUNCH/LAUNCH CONTROL FACILITIES.

AT THE DISCRETION OF LOCAL COMMANDERS, UNITS WILL IMPLEMENT AN APPROPRIATE SECURITY POSTURE UPON DETECTION OF SIMILAR CIRCUMSTANCES.

3. ACTIONS SHOULD ALSO BE TAKEN TO RE-ESTABLISH LIAISON WITH LOCAL LAW ENFORCEMENT AGENCIES AND FEDERAL AVIATION AGENCIES WHICH COULD BE MOBILIZED TO ASSIST IN THE IDENTIFICATION OF UNIDENTIFIED AIRCRAFT/HELICOPTERS HERE ALL PERSONNEL ARE FAMILIAR WITH ACTIONS TO TAKE IAW THE HELICOPTER DENIAL PORTION OF YOUR 207-XX PLAN.

4. FOR THE FOLLOWING UNITS ONLY:

OPTION III, IMPLEMENTED BY CINCSAC/SP 2920258 OCT 75, SAME SUBJECT, IS RESCINDED.

Capt Dowman, SPOA, 3301, 10 Nov 75/op

R.F. MOTTLEY, Lt Col, SPO, 2134   UNCLASSIFIED

Documents of the Pentagon and SAC about the observation of unidentified flying objects in the immediate vicinity of U.S. Air Force missile depots. "In the interest of security of nuclear weapons, security level 3 continues during the hours of the night."

the missile silos and finally landed between them. When a number of police vehicles raced towards the object, it switched off its lights and departed. Col. Chapman informed the National Military Commando Center (NMCC) in Washington, the SAC headquarters and the chief of staff. They sent him a UH-1 Huey helicopter of the National Guard which, however, arrived long after the UFO had flown off. It then appeared above Brunswick Naval Base in Maine. *"It came in at a very low altitude, just above the treetops, coming from the direction of the ocean,"* said a witness from the Navy. *"It was like a helicopter, but also different, twice as big as a helicopter with red and white lights and capable of making 90° turns. We switched on all the lights until the base looked like a Christmas tree. The thing hovered for 5 or 10 minutes above the base and then shot off over the Atlantic."* Other SAC bases also received unexpected visits. The Malmstrom Base in Montana reported that when a UFO flew over it at a height of over 200 feet, the electric supply failed. The lights came on again when the object had gone far enough away and was a certain distance. After that, it zoomed off into the sky and disappeared.

The next day the CIA, informed about these UFO alarms, asked for immediate information about all future cases. And the next case happened the very next night. On October 31, at about 1:55 a.m. an unknown object was hovering above the SAC arsenal at Wurtsmith Air Base near Oskoda, Michigan. It had *"a white light that was beamed downwards and two red lights at the edge,"* as described in the official report. The crew of an air tanker, KC 135, flying at a height of 2,700 feet saw it and also picked it up on radar. An interceptor was sent up at once, and its crew could see the object directly as well as on radar. They pursued it until it was over Lake Huron. *"Whenever we tried to get closer, it accelerated and shot away. Finally it disappeared at a speed of about 1,100 mph,"* one of the pilots reported. But that was only a prelude.

The UFOs came again on November 7, 1975, this time above the Malmstrom Air Base near Lewiston, Montana. Malmstrom was the first air base to install Minuteman missiles. These 3-stage remote-controlled rockets were the most modern missiles at that time, which, once started, could get to a target over 6,000 miles away at a speed of over 15,000 miles per hour and with extreme precision.

The ICBM complex at Malmstrom encompassed an area of over 230 square miles and was one of the largest nuclear weapon arsenals in the country. During that evening of November 7, 2 officers had just taken over patrol at the underground control area and were going through a routine check of the ICBM launch system, when a shrill alarm sounded.

That meant there were intruders in the security zone. The commander of the rocket station called up the military police and a Sabotage Alert Team (SAT) started off to see what was happening at sector K-7. When the team reached a road leading to the missile silos, they could see a luminous object floating at about 300 feet above sector K-7. When they came closer, they realized how big it was: it was an orange-glowing disc, as large as a football field, and it illuminated the missile site. The SAT team was ordered to proceed, but was afraid to do so. The men were all armed with machine guns, but none of them even remotely thought of firing at the UFO, which was sending a beam of light, as bright as daylight, down to the silos. When it slowly started increasing its altitude, they informed the commander over the radio. At the same time, the radar system of NORAD spotted the object and started 2 F-106 interceptors from the air base at Great Falls, Montana. But before these fighters could get to that area, the UFO had risen to a height of nearly 45 miles and vanished from NORAD's radar. Whereas the military policemen had to undergo a psychological test at the base hospital, because they were obviously suffering from shock, the computer experts, technicians and officers in the underground commando center had a very different problem to deal with. The target codes of the remote control system of the ICBMs had been changed. Each Minuteman rocket was tested separately, but the result was the same in all cases. If at that moment an atomic war had broken out, the United States would have been helpless. Not one Minuteman rocket could have been started. Nobody could understand how this happened, for normally any changing of codes was a complicated process which took many hours to complete.

As can be read in the released documents of NORAD and the Air Force, during this night UFOs had been seen above 6 different missile depots at Malmstrom. The 24th NORAD Regional Senior Director's log speaks of a *"very bright object . . . (which) seems to have lights (several) on it, but no distinct pattern. The orange/gold object overhead also has small lights on it"* that stood over the silos, *"issuing a black object from it, tubular in shape."* An official National Military Command Center "Memorandum of Record," dated November 8, 1975, 6:00 a.m. EST, states:

"SAC Site L-5 observed one object accelerate, and climb rapidly to a point in altitude where it became indistinguishable from the stars. NORAD will carry this incident as a FADE remaining unknown."

FADE was an Air Force code word, short for "Faded Giant," denoting tampering with nuclear weapons. The consequences were more than disquieting. After all, the whole idea of nuclear deterrents is based on the assumption that the rockets would be in readiness to start at any minute. But somehow, unknown intruders had paralyzed the Strategic Air Command by changing highly secret data, as if it was the simplest thing in the world to do!

The next morning the Malmstrom incident was on the agenda of a meeting of the General Staff at the Pentagon. The generals of the Department of Defense were suddenly confronted with the situation that the UFOs clearly caused a security risk. Someone who was more powerful than they were was in a position to deliver a decisive blow to the central nerve of American national defense, with America's own scientific wizards being unable to find any kind of explanation for it. They were completely helpless—the aliens could enter into the most painstakingly guarded areas of the U.S. security system and manipulate their nuclear weapons as and when they pleased and nobody could do anything about it. *"We must be kept constantly informed,"* said the Air Force Chief of Staff, David C. Jones of NORAD, *"and we must find a way to stop this from happening again."* And then they decided on a difficult step: *"We must inform the President."* The next day in the daily letter, the highly secret report about the world situation which is handed over to the president of the United States each day at breakfast time, Gerald Ford was informed about the events at the SAC bases.

On the previous evening, November 8, the nocturnal siege had continued. UFOs appeared again at 7:45 p.m., this time 7 of them together as blips on the radar screen of the 24th NORAD region. Two F-106 interceptors were started, but when they got even close to the UFOs, the intruders turned their lights off and became invisible, only to turn them on again after the jets left the area.

SAT units of the Malmstrom base saw the UFOs again hovering above the Minuteman silos. Then they flew towards the southwest and were seen later above 2 other high-security zones. At 9:53 p.m. they finally accelerated and vanished into the night sky. At 3:20 in the morning, three ICBM crews reported again *"an orange-white disc-shaped object."* A day later another remote-controlled missile arsenal was the target of an "unknown operation." The logbook of the 24th NORAD region says that a *"bright star-like object in the west, moving east, about the size of a car . . . passed over the radar station, 1,000 feet to 2,000 feet high, no noise heard. Three people from the site or local area saw the object."*

On November 11, the UFOs appeared over Canada. Officers of the Royal Canadian Air Force at Falconbridge, Ontario, picked up the *"radar track of an unidentified object about 25–30 nautical miles south of the site, ranging in altitude from 25,000 to 72,000 feet."* And eventually, the Commander-in-Charge of NORAD sent the following message to all NORAD units in North America:

"Since 28 Oct 75, numerous reports of suspicious objects have been received at the NORAD Central Command; reliable military personnel at Loring AFB, Maine; Wurtsmith AFB, Michigan; Malmstrom AFB, Montana; Minot AFB, North Dakota, and Canadian Forces Station, Falconbridge, Ontario, Canada, have visually sighted suspicious objects . . . To date efforts by Air Guard helicopters and NORAD F-106s have failed to produce positive identification . . . Be assured that this command is doing everything possible to identify and provide solid factual information on these sightings . . ."

But all these attempts were in vain and the UFO flights went on. On January 21, 1976, 2 UFOs appeared above the nuclear weapons complex of Cannon Air Force Base in New Mexico. *"Security police observing them reported the UFOs to be 25 yards in diameter, gold or silver in color with a blue light on top, a hole in the middle and a red light on the bottom,"* says a memorandum of the NMCC (National Military Commando Center), written by Rear Admiral J. B. Morin USN to the Deputy Director for Operations. Six months later, at 2:55 a.m. on July 30, 1976, renewed UFO activities were reported above Fort Ritchie, Maryland: *"Two different patrols from Sector R reported the sighting of 3 long objects, red in color, moving from east to west."* Five minutes later a sergeant checking on this report saw a UFO hovering at a height of 300 to 500 feet above the arsenal. Forty-five minutes later another sergeant, on his way to his duty, saw an object *"as big as a 2½-ton truck."*

That the terrestrial defense technology was indeed helpless against the unknown visitors was shown during an incident that occurred on September 19, 1976, and drew worldwide attention. Newspapers in Teheran reported this incident based on information given by the Iranian Royal Air Force. During that night a UFO was picked up by radar, flying at an altitude of about 5,500 feet. Two fighters of the type F-4 Phantom were launched to intercept the unknown intruder. When they pursued the object a smaller flying object shot out of the UFO and started pursuing one of the interceptors. When the pilot of the fighter tried to shoot at the object, his automatic firing system failed, before the entire electronic board including the radio communication system went dead. The pilot had no other choice but to dive down and escape. The mini-UFO returned to its mother ship which then ejected a disc-shaped object of about 14 feet in diameter, which landed south of Teheran. The next day Shah Reza Pahlevi ordered the Air Force to compile a detailed report of the incident, a copy of which was given to the U.S. embassy in Teheran. The Embassy sent the report not only to the State Department, but also to the White House, CIA, DIA, NSA, the Joint Chiefs of Staff at the Pentagon, as well as the commanders of the U.S. armed forces in Europe and in the Middle East. In September 1977 this report, originally classified as confidential, was released under the Freedom Of Information Act. It says:

This report forwards information regarding sighting of a UFO in Iran on September nineteenth, 1976.

A. At about 12:30 AM on 19 Sep 76, the——[words here are blacked out] received 4 telephone calls from citizens living in the Shemiran area of Tehran saying that they had seen strange objects in the sky. Some reported a kind of bird-like object, while others reported a helicopter with a light on. There were no helicopters airborne at that time.——[blacked out]

After he told the citizen it was only stars and had talked to Mehrabad Tower, he decided to look for himself. He noticed an object in the sky similar to a star, bigger and brighter. He decided to scramble an F-4 from Shahrokhi AFB to investigate.

B. At 1:30 on the 19th the F-4 took off and proceeded to a point about 40 nautical miles north of Tehran. Due to its brilliance, the object was easily visible from 70 miles away. As the F-4 approached a range of 25 nm, he lost all instrumentation and communication (UHF and intercom). He broke off the intercept and headed back for Shahroki. When the F-4 turned away from the object, and apparently was no longer a threat to it, the aircraft regained all instrumentation and communications. At 01:40, a second F-4 was launched. The back-seater acquired a radar lock-on at 27 nm, 12 o'clock high position with the VC (rate of closure) at 150 nmph. As the range decreased to 25 nm, the objects moved away at a speed that was visible on the radar scope and stayed at 25 nm.

C. The size of the radar return was comparable to that of a 707 tanker. The visual size of the object was difficult to discern because of its intense bril-

Iranians open fire on shining UFO

BEIRUT, Lebanon (UPI) — Anti-aircraft batteries opened fire on an unidentified flying object as it shone over northeastern Tehran, but apparently missed it, Iran's official Islamic Republic News Agency reported yesterday.

The shining object that flew from west to east about 8:15 p.m. on Monday had not been identified, but some reports said it might be a satellite.

Tehran's anti-aircraft unit believed that the object was an Iraqi warplane and opened fire on it. There was no immediate comment on the report, and there were no reports that the flying object had been hit or shot down.

A Middle East newspaper report about the Teheran incident.

liance. The light that it gave off was that of flashing strobe lights arranged in a rectangular pattern and alternating blue, green, red and orange in color. The sequence of the lights was so fast that all the colors could be seen at once. The object and the pursuing F-4 continued on a course to the south of Tehran, when another brightly lit object, estimated to be one-half to one-third the apparent size of the moon, came out of the original object. The second object headed straight towards the F-4 at a very fast rate of speed. The pilot attempted to fire an AIM-9 missile at the object, but at that instant, his weapons control panel went off and he lost all communications (UHF and interphone). At this point the pilot initiated a turn and Negative G dive to get away. As he turned, the object fell in trail at what appeared to be about 3–4 nm. As he continued in his turn away from the primary object, the second object went to the inside of his turn, then returned to the primary object for a perfect rejoin.

D. Shortly after the second object joined up with the primary object, another object appeared to come out of the other side of the first object going straight down at a great rate of speed. The F-4 crew had regained communications and control of the weapons panel and watched the object approach the ground anticipating a large explosion. This object appeared to come to rest gently on the Earth and cast a very bright light over an area of about 2 miles.

The crew descended from their altitude of 26 M to 15 M miles and continued to observe and mark the object's position. They had some difficulty in adjusting their night visibility for landing, so after cir-

Report of the U.S. Embassy, Teheran, to the State Department about the incident.

cling Mehrabad a few times, they went in for a straight landing. There
was a lot of interference on the UHF and each time they passed
through a magnetic bearing of 150 degrees from Mehrabad they lost
their communications (UHF and interphone) and the INS fluctuated
between 30–50 degrees. The one civil airliner that was approaching
Mehrabad during this same time experienced communications failure
in the same vicinity (Kilo Zulu), but did not report seeing anything.
While the F-4 was on a long final approach the crew noticed another
cylinder-shaped object about the size of a T-bird at 10 M with bright
steady lights on each end and a flasher in the middle. When queried
the tower stated there was no other known traffic in the area. During
the time that the object passed over the F-4, the tower did not have a
visual on it but picked it up after the pilot told them to look between
the mountains and the refinery.

E. During daylight, the F-4 crew was taken out to the area in a helicopter
where the object had apparently landed. Nothing was noticed at the
spot where they thought the object landed (a dry lake bed), but as they
circled off to the west of the area they picked up a very noticeable
beeper signal. At the point where the return was the loudest was a
small house with a garden. They landed and asked the people there if
they had noticed anything strange last night. The people talked about
a loud noise and a very bright light like lightning. The aircraft and the
area where the object is believed to have landed are being checked for
possible radiation. More information will be forwarded when it
becomes available.

What makes this case particularly remarkable is the fact that during the
same night, UFOs had been seen above Morocco and Lisbon. The circumstance seems to have drawn the attention of the then-U.S. Secretary of State
Henry Kissinger, as a telex sent out by the State Department shows.
Between 1:00 and 1:30 a.m., the headquarters of the Moroccan police station received dozens of calls from Agadir, the area around Marrakesh and
Casablanca, Rabat and Kenitra, all referring to a silvery shining round
object flying over Morocco towards the northeast. The UFO flew at a
height of 3,000 feet, was silent but threw out bright sparks at intervals.
When seen from the side, it resembled a tube. The copy of the telex sent to
the U.S. State Department from Morocco includes a report from an officer
of the Royal Moroccan Police who had been on his way from Kenitra to
Rabat at 1:15 in the morning. When he saw the UFO, it was flying relatively slowly and parallel to the coast. At first, it seemed to be disc-like,
until it came nearer and he recognized that it had a tubular shape. Henry
Kissinger then addressed the Moroccan Government personally for further
information.

On January 20, 1977, Jimmy Carter was sworn in as the President of
the United States. A few weeks later, top ranking officers of the intelli-

gence services briefed him on the latest UFO cases in the United States. *"Agents are collecting reports of UFO/IAC sightings and incidents occurring on or near sensitive governmental installations . . . Aliens have been extremely interested in our nuclear weapons and nuclear research. Many reported military sightings and incidents occur over nuclear weapons bases. The aliens' interest in our nuclear weapons can only be attributed to the future threat of a nuclear war on Earth. The Air Force has initiated measures to assure the security of the nuclear weapons from alien theft or destruction. M12 feels confident the aliens are on an exploration of our solar system for peaceful purposes. However, we must continue to observe and track the aliens' movements until it is determined that the aliens' future plans contain no threat to our national security and the civilizations on Earth."*

After this briefing, Carter knew that he could keep his promise made during the elections only to a limited extent. Had he told the public the whole truth about UFOs, everything he had learned during that day in February, there would have been a panic. How could he, the newly elected president, stand before his people and concede that there was a power whose intentions seemed to be peaceful, but at whose mercy one stood for survival? On the other hand, one could not keep telling lies forever. In his heart, Carter hated the policy of silence, the stultification of the public's right to know, the ridiculing of eyewitnesses who, in all honesty, were only trying to describe what they had experienced. The magic words for the solution to this conflict were once more "an educational program."

But this time its aim was different from what it had been in 1953: a gradual step-by-step release of information to make the public get accustomed

```
                              DECLASSIFIED
PASEK MICHAEL S
76 STATE 244918
                      UNCLASSIFIED
UNCLASSIFIED
PAGE 01         STATE  244918
65
ORIGIN OES-06
INFO  OCT-01  NEA-10  ISO-00  /017 R
DRAFTED BY OES:FIRVING
APPROVED BY OES:FIPVING
                                              030035
P 020427Z OCT 76
FM SECSTATE WASHDC
TO AMEMBASSY RABAT PRIORITY
UNCLAS STATE 244918
FOR AMB ANDERSON FROM ASST SEC IRVING
E.O. 11652: N A
TAGS:TSPA:EAIR:MILI:MO
SUBJECT:MOROCCAN REQUEST FOR INFO -- UFOS
REF:   RABAT 5209
HOPE TO HAVE ANSWER FOR YOU NEXT WEEK. REGARDS.  KISSINGER
UNCLASSIFIED
```

Document showing Kissinger's direct involvement in the investigation about the Morocco UFOs.

to the idea that we are not alone in the universe and that UFOs and extraterrestrials were real. Actually, similar plans had been made even during the Nixon administration, but the Watergate scandal interfered, and it was left to Carter to put the plans into practice. On his instructions, NASA subsidized with millions of dollars the production of Steven Spielberg's film *Close Encounters of the Third Kind*, a film which, like no other, drew the attention of the public to the fact that "we are not alone," as the subtitle of the film announced. The first copy of the movie was flown in 1978 from Hollywood directly to Washington, to be shown privately to President Carter.

But before that, on January 18, 1978, there was an actual encounter of the third kind on McGuire Air Force Base, in New Jersey. What happened during that night at 3:00 a.m. we learn through the report of an Air Force security policeman, who had been on a routine patrol when the UFO was sighted above the base:

NJ State Police, and Fort Dix MPs were running code in the direction of Brownsville, NJ A state trooper then entered Gate #5 at the rear of the base requesting assistance and permission to enter. I was dispatched and the trooper wanted access to the runway area which led to the very back of the airfield and connected with a heavily wooded area which is part of the Dix training area. He informed me that a Fort Dix MP was pursuing a low flying object which then hovered over his car. He described it as oval-shaped, with no details, and glowing with a bluish-green color. His radio transmission was cut off. At that time in front of his police car, appeared a thing, about 4 feet

Carter's executive order of 1977, mentioning the aliens' interest in nuclear weapons.

tall, grayish, brown, fat head, long arms, and slender body. The MP panicked
and fired five rounds from his .45 caliber into the thing, and one round into
the object above.

The object then fled straight up and joined with eleven others high in the
skies. This we all saw but didn't know the details of at the time. Anyway, the
thing ran into the woods toward our fence line and they wanted to look for it.
By this time several patrols were involved. We found the body of the thing near
the runway. It had apparently climbed the fence and died while running. It was
all of a sudden hush-hush and no one was allowed near the area. We roped the
area and AFOSI (Air Force Office of Special Investigations) came out and took
over. That was the last I saw of it. There was a bad stench coming from it, too.
Like ammonia smelling but it wasn't constant in the air. That day, a team from
Wright Patterson AFB came in a C-141 and went to the area. They crated it in
a wooden box, sprayed something over it, and then put it into a bigger metal
container. They then loaded it in the plane and took off.

The events of 1975 repeated themselves during Carter's period in
office. Between August 8–20, 1980, UFOs landed at least 3 times at a
high security area, the Manzano weapons depot in Coyote Canyon, at the

Part of Jimmy Carter's educational program to prepare the public for
an ET contact? Steven Spielberg's *Close Encounters of the Third Kind*.

southeast end of Kirtland Air Force Base near Albuquerque, New Mexico. Kirtland AFB, where the Sandia Laboratories are located, was
already during the 1940s the headquarters of the Atomic Energy Commission and controlled one of the largest underground nuclear weapon
arsenals of the United States. Today the Manzano area is, according to a
government document, *"part of a large restricted test range used by the
Air Force Weapons Laboratory, Sandia Laboratories, Defense Nuclear
Agency and the Department of Energy."* The arsenal consists of a row of
tunnels which lead from Coyote Canyon into 3 mountains of the Manzano
range. This area is surrounded by a double fence of steel meshwork, both

Official AFOSI document regarding the Fort Dix incident.

electrified, additionally topped with barbed wire, and is constantly watched by security patrols.

SSGT Stephen Ferenz, A1C Martin W. Rist and AMN Anthony D. Frazier, were patrolling the fence on the night of August 8, 1980. At 11:50 p.m., according to their duty report, they saw "*a very bright light in the sky, approximately 3 miles north northeast of their position,*" on the east side of the Manzano arsenal. "*The light traveled with great speed and stopped suddenly in the sky above Coyote Canyon.*" They had at first taken it to be a helicopter, but its "*strange maneuvers (stop and go)*" convinced them quickly that it could be no such thing. The object descended slowly and apparently landed in the area of Coyote Canyon. At once, Senior Sgt. Ferenz grabbed the phone and radioed

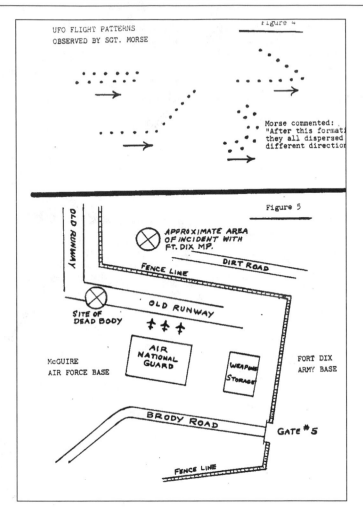

Sketches of eye witnesses of the UFO formation, the base and the
dead extraterrestrial.

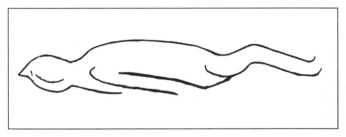

Reconstruction of the Fort Dix incident on January 18, 1978.

his observation to the security control center of the Manzano area, which again informed Sandia security. There they had already sent someone to inspect *"two alarmed structures in the area."* That could only mean one thing—the flying object had landed in the security area and had caused the alert.

The security officer—his name does not appear in the report, at his express request, to avoid harassment—drove on the road leading to the atomic arsenals of Coyote Canyon towards the shelters behind the left end of the installation, which were under alarm. When he approached them at about 12:20, he saw *"a bright light near the ground behind the structure. He also observed an object he first thought was a helicopter. But after driving closer he observed a round disc-shaped object. He attempted to radio for a backup patrol but his radio would not work."* He therefore decided to get nearer to the object on foot, armed with his machine gun. But hardly had he gotten out of the car when *"the object took off in a vertical direction at a high rate of speed."* At the same time, the security patrol of Senior Sgt. Ferenz saw this too; how it started again and rose into the sky at a high speed, to finally disappear.

And that was not a solitary case. Two nights later, on August 10, 1980, patrolmen of the state of New Mexico saw a flying object which landed in the Manzano area between Belen and Albuquerque. And again on August 22, 1980, *"three other security policemen observed the same aerial phenomenon described by the first three. Again the object landed in*

Master Sergeant Richard C. Doty wrote the AFOSI report about the UFO landing at Manzano nuclear arsenal in December 1993.

The official AFOSI document.

Coyote Canyon. . . . They did not observe it take off." After a local investigation carried out by Maj. Ernst E. Edwards of the Sandia security had brought no results, he called in special agent Richard C. Doty of the AFOSI from Kirtland AFB for help on September 2, 1980. Doty's research showed that during the nights in question no test flights had been carried out in the Manzano area. In his official report to the division for security problems of the office of counterespionage at the AFOSI headquarters, he wrote that "*the two alarmed structures located within the area contain HQ CR 44 material.*" HQ CR 44 is the "*Headquarters Compilation of Requirements # 44, redirective 5210.41 of the Department of Defense, i.e., 'Security Criteria and Norms for the Protection of Nuclear Weapons.'*" CR 44 deals mainly with the sabotage of atomic weapons by *"subjects which are not under the Department of Defense."* Had somebody again changed the launch or target codes? The use of the code word CR 44 indeed seems to be an indication that something like this happened.

About 6 months later, the United States had a new president, Ronald Reagan. Reagan, too, believed in UFOs and had had a personal sighting in 1974, when he ordered the pilot of the governor's plane to follow it. But he also listened to his national security, military and intelligence advisors, and began to ask himself, "What if the aliens don't have such peaceful intentions after all?" Perhaps they did mean a threat. That one could not counter them with the available weapons systems had already been proved by the incidents of the 1970s. The 1967 NSA study "UFO Hypothesis and Survival Questions" already recommended *"developing adequate defensive measures."* In 1978 Michael Michaud, Deputy Director of the U.S. State Department's Office of International Security Policy declared: *"Aliens from other solar systems are a potential threat to us, and we are a potential threat to them. Even if an alien species had achieved true peace within its own ranks, it would still be worried about us and would take the measures it felt were necessary to protect itself. This includes the possibility of military action."*

"The President is well aware of the threat you document so clearly and is doing all in his power to restore the national defense margin of safety as quickly and prudently as possible," wrote Maj. Gen. Robert L. Schweitzer of the National Security Council in Washington November 21, 1981, in reply to a letter from the UFO researcher Maj. Colman VonKeviczky to President Reagan, in which he asked for the President's comments on Michaud's statement. How seriously this was meant, was shown in the following years. On March 23, 1984, Ronald Reagan held his historic "Star Wars Speech" in which he announced the buildup of "a protective shield in space," consisting of satellites armed with laser guns, programmed to detect and destroy foreign nuclear missiles. Reagan made it clear to the Russians at every possible opportunity that this *"hopeful vision of the future"* and *"new hope for our children in the 21st century"* called SDI (Strategic Defense Initiative), had nothing to do with *"the threat from the east,"* but with the defense of a *"high frontier,"* against intruders from out there.

During the Geneva Summit on November 19–20, 1985, he told Secretary-General Gorbachev *"how easy your task and mine would be in these meetings that we hold, if suddenly there was a threat to this world from some other species from another planet outside in the universe! We would forget all the little local differences that we have between our countries and we would find out once and for all that we really are all human beings here on this earth together."* That this was not just a rhetorical statement is shown by the fact that President Reagan repeated this in 4 more speeches at international gatherings. On September 21, 1987, giving a speech to the General Assembly of the United Nations, he

Ronald Reagan and Mikhail Gorbachev, at the summit in Geneva in 1985.

ENCLOSURE # 19

NATIONAL SECURITY COUNCIL
WASHINGTON, D.C. 20506
November 21, 1981

Dear General S. VonKeviczky:

Thank you very much for your kind letter which came at a difficult time. I regret the delay in responding which was occasioned by the circumstances and large volume of mail.

The President is well aware of the threat you document so clearly and is doing all in his power to restore the national defense margin of safety as quickly and prudently as possible.

Sincerely,

Robert L. Schweitzer
Major General, US Army

Mr. Colman S. VonKeviczky
35-40 75th Street
Suite 4G
Jackson Heights, New York 11372

"The President is well aware of the threat ..." Letter from Maj. Gen. Schweitzer to the UFO researcher Col. Coleman S. VonKeviczky (here erroneously addressed as General).

said *"I occasionally think how quickly our differences worldwide would vanish if we were facing an alien threat from outside this world."* The next time he used this formula was on September 15, 1987, when he met the Soviet foreign minister, Schevardnadze. As the media reported, *"near the end of his lunch with Shevardnadze, Reagan wondered aloud what would happen if the world faced an 'alien threat' from outer space. "Don't you think the United States and the Soviet Union would be together?' he asked. Shevardnadze said yes, absolutely. 'And we wouldn't need our defense ministers to meet,' he added."* Once more he mentioned it on May 4, 1988, before members of The National Strategy Forum in Chicago: *"I've often wondered what would happen if all of us in this world discovered that we were threatened by a power from outer space—from another planet. Wouldn't we all of a sudden find that we*

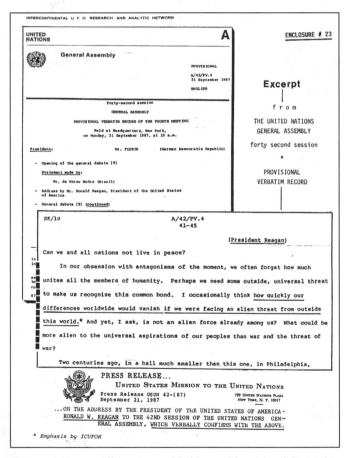

INTERCONTINENTAL U.F.O. RESEARCH AND ANALYTIC NETWORK

UNITED
NATIONS

A

General Assembly

PROVISIONAL

A/42/PV.4
21 September 1987

ENGLISH

ENCLOSURE # 23

Excerpt

from

THE UNITED NATIONS
GENERAL ASSEMBLY

forty second session

*

PROVISIONAL
VERBATIM RECORD

Forty-second session

GENERAL ASSEMBLY

PROVISIONAL VERBATIM RECORD OF THE FOURTH MEETING

Held at Headquarters, New York,
on Monday, 21 September 1987, at 10 a.m.

President: Mr. FLORIN   (German Democratic Republic)

- Opening of the general debate [9]

Statement made by:

Mr. de Abreu Sodre (Brazil)

- Address by Mr. Ronald Reagan, President of the United States
of America

- General debate [9] (continued)

SK/10   A/42/PV.4
                         41-45

(President Reagan)

Can we and all nations not live in peace?

In our obsession with antagonisms of the moment, we often forget how much unites all the members of humanity. Perhaps we need some outside, universal threat to make us recognize this common bond. I occasionally think how quickly our differences worldwide would vanish if we were facing an alien threat from outside this world.* And yet, I ask, is not an alien force already among us? What could be more alien to the universal aspirations of our peoples than war and the threat of war?

Two centuries ago, in a hall much smaller than this one, in Philadelphia,

PRESS RELEASE...
UNITED STATES MISSION TO THE UNITED NATIONS

Press Release USUN 42-(87)   799 UNITED NATIONS PLAZA
September 21, 1987   New York, N.Y. 10017

...ON THE ADDRESS BY THE PRESIDENT OF THE UNITED STATES OF AMERICA -
RONALD W. REAGAN TO THE 42ND SESSION OF THE UNITED NATIONS GEN-
ERAL ASSEMBLY, WHICH VERBALLY CONFIRMS WITH THE ABOVE.

* Emphasis by ICUFON

"How quickly our differences worldwide would vanish ..." Reagan's speech before the UN, official minutes.

didn't have any differences between us at all, that we were all human beings, citizens of the world, and wouldn't we come together to fight that particular threat?"

That Reagan was, in fact, articulating a serious concern of his was revealed by his personal astrologer Carrol Righter, in an interview with the *Las Vegas Sun* of May 31, 1988: *"One idea Reagan said he would seriously consider was turning Star Wars from a defense against the Soviet Union to a planetary shield against alien forces. . . . he might be willing to share Star Wars data with Gorbachev, if it meant saving the earth from outside beings."*

Then, towards the end of Reagan's presidency, something happened that finally convinced his vice president and successor, George Bush, to continue this policy. On December 28, 1988, a huge triangular UFO kidnapped two interceptor aircraft of the U.S. Navy, stationed at the Roosevelt Roads Naval Base on the coast of the U.S. protectorate Puerto Rico, in the Caribbean Sea.

It had been dark for quite some time when hundreds of people living in the Cabo Rojo region in the southwestern part of the island saw, at about 7:45 p.m., a blue light flying over the Sierra Bermeja mountains. Shortly after that the light changed in color and became orange-yellow and the witnesses could now make out that it was only a semi-spherical bulge in the bottom of a big and dark, metallic gray triangular craft the size of a football field. Then they heard a thundering noise. Two jet fighters, F-14 Tomcats of the U.S. Navy, raced towards the UFO to take up pursuit. The triangle tried again and again to escape pursuit by changing its direction of flight. It went in a circle and came back, dived down, and thereby looked bigger and more threatening. When it then turned towards the west, one of the interceptors attempted a head-on confrontation and positioned itself in front of the space vessel. But the alien vessel escaped by a hair's breadth by turning suddenly to the left and making a sharp U-turn. In spite of its size, it was much quicker than the airplane.

Three attempts at interception were made before the UFO finally slowed down and just hovered in the air. Now one of the fighters which had come fairly close to it on the left was flying towards the object, and a collision seemed imminent. The people on the ground who were watching the spectacle in the sky either held their breath or cried out aloud. They all believed that an explosion would take place any moment, but there was no collision, no explosion: the jet fighter just disappeared. Now the second F-14 approached the UFO from the right and it, too, was just as suddenly "swallowed up," like its predecessor. The UFO then turned around and flew over Dissamen Lake, a lagoon surrounded by innumerable palms. Then there was a bright but silent explosion. The triangle split itself into two. One half flew off towards the north and the other disappeared behind the horizon at a high speed.

The Puerto Rican journalist Jorge Martin, who had interviewed over a hundred witnesses, told me that a pilot in a third jet fighter had watched the situation from a safer distance and had then turned back. But before he could get away, three balls of red light shot out of the UFOs and followed him until both the balls and the fighter disappeared somewhere in the north. None of the witnesses could say what happened to the plane.

The Sierra Bermeja incident caused much consternation at the Roosevelt Roads naval station. During the following months, U.S. intelligence agents conducted thorough investigations of all UFO encounters in the Antilles area. The results led to the unanimous decision to keep Puerto Rico, and especially the area of Cabo Roho where UFO researchers suspect an alien base, under constant observation. Finally, Col. José A.M. Nolla, director of the Puerto Rican State Authority for Civil Defense and liaison officer of the U.S. Defense Intelligence Agency (DIA), after consultation with the Pentagon, gave instructions "*to examine cases of sightings of unidentified flying objects, to find out whether it can be guaranteed that there is no threat to the Puerto Rican public from these objects. The study . . . comes under the responsibility of a special committee consisting of the director of the state, his deputy, the chief of the geographical intelligence service, the head of the government, representatives of the observatory at Arecibo, the minister for natural and ground resources and a representative of the national guard of Puerto Rico . . .*"

In Washington, too, incidents like the one in Puerto Rico were very seriously, so there was no doubt that the SDI program had to be continued without any curtailment, even when the Cold War era finally ended under Reagan's successor George Bush. If we are to believe the official version, after The Cold War there actually should not have been any reason for the continuation of the SDI program. Nevertheless, the creation of a global space shield, now with the Russians and not against them, was one of the main topics of the summit meeting at Camp David, January 21–27, 1992. Four days later, speaking to the United Nations Security Council, CIS president Boris Yeltsin announced their plans for the "*creating of a global defense system for the world community. It could be based on a reorientation of the United States Strategic Defense Initiative (SDI), to make use of high technologies developed in Russia's defense complex.*"

Half a year before, on April 3, 1991, the *New York Times* had reported new plans of the Pentagon to place nuclear weapons in space. Against which enemy, one wanted to ask. But one such was soon found, as well as the reason why these weapons were to be directed "upwards." The new enemies were killer asteroids, rocks from the asteroid belt of the solar system which could collide with the earth, an occurrence which probably led to the extinction of dinosaurs 64 million years ago. Whereas a NASA panel calculated that the possibility of such a catastrophe was about one in 100,000 years, the scientific advisor to the U.S. government, Prof. Edward Teller, presented plans for changing "Star Wars" into a "War against Stars." Teller's war, as the *New York Times* called his project, would cost about $50 million plus $10 million yearly for its upkeep. Through this program, killer

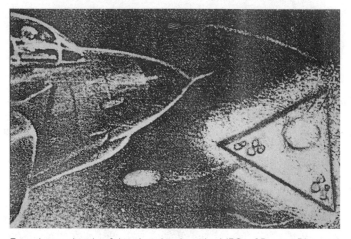

Eye-witness sketch of the gigantic triangular UFO of Puerto Rico and the interceptor plane. Other sketches by eye witnesses, below and on facing page

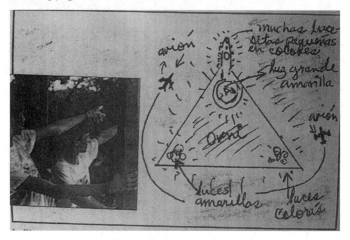

satellites could detect and destroy big objects from space, by means of nuclear or laser weapons.

How successfully the new defense technique could be employed against extraterrestrial intruders was shown by 3 cases that occurred between 1989 and 1992, in which unidentified flying objects were shot down.

During the night of September 28, 1989, at about midnight, the super-secret Brookhaven National Laboratory on Long Island succeeded in shooting down a boomerang-shaped UFO which had been seen by dozens of witnesses and now crashed in the Moriches Bay. Brookhaven shot down a second UFO on November 24, 1992, at about 7:12 p.m. The object crashed in South Haven Park, close to the Laboratory, which was at once sealed off

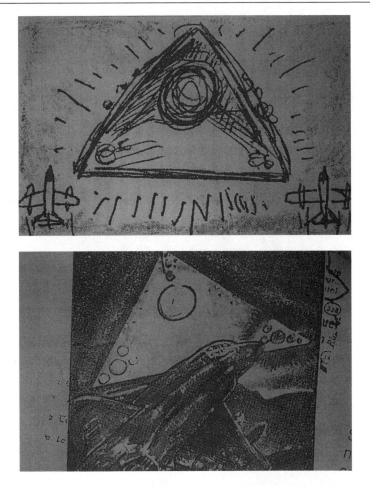

by the police, fire department and the Army. A video film made by the fire department which shows burning bits of wreck and three corpses of small beings with big almond-shaped eyes was passed on to the UFO researcher John Ford of the Long Island UFO Network by an employee of the Brookhaven Laboratory. But these two were not isolated cases.

According to a secret report of the South African Air Force which had been passed on to the British UFO researcher and ex-police officer Anthony Dodd, two Mirage FIIG of the Valhalla Air Force Base near Pretoria shot down a UFO on May 7, 1989, which had entered South African air space. They, too, used SDI technology—*"the experimental aircraft-mounted Thor-2 Laser Cannon"* which South Africa had acquired from the United States via Israel. The UFO wreck was discovered on the other side of the border in Botswana in the Kalahari Desert by search helicopters and brought to Valhalla Air Force Base near Pretoria. The object was 60 feet long, shaped like a football with ports on the sides and one protruding landing strut. On its sides it bore an insignia, an arrow pointing upwards, surrounded by a semi-circle and three dots, quite similar to what Lonnie Zamora had seen in 1964 on the Socorro UFO.

A "Project Blue Fly" retrieval team was flown in from the United States and opened the UFO. On board were two beings, still alive, about 4 feet tall, with gray-bluish skin, unusually big heads and big black almond-shaped eyes. Two Galaxy C-5 transporters of the U.S. Air Force brought both the humanoids—in a special habitat—and the wreck on June 23, 1989 to Wright Patterson AFB in the United States. The experience the American retrieval team demonstrated in handling the wreck, deciphering the hieroglyphics, and treating the humanoids, convinced the South Africans that this was not the first recovery of an alien spacecraft carried out by the U.S. Air Force.

CHAPTER 16

Majestic 12

When the American film producer Jaime Shandera of North Hollywood took the mail out of his mailbox on the morning of December 11, 1984, his attention was attracted by a brown manila envelope. It bore no sender's address, but 12 20¢ stamps and a postmark from Albuquerque, New Mexico. When Shandera opened the envelope he found a second envelope in it, half the size of the outer one, and stuck all over with packing tape. Inside that was a long white envelope with the emblem of a Marriott hotel and inside this at last Shandera found a black plastic cassette containing an undeveloped Kodak 35mm film, which Shandera, obviously curious about its content, brought to the next photo lab. He was even more surprised when he collected it the next morning. Only 8 frames had been exposed, and these were photographs of pages of an apparently very official document, bearing the stamp: "TOP SECRET/MAJIC-EYES ONLY."

This meant that the document had been put under the highest level of classification, being "Sensitive Compartmentalized Information" (SCI). Only those possessing a special access permit, designated "MAJIC," would be allowed to see the document. Furthermore, its "eyes only" classification meant that the document could only be read: the reader was not allowed to copy it, or even make notes when reading it.

The 8 reproduced pages contained, according to their title, a "Briefing document: Operation Majestic 12—Prepared for President Dwight D. Eisenhower (Eyes Only), 18 November, 1952" and, as "Addendum A," the copy of a "Memorandum for the Secretary of Defense," James Forrestal, dated September 24, 1947 and signed by president Harry S. Truman ordering the establishment of OPERATION MAJESTIC 12. Shandera read the documents, and the more he read, the clearer it became to him that they were either the most explosive documents in the files of the U.S. govern-

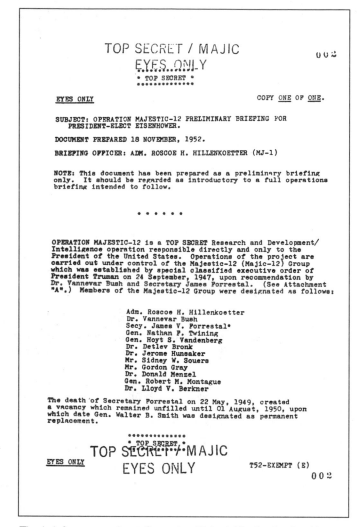

TOP SECRET / MAJIC
EYES ONLY
* TOP SECRET *
****

EYES ONLY   COPY ONE OF ONE.

SUBJECT: OPERATION MAJESTIC-12 PRELIMINARY BRIEFING FOR
       PRESIDENT-ELECT EISENHOWER.

DOCUMENT PREPARED 18 NOVEMBER, 1952.

BRIEFING OFFICER: ADM. ROSCOE H. HILLENKOETTER (MJ-1)

NOTE: This document has been prepared as a preliminary briefing
only. It should be regarded as introductory to a full operations
briefing intended to follow.

. . . . . .

OPERATION MAJESTIC-12 is a TOP SECRET Research and Development/
Intelligence operation responsible directly and only to the
President of the United States. Operations of the project are
carried out under control of the Majestic-12 (Majic-12) Group
which was established by special classified executive order of
President Truman on 24 September, 1947, upon recommendation by
Dr. Vannevar Bush and Secretary James Forrestal. (See Attachment
"A".) Members of the Majestic-12 Group were designated as follows:

        Adm. Roscoe H. Hillenkoetter
        Dr. Vannevar Bush
        Secy. James V. Forrestal*
        Gen. Nathan F. Twining
        Gen. Hoyt S. Vandenberg
        Dr. Detlev Bronk
        Dr. Jerome Hunsaker
        Mr. Sidney W. Souers
        Mr. Gordon Gray
        Dr. Donald Menzel
        Gen. Robert M. Montague
        Dr. Lloyd V. Berkner

The death of Secretary Forrestal on 22 May, 1949, created
a vacancy which remained unfilled until 01 August, 1950, upon
which date Gen. Walter B. Smith was designated as permanent
replacement.

****
* TOP SECRET *
****
TOP SECRET / MAJIC
EYES ONLY

EYES ONLY   T52-EXEMPT (E)
                            002

The briefing paper about Operation Majestic Twelve for President Eisenhower, dated November 18, 1952.

ment, at least from the Truman era, or part of a hoax hatched by a contemporary with quite a strange sense of humor. For the papers dealt with "flying saucers." The documents were apparently intended to inform the new president, Dwight D. Eisenhower, before he was sworn in, about the status of the investigations which the U.S. government had been conducting in the matter of UFOs and extraterrestrials since 1947. But it did not deal with the Projects Sign, Grudge or Blue Book, which, according to the document,

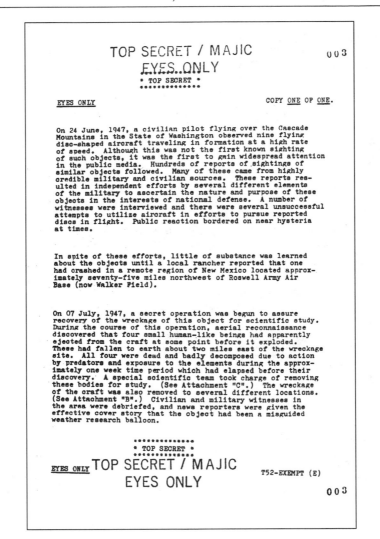

TOP SECRET / MAJIC
EYES ONLY
* TOP SECRET *

EYES ONLY   COPY ONE OF ONE.

On 24 June, 1947, a civilian pilot flying over the Cascade Mountains in the State of Washington observed nine flying disc-shaped aircraft traveling in formation at a high rate of speed. Although this was not the first known sighting of such objects, it was the first to gain widespread attention in the public media. Hundreds of reports of sightings of similar objects followed. Many of these came from highly credible military and civilian sources. These reports resulted in independent efforts by several different elements of the military to ascertain the nature and purpose of these objects in the interests of national defense. A number of witnesses were interviewed and there were several unsuccessful attempts to utilize aircraft in efforts to pursue reported discs in flight. Public reaction bordered on near hysteria at times.

In spite of these efforts, little of substance was learned about the objects until a local rancher reported that one had crashed in a remote region of New Mexico located approximately seventy-five miles northwest of Roswell Army Air Base (now Walker Field).

On 07 July, 1947, a secret operation was begun to assure recovery of the wreckage of this object for scientific study. During the course of this operation, aerial reconnaissance discovered that four small human-like beings had apparently ejected from the craft at some point before it crashed. These had fallen to earth about two miles east of the wreckage site. All four were dead and badly decomposed due to action by predators and exposure to the elements during the approximately one week time period which had elapsed before their discovery. A special scientific team took charge of removing these bodies for study. (See Attachment "C".) The wreckage of the craft was also removed to several different locations. (See Attachment "B".) Civilian and military witnesses in the area were debriefed, and news reporters were given the effective cover story that the object had been a misguided weather research balloon.

* TOP SECRET *

EYES ONLY TOP SECRET / MAJIC   T52-EXEMPT (E)
EYES ONLY

003

only had the tasks of collecting information, but with a supersecret project which had been called to life by President Truman personally, after the U.S. Army Air Force had discovered the wreckage of a crashed UFO and its dead crew. Coordinator of the project and compiler of this report for Eisenhower's information was nobody less than Admiral Roscoe H. Hillenkoetter, the first director of the CIA. The CIA had also been established in September 1947. According to the cover page of the document, it contained *"compartmentalized information essential to the national security of the United States."*

What had happened? During the night of July 4, 1947, only ten days after

The rancher William W. "Mac" Brazel discovered UFO fragments on his ranch.

Major Jesse Marcel

Kenneth Arnold's sighting, a flying saucer crashed within the territory of the United States. That night, a thunderstorm was raging in Lincoln County, halfway between Corona and Roswell in arid southwest New Mexico. William W. "Mac" Brazel, owner of a sheep ranch, and his two children heard a loud explosion which sounded different from thunder. The next morning, Brazel rode over to his grazing land to see how his sheep had weathered the storm. There, beside an arroyo, he found metallic fragments strewn over a strip of land, nearly a mile long and 200 yards wide. At first he thought they were pieces from a wrecked weather balloon but a closer look made him feel that they must have been from something quite different. The same day, he loaded his truck with some of the fragments and took them to the shed near his house. He found that some of the pieces had very remarkable properties, which he had never seen in any material before. He showed the metal to some of his friends and they all agreed that he should report his find to the local authorities.

Mac had no telephone at his ranch, but the very next day, on the morning of Sunday, July 6, he drove to Roswell, taking a few of the fragments with him on his truck to show them to Sheriff Wilcox. The sheriff at once called the Roswell Army Air Base, the headquarters of the 509th bomb group, the only atom bomb unit of the United States. The sheriff knew that, if there was anyone who could identify what had come down from the sky, then it would be this elite unit. In the early afternoon Major Jesse Marcel of the Intelligence Corps came down to the sheriff's office, had a look at the fragments, and took them back with him to the base. There he showed them to the commander, Col. William H. Blanchard. The material was so strange that it called for immediate and further investigation. Col. Blanchard ordered Marcel and another officer, Sheridan Cavitt of the counterespionage unit, to go at once with Brazel to his ranch to have a closer look at the wreckage and bring back as much of it as they could. So Marcel and Cavitt drove to the sheriff's office, each in his own vehicle, to pick up Mac Brazel and proceed with him to Brazel's ranch.

Meanwhile, Blanchard ordered an aircraft to take the fragments that were there to Gen. Roger Ramey, the commander of the 8th Air Force at Fort Worth, Texas.

Brazel, Marcel and Sheridan arrived at the ranch rather late and spent the night there. Early the next morning the three men went to the "debris field." It was strewn with bits of very thin metal-like foil and a kind of extremely tough parchment, as well as numerous little struts or "I-beams," bearing script characters that looked like hieroglyphics to them. The officers spent hours trying to figure out what had crashed there and how it could have happened. During the rest of the day they collected hundreds of fragments and loaded them into their vehicles, before driving back to Roswell that night. *"Before we get back to the base, I want to show my boy what we've found,"* said Marcel to Cavitt, *"because it is perhaps something that he will never forget all his life."* Cavitt agreed, so they stopped at Marcel's house, woke up his 12-year-old son Jesse Jr., who then, fascinated, examined all the pieces for over an hour.

The next morning, Lt. Walter Haut, Press Officer of the base, acting on the orders of Col. Blanchard, informed the press about the discovery. The proud statement given to Associated Press announced: *"The many rumors regarding the flying disc became a reality yesterday when the intelligence office of the 509th Bomb Group of the 8th Air Force, Roswell AAF, was for-*

The report about the Roswell incident in the *Roswell Daily Record,* and the following denial

tunate enough to gain possession of a disc through the cooperation of one of the local ranchers and the Sheriff's office of Chaves county. The flying object landed on a ranch near Roswell sometime last week. . . . Action was immediately taken and the disc was picked up at the rancher's home. . . ."

In the meantime an aerial surveillance, ordered by Col. Blanchard, discovered the main part of the wreckage at a bluff southeast of the debris field, just 35 miles north northwest of Roswell. It was a heel-shaped craft near which 5 small bodies were lying, each about 4 feet tall. After examining the first fragments Brazel had brought into the town, it was soon quite clear that what had been found was not the product of any terrestrial technology. It meant nothing less than the unexpected opportunity to examine a spacecraft of a highly developed civilization and acquire knowledge which could be used for the improvement of one's own armament technology. That decided what was to be done. The wreck and the debris had to be salvaged immediately and under the greatest secrecy.

Even before Marcel and Cavitt returned, a large-scale retrieval operation was started. All roads and ways leading to the ranchland northwest of Roswell were cordoned off by the military. Brazel's ranch itself was converted into a commando post and every square foot of the grazing land on the ranch was combed by servicemen to pick up every piece of debris they could find. At the same time, an airplane landed at Roswell bringing a special team of photographers from Washington.

But before Col. Blanchard himself could drive out to the site of crash, he had another problem to solve. It had to do with the press information given out in the morning. Shortly after the Associated Press started sending out the announcement of the press information officer to newspapers all over the country by telex, the Pentagon got wind of it. We can well imagine how a roaring red-faced general demanded that "every goddamned security gap be closed so that nothing about this goddamned shit can get out." Action was taken immediately.

That afternoon, Johnnie McBoyle, reporter and part owner of the private broadcasting station KSWS at Roswell, called the somewhat bigger broadcasting station KOAT in Albuquerque, New Mexico. Bursting with excitement, he begged the KOAT secretary Lydia Sleppy to send out a hot bit of news to all other broadcasting stations, through her telex, for he himself did not have one.

"A flying saucer has crashed," said McBoyle, describing his scoop, *"No, I'm not joking. It has crashed in the neighborhood of Roswell. I have just been there and seen it with my own eyes. It looks like a battered cooking pot. One of the ranchers found it. The Army is there—they want to take it away. The whole area is now hermetically sealed off. And now, listen carefully, they're talking about little men on board. Start sending the telex and stay on the line."*

Holding the telephone receiver between ear and shoulder, Lydia started typing the first lines on the telex. She had hardly typed 3 sentences when the machine stopped. There could be many reasons for that, as Lydia knew only too well, and she didn't take it too seriously. Then the machine started running again, but it was now receiving a message directly meant for her, brusque and unequivocal:

"*Attention, Albuquerque. Stop transmitting. Repeat. Stop transmitting. Matter of national security. Do not send. Wait for further instructions.*"

Lydia read out this message to McBoyle over the telephone and asked him what she could now do about it. His answer was as resigned as it was unexpected. "*Just forget it, you've never heard it, don't talk to anybody about it.*" When her boss Merle Tucker returned a week later from a business trip, Lydia told him about the incident. Tucker naturally wanted to get to the bottom of things, but no matter where he tried to inquire, he was met with silence.

The press release given out by Walter Haut, which also had been printed in a number of evening papers on July 8, was retracted on the very same day. At an official press conference held by Gen. Roger M. Ramey at Fort Worth Air Base, the general declared to the journalists that the wreckage

General Ramey and Colonel Dubose, with the the alleged wreckage of Roswell.

that had been recovered was that of a crashed weather balloon. As proof of that, he held in his hands fragments of one such balloon and allowed the reporters to take photographs of it. The nation could now smile with amusement, and the Roswell incident had never taken place—at any rate, nothing of significance had occurred there.

Or at least, as long as UFO researchers did not pursue the matter. . . .

After years of research, the author William Moore, coauthor with Charles Berlitz on the book *The Roswell Incident*, the nuclear physicist Stanton Friedman, the ex-Air Force intelligence officer Kevin Randle, and researcher Don Schmitt succeeded in finding more than 400 witnesses to the Roswell incident, including those who had actually taken part in the recovery operation. Amongst these witnesses one finds generals, high-ranking officers and ordinary servicemen, intelligence agents, locals and eventually Mac Brazel's children and neighbors who lived near his ranch at that time. During the 1980s, Moore and Jaime Shandera planned to make a documentary film about the Roswell incident, but this project was put on ice for a period owing to lack of finances. (This explains why, out of all people, it was to Shandera that the sensational MJ-12 material had been passed on.) In their stead, half a dozen documentaries, most of them based on Schmitt and Randle's work, and a television miniseries about Roswell came out in the 1990s. (For further details, see: Hesemann/Mantle: *Beyond Roswell*, Marlowe & Co., New York, 1997.)

According to the Operation Majestic-12 Briefing Document, after the recovery of the craft the best scientists in the country, most of whom had two years before that been working on the Manhattan Project developing the atom bomb, were called together to analyze the findings. Gen. Nathan F. Twining, commander of technical intelligence of the Air Force, then AMC and later ATIC, broke off his planned journey to the west coast and flew to New Mexico to supervize the action. The scientific side of the project was put under the direction of Prof. Dr. Vannevar Bush, the man best suited for a task of this caliber at that time. Dr. Bush had been the scientific advisor to the President since the beginning of the second World War. In 1941 he had been chairman of the National Defense Research Council; then in 1943, Director of the Office of Scientific Research under which the Manhattan Project was conducted. If there was anyone who was capable of using the information gathered from the Roswell wrecks to make America the first and biggest power in space, then it was Dr. Vannevar Bush.

Dr. Vannevar Bush

On September 19, 1947, a status report of the investigation was sent to the President.

In it, experts came to the conclusion that the wrecked vessel must have been a short-range reconnaissance craft, apparently of nonterrestrial origin. On September 24, 1947, Dr. Bush and the defense secretary Forrestal were invited to the White House. This meeting, which took place in the Oval Office, is not only mentioned in the Majestic-12 files, but also documented in the records of the Truman era, archived in the Truman library. During this secret meeting, and at the behest of Bush and Forrestal, the establishment of the Majestic-12 group was decided upon. Its list of members reads like a Who's Who of the top brass of the day. Besides Bush, Gen. Twining and Forrestal, the following were members:

1. Vice-Admiral Roscoe H. Hillenkoetter, Commander of the Intelligence Corps in the Pacific theatre during World War II and, since September 1947, first director of the Central Intelligence Agency (CIA);
2. Gen. Hoyt S. Vandenberg, Chief of Staff of the U.S. Air Force and former Director of Central Intelligence (DCI);
3. Dr. Detlev Bronk, internationally known biophysicist and physiologist, Chairman of the National Research Council and member of the Medical Advisory Board of the Atomic Energy Commission;
4. Dr. Jerome Hunsaker, a brilliant aircraft designer of the Massachusetts Institute of Technology and Chairman of the National Advisory Committee for Aeronautics;
5. Rear Admiral Sidney M. Sauers, former Director of Central Intelligence, then Executive Secretary of the National Security Council of the United States;
6. Gordon Gray, Assistant-Secretary, later Secretary of the Army;
7. Dr. Donald Menzel, Director of the observatory of Howard University, who had been involved in top secret research projects, later with the National Security Agency (NSA) with access level "top secret ultra." Menzel became the chief debunker of UFOs and tried, apparently acting on orders from above, to find for every UFO sighting a natural explanation;
8. Gen. Robert M. Montague, commander of the of the Atomic Energy Commission installation at the Sandia Base, Albuquerque, New Mexico, weapon testing grounds, and
9. Dr. Lloyd V. Berkner, Executive Secretary of the Research and Development Board and cofounder of the development and evaluation group for weapons systems.

In a memorandum dictated on the same day to Defense Secretary Forrestal, Truman authorized MJ-12 to *"To proceed with all due speed and caution upon your undertaking. Hereafter this matter shall be referred to only as Operation Majestic Twelve."*

The study of the Roswell wrecks went on. In a secret report dated November 30, 1947, Dr. Bronk presented the results of the work done by his group, which had conducted autopsies on the 4 bodies that had been found. The report says *"although these creatures are human-like in appearance, the biological and evolutionary processes responsible for their development has apparently been quite different from those observed or postulated in Homo Sapiens."* Dr. Bronk suggested that *"the term 'Extraterrestrial Biological Entities' or 'EBEs' be adopted as the standard term of reference for these creatures until such time as a more definitive designation can be agreed upon."* Another report dealt with the evaluation of the writing which was found on the fragments as well as on board the vessel. All attempts to decipher this writing were unsuccessful. The propulsion system of the spacecraft was no less difficult to understand. *"Equally unsuccessful have been efforts to determine the method of propulsion or the nature or method of transmission of the power source involved. Research along these lines has been complicated by the complete absence of identifiable wings, propellers, jets, or other conventional methods of propulsion and guidance, as well as a total lack of metallic wiring, vacuum tubes, or similar recognizable electronic components."*

Now, according to the Majestic-12 document, it became important to collect as much information as was possible. It was with this in mind that Gen. Twining wrote his memorandum to Gen. Schulgen on September 23, 1947 (see Chapter 3) in which he described the basic characteristics of UFOs so aptly. Since this memorandum only defines the expression "UFO" and lays down the criteria for what sort of information is to be collected and looked for in the future, no mention is made there of the Roswell wreck. On the

Memorandum written by Brig. Gen. Schulgen about the collection of data, regarding "flying saucer-type aircraft." It revealed a knowledge of the construction of UFOs which the USAF could have obtained only by examining a crashed UFO, probably the one from Roswell.

contrary, it even speaks of *"the lack of physical evidence in the shape of crash-recovered exhibits which would undeniably prove the existence of these objects."* No wonder that this AMC opinion is classified only as "secret," a level below the "top secret" classification, whereas the Roswell investigations were classified as "top secret." This prevented officers and personnel of lower ranks, engaged in less sensitive detection projects, from knowing about the existence of the much higher classified and much more secret "Operation Majestic Twelve."

But when Brig. Gen. George F. Schulgen of the General Staff at the Pentagon wrote his memo on October 30, 1947, also classified "secret," titled *"Intelligence requirements on flying saucer aircraft,"* he was less cautious. Here, instructing all Air Force intelligence agencies to collect all available information regarding aircraft of the type "flying saucer," he not only said, *"it is the considered opinion of some elements that the object may in fact represent an interplanetary craft of some kind,"* but was also in a position to give very special characteristics. For instance, *"composite or sandwich construction utilizing various combinations of metals, metallic foils, plastics, and perhaps balsa wood or similar material,"* and *"unusual fabrication methods to achieve extreme light weight and structural stability."* This is only too reminiscent of the description given by the farmer's son, Bill Brazel of Roswell, about the material which he had seen—particles like balsa wood, metallic foil, light as a feather and extremely tough. . . .

The first outsider to know about operation Majestic 12 was the Canadian Wilbert B. Smith. In his memorandum to the Controller of Telecommunications at the Canadian Department of Transport, dated 11/21/1950, he mentioned *"a small group in the U.S. headed by Dr. Vannever Bush,"* which was to study the UFOs under a level of secrecy *"rating higher even than the H-bomb."* Meanwhile the United States was in possession of at least 3 more UFO wrecks, the first of which crashed on May 31, 1947, 5 weeks before the Roswell incident in a canyon southwest of Socorro, New Mexico; another one which came down in Hart Canyon, east of Aztec, New Mexico, and the third in Paradise Valley near Phoenix, Arizona. The three crashes in New Mexico are mentioned in an FBI memorandum of March 22, 1950, which was released in 1977 under the Freedom Of Information Act. In that, FBI special agent Guy Hottel, chief of the Washington office of the FBI, reports to FBI director J. Edgar Hoover:

"An investigator for the Air Force stated that 3 so-called flying saucers had been recovered in New Mexico. They were described as being circular in shape, with raised centers, approximately 50 feet in diameter. Each one was occupied by three bodies of human shape, but only three feet tall, dressed in metallic cloth of a very fine texture. Each body was bandaged in a manner similar to the blackout suits used by speed flyers and test pilots. According to Mr.——, informant, the saucers were found in New Mexico due to the fact that the government has a very high powered radar set up in that area and it is believed that the radar interferes with the controlling mechanism of the saucers."

Wilbert Smith also learned from Prof. Robert I. Sarbacher, a top scientist of the Pentagon, that the rumors going around at that time about crashed saucers were true in substance. This was actually the basis for Smith's memorandum to the Department of Transport, but Smith never revealed his source of information. It was only 33 years later, long after Smith's death, when his secret records were published, and the name of his informant came to light. The first person to pick up the track and follow it was the Californian UFO researcher William Steinman. Sensing that Sarbacher knew more, he wrote to the professor, who was now chief of the Washington Institute of Technology, and presented him with a list of questions for the first time, and the second time, and finally for the third time. He had almost given up hope of getting an answer when an answer did arrive:

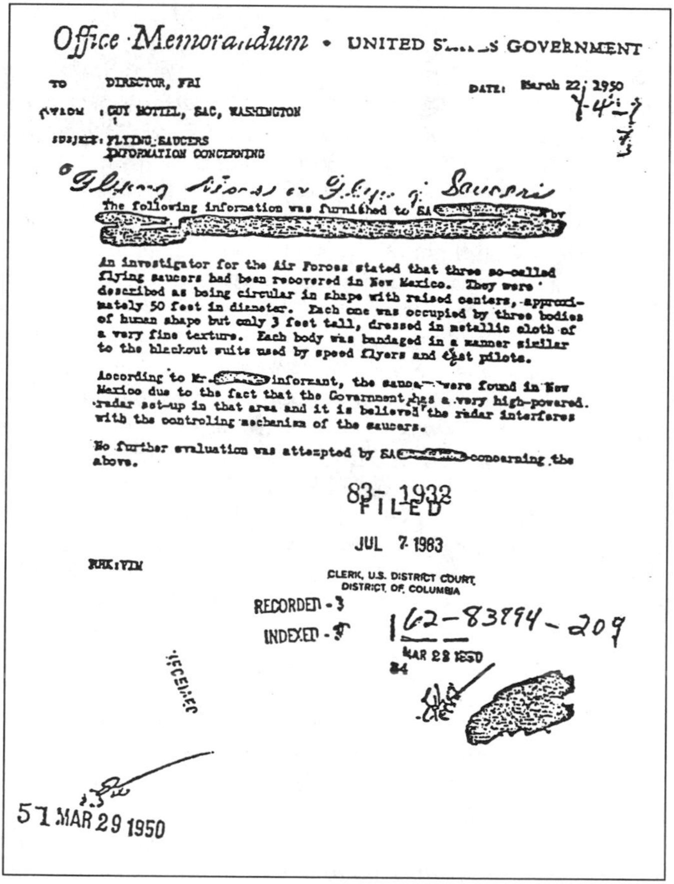

Memorandum to FBI Director J. Edgar Hoover, showing the U.S. Air Force was by 1950 in possession of 3 crashed flying saucers. This was released on July 7, 1983, on court order.

Dear Mr. Steinman:

I am sorry I have taken so long in answering your letters. However, I have moved my office and have had to make a number of extended trips.

To answer your last question in your letter of October 14, 1983, there is no particular reason I feel that I shouldn't or couldn't answer any or all of your questions. I am delighted to answer all of them to the best of my ability.

You listed some of your questions in your letter of September 12th. I will attempt to answer them as you had listed them.

1. Relating to my own experience regarding recovered flying saucers, I had no association with any of the people involved in the recovery and have no knowledge of the dates of the recoveries. If I had, I would send it to you.

Prof. Robert I. Sarbacher

2. Regarding verification that persons you list were involved, I can only say this: John von Neuman [sic] was definitely involved. Dr. Vannever [sic] Bush was definitely involved, and I think Dr. Robert Oppenheimer also.

My association with the research and development board under Compton during the Eisenhower administration was rather limited so that although I had been invited to participate in several discussions associated with the reported recoveries I could not personally attend the meetings. I am sure that they would have asked Dr. [Wernher] von Braun . . .

But the only thing I remember at this time is that certain materials reported to have come from flying saucer crashes were extremely light and very tough. I am sure that our laboratories analyzed them very carefully.

There were reports that instruments or people operating these machines were also of very light weight, sufficient to withstand the tremendous deceleration and acceleration associated with their machinery. I remember in talking with some of the people at the office that I got the impression that these aliens were constructed as certain insects we have observed on earth . . .

Sarbacher told the nuclear physicist Stanton Friedman later, on the telephone, that his colleagues had been convinced that the crew of the UFOs had actually been biological robots. He also recalled the name of another top scientist who had taken part in the project, the electrical engineer Dr. Erich A. Walker, also a member of the research and development board of the Pentagon and dean of Pennsylvania State University. Dr. Walker had been decorated for his contribution to the development of torpedoes at the underwater laboratories of Howard University. William Steinman called Dr. Walker on August 30, 1987, and the following conversation took place:

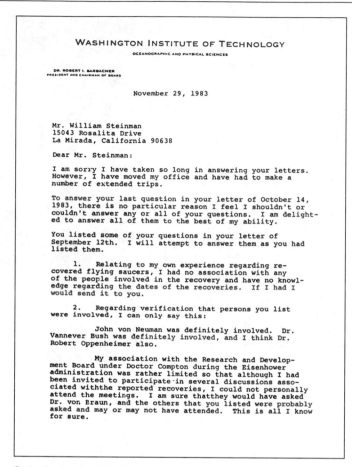

WASHINGTON INSTITUTE OF TECHNOLOGY
OCEANOGRAPHIC AND PHYSICAL SCIENCES

DR. ROBERT I. SARBACHER
PRESIDENT AND CHAIRMAN OF BOARD

November 29, 1983

Mr. William Steinman
15043 Rosalita Drive
La Mirada, California 90638

Dear Mr. Steinman:

I am sorry I have taken so long in answering your letters.
However, I have moved my office and have had to make a
number of extended trips.

To answer your last question in your letter of October 14,
1983, there is no particular reason I feel I shouldn't or
couldn't answer any or all of your questions. I am delighted to answer all of them to the best of my ability.

You listed some of your questions in your letter of
September 12th. I will attempt to answer them as you had
listed them.

    1.   Relating to my own experience regarding re-
covered flying saucers, I had no association with any
of the people involved in the recovery and have no knowledge regarding the dates of the recoveries. If I had I
would send it to you.

    2.   Regarding verification that persons you list
were involved, I can only say this:

        John von Neuman was definitely involved. Dr.
Vannever Bush was definitely involved, and I think Dr.
Robert Oppenheimer also.

        My association with the Research and Develop-
ment Board under Doctor Compton during the Eisenhower
administration was rather limited so that although I had
been invited to participate in several discussions associated withthe reported recoveries, I could not personally
attend the meetings. I am sure thatthey would have asked
Dr. von Braun, and the others that you listed were probably
asked and may or may not have attended. This is all I know
for sure.

Sarbacher's astonishing letter.

Walker: *Hello.*

Steinman: *Hello . . . this is William Steinman of Los Angeles, California. I am calling in reference to the meetings that you attended at Wright-Patterson Air Force Base around 1949–1950, concerning the military recovery of flying saucers and bodies of occupants. Dr. Robert I. Sarbacher (now deceased) related this to me. You and Sarbacher were both Consultants to D.R.B. in 1950; you were Secretary in 1950–51.*

Walker: *Yes, I attended meetings concerning that subject matter; why do you want to know about that?*

Steinman: *I believe it is [a] very important subject matter. We are talking about the actual recovery of a flying saucer (spacecraft) not built or constructed on this earth! And furthermore, we are talking about bodies of the*

3.   I did receive some official reports when I was in my office at the Pentagon but all of these were left there as at the time we were never supposed to take them out of the office.

4.   I do not recall receiving any photographs such as you request so I am not in a position to answer.

5.   I have to make the same reply as on No. 4.

I recall the interview with Dr. Brenner of the Canadian Embassy. I think the answers I gave him were the ones you listed. Naturally, I was more familiar with the subject matter under discussion, at that time. Actually, I would have been able to give more specific answers had I attended the meetings concerning the subject. You must understand that I took this assignment as a private contribution. We were called "dollar-a-year men." My first responsibility was the maintenance of my own business activity so that my participation was limited.

About the only thing I remember at this time is that certain materials reported to have come from flying saucer crashes were extremely light and very tough. I am sure our laboratories analyzed them very carefully.

There were reports that instruments or people operating these machines were also of very light weight, sufficient to withstand the tremendous deceleration and acceleration associated with their machinery. I remember in talking with some of the people at the office that I got the impression these "aliens" were constructed like certain insects we have observed on earth, wherein because of the low mass the inertial forces involved in operation of these instruments would be quite low.

I still do not know why the high order of classification has been given and why the denial of the existence of these devices.

I am sorry it has taken me so long to reply but I suggest you get in touch with the others who may be directly involved in this program.

Sincerely yours,

Dr. Robert I. Sarbacher

P. S.   It occurs to me that Dr. Bush's name is inccorrect as you have it. Please check the spelling.

occupants from the craft who were analyzed [to be] like beings not of this world!

Walker: *What are you getting all excited about? Why all the concern?*

Steinman: *I'm not excited, just very concerned. Here we are talking about a subject that the U.S. Government officially denies, even going as far as actually debunking the evidence and discrediting the witnesses. Then you sit there and say, 'What are you getting all excited about?' and 'Why all the concern?' Dr. Vannevar Bush, Dr. O. W. Bronk, and others thought it was very important and were concerned enough to classify the subject Above Top Secret, in fact the most highly classified subject in the U.S. Government!! Did you ever hear of the 'MJ-12 Group' and their 'Project Majestic-12' which was classified as TOP SECRET/MAJIC? I have a copy of President Eisenhower's briefing paper on that project, dated November 18, 1952."*

Walker: *"Yes, I know of MJ-12. I have known of it for 40 years. I believe that you're tilting at windmills!"*

Steinman: *Why do you say that?*

Walker: *You are delving into an area that you can do absolutely nothing about. So, why get involved with it or all concerned about it? Why don't you just leave it alone and drop it? Forget about it!*

When Steinman's colleague T. Scott Crain Jr. wrote to Walker on April 24, 1988, he received his own letter back with the handwritten note on it from the professor: *"Why say anything?"*

As a matter of fact, the first rumors about the participation of top-ranking scientists in the investigation of crashed saucers had already come out during the late 1940s. In November, 1949, the businesswoman Alma Lawson told the *Los Angeles Free Press* that she had met *"a reliable and conservative scientist"* by chance during a journey to Mexico, and that he had told her about a UFO crash in the Sierra Madre highlands of Mexico. Since she did not believe him, he took her with him when he went *"with 15 other scientists of the University of California"* to the crash site. Alma Lawson described the disc which she saw there being recovered as brown in color, about 100 feet wide and shaped like the back of a tortoise. Inside it they found the charred bodies of six small beings, the crew of the ship.

When Steinman called her in 1986 she revealed the name of the scientist: it was Prof. Dr. Luis Alvarez, at that time professor of physics at the University of California. Alvarez, too, had had an interesting past. He had worked on the Manhattan Project at Los Alamos and was nominated for the Nobel Prize in physics in 1958. Like Prof. Berkner of the Majestic-12, he too had been, in 1953, a member of the Robertson Panel of the CIA, which had imposed the rigorous policy of strict secrecy. Investigations showed that Alvarez had indeed been in Mexico City at that time mentioned. And when Steinman called Alvarez in 1986, he confirmed that he had taken part in the recovery of a saucer in Mexico, but refused to give further details. Prof. Alvarez died in September 1988.

Four months after the reports about the Mexico crash went out, the American geophysicist Dr. Silas Newton gave a lecture before a group of students at the University of Denver in Colorado. During this lecture, held on March 8, 1950, he mentioned that 3 flying discs had crashed in Arizona and New Mexico and had been recovered by the Air Force. Newton was considered an expert on magnetism and, with the help of an instrument he constructed, he was able to discover oil fields, which brought him millions of dollars. Since the Air Force had found out that the saucers were propelled on some electromagnetic principle, they had consulted him.

Later on, Newton related this story to the journalist Frank Scully of the showbiz magazine *Variety*. Scully made further researches and finally wrote a book about the UFO crashes. For months Scully's book *Behind the Flying Saucers* was a national best-seller until a reporter of the magazine *True* attempted to expose Dr. Newton as a con artist and the contents of the book as a big hoax. This was a welcome development for the authorities, particularly Majestic-12. Other publications took over the attack against Scully and Newton, and for the next decades crashed saucers became a taboo theme, not only for semi-serious journalists, but also for the UFO community itself.

It was only in June 1978, 18 years later, that the ice was broken. And it was broken by Leohnard Stringfield, veteran of American UFO research with, at that time, 25 years of experience in the field. At the annual meeting of the American UFO organization MUFON, Stringfield spoke about what he called *"Retrievals of the third kind—a case study of alleged UFOs and their occupants in military custody."* About 20 witnesses had given him first or second hand information, and he had come to the conclusion that, in spite of the Scully scandal, the "crash/recovery syndrome" definitely deserved serious attention. Stringfield's presentation set off an avalanche of interest and, when the press reported about the meeting, other witnesses came forward—retired Air Force personnel including high-ranking officers, scientists, and intelligence personnel. The material that Stringfield has collected since then fills 7 status reports. According to Stringfield, who passed away in 1995, between 1947 and 1990 there were at least 20 UFO crashes over the territory of the United States and at least 12 in other parts of the world. But it was actually another UFO researcher, Raymond Fowler, who had put Stringfield onto the track of UFO crashes with an extremely well documented case. . . .

CHAPTER 17

The Secret of Hangar 18

Fritz Werner (pseudonym) is an American scientist of German origin with the highest credentials. He has studied mathematics, physics, and engineering sciences, is a member of a number of faculty organizations, and an author of important technical papers. During his career in the United States, he had since 1949 worked on various government research projects. His job during those days was to investigate the effects of atomic bomb explosions, including the blast effects of various types of buildings, at the nuclear test site in Nevada. He was working as a project engineer for "Operation Upshot-Knothole" of the Office of Special Studies, later called the Installation Division, of the Atomic Energy Commission (AEC), led by Prof. Eric Wang, an ex-Austrian.

Werner's work kept him in Frenchman's Flat on the Nevada test site most of the time. On May 20, 1953, he received a call during the evening from his boss, test director Dr. Ed Doll, who told him that he had been assigned to a special mission the next day. At the appointed time, about 4:30 p.m., he reported for special duty and was driven to Indian Springs AFB near the proving grounds. There he found 15 other specialists, all waiting for instructions. They were told to leave all valuables in the custody of the military police. Then they were taken to a military aircraft which flew them to Phoenix, Arizona. There they got into a bus in which other men were also waiting and were told by an officer that no contact between the members of the group was permitted. The windows of the bus had been blacked out, so that they couldn't see where they were going. They drove about 4 hours and Werner was sure that their destination was near Kingman, Arizona, that lay about 4–5 hours' drive northwest of Phoenix. During their bus trip, a colonel of the Air Force informed them that a supersecret aircraft had crashed and they, as specialists in certain fields, were to investigate the cause of the crash.

The bus stopped and they were asked to come out one at a time as their names were called, to be escorted by the military police to the spot where the investigation was to be made. Two glaring floodlights had been put up and directed at the crashed object which was surrounded by guards. The lights were so bright that it was impossible to see the surroundings. The crashed object was oval and looked like 2 saucers, one inverted upon the other, with a diameter of about 30 feet and about 20 feet high.

It was made of some kind of dull silvery metal like brushed aluminum. The rims of the basins formed a ring which had small slits in it. There was an opening from which a peculiar light came out and from which a twisted access ramp was hanging. It was Werner's task, based on the angle of impact and the depth at which the object was sticking in the sand, to calculate the speed of the object at the time of impact. That gave him the opportunity to get a closer look at the wreck. It had dug 20 inches into the earth. Werner could see no landing gear, markings or protuberances on its upper surface; there was not even a scratch on it.

The Kingman scenario after descriptions given by "Fritz Werner."

Near it there was a tent with a guard outside, but Werner, while passing by, was able to have a quick look inside. Lying on a stretcher was an apparently nonhuman being, about 4 feet tall, with dark brown skin, clothed in a silvery metallic-looking suit, with a cap on the head.

After Werner had finished his task he was asked to make his report and record it on a tape, and then he was escorted back to the bus. During a moment when he felt he was unobserved, he spoke to a scientist colleague and told him what he had seen. The other answered shortly "I was inside. I saw 2 swivel-like chairs and a number of instruments and apparatus." An airman noticed the short conservation, separated the men and gave them a warning not to talk with each other. In the bus, they were all put under oath by the colonel and asked to swear that they would not speak about this mission to anybody. But 20 years later Fritz Werner broke this oath. He came into contact with the well-known UFO researcher and author Raymond Fowler, and told him about his experiences. To vouch for what he said he even signed an affidavit on July 7, 1973, witnessed by Fowler. In this affidavit he stated:

"The object was constructed of an unfamiliar metal which resembled aluminum. It had impacted 20 inches into the sand without any sign of structural damage. It was oval and about 30 feet in diameter. An entranceway hatch had been vertically lowered and opened. It was about 3½ feet high and 1½ feet wide. I was able to talk briefly with someone on the team who did look inside only briefly. He saw 2 swivel seats and a lot of instruments and displays.

A tent pitched near the object sheltered the remains of the only occupant of the craft. It was about 4 feet tall, with a dark brown complexion and it had 2 eyes, 2 nostrils, 2 ears, and a small round mouth. It was clothed in a silvery, metallic suit and on its head wore a cap of the same material."

Fowler, a well-known UFO researcher and author, gave this document, along with a 65-page report, to the "National Investigation Commission for Aerial Phenomena" (NICAP). The investigation of this case led Fowler to the offices of the Atomic Energy Commission, the Stanford Research Institute and to various Air Force bases. Although he could find no further witnesses, all the information given by Fritz Werner regarding persons, projects and locations were confirmed. In Werner's diary he found the fol-

Len Stringfield

lowing entries:

"May 20: Well, pen's out of ink. Spent most of the day on Frenchman's Flat, surveying cubicles and supervising welding of a plate girder bridge sensor which cracked after last shot. Had a beer in the evening. Read. Got funny call from Dr. Doll at 10:00. I'm going on a special job tomorrow.

May 21: Up at 7:00 a.m. Worked most of the day on Frenchman with cubicles. Letter from Bet. She's better now—thank goodness. Got picked up at Indian Springs AFB at 4:30 p.m. for a job I can't write or talk about."

When Fowler permitted Len Stringfield to include the story in his book *Situation Red: The UFO Siege*, he had no notion as to what it would set off. The book became a best-seller and the author received from then on dozens of readers' letters from people who had themselves taken part in this or in similar activities. Further, other UFO researchers who did not quite know how to evaluate the situation sent Stringfield a number of eyewitness reports. And all this formed the basis of his lecture at the MUFON conference in 1978.

One of the witnesses who came forward was Maj. Daly of the U.S. Air Force, who had been a specialist in meteorology at the Wright Patterson AFB during 1953. Just like Werner, he too was taken to an unknown place where it was very hot and sandy, during April or May of 1953, to investigate a crashed UFO. When he had landed at an Air Force base, he was first blindfolded and then taken on a drive which lasted for about half an hour. When he got out, he found himself in the desert, and the first thing he saw was a tent pitched in the sand. The next thing that caught his attention was a silvery metallic flying craft of about 30 feet in diameter. The metal had not been damaged, and the tests he carried out on it, which lasted 2 days, showed that it was not made of any alloy known on earth. He was not allowed to enter the craft, but he saw that it had an opening about 4 feet high and about 25 inches wide, flanked by a ramp.

Richard Hall, director of MUFON, sent Stringfield a letter on April 8, 1964, written by a soldier who was still under training:

> Here at school there is an instructor who, during the Korean conflict, was an adjutant to an Air Force General at one of our New Mexico testing grounds. I got the following story from him: In 1953 a flying saucer crash-landed near the testing grounds. Air Force personnel immediately rushed to the area and found the saucer, unharmed and unoccupied with doors open. Upon searching the surrounding area, they came upon the bodies of the saucer's 4 occupants, all dead . . . whom he described as from 3 to 4 feet tall, hairless and otherwise quite human in appearance . . . I can vouch for the validity of this information as well as the reliability of the person I got it from.

"I am almost positive it happened in 1953," said another witness who, at that time, had had a long career as a military pilot and in the 1970s served in the Air National Guard. When Stringfield visited him at his office at Lunken Airport in Cincinnati, Ohio, there was a map of the United States hanging on the wall. He pointed to an area in Arizona on the map. *"Here's where it happened, approximately. It was in a desert area, but I don't have the name of the location."* He was stationed at Wright Patterson AFB at that time and present when 5 crates arrived, flown in from the crash site. *"I stood at a distance of about 12 feet. A number of Air Police were standing silent guard when I caught a glimpse of what appeared to be hastily prepared wooden crates. In these, little humanoids appearing to be 4 feet tall were lying unshrouded on a fabric, which prevented freeze burn from the dry ice packed beneath. Their heads were disproportionately larger than their bodies with skin that looked brown under the hangar lights above. The heads appeared to be hairless and narrow. The eyes seemed to be open, the mouths small and noses, if any, were indistinct. The humanoids' arms were*

positioned down alongside their bodies, but the hands and feet were indis-
tinct. They appeared to be wearing tight-fitting dark suits, and, because of
the tight-fitting suit, there was one revealing feature—a surprising feature.
One of the humanoids appeared to be female. Either one of the aliens had
an exceedingly muscular chest or the bumps were a female's breasts.

I later heard from a crew member that one of the little humanoids was
still alive aboard the craft when the U.S. military team arrived. Attempts
were made to save its life with oxygen, but these were unsuccessful." But
how did the military know about the crash? According to the witness he
heard from the same crew member that it was picked up by special tracking equipment at Mt. Palomar in California. The coordinates were provided
to the military to determine the crash area. The retrieved craft was found
intact and later sent to Wright Patterson, too.

Stringfield was now onto a new track. He knew now where crashed
saucers and their occupants were taken to and kept. Indeed, according to
Air Force Regulation AFR 200-2, photographs, radar pictures and UFO-

Photograph of a charred corpse, about 4 feet tall, allegedly recovered from a UFO
that crashed on Mexican territory, south of Laredo, Texas, recovered by the U.S.
Army.

related material were to be taken to the ATIC headquarters at Wright Patterson AFB. And Stringfield also found witnesses to the transporting of these articles to that place. One married couple said that in the summer of 1953, when they were driving near the Wright Patterson base, the road had been blocked by a military convoy. A few minutes later, a very impressive escort drove past, consisting of dozens of military policemen on motorbikes, followed by a truck, on the trailer of which was a huge oval thing packed in tarpaulins. This information was confirmed by a close friend of the family of MUFON director John Schuessler, an engineer for McDonnell Douglas at NASA, who served as a guard at the Receiving Gate for internal security at Wright Patterson. One day while on duty "in 1952 or 53," he witnessed a large tractor with a trailer hauling a tarpaulin-covered craft into a tight security area at the base. At this time the base was put on highest security alert. A little later the guard saw the uncovered corpses of very small humanoids. According to a soldier, they were *"recovered from the crashed UFO at a site vaguely referred to as somewhere in the U.S. southwest."*

Another one of Stringfield's informants, Charles Wilhelm of Cincinnati, Ohio, related the following: Around 1959, he often visited a single woman, Mrs. Norma Gardner, who suffered from cancer, to help her with the garden and other repairs. Once he told her about his interest in UFOs. But what he had never reckoned with was, that before she retired from service for health reasons, she had been working in the UFO department at the Wright Patterson AFB. And one day she told her story in full.

In 1955 she had been assigned to a post to catalogue all incoming UFO material that her department was working on, about 1,000 items. Amongst these were a number of objects which had come from the inside of the crashed craft, which were carefully photographed and tagged. After a few months her boss sent her to a very high security area, to a hangar with the code number 18, to list material from 2 saucer-shaped flying objects. There, for the first time, she saw actual UFOs with her own eyes. They were round and disc-shaped; one was bigger than the other, the first damaged but the other intact. Shortly afterwards she saw 2 corpses from their crew, preserved in a chemical solution. They were about 4 to 4½ feet tall, with markedly large heads and enormous black eyes.

"I have taken an oath not to talk about it. It is all strictly secret," she had said, adding hesitatingly, *"but I don't have much longer to live and Uncle Sam can do nothing to me when I am in the grave."*

Some years later Wilhelm found confirmation for Norma's story: one of his school friends, whose father had been stationed at Wright Patterson, had on his death-bed spoken of 2 disc-shaped flying objects and 4 small corpses. *"The bodies were about 5 feet tall, had big heads, slanting eyes and looked quite human. He thought their fingers were longer than those of a human being, but he was not sure."*

Stringfield later found 2 more people whose relatives had worked at Wright Patterson AFB and seen the aliens' bodies. His informants vouched for the reports, but refused to give further details, *"being bound by oath."* One major of the Air Force, however, promised to leave a sealed detailed report in a safe, to be opened and published after his death.

On June 29, 1978 Stringfield learned from his son-in-law Dr. Jeffrey Sparks, professor at St. Leo College in Dade City, Florida, that he had found another witness. This witness "JK" had been stationed at Wright Patterson in 1966 as a member of the Army Intelligence Corps and while there had seen 9 alien bodies kept deep frozen in glass cases. Their bodies were slender, some 4 feet tall, gray in color. The rooms where they were kept were heavily guarded. He had learned that the base had a number of wrecks and 30 bodies. The Air Force had formed a special unit, the "Blue Berets," trained to salvage and examine crashed UFOs, stationed at certain important bases. (See Chapter 11). Their work was highly secret. All data gathered about UFOs by the Air Force was stored in a computer at the data processing center at Wright Patterson.

With JK's aid Stringfield was able to find a member of the "Blue Berets," who had himself never taken part in the recovery of a UFO, but had learned

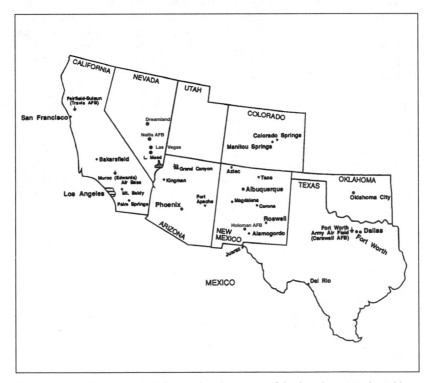

Map of the southwest United States, showing some of the locations mentioned in this chapter.

from a colleague about the transport of a "bighead" from an alien spacecraft.

In June 1978 Stringfield met a physiologist who had been stationed at Wright Patterson AFB as a physician and claimed to have examined a number of UFO occupants during the 50s. The doctor put down his observations as follows:

- The approximate height of the alien humanoid is 3 to 4½ feet tall. One source approximated 5 feet. The weight is approximately 40 pounds.
- Two round eyes without pupils. Under heavy brow ridge, eyes described variously as large, almond-shaped, elongated, sunken or deep set, far apart, slightly slanted, appearing "Oriental" or "Mongoloid."
- The head, by human standards, is large when compared with the size of the torso and limbs. "Take a look at a 5-month human fetus," I was told.
- No earlobes or protrusive flesh extending beyond apertures on each side of head.
- Nose is vague. Two nares are indicated with only a slight protuberance.
- Mouth is indicated as a small "slit" without lips, opening into a small cavity. Mouth appears not to function as a means of communication or as an office for food ingestion.
- Neck described as being thin; and in some instances, not being visible because of garment on that section of body.
- Most observers describe the head of the humanoids as hairless. One said that the pate showed a slight fuzz. Bodies are described as hairless.
- Small and thin fits the general description of the torso. In most instances, the body was observed wearing a metallic but flexible garment.
- Arms are described as long and thin, and reaching down to the knee section.
- One type of hand has four fingers, no thumb. Two fingers appear longer than others. Some observers had seen fingernails; others without. A slight webbing effect between fingers was noted by 3 authoritative observers. Other reports indicate types with less or more than 4 fingers.
- Legs short and thin. Feet of one type described as having no toes. Most observers describe feet as covered. One source said foot looked like an orangutan's.
- Skin description is NOT green. Some claim beige, tan, brown, or tannish or pinkish gray and one said it looked almost "bluish gray" under deep freeze lights. In two instances, the bodies were charred to a dark brown. The texture is described as scaly or reptilian, and as stretchable, elastic or mobile over smooth muscle or skeletal tissue. No striated muscle. No perspiration, no body odor. In November 1979, additional word was received from the medical authority concerning the nature of alien skin. Under magnification, I was told, the tissue structure appears mesh-like, or, like a grid's network of horizontal and perpendicular lines. Clarifying an earlier reference which describes the skin of the entity as "reptilian," this new information suggests that the texture of the granular-skinned lizards, such as the iguana and chameleon, may be similar to at least one type of alien humanoid.

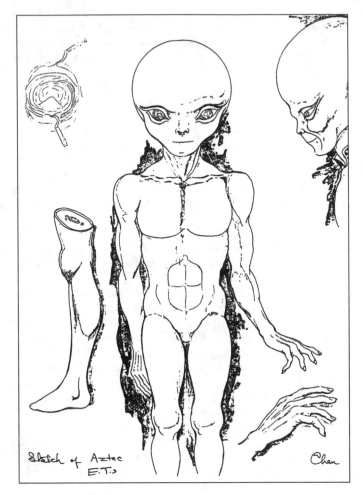

Sketch of Aztec E.T.s

Chen

Above and on facing pages, two different kinds of alien that have been discovered in UFOs, drawn according to information given by doctors who had taken part in the autopsies.

- No teeth.
- No apparent reproductive organs. Perhaps atrophied by evolutionary degeneration. No genitalia. In my non-professional judgment, the absence of sexual organs suggests that some of the aliens, and perhaps all, do not reproduce as do the Homo sapiens—or that some of the bodies studied are produced perhaps by a system of cloning or other unknown means.
- To most observers the humanoids appear to be "formed out of a mold," or sharing identical facial characteristics.

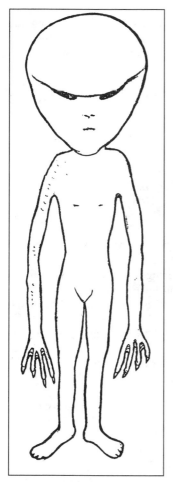

- Brain and its capacity, unknown.
- Colorless liquid prevalent in body, without red cells. No lymphocytes. Not a carrier of oxygen. No food or water intake is known. No food found aboard craft in any known retrieval. No digestive system or GI tract. No intestinal or alimentary canal or rectal area described.
- More than one humanoid type. Life span unknown. Descriptive variations of anatomy may be no more diverse than those known among Earth's Homo sapiens. Other recovered alien types of human or other grotesque configurations are unknown to me. Origin unknown.
- The bodies were sent for further investigations to medical institutes farther east, such as in the states of Indiana, Illinois and Texas.

Further details were given to Stringfield on July 2, 1979:

- The eyes were recessed into the head. There seemed to be no visible eyelids, only what seemed like a fold. The nose consisted of a small fold-like protrusion above the nasal orifices. The mouth seemed to be a wrinkle-like fold. There were no human type lips as such—just a slit that opened into an oral cavity about 2 inches deep. A membrane along the rear of the cavity separated it from what would be the digestive tract. The tongue seemed to be atrophied into almost a membrane. No teeth were observed. X-rays revealed a maxilla and mandible as well as cranial bone structure. The outer "earlobes" didn't exist. The auditory orifices present were similar to our middle and inner ear canals. The head contained no hair follicles. The skin seemed grayish in color and seemed mobile when moved.

There is much evidence to show that the Air Force or the Blue Berets had made a documentary film about the recovery in Arizona, which was shown at air force bases to specially chosen groups of people. Stringfield's informant in this case was Mr. T. E. who, in 1953, had been a radar specialist for the Air Force on a secret mission in Fort Monmouth, New Jersey. One day in the spring of 1953 he was called, along with other chosen radar operators, to the film theatre of the base. Without any introduction or comments, a 16mm film projector was set up and a film was shown. The first thing that they saw was a desert scene with a silvery disc-like object stuck in the sand with a door-like opening, from which a ramp led downwards to the ground. The next scene showed the object, which had a diameter of about 24 feet, surrounded by about a dozen soldiers. The witness remembers having wondered why they were showing him this film. Then pictures of the inside of the object followed.

After the last interior shot, the scene changed to 2 tables inside a tent upon which 2 dead bodies were lying. Now T. E. started looking with greater attention. The beings there seemed to be small and slim, had prominently big heads, identical facial characteristics and an ashy complexion. The facial features were mongoloid-type. They had small noses, thin, lipless mouths, and their deep-set eyes were shut. They were wearing tight fitting bright suits. At that moment, the film ran out and the lights went on. *"Just think about the film,"* said the officer present, *"but don't talk about it to anybody."* And T. E. was particularly surprised when, 2 weeks later, he was told by an officer, *"Forget the film that you saw, it was only a joke."*

After Stringfield cited T. E.'s report during his talk in Dayton, he received a letter from MUFON member John Jeffers on February 6, 1979. Jeffers had gotten to know a former Air Force colonel, who had been stationed at the Maine Air Force radar post. Once a week, the commander held a meeting with the officers and during one of these meetings in 1956, they showed them, without any comment, *"a film from the Air Force."* *"The film showed a round metallic object which lay on the ground. Its insides were well-illuminated. The scene changed and showed 3 bodies lying on a table. Their color was ash gray."*

The third confirmation came from a major of the Air Force who, during his service period, had been put on various special jobs. On one occasion, he had been ordered to go to Wright Patterson for a very strictly secret discussion of a special situation. The officers present were taken to an underground chamber in which the corpse of one of the crashed aliens was to be seen in a glass coffin. A little later, they sent him to an underground complex of the archives of the U.S. Air Force at Colorado Springs, where he was shown a film. The strip showed a spaceship wedged into the sand of the desert and the recovered bodies.

During the summer of 1980, it seemed almost as if the riddle of Hangar 18 at Wright Patterson and the UFO recovery actions were on the point of being solved. Stringfield now had contact with 20 eyewitnesses and 2 persons who had second-hand information. The accounts of the witnesses gave him a complete and gapless picture of the salvage action at every one of its stages and practically the only thing that he still lacked was concrete evidence. Some of the witnesses had even given him copies of official photographs of the humanoids which he, however, wanted to publish only after thorough analysis. But, with his second status report of January 1981, he must have touched a very sensitive nerve of the secret services.

The Wright Patterson Air Force Base, Dayton, Ohio.

Only 3 months after Stringfield had declared at the annual meeting of MUFON that he was in possession of photographs, suddenly and overnight all of his 20 witnesses became silent. To be more exact, he received no more letters from them. Writing to me on July 14, 1981, he said *"29 further potential informants also wouldn't talk anymore, or simply disappeared. My medical source also told me he could not give me any more information. I cannot imagine that 49 people can suddenly change their minds overnight. I rather believe that they had been advised to do so and, strangely enough, at that time, I came under heavy attack from various people, who tried to raise doubts about my integrity. And other alleged witnesses made the wildest of statements about living aliens in the cellars of Wright Patterson and sent primitive faked photographs."*

In fact, a very different kind of person also failed in his attempt to pierce this veil of secrecy around Hangar 18. In 1962, the Republican U.S. senator and ex-governor of Arizona, Barry Goldwater, stopped over at Wright Patterson AFB on his way to California. Goldwater had long been interested in UFOs and had heard rumors about Hangar 18 and the Blue Room, the

Senator Barry Goldwater

BARRY GOLDWATER
ARIZONA

United States Senate
WASHINGTON, D.C. 20510

COMMITTEES:
INTELLIGENCE, CHAIRMAN
ARMED SERVICES
TACTICAL WARFARE, CHAIRMAN
PREPAREDNESS
STRATEGIC AND THEATRE NUCLEAR FORCES
COMMERCE, SCIENCE, AND TRANSPORTATI
COMMUNICATIONS, CHAIRMAN
AVIATION
SCIENCE, TECHNOLOGY, AND SPACE
INDIAN AFFAIRS

October 19, 1981

Mr. ▆▆▆▆▆▆▆▆
▆▆▆▆▆▆▆▆▆▆▆▆▆

Dear Mr. ▆▆▆▆

First, let me tell you that I have long ago given up acquiring
access to the so-called blue room at Wright-Patterson, as I have
had one long string of denials from chief after chief, so I have
given up.

In answer to your questions, one is essentially correct. I don't
know of anyone who has access to the blue room, nor am I aware of
its contents and I am not aware of anything having been relocated.
I can't answer your question six, in fact, I can't find anyone who
would answer it.

To tell you the truth, Mr. ▆▆▆▆▆, this thing has gotten so highly
classified, even though I will admit there is a lot of it that
has been released, it is just impossible to get anything on it.

I am returning your papers because I know they are of value to you.

Sincerely,

Barry Goldwater
Barry Goldwater

Senator Barry Goldwater's letter, "This thing has gotten so highly
classified, even though there is a lot of it that has been released."

archive for UFO fragments. So he requested permission from his old
friend, the commander of the base, Gen. Curtis LeMay to see the wreckage. LeMay's answer was very sobering, *"Oh Hell! No! I can't go there,
you can't go there and don't ever ask me again!"* On October 19, 1981,
Goldwater wrote to the UFO researcher, Lee Graham, *"First let me tell you
that I have long ago given up acquiring access to the so-called blue room
at Wright Patterson, as I have had one long string of denials from chief
after chief. So, I have given up. . . . To tell you the truth, Mr. [Graham,]
this thing has gotten so highly classified, even though I will admit there
is a lot of it that has been released, it is just impossible to get anything
on it."*

The explanation for this extremely high secrecy classification—Goldwater described it in another letter as "above Top Secret"—we find in the
Majestic-12 documents of 1952: *"Implications for the National Security
are of continuing importance in that the motives and ultimate intentions of
these* [alien] *visitors remain completely unknown. In addition, a significant
upsurge in the surveillance activity of these craft beginning in May and*

continuing through the autumn of this year has caused considerable con-cern that new developments may be imminent. It is for these reasons, as well as the obvious international and technological considerations and the ultimate need to avoid a public panic at all costs, that the Majestic-12 Group remains of the unanimous opinion that imposition of the strictest security precautions should continue without interruption into the new administration."

The result was, as we've already seen, the Robertson Panel, which included 2 scientists from the Majestic-12 circles.

But even the attack against Stringfield could not stop the truth from leaking out. The release of FBI documents of 1950, which confirmed the recovery of 3 so-called flying saucers, convinced UFO researchers that they were not on a wild goose chase. During that same year, the book *Roswell Incident* by Charles Berlitz and William L. Moore came out and became an international best-seller. And, in official circles, one had to reconsider whether the policy followed hitherto could be sustained any longer.

Two years later, after his taking part in a radio broadcast, Moore received a call. *"You are the only person I can talk to on this subject, who seems to know what he's talking about,"* said the caller. During the following months, he convinced Moore that he was an official of the government who wanted to give the public information through Moore. His cover name was to be Falcon. Moore met the film producer Jaime Shandera and together, during their work with Falcon, they often went through situations which were reminiscent of a third-rate espionage film. Once, Moore went from one airport to another, only to get new instructions each time over the telephone. He was sent to hotels, to particular windows in particular restaurants and then finally to a hotel room, at which a secret agent met him with a pile of files under his arm. Moore was given 17 minutes to do what he wanted to do with the files, after which they would be taken away. The UFO researcher photographed what he could. There were sensational documents, short reports about UFO crashes, the recovery of their occupants and about Project Aquarius, which had all been put together for the briefing of President Jimmy Carter, in 1977.

According to this document, Project Aquarius was created to *"coordinate ·and collect all available scientific, technical and medical information relevant to intelligence regarding sightings of UFOs/IACs (Identified Alien Craft), and contact with extraterrestrial life-forms."* It was divided into four subprojects:

1. *Project PANDO (code name: RISK) Originally established in 1949. Its mission was to collect and evaluate medical information from the surviving alien creatures and the recovered bodies. Physicians in this project medically examined EBEs and provided U.S. medical researchers with certain answers to the evolution theory. (OPR: CIA) (Terminated in 1974)*
2. *Project SIGMA (code name: MIDNIGHT) Originally established as part of Project GLEEM in 1954. Became a separate project with positive*

*success when in 1959 the U.S. established primitive communications
with the aliens. On April 25, 1964, a USAF intelligence officer met 2
aliens at a prearranged location in the desert of New Mexico. The contact lasted for approximately 3 hours. Based on the alien's language
given to us by an EBE, the Air Force officer managed to exchange basic
information with the 2 aliens. (Atch: 7) This project is continuing at an
Air Force base in New Mexico. (OPR. MJ12/NSA)*

3. *Project SNOWBIRD (code name: CETUS) Originally established in
   1972. Its mission was to test fly recovered alien aircraft. This project is
   continuing in Nevada. (OPR: USAF/NASA/CIA/MJ12)*
4. *Project POUNCE (code name: DIXIE) Originally established in 1949.
   Its mission was to evaluate all UFO/IAC information regarding space
   travel technologies. This project is continuing. (OPR: NASA/USAF)*

But that was not all. Falcon arranged for the sending of the Majestic-12
documents to Shandera, and declared that he was ready for an interview
with the film producer in front of a running camera, provided he was filmed
in silhouette and recorded with his voice distorted.

The real sensation came when Falcon, together with another intelligence
agent, "Condor," repeated his statements on TV before millions of viewers.
In fact, it was a major breakthrough in UFO research when, on October 14,
1988, the 2-hour TV feature, "UFO Cover-up Live" was shown nationwide
on CBS.

For the first time, UFO sighting witnesses, amongst them top-ranking
military officers and airline pilots, were presented without the usual and
obligatory skepticism. Authentic photographs and films were shown to the
public and a group of experts came on to inform them about the current
state of UFO research. Through satellite, the viewers experienced the first
UFO glasnost in TV history: Sergei Bulantsev, from "Tass," and Leonhard
Nikishin of the Academy of Sciences, sat in the Moscow studio and
described the most interesting sightings and encounters in the Soviet
Union.

But the most impressive part of the broadcast was perhaps the description given by two elderly ladies, who had come to the TV studio in Washington.

On December 29, 1980, Betty Cash and Vickie Landrum, along with her
7-year old grandson, Colby, were on their way home from Houston, Texas,
where they had spent the evening playing Bingo. They were driving at a
speed of about 45 mph long a narrow country road and were just looking
around at the emptiness around them, when Betty suddenly saw a light
moving in the sky. She thought nothing more of it and soon lost sight of it,
but shortly after that, a huge fiery object in the shape of a rhombus appeared
a bit ahead of them, and hovered above the road. Vickie, being religious,
thought at once that biblical prophecy had come to fulfillment. *"That's
Jesus!"* she called out to Colby, *"Don't be afraid, he's coming from Heaven
and will lead us human beings to a better world."*

Flames were shooting out of the object which was approaching them threateningly. Its flight was unsteady and it seemed to stagger. Betty, quickly realizing that they were in danger of soon being burned alive in the car, drove off to the side and parked. The 3 of them got out of the car at once and ran on to the road from where they could see the phenomenon better. It was a huge flying craft, like none that they had ever

Vickie Landrum and Betty Cash.

seen before, a diamond glowing in orange color, from which a fiery trail went out. It was being followed at a safe distance by a squadron of helicopters. The noise of the helicopters was in sharp contrast to the majestic silence of the object itself.

Colby was frightened and ran back to the car. The 2 women followed him and they watched the thing from inside the car. Soon it became so bright that they had to close their eyes and, at the same time, they felt an intensive wave of heat going through them. *"I seemed to be burning,"* said Vickie in "UFO Cover-up Live." Then it was only a few minutes before the UFO disappeared at the other end of the road. Terribly frightened, the 3 continued their journey home. Once more, from the highway, they were able to see the strange squadron with the bright diamond ahead of it. Then they arrived home.

The next day they all felt sick. Vickie complained about a headache,

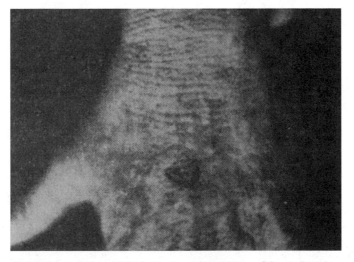

Cancerous tumor on Vickie's hand, a consequence of the radioactivity of the UFO.

Betty had nausea and her neck began to swell. Red dots started appearing on her face and Colby also showed the same symptoms.

Overnight, from being two elderly but active women, they had turned into sick and suffering people. Betty, who was planning to open a restaurant during the coming year, was now a complete wreck. Her eyes were swollen and the red dots on her face became pustules. For days on end she was plagued by nausea and diarrhea. Her hair fell out in bunches. Afraid that Betty was going to die, Vickie called a doctor and had her taken to a hospital, where she stayed for 12 days. Finally, she became blind in one eye. During that week, Vickie and Colby also suffered from reddening of the skin, swelling of the eyes, stomach aches, nausea, loss of appetite, falling hair—all the typical symptoms of exposure to dangerous radiation.

Betty, in the "UFO Cover-up Live" broadcast in 1988, said: *"Now I have cancer. I was operated on in March 1983. The doctors were not sure whether they could get it all. Some days I feel OK, on other days, awful."* Vickie is also a cancer patient now.

The American UFO research group MUFON investigated this case and described it as one of the most significant UFO encounters in the history of the phenomenon. They were successful in finding 35 witnesses to the incident. But when the two women sued the government—after all, United States military helicopters were involved—and asked for compensation, this was completely refused on the grounds that they were not in the least responsible. *"I am very disappointed with the government of our country,"* said Vickie during the broadcast.

After that, Falcon was presented. Filmed under shadows and his voice made unrecognizable, he declared that *"the object which was observed in the Cash/Landrum case was an extraterrestrial craft that was flown by one of our military pilots. Although he had been trained in this ship and was familiar with it, it happened to get out of his control. The crew radioed that they believed the ship would crash. It is the usual procedure in military traffic to send recovery helicopters when a crash is imminent. These helicopters followed the craft. The craft went through various problematic phases, but did not crash because the pilots were able to get it back under control."*

An alien space ship piloted by U.S. military pilots? That sounds unbelievable. But the revelations of Falcon in the broadcast went much further. *"Inside the MJ-12 community there is a book . . . This book, or as it's called within the MJ-12 community, "the bible," contains historically everything that has occurred from the Truman era up to the 3 aliens being guests of the United States government. It includes technological data gathered from the aliens, medical history gathered from dead aliens that were found in the desert, autopsy information, information gathered from the aliens about their social structure and the universe. Presently, as of the year 1988, there is one extraterrestrial being here as a guest of the United States government and he's remained hidden from public view. The "Yellow Book" is a book that was exclusively written by the second extraterrestrial being. It contains information about the planet of the aliens, their solar system, their dual suns, their culture, their social makeup and structure, and their life among earthlings. But what I found most intriguing in my experience with the aliens was an octahedral crystal which, when it was held in the aliens' hands, showed pictures either of the aliens' home planet or of Earth, many thousands of years ago."*

As incredible as these statements sound, there are enough reasons to take Falcon seriously. William Moore came into contact with 9 more government officials, all through Falcon. Moore and Shandera were able to verify their identities and positions inside the Secret Service and get these data confirmed. In 1983, Moore introduced Falcon to a CBS reporter, Peter Leone. Leone said in "UFO Cover-up Live:" *"It was possible for me to verify Falcon's credentials. In 1987 I met Falcon again and once more I could confirm his references. It became clear to me that he was what he claimed to be."*

Falcon went on: *"(The aliens' home planet) was in the Zeta Reticuli star group. Since 1948 until today 3 aliens have been guests of the U.S. government. The first alien was captured in the New Mexican desert after its craft crashed. The alien, named EBE (Extraterrestrial Biological Entity) by the government, was kept in captivity for 3 years. We learned a great deal about the alien's race, culture and spacecrafts.*

The second alien came as part of an exchange program. I can't recall the exact year of his visit. The third one also came as part of the exchange program and has been a guest of the U.S. Government since 1982."

According to Falcon the aliens were 3 feet, 4 inches to 4 feet 3 inches tall, had slender bodies and disproportionately large heads. Their life span was 300 to 400 earth years and their IQ was over 200. *"They have a religion, but it's a universal religion; they believe in the universe as a supreme being."* They consider and believe in the reincarnation of souls as an essential factor.

They came to the earth with peaceful intentions, but did not think that it was right to interfere directly with our evolution. All that they could do—and had already done—was to influence our moral and cultural development by indirect means.

That breakthrough had a signal effect. Encouraged by the revelations of Falcon and Condor on "UFO Cover-up Live," other ex-Secret Service men and government scientists began to lift the curtain of silence. One of them was Robert Lazar, 31, a courageous young scientist who had worked on one of the most secret projects of the United States. Physicist and research engineer, Lazar had been working in Dreamland, a particularly guarded security area on the even more secure supersecret air force and naval testing grounds at Groom Lake in the desert of Nevada.

During an exclusive broadcast of KLAS-TV in Las Vegas, Nevada, presented by George Knapp on November 6, 1989, Lazar talked. He claimed that the U.S. Air Force had a total of 9 flying saucers in their possession. The majority of them had crashed in and been recovered from the south-

Bob Lazar in June 1993

west United States during the 40s and 50s. *Our top scientists have been studying their propulsion mechanism for 40 years, but it's hardly been a decade since we began to understand the basic principles of their propulsion system."*

According to Lazar, he has a degree in engineering sciences from the California Institute of Technology and another in nuclear physics from the Massachusetts Institute of Technology. He had worked in the Los Alamos National Laboratories before his work at Groom Lake began in 1988. Lazar was employed by the Department of Naval Intelligence to work on the development of advanced propulsion systems. He did not have the faintest idea as to how advanced his new field of work would be when he was sworn to silence.

On his first working day, he was given various secret reports and was told to study them carefully. The papers dealt with an antimatter reactor which served as a source of energy. *"They described a gravity amplifier. It was a dual element propulsion system, a strange technology. There was no physical connection between the two systems. They used gravitation as a wave, used wave conductors, such as with microwaves."* There was a poster hanging in one of the offices, which showed a disc-like flying craft hovering about 3 feet above the dried-up lake. A new kind of test craft, thought Lazar. The thing that irritated him about the poster was what was written underneath: *"They are here."*

Photograph of a disc above the Area 51, taken on Feb. 28, 1990, by Gary Schultz.

A little later he was taken to see this very craft. It was standing in a hangar. His colleagues asked Lazar to have a look at the mysterious object, also from the inside. Lazar was astonished when he climbed into the disc. There were tiny pilots' seats, too small for normal people, and at once he knew that the vessel was not from this world.

"There they stood, all of them. The hangars were all interconnected and each one harbored such a disc. There were 9 in all. And each one was different. Three had been taken apart for investigation, one was damaged, one had crashed only in August 1981 and the rest were intact." The damaged disc stood tilted and had a big hole in the underside, as if it had been shot down. *"To keep track of them I gave them simple names: 'the hat,' 'the cake tin,' 'the sports model'—this one looked freshly polished and like what I thought a newly built space vessel should look like."*

He studied this sports model thoroughly, and when he saw it in the air he was absolutely sure that "it was certainly not from here." Its flying characteristics were absolutely different from that of usual aircraft, its drive absolutely unconventional. It was not based on the principle of action and reaction. It did not push out any gas like a jet. It did not have any propeller, made no noise. It looked like magic.

When it started, its underside started glowing. It began to hiss like a sphere loaded with high voltage current. *"It is my impression that that is the reason why the discs were round, with no corners or edges: in order to discharge high voltage. If you have seen an insulator of a high voltage system, it's also round or at least rounded so that a coronal all-around discharge is possible. In any case, it began to hiss as if under high voltage, stayed in the air, and then lifted up softly and silently to hover again, this time at a height of about 30 feet."*

It was a short demonstration flight with the aim of showing the mechanism of the disc to Lazar and the other technicians. Then Lazar was shown the propulsion unit, an antimatter reactor. It consisted of a plate 18 inches in diameter with a sphere in the middle. The sphere had a removable cover. The reactor was in the middle of the disk. In this reactor, according to Lazar, there is a chip of the element 115. When it is bombarded with protons, the element 115 changes, disintegrates and thereby sets antimatter and gravity waves free. Wave conductors and gravity amplifiers channel the gravity waves, and build a strong gravitational field around the ship out of it.

Since it is thus independent of every other gravitational field such as that of a planet, the craft can reach enormous speeds, change its direction of flight and also stop in flight—the flight characteristics which have been associated with for literature for decades.

This mysterious element 115 does not occur on earth. According to Lazar, however, the United States government has over 500 pounds of element 115 taken from the recovered wrecks. It is an extremely heavy element which can be transported only in leaden chests. It cannot be made synthetically. *"Synthetic elements reach the highest level of 92 in the Peri-*

*odic table of elements. Above 103 and everything else higher than Pluto-
nium, they disintegrate too fast,"* explained Lazar. *"Let's take element 106.
It can be kept only for a limited period. Scientists speculate that the elements from around 113 to 116 will again be stable and that is true. Element
115 is the proof of that."*

Lazar believes that there is only one natural source for 115: a super-
heavy star, shortly before turning into a supernova, or a binary star system. One such system with two suns, a yellow dwarf sun and a red giant,
is Zeta Reticuli, the home planetary system of the aliens of whom Falcon
spoke.

Actually, Lazar and his colleagues were given various briefing documents to supply them with the necessary background information for their
work. These reports, according to Lazar, contained all possible details
about the aliens, even about their religion. They contained photographs of
the extraterrestrials and autopsy reports. They were full of information. The
extraterrestrials were described as being between three feet eight inches and
four feet two inches tall with brown-gray skin, big hairless heads, slit eyes,
and long thin arms. Their native planet had been designated Reticulum 4,
the fourth planet in the system Zeta Reticuli.

The perpetual secrecy and security measures at every step and turn was
one of the reasons Lazar gave up his job at Groom Lake. *"I was again and
again reminded that I was under a secrecy oath. More than once, the military personnel threatened me with their weapons, saying that I would die if
I talked. They listened to all my telephone conversations. At some point or
other, I found myself unable to bear this continuous stress."*

Psychologists and psychiatrists examined Lazar for KLAS-TV and were
even convinced that the physicist had been influenced mentally, perhaps
put on drugs. The hypnosis therapist Layne Keck said *"the man is under
tremendous pressure. Apparently he has been subjected to massive psycho-
terror for a long time."* When the TV reporters investigated further, they
found that Lazar had become "persona non grata." The universities at
which he claimed he had studied said that they knew nothing about him.
The Los Alamos Laboratories denied categorically that there had ever been
a Robert Lazar in their employment. Even the hospital where he was born
suddenly denied his birth. Was Lazar a swindler?

The journalists did not give up. They managed to find an old copy of an
internal telephone book of the Physics Department of Los Alamos laboratories. There, all of a sudden, Lazar was listed. An article in the *Los Alamos
Monitor* of 1986 reported his construction of a jet car and described him as
*"a physicist at the Los Alamos Meson Physics Facility . . . who had worked
on this technology with NASA scientists."* And he was able to produce his
W2 income tax declaration form, which showed him to be an employee of
the Department of Naval Intelligence.

After his dismissal, according to Lazar, the pressure went on. *"They
threatened me and my wife during various unexpected visits to our house.
I just had to talk to get rid of the pressure. Now at least they have no rea-*

son to threaten me. I have already said everything and nobody can stop that anymore."

They could not stop him talking, so they tried to discredit him. After leaving his job in Groom Lake, Lazar opened a private consulting firm for electronics. In January 1990 he was taken to court for having designed a computer and an alarm system for "an illegal bordello" in the vicinity of Las Vegas. After months of detention while awaiting trial, he was finally sentenced to 3 years of probation for having *"supported illegal prostitution"* although his lawyer had tried to argue that it was not Lazar's responsibility, when providing technical advice and installation, which was legal, to investigate the background of his clients. Lazar was forced to plead guilty in order to get amelioration of sentence. . . . His opponents had succeeded in discrediting him.

It looks as if the research at Groom Lake was started shortly after the recovery of the first 4 saucers. An ex-member of the medical corps of Nellis Air Force Base, which lies close to Groom Lake, told the UFO researcher and ex-ATIC-officer, Lt. Col. Wendelle C. Stevens, that the rebuilding of the base and the provision of huge underground constructions was begun in 1951. Towards the end of 1951, according to that witness, project Red Light moved in, with a crew of 800 to 1,000 men, all highly qualified technicians, some of them from the Manhattan Project and others from the Los Alamos National Laboratories. Rumors went around the base that project Red Light was engaged in investigating UFO technologies and that actually UFO wrecks had been brought to the hangars in the testing area. There was even talk that secret test flights had been tried with the captured UFOs. Some of them had been successful, but in some other a flights the spaceship exploded in flight and two U.S. test pilots were killed.

The most incredible story which came to Stevens's ears, however, was that a living alien had been brought to Groom Lake and kept in a special habitat. He is supposed to have died shortly after that. That tallies, at least regarding the dates, with Falcon's statements about EBE 1.

And what about the alleged experiments with UFO technology? It is said that the most advanced aircraft of the U.S. Air Force at the present time is the Stealth Fighter. Stealth was first built during the 70s but shown to the public only in 1989. Are we to believe that over a period of 20 years and with billions of dollars given out for research, nothing new has been developed? Stealth was also considered a legend, until the Air Force invited the press for a demonstration flight.

> For months now reports have been piling up about flying craft that look as if they came out of science fiction, rising up from the strictly guarded test bases in Nevada and California. Observers saw glowing supersonic jets by moonlight and others triangles or bulging surfboards flitting around the desert sky,

reported the German news magazine *Der Spiegel*, 47/1990.

Area 51, satellite photograph. Clearly recognizable: the landing ramp, which goes deep into the dry Groom Lake.

The state of Nevada, strewn with boulders and furrowed by salt lakes, almost as big as Italy but with a population of only 800,000 people, has always been the center of so-called "Black World Research"—classified armament programs of the army, carried out without public control and financed by the secret funds of the Pentagon. The black 'birds,' secret prototypes, take off mostly during the night or the early morning hours for test flights and land, unnoticed if possible, behind the barbed wire fences of restricted areas.

The journal *Aviation Week and Space Technology* has evaluated a total of 45 eyewitness reports, some of them containing very accurate and detailed information, in order to get an insight into the *"deep black"* aeronautical arsenal of the army. *"One of the craft that has been observed is shaped like a triangle with rounded corners. It is flat like a manta ray and glides almost silently through the air."*

Data regarding such a hitherto secret aircraft has been released by the U.S. Navy, at whose Groom Lake laboratories Lazar had been working: "The new flying triangle" will be called the new A12 "Aurora" intercepting bomber, according to experts. *"A perfect triangle on which the cockpit is enthroned as a long glass dome. Six of these naval flounders are already being built, and a total of 620 have been ordered. Towards the end of 1995 they will be hooked on to the starting catapults of aircraft carriers."*

But that, too, is only the tip of the iceberg. *"Out there in Nevada there are bigger and better things in progress,"* said an insider, for instance, the Aurora Air Breather, a further development of the A12, an unmanned robot aircraft which can fly at speeds of over 6,000 mph. There is also talk of *"exotic propulsion systems and aerodynamic forms which could not be properly explained until now,"* and of a *"whole arsenal of black proto-*

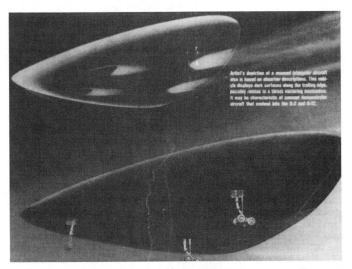

Reconstruction of a manned triangular aircraft, drawn according to information given by eye witnesses from the black world—Reconstruction by *Aviation Week & Space Technology*.

types." Some of them are so secret that *"whenever they come out of the hangar or are coming down to land, a siren goes off and the entire ground personnel, except for a few chosen ones, have to lie face down on the ground so as not to see any details."*

"*At our place there are things flying around that would make George Lucas envious,*" said a Lockheed engineer to the army newspaper *Gung-Ho*. And an Air Force officer who had been working on the Stealth program said, "*we are testing machines here that will defy all descriptions. To compare them with Stealth would be like comparing a space shuttle with Leonardo da Vinci's parachute construction.*"

Gung-Ho confirmed the existence of an "Alien Technology Center" at Groom Lake and asked whether they were really studying the technology of the Mexicans! According to the report in *Aviation Week*, "*some of the aircraft are propelled by technologies that are far beyond those that are used by engineers today who build traditional aircraft.*" As a matter of fact, the U.S. Air Force, Navy and NASA have recently started to take a surprisingly deep interest in such exotic propulsions as antimatter reactors. Thus in August 1990 a circular called upon all important scientists working on government-sponsored projects to immediately coordinate their findings in the direction of "*advanced propulsion technology—especially in the field of antimatter reactors, cold fusion and anti-gravitation propulsion*" with one of the NASA offices. Also in issue No. 38, 1990 of the weekly journal *Aerotech News and Review* it was said that the U.S. Air Force was now working on antimatter propulsion systems like the ones Lazar had already described a year before:

"If antiprotons could be preserved and combined with protons in a safe manner then the Air Force would have an unbelievably strong source of energy."
In a report written for the magazine *UFO Universe* of June 1991, the expert author William F. Hamilton III writes, *"various companies involved in government projects have been doing research in the fields of gravitation and gravitational propulsions since 1955 . . . a CIA memorandum of February 1956 calls for all UFO files of government offices to be sent to the department for applied sciences."* According to Hamilton, this was a direct result of the investigations of UFO wrecks which had been recovered between 1947 and 1953.

Indeed, the year 1948, one year after Roswell, was a turning point in American aircraft manufacture. It was in those days that Jack Northrop—whose firm later developed the Stealth aircraft—built the YB-49 for the Air Force, an aircraft with revolutionary design. It looked like a huge boomerang with a dome-like a cockpit on the nose of the triangle. The tests with the YB-49—actually a forerunner of Stealth with exactly the same wingspan—lasted only 4 years. In 1952 all prototypes were destroyed. The suitable propulsion was still missing.

Between 1952 and 1958 they experimented with the saucer-shaped AVRO disk, which, apparently, did not develop the required flight capacity. In 1972 work was started on the Stealth bomber, and in January 1981, Jack Northrop, now 85, was able to see the first successful demonstration flight. In October 1989 the residents of Lancaster in eastern California could see glowing objects rising up into the sky, which could remain stationary in the air or glide as if they were not affected by gravity, above the testing grounds in Edwards Air Base in the Mojave Desert, the second supersecret testing ground of the U.S. Air Force.

And all this began at Roswell. Will that July 4, 1947, go down in history as the dawn of a new era? Was it the day mankind was released from his cosmic isolation? Is the United States Government already in contact with aliens from the planet Reticulum 4? Everything indicates that behind the veil of silence, things are happening that are far beyond our imagination. Perhaps it is only a question of time before we finally know the truth . . .

In October 1993 the Republican congressman Steven Schiff of New Mexico petitioned the General Accounting Office (GAO) to investigate whether the government was covering up the recovery of alien bodies from a crashed flying saucer near Roswell in 1947. Schiff was a member of the House Government Operations Committee under whose jurisdiction the GAO operates. As GAO spokeswoman Laura A. Kopelson explained later, this investigation was started when Schiff met GAO chief Gen. Charles A. Bowsher and complained to him about the reluctance of the Pentagon to reply to his requests. As a result of correspondence which he had had from UFO researcher Sgt. Clifford Stone, a resident of Roswell, New Mexico, Schiff had written in March 1993 to the then Defense Secretary Les Aspin, requesting a personal briefing on this subject. But that request was not granted. Instead, the Pentagon office for legislative matters answered and advised Schiff to approach the National Archives, where the Blue Book files were kept. Peeved by this indifferent treatment, Schiff again wrote to Aspin on May 10, 1993, and received an answer from him with more or less the same content. During a routine meeting of the GAO in October 1993, Schiff complained about the behavior of the Defense Secretary and the GAO declared itself ready to start an official investigation.

GAO's spokeswoman Kopelson said in January 1994—when the press heard for the first time about the GAO investigation—that an experienced GAO official was conducting the research, but found himself "stonewalled" by the Pentagon. Meanwhile the U.S. Air Force published its own "Report of the Air Force Research Regarding the Roswell Incident," written by Col. Richard L. Weaver, director for Security and Control of Special Programs. After 22 pages, Weaver came to the conclusion that whatever crashed in Roswell in 1947 was not a weather ballon—as claimed by the Air Force in 1947—but a weather ballon with a very special mission: This supersecret mission had the code name "Project Mogul." Its purpose was to detect disturbances in the atmosphere, which would betray Russian atomic tests. Alien bodies, of course, were not found, since *"the recovered wreckage was from a Project Mogul balloon. There were no 'alien' passenger[s] therein."* Naturally, besides the fact that "Project Mogul" indeed launched balloons in the summer of 1947, Weaver presented no evidence at all for his hypothesis, not one single USAF report confirming his "identification," and, of course, his report satisfied neither the GAO nor Senator Schiff.

But when in July 1995 GAO published the report *"Results of a Search for Records Concerning the 1947 Crash Near Roswell, New Mexico,"* they had to admit their failure to penetrate the veil of silence. *"We conducted an extensive search for governmental records related to the crash near Roswell,"* it said. *"In our search . . . we learned that some government records covering Roswell AFB activities had been destroyed . . . the document disposition form does not indicate what organization or person destroyed the records and when or under what authority the records were destroyed."* *"The missing documents leave unanswered questions,"* Schiff replied. *"These outgoing messages were permanent records, which never should have been destroyed."* But someone obviously ignored all Air Force habits and made the "smoking gun" of the Roswell crash simply disappear. . . .

Then, 2 years later, just in time for the 50th anniversary of the Roswell events—celebrated by an international festival sponsored by the city of Roswell—the Air Force finally solved the mystery. On a televised Pentagon press conference on June 24th, 1997—the anniversary of Kenneth Arnold's sighting—U.S. Air Force spokesman Col. John Haynes presented the "final last word" in the Roswell case. "The Roswell Report—Case Closed," compiled by Capt. James McAndrew of the USAF. This time the Air Force changed policy. Yes, indeed, they admitted, all the witnesses who described "alien bodies" told the truth. But, to quote Col. Haynes, these bodies *"were probably test dummies that were carried aloft by United*

States Air Force high altitude balloons for scientific research." Case closed, mystery solved, isn't it?

Is it? Indeed, the U.S. Air Force performed experiments with crash test dummies in New Mexico. Maybe indeed *"anthropomorphic dummies were not widely exposed outside of scientific research circles and easily could have been mistaken for something they were not."* But, to quote the McAndrew Report: *"These abstractly human dummies were first used in New Mexico in May 1950 . . ."* 3 years after the Roswell incident! Moreover, according to McAndrews, the test series in which those dummies were *"carried aloft by USAF high altitude balloons"* as part of the high altitude aircraft escape projects High Dive and Excelsior, took place *"between June 1954 and February 1959,"* at a time when most of the witnesses of the Roswell Incident had long since been transferred to other bases or to the Pentagon in Washington D.C., as in the case of Major Marcel and Col. Blanchard. Does the Air Force expect us to believe that "time traveling crash-test dummies" materialized by coincidence on top of a Mogul balloon in July 1947 and caused it to crash?

To top off this remarkable hypothesis, Col. Haynes invited the journalists to study video footage from the USAF archives which indeed show dummies being dropped from an altitude of 90,000 feet during *"the 1950s,"* plus clear images of a disc-shaped craft being launched as well as resting on the ground, identified as an experimental vehicle built by NASA for its Viking project in 1972.

"Colonel, how do you counter the UFO enthusiasts who say that they're talking about 1947, when you are talking about dummies used in the 50s, almost a decade later?" a journalist asked. *"Well, I'm afraid that's a problem we have with time compression,"* the Colonel replied, *"I don't know what they saw in 1947, but I'm quite sure it probably was Project Mogul."*

A week later the veil of silence and feigned ignorance was in fact penetrated by a courageous individual who once had his desk in the Pentagon, after an outstanding career in a key position as Army Intelligence officer under General MacArthur in Korea and on President Eisenhower's National Security Council, with a desk at the White House. This remarkable person, honored with 19 medals, decorations, and ribbons during his 21 years of service, was Col. Philip Corso. His book *The Day After Roswell*, which was placed on the national best-seller lists within 2 weeks after publication, became a thorn in the sides of the UFO antagonists. For Corso not only claimed that, while on duty at Ft. Riley, Kansas, in July 1947, he himself had handled the alien bodies which were on their way from Roswell to Wright Field, but also went much further in his revelations. In 1961, as Lt. Col. at that time, Corso was entrusted with one of the Pentagon's most classified weapons development budgets. Under General Trudeau he became head of the Foreign Technology Desk in the U.S. Army's Research & Development department, and in this position, he handled artifacts and technology retrieved from the Roswell disc. Corso claims that as part of the Army's reverse-engineering project, these artifacts were handed over to private companies such as IBM, Hughes Aircraft, Bell Labs and Dow Corning—without revealing the source of those objects. *"We told them, 'That's what we got. No questions. Find out how it works, build it, claim the patent, make the money,'"* Corso said to me when I interviewed him in July 1997. That is how, according to Corso, today's integrated circuit chips, fiber optics, lasers and super-tenacity fibers were developed. If Corso's story is true, we must indeed rewrite the history of the twentieth century—the century during which we learned that we are not alone in the Universe.

CHAPTER 18

No Defense Significance?

France

The nation listened with astonishment when the French Defense Minister Robert Galley spoke about the UFOs on February 21, 1974, at 8:30 p.m. at the radio station FRANCE INTER. It was the first time in history that a minister of the government informed the public about UFOs openly:

" . . . *in 1954 a department for collecting and studying reports about unidentified objects was established under the defense ministry. I have read*

Robert Galley, former French Defense Minister, in his historical interview with Jean-Claude Bourret, reporter of the radio station France-Inter, broadcast on February 21, 1974. Galley conceded that the French Government had been conducting UFO research secretly for the past twenty years.

a number of these eyewitness reports over a long period of time, I think over 50 reports up to 1970. One of the earliest comes from November 20, 1953, the observation of a Lt. Jean Demerry of the Air Force base 107, near Villa-Coublay. There were also reports from the police. Further, there are sighting reports made by pilots and commanding personnel of various Air Force bases with a long list of details which all tally with one another in a

This UFO photograph taken by Mr. Didier, of St. Vallier-de-Thiey, in the French province Alpes Maritimes, was taken on January 7, 1974, at 8:45 p.m., and was considered to be genuine by GEPAN and the Gendarmerie.

rather disquieting fashion, all of them during the year 1954. I am therefore of the opinion that one should have an open mind about these phenomena. That is, our stand should not be disbelief or automatic dismissal. I want to go as far as saying it is an undeniable fact that today, there are things which cannot be explained." This sensational revelation made headlines in France the following day. The papers, *France Soir, L'Aurore, Le Figaro,* and *Le Parisien Libre* reported this on their title pages. Until then, one had to be content with semi-official information.

Already in 1971, *L'Aurore* had reported under the headline "The Hunt for Flying Saucers" that the entire French police force had been instructed to register UFO sightings and to investigate them. Cited therein was a report written by Police Chief Kervendal, as the official representative of the 61,000 French upholders of the law, a force which stood directly under the Defense Ministry. *"On account of their being spread out over the entire state territory, and owing to their mobility, our police as a unit is a particularly well-suited helper in the search for truth in this matter."* A specially compiled questionnaire reminded the officer to observe and register not merely such facts as the weather, the place of occurrence, names of witnesses, time, and the shape of the object, but he was also to:

1. Have a careful look at the spaceship, note down exact data about the size, color and changes thereof, and construction of the landing gear;
2. Pay attention to noises: Does the object make a noise? If so, how loud? What did the witness feel afterwards? Heat, itching, gusts of wind? Did he later suffer from sleeplessness or other problems?
3. Keep a lookout for visitors from space: In case beings are seen on board or in the vicinity of the flying object, note down the size and stature, the appearance of the head, arms and feet and legs, the hair and clothing.

That was not enough; the policeman was to check for possible radioactivity and also note the behavior of animals in the area. Possible landing sites were to be photographed with infrared film at a height of 30 feet, by means of a helicopter.

Soon after that, an incident occurred that offered the police department the chance to carry out such an investigation. On July 1, 1965, at 5:30 in the morning, a UFO landed on a field of lavender near Valensole, in the Department Alpes-de-Haute-Provence. At this time, the farmer Maurice Masse (41), had begun his day's work and was just about to start up his tractor when he heard a whistling noise. He looked in the direction from which the noise came and saw, at a distance of about 300 feet, a strange-looking machine that had apparently landed on his field. Masse thought it was a helicopter that had gotten into trouble and ran to it to help the pilot. But then, he recognized that what stood there was no helicopter. *"It looked far more like a rugby ball but had the size of a Renault Dauphine, with a dome that looked like Plexiglas; and it was standing on 6 struts,"* said the farmer later.

The UFO landing site at the lavender field near Valensole was thoroughly investigated by the police, scientists and UFO researchers.

Maurice, still unruffled, went towards the craft. When he was about 30 feet away from it, he discovered 2 small humanoid creatures which were bending over a lavender bush. Suddenly they noticed his presence and were apparently startled by it. One of them quickly pointed a staff-like gadget towards him. Instantaneously, Maurice felt as if he had been paralyzed, as if he were stuck to the ground, and was capable of no movement except with his eyes. *"I just quietly watched the 2 little men with their child-like bodies and huge heads, which were 3 times as big as those of normal human beings,"* said the farmer later to the police. *"I noticed that they were completely hairless and had smooth white skin, like a baby's, at least on the face and on the head. The rest of their bodies were covered in dark and close-fitting suits. The facial features and proportions were roughly the same as human beings'; they had a sharp chin and big slit eyes, but the mouths didn't have lips, they were more like holes."* They seemed to communicate with each other in guttural sounds and they took stock of the farmer pretty thoroughly, almost with amusement. Their facial expressions were *"in no way unfriendly, rather the contrary. I felt an intense feeling of peace coming from these beings,"* said Maurice Masse.

After a few minutes, the visitors returned to their ship with rather astonishing agility. They entered the ship through a sliding door. He saw the heads once more through the Plexiglas dome. Then the object flew off with a shrill whistling noise, towards the west. It was only after another quarter-hour of paralysis that the farmer could move once again.

At the site of the landing the first thing he noticed was a shallow depression of about 4 feet in diameter, with a cylindrical hole of 7 inches in diameter in the middle. The earth in the depression had become soft, although the weather had been dry for many days. Around this depression, he found 6 indentations of about 3 inches in width where the landing struts had stood. He informed the police the same day.

After a thorough investigation, Lt. Col. Valnet of the police department came to the conclusion that *"the witness had spoken the truth. We are dealing with a sensible, responsible man who is not trying to show off."*

But the incident had consequences for Masse. Four days later, he collapsed and would have slept for 24 hours if his wife had not woken him up. During the following months, his sleep requirements increased from the usual 5–6 hours to 10–12 hours per day. The lavender bushes at the site of landing withered. During the next ten years, nothing would grow within a circle of about 30 feet surrounding the landing spot, no matter how often Masse tried to replant the area.

The Valensole landing was not a unique event. Between the years 1973–74, 18 UFO landings had occurred, *"the majority of them without explanation,"* as Chief Kervendal reported in September 1975 in the military journal, *Armée D'Aujourd'hui*. Scientific investigation was now necessary.

The next step was taken when, on May 1, 1977, the National Center for Space Research, CNES, (Centre National des Études Spatiales), the French counterpart of NASA, established a section for UFO research. The name of this sub-department was GEPAN, Study Group for Unidentified Air Phenomena, (Groupe d'Étude de Phenomènes Aériens Non-indentifiés). The founding of this department was the direct result of the efforts of the French Government to get to the bottom of the UFO phenomena on a scientific basis. Thus, GEPAN encompassed some 100 engineers, technicians and officials of the Space Travel Center at Toulouse who, in their own fields, were investigating the UFO sightings. A number of subgroups were busy with tracking and analyzing radar detection statistics, the evaluation of questionnaires and the study of material and physical traces left behind.

The scientific panel of GEPAN consisted of 8 independent scientists of various disciplines, amongst them an astronomer, a plasma-physicist, a high-voltage technology engineer, an expert for atmospheric physics, a meteorologist, a satellite expert, a psychologist and a sociologist. This committee was formed to help GEPAN to gain orientation over the entire spectrum of UFO appearances. This committee saw its main task in collecting UFO sighting reports from all over the country, through UFO research groups and the police, and evaluating them objectively. Until 1983, they had collected over 15,000 reports and new ones were coming in almost daily. There were around 4,000 police units in France, all of whom had official instructions to call police headquarters in Paris whenever UFO sightings of a special kind occurred, and the police headquarters in Paris would then decide whether GEPAN was to be alerted immediately or not. If that happened, GEPAN immediately put together a team of experts from the various disciplines, which then went as early as possible to the spot in question. GEPAN received about 20 such reports every month, out of which, on average, only one set off a "UFO alarm."

Two years after its being established, GEPAN presented in 1979 an analysis of 11 cases, 9 out of which showed that *"a physical phenomenon exists, whose origin, propulsion and behavior are beyond human knowledge."* And soon, their scientists could investigate a case that was more impressive than the UFO landing at Valensole.

An elderly farmer, Renato Nicolai, living at Trans-en-Provence near Nice in the south of France, was working in his big and rather neglected garden on the evening of January 8, 1981. At about 5:00 p.m. he heard a whistling noise, looked up and saw a disc-shaped air vehicle that was hovering low above the fir trees at the edge of his plot. When it looked as if it was going to land, Nikolai fled to a shed on the hill behind his house. From a safe distance of about 70 yards he watched the 4½-foot thick lead-colored disc. It looked like two saucers placed one above the other, rim to rim, with a kind of flange around it, and it landed in the middle of his garden. A minute later, it started to whistle again, rose up, went up to the height of a tree and then shot off, towards the north. When it had risen, Nikolai could see two hemispheres on its underside, each about 8 inches in diameter, which he took to be some kind of landing gear, as well as two depressions, *"like drop-doors."* When the UFO had vanished, he went home and told his wife what he had seen and, since she thought he was trying to fool her, he took her out to the garden and showed her the place where the object had landed.

There, they found 2 concentric circles of thin black stripes, one about 88 inches and the other 96 inches in diameter, encircling some lightly desiccated lucerne plants. Nicolai thought that a test vehicle of the French Air Force had made an emergency landing in his garden and informed the police, who visited the site the next day and informed GEPAN. GEPAN experts arrived on January 12. After intensive interviews and psychological tests, they were convinced that the witness was telling the truth. They then took samples of the ground and the plants and sent them to the leading expert for *plant pathology,* Prof. Michel Bounias, of the National Institute for Agricultural Research. During the next 2 years, Prof. Bounias put these samples through a series of stringent tests. Then, in 1983, GEPAN published the results of his investigation in their technical report No. 16, "Analysis of a Trace":

1. The leaves of the lucerne plants had suffered a loss of chlorophyll of about 30–50%.
2. The young leaves *"developed in a manner that is characteristic of old leaves,"* that is, they aged in a way that could not be reproduced by natural processes or in a laboratory.
3. *"Apparently, an unusual and extensive activity had taken place that had heated up the ground to a temperature between 300 and 600° Celsius and probably left behind the traces of substances like phosphates and zinc which have been found."*

That *"confirmed at least, that at that spot, a significant mechanical activity had taken place,"* said GEPAN Director Jean-Jacques Velasco in 1987. *"The effects on the plants at the spot resembled those which one sees in the case of plants grown from seeds that have been subjected to gamma ray radiation. Our data show that a considerable dose of gamma radiation must have caused the anomalies which we saw in the plants. Do we have to postulate an ionizing or perhaps nuclear radiation? Probably not, since no radioactive anomalies were found. Could it have been caused by an electromagnetic field? Probably yes."*

After they published the above information, the American UFO researcher, Mark Rodeghier, asked GEPAN, *"Why has so little evidence existed until now for the physical reality of UFO phenomena?"* The reply was, *"After having considered this case, the answer can only be 'because no one else had the means at their disposal which GEPAN had, and no one took the trouble which GEPAN did.' We can only speculate about how far advanced UFO research could be today, if the sophisticated means of investigating these cases as GEPAN has done had existed previously."* But for some people GEPAN had probably gone too far. Thus the GEPAN administration soon learned that the police had received instructions not to inform GEPAN straightaway about cases which were judged to be *"very strange."* And sometime later, the Director of CRNS at that time, Dr. Gille, expressed his opinion that *"GEPAN was nothing but an agency for public work, watched by the government. The real UFO research was most probably conducted somewhere else."* When the Socialists won the election in 1981, things gradually went downhill for GEPAN. In 1984, after various budget cuts, the group consisted of only 2 people: Mr. Velasco and his secretary. In 1988 GEPAN was closed down or rather rechristened "SEPRA" (Societé pour l'Évaluation des Phenomènes Rentreé Atmospherique), an agency for evaluating atmospheric reentry phenomena.

Although ignored by the international press, this great openness—at least in the initial stages—and the activities in this field in France, would lead to a reaction in the neighboring countries which was more or less to be expected.

The United Kingdom

On January 18, 1979, the subject of the UFOs was on the agenda of the British House of Lords. The 3½-hour debate which followed was the result of the efforts of one of the peers, the Earl of Clancarty, to learn about what Britain's defense ministry knew about UFOs. For there were indications that thorough investigations had been conducted in the matter, about which only isolated bits of information had trickled down to the public. As early as the July 11, 1954, Lord Dowding, Great Britain's prominent Air Marshall of the Second World War, had declared in an article for the *London Sunday Dispatch, "I am convinced that these objects do exist and that they are not manufactured by any nation on Earth. I can therefore see no alternative to accepting the theory that they come from some extraterrestrial source."* It was only 3 years later that the public learned that at the time this statement was made by the Air Chief Marshall of the Royal Air Force, thorough investigations had already been carried out in the matter.

On June 16, 1957, the London paper *Reynolds News* wrote about a UFO research office of the Royal Air Force. *"In Room No. 801, of what was formerly the Hotel Metropole, Great Britain's Air Ministry officially investigates flying saucers. All Royal Air Force bases in England house fighter*

The Earl of Clancarty, leader of the House of Lords UFO Study Group, with UFO researcher Col. Colman VonKeviczky.

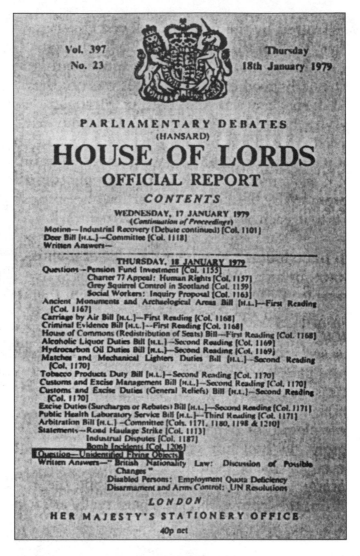

Vol. 397
No. 23

Thursday
18th January 1979

PARLIAMENTARY DEBATES
(HANSARD)

HOUSE OF LORDS
OFFICIAL REPORT

CONTENTS

LONDON
HER MAJESTY'S STATIONERY OFFICE
40p net

planes ready to intercept unidentified flying objects in airspace and, if necessary, to attack. . . . The existence of this room was revealed last night by a spokesman of the Air Ministry. He added that they had been investigating reports about flying saucers since 1947. 'We have something like 10,000 sightings in our archives,' he said."

In August 1976 the Earl of Clancarty inquired at the Ministry of Defense in respect to the UFO phenomena and whether openness in the matter, such as in France, would not be more sensible than secrecy. The answer was rather short. They had not heard about the radio interview of the French

Defense Minister and they were interested in UFOs *"only if they posed a threat to the United Kingdom."* But, Lord Clancarty was not satisfied with that answer. He then wanted to know whether in England, as in France, the police had a role in the investigation of UFOs. The Defense Minister denied this. When, shortly after that, the Earl of Clancarty gave a speech at Scotland Yard, he learned that the police had, until 1977, investigated thousands of UFO cases. He then began to discuss this subject with other members of the House of Lords and, finally, there was so much interest that the question was put on the agenda.

"It is not time that Her Majesty's Government informed our people of what they know about UFOs?" asked Lord Clancarty, as one of the 11 speakers during the UFO debate, on January 18, 1979. *". . . it is on record that both sighting and landing reports are increasing all the time. Just suppose the UFO pilots decided to make mass landings tomorrow in this country—there could well be panic here, because our people have not been prepared."* Clancarty was supported in this demand by the Earl of Kimberley, the airspace expert of the Liberals, who added that, *"It has been reported that the United States and the USSR signed a pact in 1971 to swap UFO information, but the pact stated that they were to keep the rest of the world in the dark. I believe that the pact was signed so that neither superpower would make mistakes about UFOs being atomic missiles. I am also led to understand that quite recently the 3 United States balloonists, who crossed the Atlantic, were followed for up to 12 hours by UFOs but were ordered by United States Government agents not to discuss them.*

We know that war in space, once a figment of the imagination and a subject much loved by science fiction writers, is very nearly a fact now. Both super powers have, or will have, killer satellites and laser beams operating in space . . . perhaps this may be one of the reasons the United States is not more forthcoming about its UFO information?" Two other members of the House of Lords, Lord Kings-Norton and Lord Gainford, described their own UFO sightings.

The result of this debate was the establishment of the "House of Lords UFO Study Group," a special committee under the *"able chairmanship"* of Lord Shinwell (94). Twenty UFO experts from 6 countries were invited to speak to the study group on this theme. The UFO-interested Lords knew that they did not stand alone. Prince Philip, the Prince Consort of Queen Elizabeth, is a UFO researcher. In his study, on the second storey of Buckingham Palace, there hangs a huge map on which 300 sites of UFO sightings have been marked in red. Some of them that apparently happened in close succession are shown connected together by pencil lines drawn by the Prince. *"I find this matter absolutely fascinating,"* said Prince Philip in 1975. *"I am convinced that UFOs exist. I have read many books about these objects and have learned that UFO sightings happen periodically."* His personal attendant, James Chesworth, confirms, *"He spends a lot of time every week in his study."* He was informed regularly about the latest developments by Lord Clancarty.

An inquiry about UFO information made by UFO study group member Lord Hill-Norton to the Ministry of Defense elicited the answer that until 1967, all UFO files had been regularly destroyed after a 5-year period, *"since they were of no defense significance."* His Lordship is convinced that by saying this, they were only trying to circumvent the law of the country, which mandates that all government documents should be released for public perusal after 30 years. It is certain that the Defense Ministry had conducted thorough investigations and had established an experienced group for this purpose, as is shown by a document from the year 1970:

"Unidentified flying objects reports are examined in the Ministry of Defense by experienced staff. They do this with open minds. They have access to all information available to the Ministry of Defense. They call on the full scientific resources of the Ministry of Defense and may call in expert advice as necessary from other government and non-government bodies."

How far this international cooperation in the matter of UFOs really goes, is shown by a British document released in 1978 by the Ministry of Defense Department of Aerial studies. In this document, 18 cases of sightings have been classified under certain code numbers and the service departments

```
                                                    COPY    17/   75
UFO/45/MEMO/666/78

MINISTRY OF DEFENCE    DEPARTMENT OF AERIAL STUDIES
*** CLASSIFIED TO ALL PERSONNEL BELOW   AGDO 2

CONTACTS FOR THE YEAR ENDED 22/ 2/78.  (23)  AS FOLLOWS:
K5634    J.MITCHELL        LEICESTER    559/7C    CLASS 5    23/ 5/77 0935
K5635    O.KRAMER          BRADFORD .... 11A/?    CLASS 5    24/ 5/77 1116
K5636    D.M.SMITH         LONDON (SW)  559/7C    CLASS 3    15/ 6/77 0600
K5637    F.W.SHOEMAKER
K5638    R.L.DOORS         LONDON (SW)  559/7C    CLASS 5    23/ 7/77 1755
K5639    T.BETTS           FALMOUTH     55B/0'X   CLASS 20   23/ 7/77 1721
K5640    N.M.GRANGER       LLANELLI     555/C4S   CLASS 5    1/ 8/77 0931
K5641    T.D.PATEL         SOUTHALL     6400KK/2  CLASS 16   11/ 8/77 1159
K5642    S.L.D.C'BRIEN     LEEDS        559/7C    CLASS 5    18/10/77 0445
K5643    T.MCNAMARA        BELFAST      086/23    CLASS 16   22/11/77 2350
K5644    E.F.WEST          ABERDEEN     088/23    CLASS 6    23/11/77 0020
K5645    T.BRANDENBURGER   SLOUGH       559/7C    CLASS 5    14/12/77 1807
K5646    F.K.SKINNER       BELPER       HE/44/46  CLASS 16   23/12/77 2330
K5647    K.W.WRIGHT        DERBY        559/KK    CLASS 5    31/12/77 1305
K5648    T.M.SLEFY         TRURO        559/?     CLASS 8    2/ 1/78 0435
K5649    C.M.MARLES        LFLB         1081/46   CLASS 10   23/ 1/78 1056
K5650    A.ANDREWS         GLASGOW      559SERIES CLASS 5    1/ 2/78 0945
K5651    D.T.SMEDLEY       LONDON (E)   74/7C     CLASS 23   22/ 2/78 1201
*/*ENDLIST

CLASSIFICATION NOTIFIED TO THE FOLLOWING DEPARTMENTS:
METROPOLITAN POLICE
DEFENCE (AIR FORCE)
DEFENCE (CIVIL)
SPECIAL PATROL GROUPS
B.B.C. (INTELLIGENCE BRANCH)
SUB-REGIONAL CONTROLS
COMPUTER DATA SECTION
MICROWAVE COMMUNICATIONS NETWORK
/*ENDLIST

FURTHER CONTROLS AND DATELINE NETWORK CMDAF   VIA NORC CHELTENHAM
OPERATION 23 NOTIFICATION TO SECTIONS E H W Z  VIA NORC CHELTENHAM
                                               NORAD CYBERTECH LINK F 6
DATA COMPILATION NETWORK SECTIONS    H K W
FURTHER NOTIFICATION FOR ACTION TO BE TAKEN    VIA COMM. 46 (78)
RLD CIA NORAD UFO 23
***LISTED AND CLASSIFIED

/*END COPY   17/  .75 CLASSIFIED  2296/44/C/FGOO 2/23M
```

Report of the Department for Space Studies of the British Ministry of Defense. A copy was sent to the CIA.

involved in the investigations have also been named, including a "microwave communications network." The document is addressed to the North American Air Defense Command (NORAD) and the CIA, among others. This confirms what, some years ago, a former official of the British naval intelligence service told me. *"There is a pact between the United States of America and NATO countries by which they investigate UFO cases in their respective countries and send their reports directly to the CIA, NORAD or the Air Technical Intelligence Center (ATIC). Strict secrecy is to be maintained in the matter."*

The mysterious Department of Aerial Studies naturally drew the attention of the Earl of Clancarty at once, for everything pointed to its being a secret organization of the Defense Ministry to carry out UFO research, about which, of course, the House of Lords had not been informed. A spokesman of the Ministry confirmed this and added that this Department was in continual contact with similar departments in the United States. *"They told me that between 1978 and 1981 some 2,250 cases of UFO sightings had been officially investigated there,"* said the Earl. An extensive report about UFO investigations carried out by the Government was handed over to the Earl, which, as he said, *"confirms the suspicions of millions of people that UFOs do exist and that the Government is investigating them. For years, this has been kept quiet. The report, in fact, shows that the Government has been involved in a massive cover-up policy."* The Ministry of Defense confirmed that this service department had been established *"to question whether defense was involved. Information had been exchanged with the United States whenever we thought it could be of interest to them."*

Then an incident occurred that, like no other, was packed with politically explosive implications and involved the armed forces of the United Kingdom, as well as those of the USA.

It all began quite harmlessly at an English pub, during a night in the year 1975, when the Englishwoman Brenda Butler met a young American soldier Steve Roberts (pseudonym), a security officer of the U.S. Air Force. They became friends and at some time or other, Brenda told Steve about her passionate interest in UFOs. Steve had heard a lot about these mysterious alien spaceships in the United States and knew comrades who had already had UFO experiences, mostly in service. And, when between 1975 and 1980 2 minor UFO incidents happened at Steve's base, the USAF-NATO base in Woodbridge he told Brenda about them. The UFO enthusiast received the news with great interest and Steve asked her to keep the information confidential; otherwise, he would get into trouble with his superiors.

One day, in January 1981, Steve seemed to be anxious, as if he knew something he couldn't digest and about which he was not prepared to talk. But, on Brenda's continued insistence, he finally told her about something that was really very, very secret. Shortly after Christmas Day in the year 1980, a UFO had made an emergency landing in the Rendlesham Forest near Woodbridge. It had had technical problems and had landed at a clearance in the woods. He had been part of a security patrol which had observed the proceedings and had even witnessed an encounter between the base commander, Gen. Gordon Williams, and 3 small humanoid beings who came gliding out in a beam of light from the UFO.

Brenda was skeptical. But when one of Steve's colleagues told her that on the day in question, December 27, 1980, he had seen a whole convoy moving in the direction of Rendlesham Forest, Brenda began to believe the story. The soldier had said that he too, at that time, had heard that a UFO had landed only about a half a mile from the runway of the base. During the next few days, Brenda questioned the local people at the pubs and, again and again, got the confirmation that, at the time in question, strange lights had been seen in the sky. Then she decided to investigate more thoroughly. She joined forces with a local UFO researcher, Dot Street, who again brought in the UFO specialist and author Jennie Randles for advice. It turned out that Jennie herself was just then investigating the same story. In a roundabout way, she had come into contact with a radar operator of the RAF base Wharton at Norfolk. During the night of December 27, he had spotted an unidentified object in the Rendlesham Forest area on the radar screen.

That in itself would not have been particularly unusual. But a few days later, intelligence service officers of the U.S. Air Force appeared at Wharton Air Force Base. The radar operators handed over the records in question to the Americans, on condition that they be told what had happened. The officers answered saying that a UFO had come down in the forest near Ipswich (in Suffolk), a metallic structured flying object of unknown origin. Security patrols that had come close to the object had reported that their motors had stopped running suddenly. They were forced to go on foot the rest of the way. The object hovered a few feet above the ground and it had taken some hours before it could be started again. During this time, the crew, 3 small beings, had communicated with the base commander, Gen. Gordon Williams.

An incredible story, if the research team Brenda Butler, Dot Street and Jennie Randles had not, during their further researchers, come across more witnesses. The USAF security officer James Archer (pseudonym) saw mysterious lights in the forest on December 27, 1980, at about 2:00 a.m. He reported this and was ordered to go the forest together with 2 colleagues to see what was happening there. When the 2 MPs approached the lights, their radios stopped functioning. Finally they saw a *"triangular thing standing on legs."* It then lifted off and hovered above the forest ground. The landing legs had left impressions in the ground. Archer saw something in the spaceship which he took to be a robot because it was *"not human."* According to the commander of the security police at Woodbridge, Sgt. Adrian Bustinza, after Archer's first report a second patrol consisting of 2 cars with 2 men each went to the site of landing. Bustinza was himself in one of the cars, with the deputy commander of RAF Woodbridge, Lt. Col. Charles I. Halt.

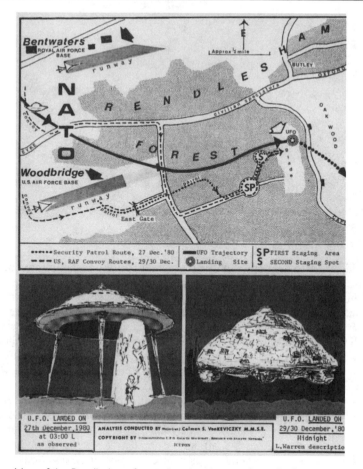

Map of the Rendlesham forest, showing the way from the base to the landing spot. Representation of the landed UFOs on December 27 and 29, according to eyewitnesses. (ICUFON).

When the 2 cars were near the site their motors also stopped running and they, too, had to walk the rest of the way. They then saw an object standing on 3 struts. It lifted off, flew a few feet above the trees and landed again. It moved up and down and had many lights in various colors. Photographers and cameramen were called for, and (Woodbridge) base commander Gordon Williams was informed. Steve Roberts affirmed that a number of security officers were present and photographs and films were taken, which were collected at once and sent for evaluation to the headquarters of the U.S. armed forces in Europe, the Main Air Force Base in Rhein, Germany. What the military men did not know was that at the same time thousands of local people observed the strange dancing lights in Rendlesham Forest, and

The clearing in the Rendlesham forest where the UFO landed.

saw the air force helicopter circling around the forest as well. In the neighboring area the animals started behaving strangely.

While the 3 UFO ladies were still continuing their research, an article that attracted much attention appeared in the popular scientific magazine *Omni* in America. The editor Eric Mischera quoted from an interview which he had had with Col. Ted Conrad, commander of the neighboring Bentwaters AFB. Conrad also confirmed the UFO landing, of which he was a witness. *"It was a large craft, mounted on tripod legs. It had no windows but was covered in red and blue lights. It definitely demonstrated intelligent control. After almost an hour it flew off at a phenomenal speed. It left behind a triangular set of marks evidently formed by the tripod legs. A later investigation proved the marks to be radioactive."* To hear that from the mouth of a high-ranking US officer—Conrad was shortly after that promoted to the rank of General—was indeed a sensation. Even though Conrad had said nothing about the 3 extraterrestrials, Butler, Street and Randles could have hardly hoped for a better confirmation of the Woodbridge incident.

But that was not all. A young security officer, Airman Larry Warren, had told the United States UFO researcher Lawrence Fawcett about a UFO landing in the forest at Rendlesham. According to Warren the incident had occurred on the night of December 29 1980, a date also named by Col. Conrad, which suggests that during that short period at the end of December 1980, two landings had taken place in the same area. Warren was at this time stationed at the neighboring air force base in Bentwaters as part of the NATO exchange program. During the night of December 29, he and a few other security officers had driven in a jeep out into the countryside.

Once outside the base, Warren noticed that animals, mostly deer and rabbits, came running out of the forest as if in panic. They drove along a road into the Rendlesham woods until suddenly the motor stopped running.

Airman Larry Warren

They got out and walked onwards, during which Warren saw a convoy leaving the base and coming towards the forest. Already at that distance he could hear the voices and noises of the radio apparatus, soon, however, to be drowned by the noisy sound of a helicopter flying over their heads. Then a group of other military personnel came, amongst them some British officers. One man in the group started shouting out loudly and hysterically and ran away. Warren had the feeling that *"World War III had just broken out."* Then he, too, saw the object. It was about 45 feet in diameter, hovered above the ground and looked like a *"transparent aspirin tablet."* It was pulsating slightly. Warren saw that a whole group of cameras was directed at the disc and that security officers were standing around at a respectful distance. He heard a voice, probably that of the pilot of the helicopter, saying over the radio *"It's coming now!"* They all looked up and saw a red object directly above them.

It was a bright red light that hovered for a short period above the "aspirin tablet" and then exploded in a rain of colors. For a moment all were blinded. When they recovered, they saw before them a big dome-shaped craft. Warren and few of his colleagues decided to get closer to the object. But when they had approached it so closely that they could almost touch it, a ray of green light shot out of the UFO and Warren lost consciousness. He came to again in the barracks. The mud from the forest expedition was still clinging to his boots and trousers. The next morning, Warren and his companions were called to see the base commander. They were told that they should under no circumstances tell the public about anything they had seen, for it was all put under extreme secrecy.

Within a year Warren was honorably discharged from the Air Force and returned to the United States. He could never forget Bentwaters. The encounter with the UFO kept repeatedly appearing in his dreams. He would wake up crying out and bathed in sweat from fear. He then started getting deeper into UFO research, and learned that there were people who had been abducted and taken to UFOs, examined there and brought back to the earth. They could not remember anything about this experience except that they had seen a UFO, and there was a long gap of time between the sighting and the next recovery of consciousness. They, too, suffered from nightmares. It was only under hypnosis that they were able to find out what they had experienced during this missing period of time.

Warren decided to get himself hypnotized. The psychoanalyst Fred Max conducted the session and made audio recordings. Under hypnosis Larry described accurately what had happened during that night. He even named the comrades who had been with him in the jeep, and one of them was James Archer, who months before that Butler, Street and Randalls had stumbled upon and whose real name was never released. Under hypnosis, Larry saw the aliens. He described them as "looking like kids," being 3 to 4 feet tall, with large heads and cat-like eyes, dressed in silvery overalls. They seemed to float in a kind of ray or beam which came out of the UFO directed at the Earth. *"All personnel seemed in a trance and just watched them,"* Warren wrote in his book *Left at East Gate*. *"After a short duration, Colonel Williams approached them slowly. Standing about 5 feet apart, they seemed to stare at each other . . . "* Larry described how Gen. Gordon Williams tried to communicate with these beings telepathically and with gestures. Then one of the aliens floated towards Larry's group. *"My God, it's coming towards us!"* cried Warren and, under hypnosis, experienced once more his blackout and recovery of consciousness in the barracks.

Another witness, Sgt. John Burroughs, confirmed certain elements of Warren's story. He told me in an on-camera interview:

> Since something was seen in the second night, on the third night we decided to go back. When we got out there they already had people in the woods and stuff had already happened. They'd already spotted some stuff and they were following some stuff. We were held up for a while at a point before we were allowed to go any further. Eventually I met up with the people already out there and then I saw some blue lights in the sky, flying around, beaming stuff on the ground. The main object had landed some distance away. The impression I got from seeing it at this distance was that it almost looked like a huge Christmas display out there in the woods. Like different colored lights doing different colored things. Another thing I can tell you is that everything seemed to have a kind of slow motion effect. It seemed like things were happening somehow slower.
>
> Sgt. Adrian Bustinza and I at one point towards the very end saw the object in the distance seem to get closer and he and I started running towards it. As we were running, he went down to the ground, and later he claimed that something held him to the ground. I remember getting very close to something and suddenly remember standing in an open field and the thing was done. I don't remember anything that happened, but there are people who said I jumped on top of the object—but I don't remember that.

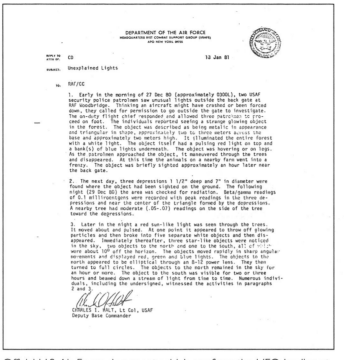

Official U.S. Air Force document, which confirms the UFO landing at Rendlesham forest.

Lawrence Fawcett applied to the Pentagon for information regarding this incident citing the Freedom Of Information Act and was given a report written about the incident by the vice-commander of Woodbridge, Lt. Com. Charles I. Halt. This report alone suffices to make the Rendlesham incident one of the strongest proofs for the existence of UFOs. Therein it says:

1. Early in the morning of 27 December, 1980, (approximately 3:00 a.m.), two USAF security police patrolmen saw unusual lights outside the back gate at RAF Woodbridge. Thinking an aircraft might have crashed or have been forced down, they called for permission to go outside the gate to investigate. The on-duty flight chief responded and allowed three patrolmen to proceed on foot. The individuals reported seeing a strange glowing object in the forest. The object was described as being metallic in appearance and triangular in shape, approximately 2 to 3 meters across the base and approximately 2 meters high. It illuminated the entire forest with a white light. The object itself had a pulsing red light on top and a bank(s) of blue lights underneath. The object was hovering or on legs. As the patrolmen approached the object it maneuvered through the trees and disappeared. At this time the animals on a nearby

farm went into a frenzy. The object was briefly sighted approximately an hour later near the back gate.

2. The next day, three depressions 1½ inches deep and 7 inches in diameter were found where the object had been sighted on the ground. The following night, (29 Dec 80) the area was checked for radiation. Beta/gamma readings of 0.1 milliroentgens were recorded with peak readings in the three depressions, and near the center of the triangle formed by the depressions. A nearby tree had moderate (.05–.07) readings on the side of the tree towards the depressions.

3. Later in the night a red sun-like light was seen through the trees. It moved about and pulsed. At one point it appeared to throw off glowing particles and then broke into five separate white objects and then disappeared. Immediately thereafter three star-like objects were noticed in the sky, two objects in the north and one in the south, all of which were about 10° off the horizon. The objects moved rapidly in sharp angular movements and displayed red, green and blue lights. The objects to the north appeared to be elliptical, through an 8–12 power lens. They then turned to full circles. The objects to the north remained in the sky for an hour or more. The object to the south was visible for two or three hours and beamed down a stream of light from time to time. Numerous individuals, including the undersigned, witnessed the activities in paragraphs 2 and 3.

Col. Halt is even today prepared to confirm without any reservations the contents of his report. Besides that, an audiotape has been released in which he describes his observations before and after the landing:

Voice: *1:48 a.m.: We're hearing very strange sounds out of the farmer's barnyard animals. They are very, very active, making an awful lot of noise . . . You saw a light? Slow down. Where?*

Halt: *I see it too. What is it?*

Voice: *We don't know, Sir.*

Halt: *"I saw a yellow tinge in it, too. Weird. It appears to be maybe moving a little bit this way. It's brighter than it has been. It's coming this way. It is definitely coming this way! Pieces of it are shooting off. There is no doubt about it! This is weird!"*

Voice: *"Two lights! One to the right and one light to the left!"*

Halt: *"Keep your flashlight off. There's something very, very strange . . . Keep the headset on; see if it gets any . . . Pieces are falling off it again!"*

Voice: *"It just moved to the right."*

Voice: *"Yeah! Strange! Let's approach to the edge of the wood up there . . . OK, we're looking at the thing. We are probably about 2 to 3 hundred yards away. It looks like an eye winking at you. Still moving from side to side. And when you put the starscope on it, it's like this thing has a hollow center, a dark center, like the pupil of an eye looking at you, winking. And it flashes so bright in the starscope that it almost burns your eye . . . We've passed the farmer's house and across into the next field and now we have multiple sightings of up to 5 lights with a similar shape, but they seem to be steady now rather than a pulsating or glow with a red flash. We've just crossed a creek and we're getting what kind of readings now? We're getting 3 good clicks on the meter and we're seeing strange lights in the sky."*

Halt, *3:05 a.m.*: *"At about 10 degrees, horizon, directly north, we've got 2 strange objects, er, half-moon shape, dancing about with colored lights on 'em . . . "*

Voice: *"They're both heading north. OK, here he comes from the south; he's coming toward us now, now we're observing what appears to be a beam coming down to the ground. This is unreal!. . . .*

Halt, *3:30 a.m.*: *The object to the south is still beaming down lights to the ground."*

Halt: *4:00 a.m.*: *"One object still hovering over Woodbridge base at about 5 to 10 degrees off the horizon. Still moving erratic, with similar lights and beaming down as earlier.*

(Note the omission between about 2:00–3:05 and 3:05–3:30 in the original tape)

The Americans and the British had tried everything to cover up the incident. Ralph Noyes, a retired under-secretary of the Defense Ministry, who had himself been for 4 years the chief of the UFO department of the Ministry of Defense, still had to learn this. During his period in that office, only conventional cases on UFO sightings up to the level of observations made by RAF pilots had gone over his desk. And now, he was so fascinated by the Bentwaters affair that he tried through all of his connections to find out the truth about it. But no matter where he asked, he was met by silence. They did confirm that during the night in question UFOs had been seen, but further details were denied. Finally he decided with resignation that the Ministry of Defense may have good reasons to keep back information about the Rendlesham Forest from the public. *"As a former official of the Ministry of Defense, I do not wish to insist upon asking questions about a matter that concerns national security . . . The Woodbridge case of December, 1980, is for me one of the most interesting and important cases during the last years, at least in England."*

Still in 1996, the Rendlesham Forest incident was subject of a Parliamentary questioning. On July 24, a written answer was delivered on request to House of Commons representative Mr. Redmond. Nicholas Soames, the Minister of State for H.M. Armed Forces, repeated the "no defense significance" formula in his answer. Mr. Soames was standing in for the Secretary of State for Defense, Michael Portillo. To quote from the official "Hansard" records:

Mr. Redmond: To ask the Secretary of State for Defense:
1. *what response his Department made to the report submitted by Lieutenant Colonel Charles Halt relating to events in Rendlesham Forest in December 1980; what interviews were held; and if he will make a statement;*
2. *who assessed that the events around RAF Woodbridge and RAF Bentwaters in December 1980, which were reported to this Department by Lieutenant Colonel Charles Halt, were of no defense significance; on what evidence the assessment was made; what analysis of events was carried out; and if he will make a statement?*
Mr. Soames: *The report was assessed by the staff in my Department responsible for air defense matters. Since the judgment was that it contained nothing of defense significance no further action was taken."*

Indeed the official statement, that the Bentwaters/Woodbridge Incident had "no defense significance," is more than questionable. As Col. Halt told UFO researcher Peter Robbins, *"light beams"* coming from the UFO *"had penetrated the hardened bunkers of the Bentwaters weapons security area,"* in which, as the Colonel confirmed, nuclear weapons were stored.
"It has been claimed that on the night of the Rendlesham Forest incident one of the UFOs fired a pencil-thin beam of light into one of the nuclear weapon storage areas. Clearly the fact that allegations like this had been made by military personnel who were there at the time is something which needs proper investigation," commented Nick Pope, a Higher Executive Officer (which equates to the rank of a Major) from the Secretariat (Air Staff 2A) of the Ministry of Defense, who was responsible for investigating UFO sightings and handling policy on this subject in an official function from 1991 to 1994. *"To the best of my knowledge that's not something that has been looked at to date. What exactly the Ministry of Defence did in the immediate aftermath of the Rendlesham Forest incident is a bit of a mystery. On one hand, nowadays, when questioned about this, the MOD says that the whole situation was looked at at the time, but nothing of any defense significance was discovered. But this is strange since there is no paper in the Rendlesham Forest file that indicates any investigation whatsoever was carried out . . ."* Pope blames MOD bureaucracy and ignorance for this obvious neglect. Another possibility is that an investigation was performed by a more secret authority, such as the alleged UFO tracking station at Rudloe Manor, headquarters of the RAF Support Command, the

Provost and Security Services and the Defense Communication Network.

At any rate, the UFO department of the British Ministry of Defense is still active and collects UFO reports, especially to clarify if there is any defense significance. The following figures were officially released by the MOD and represent the number of UFO sightings reported to the Ministry.

1977:435	1981:600	1985:177	1989:258	1993:258
1978:750	1982:250	1986:120	1990:209	1994:250
1979:550	1983:390	1987:150	1991:117	1995:373
1980:350	1984:214	1988:397	1992:147	1996:609

Total between 1977 and 1996: 6,604 sightings.

The problem with these figures is that they represent just a tiny fraction of the actual UFO sightings going on in the UK." MOD official Nick Pope told me.

A lot of people will not report to the MOD at all. The 200–300 reports the MOD receives in average each year is just the tip of an iceberg . . . about 90–95% of these sightings which I investigated did turn out to have conventional explanations: military aircraft activity, astronomical observations, weather balloon launches and various other phenomena. But there's a hard core of maybe 5–10% of the UFO sightings which even I could absolutely not explain in any conventional terms even after the most throrough investigation. It's my view that some of these may well be extraterrestrial in origin. I'm saying that not because I make a great leap of faith, but because these sightings, which are not just of lights in the sky, are of structured craft with a technology that exceeds the very best of our own in terms of speed and maneuverability. We've got something in our airspace and it is not ours.

In November 1995, the MOD informed British UFO researchers that it plans the future declassification of another 300 pages of UFO files from the years 1963–1964 under its "30-year ruling." Further, a more open policy in UFO matters was promised. Thousands of pages are accessible today in the Public Records Office (PRO) at Kew. And some of them might cast a light on one of England's most fascinating UFO events, the "Cumbrian Space Man."

On May 24, 1964, a Sunday, Jim Templeton, fire officer of the Cumbrian Fire Service in Carlisle, Cumberland, decided to go for a picnic with his wife and little daughter and spend the sunny spring afternoon in the Burgh Marsh, a popular nature resort. Being an enthusiastic amateur photographer, Jim took his camera with him. His five-year-old daughter Elizabeth was wearing her new summer dress for the first time, and, after she picked up some wild spring flowers, Jim decided to take a picture of his little princess. It was a strange day, he noticed. There was a kind of electricity in the air, as when a thunderstorm approaches. Normally the sheep and cows would have been peacefully grazing all over the place, but on this afternoon they were all pushed back at the other end of the meadow, as if they were afraid of something. The only human beings he noticed were 2 old ladies, sitting in their car in the parking lot, about 400 yards away from the spot they had chosen for their picnic.

A few days later Templeton brought his film for development to the local drugstore. "It's a shame," said the owner when Jim came to pick up the photos. "Someone just ran into your best picture." "That's impossible," countered the fire officer. "No one was there that afternoon." But he was wrong. Indeed, on the one single photograph of his pretty young daughter a tall, white figure appeared to hover behind her, dressed in something like a spacesuit, with a helmet on the head.

Templeton showed the strange picture to his colleagues and the police and finally sent it to Kodak, where they could not explain it, either, but asked for permission to use it in an advertisement, offering anyone able to solve the mystery a "lifelong, free supply of film." Nobody had an answer, and a double exposure or manipulation of the negative could soon be excluded.

A few weeks later two men in dark suits visited Templeton at work. They claimed they were with Her Majesty's government but refused to show him their identity cards. Jim had to ask, and was granted, permission by his station chief to take time off to go out with the 2 visitors. They asked him to take them to the exact spot where the photograph was taken. "And that's where you saw the man?" they asked Jim. "I didn't see any man," the fire officer replied. At that the 2 men suddenly turned around abruptly and went off, leaving him standing totally at a loss on the spot, so that he had to walk the 5 miles back to the station.

Shortly afterwards he received a call from the editor of the *Cumberland News*, asking if they could borrow the negatives from him for some time. Templeton agreed. "We will send prints to Woomera," the editor explained. 1964 was, in fact, the year when England started to build the first "Blue Streak rockets," which were launched from Woomera, Australia. These missiles were manufactured at a place on the Carlisle-Newcastle road, in the immediate neighborhood of Burgh Marsh. During one of the launchings, the editor explained to Jim, a strange thing happened. One of the technicians, while observing the launch preparations on the monitor, suddenly saw 2 tall men in white spacesuits close to the launch tower. The countdown was immediately stopped, and the launch platform searched for the two men without any success. But after the Australian press published the Templeton-picture, the technician was sure of what he had seen: "He looks like the boys I saw on the monitor!"

In 1996, shortly after the declassification of the new documents from the 1960s, UFO researcher Jenny Randles conducted research at the Public Records Office in Kew. She discovered documents from the MOD dated December 29, 1964, mentioning *"the Cumbrian Spaceman"* being investigated by the *"Department for Scientific and Technical Intelligence"*

(DSTI). Were the 2 strange visitors officials of this supersecret authority? And the Woomera connection? An internal memorandum of June 18, 1964 actually refers to a rocket launching, asking: *"What do you think of the strange object hovering near the launch pad?"* Randles was moreover able to locate many reels of film from the rocket tests in Woomera, with only one missing—the Blue Streak launch of May 25, 1964, the very day after Templeton shot his picture. This, of course, proves that as a matter of fact important evidence is still being held back by Her Majesty's Government. But, at least the tip of the iceberg is now available for the UFO research community and the public.

With this brave approach, England was not alone. At the time, another NATO country, namely Spain, had also long since opened its UFO archives. The first step towards that was made on October 20, 1976, when a lieutenant general of the Spanish Ministry of Defense in Madrid requested the journalist Juan José Benitez to come to his office in order to hand a pile of documents over to him. The file was called "Reports about UFOs" and contained 78 photocopies of official documents about 12 significant cases, in which members of the armed forces had mostly been involved. Besides that, there were photographs, radar pictures and movie reels. The first of these incidents occurred on March 20, 1964, in the province of Seville, and the latest was a UFO landing on the island of Gran Canaria in the Canary Islands on June 22, 1976. That was in itself astounding because, by that act, for the first time a European government officially confirmed a UFO landing and an encounter of the third kind.

How spectacular this case really was, I found out during my research on the spot. Since then I have been on the Canary Islands twice, in July 1982 and in November 1991. I went to the landing site and spoke to over a dozen eye witnesses and could, based upon their statements and the press reports from the local papers of Gran Canaria, which were kindly given to me by the editors of the papers, reconstruct what had happened almost without a gap. The documents from the Spanish Air Force helped add important details to the case.

CHAPTER 19

A Spanish Confirmation

It was exactly 9:27 PM when the crew of the *Atrevida*, a corvette of the Spanish Navy sailing near Punta Lantailla off the coast of the island Fuerteventura, noticed an unusual phenomenon in the sky. The "Informe 01/76 Sobre OVNIs" (Information No. 01/76 about UFOs) contains the statements of the 2 chief witnesses interrogated by the Air Force, the captain of the corvette and the senior lieutenant:

> At 9:27 p.m. on June 22, 1976, we saw a bright light with an intense yellowish-blue color rising from the horizon and coming towards us. At first we thought it was an airplane with landing lights, but then when it had reached an elevation angle of 15°–18° it stopped. The original light went out and a beam of light appeared and started rotating. It remained thus for about 2 minutes. Then a big halo of yellow and blue lights appeared and remained for 40 minutes in that position whereas the original phenomenon was no more to be seen. After 2 minutes, the beam of light broke up into 2 fields with the smaller part below. A blue cloud appeared between the fields of light and in the middle of the halo, and the envelope suddenly vanished. The upper part started ascending quickly and jerkily in a spiral path. And then that too disappeared. The original semi-circular halo remained untouched by these proceedings. It just stood there and parts of the island were illuminated by the light that came out of it, which convinced us that the whole phenomenon was taking place quite close to us.

At this time the physician Francesco Padrón León, M.D., from Guia was on his way to visit a patient in the quiet northwest of the island of Gran Canaria, an area still untouched by tourism. One of his patients, Santiago del Pino from Galdar, had picked him up with a taxi to take him to his mother, who was lying ill at her farmhouse in the little village of Las Rosas. The taxi driver was Francisco Estevez Garcia, alias "Paco," also an old acquaintance of Dr. Padrón. Dr. Padrón was sitting in the passenger seat next to the driver. They had driven past Galdar in the direction of Las Rosas which was situated on a field road that branched off from the main road leading to Agaete, engaged in excited conversation, with the radio turned on loud. When Paco turned into the side road, Dr. Padrón called out suddenly, "What is that?" Then they all saw it. "Madre de Dios!" At the same moment, the radio went silent and the 3 men were filled with a cold sense of fear. Paco began to tremble.

Only about 60 yards in front of them floated a perfect sphere about 6 feet above the field, with its periphery shining in a gray or ice blue color. The thing was transparent and, when they looked closer, they could see the stars behind it. *"It was as big as a 3 storey house,"* Dr. Padrón told reporters of the island paper *La Provincia* during his one and only interview, given later but very reluctantly: *"It looked like a gigantic soap bubble. The ball was there. It hovered quietly in one place a few feet above the ground. I couldn't believe my eyes, and said so to my companions. But it was there. The thing was quite really there, in the middle of the night. We suddenly felt cold. Our driver began to shiver, particularly when the radio which had been on the whole time suddenly became silent. Inside the sphere one could see a platform, silvery in color, and a few plates on the platform . . . without corners or right angles . . . and 2 big beings. I can describe them in the last detail, for we saw them for about 20 minutes."* The beings were between 9 and 10 feet tall, wore red overalls with black capes. Their arms ended in conical shapes, but one could not say whether they were hands or just gloves. They were standing opposite to each other, moved their hands and seemed to be operating some apparatus. *"Honestly, I was fascinated by the majestic aura they radiated and the perfect form of their bodies. I have never seen anything like that before. A salient feature was the particularly large size of the backs of their heads,"* Dr. Padrón added.

When Garcia switched on the full beams of his taxi, the object began to rise until it finally reached the height of the roof of one of the nearby houses. Then there appeared inside the sphere a kind of transparent tube out of which a bluish gas streamed; it then flowed around the sphere. And with that it began to get bigger and bigger until it had reached the size of a 20-storey building. But the platform, the plates and the beings remained in their original size. Now the thing had become far too spooky for the 3 men, and besides that, they had to get going—there was a sick patient waiting for them. Paco stepped on the gas and speeded off. They arrived at their destination 2 minutes later and found the Pino family waiting for them. They, too, were watching the strange phenomenon. When it had appeared, their televisions had gone dead, and they rushed out to see what was happening.

Meanwhile the sphere had reached gigantic proportions when suddenly the flow of gas stopped. Whereas the entire procedure until then had been absolutely silent, now they heard a shrill whistle and suddenly the sphere

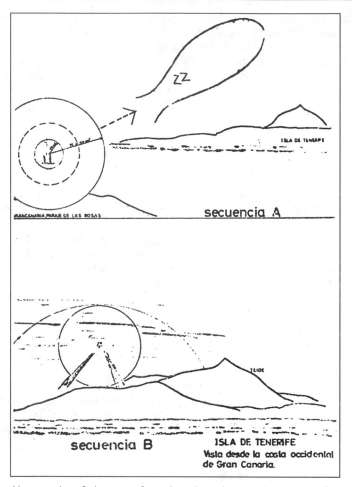

Above and on facing page, from the released secret documents of the Spanish Air Force: sketches of UFO of June 22, 1976, from different perspectives, according to eyewitnesses's information.

zoomed off into the sky with the speed of lightning, towards the nearby island of Tenerife. The object then took on the shape of a spindle, surrounded by a bright halo of light, and disappeared.

After they had all calmed down, Dr. Padrón discussed the matter with the other witnesses. *"I had noticed that we had all seen the same thing, and that nobody had been the victim of an optical illusion,"* said the doctor. *"Then I mentioned that the beings had all been blue. I said this to test whether I myself had suffered from optical illusions. But the others answered saying that I was mistaken: the clothing was red. Then I knew that what I had seen was real."*

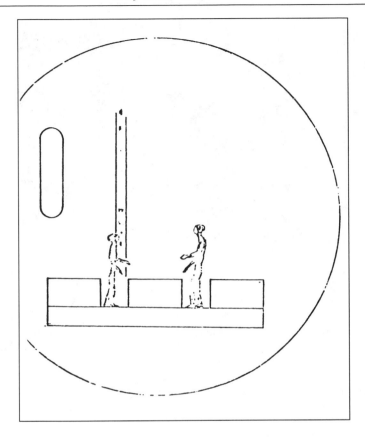

On Friday, July 23, 1982, I interviewed Dr. Padrón León in his house in Guia to get more details about this incident. His children told me about how distraught and shocked their father had been when he came home that night. Even months later he had nightmares in which again and again he saw the UFO and its crew. Subsequently he felt a compulsion to go back to the spot where it had happened. The taxi driver Paco had to be taken to a psychiatric clinic after the incident. He had suffered such a shock that afterwards he became anxious and superstitious and had to give up his job. Padrón told me that investigators from the Spanish Air Force had come to him and after hearing his story, declared they knew that everything he had said was true, which, however, they denied before American journalists. But in the released files there is a 2-page statement made by Dr. Padrón.

I was able to find more witnesses as well. A second taxi driver José Luis Dias Mendosa, who was at the time driving a customer, had seen the sphere as well. *"It was big and round some 60 feet high. It hovered almost stationary,"* he told me, *"inside of it I could see 2 red figures. The outside of the object was gray."* When I asked him how long he was able to observe

Dr. Francisco Padrón León, with family, at his house in Guia, Gran Canaria.

the object he answered, *"about a quarter of an hour. Then it went up slowly into the sky."* A group of villagers in Las Rosas remembered that the two red figures moved their hands *"as if they were greeting us. Then the thing rose up at a high speed."*

The architect Domingo Alamo and his wife and a couple who were visiting them were sitting on the terrace on the roof of their house at Galdar, when they saw at a distance the big spherical object. *"It was as big as the village church,"* said Alamo.

The witness Claudio Ramos told reporters of the local paper La Provincia: *"Shortly after 10:00 I saw something. I was watching television when the picture suddenly went bad. Everything was doubled and I couldn't get a proper picture anymore. My wife was busy packing some food for my brother-in-law. Suddenly I heard her cry out. She told me that she had seen something strange near the house. We went out just at the moment when this thing was changing its position."* He, too, saw the 2 figures *"who had a shining red color and looked as if they were people."* A total of about 30 witnesses had seen the landing. But thousands had that evening experienced the video and audio disruptions. *"Many acquaintances have affirmed that the [TV] picture was totally ruined by black stripes, whereas the sound was audible but squeaky and distorted,"* wrote Carl-Wilhelm von Siemens to the UFO researcher Adolf Schneider of Munich. For von Siemens, who was on the island at that time, *"there were no doubts whatsoever about the object being real,"* particularly because he had spoken to eyewitnesses, *"all of whom had seen the same object from various places and gave the same description."*

Hundreds of people saw the UFO when it flew over the island. Manollo, the driver of Taxi No. 10 in the island's capital Las Palmas, told me he had been sitting on the terrace of his house that evening, when he saw a bright spot in the sky. The light came from the northeastern direction and became bigger and bigger, then it disappeared in the direction of Galdar. German tourists saw it, too. One of them is Mrs. G—— from Frechen. At 10:00 p.m. she had been sitting on the terrace of her holiday bungalow. She saw an object shining orange, which started moving towards the center of the island. At the time of the sighting she noticed that there were disturbances in the radio and TV "*as if somebody were using an electric razor nonstop in the next room.*" At the same time another German tourist took 36 color photographs of a gigantic ball of light in the area around Maspalomas and Playa des Ingles in the southeast of the island. The Civil Guard was informed about this by the photolab and they immediately confiscated the pictures and negatives. The tourist was asked to keep quiet about the incident. Finally the Air Force released one of the pictures with the statement that thorough investigation done by expert laboratories had confirmed its authenticity.

At about 10:00 p.m.—the same time the pictures were taken—Horst Barthel, ex-German owner of the discotheque "Club 25" in Playa des Ingles, was sitting in an airplane that was just about to land at Las Palmas. Barthel looked out of the window and saw in the northwest, roughly in the direction of the island Tenerife, a bright light. At first he thought that the volcano Pico de Teide had erupted, but soon he recognized that it was a spindle-shaped flying craft. The object, which was yellowish-blue and "*relatively big and bright as a welding flame,*" looked like a slim cone surrounded in the middle by a ring of light.

The most impressive evidence for the incident certainly was the onion field just outside of Las Rosas over which the UFO had hovered. It belongs to the farmer Don José Gil Gonzáles, whom I was able to interview. He confirmed the report of the local paper *La Provincia*, published 2 days after the landing, according to which within a circle of about 100 feet diameter the onion plants had all been pressed down spirally and were found to be partly burned. Particularly at the edge of the circle the journalists found a strange grayish-white powder. Shortly after the newspaper reported this finding, the field was cordoned off for two days, during which experts of the Air Force and a group of Americans—allegedly NASA scientists—collected samples of the earth and measured the radiation. The physical traces described in *La Provincia* were confirmed 4 weeks later by UFO researcher Rolf Tobisch of Frankfurt, who was able to photograph the burned and crushed plants.

When I visited Las Rosas in July 1982, this patch on the field was still barren. Contrary to the early expectations of many, no attempt whatsoever was made to commercialize the UFO incident or the landing site, although a lot of tourists had shown great interest in the matter, since "UFO landing on Gran Canaria" was the front page headline of *Bild am Sonntag*, Germany's largest tabloid. No hotel was ever built in Las Rosas, no signs show or lead to the spot and even tips are refused strictly, which is a rare thing in Spain. Apparently no one wants any publicity. I had the luck to find a friendly elderly taxi driver who, following the instructions given by Dr.

The landing site shortly after the incident: Many of the plants show signs of burning. Photos: Rolf Tobisch.

The landing site today; the author speaking to the farmer Don Jose Gei Gonzáles.

Padrón's lovely daughter Celia, took me by a direct route to the landing site. We drove some 20 minutes from Guia—the road almost goes into Galdar—to Las Rosas, past stony fields and miserable looking farm houses. As a backdrop to the perpetual reddish-brown of the Gran Canarian landscape the rocky volcanic mountain, which a poet once called a "thunderstorm in stone," reared up in the distance.

It was a hot scirocco day: the air was not the fresh salty breeze of the sea, but heavy and laden with yellow dust. When we approached Las Rosas, there were 2 elderly men sitting on a bench near the field path. We asked them the way and mentioned the OVNI (UFO). Yes, they had seen it too. We took them with us to their houses and they showed us where they had observed it from at that time. I asked Gonzáles' farmhand about the site of the landing and he showed me a field, which was only a few yards from the road. On the way back we stopped there once more. Meanwhile Gonzáles had been told about our arrival, and naturally he did not want to miss the opportunity of greeting me and taking me personally to the landing site. I told him that I was a journalist from Germany and asked him whether I could take a few photographs of him. I could. He joked saying that he would not look so handsome now as when *La Provincia* had photographed him, since he had not shaved himself that day, but that made no difference to me. All my efforts to give the farmer's boy a tip were in vain. "Oh no, señor!" It was already twilight and we started on the way back. The visit to the suburb had lasted for almost two hours, and the taxi bill was just under $15. I was astonished by the big heartedness of these simple people. They were all quite happy to talk about OVNIs. In fact, in that part of the world, UFOs are something that one takes for granted, so much so that some UFO researchers have even speculated about whether there is a UFO base in the Canary Islands.

During that night of June 22, the said UFO flew on further, as is revealed by documents of the Spanish Air Force. Dozens of witnesses saw it from the ferry *Ciudad Agaete*, going from Agaete to Tenerife. Astronomers of the observatory of Izana on Tenerife tried to get a better look at the object through their telescopes. Thousands of people in Tenerife's capital Puerto de la Cruz were panic-stricken when they saw the spindle of light passing over their town. Witnesses described it as a big light which seemed to ascend and was pointed at the sky like a searchlight. Surrounding it was a radiant blue ring. An employee of the mayor's office said, "*at 10:15 p.m. I was standing at the window when I saw a lot of people looking up into the sky. When I too looked in the same direction I could only see a point of bright light, which then disappeared. But then after a few minutes it came back and was definitely much bigger. Then it became pretty big, blue in color and sent out flashes 2 or 3 times. Occasionally one could see a kind of trail. I could watch it for a few minutes before it disappeared slowly.*"

Many compared it to a gigantic shining mushroom and some witnesses even believed they saw 2 fuzzy reddish figures. The UFO had first flown in a zigzag manner, and then taken a spiral path. Here, too, there were disturbances in radio and television reception. After that, hundreds of inhabitants of the western islands Gomera, La Palma and Hierro also saw the phenomenon. Dozens of people called the papers, the broadcasting stations and the authorities. During the whole period the personnel of the air traffic control tower were watching the UFO on radar, according to the official report. Previously, the officials had denied this fact to the press.

But despite the original official denial, shortly after the Gran Canaria incident General Carlos Castro Cavero, division commander of the Canary Islands Air Command told the press that *"for some time I have been convinced that these UFOs are extraterrestrial spacecraft."* He also revealed that UFOs are taken seriously at the highest levels. The Defense Ministry, he revealed, had files on more than 20 cases *"which the best experts could not explain."* One of them was the landing on Gran Canaria. General Cavero's statement was confirmed by the documents handed over to Benitez. In them, a reporting officer of the Air Force came to the conclusion that, after going through all the eyewitness reports, *"one is confronted seriously with the necessity of possibly accepting the hypothesis, that a spacecraft of unknown origin, driven by an unknown energy, had maneuvered above the Canary Islands."*

During my investigations on the Canary Islands, I came upon another remarkable incident that occurred three years later. When the professional photographer Antonio Gonzáles Llopis set up his camera on a tripod on a road leading to the Hotel Riviera in the neighborhood of Puerto Rico on Gran Canaria, all he intended to do was to photograph a picturesque sunset. The radio in his car was on and he was listening to the sports report. It was March 5, 1979, at about 8:10 p.m. The setting sun was veiled by a bright red cloud and surrounding it were beautiful concentric rings of clouds in all the colors of the rainbow. The photographer took five shots of the splendid spectacle in the sky, then took some pictures of the fishing boats that were sailing before the coast. He was about to dismount his camera when he suddenly saw something emerging from the ocean. *"The light was not at all white, more like old ivory, and very shiny. It came out of the water, absolutely. I can swear to that. It rose into the sky at a tremendous speed. The big ball of light looked like suddenly released energy. On the top the UFO was shaped like a pyramid."*

Llopis at once took a few pictures of it. The object became bigger and bigger, and then suddenly dissolved into the sky, and was no longer visible. It was 8:15 p.m.—the sports report on the radio had just come to an end. The ascent of the UFO had lasted about 3 minutes. Meanwhile, other people had also collected on the beach road, who had come to watch the grand sunset and had now seen the UFO as well. At the same time, thousands of people on the islands of La Palma, Gomera, Tenerife, Hierro and Gran Canaria saw this and got into a panic. The people of the little island of Guia de Isora, at the extreme western end of the archipelago, were closest to the phenomenon. Women fainted; some thought the end of the world had come and started praying; many had nervous breakdowns and became hysterical. The searchlights of vehicles went out and, in many cases, the motor stopped running.

At this time, an airliner of the charter company NAYSA was on its way from Las Palmas to Mauritania. The pilots of the airplane saw the object. Flight Captain Eufronio Garcia Monforte said, "*It rose up with a speed of over 13,000 mph. At first, it was only a bright light that changed in color from orange to red. Then, we saw that it was a rotating cone. Finally, it took on the shape of a sphere of about 1,200 feet in diameter and its colour became a bluish green.*" After 20 minutes, during which period the pilots could observe it directly as well as on radar, the UFO vanished into the evening skies. Meteorologists confirmed that it could not have been a natural phenomenon. UFO researchers have found certain similarities between this event and the UFO appearance of June 22, 1976.

Besides Llopis, there are 2 other photographers who captured the UFO on film: Gilberto Narranjo, employee of the television receiving station of Izana, and the Dutchman William N. Lijtmaer who was on holiday in Tenerife.

During the following weeks, the Spanish Air Force conducted extensive investigations, which was confirmed by the Commander of the Second Division of the Air Force Staff. Llopis was also interrogated and he said that he was "*quite convinced that it had been a UFO, which had its base under the ocean near the Canary Islands.*" But this time the Air Force kept quiet about the results of the investigation.

On November 11, 1979, a Super Caravelle of the Spanish Airlines TAE started from Palma de Mallorca with 109 passengers on board. The aircraft was on its way from Salzburg to Tenerife with stopover at Mallorca. Until then, everything had gone smoothly. Above Evisa however, the crew discovered on the radar that strange signals were approaching them very rapidly. Flight Captain Tejada called the control tower at Valencia and asked "are there airplanes on our route?" Answer: "No, no announcements." Then Tejada and his copilot saw glittering red lights that were somehow behaving crazily. They were on a collision course. The lights were flying at a speed that no conventional aircraft reaches. Suddenly they stopped close ahead of the Caravelle. For 10 minutes they kept playing with it, then they readjusted their course once more for a collision, more precisely than before. Now for Tejada the situation was too dangerous, so he dove and reduced his altitude from 29,000 feet to 16,000. He then requested from the control tower near Los Manises near Valencia permission to land, owing to pursuit by unknown flying objects and danger of collision. There was panic on board. The passengers were crying and weeping, others began to pray. They thought the airplane was going to crash owing to mechanical defects.

After landing, the personnel at the tower as well as the ground crew confirmed everything that the pilots had seen. Even then, at an altitude of about 10,000 feet, a red light hovered over the control tower, a second one over the runway, a third one over the nearby military airport and a fourth one circled around high above the town. Captain Tejada showed these lights to one of the passengers, Norbert Zauner-Stürmer, an engineer from Salzburg, in order to put an end to speculation among the passengers about the airplane having technical defects. The engineer said: *"I had always considered all this talk about UFOs to be utter nonsense, but now I concede that there was something in it. I saw it with my own eyes."* At once, the Valencia airport was alerted and the next Air Force base informed. A few minutes later, 20 fighters were sent up to intercept the UFOs—without success. *"They maintained a constant distance ahead of us, although our fighters had reached a speed of 1,500 mph,"* said one of the fighter pilots to his superior. Actually, as was revealed at Valencia, the UFOs had been spotted on the radar screens of the airport and the airport base. Many civilians were also able to see this, and the Spanish press even published some photographs.

The Spanish transport minister Salvador Sanchez Teran took the matter so seriously that he at once flew to Valencia in order to form an investigative commission consisting of military personnel and civilians. Although in the Spanish press there were rumors that the fighter pilots had taken some pictures of the objects while in the sky, the results of the official investigation were kept secret for 15 years. A question put to Parliament by the assistant chairman of the defense commission to the government

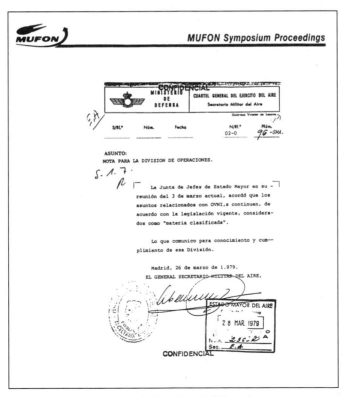

This order, dated March 3, 1979, declared UFOs to be a secret matter.

brought no results at that time. What had led to the change of policy in the defense ministry? One year before this, in December 1978, the Spanish UFO researcher Pedro Redon wrote to King Juan Carlos requesting the release of further UFO files. The King of Spain gave the letter to the Chief of Staff, and he ordered, in 1979, a review of UFO data. Eventually, on March 3, 1979, the General Staff decided *"to keep secret everything that affected national security"* and therefore to *"treat the UFO files as a secret matter."*

They were, moreover, taken away from the Air Force and put directly under the General Staff so that they would come under the law for state secrets, and release would be considerably more difficult. Now, any release would require the sanction of the highest military commission. Insiders suspected that the change of policy was affected or caused by the negotiations which were then going on regarding the entry of Spain into NATO, which happened in May, 1982. A day before this decision was made, the first free elections in Spain since the Franco era had taken place, and the new democratic institutions restricted the freedom of the army considerably. Autonomous actions of the generals without consulting the government—which was very intent on gaining the respect of foreign nations for their "new Spain"—was no longer possible. The Defense Ministry answered inquiries about UFO files from then onwards laconically with the phrase *"UFOs are a secret matter, and therefore no information is available."*

And so it remained for some time to come: *"Your request has been considered by the Staff of the Air Force and the General Staff, and it has been decided to extend the classification of 'top secret' for documents concerning the subject of UFOs,"* wrote a state secretary of the Defense Ministry almost a year later, in answer to a request from the UFO researcher Vincente-Juan Ballester Olmos for the release of UFO files of June 1984. On March 26, 1985, Senator Juan Francisco Serrano of the political party "Grupo Popular" asked the government in Parliament:

1) Whether UFOs are being officially investigated in Spain;
2) If the subject of UFOs is being treated as a state secret, and
3) Which ministry is responsible for this matter."

The answer of the government was published in the official bulletin of the senate:

1. There are standard procedures for the investigation and pursuit of UFOs in Spanish airspace.
2. The General staff of the Air Force gave out instructions for the procedures to be followed when UFO sightings are reported in December 1968.
3. According to Article 31 of the code of laws 6/1980 in which the basic criteria for national defense have been laid down, the Air Force is

responsible for the control of national air space. Therefore it is the Defense Ministry which is responsible for the matter of UFOs.

The instructions and standards set up in 1968, to which the Spanish government referred, were the direct reaction of one of the most spectacular UFO incidents in the history of the country. On the evening of September 5, 1968, all traffic came to a standstill in Madrid, when thousands of citizens stood watching a tetrahedral object flying at a great height above the city. At once an F-104 jet fighter took off to take up pursuit, but when the plane went up, the UFO accelerated and increased its altitude. At an altitude of about 45,000 feet, the Air Force pilot had to give up. The UFO was beyond reach, and had, according to the radar screens, reached an altitude of 75,000 feet. The next day the papers were full of reports about this UFO and speculation about the role of the army under such circumstances. On December 5, 1968, the press department of the Air Force Ministry called upon the citizens in the future to report all UFO sightings to the nearest Air Force installation. At the same time, Gen. Mariano Cuadra, Vice-Chief of Staff, instructed the air sec-

Thousands of the citizens of Madrid observed this tetrahedral-shaped UFO on September 5, 1968. It maneuvered above the city at an altitude of 30,000 feet.

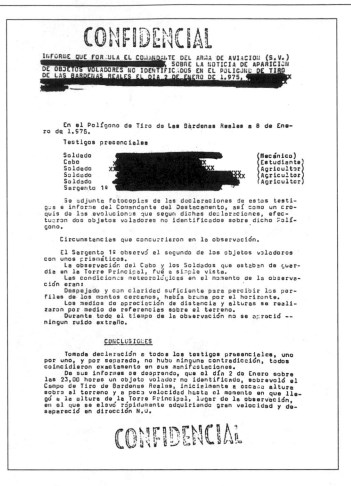

tors to investigate UFO sightings at once and collect data. Following this, on December 26, 1968, the instruction *9266 CT* ("C" stands for "confidential") was issued, giving details for investigation procedures such as the circumstances of sighting, weather conditions, air traffic, radar detection, etc . . . including a questionnaire for use during investigations.

This paper had its validity until, in January 1975, a UFO landed at the army exercising grounds of Poligono de Tiro de las Bardenas Reales near Navarra. During the night of January 2, at about 11:00 p.m. a 4-man patrol noticed 2 bright lights on the northeastern side of the terrain. One seemed to land near the watchtower, whereas the other one rose up just before reaching the watchtower and flew off in a northwestly direction. The patrolmen radioed to the sergeant on duty who was able to observe the second object through binoculars. He described it as *"an inverted bowl of the size of a truck, with a cone of light coming out of it, shining down to the*

Official report and illustration from the Air Force documents about UFO maneuvers on Army exercise grounds at Bardenas Reales, near Navarra.

ground." When the press learned about the incident and made inquiries, the Air Force brusquely stated that the soldiers had suffered from an optical illusion and the UFO had only been the moon. But the UFO files which were given to Benitez in 1976 came to a very different conclusion:

All witnesses were interrogated one after the other and separately. Contradictions could not be found. All descriptions were identical. From their reports, the fact emerges that . . . unknown flying objects . . . flew at a low height and a low speed . . . ascended quickly and disappeared at high speed in the northwest."

These files are the only ones to reveal that the incident repeated itself three days later. Again a 4-man patrol saw a UFO at the same spot. When it had flown away, an armed patrol examined the landing site and found a circle of burned grass.

The Air Force reacted quickly. On January 10, new *"instructions for information about alleged UFO sightings,"* this time more detailed than those of 1968, were issued by Gen. Mariano Cuadra, now State Secretary for the Air Force, and sent to the Chiefs of Staff.

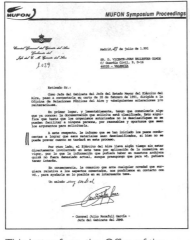

This letter, from the Office of the Chief of Staff to V. J. Ballester Olmos, announces the release of UFO files.

One year later, the 16 UFO files were given to Benitez. But it was only in the 1990s that the real breakthrough came. The new openness of the Belgian and Soviet military in the spring of 1990 (see chapter 2) encouraged the Spanish UFO researcher Vincente-Juan Ballester Olmos to try a new strategy.

He decided on direct communication, and therefore sought appointments with officers of the public relations departments, the air security section and finally members of the general staff, to present his request personally. Then in February 1991 he wrote a memorandum to the Chief of Staff in which he offered the cooperation and help of his own organizaton in the matter of solving the UFO mystery, giving as an example the cooperation between the Air Force and SOBEPS in Belgium. He furthermore requested the release of classified UFO files to enable researchers to follow up historical cases. That started the ball rolling. On May 22, 1991, the Defense Ministry confirmed the existence of 55 files about UFO cases covering the period 1962 to 1988 and conceded, *"it could be considered as suitable for the General Staff to open the archives of their security to persons with genuine interest in the matter."* Two months later Ballester Olmos received a letter from the Chief of the Cabinet of the Air Force's Chiefs of Staff announcing *"suitable steps for the release of UFO material have been initiated."* A circular was sent to various air commands of the defense regions of Spain to send their UFO files to the Defense Ministry in Madrid *"for purposes of centralization."* In December, 1991, the Air Force Staff presented the Defense Minister 60 UFO reports, seeking his approval for their intention to release them.

On January 15, 1992, the files were sent to the air operations commando MOA, the Spanish equivalent of the ATIC (Air Technical Intelligence Center) for final checking before release. On April 14, 1992, the General Staff met and decided, on the recommendation of the MOA, to reduce the classification of the UFO files concerned from 'top secret' to 'confidential,' whereby they would then come under the jurisdiction of the Air Force. And with that the decision of March 3, 1979, became inoperative. It also set up a precedent. Thereafter, each single sighting would be checked by intelligence services to see whether publishing it would affect national security. If not, the Staff of the Air Force could decide about its release. These instructions were made concrete in June 1992 with the directive IG-40-5 of Air Force Intelligence:

When a UFO sighting is reported by civilians the case should be forwarded to the regional Air Force authority and the MOA headquarters. If the regional office decides that an investigation is necessary then a clerical officer must be entrusted with the task of carrying out investigations. In important cases the MOA will name a specialized investigation officer from the intelligence services to observe the investigation. All information shall be classified as confidential. The intelligence service of the MOA staff shall keep the files and records and decide about possible release.

After that the instructions for dealing with UFO sightings from 1968–1975 were revised. The new instructions were much more thorough and extensive. Now every officer conducting such an investigation had to collect exact data about weather conditions, flight activities at that time, radar sightings at that time, observations made by pilots during radio communication with air traffic control, etc. If he considered it necessary, he could also appeal to the public through the media to give more information about possible sightings. On completion of the investigation, the credibility of the report would be assessed according to a scale from A to D, its quality from 1 to 4. In addition there are instructions for the handling of UFO photographs and fragments. An example of the layout for such a report is also given, including a 16-page questionnaire which covers all possibilities which one could think of in connection with UFOs.

The Spanish Air Force did not wait long before releasing the UFO files. Since the autumn of 1992, the first UFO reports have been available for study by the public in the library of the Air Force headquarters in Madrid. Towards the end of 1993, the UFO files from the time period 1967–69 were declassified. And more would follow.

On July 11, 1994 at 8:30 a.m. MOA sent out a telex to all units of the Spanish Air Force. Under the heading "Sightings of strange phenomena in national airspace" it reads as follows: *"In spite of MOA's painstaking efforts to centralize UFO documentation at headquarters since July 1991 and MOA's instructions to all Commands in this respect in November 1992, it still appears there is some Air Force information which is not yet in the hands of MOA and must be sent in without delay. Such information has been mentioned by journalists in the media, reinforcing the public conviction that the Air Force is hiding UFO information."* This order led to the most extensive search for UFO files in Spanish history.

Whereas most units reported that they had no relevant documents in their files, others came up with more promising results. MACEN (Centers Air Command) in Madrid forwarded a file regarding the incident of November 11, 1979 with the reports of the pilots and the radar ground control operators. GRUCEMAC (Central Group of Command and Control), site of the mainframe Air Defense Radar, supplied copies of control logbooks for specific dates in 1986 and 1990. Several EVAs (Air Surveillance Squadrons) sent further information on radar cases, for example EVA-5 in Alicante, which had 3 UFO detections on radar in 1986. But the most prolific information was supplied by MACAN (Canary Islands Air Command) in the form of a 3-page summary of 15 sightings which happened between 1977 and 1991.

With this additional information the number of files released under declassification grew from the original number of 55 in May 1991 to 60 in July 1991, to 62 in March 1992, to 81 Air Force files plus 41 from the Army and Navy—a current total of 122 cases altogether! Of these, 88 are from the Spanish mainland, 28 from the Canary Islands and 6 from the Baleareic Islands. Forty-five occurrences involved aircraft: 60% commercial airliners and 40% military jets. And 20 of the cases were investigated by the Spanish Air Force officially and remained "unexplained" even after the most careful study. One of them, classified as "UFOs/Aliens," is the Gran Canaria landing of 1976.

Since March 1997, the complete UFO files of the Spanish Air Force have been open for public inspection in the library of the Air Force Headquarters in Madrid. One of the most spectacular cases was the UFO encounter of the former Spanish Prime Minister Adolfo Suarez in February 1980. On his flight back from a state visit to Germany, he and the whole crew of his airplane as well as that of a second aircraft observed a multicolored, luminous sphere which passed by. The pilots of both aircraft located the object on radar. Further investigation revealed that there was no known traffic in the region at the time in question besides those two airplanes.

Greece

Prof. Paul Santorini is one of the few Greek physicists of international fame. He was a student and friend of Albert Einstein (with whom he played violin duets) and did pioneer work in the development of radar systems, the atom bomb and the napalm bomb. He possesses 2 patents for the control systems which are used in the U.S. for remote control rockets and missiles, and has written over 190 scientific papers. He has represented Greece at 23 international scientific congresses and is member of the Academy of Sciences in New York. His homeland honored him with both its highest orders, the "George I" and the "Phoenix." He retired as director of the Experimental Physics Laboratory of Athens Polytechnic in 1964. Prof. Santorini is no dreamer and he is sure of what he says when talking about UFOs, as he did in a lecture to the Greek Astronautical Society on February 24, 1967: *"My own observations of flying saucers over Athens, and the investigations I conducted, have led me to the conviction that flying saucers are continually keeping a watch on the earth, and are taking samples of our flora and fauna."* His personal experience with them began in 1947, when the army was given a team of scientists and engineers to investigate objects which were flying over Greece, and were taken to be Russian rockets. *"We found out that they were not rockets, but before we could undertake anything more, the chiefs of the army, after consultation with officials of the Pentagon, told us to break off all further observations."*

Two decades later they were a little more open. After the NATO air base Larissa had become the target of unknown flying objects on 7 occasions between 1974 and January 18, 1978, Gen. Constantinos Margaritis, former chief commander of the Greek Air Force, declared that the UFOs could be a serious threat to the security of the country. During that period, the Theta UFO Study Group, with headquarters in Athens, could study 117 UFO cases. Robert D. Shorter, an American engineer living in Athens, member of Theta, learned from Air Force circles about a 16mm UFO movie which had been shot from an interceptor plane and examined by the Air Force. *"A reliable informant told me that a thorough study of UFOs is going on in the highest military circles, and that some of the top people have come to the conclusion that UFOs are alien spaceships."* Staff Sgt. William S. Baker, who had belonged to the American NATO unit in Greece goes even further: *"I could name high-ranking Greek officers who had UFO sightings and who described them as very threatening, but the official policy in this matter compels them to silence."* Besides that, Baker, owing to the information that he has, is convinced that the Greeks and Americans are working together at a secret level in the surveillance of UFO operations. On August 11, 1977, when the English-language newspaper *Athens Courier* reported a UFO sighting above the Acropolis, a high-ranking security official was cited who had spoken about Greco-American cooperation in UFO matters. Shorter also knew *"that both countries discuss these matters during secret meetings and that RF-4C jet interceptors have been equipped with special cameras. These stand in constant readiness to take up the pursuit of UFOs and to film them as soon as they are sighted over the country."*

An incident occurred sometime during the middle of 1977 above the Aegean Sea, off the coast near the town of Velos. The exact time, date and names of the witnesses have been put under strict secrecy by the authorities. We only know that it was a 26-year-old flight lieutenant who was on a routine flight, shortly after the sun had set. His airplane was a Vought A7H Corsair II, a type which had once been in operation in Vietnam, having been used there by the U.S. Air Force for its swiftness and high maneuverability, and which had later been sold to the Greeks under the NATO program of mutual aid. The lieutenant had already accrued years in active service, and had had over 700 flight hours. During the flight he suddenly noticed a flash of light at the end of the right wing of his aircraft. At first he thought it was another fighter plane, but a few seconds later he saw that it was a disc-like object. The UFO turned and shot towards him.

His report: *"when it approached I saw a spherical object of about 30 feet in diameter with a smooth silvery surface and a slightly raised center."* The pilot was frightened and swerved to the left, accelerated and started diving. The UFO followed him. *"I was frightened, but at the same time impressed by its maneuvering ability. It was clear that the object was controlled by intelligence. I went down from an altitude of 16,000 feet to about 9,000. The object did the same and stayed at that angle so I could not fire at it."* For the next 7 minutes the young lieutenant tried in vain to shake off his pursuer. It was only when he had almost given up, when escape seemed almost impossible, that the hunt suddenly came to an end. The UFO turned, sped towards the south and disappeared.

In 1978 the Greek Defense Minister E. Avaroff Tositas declared before the NATO General Staff in Brussels that the UFO operations represented a potential danger for the European continent. *"I recommend an immediate investigation into the origin and identity of these unknown phenomena in the air."* At a press conference after this held at an exclusive hotel in Athens he told the reporters *"I once had my doubts whether there were UFOs, but now I don't have any."*

UFOs—even today a problem for NATO? Already in 1961 Gen. L. M. Chassin, the NATO Air Defense coordinator at that time, said *"flying saucers are of great importance to us. I have demanded that the governments take initiatives, and instead of ridiculing those who believe in saucers, to start investigation commissions and that, in as many civilized countries as possible. We must seriously make sure that the conspiracy of silence does not suppress news about phenomena of great importance, for that would have consequences which are incalculable for the whole human race."*

CHAPTER 20

Abductions, The Key To Understanding?

Something happened in Stendal in East Germany, the former communist German Democratic Republic, on a cold January evening in the year 1962 at about 6:30 p.m. Norbert Haase, age 18, his brother, and a few friends had been skating on the lake in the town, as they had done almost every afternoon since the lake froze. Now the boys wanted to go home, except Norbert, who loved to skate under the starry sky and wanted to stay longer. His brother insisted on his coming home with them but Norbert kept looking at the sky longingly. Suddenly he saw something strange. "Hey, look! There's a star flying up there!" he cried out to his brother. But the latter only laughed and said "It's only a plane, don't dream so much." Soon the boys were almost out of sight and Norbert felt a bit sorry that he had not gone with them. But something held him back. He wanted to glide once more across the lake to the little island on the far side, which was a haven for ducks and swans. It was circular and had a diameter of about 36 feet. Norbert was only about 50 yards from the island when suddenly from behind it a bright light shot up.

"It was as if someone had suddenly switched it on," he explained later. *"It just flamed up suddenly. I found it rather frightening. It was actually beautiful, but I was overwhelmed—it was so bright and radiant, bluish white in color. Then it hovered about 15 feet above the trees of the island and was twice as broad as the island. It was long and flat, surrounded by rays of light rather like a cross around the bright core."* Norbert stood still, was blinded by the light, felt a kind of prickling sensation all over his body and then fell unconscious.

When he came back to himself, he found himself lying at the edge of a slope on the bank of the lake, about 500 feet away from the island. He was confused and did not know how he had gotten there. He had a severe headache and his eyes hurt him. His skates were lying near him. He looked

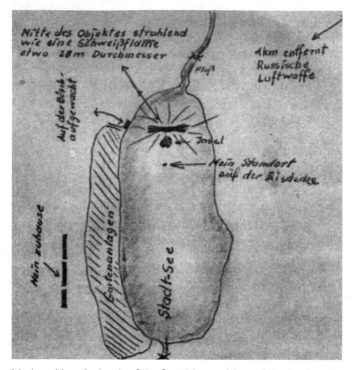

Norbert Haase's sketch of the Stendal town lake and the landing site of the UFOs.

at his watch and saw that it had stopped at 6:40 p.m. He then went home. His parents lived in a little railwayman's colony not far from the lake. When he reached home it was midnight. His mother had been greatly worried about him for he had never been so late in coming home, and when she saw him she had a fright. His skin was bright pink as if he had gotten a bad sunburn. On the right side of his nose he had a small wound where the top layer of the skin had been removed. Norbert still has the scar today.

The next day, Norbert's father took him to the doctor, who had known Norbert from his childhood. The physician, Dr. Boos, was unable to make any diagnosis. So he sent Norbert to the polyclinic at Stendal. There too, Norbert could only relate what he remembered. During the first 2 nights, he had bad nightmares, kept talking in his sleep, or woke up bathed in sweat. *"They told me later that I had talked about astronomy, space, time, and God. Naturally, they told the doctor about this and he then questioned me. I said it was impossible, I had never thought about God."*

On the fourth day at the polyclinic, Norbert was visited by two STASI officers (Secret Service of East Germany). They asked the boy to fill out a questionnaire which had the heading, *"Unidentified and Other Kinds of Phenomena."* They asked him a lot of questions, but again, he could remember only the light. Even when they asked him if he knew what a UFO was, he said, "No." In the communist German Democratic Republic of those days the word was unknown.

A few days later, 2 psychologists from Leipzig came to see him at the clinic. They said they wanted to put him under hypnosis. Norbert didn't know what that was, but upon hearing the explanation, and that it would not hurt him but would probably help him to remember, he agreed. He was hypnotized for 3 days and questioned each time for 2 to 3 hours under hypnosis. Seven or 8 audiocassettes were recorded. On the last day of the therapy, they played for him a 5-minute extract of the first cassette.

"To their question as to where I was, I answered saying that I was lying on a table. Then, there were other questions like, 'Were there people there?' and I answered 'Yes, beautiful slim people with long hair and white overalls. I had also seen a symbol, the tree of life from mythology, but without the snake. That was somewhere on the collar, a kind of stand-up or turtleneck collar."

The same symbol of the tree of life was seen by an American contactee, the late Dr. Daniel Fry. At that time, in 1950, one of the extraterrestrials explained to Fry, *"This is well-known to us in our history as well. Our explanation is that we had, at least in part, the same ancestors."* Norbert Haase did not know the term UFO when he was asked by the STASI and besides that, it can be ruled out that a copy of Dr. Fry's book, which was published in West Germany in 1956, in a very limited edition, had been smuggled into East Germany. Norbert was astonished when I told him about this correlation in 1981.

The contact with the spaceship has, at any rate, changed Norbert's life. He was never again the same after that, was no longer happy in the company of his friends. He began to think about God and the universe. In 1968, he was sent with the National People's Army for maneuvers to the former Czechoslovakian Socialist Republic (CSSR). During the People's Revolution in Prague he was ordered to shoot at the people, but along with 132 comrades, he refused. For this, he had to spend 4 years in military prisons. From there, he repeatedly appealed for permission to leave the country until, in 1974, he was finally extradited to the Federal Republic of Germany.

The abduction case of Norbert Haase was not the only one and the STASI was not the only secret service which had to deal, worried and helpless, with the new phase in the approach strategy of the extraterrestrials. For they suddenly started kidnapping people. This had drawn the attention of the official UFO researchers since the encounter of the policeman Herbert Schirmer in 1967—one of the cases investigated by the Colorado Study. (See Chapter 9) During the following decades this new development assumed an alarming international dimension. For the supporters of the cover-up policy, this was a good argument for the continuation of the policy of silence, since the thought that extraterrestrials could snatch people away from their everyday lives, take them on board their spacecraft to examine them physically, and perhaps even manipulate them, could give rise to anxiety, unrest and panic.

Apparently, the visitors did everything to show those with political responsibilities their capabilities and possibilities. Not only were a number of military personnel abducted, but one case of kidnapping actually happened before the eyes of a politician of international status . . .

In New York City, November 30, 1989, the security agents Dan and Richard were performing a routine job. They were to escort the UN Secretary-General Xavier Perez de Cuellar from his office to the nearby heliport. The helicopter was to be ready at 3:30 a.m. for Perez, and he left at 3:00 a.m. in his limousine, accompanied by the security men. There was little traffic on the streets by the East River. A few shops on the East Side had already put out Christmas decorations. The night was clear, quiet and peaceful, befitting the season of Advent.

The limousine had just gone under an overpass when the motor stopped and the headlights went out. Richard, who was driving the car, and Dan, who was sitting next to him, looked at each other. Whatever it was, it meant danger. Dan grabbed his mobile radio. It didn't work. The telephone in the automobile was also dead. They were left completely to their own devices. Now it meant putting into practice what they had been trained for over the years, specifically, how to deal with dangerous situations.

Richard pushed the car back under the overpass to a position that seemed to offer the best protection, while Dan, revolver in hand, scanned the surroundings for a possible source of attack.

But what he saw robbed even the very experienced and hardened security agent of his breath. There, above a multi-storeyed residential building about two blocks away from him, an oval object, glowing reddish-orange, was hovering in the sky. "Get the binoculars! There's something very strange flying up there!"

The apartment house in Manhattan, above which the UFO hovered on November 30, 1989, photographed from the position in which Perez de Cuellar's limousine was standing.

UFO above a building in Manhattan, photographed on November 9, 1965, during the big blackout.

It was something huge in size, two-thirds the width of the building. A beam of whitish blue light came out of its bottom, aimed at a window on the twelfth floor. The back door of the limousine opened, and Perez de Cuellar asked, "What's going on?" "Come out, Sir! This you've gotta see!" called out Dan.

The ghostly scene developed before the eyes of the 3 men, who watched it alternatingly through a pair of binoculars. At first, a small being, with a big head and gray-white skin, slid out of the window, followed by a woman with black hair, dressed in a white night dress, rolled up in a fetal position. Behind her were two more of the little gray beings. "The poor woman," said Perez de Cuellar, with a strong South American accent, "it looks like they're kidnapping her! And we can do nothing to help her!"

Now the beam withdrew. The oval disc lit up its original color of orange-red. It then glided off at high speed above the heads of the 3 men over the overpass, the entrance to the Brooklyn Bridge. Finally, it dove down in a wide curve into the East River, not far from Pier 17, behind the bridge. Richard went to the car and started it. Everything functioned now without any problems.

"We can go, sir," he said. But Perez still looked thoughtfully into the distance where the UFO had disappeared. "Drive to the side of the road. We'll wait here. I want to see that thing when it comes out again." They waited 45 minutes. Nothing happened. The East River was flowing silently, showing no signs of anything unusual having happened there. The radio kept calling, "Where are you? The helicopter is waiting for the Secretary-General." They had to go. A schedule of important appointments was waiting for Xavier Perez de Cuellar, Secretary General of the United Nations.

For more than 20 years, Budd Hopkins had been studying reports of people who had encountered the unbelievable. He is actually a painter and a sculptor, a celebrated contemporary artist whose works are exhibited in the most important museums of his native city, New York, such as the Guggenheim and the Museum of Modern Art. Many articles have been written about him in the leading art magazines in the United States, and he was honored by being included in the Board of Trustees of the Guggenheim and the National Arts Trusts. But then, his life took a turn.

In the summer of 1964, he and his wife, together with a friend of the family, saw a metallic disc that hovered in the air, carried out incredible maneuvers and then went off at incredible speed. Then in 1975, a friend who had been the witness to UFO landing in New Jersey, reported this to him. Hopkins did not believe him, but decided to investigate the matter thoroughly.

He found signs of landing and found more witnesses, amongst them one who had reported it the same night to the police. Hopkins wrote a report about this mysterious encounter for the New York newspaper the *Village Voice*. Since he was a well-known personality, *Cosmopolitan* reproduced this report and other papers published extracts from it. The response was phenomenal. Not only did other witnesses of the New Jersey landing send in their reports, but he was also literally overwhelmed by letters from people who had had similar UFO experiences. The painter noticed again and again the similarities in the experiences, and one common fac-

Budd Hopkins.

tor drew his attention in particular. Many of the witnesses had, after their UFO sighting, noticed a gap in time. There was a period of one, two or three hours, about which they could remember nothing. That reminded Hopkins of a particular case that had happened in 1961, and which, since then, has become one of the classic cases of UFO abductions.

During the night of September 19, 1961, the married couple Betty and Barney Hill, returning from a vacation in Niagara Falls, were driving back home to Portsmouth, New Hampshire. It was shortly before midnight when they saw in the southwestern sky a bright star-like object that was crossing the heavens. They drove on and the flying object appeared once more, this time much closer. At first, it was flying west, then turned suddenly and started moving towards the couple. While Hill reduced speed, his wife tried to make out details by

Betty and Barney Hill.

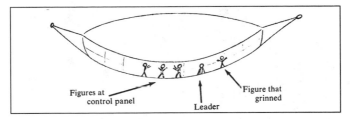

Figures at control panel

Leader

Figure that grinned

The Hills' sketch of the UFO.

looking through a pair of binoculars. Soon she could see a a disc-like object, surrounded by a brightly shining ring. Then, Barney could also see it with his naked eyes and finally the UFO stopped about 300 yards ahead of the car, at a height of about 100 feet, and hovered there. The ring of light could now be recognized as a row of windows behind which a bluish white light was burning.

Barney stopped the car and got out to have a better look at the object, taking the binoculars with him. Behind the windows, he could recognize sketchily the silhouettes of human-like beings in black uniforms, with black capes above about their heads, who then turned around and went back. During this time, Betty Hill was also looking at this from the car and heard her husband saying again and again *"I can't believe it, I can't believe it."* When the UFO started moving once more, towards them, they got frightened. *"They want to get us,"* he shouted, and ran back to the car. Then, they both heard a strange humming sound.

The next thing they could remember was that they were driving on the interstate road about 40 miles further, roughly near Ashland. "Do you believe in flying saucers?" Betty asked her husband. "Don't be ridiculous," replied Barney, "that wasn't a flying saucer." Again, they heard the same humming noise. "What's the time?" asked Betty. Barney looked at his watch. "That's impossible," he said, looking at Betty helplessly. "The watch has stopped."

When they got home, they calculated that they had been on the road 2 hours longer than they had planned.

The next day, Betty felt a strange sensitivity in her neck. She had the feeling that this could have something to do with the UFO sighting. She was afraid that she had been exposed to radioactive radiation. Her sister advised her to test the car with a compass to see whether magnetic anomalies were present. They found that there were some spots at which the compass needle reacted abnormally. During the following weeks Betty was plagued by nightmares about being abducted with Barney and taken into the UFO, and examined there. Barney developed a stomach ulcer and his blood pressure went up. His physical condition generally became worse. A regular circle of dark spots appeared in his groin. Finally, their doctor advised them to go to a psychiatrist.

At the same time, they contacted a local UFO researcher, Walter Webb, a

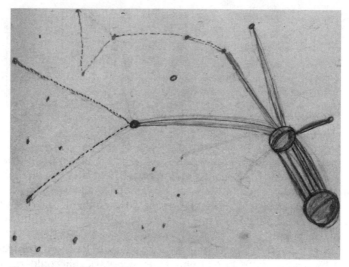

The starmap of Betty Hill.

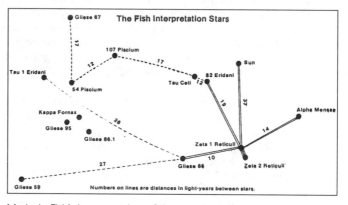

Marjorie Fish's interpretation of the starmap.

teacher at the planetarium in Boston, in the hope of getting some clarification and advice. Both Webb and the psychiatrist advised them to undergo hypnosis. On December 14, 1963, the hypnotic therapy was started at the practice of Dr. Benjamin Simon, a psychiatrist and neurologist who specialized in hypnosis. What came out of these sessions was amazing. Under hypnosis, they both related independently of each other, but completely in sync, the story of how they were taken to the space ship and examined there. Betty said that one of the aliens, about 5 feet 6 inches tall and apparently the captain of the crew, showed her a 3-dimensional model which he said was a map of the skies. During the posthypnotic sitting, Betty drew the map.

Between 1968 and 1973, the amateur astronomer Marjorie Fish attempted to interpret the map drawn by Betty. Working together with the astronomer Prof. Walter Mitchell, of Ohio State University, and Mark Steggart, of the University of Pittsburgh, she entered the data of the map into a computer and made it look for parallels between known positions of stars. The result was astonishing. The map showed our Sun and its neighboring stars, as seen from the constellation Zeta Reticuli and at a distance of 37 light years. And there were stars and constellations to be seen that astronomers had discovered only after 1968.

A further confirmation for Betty and Barney Hill's mysterious encounter came from NORAD. At 11:50 p.m. during that particular night, they had picked up an unknown object trying to land on the radar screen, as well as its departure 2 hours later.

Just like the Hills, the UFO witnesses who wrote to Budd Hopkins also complained about nightmares. So he contacted Dr. Aphrodite Clamar and Dr. Girard Franklin, 2 New York psychotherapists, and made arrangements for the witnesses who were willing to undergo hypnotic regression. It became clear that this UFO experience was often not the first in the lives of the abductees. A further regression showed that many of them had, during their childhood or youth, met the aliens. After 5 years Hopkins had become convinced that human beings were objects of research for the extraterrestrials; that they took human beings to their space vessels and examined them medically, took samples of tissue and genetic material from them, and kept some of them under observation right through their lives. The results of his study were published first in his book *Missing Time*, a documentary investigation of UFO abductions.

His book stayed on the U.S. best-seller lists for weeks. In this book, Hopkins describes 3 cases in which the witnesses had been abducted first at the age of 7, and then, at the ages of 16 or 17. What impressed and convinced Hopkins most were the circumstances of these experiences, that they all followed a clear pattern. The 37 people whose experiences he describes in the book came from all branches of life, and were of different ages and social levels. These included 2 nurses, a professional golfer, students, a lawyer from Wall Street, a painter, a journalist, a retired headmaster, an insurance salesman and a high school teacher. *"It almost looks as if we have here a kind of invisible epidemic,"* concluded Hopkins, and estimated the number of yet undiscovered cases as "at least 500," a number about which he can now, today, only laugh . . .

Soon after the publication of *Missing Time*, over 2,000 letters came from people who at least believed that they had had similar experiences. Hopkins was able to investigate closely some 180 of these cases. One of them was the story of Debbie Thomas, alias Kathie Davis, from Copley Woods, near Indianapolis, Indiana. For Hopkins, this case was so important that he devoted his second book, *Intruders,* to it, which in 1987 also became a bestseller. In addition, it provided material for a television program in 2 parts, which was shown nationwide on U.S. television in May 1992.

The Kathie Davis experience began on June 30, 1983, when at about 9:00 p.m., she looked out of the kitchen window and saw a light in the garden. A

The landing site at the farm of Debbie
Thomas, during August 1983; during January
1984 (the snow melts here first, because the
dehydrated earth cannot hold any moisture),
and in June 1984

little later, her mother noted a bright sphere only about 12 feet away from the house. She took her father's small caliber gun and went out into the garden. She found nothing there, and believed that she had been there for only 10 minutes. Then she drove over to see her friend Dee Ann, who lived about 5 minutes away, to invite her and her daughter Tammy for a night swim in their swimming pool. At Dee Ann's house, the 3 women changed quickly and drove back to Davis's house where, in the meanwhile, Kathie's father had returned from work. Kathie was surprised. Robert Davis had night duty and never came home before 11.30 p.m. She, on the other hand, could swear that it was not later than 10.30 p.m. What then had happened to this missing hour? Then, Tammy happened to put her foot on a spot where there was no grass, and it felt as if it was a warm slab of cement. Her foot went numb and she felt dizzy. It became slowly clear to the women that something was wrong. They both felt sick; Kathie's eyes were burning and inflamed.

The next morning, they had a closer look at the grass-free patch. It was a circle 7½ feet in diameter, within which the grass had become brown and dry. From this circle went a perfectly straight strip of dead grass 45 feet in length. Neighbors, too, had seen something unusual in the Davis's garden. At 10:30 they saw a flash of light and heard a low vibrating noise. The picture on their televisions changed to red. All the bulbs in the house started flickering. They believed it was an earthquake or a streak of lightning somewhere. At 10:45, things were back to normal. During Hopkins' on-site research, he found that another neighboring family had had a loss of power after hearing a droning and vibrating noise. He decided to put Kathie Davis under hypnosis. *"I guess I'm still in the garage standing in the doorway, looking out. I saw a round ball of white light looking right at me. . . . I'm just standing here looking at the light and it's looking at me,"* described Kathie under hypnosis. *"There's a lot of dark things in the yard . . . they are coming towards me, but not directly at me. Now they are gone, except one."* *"How close were you . . . ?"* Too close! . . . *I hear my name . . . It said 'Kathie'. . . . Something touched me! But I didn't think it was close enough . . . On my neck . . . it made me cringe . . . there's just the light now . . . I can't see! . . . It feels like it's going all through my body . . . "* *"Are you still holding your gun?"* *"No, I'm not holding anything . . . I'm just standing . . . and there's something holding my arm and it feels like somebody's poking my ear with a pencil or something . . . it feels like I've got an infection . . . and my ear hurts real bad! I want to touch it but someone holds my arm tight . . . I want to keep moving my arm out to touch my ear but someone's holding my arm, and I can't walk. I can't see because everything's all white and my eyes are shut . . . I think I don't want to see."*

In other cases, abductees described how implantations had been put into their ears. Is that what happened to Kathie? The fact is, during the following weeks, the young woman suffered from a bad inflammation of the eyes, frequent nausea and loss of hair. Had she been exposed to some kind of radiation?

The traces in the grass were also a mystery. There, apparently, the original clay earth had been baked into a hard stone-like mass, effected by high temperature. A chemist employed by Hopkins was able to produce a similar effect when he took a sample of the earth and subjected it to a temperature of 460°C for six hours.

Kathie's case was the most impressive one for Hopkins for 2 reasons. For the first time, there was physical proof. The traces of the landing, and the scars—which almost all the abductees had—showed that the mysterious encounter in Copley Woods was not something that had happened only in the imagination of the witness. The whole family was involved and there were other witnesses, like Kathie's mother and the two neighboring couples. The scenario, which had been sketched in broad outline in *Missing Time*, was now getting fuller.

Linda Cortile

And once again, Hopkins received letters, more than 3,000 this time. One of them came from a woman in Manhattan, Linda Cortile. A series of hypnotic sessions showed that Linda, too, an attractive brunette in her mid-thirties, had been abducted many times as a child, teenager and as a young woman in her twenties. Just one of the many hundreds or thousands of cases, as it appeared at first. And then came a call, towards the end of November, in 1989. Linda had been abducted again only 6 or 7 hours ago. Linda had gone to bed late that night, after 3:00 a.m. She was a night owl and utilized the time after her husband had gone to sleep to do the washing. A few minutes after she had laid herself down, she felt a prickling sensation and a sort of paralyzing numbness going through her whole body. She knew somebody had entered the bedroom. She tried to wake her husband, but in vain. Then she saw a small figure with a big head and big black eyes coming towards her. Her arms and torso were not yet fully paralyzed and, in a desperate effort, she threw her pillow at the intruder. At that moment, she was completely paralyzed. The only thing that she then remembered was that she was lying on a table and small hands, or instruments, were stroking her spinal column softly up and down. Budd Hopkins tried to calm her down and fixed the date for a hypnosis session.

Under hypnosis, Linda described how 3 small beings lifted her up from her bed, brought her to the living room and from there put her in a blue-white beam of light, through the closed window. She slid up slowly, in a kind of squatting position, from the twelfth floor, above the lights of Manhattan. Then she went through a circular opening on the underside of a big object that was hovering at a tilt above the building. After that, there was a medical examination on board the ship, during which the small hands were stroking and tapping on her spinal column. The return was less gentle. She experienced how she fell on her bed from a height of about a foot. Panic-stricken, she looked around, and only when she noticed that nothing had happened to her husband or to her children, could she go to sleep again.

It was certainly a wonder that the woman could be abducted in that manner right in the middle of Manhattan, but the chances of finding witnesses for this seemed, at least to Hopkins, extremely low. Judging from other cases, the UFO crew would have chosen to camouflage themselves somehow. But then, 15 months later, he received a letter from 2 alleged policemen named Dan and Richard who said they were security agents. They claimed that during that particular night they had escorted no less a personage than the Secretary-General of the United Nations Perez de Cuellar to the New York heliport and that, on the way, all 3 of them had been helpless witnesses to the abduction. Hopkins had extensive correspondence with these 2 police officers. But they became even more involved when they met Linda Cortile and identified her as the woman in the white nightdress, who had been "beamed" up to the spacecraft. Hopkins then stumbled upon another completely independent witness. A woman whose car had been under the same bridge as the limousine of Perez de Cuellar and whose engine had also stopped functioning, and who had also seen the abduction.

"And so, I was able to interview a total of 7 witnesses for the different aspects of the case," said Hopkins at the annual conference of the UFO research group, MUFON, at Albuquerque, New Mexico in July 1992. *"I have videotapes, relevant license plate numbers that have been verified, all aspects checked. Much of it was done with the help of FBI officers having expert knowledge in all the points that are important here. I have the expert opinion of two psychiatrists and two psychologists who investigated different aspects of the case. Dan's psychological crisis after the incident, Linda's emotional stability and reliability, Richard's reaction and that of the third man (de Cuellar) and of Linda's family. They all permit only one conclusion: The witnesses are speaking the truth about what they experienced. These things really did happen."*

One more piece of evidence was the X ray picture of an implant in Linda's nose, which had apparently been put in during the night in question, and was removed during a later abduction. It is only a question of time before ex-Secretary-General Perez de Cuellar gives an open statement about his experience. The case of Linda Cortille will then really become that which the participants of the Albuquerque conference had long declared it to be: the abduction case of the century, the decisive evidence that extraterrestrials are here and are carrying out a systematic program of abducting human beings, whatever their purpose may be.

And with that, the year 1992 indeed had the likelihood of going down in history as the "year of abductions." It was not only Hopkins's sensational revelations at the Albuquerque conference, or the CBS-TV mini-series that brought the breakthrough. For the first time, the subject was reported in a serious newspaper, the *Wall Street Journal,* on May 14, 1992 in an earnest tone. The headline on the front page said: *"Harvard doctor offers trauma-treatment for UFO abduction witnesses"* and referred to the work of Prof.

Prof. John E. Mack

John E. Mack, psychiatrist at Harvard Medical School, who started taking an interest in the phenomenon after a colleague of his had introduced him to Budd Hopkins. Said Mack: *"I told myself, if he believes that these were real experiences, then there must be something wrong with him."* It was only after Hopkins had introduced him to a few dozen abductees that the doctor started changing his opinion. *"What I noticed was that the stories came from people who did not know each other at all, but the stories were consistent with one another even in the details,"* said Dr. Mack. *"It is not mass hysteria. These people have no reason to tell lies and had hesitated for a long time before they started doing anything about what happened."* And what do his colleagues think about the UFO interests of the Harvard doctor? *"Many great ideas appeared in the beginning to be improbable,"* said Malkah Notman, chief of the department of Psychiatry at Harvard, to the *Wall Street Journal*.

In 1994, Prof. Mack published his study *Abductions: Human Encounters with Aliens* which became an international success. As important as Budd Hopkins's pioneering work has been, the nimbus of a Harvard Professor of Psychiatry and Pulitzer Prize winner (for his T. E. Lawrence biography *Prince of Our Disorder*) gave the subject the attention and respect it deserved. Mack, through a careful study, proved all alternative (debunking) explanations wrong and diagnosed: *"Efforts to establish a pattern of psychopathology other than disturbances associated with a traumatic event have been unsuccessful. Psychological testing of abductees has not revealed evidence of mental or emotional disturbance that could account for their reported experiences."* But what impressed him most was the consistency of the experiences of people with completely different social, cultural and educational backgrounds, who had neither met nor had knowledge of one another before. *"Psychological, or unconscious or inner experiences, or past experiences which determine present experiences, are very private,"* said Prof. John Mack when I interviewed him in May 1995 in Washington D.C., *"they differ among people enormously. If you are having a symptomatic expression of something that happened to you when you were a child or if you have been abused or if you're having dreams or some kind of fantasy this will be very personal, very variable among individuals. You will not have a consistent complex narrative which is similar from one person to another from the beginning to the end. If anyone behaves like that, it's real experience. Something which is generated internally does not have this quality."* Dreams and fantasies are as individual as humans are, but the abductees all described the same details. More than that, they react to their abduction just like people react to real experiences. Some were even trauma patients, showing symptoms of a post-traumatic stress disorder (PTSD), as it was diagnosed in the cases of veterans of the Vietnam war, a psychological reaction to a severe traumatic experience.

For Mack, the abduction phenomenon has the potential to revolutionize our world view. He concluded: *"The abduction phenomenon has important philosophical, spiritual, and social implications . . . What the abduction phenomenon has led me (I would now say inevitably) to see is that we participate in a universe of universes that are filled with intelligences from which we have cut ourselves off, having lost the senses by which we might know them."*

Dr. Mack is not the only renowned U.S. scientist who took up this rather sensitive subject. Dr. Leo Sprinkle, Professor of Psychology at the University of Wyoming and member of the renowned American Association for the Advancement of Science, examined 2,000 abductees and made personality profiles of each one of them. The result was that they were quite representative of the average personality of the grown-up American of today. They could not be classified as persons given to fantasy and nothing pointed to their *"tending to neurotic or psychotic reactions. Everything seems to point towards a program of conditioning our cosmic consciousness. The purpose of these encounters seems to be to initiate individuals and to stimulate the entire society."* Physics professor Dr. James Harder from the University of California in Berkeley interviewed over 150 abductees under hypnosis, and Dr. Thomas E. Bullard of Indiana University evaluated over 3,000 abduction cases. Of 193 cases where the same person had been involved in more than one episode, Bullard found that 163 showed an identical sequence of procedure:

- Capture
- Examination
- Conference (period of communication)
- Tour (to show the spacecraft)
- Otherworldly journey
- Theophany (messages of a spiritual nature)
- Return
- Aftermath (experiences thereafter)

In about two-thirds of the cases, the kidnappers were described as humanoid, about 4 feet tall, with big, hairless heads, huge slanting black eyes, small mouths and noses, slim bodies and long arms. The communication took place telepathically, that is, the abductees heard the voices of the aliens in their heads. In most cases, they glided up a beam of light into the UFO or were carried to the space vessel by the crew. In 80% of the cases, the UFOs were disc-shaped with a dome on top. The inside was usually cold and clammy, with a diffused light. The abductees were laid on a table, which resembled an operating table, and examined with the aid of instruments. The reproductory organs seemed to be of great interest. Often, samples of the hair, the skin or body fluids were taken, or needles were pushed into the bodies of the abductees, sometimes for the implanting of small objects. Then, in most cases, there followed a telepathic communication, sometimes a tour of the spacecraft, or the showing of pictures from another planet. In some cases a desert planet was shown, where the sky was dark and the people there lived only in subterranean spaces. Then, they were warned about the ecological destruction of the Earth. Over-population was, they said, one of the biggest problems. According to the aliens, our Earth is suitable only for 3 billion people.

But how many human beings are abducted? "One out of 40" estimated the former CIA and USAF advisor and later "UFO pope" J. Allen Hynek, who died in 1986. At that time it sounded fantastic. Then a Gallup poll among 6,000 U.S. citizens brought up similar figures. The poll was conducted by the Roper Organization in 1992, a demographics institution moderately well-known in the United States. Eleven questions were asked, 5 of them with the aim of identifying probable abductees. Whoever answered 4 or more of these questions with a "yes" had grounds to assume that he or she had been abducted in the past. The relevant questions asked were:

1. Have you ever awakened paralyzed, sensing a strange figure or presence in the room?
2. Have you ever experienced an hour or more of "missing time"?
3. Have you ever felt like you were actually flying through the air without knowing why or how?
4. Have you ever seen unusual lights or balls of light in a room, without understanding what caused them?
5. Have you discovered puzzling scars on your body, without remembering how or why they got there?

The results were astonishing. 18% of the Americans said "yes" to the first question, 13% to the second, 10% to the third and 8% each to questions 4 and 5. Two % of the 6,000 Americans questioned answered 4 or more questions with a "yes"—or, one in 50! But that would mean 3.7 million adult Americans had been abducted. Besides that, Roper found that the last mentioned group of affirmers were people with above average education and who were politically or socially more active than the average citizen. The term "invisible epidemic," postulated by Budd Hopkins, had obviously become a fact.

This evoked the interest even of established scientific institutions. In June 1992 a group of open-minded scientists organized the "Abduction Study Conference" at the Massachusetts Institute of Technology (MIT), one of the most respected scientific institutions in the United States. It was perhaps the highlight of the "year of abductions" and was, doubtlessly, an historic event. Host of the conference was the MIT Physicist Prof. David E. Pritchard, with Prof. John E. Mack as co-chairman. Eight of the 54 speakers were professors of leading universities, 23 had a Ph.D. or M.D. after their names, 21 were professional psychiatrists or psychologists. They all presented scientific papers with titles like "Methodological Problems in Abduction Work to Date," "A Comparative Study of Abduction Reports," "Medical Examination and Subsequent Procedures," "The Hopkins Image Recognition Test (HIRT) for Children," "Are UFO Abductions a Universal or Culturally Dependent Phenomenon?", "An Experimental Study of the Reliability of Hypnotic Abductee Data," "Follow-up of Diagnostic Positives," "Validating the Roper Poll: A Scientific Approach to Abduction Evidence," "Investigating and Correlating Simultaneous Abductions," "Personality Characteristics of UFO Abductees," "Comparisons with Psychological Indicators of Other Anomalous Phenomena," "Resolution of Phobias from Recall of Abductions," "The Relationship of Abduction Reports to Folklore Narratives" and "Avoiding Abductee Contamination and Therapist/Abductee Relations." The results of the conference, published in its 683-page Proceedings, confirmed the reality of the abduction phenomenon and set a milestone in its public acceptance, at least in the United States.

One of the more spectacular revelations made at the conference proceedings was the discovery of "brain scan anomalies of 2 abductees," as presented by Pat Marcattilio. Working with two abductees whose case was also studied by Prof. David Jacobs of Temple University, Marcattilio learned about their memories of implants put into their heads through the nose by their alien abductors. In an attempt to verify their claims, he organized a Magnetic Resonance Imaging (brain scan) of their heads at a neurological practice in New York City. Indeed, the MRI scan located *"a 3 mm zone of high intensity within the posterior sella turcica"* in one case, a *"3 mm module in the left lobe of the pituitary gland"* in the other case. His was the first evidence that there seems to be a physical reality behind an important aspect of the abduction phenomenon.

But this discovery was just the beginning. In the following years, researchers reported a few more cases of implants, either located by CAT scans, MRI or, in other portions of the body, X rays. In 3 incidents, implants were retrieved. In one case an implant was sneezed out; in another case it slowly started to protrude through the skin and came out completely a couple of weeks later. But then in 1995, several implants, located through X rays in the area where the abductees remembered their injections, were surgically removed under controlled conditions. Houston-based pediatrician Dr. Roger Leir learned about these cases from Derrel Sims, a hypnotherapist and head of the Houston UFO Network (HUFON) and offered his voluntary help for such extraordinary operations. On August 19, 1995, he removed 2 implants from the big toe of a woman and another one from the area between the thumb and the index finger of a man. The surgical procedure was unusually painful for the patients, indicating that the implants were connected with the nervous systems. As Dr. Leir explained: *"Before removal of the object in the hand, an electromagnetic energy detector was used to examine the affected area. The resultant field was so strong that the patient had to be taken into the parking lot where there were no electromagnetic energy sources and checked again. The repeated examination also revealed the same type of signal strength. The same test was carried out after the object was excised and in its container. There were no field emissions whatsoever."*

The first implant was flat and triangular, each side 5 mm long. Although metallic, it was wrapped in a very tight membrane. The other 2, also wrapped in the same type of membrane, were smaller and resembled cantaloupe seeds, 2 × 4 mm in size. Under black ultraviolet light, all 3 objects fluoresced in a bright green color. Moreover, they turned out to be magnetic. Under analysis, the black metal core turned out to consist of an interesting alloy with a high degree of silicon. The analysis of the membrane revealed *"proteinaceous coagulum (made from blood protein) and keratin (a protein that toughens the hard epidermal tissues, the hair and nails)."* Soft tissues from the area surrounding the implants were sent for pathological analysis, which revealed *"numerous peripheral nerves and pressure receptors; no evidence of inflammation, either acute or chronic, no inflammatory cells or infiltrates, no fibrosis."* This is absolutely unusual for the presence of any foreign body in human tissue, since an inflammation is the usual physical reaction to any "intruder."

The conclusion is fascinating. Whoever implanted the objects obviously wrapped them in a membrane of keratin taken from the abductee's body. Averting inflammation may be the explanation behind the "scoop marks" so often reported in cases of abduction. Further, the implant is somehow connected with the nervous system, obviously to retrieve data. This, of course, is evidence for a technology at work—a technology far beyond our accomplishments so far.

The abduction syndrome is by no means a purely American phenomenon. The British writer Jenny Randles can document 12 cases in Great Britain. One of them was the mysterious encounter of police officer Philip Spencer in the North, who was going through the Ilkley Moor early in the morning of December 1, 1987. When he came back 2 hours later than planned, he remembered only having seen a being about 4 feet tall with long arms and a big head and having photographed it. He had followed this little man to the top of a hill, looked down and seen for a few seconds, a silvery disc about 36 feet in diameter, which suddenly ascended and disappeared in the sky. *"I am being laid on a table. There's a ray over me . . . like a pillar. It's coming down to me. I hear again this voice . . . it says 'we won't harm you, don't be afraid,' "* said the policeman later under hypnosis.

The physicist Prof. Thales Shonya and his brother Prof. Gela Shonya, chief physician of a clinic of the Academy of Sciences in Tblissi, capital of the Georgian Republic in Russia examined over 200 cases of abduction. The Shonya brothers estimated the total number of cases to be about 2,000.

One case of abduction in Russia had already been mentioned in Prof. Zigel's reports (See Chapter 13). The witness was a Lt. V. G. Palzev, who after 2 years finally decided to talk about his experience, which had happened on the night of June 15 in 1975. Palzev was hitchhiking to his home town of Borisoglevsk where he was going to visit his sick son. In the village of Gribanovka he got out of the truck because it was going in a different direction. As the lieutenant was standing on the lonely country road hoping for a lift he noticed that the night was bright and lit by the moon. The road was flanked on both sides by trees and, at about 1:50 a.m. he saw a light between the trees. He thought that it might be a parked car, just the opportunity he had been waiting for. He ran towards this supposed car which, he soon noticed, seemed to be standing on a newly ploughed and freshly sown field. But when he got to a distance of about 300 feet from it, he was surprised to see it was not a car at all. It was an object like nothing he had ever seen before, a disc with a transparent and partly lit dome, hovering above the ground. When he was about 150 feet from it, Palzev could see the silhouette of 3 small humanoid figures *"with heads like ostrich eggs"* inside the vessel. When he was within a hundred feet of the disc, he suddenly felt a force like an invisible net which pressed him together. He felt this pressure all over his body and tried to overcome it, but lost consciousness. When he woke up again, Palzev found himself about 300 feet away from the place where he had started. His cap lay near him, his new leather briefcase looked suddenly old and dirty. The object was still there. It lifted up to a height of about 10 feet and Palzev felt a gust of wind blowing past him. Then it ascended higher and, when it was about 60 feet above the ground, glided off at an angle over the road. The object was silent and after a few seconds it finally shot off into the sky at a very high speed. Some minutes later a motorcycle appeared, but by then the object was out of sight. Palzev looked at his watch. It was 2:45 a.m. and he had thought that hardly 15 minutes had gone by, not the 50 shown by his watch!

During the next couple of years, Palzev was repeatedly the victim of nightmares and again and again felt the desire to relate his experience to someone. In May 1977, Palzev and Zigel visited the landing spot. The ground had not been ploughed for a long time but, compared to the rest of the field, all the plants within that spot showed extremely poor growth. Zigel wrote a report about this and recommended a hypnosis session as the best way to find out what had happened during the missing 40 minutes. This was unfortunately never carried out.

In Germany there are, meanwhile, over 120 documented cases which are being investigated by me and the UFO researchers of MUFON-CES. Similar incidents have occurred in Italy, Spain, France, Belgium, Sweden, Finland, Venezuela, Argentina, Chile, Brazil, Puerto Rico, Australia, New

Zealand, South Africa, Zimbabwe, Japan, and yes, even in China, Java and Malaysia. Even if the pattern and the description of the kidnappers differs sometimes, one thing is certain: we are dealing here with a global phenomenon and abductions are physical occurrences for which there have been witnesses.

There was the case of the lumberjack Travis Walton which brought about a turning point in the study of abductions. If there had been only speculation until then that abductions were only psychological phenomena, this case proved their physical reality, for Travis was abducted in front of 6 witnesses who saw a beam of blue light lift him up to the UFO. Although it belonged to one of the best documented UFO cases, the Walton case did not earn the attention that it deserved for a long time. But that changed in 1992 when the producer of "Intruders," Tracy Torme, announced for 1993 the

Travis Walton

filming of *Fire in the Heavens, the True Story of Travis Walton*. This Paramount film, however, unfortunately proved to be a complete distortion of the Walton case.

Way back in 1975, on November 5, Travis Walton (22) belonged to a 7-man team of lumberjacks and was working at the Apache-Sitgrea National Park. At 6:00 p.m. they stopped work. The men had had a hard day, were tired, and drove home in silence along a lonely mountain road. Suddenly they saw "a fire in the sky;" a big shining thing hanging over a clearance not far from the road. They stopped to have a better look at it. It was a luminous disc, vibrating and shining in an orange yellow light. Travis jumped out of the car and ran out towards the craft. His colleagues tried to stop him, calling out, "Come back, you idiot!" but he went ahead anyhow, disregarding their warning. He reached the craft, stood almost underneath it, when suddenly a blue beam of light came out of its underside and knocked him down. Travis fell back and lay as if dead on the ground. This was enough for his co-workers. "They killed him! This goddamned thing killed him!" they shouted, and Mike Rogers, foreman of the team, stepped on the gas, to "get out of here, before it comes and kills us, too."

He did not stop before they reached the safe distance of nearly a mile and were sure that the UFO was not following them. The men looked around and saw a flash of light between the trees, which seemed to suggest that the strange craft had departed. Hoping so, they went back to the spot, to save the body of their colleague, but found no trace of Travis. After a long search, they drove back and told the Sheriff about what had happened, who said mildly that he found it difficult to believe them. Nevertheless he initiated an extensive search without any success. He then arrested the 6 men on suspicion of murder. But when he put them through a lie-detector test, they all passed, with the exception of 17-year-old Steve Pierce who was too excited and jittery. But this still didn't convince the Sheriff who was quite sure the lumberjacks had killed Travis.

Five days later Walton found himself at the edge of a road near Heber, Arizona, 30 miles away from the place where he had disappeared. Still slightly giddy, he staggered to the nearest gas station, called his mother and got himself picked up. He was thoroughly distraught, felt as if he had been dried out, and had strange prick marks on his right arm. He, too, had to go through a lie-detector test and he finally agreed to undergo a hypnotic regression. Under hypnosis he described how he had become unconscious under the beam of light, how he had lain on a table in a room with gray metal walls surrounded by slim chalk-white little men, about 4 feet 8 inches tall, dressed in brown overalls. They looked like well-developed fetuses, with disproportionately large heads and big dark eyes. Later he was in another room which had the shape of a dome. He went around rather aimlessly until he met a man with blond-brown hair and gold-brown skin, dressed in a radiant blue space suit, black boots and a helmet. Travis tried to make contact with him but without success. The stranger just did not react. It looked as if Walton was inside a mother ship, for the man led him silently to a dimly lit, clammy room in which a number of vehicles were standing, which resembled the one he saw in the forest. Then in another room he found himself in front of 2 other men and a good-looking woman. She instructed him in sign language to lie down on a table, then she put a mask over his face, and he became uncon-

Alien sketched by Travis Walton.

scious. The next thing that he remembered was lying on the ground near the road to Heber, watching a luminous disc just disappearing in the sky.

But as spectacular as this case was, the real impact on public awareness of these experiences was made by an abduction case that Budd Hopkins would have preferred to file away as being of little importance. But the victim was too well-known for that—the abductee was Whitley Strieber, the famous author of thrillers and horror novels. Strieber wrote about his experience with aliens, and what makes his megahit *Communion* worth reading are his reflections about his experiences. In its sequel *Transformation*, also a best-seller, Strieber described in more details how the abduction experience changed his life and widened his consciousness.

For 6 months *Communion* was at the top of the *New York Times* best-seller list in 1987, before the film version was released 2 years later.

Strieber's experience started on December 26, 1985, when he was spending the Christmas holidays with his wife in a log cabin in a remote area of

New York state. Shortly after he had gone to sleep that night, he heard funny noises. He got up and looked around. He saw the bedroom door being opened slowly and a small figure creeping through the half-opened door. Strieber could not move at this point. The being was perhaps about 3 feet 10 inches tall, wore a kind of helmet and a breastplate. Strieber became unconscious and remembered later—only under hypnosis—that he was carried out of the cabin. He wanted to defend himself but couldn't. He then realized that he was sitting in a clearing in the forest and was astonished that he did not freeze, although he was naked. To his left he saw a small being, dressed with in overalls, whose face looked like a mask. Suddenly he was floating and he saw trees below him. Then a dark floor came sliding under his feet and covered this view. He found himself sitting in a circular room with a dome-like ceiling. The air in the room was stuffy and dry; the predominant colors were gray and brown.

The light was diffuse without there being any clear source of illumination. There was one being on the left and one on the right. One of them took a shining needle about as thick as a hair out of a box and explained to Strieber telepathically that the needle would be pushed into his brain. Strieber got into a panic. But he endured the procedure without suffering any damage. Then he was taken to another room which looked like a small operation theater, with a table in the middle and 3 rows of benches fully occupied by crouching figures, some with round, others with slit-shaped eyes. The most impressive one was also the biggest, being about 5 feet tall, delicate and with hypnotizing, slanted eyes. It had something insect-like about it.

The next day Strieber felt pretty awful. When neighbors were telling his wife about having seen strange lights during the previous night, he paid only very casual attention to their conversation. During the following days, he suffered from attacks of weakness and fever, pain in the head and ears. Early in January the local paper reported UFO sightings at the time in question. Then Strieber noticed that one of the books that friends had presented to him at Christmas dealt with UFOs. He started reading and got frightened. He read about visits to the bedroom like he had had, and learned that Budd Hopkins, whom he knew as a painter, was one of the leading experts in the field. Back in New York he called Hopkins. He wanted to get to know him and wanted to find out what had happened.

Through hypnosis he learned that his contact with the aliens on December 26 had not been the first one. He had been abducted once before October 4, 1985, also from the same log cabin, when he had woken up seeing a blue light on the roof of the living room. After that, a figure wearing a kind of cape came into the bedroom. Strieber could vaguely see its bald head and big, insect-like eyes. The being touched his head with a staff, showed him pictures of a doomsday catastrophe and gave him warnings about the ecological destruction of our planet.

Friends who were staying with the Striebers in the log cabin during that weekend remembered seeing a bright light coming in through the window and hearing a loud bang, followed by *"the patter of little feet in your bedroom."* But they thought the noise came only from the cats.

Strieber's son had also been abducted that night. Later he dreamed that *"a number of little doctors carried me out to the veranda on a stretcher. I was afraid and they said 'we won't hurt you.' "*

On March 21, 1986, back in the log cabin, Strieber woke up once more in the night. He was paralyzed and unable to open his eyes, but he felt something being stuck into his nostril and slowly pushed upwards. During the following days he suffered from nosebleeds and, after March 25, his wife and son also started suffering from nosebleeds. A doctor diagnosed a slight lump. During a further encounter 2 triangles were scratched on his arm. The beings warned him about the consequences of the hole in the ozone layer and taught Strieber to recognize his fears and to overcome them.

"The visitors have said 'we recycle souls,' and—of the earth—that 'this is a school' " wrote Strieber. *"It may be exactly that—a place where souls are growing and evolving toward some form that we can scarely begin to imagine."* But Strieber asks himself why he had been chosen. Together with Hopkins and various hypnotists, he decided to fish in the past. With their help he discovered indications of abductions during his childhood, at the age of 12 and later as a teenager. The communion with the visitors seemed to have stretched right through his life.

Today Strieber is convinced:

> If visitors are really here, one could say that they are orchestrating our awareness of them very carefully. It is almost as if they either came here for the first time in the late forties, or decided at that time to begin to emerge into

The alien, which was sketched according to Whitley Strieber's description, has a very ancient double: a mask from Vinca, Bosnia, dated approximately 5,000 BC.

our consciousness. People apparently started to be taken by them almost immediately, but few remembered or reported this until the mid-sixties. Their involvement with us might have been very intimate, though, right from the beginning. Many of those who have been taken report very early childhood experiences, some dating considerably earlier than the first reported sightings of discs, which began right after World War II.

What may have been orchestrated with great care has not been so much the reality of the experience as the public perception of it. First the craft were seen from a distance in the forties and fifties. Then they began to be observed at closer and closer range. By the early sixties there were many reports of entities, and a few abduction cases. Now, in the mid-eighties, other people and myself—for the most part independent of one another—have begun to discover this presence in our lives. Even though there has been no physical proof of the existence of the visitors, the overall structure of their emergence into our consciousness has had, to my mind, the distinct appearance of design."

Perhaps Strieber had been chosen because he was in an excellent position to initiate millions of people into this deeper message of the UFO phenomenon. Perhaps the abduction of Linda Cortile had also been staged to involve one of the top politicians of our planet, and possibly to induce him in the near future to break his silence and tell the public officially about the presence of aliens. Strieber asks,

Will the visitors emerge into our world in a flood of memory? and if so, then why? Why not simply land, open the hatch and come out? It could be that they wish to avoid what Cortez did with such eagerness. It is not difficult to crush the flowers of a culture's spontaneity. A friend of mine sat in a Native American medicine circle within hearing distance of a hissing interstate highway—and he heard the emptiness in the old chants, the sadness where conviction once rang. And no new stories are being woven in Papua, New Guinea. The streets are becoming a ramshackle version of Lansing, Michigan. It's all turning into rock 'n' roll. The scepters of the kings are being broken up for firewood and the old, rich truths of that culture now seem to its inheritors an embarrassment.

Would we not all risk being lost in nonmeaning if an apparently superior visitor culture emerged suddenly into the open? Science, religion, even the arts might be shattered by the appearance of a culture that already knew everything we want to know about the universe. Unless, of course, it were to emerge by giving us understanding of its truth and its strengths as well as its weaknesses, rather than overwhelming us into a state of blind awe.

Maybe that is why 2 triangles were inscribed on my arm: to symbolize that we are each a tiny, complete universe, a small but valid version of the whole; that the smaller is not less perfect than the greater, but only less mature.

Budd Hopkins even believes that there is something the aliens could learn from us, namely the beauty and depth of emotions which control human life.

"Our unbelievably rich emotional life, our inner life, our feelings for our children, all these human emotions which they apparently lack: that seems to be something that they find interesting in us. It looks almost as if we were at least in this aspect their teachers, that they are here to learn something from us, since we are their brethren in space. And that is one of the most important things that we can learn from all these experiences of humans with UFO crews—that it is absolutely wonderful to be a human being."

One of the earliest known cases perhaps gives us the key to understanding the strategy of the extraterrestrials. It happened on August 13, 1975, and typically enough, the abductee was a sergeant of the U.S. Air Force, Charles L. Moody.

Moody, a veteran of the Vietnam war who had served in the Air Force for 14 years, had just come home from night duty at the Holloman AFB in New Mexico. It was 11:30 p.m. That afternoon he had read that during the following night there would be a meteor shower and the best viewing time would be 1:00 a.m. After a wash and change, Moody switched on the TV and watched the "Tonight Show." When the show ended at 12:30 a.m., he got into his car and drove out into the desert to watch the night sky unhindered by the lights of the town of Alamogordo. Since the papers had spoken of a shower of meteors, he was rather disappointed when all he saw was one single shooting star. He sat in his car smoking a cigarette when suddenly he got the shock of his life.

A large metallic, partly lit, disc-shaped craft came shooting down from the sky only about 100 yards away from him. Sgt. Moody, who believed that he knew every type of aircraft, was surprised. He had never seen anything like this one before. It was about 55 feet wide, 18–20 feet high and hovered about 20 feet above ground. It fluttered a bit, then stabilized itself and came slowly towards Moody. It was getting a bit too weird for Moody, so he rolled up the window and was about to start his car, but the motor would not work, in fact, the entire instrument panel was dead. It couldn't be the battery that was causing trouble, since he had changed it only the month before. Keeping an eye on the object that was still coming towards him, he tried again and again in vain to get the motor going. When the object was about 30 feet away from him, still hovering in the air, he heard a high-pitched hum and could make out a long window of about 3 feet in width, behind which he could see shadowy forms of human-like beings. Moody then lost consciousness.

The next thing he remembered was that he was still sitting in his car, watching the object disappear in the sky. On turning the ignition key, the motor started. He stepped on the gas and drove off, half-dazed. Back home, he went into the kitchen and looked at the clock. It was 3:00 a.m. Moody couldn't believe it. The last time that he had looked at the watch it had been 1:15 a.m., and that was only a few minutes before the strange object appeared. Now his wife Karen woke up and he told her all that had happened. They didn't pursue the matter further.

But during the next few days, Sgt. Moody had pains in the lower part of his body and also eruptions on his skin. He confided his experience to a former colleague, Dr. Abraham Goldman, who was now a psychological and neurological counseler. The doctor showed him a method of self-hypnosis and meditation through which he himself could get information about the lost hour. Further, Moody came into contact with Coral and Jim Lorenzen, the founders of APRO (Aerial Phenomena Research Organization), America's oldest UFO research organization, whose special field was encounters of the third kind. During the following weeks Moody told the Lorenzens that the experiences of August 13 came slowly back into his conscious memory. At first he remembered the beings, 5 feet tall, humanoid, with disproportionately large bald heads, small noses and ears, thin lips, all dressed in black overalls, with the exception of the one who was apparently their chief and wore silver white overalls.

Shortly after, Moody started to remember details of the abduction. He almost had the feeling that "they" were controlling the return of his memories. At first he saw 2 beings coming towards him while he sat paralyzed in the car. The next thing he remembered was lying on a dull metallic table. He felt numb, couldn't move, but was aware that the "chief" in white silvery overalls came to him. The being "spoke" to him, or rather he heard his voice in his head without the being moving his lips. Whereas until then he had been terribly frightened, the friendly, almost fatherly, manner of the chief calmed him down. He asked him how he felt and promised, "We won't hurt you, Charles." Moody wondered that the being knew his name, but did not address him by his nickname "Chuck." He then stood up and could see the details of the room. He was a bit perplexed by the "indirect lighting." The leader explained to him that he had no need to feel anxious and soon Moody noticed that the leader could obviously read his thoughts. His questions were answered before he ever asked them.

He was taken to another room and the alien touched Moody's back with a staff-like gadget *"to heal his wounds."* The sergeant looked around. The room was *"clean as an operating theater."* The walls and furniture were made of a kind of dull metal or perhaps plastic. The lighting was indirect here too, without any visible source of light. Moody thought *"if I could only have a look at the engine room of the spacecraft, that would be wonderful."* The chief alien put his hand on his shoulder and asked him to follow him. They went into a small, empty and dimly lit room which seemed to be a kind of lift. When its sliding doors opened again, Moody was standing in a room of about 25 feet in diameter with thin pillars in the middle which seemed to go through its ceiling. Surrounding the pillars were 3 cavities, covered by small glass domes, in which were big crystals with 2 rods. In the corner was a big black box, but he could see no sign of cables or wires. The alien explained to Moody that this was not their main ship, but only a kind of reconnaissance craft and that the mother ship was circling around the earth in an altitude somewhere between 400 and 6,000 miles. After some time, they got into the lift again. The alien now told Moody that it was time to leave. He put both his hands on Moody's head and said that he was to forget everything he had seen on board for 2 weeks. After this period he would understand and remember. A moment later Moody found himself back in his car.

Unfortunately, before the Lorenzens were able undertake a thorough investigation of this case, Moody was transferred to Europe. At first he was told that he was to leave the United States on November 29, 1975, but then the date was changed to October 29. Before that Moody told the Lorenzens that he was willing to undergo a hypnotic regression—which now became impossible. However, the Lorenzens visited Moody in Europe with the lie-detector expert Charles McQuiston, who analyzed the statements of the sergeant and came to the conclusion that he was telling the truth.

The Lorenzens were even more impressed when, at the same time they investigated the Moody case, they learned about the Travis Walton abduction. The description of the aliens as given by Moody and Walton were identical, but Walton could not have known about Moody. It was only in December 1975, two weeks after Walton's return, that the *APRO Bulletin* published Moody's story.

The visitors had told Sgt. Moody on board their craft that man would misunderstand their presence and their intentions. They were not the only extraterrestrial race that would visit Earth to study the planet and the human culture, but there were many races who worked in friendly cooperation, although their native planets were light years apart. "*It is not our problem to accept you, but yours to accept us.*" Their task on Earth is not without danger for them. Their spaceships could be destroyed by atomic weapons, and even conventional weapons could do a lot of damage. They had further problems with our radar, for it disturbed their propulsion mechanism and could block the system by the ultra-high frequency electromagnetic waves it sends out. This statement is confirmed by an FBI memorandum released in 1980 and dated March 22, 1950, in which crashed UFOs are explained. "*The government is using a strong radar system in this area and it is believed that radar disturbs the control mechanisms of the saucers.*" Sgt. Moore continued: "*They, too, are afraid for their lives and do everything to protect themselves, but they come with peaceful intentions.*" Their plans for the future, as Sgt. Moody told the Lorenzens on October 6, 1975, is that "*in about 3 years they will make themselves known to all mankind. It won't be a friendly meeting but a warning for the whole of mankind. Their plan is for limited contact, and only after 20 years of deeper investigation could a closer contact take place. Only then would we be in a position to understand them fully, who and what they are.*" Three years later, in 1978, there was a unique UFO demonstration. It was not an open contact, and no mass landing but simply, as Moody had announced, a global demonstration of their presence. Twenty years later would be 1998. Let's wait and see if mankind is now ready for open contact.

CHAPTER 21

A Challenge for the United Nations

On December 18, 1978, UFOs were at last on the agenda of the plenary session of the United Nations. It was to be decided whether to accept or reject the proposal 33/426 which, though called *"Establishment of an agency or a department of the United Nations for undertaking, coordinating and disseminating the results of research into unidentified flying objects and related phenomena,"* contained in its actual text no specific plans for such an institution. Instead of that, it initially called upon the member states to investigate UFO phenomena at a national level and forward the results to the Secretary-General of the UN, who would then decide whether he would merely put them into the files or forward them to one of the United Nations' bodies. Further, the proposal recommended that the United Nations Committee on the Peaceful Uses of Outer Space (UN-CPUOS) should take specific steps during the following year, 1979, in the matter of UFOs. Proposal 33/426 was accepted by the plenary session but the UN did not act according to it and the proposed activities of the Outer Space Committee were not implemented. Observers of the situation, especially ex-UN employee Maj. Colman S. VonKeviczky, spoke of a conspiracy of the United States which did everything behind the scenes to obstruct the formation of a UN UFO department, as was shown by his own personal experience; a similar proposal made by him in 1967 had cost him his job at the UN.

Col. Colman S. VonKeviczky, M.M.S.E., born in Hungary, finished his studies at the Royal Hungarian Maria Ludovika Military Academy in 1932, graduating with a Master's Degree in Military Sciences and Engineering. He studied 2 more years at the UFA Motion Picture Academy in Berlin. He then joined the Royal Hungarian Army, where he attained the rank of Major. In 1992, the Defense Ministry of the now democratic Hungary promoted him to the rank of a full Colonel. From 1938 until 1945 he was chief

The UN headquarters in New York. Is the United Nations prepared for a contact with extraterrestrials?

of the audiovisual department of the General Staff and Defense Ministry. When Russia invaded Hungary he fled to Bavaria in Germany and was soon employed by the U.S. Army as a cameraman. It was not long before his expertise was rewarded and he became a director for the production of army documentary films. When he emigrated to the U.S. in 1952 his attention was drawn for the first time to UFOs. It was the year of one of the first big sighting waves. He obtained copies of the first snapshots and movies taken of UFOs to evaluate them, being himself an expert in photography. After studying them, he was surprised to see that evidently authentic photographs were being pooh-poohed by the Pentagon and the Air Force. His interest in UFOs grew and he started studying their types and modes of operation as reported from all over the world; and was surprised by the "*apparent uniformity of their behavior.*"

Major Colman S. VonKeviczky, MMSE

After being sworn in as a citizen of the U. S., VonKeviczky took up a post in the Public Information Office of the UN in New York. In 1965 there was another wave of UFO sightings in the U.S. Now that was he an employee of the UN, VonKeviczky thought that his hour in connection with UFOs had come. He compiled a memorandum consisting of 124 documents, addressed to U Thant, Secretary-General at that time. On February 9, 1966, U Thant invited VonKeviczky to his office for a personal discussion of the situation. During this meeting VonKeviczky pointed out to the Secretary-General that both the Russians and Americans had opened fire at UFOs and that this policy was a major threat to international security. *"The most important thing to do is to inform the people,"* he had said. *"The UN should create an agency, whose task would be to try to establish contact and cooperation with the aliens."*

U Thant was so impressed by the documentation that he told VonKeviczky to work out a plan for the starting of such a project. Further he invited another supporter of the "extraterrestrial visitors" theory, Prof. James McDonald of the University of Arizona, to speak before the UN Committee on the Peaceful Uses of Outer Space (CPUOS). According to the *New York Post* of June 27, 1967, U Thant *"confided to friends that he considers UFOs the most important problem facing the UN next to the war in Vietnam."* At once both superpowers intervened with unusual unity of purpose. Whereas the Soviet ambassador to the UN, Nikolai Trofimirovich Federenko, declared that UFOs were *"merely the nightmares of imperialistic and capitalistic nations,"* the U.S. comforted the Secretary-General by saying they intended to give the envisaged task to one of the bigger universities, so that an agency under the UN would be superfluous. The university that was finally commissioned was that of Colorado. And at the insistence of the U.S. government Maj. Colman S. VonKeviczky was relieved of his post at once. But the ex-Hungarian did not give up. Shortly after that he was the keynote speaker at an international UFO congress.

The Seventh International Congress of UFO Researchers, organized by Karl and Anny Veit and the German UFO Study Society (DUIST), was held at Mainz, Germany from November 3–6, 1967, under the chairmanship of the DUIST honorary president, Prof. Hermann Oberth, the "father of space travel" and former teacher of Wernher von Braun. On November 5, 1967, the 800 participants who attended the congress, including delegates from 24 nations, passed the so-called "Mainz Resolution," addressing the governments of 124 nations. The resolution stated: *"All nations must unite in mutual research and scientific cooperation to investigate and solve this*

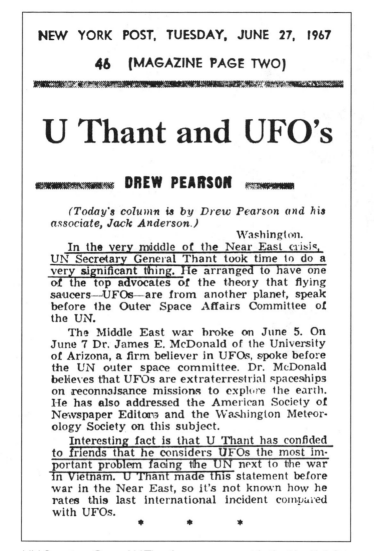

NEW YORK POST, TUESDAY, JUNE 27, 1967

46 (MAGAZINE PAGE TWO)

U Thant and UFO's

DREW PEARSON

(Today's column is by Drew Pearson and his associate, Jack Anderson.)

Washington.

In the very middle of the Near East crisis, UN Secretary General Thant took time to do a very significant thing. He arranged to have one of the top advocates of the theory that flying saucers—UFOs—are from another planet, speak before the Outer Space Affairs Committee of the UN.

The Middle East war broke on June 5. On June 7 Dr. James E. McDonald of the University of Arizona, a firm believer in UFOs, spoke before the UN outer space committee. Dr. McDonald believes that UFOs are extraterrestrial spaceships on reconnaisance missions to explore the earth. He has also addressed the American Society of Newspaper Editors and the Washington Meteorology Society on this subject.

Interesting fact is that U Thant has confided to friends that he considers UFOs the most important problem facing the UN next to the war in Vietnam. U Thant made this statement before war in the Near East, so it's not known how he rates this last international incident compared with UFOs.

*　　*　　*

UN Secretary-General U Thant's announcement in the *New York Post* that UFOs are the most important problem facing the UN, next to the war in Vietnam.

problem for the common cause and for the mutual advancement of our peaceful relationship in outer space."

One answer to the dispatch of this proclamation came from the Austrian ambassador to the UN, Dr. Kurt Waldheim, who was himself later Secretary-General of the UN. Waldheim said, "*I take pleasure in acknowledging receipt . . . and can assure you that the contents of your communication*

UN Secretary-General U Thant

have received full attention. I have also not failed to bring them and in particular the Resolution of the seventh International UFO Congress to the attention of the Outer Space Affairs Group to the Secretariat of the United Nations." What came out of that was never revealed. Only the fact that some of the items in the "Treaty on Peaceful Uses of Outer Space" are almost identical with items in the "Mainz Resolution," indicating that the resolution had found some attention.

When the journalist Ilse von Jacobi interviewed U Thant during the International Conference of World Federalists in Ottawa (August 23, 1970), she broached the subject of UFOs: his opinion about them and whether the UN would take up the problem. All that she could elicit from him was, "*There are things about which I neither can, nor am permitted, to speak. . . . Yes, it is certainly possible. As soon as one of the governments represented at the UN officially presents a motion to investigate these things, we shall set up a department to deal with the study.*"

A. H. Abdel-Ghani, chairman of the UN space committee (CPUOS) expressed himself in the same strain in answer to a letter written by Maj. VonKeviczky: "*It must first be decided by one of the member states that this is a subject which should be brought before the committee, for it to be taken up officially.*"

One year later the UN had to tackle the UFO problem again. In front of the First Committee of the General Assembly, Twenty-Sixth Session, Grace S. K. Ibingira, Ambassador of Uganda, declared, "*there is a lot of evidence for their existence and there are a number of eminent scientists in the USA, the Soviet Union, Great Britain and in many other countries who believe that a number of these 'unidentified flying objects' are interplanetary spaceships. . . . I propose that the commission consider the possibility of including a clause, or statement in the preamble of the Convention of Liabilities, enjoining all nations indulging in space research, to take care that their spacecraft and other space objects do not react in a provocative or inimical manner on encountering other space objects, which are apparently controlled by an intelligence. I have already emphasized that this is not an acknowledgement of extraterrestrial life. It is, I think, nevertheless a matter of prudence.*"

On February 23, the ambassador expressed his disappointment about the reaction of the UN to his suggestion. It seemed to him, "*that a strong pressure is being exercised within the UN, which prevents this matter from receiving the attention it deserves.*" Already on April 13, 1971, the Canadian Foreign Department had declared in answer to a query, "*The Canadian Government does not underestimate the seriousness of the question of*

UFOs, and this matter is being considered and studied in a number of departments and agencies. Canada's representatives at the UN have maintained a close liaison with the Secretariat and other missions in New York on this subject. But we do not consider that the prospects for the adoption of a resolution by the General Assembly at the present time are encouraging." Who was putting pressure on the UN?

Uganda's UN Ambassador Grace S. K. Ibingira and delegation.

Ibingira, in a letter to Colman S. VonKeviczky, mentioned the *"great apathy"* of the UN in the matter and suggested for the future the starting of a strong lobby at the UN. *"I believe that the time is coming when efforts of organizations like yours will no longer be ignored by the world body."*

The first step in this direction was taken by the tiny Caribbean state of Grenada and its Prime Minister Sir Eric Gairy. On October 7, 1975, he appealed to all nations at a plenary session of the General Assembly to establish an *"agency to investigate the numerous unknown phenomena, which at present are still awaiting a solution."*

During a second speech, exactly one year later, on October 7, 1976, Gairy again repeated his appeal. At once he received enthusiastic and congratulatory letters from UFO organizations from all over the world. He was invited to speak at a UFO Congress in Acapulco, Mexico from April 22–24, 1977. Gairy addressed the delegates with these words:

"In the same way that this planet is the accepted inheritance of all humanity, knowledge is also to be shared for the benefit of all mankind, and, in this

light, one wonders why the existence of UFOs or flying saucers, as they are sometimes called, continues to remain a secret to those in whose archives repose useful information and other data. While we appreciate that some countries consider this to be in the interest of military expedience, I now urge that a different view be taken because it is my firm belief that the world is ready, willing and mature enough to accept these phenomena." Enthusiastic applause. The 400 delegates from 16 countries, amongst them numerous scientists, unanimously declared their support for him.

In a letter to Secretary-General Waldheim written on July 14, 1977, Gairy requested including the question of *"establishment of an agency or a department for undertaking, coordinating and disseminating the results of research into unidentified flying objects and related phenomena,"* in the agenda of the 32nd plenary session of the UN.

A week later Gairy's draft resolution A/32/142 followed, calling upon the Assembly to accept that it:

1. Considers it desirable to establish, as a matter of priority, an agency or a department to conduct and coordinate research into unidentified flying objects and related phenomena;
2. Requests the Secretary-General to examine this matter with a view to recommending to the General Assembly at its present session an organizational structure within the United Nations, through which the objectives set out could be most effectively achieved.
3. Declares 1978 'International Year of Unidentified Flying Objects,' during which the following action would be undertaken:
   a. Holding of the Second International Congress on UFO Phenomena in Grenada, which was unanimously approved by the First International Congress held at Acapulco.
   b. Issue of a special commemorative stamp series by Grenada and the United Nations . . . illustrating the milestone events of international research into UFOs

In his third speech before \the UN, on October 7, 1977, Gairy declared that he had himself already seen a UFO and had been *"overwhelmed by its appearance." His demand for "the establishment of a department or agency of the United Nations to study the UFO phenomenon"* was at first presented to the plenary session for discussion. A special political committee, under the chairmanship of Bernhard Neugebauer, the East German ambassador to the UN, was entrusted with the task of examining the problem internally at first. *"There are good possibilities for contact between terrestrial spaceships and spaceships of an extraterrestrial origin,"* declared Grenada's Minister of Education, Dr. Wellington Friday, Dean of the University of Grenada. *"As human beings we should give serious consideration to preparing ourselves as earth people for the psychological and philosophical contact or communication with alien intelligent life."* Addressing the major powers he added, *"All countries have a legitimate right to all*

Grenada's Prime Minister Sir Eric Gairy (right) with Colman
VonKeviczky.

*data derived from the UFO research . . . and just because Grenada is a
small and young nation, we can develop new initiatives in the direction of
this interplanetary matter, whereas the superpowers hide the true evidence
about UFOs."*

Something strange happened after that. At the second meeting of the
Special Political Committee, held to discuss Gairy's petition, Grenada suddenly changed course, steered away from concrete proposals and went over
to making general suggestions. Draft resolution A/32/142 was being
superceded by a new one, number A/SPC/32/L.20. Friday announced that,
*"in view of the baffling nature of the problem, and the fact that some dele-
gations might need more time to study it,"* he now believed that it, *"would
be preferable to refrain from pressing for the establishment of a UN agency
at present, and to seek instead to have the Secretary-General study the
scope of the various aspects of the item and undertake a study for consideration by the General Assemby at its 33rd session."*

There was suddenly no more talk about the proposals contained in the
resolution A/32/142 to declare 1978 as the year of UFOs, to convene a
world UFO congress or to bring out a series of postal stamps. During the
third session of the Special Political Committee, it was decided to get the
"recommendations of the SPC"—not the draft A/SPC/32/L.20 itself—
adopted by the General Assembly by consensus (general consent by apparent majority, but without actual counting of votes). The "recommendations"
left all future action to the sole decision of the Secretary-General. Who was
at the back of this change in position can be inferred from a remark made
by Dr. Friday: *"I would like to thank those delegations, particularly the del-*

In 1978, commemorating the "Year of UFOs," Grenada brought out a series of stamps to honor "the attempt to find out more about UFOs and related phenomena."

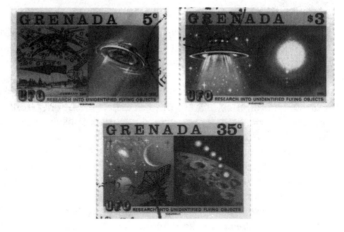

egation of the United States, for having modified their stand so that the draft recommendation (not the draft resolution) *could be adopted by consensus.*" But it was Washington that, according to the news agency Associated Press, had declared on November 30, 1977, "*that the U.S. government was expressly against the establishment of a UN department for investigating UFOs*" and did everything to thwart it.

On December 13, 1977, the General Assembly adopted only the decision 32/424, which requests the Secretary-General to "*transmit the the text of the draft resolution . . . to the member states and to interested specialized agencies, so that they may communicate their views to the Secretary-General . . . and to bring their replies to the attention of all the member states and inter-*

ested specialized agencies." This watered down version of the original resolution A/32/142, being quite in line with the unofficial motto of the UN "Do something for nothing," remained a sort of goodwill declaration until Gairy realized that his initiative was sinking into quicksand. It was only when Francis M. Redhead, Grenada's deputy ambassador to the UN, sent a letter to Secretary-General Waldheim on July 7, 1978, requesting Waldheim to at least inform Redhead about the matter, that something started happening.

Waldheim arranged a private meeting for July 14, 1978, at which Gairy was to present a number of international UFO experts and 2 well-known witnesses, amongst them VonKeviczky, the Blue Book advisor Prof. J. Alan Hynek, the French astrophysicist Jacques Vallee, Claude Poher from France, Leonard Stringfield, David Saunders, science reporters Lee Spiegel from the USA and Martin Gleisner of the special political committee. But, through the machinations of Hynek and Vallee, Colman VonKeviczky was struck off the list, as persona non grata of the U.S. government. Since his initiative in 1966 he was not welcome, and these 2 gentlemen, whose governmental associations were only too obvious, threatened to boycott the meeting if VonKeviczky took part in it. This is not surprising when one remembers that Hynek, already in 1953, was an advisor to the OSI (Office of Special Intelligence) of the CIA in UFO matters, and that Vallee coordinated the satellite tracking system of the French Ministry of Defense.

Thus, the invitation sent to VonKeviczky was withdrawn on July 13, 1978, a day before the meeting. Gairy wrote to him, saying, *"My government knows that ICUFON possesses the best evidence for the existence of UFOs and their operation, but, my cabinet and I, and the scientists who are supporting us, will never agree to the presentation before the General Assembly of facts and evidence that would show that the UFOs are a matter concerning International Security."* VonKeviczky's comment to that was, *"The United Nations was created by nations in order to guarantee worldwide security and peace and not to support the scientific investigation of UFOs."*

Instead of that, Vallee, addressing the Special Political Committee on November 27, 1978, declared UFOs to be "psycho-physiological phenomena," *"Although the UFO phenomenon is real and appears to be caused by an unknown physical stimulus, I have so far failed to discover any evidence that it represented the arrival of visitors from outer space."* He then referred to indications for their physical manifestation which certainly required investigation and went on to talk about *"psycho-physiological effects on the witnesses"* and *"social belief systems generated in all the nations represented here by the expectation of space visitors,"* a belief he claimed to be *"independent of the physical reality of the UFO phenomenon."* Also, he said, *"the belief in the imminence of UFO contact is an indication of a widening gap between the public and science."* Of course he *"did not think that these things were part of the task or the budget of the United Nations."* Naturally, with such "expert recommendation" the subject was quickly wiped off the table, although the 2 UFO witnesses who had taken part in the Waldheim Meeting of July 14 gave quite a different picture.

One of them was the U.S. Army Col. Lawrence E. Coyne. While piloting an army helicopter on October 18, 1973, Coyne and 2 other witnesses who were with him had a close encounter with a cigar-shaped UFO (See Chapter 17). But, as spectacular as this Coyne case was, the really sensational revelation made at the secret conference came from one of the first men in space, the U.S. astronaut and Air Force Lt. Col. Gordon Cooper. After he had had his own UFO experiences, Cooper had come to the conclusion that UFOs exist and are of extraterrestrial origin. He had also developed some remarkable ideas which he hoped could be put into practice through the UN.

As early as August 15, 1976, during an interview with the *Los Angeles Herald Examiner*, Cooper had said: "*Intelligent beings from other planets visit our world in an effort to make contact with us. During my flights I have encountered various space vessels. NASA and the U.S. government know this and possess a great deal of evidence. Nevertheless they are keeping silent, so as not to alarm the public.*"

Lt. Col. Gordon Cooper, born on March 6, 1927, at Shawnee, Oklahoma was chosen in 1959 to be one of the first of 7 astronauts of the United States who were trained to fly in the Mercury capsule. In 1945 he had joined the Army Air Corps, as the U.S. Air Force was called then. From 1949 to 1956, he was stationed at Neubiberg Air Force Base in Bavaria; from there he went to Edwards Air Force Base in California. He started on his first flight into space on May 15, 1963, in the *Faith 7* and proved, by staying in orbit for 34 hours and 20 minutes, during which the capsule went 22 times around the earth, that human beings could stay in space for longer periods. The second flight, from August 21–29, 1965, was with Charles Conrad in the *Gemini V* space capsule, which went 120 times around the earth, during a period of 190 hours and 56 minutes. In 1970 he left NASA and retired from the USAF as Lieutenant Colonel. After that, he was technical director of Walt Disney Productions in California and engaged in obtaining financial support for a private center for new technologies. He is now president of the Galaxy Aircraft Corporation in Van Nuys, California.

Cooper revealed his story for the first time in May 1978 to the science reporter Lee Spiegel of the popular science magazine *Omni*. He had had his first UFO encounter in 1951 at Neubiberg in Bavaria, Germany. UFO squadrons flew over the air force base there for a period of 2 days. "*The first day, a weatherman spotted some strange objects flying at high altitude and, before long, the entire fighter group was out looking at these groups of objects flying over. But, unlike jet fighters, they would stop in their forward velocity and change 90 degrees, sometimes in the middle of their flight path.*" The maneuvers repeated on the following day, when Cooper and the other pilots started their jets and tried to pursue the strange, otherworldly craft. Cooper said: "*We never could get close enough to pin them down, but they were round in shape and very metallic looking.*" When I interviewed Cooper personally on December 14, 1993, at Van Nuys, he told me "*the objects were lenticular-shaped and flew in formation from east to west.*"

Six years later, in May 1957, Cooper was a Project Manager at Edwards

The historic UN UFO conference, under the chairmanship of Secretary-General Kurt Waldheim (middle); (from L to R) the astronaut Gordon Cooper, Jacques Vallee, Claude Poher, J. Allen Hynek, the Prime Minister of Grenada Sir Eric Gairy; (right) Morton Gleisner, Lee Spiegel, Len Stringfield, David Saunders. (United Nations photo.)

Air Force Base. After lunch on this particular day, Cooper assigned a team to photograph the vast dry lake beds near Edwards. As Cooper told me during our on-camera interview, the "*crew was filming the installation of a precision landing system out on a dry lake bed. They made stills and movies and were filming the whole installation and then they came running in to tell me that there was a UFO, a little saucer that came right over them and put down a three-gear and landed about 50 yards from them. And as they proceeded to go and get a closer shot of it, it lifted up, pulled the gear in again and disappeared at a rapid rate of speed.*"

"*There were varied estimates by the cameramen on what the actual size of the object was,*" Cooper confessed to Lee Spiegel, "*but they all agreed that it was at least the size of a vehicle that could carry normal-sized people in it.*" Unfortunately, Col. Cooper did not have the luck to have been there personally during that sighting, but he saw the film as soon as it was developed. "*It was a typical circular-shaped UFO,*" recalled the astronaut, "*but not too many people saw it because it took off at quite a sharp angle and just climbed straight on out of sight.*" He didn't ask any more questions about who had seen the UFO "*because there were always strange things flying around in the air over Edwards. People just didn't ask a lot of questions about things they saw and couldn't understand. They would just shrug their shoulders and simply chalk up what they had seen to another experimental aircraft that must have been developed at another area of the airbase . . . but it wasn't that. I think it was definitely a UFO. However, where it came from and who was in it is hard to determine, because it didn't stay around long enough to discuss the matter—there wasn't even time to send out a welcoming committee!*"

"I had to follow my directions as a military man; I looked into my directions about who I was to call and report this, which I did, and they ordered me to get the film developed and send it in with one of our general's airplanes to Washington, which I did, and that was the last time I heard about it," Cooper told me. Although originally he was certain that within a few weeks he would get an answer about what his people had seen, the film disappeared officially—into some dark corner. *"I am sure there is a great deal of information in Washington if only somebody could just find it. I don't think a great deal of UFO information was ever classified. As a rule, if you really want to keep something secret, you don't classify it. I'm sure that a lot of that stuff was probably just thrown into a file someplace in Washing-*

WED ENTERPRISES • A Division of Buena Vista Distribution Co., Inc., subsidiary of Walt Disney Productions

imagineering®

GORDON COOPER
Vice President
Research and Development

November 9, 1978

Ambassador Griffith
Mission of Grenada to the United Nations
866 Second Avenue
Suite 502
New York, New York 10017

Dear Ambassador Griffith:

I wanted to convey to you my views on our extra-terrestrial visitors popularly referred to as "UFO's", and suggest what might be done to properly deal with them.

I believe that these extra-terrestrial vehicles and their crews are visiting this planet from other planets, which obviously are a little more technically advanced than we are here on earth. I feel that we need to have a top level, coordinated program to scientifically collect and analyze data from all over the earth concerning any type of encounter, and to determine how best to interface with these visitors in a friendly fashion. We may first have to show them that we have learned to resolve our problems by peaceful means, rather than warfare, before we are accepted as fully qualified universal team members. This acceptance would have tremendous possibilities of advancing our world in all areas. Certainly then it would seem that the UN has a vested interest in handling this subject properly and expeditiously.

I should point out that I am not an experienced UFO professional researcher. I have not yet had the privilege of flying a UFO, nor of meeting the crew of one. I do feel that I am somewhat qualified to discuss them since I have been into the fringes of the vast areas in which they travel. Also, I did have occasion in 1951 to have two days of observation of many flights of them, of different sizes, flying in fighter formation, generally from east to west over Europe. They were at a higher altitude than we could reach with our jet fighters of that time.

I would also like to point out that most astronauts are very reluctant to even discuss UFO's due to the great numbers of people who have indescriminately sold fake stories and forged documents abusing their names and reputations without hesitation. Those few astronauts who have continued to have a participation in the UFO field have had to do so very cautiously, There are several of us who do believe in UFO's and who have had occasion to see a UFO on the ground, or from an airplane. There was only one occasion from space which may have been a UFO.

If the UN agrees to pursue this project, and to lend their credibility to it, perhaps many more well qualified people will agree to step forth and provide help and information.

I am looking forward to seeing you soon.

Sincerely,

L. Gordon Cooper
Col. USAF (Ret)
Astronaut

LGC:jm

NOV 1 5 1978

Astronaut Gordon Cooper's letter to Granada's UN Ambassador
Griffiths.

*ton and forgotten. I'm certain there are roomfuls of such movies that have
things in them that people don't even know about. As soon as you classify
something, every Congressman in the U.S. tries to get a hold of it, and
broadcasts it all over the country. Our classification system isn't always the
best way to keep something a secret."*

Four months after his confidential talk with Secretary-General Waldheim, Cooper formulated his point of view regarding the UFOs once more in writing, in a letter to Grenada's ambassador to the UN, Griffiths.

I wanted to convey to you my views on our extraterrestrial visitors, popularly referred to as UFOs, and suggest what might be done to properly deal with them. I believe that these extraterrestrial vehicles and their crews are visiting this planet from other planets which obviously are a little more technically advanced than we are here on earth. I feel that we need to have a top-level coordinated program to scientifically collect and analyze data from all over the earth concerning any type of encounter, and to determine how best to interface with these visitors in a friendly fashion. We may first have to show them that we have learned to resolve our problems by peaceful means rather than warfare, before we are accepted as fully qualified universal team members. This acceptance would have tremendous possibilities of advancing our world in all areas. Certainly then it would seem that the UN has a vested interest in handling this subject properly and expeditiously.

I should point out that I am not an experienced UFO professional researcher. I have not yet had the privilege of flying a UFO nor of meeting the crew of one. I do feel that I am somewhat qualified to discuss them since I have been to the fringes of the vast areas in which they travel. Also, I did have occasion in 1951 to have two days of observation of many flights of them, of different sizes, flying in fighter formation, generally from east to west over Europe. They were at a higher altitude than we could reach with our jet fighters of that time.

I would also like to point out that most astronauts are very reluctant to even discuss UFOs due to the great numbers of people who have indiscriminately sold fake stories and forged documents, abusing their names and reputations without hesitation. Those few astronauts who have continued to have participation in the UFO field have had to do so very cautiously. There are several of us who do believe in UFOs and who have had occasion to see a UFO on the ground or from an airplane. There was only one occasion from space which may have been a UFO.

If the UN agrees to pursue this project, and to lend their credibility to it, perhaps many more well qualified people will agree to step forth and provide help and information.

Astronaut Gordon Cooper, 1993

Meanwhile, some of the member states of the UN had replied to Waldheim's invitation. India proposed that the subject of UFOs be put under the global designation, "Search for Extra Terrestrial Life/Intelligence" and passed on to the Committee on Peaceful Uses of Outer Space, which could then commission scientists to investigate the nature of UFOs. India recommended "setting up a panel of scientists to study and analyze data on the (UFO) question." Seychelles supported the proposal of Grenada without any reservations.

After the Secretary-General had taken up the recommendations of A7SPC/32/ L20, there followed on November 27, 1978, at the 35th session of the Special Political Committee, a new attempt of Gairy's. With the draft resolution A/SPC/33/L.20, he now proposed that the Assembly:

1. Recommend that, in consultation with appropriate specialized agencies, the UN initiate, conduct and coordinate research into the nature and origin of UFOs and related phenomena.
2. Request the Secretary-General to invite member states, specialized agencies and nongovernmental organizations to transmit to him by 31 May 1979 information and proposals which could facilitate the proposed study.
3. Further request the Secretary-General to appoint at the earliest possible date a 3-member group of experts under the aegis of the CPUOS (similar to the suggestion of India), for the purpose of defining guidelines for the proposed study.
4. Decide that the group of experts should meet during the sessions of the CPUOS to study information and proposals submitted to the Secretary-General by member states, specialized agencies and nongovernmental organizations.

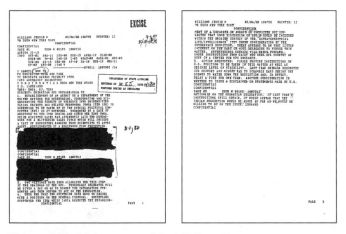

This confidential document of the U.S. State Department was sent to the CIA, NSA, Pentagon, Air Force and NASA, and reveals the U.S. policy against attempts by Grenada to investigate UFOs.

5. Further decides that the group of experts should report on its work through the CPUOS to the General Assembly at its 34th session.
6. Decides further to include in the provisional agenda of the 34th session of the General Assembly an item entitled, "Report of the group of experts of CPUOS for the defining of guidelines for the study of UFOs and related phenomena.

But once more, this concrete advance ended up as a nebulous "recommendation" of the committee to the General Assembly: *"The General assembly invites interested member states to take appropriate steps to coordinate on a national level scientific research and investigation into extraterrestrial life, including UFOs, and to inform the Secretary-General of the observations, research and evaluation of such activities; the General Assembly requests the Secretary-General to transmit the statements of the delegation of Grenada and the relevant documents to the Committee on the Peaceful Uses of Outer Space, so that it may consider them at its session in 1979; the CPUOS will permit Grenada, upon its request, to present its views to the Committee at its session in 1979. The Committee's deliberation will be included in its report which will be considered by the General Assembly at its 34th session."*

On December 18, 1978, the General Assembly accepted this recommendation of the SPC by consensus, as "Resolution 33/426." But even this diluted version was ignored by the Committee on Peaceful Uses of Outer Space. Instead of giving Grenada the chance to present its views to the committee—as was stipulated—it was merely requested by the Secretary-General that the records of the hitherto presented proposals of the Caribbean State regarding the UFO phenomena be submitted. And soon, the "Gairy-problem" was also solved. In March 1979, the democratically elected Prime Minister of a commonwealth country was deposed by a communist guerrilla movement under the leadership of the terrorist Maurice Bishop, which, surprisingly enough, had the support of the United States of America. And with that, the subject of UFOs, in spite of Resolution 32/426, was removed from the UN agenda.

Colman VonKeviczky was the only one who did not give up. As a true modern-day hero, a man with a vision, he was not at all impressed by the opposition of the United States Government against his initiative. In his "Blue Memorandum," which he sent to representatives of all members states of the United Nations General Assembly, he proposed "Project WASA," the World Authority for Spatial Affairs," an *"independent spatial authority of volunteer and interested nations to contact and communicate with the exploring extraterrestrial (UFO) forces, to maintain and endure the global peace, and secure an evolutive progress of all the nations toward the interplanetary age."* Since then, he keeps asking UN representatives regularly to do something about the UFO question. His plan which he outlined at the UFO World Conference, Dialogue with the Universe, at Frankfurt in October 1989 was to:

Call an International Security Congress of the nations, attended by official representatives from the military, scientific fields, space exploration programs and UFO pioneer researchers to build a World Authority for Spatial Affairs, for the following reasons:

a. An immediate cease-fire on alien spacecraft and aliens is necessary;
b. To contact and communicate with the UFO forces;
c. To inform the nations on the problem and ask for their cooperation;
d. To start to educate the "Space Age" generation, within the framework of the United Nations University.

United Nations! Prevent humanity's cataclysmic 'star wars' inferno and solve the UFO problem . . . before it is too late . . .

His proposal, the "Frankfurt UFO Resolution," was signed and supported by all the participating experts, including the author of this book.

In fact I agree with VonKeviczky and consider his proposal the only logical series of steps to end the international cover-up and prepare mankind for a new, cosmic age. Without a doubt the UN would be the ideal starting point for the establishment of contact with extraterrestrials. It is, after all, the only political organization that represents the total humanity of the planet Earth. And, in fact, just recently, something actually started happening at the UN. On October 22, 1992, in the auditorium of the UN library at its headquarters in New York, a symposium was held under the chairmanship of the UN official Mohammed Ramadan and the diplomat Michael Geoghegan. It was called "Symposium about extraterrestrial/human interaction, and the future of humanity." During this symposium, 3 prominent UFO researchers and 2 abductees briefed UN representatives and officials about the matter. At the end of the conference, the speakers sent an open letter to the UN Secretary-General Butros Butros-Ghali and the Committee for Peaceful Utilization of Space, in which they referred to the UN resolution 32/426: "*The UFO problem is the most important matter in this century and has great scientific and technological significance, for it inherently poses innumerable implications arising from the existence of alien intelligence. We, therefore, call upon the UN to establish an agency or a department for undertaking, coordinating and disseminating the results of research into unidentified flying objects and related phenomena. When the first open contact with an extraterrestrial intelligence occurs, one of the first questions they will ask will be, 'Who speaks for the people of planet Earth?' We must then answer, 'We, the United Nations Organization!'* "

And, in fact, at that time, extensive preparations had already been made for this occurrence, which could prove to be the greatest adventure in the history of mankind.

CHAPTER 22

A Chance for Humanity

Where the mind is without fear, where the head is held high,
Where knowledge is free,
where the world has not been broken up into fragments by narrow
  domestic walls,
Into that Heaven of Freedom, my Father, let my country awake!
                                    —Rabindranath Tagore, "Prayer"

The largest radio telescope in the world, at Arecibo, Puerto Rico. It was here that on October 12, 1992, Project SETI was initiated.

It was a rather simple ceremony, far from being as spectacular as a rocket launch and without any countdown. And yet, it symbolized a decisive step for mankind's exploration in space. On October 12, 1992, at 3:00 PM, the astronomer Jill Tarter, in front of the TV cameras from all over the world and bombarded by photographers' flashes, leaned over a panel at Arecibo, Puerto Rico, and pressed a button which put the most powerful radio telescope in the world (with a bowl-antenna 100 feet in diameter) into operation. At the same time, one of her colleagues activated a second radio telescope at the Goldstone tracking station near Barstow in the Mojave Desert. Perhaps the future will prove that this October 12th was a far more important day for humanity than the day Columbus discovered America, the 500th anniversary of which was marked and honored by this ceremony. For, with that ceremony, the NASA project SETI was launched: mankind's largest scale search yet for intelligence in the universe. Equipped with a budget of 100 million dollars, over 100 physicists, astronomers, computer programmers and technicians started the "Search for Extraterrestrial Intelligence," Project SETI.

At that time, it was said that these experts were to search for signals coming from extraterrestrial civilizations on all frequencies for a period of 10 years, at the behest of the space administration, NASA. The radio telescopes were equipped with newly developed Multichannel Spectral Analyzers (MCSAs), which were capable of receiving and analyzing millions of radio frequencies simultaneously. They were so sensitive that they could receive signals even from the other side of the galaxy. And they were capable of separating out those signals possibly of artificial origin, such as background cosmic radiation, gas cloud and pulsar signals.

The father of the SETI project, the American astronomer Prof. Frank Drake, had been looking out for radio signals from extraterrestrials ever since he started Project OZMA in 1960, with the Green Bank Observatory's 92-foot radio telescope in the forests of the Appalachians in West Virginia. This forerunner of the SETI project had been named after the beautiful queen of the wonderland in *The Wizard of Oz*, among whose subjects were beings with very long ears who could hear sounds coming from thousands of miles away. The ears of the Green Bank Observatory were directed at 2 stars about 15 light years away, Tau Ceti and Epsilon Eridani. It was believed possible that these stars could have earth-like planets circling around them. Soon, however, the Green Bank radio telescopes were found to be insufficient. The program was therefore terminated in July 1960, after 150 listening hours.

Professor Drake then tried to prove the plausibility of extraterrestrial life by means of a mathematical formula. The "Drake formula" ($N = R \times Ne \times Fl \times Fi \times Fc \times L$) is supposed to be an equation showing the number of intelligent civilizations in the galaxy (N = number of intelligent civilizations in a galaxy, R = mean rate of formation of stars, Fp = proportion of stars with planets in the galaxy, Ne = number of planets per solar system where life can exist, Fl = proportion of inhabitable planets with life, Fi = proportion of planets with intelligent civilizations, Fc = proportion of planets with intelligent civilizations who have developed ways and means of interstellar communication, L = the life span of such civilizations). According to this formula, depending on the values of the factors, there could be between 40 and 50 million intelligent extraterrestrial civilizations in our galaxy alone. This sounded so promising that OZMA was continued from 1972 to 1976, followed by about 50 more projects, some of which, in fact, did receive unusual radio signals.

When NASA included Project SETI in its budget in 1978, it received from U.S. Senator William Proxmire the notorious "Order of the Golden Fleece" for the most extravagant waste of the taxpayer's money. *"If they're looking for intelligent life, then they should start here in Washington,"* said Proxmire mockingly, *"and that is difficult enough, perhaps more difficult to find than anywhere else out there in the universe."* Following that, the famous late astronomer Carl Sagan met Proxmire and showed him pictures of the galaxy. He told him that there were billions of stars in our galaxy alone, which itself is one of billions of galaxies in the universe. *"We scientists have good grounds to assume that there are also billions of planets out there. It would be presumptuous to believe that we are the only intelligent form of life in the endlessness of the cosmos."* Proxmire took back his words.

Professor Frank Drake, father of the SETI project.

Sagan sent out an appeal in 1982, requesting the support of well-known scientists for the Project SETI. Fifty signatures were collected, amongst them those of Linus Pauling and Stephen Hawking. *"Intelligent organisms are just as much part of the universe as stars and galaxies,"* said a group of well-known astronomers and astrophysicists during the same year. *"One can imagine no discovery that would have a greater effect on the knowledge of mankind about itself, than the discovery of extraterrestrial intelligences."* And, therefore, despite the high costs and meager results, SETI managed, again and again, to find a place in the NASA budget. For SETI

Cartoon in the *Financial Times* on the SETI project.

carried in it the vision of a cosmic future for mankind. *"We feel there are other planets already communicating with one another,"* NASA scientist Dr. Ichtiaque Rasool stated. *"Our dream is to make Earth a part of that interstellar communication network . . . When we make contact . . . it'll be the biggest breakthrough in the history of mankind. These advanced civilizations could help us conquer problems like disease, pollution, food and energy shortages, and natural disasters."*

There was one more reason why SETI was kept alive and repeatedly supported with a budget of millions: SETI was the perfect cover-up project for the intelligence services. It conveniently diverted the attention of the public from secret UFO projects by permitting leading scientists to openly discuss the ways and consequences of communications with extraterrestrials, without awakening the least suspicion that such things had already taken place.

Howard Blum, an award-winning journalist of the *New York Times*, investigated the background of the SETI project. His work on the spectacular case of espionage of the double agent John Walker had given him access to intelligence circles in Washington, and therefore it was no coincidence when, in the spring of 1989, one of his informants contacted him. *"I've got a story for you,"* said the intelligence official, *"It has to do with unidentified flying objects."* Blum's initial skepticism was overcome when his research showed that the credentials of his informant were genuine. Documents were then passed on to him, and people involved started talking. Blum, in his best-seller *Out There*, revealed not only the existence of a UFO working group within the Defense Intelligence Agency (DIA), but also the involvement of the supersecret National Security Agency (NSA) in the SETI project.

As a matter of fact, American UFO researchers had long suspected that it was not the CIA that coordinated the secret UFO projects of the Government (its jurisdiction being mainly in foreign politics) but the NSA. Ever since its establishment on November 4,1952 the public had known not much more than the name of this organization, and because of a history of secrecy and denials its initials were either read as "No Such Agency," or "Never Say Anything." Even insiders knew very little about the NSA— only that it had been founded with $2.5 billion; that its headquarters at Fort Meade, Maryland, near Washington ("The Puzzle Palace," as insiders call it) was twice as big as CIA headquarters; and that its official annual budget totals, as a rule, above $2 billion, plus "a black budget" of $5 to $10 billion per year. *"For the CIA it's cloak and dagger, but for the NSA spying is* Star Wars," wrote Robert Parry of the Associated Press in 1982.

The journalist James Bramford, in his best-seller *The Puzzle Palace*, revealed that over 60,000 employees work for the NSA, more than for all the other U.S. intelligence services put together. In addition, the NSA has the biggest and most modern computer system of the USA, its own college with 18,000 students, its own power station and its own TV studio. All over the world, NSA listening posts eavesdrop not only on military but also civil communications. Besides that, all foreign telephone conversations between the USA and the outside world go through the NSA computers and, in case certain key expressions are used, are automatically recorded. "Big Brother is watching you"—George Orwell's vision of the future in his novel *1984*—had long been a reality for the NSA.

Since the NSA was on the distribution list of practically all relevant documents and reports released under the FOIA, UFO researchers were soon convinced that the NSA was closely following all UFO sightings. In fact, the records of the Robertson Panel, which was organized by the CIA in 1953, mention a "group meeting" of the NSA, to discuss the subject of UFOs and its security aspects, to which H. P. Robertson was invited. Edward J. Ruppelt, the head of the Blue Book team, also mentioned instructions that came from the Puzzle Palace. But when UFO researchers, invoking the FOIA, asked the NSA for UFO files, the agency gave them the cold shoulder. *"Please be informed that the NSA has no interest whatsoever in UFOs,"* was the answer given by an employee of the NSA to an enquiry from Robert Todd in 1976. Only a lawsuit brought about the release of 2 documents in January, 1979. One of them was the already mentioned "UFO Hypotheses and Survival Questions," compiled by no one less than Lambros D. Callimahos, the gray eminence of the NSA and founder of the Dundee Society, a brotherhood of elite scientists and top officers of the agency. According to Howard Blum the NSA, *"contrary to all its public statements, has been secretly monitoring and often assessing worldwide allegations of UFO activity since 1972. For the past 18 years, NSA listening posts throughout the world have operated under standing order. It is mandatory to report to Fort Meade immediately on all intercepted foreign government signals indicating intelligence that pertains to unidentified flying objects. These listening installations are required to track and report on any signals or electronic intelligence that might have an extraterrestrial origin."*

According to Victor Marchetti, one of the earlier assistants of the deputy director of the CIA and later renegade of the intelligence community, rumors were indeed going around in intelligence circles about strange, probably extraterrestrial signals the NSA had picked up. Marchetti, who had himself been employed by the NSA for some time, was at that time working as liaison officer to the NSA. But when he was asked to investigate the rumors for the CIA Deputy Director, he was met by a wall of silence. Even for SIGINT (signal intelligence) relations, the story was handled with extreme secrecy.

Encouraged by Marchetti's revelations, the American citizens' initiative, "Citizens Against UFO Secrecy," filed a lawsuit against the NSA on January 23, 1980, demanding the release of UFO documents. On March 24, the suit was dismissed. The NSA confessed to having 79 UFO files under lock and key—later this number was officially increased to 135 and then to 239—but did not find itself in a position to release them, owing to reasons of national security. Following that, CAUS lawyer Peter Gersten applied for an on-site investigation of the documents, to verify their relevancy to national security, to be carried out by the judge of a district court. Finally the court ordered the NSA representative Eugene F. Yeates to make a statement under oath, behind closed doors, in the sole presence of the judge, and to the exclusion of the lawyers. For that the judge Gerhard Gesell had to undergo a security check and was given a top-secret clearance.

At last, on October 10, 1980, Yeates made his statement, and based on this, the court came to the conclusion "*that release of this material could seriously jeopardize the work of the agency and the security of the United States.*" Thus the UFO files had to remain locked up. CAUS appealed to the Supreme Court of the United States and suffered its next defeat. On March 8, 1982, the decision of the highest court of the nation was announced: the case was not to be brought up again. The NSA was therefore allowed to hold back UFO information "for national security reasons." When finally, on April 27, 1982, CAUS asked for the release of the court records, UFO researchers received a copy of the affidavit of NSA official Yeates. Marked "top secret umbra," the highest level of secrecy for SIGINT documents, and higher than "top secret," the release of this paper was more valuable for its appearance than its content. Out of the 21 pages, 14 were completely blacked out!

Early in 1987, according to Howard Blum, the UFO Working Group of the DIA received a secret briefing paper prepared by the "*President's Office of Science and Technology,*" in which the plans for the NASA-SETI project scheduled for 1992 were outlined. "*Time had come for the Working Group to launch its first field operation,*" wrote Blum in *Out There. "Since the inquiry would involve a knowledge of signal detection procedures and electronics, it was recommended that the operatives be 'borrowed' from the National Security Agency.*" And with that 2 aims could be followed simultaneously. For one thing, NSA officials were right at the front if signals were captured. And then they were in a position to stop the information from being made public.

"Never say anything": Pages from the heavily censored transcript of the NSA representative Yeates' declaration under oath regarding the subject of UFOs.

The first step, at least towards delaying the publication of any radio contact that might be made, was the "SETI Post-Protection Protocol" which was passed at the 38th congress of the International Astronautical Federation at Brighton, England, in 1987. It was drafted by Michael Michaud, the Deputy Director of the State Department's Office of International Security Policy, who had already in 1978 stated that *"aliens from other solar systems are a potential threat to us, and we are a potential threat to them."* In this document *"Declaration of Principles Concerning Activities Following the Detection of Extraterrestrial Intelligence,"* the institutions and individuals that take part in the search for extraterrestrial intelligence, agree to deal very cautiously with the signals received. *"Every individual, public or private research institution, or governmental agency that believes it has detected a signal from or has other evidence of extraterrestrial intelligence, should . . . prior to making a public announcement that evidence of ETI has been detected . . . promptly inform all other observers or research organizations that are parties of this declaration . . . (and) his/her or its relevant national authorities . . . These will then form an international scientific commission, which will discuss the release of the information to the public."* These individuals also agreed not to answer such a signal *"before suitable international consultations had taken place."*

But even this SETI Protocol document that puts a number of hurdles on the path to publicizing, did not go far enough for the officials of the NSA. They considered the idealism of some SETI employees, like the astronomer Jill Tarter, (who openly promised to inform the public *"as soon as we are sure that it is ETI and nothing else"*)" as being *"foolish and dangerous."* For them the reception of extraterrestrial signals was clearly only a matter of national security.

A number of nightmarish eventualities were discussed by the NSA scientists, ranging from the possibility of a response to an alien signal betraying the location of the earth to the alien invader, to the danger of a cultural shock for the peoples of this earth. Should the aliens then make open and peaceful contact, it was by no means a group of international scientists or the Secretary-General of the United Nations who were to represent humanity. Under such circumstances, according to an NSA document cited by Blum, *"the government of the United States must exclusively supervise, monitor, and control all communication with other planets."* That was not merely a matter of national pride: military considerations played a big role in it. Perhaps one could talk the aliens into signing a treaty of military alliance or a commercial agreement with the United States alone, which would then guarantee the leading role of the United States of America on this earth for the third millennium. The said document goes on to say *"In conclusion we strongly urge that responsible government authorities immediately assume effective control of the SETI program."*

Apparently, this attempt of the NSA to take over effective control of the project met with the opposition of the idealistic SETI scientists and, therefore, NASA-SETI had to die before it did more damage. In October 1993, only a year after it was started, the SETI budget was reduced drastically when the NASA budget was cut down by the U.S. congress. It was only with the donations of private sponsors—amongst them the computer technology firms Hewlett-Packard, Microsoft and Intel—that Prof. Frank Drake, the father of SETI, could keep up the search for alien intelligence. This has been ongoing since January 1994, under the name PROJECT PHOENIX.

This again supported the beliefs of those who, right from the beginning, had held SETI to be a camouflage operation only, making use of the idealism of scientists like Drake and Tarter to further quite different aims. For SETI offered an excellent façade for obliging world-famous scientists to write papers on the possible intentions of the aliens and the possible results of publicizing an effected contact—subjects which had been taboo in scientific circles under other circumstances. These articles, written by well-known astrophysicists, political analysts and sociologists, however, allow us to get acquainted with the well-founded thoughts and ideas regarding our relationships with alien visitors, and also show why, now as before, secrecy is maintained in the matter of UFOs. Thus between 1986 and 1988, 3 congresses were held in Brighton, England, Innsbruck, Austria and Bangalore, India, organized by the International Astronautical Federation to discuss the *"legal, political and social implications of the discovery of intelligent extraterrestrial signals." "The discovery of an alien signal will be a profound event in the history of mankind,"* said Washington political analysts J. M. Logsdon and C. M. Anderson at the Brighton conference. In their lecture *"Announcing the First Signal: Policy Aspects,"* they declared that *"procedures for announcing to the world that such a signal has been detected and verified should be developed with probable global impacts of that announcement in mind. There almost certainly will be an intense reaction in many sectors of society in many countries. Questions of perceived security threats are likely to arise. There will be political, social and philosophical impacts on key institutions: the church, policy, the media, and cultural, scientific and intellectual organizations. The general public will certainly seek explanations, and various elites are likely to compete in providing such explanations."*

Allen Tough, professor of pedagogics at the University of Toronto, discussed "Factors that Might Encourage Secrecy." Amongst these were

the belief that people may panic; the fear of a negative impact on religion, science and culture; embarrassment; the individual and national competitive urge; avoiding a harmful premature reply; a national trade or military advantage; and the fear of a 'Trojan Horse' . . . (that) an alien race, under the guise of teaching and helping us join the cosmic community, might actually trick us into building devices that allow 'Them' to conquer 'Us' . . .

Tough leaves no doubt that governments

might also worry about the longer term effects on the culture and economy of that nation and to the whole world . . . they might believe and fear that religion, philosophy and science would . . . be ruined, outmoded, or at least demoralized. Current technology, such as transportation and space exploration, could be superceded; many jobs and the economy could be disrupted. In general, a culture can suffer from contact with a stronger and more advanced culture.

Furthermore, according to Tough,

the army and intelligence services of the nation receiving the signal could get the notion, that detailed extraterrestrial information would enable it to produce highly developed weapons, aircraft or spacecraft.

The Italian sociologist Dr. Roberto Pinotti, of the Instituto Futuro in Florence.

Tough quoted the astrophysicist Ronald Bracewell of Stanford University, who had said that it would be naïve to believe that governments would inform the public about contact with aliens. *"Every authority which is in a position to keep this a secret will try to do so at all costs, no matter what the message itself is . . . a contact with another civilization is automatically 'the most strictly guarded and best evaluated military state secret in the history of the earth.'"*

As the Italian sociologist Dr. Roberto Pinotti of the Instituto Futuro in Florence said at the Brighton conference, *"the problem of mass behavior after man's future contacts with other intelligences in the universe is not only a challenge for social scientists and political leaders all over the world, but also a cultural time bomb as well. In fact, because the impact of CETI (Contact with ETI) on human civilization, with its different cultures, might cause a serious socioanthropological shock, a common and predetermined worldwide strategy is necessary in releasing the news after the contact, in order to keep possible manifestations of fear, panic and hysteria under control. . . .*

The modern world is proud of its achievements. In spite of the fact that Copernicus showed that the Earth was not the center of the universe, man has continued to believe that even though he was not geographically in the center of the universe, he is in essence its center. This common belief would be shattered by the presence of ETI, even though there would be no evidence that the alien culture might be malevolent, and the masses would be swept into a state of fear."

Perhaps the father of Soviet cosmonautics, Constantin Tsiolkovsky, was right when he wrote: *"Perhaps life on Earth is not yet ready for contact with extraterrestrial beings . . . Such a contact will, perhaps, only damage mankind. . . . Up until recently, we have denied the possibility of alien influence in our lives. It is difficult for us to imagine that there is something which is superior to mankind."*

In other words, ignorance gives rise to anxiety; anxiety causes panic, mass hysteria and anarchy.

The Swiss psychoanalyst Carl Gustaf Jung came to the same conclusion. In 1954, he wrote an article for the Zurich newspaper *Weltwoche*. *"Should the phenomenon . . . turn out to be of extraterrestrial origin it would prove an intelligent, interplanetary connection. It cannot be foreseen what such a thing would mean for mankind. But without a doubt it would bring us into a most critical situation, comparable with that of a primitive tribal society confronted with our superior western culture . . . we would lose control, and we would, as an old medicine man once told me with tears in his eyes, 'loose our dreams.' In other words, our currently high-flying intellectual pursuits would be hopelessly anticipated and thereby paralyzed. Our science and technology would become junk. The moral meaning of such a catastrophe can be understood by observing the tragic end of primitive cultures happening in front of our eyes."*

In 1961, a study was prepared for NASA by the Brookings Institute. Entitled *"Proposed Studies on the Implications of Peaceful Space Activities for Human Affairs,"* we read on page 79 about the implications of a discovery of extraterrestrial life, quoting the well-known ethnologist Margaret Mead. *"Anthropological files contain many examples of societies, sure of their place in the universe, which have disintegrated when they had to associate with previously unfamiliar societies espousing different ideas and life ways; others that survived such an experience usually did so by paying the price of changes in values and attitudes and behavior."* That's why the study recommends *"historical and empirical studies of the behavior of peoples and their leaders when confronted with dramatic and unfamiliar changes or social pressures. Such studies might help to provide programs for meeting and adjusting to the implications of such a discovery. Questions one might wish to answer by such studies would include under what circumstances and how might such information be presented or withheld from the public for what ends?"*

"Culture shock" is an expression coined by sociologists and cultural anthropologists to describe the consequences of unprepared confrontation between two fundamentally different cultures. *"It leads,"* if we believe the sociologist Alvin Toffler, to *"bewilderment, frustration and disorientation . . . the breakdown of communication, a misreading of reality, the inability to cope. Yet culture shock is relatively mild in comparison with the much more serious malady, future shock. Future shock is the dizzying disorientation brought on by the premature arrival of the future."*

This, according to sociologists, is a cause of the worldwide wave of civil wars and racist violence in the 1990s. The world is changing too fast. Certain groups of people try to hang on to outmoded values like religious fundamentalism, tribalism or chauvinism in order to create stability. It is the senseless behavior of people who have been overtaken by time. And, for Pinotti, that is a time bomb which can explode at any time. As Pinotti stated, *"In any case it is evident that our culture is in constant turmoil. Its values are incessantly changing and a dominating sense of general disorientation prevails, involving the weakest, less intelligent and most irrational—and they are surely the majority—members of society. In this global situation the news of the existence of ETI could prove to be devastating. In fact at this particular moment what mankind needs is psycho-sociological balance and rules to follow".*

One of these socio-psychological stabilizers is the belief in man's ability to master and control the future. Politics, 5 year plans, insurance policies, social security, investments, the stock market—all are based on the concept of safe-guarding the future. The encounter with an ETI would confront us with what might turn out to be the most important factor for our future—that which turns out to be a great unknown, an undeterminable, uncontrollable factor. On a sociological scale this means a crisis of rules, values and authorities—the basics of security and the fundamentals of every society. A global attempt of "breaking with the past" would make this CETI the most exciting and maybe dramatic event in human history, causing a sudden lack of rules or anomie, usually associated with the disintegration of social structures.

Surely a "revision process" would affect every field of human activity and thought in the light of what would be defined as "The Second Coper-nican Revolution." Science would be criticized and *"new philosophical schools and cults would arise, along with traumatic theological debates on all the churches and religions; the arts would be inspired while socioeco-nomic structures as we know them today would be doomed,"* as Pinotti pre-dicts. The momentary crisis of ideologies would continue into a breakdown of political systems. Instead of these, 2 general attitudes would polarize people. There would be those who would develop a more global attitude—surely the more intellectual classes—and those who would withdraw into the snail's shell of their ethnic traditions, causing new "tribal wars" and eth-nic conflicts by trying to save their cultural identity. Surely, modern day society has everything to lose from any form of sudden contact with ETI. Everyday life as we know it would be the first victim of this frontal colli-sion . . . if we did not take the chance to let the knowledge about alien cul-tures slowly leak into our common consciousness. But since the birth of the UFO phenomenon this sword of Damocles has been hanging over our cul-ture, so we have to prepare and develop adequate measures to control the damage and make the best of it.

"If we wish to avoid such a catastrophe, the authorities in possession of important information should not hesitate to enlighten the public as soon and as completely as possible and should, above all, stop these ridiculous antics of mystery and vague allusions. But instead of that, a fantastic and false publicity has been allowed to grow up: the best form of preparation for creating panic and psychic epidemics according to Carl Jung."

Pinotti, too, sees the solution in initiating a long-term strategy: an edu-cational program to get the masses gradually accustomed to the thought of alien existence and integrating this into the world concept developed by the younger generation, at least.

"In 1974, the American film producer Robert Emenegger attempted to gauge the reaction of the public towards extraterrestrial presence by get-ting the opinions of 5 leading American social psychologists. Although they differed in their opinions regarding the premise itself that ETI visit our Earth, they were all unanimous in saying that panic was not the one and only possible reaction. The reaction would depend very much on the exist-ing belief of the public. The psychologists also said that the negative reac-

tions could be ameliorated to a great extent by the knowledge that we are masters of the situation."

"Contact-educative" films like *E.T.* and *Close Encounters of the Third Kind* by Steven Spielberg, *Starman* by John Carpenter, and *Cocoon* by Ron Howard, in addition to television series like "Star Trek" and the "X-Files," have rendered good service. Pinotti, however, leaves it open as to whether this has been pure coincidence or deliberately manipulated from above. These films, according to the sociologist, *"changed the feelings of the public in a positive sense. Unconfessed fears were replaced by hope reducing the possibility of negative consequences."*

Pinotti says,

> In other words, a long-term strategy is required, by which SETI should be integrated into a global educational program aimed at developing a common understanding of the role of mankind in the universe. This "universal consciousness" amongst the future generations is the only way by which, with our limitations and possibilities, we can hope to survive the effects of a contact. From this point of view, and in a purely psychological sense, more "universal consciousness" is present in the unconscious and uncritical belief of a child in "science-fiction aliens," than in the extensive knowledge and responsibility-conscious "wisdom" of a renowned scientist about the possibilities of extraterrestrial life.
>
> It will, in any case, be necessary to prepare the public about a contact before the news of contact is publicized. We must develop a long-term policy in which the attempts of scientists, political leaders, news reporters and media are united to create the conditions under which a confrontation with ETI will prevent traumatic results. This is an historic obligation for all of us.

Contact with a superior civilization could be the greatest chance for humanity, as we stand at the threshold of the third millennium—if we are prepared for it. It would open up new perspectives for us, a new concept of the universe and bring in a new cosmic era just as the Copernican revolution did 500 years ago, when the knowledge that the earth was not the center of the universe changed the world. That redefinition of our place in the universe led to the beginning of the era of discovery. The Renaissance led to the understanding of physical occurrences through the natural sciences, a turning away from the mythical world concept of the Middle Ages that had been spread by ill-conceived religion and its power-hungry institutions. Meanwhile, man has charted the earth to the last square foot and is yearning to explore new shores, the shores of the cosmic ocean. Men have set their feet on another heavenly body, the moon; unmanned space probes have reached the outer fringes of the solar system. The man of the future is "homo cosmicus," who is destined one day to give up his planetary isolation and to leave the lap of Mother Earth, to become an accepted member of the societies of space. How insignificant our differences on this earth are, if only we think in cosmic dimensions! Are we not all one people, children of this earth, who can solve our global problems together? The united action of all humanity is an indispensable prerequisite for solving such difficult problems as overpopulation, world hunger, the hole in the ozone layer, the greenhouse effect, restoration of destroyed ecology, etc., problems whose solutions are essential for the survival of humanity, for its continued existence in the third millennium.

No, the aliens will not steal from us the golden opportunity to learn how to help ourselves, to grow up as one united people and bear the responsibility for our home planet and its future. But the mere recognition of their existence, the encounter and communication with them could give us a new perspective, a holistic view of creation and our role in the universe. That would be the first step in the next phase of our evolution: the birth of "homo cosmicus," the cosmic man who stays in dialogue with the universe because he knows that he is part of it. This alone probably makes the UFO phenomenon the secret key to our entrance into the 21st century.

CHAPTER 23

Breakthrough

What the 1989/90 wave of sightings all over Europe seemed to promise, indeed came true in the following years. The sightings were just the beginning, the first of many waves occurring all over the planet. The 1990s have become the "decade of the UFOs." For the first time in history, large spaceships appeared over major cities and landings have happened in front of dozens of witnesses. This has caused a change in the mass consciousness. UFOs and extraterrestrials, once a ridiculed subject pursued only by freaks, suddenly became a part of pop culture. The "X-Files" has become one of the most successful TV series of the decade, not only in the U.S. but all over the world. Two of the most successful movies of the nineties, *Independence Day* and *Men in Black*, both dealt with UFOs and extraterrestrials.

If we believe in the ancient predictions and prophecies of the Mayas of Mexico, a culture known for its deep knowledge of astronomy, the nineties were the beginning of a new era, the "Era of the Sixth Sun." According to the Dresden Codex, one of the few Mayan astronomical manuscripts which survived the Spanish *Conquista*, this era began on July 11, 1991 with the great solar eclipse over Mexico, at 6 minutes and 45 seconds one of the longest in history. It was supposed to announce the beginning of great changes on the planet—and the return of the "masters of the stars."

When the total eclipse occurred, millions of Mexicans were out on the streets to witness the historic event. Whoever had a camcorder tried to film the celestial show, and of course there wasn't a single TV station in the whole country which didn't have its crews out there to report the cosmic carnival it caused in the streets of Mexico.

Jaime Maussan had had substantial experience as a television journalist at that time. He was anchorman of Mexico's "Sixty Minutes" on Televisa, the largest private network in the country. His "Programas de Investiga-

Jaime Maussan

cion" uncovered so many political and ecological scandals that Maussan received numerous international awards for his work, including an election to the Global 500 roll of honor by the United Nations Environmental Program. On the day after the eclipse, Maussan learned from his colleagues of the news programme "24 horas," that a man who filmed the eclipse had discovered a strange object on his footage. Just a week later Maussan took part in a program on UFOs and aired this video, asking the people, "If you have filmed the eclipse, look carefully, maybe you have it on your tape, too." Many did—and Maussan received 14 other tapes, all showing the same reflective, disc-shaped craft in the unusually clear, blue sky of the mostly smog-covered Mexican capital. In one of his regular programs, Maussan presented a scientific analysis of these films, proving they did not show planets or balloons, as skeptics reckoned. From that moment on, he received hundreds of videos from all over the country—documenting the largest UFO wave in the history of the phenomenon.

But already 4 days before the first video came to him, as Maussan learned later, the events of July 11 had had preview. In the evening of July 7, 1991, at about 8:00 p.m., when 4 federal policemen were driving on the Atlixcoyotl Highway from Puebla to Atlixco, they encountered a "flying light" just before they passed the El Mirador heights. The object flashed in green, red, blue and orange and approached them at treetop level. The policemen feared a collision, when it suddenly stopped and hovered absolutely silent in front of them in a safe distance. Had they until then believed it was an unknown new type of aircraft, now all doubts were gone.

The commander of the *Federales* ordered one of his men to take a picture of the object, hoping they could identify some insignia later. Just after the picture was shot, the disc made a turn and flew away at very high speed, to disappear in the direction of El Tecajete mountain, close to Mexico's largest vulcano, the Popocatepetl.

Three months later, on October 31, 1991, Prof. Olquin and Dr. Carlos Perez observed the same type of craft in Zacatelco, a small village between Tlaxcala and Puebla, not too far from Atlixco. Dr. Perez managed to take 2 pictures when the reddish-glowing disc with "windows" or ports hovered in front of them, before it speeded up and shot away over their heads. These sightings and the excellent pictures taken by credible witnesses caused a team of Nippon TV, a Japanese station, to investigate the events. For three days the Japanese TV journalist Yunicho Yaoi interviewed witnesses in Atlixco and Zacatelco, including the police commander and the Alcalde (mayor) of Atlixco. At night, the team took up a position on a mountain above Atlixco, and actually managed to film a rotating disc with yellow-white ports from a distance. This amazing confirmation was shown on Japanese TV shortly after and made the Mexican sightings known outside of the country for the first time.

On July 28, 1994, at 9:55 p.m., Aeromexico Flight 129, en route from Guadalajara, approached Mexico City's International Benito Juarez airport. The pilot of the DC-9, flight captain Raimundo Cervantes Ruano, entered the final level of approach, extended the landing gear and made a final turn. He and his 109 passengers aboard expected a smooth landing, when suddenly the aircraft hit something and shook. *"What was that?"* he yelled in the microphone, *"Tower, we have an emergency!"* *"Confirm. You've had a collision,"* an equally breathless air traffic controller confirmed, *"prepare for an emergency landing."* Fire fighters and ambulances were ready when the airplane set down. When the aircraft mechanics looked for the damage caused by the collision, they found a part of the landing gear cleanly cut off. Later, the air traffic controllers confirmed that in fact an "unknown" appeared on the radar screen when Capt. Ruano headed for landing, and crossed his course so suddenly that any forewarning was impossible. At the same time, a Mexican filmed a luminous object flying over the airport area.

During the next 11 days, 5 more airplanes had near-collisions with unidentified flying objects while approaching Mexico City. The last one happened on August 8, 1994, in the afternoon, when Aeromexico flight 305 from Acapulco was on its way to the capital. The pilots, flight captain Fernando Mesquita and copilot Carlos Corzo, checked with the tower and were asked by the air traffic controllers to take "heading 340 and maintain 13,000 feet." Shortly after, they requested Flight 305 to "turn left, intercept the final approach and descend to 11,500 feet." It was a cloudy day, and just when the aircraft came out of a cloud, the pilots saw a big, shiny object immediately in front, heading towards them. *"We're gonna die!"* Corzo screamed in the microphone. At this moment, when his heart seemed to stand still, the disc evaded them and shot away right under the left wing of the aircraft. *"What other traffic was around here?"* he asked the tower, his heart still beating faster. *"How could it be that we had an object just in front of us?"*

"You are the fifth one to report a near-collision with unknown traffic," the confused air traffic controller replied, *"we don't know what's going on out there." "It was oval-shaped, about 75 feet in diameter,"* Captain Corzo told me when I interviewed him in April 1996, *"and it was shiny, like polished metal."* But, as the air traffic controllers told him, it was not seen on radar.

This frightening situation caused the Mexican airport authorities to act. Within 4 weeks they ordered and installed a new, more sensitive radar system, which would not, unlike most civilian radars, filter out any unconventional signals, but show all targets in the air as military radar systems do. Since then, they have recorded UFOs over Mexico at least 5 times a week—and sometimes half a dozen a night. On the invitation of 2 friends, I spent a night in the radar room of the Mexico City International Airport in February 1996 and was present when four UFOs, some of them flying at double the speed of sound, were located on the radar screens.

But the most spectacular case happened during the night of September 15, 1994, when the air traffic controllers observed an object over the village of Metepec near Toluca, west of Mexico City, on screen for 5 hours, between 8:00 p.m. and 1:00 a.m. They were puzzled but believed the echo might have a conventional explanation, until they learned that in the very same night, literally hundreds of people saw the object, hovering over a cornfield.

Among the witnesses were housewife Sara Cuevas and her sister Erika, who, driving home from Toluca at about 8:00 p.m., saw a luminous object hovering over Metepec. At first, they believed it was an airplane, until it came

Erika and Sara Cuevas

down and turned out to be a reddish disc of about 75 feet in diameter. The 2 sisters drove home quickly, to observe the object from the roof of their home. When they arrived there, they saw that the disc was floating at an altitude of about 600 feet over a cornfield bordering their suburban town. They alerted the neighbors, who saw it too. Then Sara got her video camera and tried to film the UFO—without success, for the camera failed to work. Suddenly 2 reddish objects shot out of the main craft, came down and whirled through the cornfield. When they returned, both the little objects and their mother ship moved away, and hovered over the Metepec Hill for 2 hours. Then the big craft returned, 7 little red discs, 1–2 feet in diameter, shot out of it and whirled through the cornfield, to create a strange pattern of flattened plants. Dozens of neighbors observed the spectacle, when one of the little discs exploded and about 500 little balls like eyes appeared, going down between the plants and illuminating the field, before they disappeared. Hell broke out among the witnesses. Some started shouting hysterically, others cried, others were paralyzed and under shock. Eventually the little discs returned to their mother ship, which continued to hover over Metepec for another 2 hours.

The next morning, Metepec was besieged by reporters of the local media, including Jaime Maussan, who extensively interviewed the witnesses. Investigators found out that many of the corn plants were burned and that the ground temperature within the pattern was still higher than in the surrounding field. Further, they measured a radioactivity there, about 350% above the average readings from the field. Still, Sara Cuevas's German husband, a technician, did not believe her. Disappointed by his skepticism, she decided to try everything to film the UFO, in case it came back.

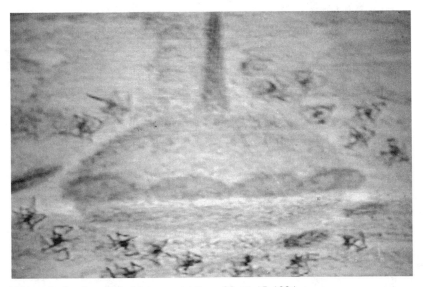

Witness's drawing of the Metepec sighting of Sept. 15, 1994

The Metepec corn pattern, after thousands trampled it down. Center—top: Sara Cuevas' house.

It did not. But instead of the UFO, she and her sister, who accompanied her on her vigil, saw something else. In the middle of the cornfield pattern, about 100 feet away from her, stood a luminous figure which obviously inspected the formation. For about 3 minutes, Sara was able to film the dwarf like entity, before it slowly turned around and disappeared.

The film was analyzed by computer expert Prof. Victor Quesada of the "Grupo Sol" of the Polytechnical Institute/University of Mexico who concluded that the luminous figure was much too bright to be, for instance, an electrically illuminated mannekin.

For the air traffic controllers of Mexico City's international airport, the Metepec case was a revelation. It showed that their radar system had not been wrong, since in fact a large object had hovered over Metepec at the time in question. When Jaime Maussan interviewed them, they agreed to contact him in case of a future, similar event. It happened just the following night; again they had an object for a long period of time on the screen in another area west of Mexico City. When Jaime Maussan learned about it the next morning, he rented a helicopter and flew there—to find another "corn pattern" of a field. This repeated itself for the next 5 days—every night an "unknown target" on the radar screen, every morning a strange formation in a crop field—(on one occasion a pumpkin field) in the area in question.

But what makes the Metepec incident even more significant is that at the same time the object disappeared over the hill, at 1:00 a.m. local time, a

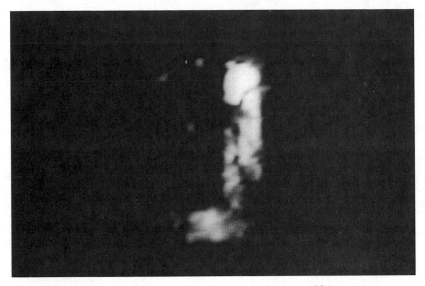

The "Metepec spaceman," filmed by Sara Cuevas on Sept. 16, 1994

similar craft landed in Ruwa, Zimbabwe, 9 time zones east, and was seen by nearly a hundred schoolchildren.

On Wednesday, September 14, 1994, at exactly 9:04 p.m., thousands of citizens of Harare, the capital of Zimbabwe, were shaken by a loud explosion, followed by a vibration of the windowpanes. Those who rushed out of their houses saw nothing but the cloudy sky. They could not know that the explosion was a supersonic bang, caused by mysterious objects which entered the earth's atmosphere over the south of Africa at that very moment. And in fact, millions who lived under a clear sky saw them that night, from Botswana to Mozambique, the south of Zambia and South Africa and the whole of Zimbabwe. Astronomers originally believed that a meteorite shower had caused the celestial show, but they later learned that the glowing objects were parts of a Russian satellite, launched on August 24. But some witnesses, especially in the area around Lake Kariba at Zimbabwe's northern border, claimed in addition to the reentering fragments, they saw conical objects "which changed their course," making them a completely different sky phenomenon.

Whatever it was that entered the Zimbabwean airspace that night, "something" came back. The next morning, September 15, about 10:00 a.m., a group of pupils of the Ariel school at Ruwa, a suburb of Harare, were playing together during the morning break. Suddenly, they saw a cigar-shaped craft hanging low in the sky, just above the bush which was nearly bordering the schoolyard, separated by just a swampy area. It was metallic-looking, reflected the morning sun brightly, and disappeared after just a few seconds behind some tall trees.

Ariel School in Ruwa, Zimbabwe

The children wondered what it might have been. Of course they had heard about UFOs, had seen them in the movies and on Television, so they didn't have a shadow of a doubt that what they had seen was an extraterrestrial spacecraft. It was exciting, yes, but the sighting was too short to make a great deal out of it.

On the following day, Friday, September 16, 1994, Alisa Stevens, who lived at a farmhouse adjacent to the school grounds, woke up early in the morning. She got up and looked out of the window when she saw "a large, glowing thing" hovering just over the chicken coop. She went back to get her husband, but when she looked out of the window again, it had disappeared.

But this was only the beginning of an event, which turned out to be the best documented and best witnessed close encounter of the third kind of all times. It was again 10:00 a.m., time of the morning break, and with the ring of the bell children started to pour out of the little classrooms of the Ariel School.

That morning they were alone on the playground, without the supervision of their 13 teachers, who had a meeting in the conference room of the office of the headmaster, Mr. Colin Mackie. Some of the children suddenly saw a purple light in the sky above the forest, which kept coming and going. And then, a disc appeared, a huge, shiny craft with a flat dome on top, surrounded by yellow lights or portholes and extending tripod landing gear. It came down close to a rock on the other side of the marsh area, between the trees on the edge of the forest. Balls of light or miniature discs appeared and flew around for a short while. The pupils who saw it now

View on the zone in which a UFO landed on Sept. 16, 1994 (with enlargement of the specific area)

started to scream out of surprise and fear. This drew the attention of nearly everyone on the playground, and within seconds the limit of the schoolyard on that side was thronged by about a hundred pupils who all watched the incredible spectacle.

Now all the children who were close by observed something coming out of the disc. First one, then a second, finally a third figure exited the craft from the back of its dome, beings in shiny, tight-fitting black overalls with dark faces, two of them bald, the third with long, black hair, about 4–5 feet tall. They had big black eyes, which some of the young witnesses described as "like a cat's eyes," tiny little mouths and small noses. Some of the children could see a metal band around the head. All the younger children were scared and started crying. The entities—some saw only 2 of them, depending on the perspective—jumped down from the top of the saucer and moved slowly and wobbled. Whereas one of them went behind a tree, another one came closer and stared in the direction of the children who all started screaming at once. "Look at its eyes," one of them shouted, "they are so ugly." But a few of them were unusually silent. Deep inside themselves they heard a voice, telling them there was nothing to fear. They had just come to warn them that Earth was going to be destroyed by mankind itself . . .

At that moment, some of the children ran to the headmaster's office to tell the teachers what had just happened on the playground. But nobody wanted to believe them. One boy ran to the only adult on the playground, Mrs. Alyson Kirkman, a mother who was on voluntary duty at the snack bar on this day. But when the boy told her about the UFO and the aliens, she just said: "Pull my other leg." She could not believe him, nor was she ready to leave the snack bar with the money in her cash box, nor could she leave her stock of sweets and cookies alone.

After about 3 minutes the creatures went back to the ship, and lights started to flash, before the disc itself disappeared in a burst of light.

Now, after they finished their meeting, the first group of teachers came out, to see what was going on, after more and more children had come into the conference room to tell them about the strange encounter. But when they finally appeared on scene, everything was already over. What remained was excitement for many and trauma for some. Some children suffered from nightmares for the next few weeks or months, in some cases years. One boy underwent a psychological crisis and started bedwetting because his parents did not believe him. Others had dreams of aliens coming into their homes at night to abduct them. Others saw balls, circles and triangles of light in their bedroom. Some children believed the creatures were "tokoloshes," the gnomes of African mythology.

After the children went home, most of them told their parents about what had happened at school. Some of them informed the press, and when school started again on Monday, it was besieged by the reporters, just as Metepec in Mexico had been during the days before. One class went to the landing site with their teacher, to find dead birds, strange footprints, burning marks, an indentation in the grass and heaps of dead ants.

Two children's sketches of the Ruwa landing

About half a year after the incident, Prof. John E. Mack, psychiatrist of the Harvard Medical School and Pulitzer prize winner, visited the Ariel school and questioned some of the children, to conclude that they certainly had had a real experience which had left a very deep impression upon them.

Since I was very impressed by his report, I visited the school twice in March 1997 and interviewed 44 children, as well as the headmaster and 2 teachers of the school, some parents and also Cynthia Hind, Africa's leading UFO researcher, who carefully investigated the case right after it happened. Although Cynthia could not verify the physical traces, she agrees with John Mack and myself that this is most certainly one of the most significant cases in the history of the UFO phenomenon.

The landings at Metepec and Ruwa were not the only ones. In fact, a series of landings took place between 1993 and 1995 in a country which might have one of the oldest traditions of alien contact: in Israel, in the village of Kadima, east of Netanya.

The UFO wave in Israel began in 1987, 40 years or one biblical generation after the foundation of the country. Three times, on September 28, 1987, May 20, 1988 and April 21, 1989 witnesses saw a strange craft over Shikmona Beach south of Haifa. In the course of the first and second incidents, the bat-shaped object caused a whirlwind and shot a red beam of light onto the beach, to burn its shape into the sand. In the third case the object changed into a pillar of fire and left behind a grayish powder.

On December 6, 1991, the most remarkable military UFO encounter in Israel's history took place. It all started at about 3:00 a.m., when an excited taxi driver called the police to report a UFO sighting just outside of the city of Bet Shean in the Jordan Valley. The officer on duty went outside and saw it with his own eyes: a brilliant light hovered over the industrial zone of his town. Believing it might be a sort of glider carrying terrorists from nearby Jordan to perpetrate an attack, he immediately called his superior, Chief Inspector Yitzhak Mordechai at home, woke him up and implored him to rush over. "I am on the way," Mordechai replied, "in the meantime, call the Army!" The officer did. By the time the chief inspector arrived on the site, the industrial area was crowded with armed men, soldiers of the Army, border guards and police. They all stared at a boomerang-shaped craft which hovered at an altitude of only 450 feet, illuminated by a bright light in the center. Then it started to move. A hundred men jumped into their cars and turned on the motors, to follow the strange craft which slowly flew in an eastern direction. After about half an hour, the convoy of jeeps and police cars reached the border of the kingdom of Jordan, where it stopped, only to fly back to Israel and hover at one spot, again surrounded by the soldiers and policemen, who had meanwhile realized that this invader was definitely not from this world.

At about 5.00 a.m., someone gave the order to shoot. Later, the police blamed the Army for the shooting, whereas the Army claimed it was the police who gave the order. The object however did not answer the fire but just rose up into the sky and disappeared.

On September 26, 1991, at the village Zur Moshe, 2 miles north of Kadima, Eli Cohen woke up at 3:00 a.m., because a bright light shone into his bedroom. He grabbed his rifle, checked every room and found that the power had failed, then went into the garden, and saw a luminous object moving back and forth above a group of orange trees. In the meantime, Eli's wife woke up, and came down to join him. Together they observed 3 beams of light shooting out of the craft, which stayed over their house until dawn. The following night it returned. On the third night, Eli invited friends over and borrowed a camcorder. He was able to film it for 10 minutes before it again disappeared at dawn. The film clearly shows a dome-shaped, structured craft.

On Saturday morning, March 20, 1993, Ziporet Carmel of Kadima, niece of the well-known Israeli poet Avigdor Hameira, woke up at 6:30 a.m., because a bright white light shone into her bedroom. Her Great Danes got

Ziporet Carmel

nervous, so she decided to get up and see what was going on. She went outside and saw, about 450 feet behind the house, something like a big, metallic crate, about 15 feet tall. Believing that someone used it to harvest oranges, she turned around to go back into the house and get back to bed. But just as she opened the door she had the feeling that someone was looking at her, and the dogs started to bark and behave frantically. She turned around again, and saw a man, standing next to the crate which was now even higher. The man was extremely tall, more than 8 feet, and dressed in silver metallic overalls and sombrero-like headgear, from which a veil hung down and covered his face. "If I could only see his face," Ziporet thought, when she heard a voice inside of her, saying: "That's all you will see for today." At this moment, both the tall man and the crate disappeared in a flash of light. Two days later, she went with her girlfriend to the spot were the "crate" had stood, and saw a circular impression in the grass, 15 feet in diameter, surrounded by 3 smaller, circular imprints. The plants were covered by a reddish, strong-smelling substance, containing cadmium, as researchers found out later. They further found out that the roots of the plants were obviously burned. Ground samples, put in a glass of water, swam on the surface, whereas normal samples sank to the bottom. Moreover, pieces of a silvery metal were found, which when later analyzed by Dr. Henry Fohner of the Geological Institute of Israel, turned out to be 99.9% pure silicon.

Ten days later, on March 31, 1993, one of Ziporet's neighbors felt her house tremble during the night. When she opened her eyes she saw "a bald giant, 7 to 8 feet tall, with round, yellow eyes and a small flat nose, dressed in gray metallic overalls," standing next to her bed. "Don't be afraid. I will not harm you," she heard in her mind and saw the being gliding through the room. The next morning, 2 more circles were found, 20 and 11 feet in diameter and "pressed down by a centrifugal force," with the same characteristics as the first one. In May, another woman, Batya Shimon, of Rishon-le-Zion south of Kadima, reported a similar experience with an eight-foot-tall creature "with fascinating blue eyes," dressed in silver overalls, that appeared in her bedroom and glided through her apartment. The incident repeated itself the next night, when Batya followed the creature and saw "a mushroom-

Israeli "landing circle" in Kadima, January 1995.

shaped craft, surrounded by searchlights" hovering outside. A hatch opened, which looked like dark glass, and 2 beings stepped out. The next thing she felt was a pressure on her shoulders. She was blinded by the bright light—and found herself back in her bed, with one of the creatures standing next to her, the other one further away. "Don't be afraid," she heard inside her head. She could not reply, since she was paralyzed. Her husband was sleeping deeply next to her. The beings glided, surrounded by a fluorescent light, out of her bedroom window, back to their craft. The next morning Batya found a powder containing mainly cadmium on the floor of her flat. On May 30, 1993, Hannah Somech of Bourgata, north of Kadima, woke up at 3:00 a.m. when she heard her dog barking. She got up and went down the stairs from her bedroom to the kitchen and looked out at the garden through the glass door when she saw her dog literally flying through the air against a wall. Shocked and terrified she bravely opened the door but was confronted by an invisible wall: she could not go any further. Then she saw an eight-foot-tall creature in bright overalls. A thief, she thought. "You think I am a thief?" she heard inside of her. "What did you do with my dog," she asked furiously. "He disturbed me, as you do now," the giant spoke telepathically, without moving his lips. "I could do the same with you, but I don't want to. Just leave me alone, I am busy." The woman ran back to the bedroom to wake up her husband, but when both came down, the creature had disappeared. In the garden, they found huge footprints, 1 foot, 4 inches in length. Later, circles appeared too, again covered by the reddish cadmium-based liquid. After the encounter, Hannah suffered severely from fatigue, headaches and muscle pain.

Two years later, in January 1995, the events occurred once more. Again, Hannah woke up in the middle of the night to so see "something like a crystal" hanging in the sky, a beam of light coming out of it. On the next morning, a new set of circles was found on her land. Other circles, one of them 135 feet in diameter, were found at Kadima, covered by the same reddish liquid. But the most significant humanoid encounter took place further south in the country, at Yatzitz, 20 miles south of Tel Aviv. On the evening of January 3, 1995, Hertzl Casatini, security chief of the village, visited the house of his friend Danny Ezra when the house started trembling. Casatini believed it was an explosion, maybe a terrorist attack. He immediately opened the garden door to have a look outside, when he was shocked by what he saw: a huge creature, about 11 to 12 feet tall, was running over a field. *"He had a very round face,"* Hertzl told me when I interviewed him in November 1996. *"It was very difficult to distinguish features except for 2 huge round eyes and an oval face, but there was a haziness emitted from the face, it radiated some kind of light, that made it very difficult to distinguish details. It wore a very smooth golden-brown one-piece suit. It was running like a human being, but maybe more mechanical, more stiff, like a robot. It was more like a threatening walk, like a monster in a movie."* Hertzl called his friend, but when he came the being had already disappeared. Both men jumped into the car and tried to follow it, but without any success. Then they drove to the security office of the village, and called the border police. The officer who picked up

"Giant's footprint," found in Yatzitz on January 3, 1995

the call, a man called Biton, did not believe him, but Casatini did not leave any doubt that he knew what he had seen. "Stop laughing and come over immediately," he yelled into the receiver. When the police finally arrived, they found tracks—footprints 1 foot, 4 inches in length, some at a distance of 3 feet, some 36 feet away from each other. Obviously the creature had literally jumped in a tiptoe fashion, since the sole of the shoe had made a far deeper impression in the front rather than in the heel; it had pressed up to a depth of one foot into the dry soil. This, as investigators calculated, indicated that the entity weighed over 1,000 pounds. The case created a stir in Israel, nationwide headlines and television reports. But Casatini became the victim of after effects of a different kind. The day after the incident he had a high fever. When he went to the shower he noticed his gonads were swollen. He was sick for 2 days and had to take antibiotics until the fever and the swelling went down.

With these events, a major wave of UFO sightings started in Israel in the years of 1995–96, when thousands of eyewitnesses saw and filmed strange craft over the country. It reached its peak on September 17, 1996, when at 2:00 a.m. the traffic on the Ramat High Road in the suburban area of Tel Aviv stopped for some time; hundreds of motorists saw a "luminous UFO" flying over the city. Dozens of people called the police with their mobile phones, and shortly after, police officers joined the witnesses. When a soldier from the Border Police wanted to shoot at the UFO, others stopped him. "*Are you crazy?*" they yelled, "*do you want to provoke an interplanetary war?*" About one hour before dawn the UFO ended its loopings over the city and flew eastwards, following the Shaul-Hamelech Boulevard.

The three Varginha witnesses: Valquiria, Katia, Liliane on the site of their close encounter

Some motorists tried to follow it, but the craft made a turn, flew back to Ramat Aviv and disappeared into the morning sky.

The year 1996 saw a major UFO wave for Brazil as well. Here, humanoid creatures were not only observed by credible witnesses, but also captured alive by the military.

On January 20, 1996, one of the most significant UFO cases of the 1990s happened in Varginha, an industrial city in the south of the Brazilian state of Minas Gerais with a population of 180,000. On this day, the Brazilian Army captured 2 extraterrestrial beings, according to dozens of eyewitnesses interviewed by the local UFO researchers Dr. Ubirajara Rodrigues and Vitorio Paccaccini, who investigated the case and presented it to the Brazilian media.

It all began that Saturday afternoon when 3 girls, the sisters Liliane de Fatima (16), Valquiria Aparecida Silva (14) and their older friend Katia de Andrade Xavier (22) were on their way home and saw a strange creature cowering near a wall. It was about 4 to 5 feet tall and naked, with brown skin covered by a greasy, dark oil, a large, hairless head, small mouth and tiny nose. Since its large eyes had no pupils and it had 3 little bumps on its hairless head, the girls believed they had met with the devil and ran home as quick as they could.

Hearing her daughters screaming outside, Luiza, the mother of Liliane and Valquiria, came out of the house and tried to calm them down. Then she decided to take the girls back to the spot to see the strange creature with her own eyes. When they got there, however, they could not find the being anymore. Instead of that, Luiza noticed a strange, intense stench.

The story about the girls' strange encounter quickly traveled throughout Varginha and reached Dr. Rodrigues, a lawyer and local UFO researcher. After he interviewed the girls he was absolutely sure they were telling the truth. And in fact, when he spoke to people living in the area where the creature was seen, he located 2 eyewitnesses, a girl and an elderly lady. Both had heard the screams of the girls and gone out, and had then seen how minutes later local firemen and soldiers captured "a strange animal" and dragged it away.

But this was not the first capture, as Rodrigues learned. At about 10:00 a.m. a city fire truck arrived, after locals reported seeing a "strange creature" in a park in the Jardim Andere district of the city. It is not unusual in Brazil for wild animals to wander into populated areas, and it is usually the responsibility of the Fire Department to deal with them. The vehicle parked atop a brow overlooking the park, and firemen with cages and nets jumped out of it. Eventually they located the creature—it was nothing they had ever seen before. It was small, a 3½ foot tall biped, with blood-red eyes and a strange, oily-brown skin. Apparently injured, the creature had 3 distinguishable raised humps on its forehead. The firemen threw their nets and when, after some difficulty, they finally caught it and carried it away, a strange "buzzing sound" came out of its small, slit-like mouth. According to the researchers, a young policeman who assisted in the capture was heavily injured by the entity and died in a local hospital some days later. The cause of death was officially given out as "pneumonia," which his family found hard to believe.

The commander of the Fire Department shortly afterwards informed the closest military installation, the Escola de Sargento des Armas (School of Army Sergeants) at Tres Coracoes, 15 miles away. Its commander, General Sergio Coelho Lima, immediately ordered troops to the area. The firemen put the creature into a wooden box and handed it over to the soldiers, who, after warning them not to talk to anyone about the incident, took it to the base at Tres Coracoes.

The second being was not brought to Tres Coracoes, but first to the Regional Hospital and then to the better-equipped Humanitas Hospital. Nurses of both hospitals confirmed a "secret military operation" at the time in question. A whole wing of the Humanitas Hospital was taken over, the patients removed to other wards. On Monday, January 22, 3 military trucks were seen parked outside Humanitas Hospital between 3:00 and 6:00 p.m. Medical sources have revealed that by 6:00 p.m. the creature was dead. As several witnesses described, it was taken out in a small wooden casket, which was loaded on one of the trucks. All three Army trucks then drove to Campinas in the state of Sao Paulo, about 200 miles away from Varginha. The University of Campinas is one of the best scientific institutions of the country. There, an autopsy was performed by Prof. Dr. Badan Palhares, the leading pathologist of the country. He had made headlines 10 years before when he

Valquiria's drawing of the creature

identified the remains of Dr. Mengele, the Nazi "Dr. Frankenstein" who performed cruel and indescribable experiments on concentration camp prisoners.

After reports about the Varginha incidents appeared in the newspapers, Prof. Palhares was asked in public by one of his students if he had indeed autopsied an extraterrestrial. His reply was, "*I cannot talk about it now, maybe in 10 years.*" The surviving entity, as the researchers learned, was handed over to a "Blue Fly" Team from the United States and flown to the Wright Patterson Air Force Base in Dayton, Ohio. We can assume that from there it was brought into the mysterious Area 51 in the heart of Nevada.

But where did the 2 creatures originate from? In the early hours of January 20, farmer Eurico de Freitas and his common-law wife Oralina Augusta were roused from their beds by the noises made by their horse, who had obvviously been disturbed. The couple's 3 dogs were barking furiously. When they nervously made their way outside, they were greeted by an unexpected sight. A grayish craft, shaped like a submarine and the size of a small bus, was crossing their meadow at a height of only 15 feet. White smoke was pouring out of the flying cigar, which they were able to observe for 45 minutes. Similar craft were seen over Varginha in the weeks before the incident, but this one obviously had some trouble. Eventually it disappeared behind some trees, and the farming couple went back to bed. Shortly after, a couple of local witnesses saw Army trucks parked at the edge of a street. Soldiers came out of a forest and loaded metallic debris onto the backs of the trucks.

And if we believe a radar operator of the Forca Aerea Brasileira (FAB— Brazilian Air Force), the crash in Varginha was not unexpected at all. As he told UFO researcher Vitorio Pacaccini, the Brazilian Armed Forces (CIN-

DACTA) were alerted by the United States that they had tracked a UFO entering Brazilian airspace. The advance warning came complete with latitude and longitude coordinates. According to an American source, the craft was actually shot down by the U.S. Space Command.

Whatever happened in Varginha, the officials tried everything to cover up the events. Rodrigues and Pacaccini received numerous threats by telephone, soldiers who spoke to them were arrested or transferred to other installations. The girl's mother, Luiza Silva, was offered a huge amount of money, if all of them agreed to retract their original statement. But the forces behind the cover-up did not succeed this time. The case caused a stir all over the country, and even the the news magazine *Istoe*, a kind of Brazilian *Time* or *Newsweek*, dedicated a cover story to the case and reported it on 6 pages.

But more than that, the events in Varginha were the beginning of a major series of sightings throughout the country. They reached their peak between October 16 to 18, when thousands of witnesses saw UFOs over the state of Paraiba in the northeast of Brazil. During the night of October 16, a large rectangular craft, 200 to 300 feet long, thoroughly frightened about 300 residents in the capital city of Joao Pessoa (population: 498,000) when it flew over its main street, the Avenida Rui Carneiro. Shortly after, it was observed over 10 other cities of Paraiba, including Oatos, about 110 miles west of the capital.

On the following night, "un gigantesco OVNI triangular" (a gigantic triangular UFO) was seen over Campina Grande, the second largest city of the state. In the same night, the people of Joao Pessoa saw formations of "luminious, greenish spheres with flashing yellow lights" passing over the city 3 times. One of the witnesses, Dr. Jacipa Lucena de Farias, professor at the University of Paraiba, counted 11 UFOs during the second passby and 30 at the third. Shortly after, about 40 greenish lights were seen over the small town of Jaguaribe.

During the third night, on October 18, a large cylindrical craft appeared over Guarabira, north of Campina Grande. It was shining brightly and moved both horizontally and vertically. Further sightings were reported from the villages of Pilozinhas and Mamanguape as well as from the city of Sao Neves.

Other mass sightings were reported from Santiago, Chile, San Juan, Costa Rica, Las Vegas, Nevada, Zaragoza, Spain, Bombay, India, Seoul, Korea, and the major cities of Australia and Ecuador. A cigar-shaped mother ship, about a mile long, releasing smaller balls of light, was filmed on August 27, 1995, by Tim Edwards over Salida, Colorado. But the most impressive UFO demonstrations above major cities took place in early 1997 over 2 major cities, each one in a superpower nation: Phoenix, Arizona and St. Petersburg, Russia.

On February 19, 1997, thousands of eyewitnesses in St. Petersburg, Russia, observed a 900-foot-wide, boomerang-shaped craft which hovered over Lagoda Lake northeast of the city. Six eyewitnesses filmed the giant spacecraft. At 7:02 p.m. a strange object suddenly appeared in a flash of light over the lake. Four lights in triangular formation, with one light in the center and one corner pointing downwards, hung silently in the air. The lights were so bright that they immediately drew the attention of everyone who happened to be near the lake. Hundreds of witnesses observed them for 15 minutes. The lights separated and formed a kind of luminous boomerang. Then, for minutes the object disappeared, only to reappear shortly after, at an angle of 20–25 degrees above the horizon. The witnesses saw, and filmed, little balls of light approaching the object, which disappeared in a flash of light just before they reached it.

At the same time, the object was visually observed by the air traffic controllers of the St. Petersburg "Pulkowo" airport in the south of the city. From their perspective, the lights were hanging over St. Petersburg. Air traffic controller Viktor Lokjuschin stated,

> It was already dark, although we still saw the contours of the buildings of the city, not just their lights. I told my colleagues about the phenomenon and we all watched it. At 7:05 p.m. the first "starlets" approached these lights. I myself counted 3 of them, others saw five. I radioed an aircraft which was waiting for permission to take off, a TU-134 on the way home to Kaliningrad, about whether they saw an unidentified flying object in front of them. The pilot replied, "Yes, we see it, too." At the same time, one of our (Pulkowo-based) aircraft, a TU-154, was landing, and they radioed that they had observed it the whole time. At 7:07 the clearly visible lights disappeared, only to reappear in a different position at 7:08 again.

The weather at 7:00 p.m. can be described as: Visibility: Over 30,000 feet. Dense clouds in an altitude of 18,000 feet—therefore the object was lower than

The boomerang-shaped craft over St. Petersburg, February 19, 1997, through the telescope. It is estimated to be about 900 feet in diameter.

18,000 feet. The wind came from 140 degrees with 4 m/s, air pressure 766 mm, temperature 10°C. The visibility was excellent. During the second phase, 7:08–7:17, a few more 'starlets' approached the object from left to right.

Interestingly, the object was not located on the radar screen. In the area it was hovering, only instabilities were observed. According to the head of the air traffic control center of the Pulkowo Airport, this can mean anything—usually an electrically charged cloud—but not a solid craft.

At the same time, thousands of citizens of St. Petersburg, too, saw the formation of lights. Witnesses at the shores of Lagoda Lake were able to count up to 14 lights, whereas the witnesses in St. Petersburg counted a maximum of 7 lights. UFO researcher Valerii Uvarov from St. Petersburg was able to collect 6 videos of the event, including one taken by the general manager of the local TV station Sjas TV, Michail Kompa.

This evidence enabled him, together with many detailed eyewitness reports, to determine the position of the craft through triangulation. Further, he was able to calculate its size, based on the arc it subtended on the film, as being about 900 feet in diameter! Indeed, the object was so large that it was even seen from the bay south of Finland, where it was so clearly visible that sailors believed it to be just 10 miles away.

According to most eyewitnesses, after 15 minutes another "ball of light" headed towards the craft. But this one did not come from the side, as the "starlets" did, but upwards from the ground. The object tilted a little bit and its lights joined together, maybe because it rose up, and formed one bright light, before it speeded up and shot away in a northeastern direction. Did someone from the ground fire at the alien intruder?

Three weeks later, a similar phenomenon was observed over a major city in the American southwest, Phoenix in Arizona. The great UFO wave over Arizona began at 8:00 p.m. on Thursday, March 13, 1997, when a former police officer in Paulden, AZ called the *Daily Courier* to report a sighting of 5 "diamond-shaped objects." Soon after that, the phone rang at the National UFO Reporting Center, after dozens of witnesses observed "a giant craft" with "5 or 6 lights in triangular formation" moving over the city "with the speed of a blimp." At 8:23 p.m. the object reached Phoenix. Thousands of witnesses saw the formation of lights; several of them were able to discern "a huge, dark structure" connecting them. They estimated the width of the V-formation to be about 4,000 feet, maneuvering at an altitude of about 2,000 feet. During the observation, the third light from the right detached itself from the formation and circled over the city, before it returned to its original position. After passing over the capital of Arizona, the formation moved southeast and was seen over Tucson at 8:45 p.m., when one of the front lights took off, flew over the city and came back. A man watched the squadron for about 15 minutes, before it moved south, disappearing over mountains. The mother ship had obviously crossed the state from northwest to southeast, covering a distance of 200 miles in 29 minutes.

The "Phoenix lights" of March 13, 1997: Triangular craft flying over the city

Shortly before 10:00 p.m. the "giant craft" returned to Phoenix, approached the Estrella Mountains in the south of the city and released 6 "balls of light" which formed a bow-shaped configuration of about one mile in diameter. Six witnesses were able to film the formation from different perspectives, which made it possible for the local computer expert Jim Dilettoso to calculate its length and actual position. On the film, one ball of light appears after the other like pearls on a string, only to disappear again after some time in the same order. The craft itself flew to the southeast and was seen flying at a low altitude by witnesses in Scottsdale, who described it as "3 or 4 times as big as a Boeing 747" and "absolutely silent." According to the Channel 15 news, a pilot approaching Phoenix Sky Harbor Airport at that time saw the formation from the air and radioed the air traffic controllers to ask if they had the "giant craft" on radar. They denied it.

Another witness, trucker Bill Greiner, observed 2 orange lights hovering near Luke Air Force Base for about 2 hours. Finally he observed how 3 jet fighters were started from the base, to approach the first of the 2 lights, which hovered at a distance of 1 to 2 miles in the southwest, while the second one stood in the northeast. Both UFOs glowed orange and were surrounded by a pulsating, reddish ring of light. When the jets approached the first UFO it shot straight up and disappeared. The interceptors changed their course towards the second UFO, which did the same as the first one. When local UFO investigator Tom King phoned Luke AFB later to verify Bill Greiner's report, he was told that all jets were already bedded down at 7:00 p.m. Later, however, Lt. Col. Mike Hauser of the USAF confirmed that 3 jet fighters were actually started after dozens of civilians had called

Mothership (left) releasing "balls of light" over Phoenix

the base and reported their sightings. Of course, as usual, UFO skeptics had a quick explanation for the Phoenix lights. According to them, they were signal flares, part of an exercise of the U.S. Air Force. But on April 3, 1997, UFO researcher John Greenewald sent a request for information regarding the events on March 13, under the "Freedom of Information Act," to Luke AFB. In his reply, a USAF spokesman not only confirmed having received numerous phone calls at the base, but also clearly stated that "*we were not in any way involved in the incident . . . our officials never claimed air signal flares caused the sightings.*"

We do not know if these events were just another test of the public's reaction to a future contact, a rehearsal for the grand finale, or if they represent a new phase in the aliens' approach. If the latter is true, then Sergeant Moody's second prediction might indeed turn out to be as accurate as the first one—that a contact is imminent. Only one thing is sure: the UFO phenomenon is an interactive one, dependent on the public's awareness and readiness for an alien presence. An open contact will only happen when we are truly ready for it; willing to accept that we are not alone and that there are others, who are neither gods nor demons, but humans and children of the same universe as we.

"Communication," to quote Robert Anton Wilson, "is only possible among equals." There is no doubt that we can learn a lot from "them," since they are technologically superior. But "they," too, can learn a lot from us, from our achievements, our art, our culture, our spirituality, our emotions and from the human experience itself. There is not one single being in the universe which cannot learn, one way or the other, from another one. When

The Phoenix formation from a different perspective

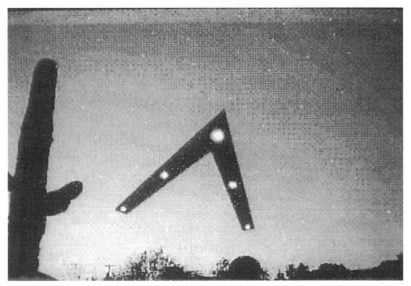

Reconstruction of the Phoenix craft by Jim Dilettoso.

we finally realize that every life form is a worthy expression of the one universe (or of God, its creator) without being superior or inferior in value, we are ready for an open contact. When this will be, it is up to us to determine. But until this happens, someone up there keeps reminding us, in a manner that is increasingly impossible to ignore, that indeed we are not alone.

APPENDIX

A Short History of the UFO Phenomenon

EARLY HISTORY

30,000 BC.:   First pictorial representation of UFOs in cave paintings in the south of France

1462 BC: UFO sighting during the reign of Pharaoh Thutmosis III.

586 BC: UFO encounter of Prophet Ezekiel

332 BC: "Flying shields" destroy the walls of Tyros

776 AD: "Flying shields" over Eresburg, Saxony

1561:   UFOs over Nuremberg

8/12/1883:   Prof. Bonilla of Zacatecas Observatory, Mexico, photographs UFO formation

8/5/1926:   Nicholas Roerich's UFO sighting in Kukunor District in the Himalayas

10/30/1938:   Orson Welles' radio play *War of the Worlds* leads to mass panic

THE 1940s:

1944/45:   Foo fighters over Europe

April 1945:   General MacArthur establishes interplanetary "Phenomenon Unit" after UFO Sighting

6/24/47:   Kenneth Arnold's UFO encounter over Mount Rainier, WA: Beginning of the era of "Flying Saucers"

7/4/47:   UFO crash near Roswell, NM

7/7/47:   First modern UFO photo by W. Rhodes, Phoenix, AZ

7/8/47:   Official announcement of the recovery of a "flying disc" near Roswell, NM

9/23/47:	AMC Commandant General Nathan F. Twining writes memorandum about "flying discs"
9/24/47:	President Truman establishes Operation Majestic 12
Sept. 1947:	First UFO detection project in Alaska started
1/7/48:	Crash of Captain Mantell during pursuit of UFO at Godman Field, KY
1/22/1948:	Start of Project SIGN
3/25/48:	UFO crash at Aztec, NM
7/24/48:	Pilots' sighting over Montgomery, Alabama (Pilots Chiles/Whitted)
9/5/48:	Project SIGN—situation report sent to Chief of Staff General Vandenberg. Conclusions: UFOs are of inter-planetary origin
2/8/49:	Project SIGN terminated
2/11/49:	Start of Project GRUDGE
2/16/49:	Secret conference at Los Alamos, NM
Nov. 1949:	UFO crash in Mexico
12/30/49:	Project GRUDGE closed. Project TWINKLE takes over the job.

THE 1950s

5/11/50:	McMinnville, Oregon: the Trent photographs
7/4/50:	First contact in White Sands, NM (Dr. Daniel Fry)
8/15/50:	Nick Montana films two UFOs over Great Falls, Montana
12/2/50:	Start of Project MAGNET in Canada
12/6/50:	UFO crash near Laredo, Texas
2/9/51:	UFO encounter over the north Atlantic (Commander Graham Bethune)
8/25/51:	Lubbock, Texas: 4 professors observe UFO formations
10/27/51:	Project GRUDGE starts working again
3/16/52:	Project GRUDGE renamed Project BLUE BOOK
April 1952:	UFO sighting by Defense Secretary Kimball
June 1952:	UFO crash at Spitzbergen, Norway
7/2/52:	UFO Fleet over Tremonton, Utah filmed
7/14/52:	Pilots' encounter over Norfolk, Virginia (Pilots Nash/Fortenberry)
7/19/52:	UFOs maneuvers over Washington D.C.
7/24/52:	President Truman orders shooting down of UFOs
7/26/52:	Second UFO wave over Washington D.C.
7/29/52:	General Samfords' press conference at the Pentagon

9/20/52:	NATO maneuvers (Operation Mainbrace) in the North Sea stopped because of UFO encounters
11/20/52:	George Adamski's first contact with an extraterrestrial in the California Desert
12/6/52:	Pilots' sighting over Florida (Pilots Harter/Coleman)
12/13/52:	Adamski photos taken over Palomar Gardens, CA
1/18/53:	Robertson Panel of the CIA Passes Educational Program
5/20/53:	UFO crash near Kingman, AZ
11/23/53:	Lt. Moncla disappears after chasing a UFO over Kinross Field, Michigan
2/15/54:	Stephen Darbishire photographs UFO near Coniston, England
2/10/54:	Contact with President Eisenhower at Edwards AFB, California
July 1954:	Project SKYSWEEP discovers two Mother ships in the Earth's orbit
8/12/54:	Start of Project MOON DUST
16/1/1958:	Navy photographer Barauna takes first official photo-series of a UFO over Trinidad Island.

THE 1960s

Feb. 1961:	UFO crash at Timmendorfer Strand, Germany
2/14/61:	NATO alarm on detection of UFO fleets over western Europe. Start of NATO study "ASSESSMENT"
9/19/61:	Abduction of Betty and Barney Hill
Jan. 1962:	Abduction of Norbert Haase, investigated by East German Intelligence
2/24/64:	UFO landing near Socorro, NM
5/24/64:	Jim Templeton photographs "spaceman" in the Burgh Marsh, in Cumbria, England. The same type of humanoid was observed during a rocket launch in Woomera, Australia the next day
2/26/65:	Madeleine Rodeffer films UFO at Silver Springs, Maryland
7/1/65:	UFO landing at Valensole, France
August 1965:	Wave of UFO sightings over the American midwest
11/9/65:	UFOs cause power failure in New York City
12/9/65:	UFO crash near Kecksburg, Pennsylvania
9/7/66:	Fred Steckling films UFO formation near Mannheim, Germany
10/6/66:	Start of the Condon study at the University of Colorado

5/17/67:	First scientific UFO study in the USSR
8/23/67:	UFO encounter of test pilot Lt. Col. Lev Vyatkin
11/10/67:	First TV broadcast about UFOs in the USSR
12/3/67:	Abduction of Patrolman Schirmer at Ashland, Nebraska
9/5/68:	Thousands see UFO over Madrid, Spain
Dec. 1968:	Colorado study publishes Final Report
7/19/69:	UFO sighting during the first moon landing
10/20/69:	Termination of Project BLUE BOOK

THE 1970s

10/11/73:	Abduction of Charles Hickson and Calvin Parker near Pascagoula, Miss.
10/17/73:	Police Chief Greenhaw photographs alien
10/18/73:	Army helicopter encounters cigarshaped UFO
11/6/73:	UFO seen over the Gulf of Mexico
2/21/74:	French Defense Minister Galley speaks openly about UFOs
1/2/75:	UFO landing on military terrain near Navarre/Spain
8/13/75:	Abduction of Sergeant Moody
Jul.–Nov. 1975:	UFOs over U.S. nuclear arsenals
11/5/75:	Abduction of Travis Walton near Snowflake AZ in front of 6 witnesses
6/22/76:	UFO landing in Gran Canaria, one of the Canary Islands
7/19/76:	Interceptor jets pursue UFO over Tehran
1/20/77:	Jimmy Carter sworn in as U.S. President. An era of openness in the subject of UFOs begins
5/1/77:	Establishment of GEPAN in France
9/20/77:	UFO over Petrosavodsk, USSR, sends out rays that bore holes in windowpanes. The incident leads to the first open discussion of the UFO phenomenon
1/18/78:	Alien shot at the McGuire/Fort Dix AFB
3/12/78:	UFO fleet flies over Brazil
5/16/78:	UFO crash near El Taire, Bolivia
7/17/78:	Airline pilots see UFO over Teheran
9/14/78:	UFO flies over Italy
10/21/78:	Pilot Frederick Valentich vanishes after UFO encounter
11/9/78:	UFO causes Kuwait's oil pumps to stand still.
Dec. 1978:	UFO wave over Italy
12/7/78:	Abduction of Fortunato Zanfretta in Genoa
12/12/78:	Policemen encounter UFO near Cononley-Moor, Yorkshire. Two hours later, the same object was seen by a woman in Burghausen, Bavaria in Germany

12/18/78:	UFOs on the agenda of the UN General Assembly
12/31/78:	TV team films UFOs over New Zealand
1/18/79:	UFO debate in the House of Lords
3/3/79:	The Spanish General Staff puts all UFO files under enhanced secrecy
3/5/79:	Thousands see UFO over the Canary Islands
11/11/79:	Passenger aircraft compelled by UFOs to land at Valencia, Spain

THE 1980s

1/14/80:	UFO over Garlstedt, Germany sets off NATO alarm
Aug. 1980:	UFOs land at US atomic arsenals in New Mexico
12/27/80:	UFO landings in Rendlesham Forest, Suffolk, England; later officially confirmed
12/29/80:	Two women, Betty Cash and Vickie Landrum, exposed to the radiation of a "UFO" near Houston, Texas, and suffer serious health damage
1/8/81:	UFO landing at Trans-en-Provence, France
5/15/81:	Russian space station Saljut 6 sights UFOs in orbit around Earth
8/23/81:	UFOs over Moscow
3/12/82:	UFO landing at Messel, former West Germany
3/27/83:	Cigar-shaped UFO over Gorki, USSR
10/4/83:	UFOs over Soviet atomic arsenals
Feb. 1984:	Establishment of "Commission for Investigating Paranormal Phenomena" in Moscow
9/7/84:	UFO escorts Flight 8352 from Minsk to Tallin
3/11/85:	Michail Gorbachev elected as Secretary-General of the CPSU. The era of glasnost begins, which encompasses "glasnost" for UFOs as well
3/26/85:	UFOs discussed in the Spanish Parliament
1/29/86:	UFO crash near Dalnegorsk, USSR
11/17/86:	Flight JAL 1628 sights 2 UFOs and a gigantic Mother ship
9/15/87:	President Reagan warns the UN about an alien threat.
11/28/87:	UFO maneuver over Dalnegorsk, USSR
10/14/88:	"UFO Cover-Up Live" on U.S. TV causes a stir
12/28/88:	Triangular UFO "swallows up" 2 jet fighters over Puerto Rico
	Alien spacecraft in orbit around the Earth reported by Discovery STS-29
3/25/89:	Mars probe PHOBOS II disappears after UFO encounter

5/7/89:	UFO shot down over South Africa
6/28/89:	UFO above missile arsenals at Kapustin Yar, USSR
9/27/89:	UFO landing in Voronesh, USSR, directs worldwide attention to a wave of UFO sightings in the Soviet Union
9/28/89:	UFO shot down over Long Island, New York
11/6/89:	Robert Lazar reveals secret UFO projects of U.S. government on KLAS-TV
10/26/89:	"Dialogue with the Universe," UFO conference in Germany. The first meeting between UFO experts from Russia and the West
11/29/89:	Police follow triangular UFO near Eupen, Belgium
11/30/89:	UN Secretary-General Perez de Cuellar witnesses an abduction carried out by a UFO

THE 1990s

3/21/90:	MIG 29 fighters chase UFO over Sagorsk, USSR. The incident leads to official recognition of UFOs by the Soviet Air Force
3/30/90:	F-16 chase UFO near Wavre, Belgium. The incident leads to official recognition of UFOs by the Belgian Air Force
8/24/90:	UFO formations filmed near Greifswald, Germany
9/13/90:	UFO destroys radar unit near Samara, USSR
9/21/90:	Police follow UFO near Frunse, USSR
9/28/90:	Space station MIR reports UFO in Earth orbit
11/5/90:	UFO sightings in the whole of western Europe
11/26/90:	Delegate di Rupo petitions for UFO study center at the European Parliament
7/11/91:	Eclipse over Mexico. Thousands see disc-shaped craft in the sky over Mexico City, begin of the largest wave of UFO sightings in history
9/15/91:	Discovery of NASA STS-48 films showing evading maneuver of a UFO in Earth orbit, when it is fired at
12/6/91:	Police and army follow boomerang-shaped UFO from Beth Shean, Israel to the Jordanian border
1/27/92:	Bush and Yeltsin decide on the building up of a global "space shield" during summit conference at Camp David
4/14/92:	Spain rescinds law of strict secrecy regarding UFO documents.
6/13/92:	Abduction Study Conference at MIT, Cambridge, MA

10/12/92:	Start of Project SETI
11/24/92:	UFO shot down over Long Island
3/10/93:	UFO landing in Kadima, Israel—the first of a series
3/30/93:	Wave of UFO sightings over Great Britain. Triangular craft fired a beam of light at RAF Shawbury.
Oct. 1993:	US Congressman Schiff petitions for GAO investigation of the Roswell-Incident
10/20/93:	Prof. Tullo Regge submits his draft report to the European Parliament
1/14/94:	Regge withdraws his recommendations upon pressure from the Socialist faction of the European Parliament.
March 1994:	The Swiss "Confederate Military Department" (CMD) opens its UFO files for a TV journalist
7/11/94:	Spanish Air Force Intelligence orders search for UFO documents.
Jul.–Aug. 1994:	Series of near-collisions of civilian airplanes with UFOs over Mexico City
9/14/94:	Thousands saw luminous objects over the south of Africa
9/15/94:	Thousands see UFO over Metepec, Mexico
9/16/95:	UFO lands in front of nearly a hundred schoolchildren near Ariel School in Ruwa, Zimbabwe.
1/3/95:	Giant alien walks over the field of Yatzitz, Israel and leaves footprints
1/6/95:	A British Airways Boeing 747 encounters a big wedge-shaped UFO. The incident was later investigated by the CAA.
9/27/95:	GAO publishes his findings on the Roswell Incident: the relevant documents had disappeared
10/21/95:	Space Shuttle astronaut Cathrin Coleman reports "unidentified flying object"
Nov. 1995:	The British MOD announces the release of further UFO documents
1/20/96:	UFO crash in Varginha, Brazil. The Army captures 2 creatures
7/24/96:	Parliamentary questioning in the British House of Commons about UFOs
9/17/96:	Thousands see UFOs over Tel Aviv, Israel
10/16/96:	Thousands see UFOs over Paraiba, Brazil
12/1/96:	Space Shuttle mission STS-80 films UFO maneuvers in the Earth orbit
2/19/97:	UFO, 900 feet wide, hovers over Lagoda Lake near St. Petersburg, Russia, and is seen by thousands of witnesses

March 1997:	The complete UFO file of the Spanish Air Force is open for public inspection
3/13/97:	Thousands see giant UFO over Phoenix, AZ, releasing balls of light
4/7/97:	Project Starlight's Washington Briefings under chairmanship of Astronaut Edgar Mitchell
6/24/97:	Pentagon spokesman Col. John Haynes presents the Roswell report of the USAF

Index

Michael Hesemann is one of Europe's leading UFO experts. He studied cultural anthropology and history at Göttingen University. He lives in Düsseldorf, Germany. Since 1984 he has published MAGAZINE 2000, which comes out in German and Czech (and will soon appear in English). It has a circulation of 100,000 copies.

His international best-sellers *UFOs: The Evidence, The Cosmic Connection, Beyond Roswell* (with Philip Mantle) and *UFOs: A Secret History* have been published in 14 countries and sold more than 700,000 copies. Hesemann has produced several award-winning video documentaries: *UFOs: The Secret Evidence, UFOs & Area 51: Secrets of the Black World* and *UFOs: The Contacts*, which have been distributed in 12 countries. He has worked for TV programs in the U.S., Germany, Mexico and Japan. He is an Associate Member of the prestigious Society for Scientific Exploration, and the Explorer Society. Like no one else in his field, Hesemann has investigated UFO incidents in 42 countries. Since 1993 he has travelled more than 300,000 miles in search of the truth "out there." He has lectured at international conferences in 22 countries on all 5 continents (invited by the Human Potential Foundation, UN–SEAT, The International Humanist Society and the Ministry of Transport of the Republic of San Marino, amongst others), and at over 30 universities and the United Nations.